La Ruta Maya

Yucatán, Guatemala & Belize
a travel survival kit

Tom Brosnahan

La Ruta Maya: Yucatán, Guatemala & Belize – a travel survival kit

1st edition

Published by
  Lonely Planet Publications Pty Ltd (ACN 005 607 983)
  PO Box 617, Hawthorn, Vic 3122, Australia
  Lonely Planet Publications, Inc
  PO Box 2001A, Berkeley, CA 94702, USA

Printed by
  Colorcraft Ltd, Hong Kong

Photographs by
  Tom Brosnahan (TB)
  James Lyon (JL)
  John Noble (JN)
  Tony Wheeler (TW)
  Front cover: Chac-Mool, Chichén Itzá, The Image Bank

First Published
  October 1991

Although the authors and publisher have tried to make the information as accurate as possible, they accept no responsibility for any loss, injury or inconvenience sustained by any person using this book.

National Library of Australia Cataloguing in Publication Data

Brosnahan, Tom

La Ruta Maya: Yucatán, Guatemala & Belize – a travel survival kit.

  1st ed.
  Includes index.
  ISBN 0 86442 105 2.

  1. Yucatán Peninsula – Description and travel – 1981 – Guide-books. 2. Guatemala – Description and travel – 1981 – – Guide-books. 3. Belize – Description and travel – 1981 – – Guide-books. I. Title.

917.28

Tom Brosnahan

Tom Brosnahan was born and raised in Pennsylvania, went to college in Boston, then set out on the road. After travelling in Europe he joined the Peace Corps, and saw Mexico for the first time as part of the Peace Corps training program. A short term of teaching English in a Mexico City school whetted his appetite for more exploration. After graduate school he travelled throughout Mexico, Guatemala and Belize writing travel articles and guidebooks for various publishers, and in the past two decades his twenty books covering numerous destinations have sold over two million copies in twelve languages. Ever since he first saw Yucatán, Guatemala and Belize, Tom had a dream of returning to follow in the footsteps of John L Stephens and write an authoritative guidebook to the Mayan lands. *La Ruta Maya – a travel survival kit* is the fulfilment of that dream.

Dedication

For Lydia Celestia, who's Mayan, in a way.

From the Author

I know of no more fascinating places, or better places to explore, than Yucatán, Guatemala and Belize. Though their fascination is eternal, their exchange rates and economies are not. I've done my best to provide detailed, exact and complete information on accommodation, meals, transportation, etc. But a swing in the world price of oil, or an economic policy decision made in Mexico City, Guatemala City or Belize City can change all of my carefully recorded information in a day. If this happens, please rest assured that the establishments recommended will still offer the best value for the price, whether that price is higher or lower than noted in this guide.

When you return from your journey along La Ruta Maya, I'm sure you'll have suggestions, recommendations and perhaps even criticisms. Please write and let me know about them so that I can improve the next edition of this guide. You'll be helping many thousands of faithful Lonely Planet readers to enjoy La Ruta Maya as you have. I'm very grateful for letters, I read each one, and I reply as soon as I can.

If you have problems with any establishment mentioned in this guide, please write to me so that I can reassess it or remove it and save future travellers from similar problems. Establishments recommended in this guide must provide you, the reader, with good, honest, courteous service at fair prices. If I receive complaints about any establishment, it will be removed from this guide.

Acknowledgements My thanks to Andy Alpers of L Martinez Associates Inc in Miami; and Bibi Rubio, Roberto Woolfolk Saravia and the rest of the staff at the Instituto Guatemalteco de Turismo in Guatemala City for their valuable assistance and ever-cheerful support in many ways; to Leif Ness of Guatemala City for inspiration as well as information; and to Jane Kendall and her colleagues at Concord Travel Inc, Concord, Mass, for help in untangling the web of airline routes which bind La Ruta Maya to the outside world. Portions of this book were adapted from Lonely Planet's *Mexico – a travel survival kit* (3rd edition) by John Noble, Dan Spitzer and Scott Wayne. I'm particularly indebted to John Noble for letting me use portions of his excellent writing on Chiapas. For courage through what seemed an endless task I must thank, as always, Jane Fisher, my wife.

From the Publisher

This first edition was edited at Lonely Planet by Rick Bouwman and Sally Steward. Thanks to Michelle de Kretser for editorial guidance and to Sharon Wertheim for help with indexing. Maps, design and cover are the work of Trudi Canavan, with some additional maps from Jane Hart, Chris Lee-Ack and Valerie Tellini. Illustrations by Trudi Canavan.

Travellers who have provided us with news and anecdotes and to whom thanks must go include:

Mhairi Baird (UK), Jessica Ballin (UK), Glenn Barker (UK), Nils Benson (USA), Jennifer Constable (Ber), Mike & Gabriella Copeman (UK), Penny Cottee (UK), Guy Deaun, Jane Ehrenreich, Mark Escott (D), Hugh Finstein (C), Kath Grigg & Delforth Pelletti (Aus), Andrew C Hilliard (CR), Steve Hoskins (USA), John L Kautter (USA), Keith A Liker (USA), Scott MacKinlay (USA), Rona McCarthy (UK), Christina Nystrom (Sw), Shirley Poffenberger (USA), Daniel Rios (Gua), Paul Smith (Tai)

Aus – Australia, Ber – Bermuda, C – Canada, CR – Costa Rica, D – Germany, Gua – Guatemala, Swe – Sweden, Tai – Taiwan, UK – United Kingdom, USA – United States of America

Warning & Request

Things change – prices go up, schedules change, good places go bad and bad places go bankrupt – nothing stays the same. So if you find things better or worse, recently opened or long since closed, please write and tell us and help make the next edition better!

Your letters will be used to help update future editions and, where possible, important changes will also be included as a Stop Press section in reprints.

All information is greatly appreciated and the best letters will receive a free copy of the next edition, or any other Lonely Planet book of your choice.

Contents

INTRODUCTION 9

FACTS ABOUT THE REGION 11

History 11   Economy 29   Religion 38
Geography 23   People 30   The Mayan Calendar System 40
Flora & Fauna 25   Architecture 32   Language 44
Government 27   Culture 36

FACTS FOR THE VISITOR 46

Planning Where to Go 46   Cultural Events 60   Women Travellers 81
Visas & Embassies 47   Post & Telecommunications 62   Dangers & Annoyances 81
Customs 51   Time 67   Work 82
Crossing Borders 52   Electricity 67   Activities 82
Motor Vehicle Insurance 53   Laundry 67   Highlights 83
Money 53   Weights & Measures 68   Accommodation 84
Climate & When to Go 57   Books & Maps 68   Food 85
What to Bring 58   Media 71   Drinks 87
Tourist Offices 59   Film & Photography 72   Entertainment 90
Business Hours 60   Health 73   Things to Buy 90

GETTING THERE & AWAY 92

Air 92   Land 95   Tours 95

GETTING AROUND 98

Air 98   Car 100   Local Transport 101
Bus 99   Hitchhiking 101
Train 100   Boat 101

MEXICO

CANCÚN & ISLA MUJERES 104

Cancún 104   Places to Eat 119
Places to Stay 111   Isla Mujeres 126

VALLADOLID & CHICHÉN ITZÁ 137

Valladolid 137   Tizimin 142   Isla Holbox 145
Places to Stay 139   Río Lagartos 144   Chichén Itzá 146
Places to Eat 141   San Felipe 145   Izamal 156

MÉRIDA 158

History 158   Entertainment 174   Progreso 180
Walking Tour 161   Things to Buy 174   West to Celestún 182
Places to Stay 166   **Around Mérida** 179
Places to Eat 170   Dzibilchaltún 179

UXMAL & THE PUUC ROUTE 184

Getting Around 184   Ticul 198   Mérida to Campeche – short
Uxmal 186   Mérida to Ticul via Acanceh   route (Highway 180) 202
The Puuc Route 191   & Mayapán 200
Uxmal to Campeche 196

CAMPECHE 204

Campeche 204
Walking Tour 207
Places to Stay 210
Places to Eat 214
Campeche to Escarcéga 213
Escárcega 214
Escárcega to Chetumal 215
Escárcega to Palenque 216

YUCATÁN'S CARIBBEAN COAST 219

Chetumal 219
Around Chetumal 224
Felipe Carrillo Puerto 226
Tulum 228
Tulum to Boca Paila & Punta
Allen 234
Cobá 234
Beaches along the Coast 237
Playa del Carmen 242
Cozumel 247

TABASCO & LOWLAND CHIAPAS 259

Palenque & Environs 259
Río Usumacinta 271
Bonampak & Yaxchilán Ruins 272
Palenque to San Cristóbal 275
Villahermosa 281
Places to Stay 288
Places to Eat 290
Villahermosa to Tuxtla
Gutiérrez 293

HIGHLAND & PACIFIC CHIAPAS 295

Tuxtla Gutiérrez 295
Places to Stay 299
Places to Eat 301
Cañón del Sumidero & Chiapa
de Corzo 303
San Cristóbal de las Casas 307
Around San Cristóbal 324
Comitán 329
Lagos de Montebello 333
The Guatemalan Border 335
The Soconusco 336

GUATEMALA

GUATEMALA CITY 346

History 346
Zona 1 352
Zona 2 353
Zona 4 354
Zona 10 354
Zona 13 355
Kaminaljuyú 355
Places to Stay 355
Places to Eat 358
Entertainment 361

GUATEMALA'S HIGHLANDS 366

A Note on Safety 366
Getting Around 367
Antigua Guatemala 368
Semana Santa 370
Places to Stay 373
Places to Eat 374
Entertainment 376
Around Antigua Guatemala 377
Lake Atitlán 379
Iximché 379
Los Encuentros 379
Sololá 380
Panajachel 380
Around Lake Atitlán 387
Quiché 389
Chichicastenango 389
Santa Cruz del Quiché 395
**South-Western
Highlands 397**
Cuatro Caminos 397
Totonicapán 397
Quetzaltenango 399
Around Quetzaltenango 405
Huehuetenango 407
La Mesilla 412
Todos Santos Cuchumatán 412

GUATEMALA'S PACIFIC SLOPE 413

El Carmen 413
Ciudad Tecún Umán 413
Coatepeque 415
Retalhuleu 415
Champerico 418
Mazatenango 418
Santa Lucía Cotzumalguapa ... 418
La Democracia 422
Escuintla 422
Puerto San José, Likín &
Iztapa 423
Lake Amatitlán 423

CENTRAL & EASTERN GUATEMALA 424

Salamá 424
Biotopo del Quetzal 426
Cobán 427
Río Hondo 430
Estanzuela 431
Zacapa 431
Chiquimula 431
Esquipulas 432
Copán 434
Quiriguá 442
Lake Izabal 445
Puerto Barrios 446
Lívingston 448

EL PETÉN 451

Getting Around 451
Flores, Santa Elena & San
Benito 451

Tikal 459
Uaxactún................................. 467
Sayaxché & Ceibal 467

Eastwards to Belize................. 469

BELIZE

BELIZE 473

Tourism in Belize 473
Belize City.......................... 473
Walking Tour............................479
Places to Stay...........................480
Places to Eat 482
Entertainment 484
The Cayes..........................487
Caye Caulker............................487
Ambergris Caye.......................493
Other Cayes 500
Western Belize 501
Belize Zoo 501

Banana Bank Ranch 501
Guanacaste Park 501
Belmopan................................. 502
San Ignacio (Cayo) 502
Mountain Pine Ridge.............. 506
Xunantunich............................. 508
Benque Viejo del Carmen....... 509
Northern Belize................ 511
Bermudian Landing
Community Baboon
Sanctuary 512
Altun Ha................................... 512

Crooked Tree Wildlife
Sanctuary 513
Orange Walk 513
Corozal Town............................. 515
Crossing the Border 518
Southern Belize 519
The Hummingbird Highway... 519
Dangriga.................................... 519
Southern Highway 520
Placentia................................... 520
Punta Gorda 521

GLOSSARY 522

MENU TRANSLATOR 525

INDEX 528

Map.............................528   Text 528

Map Legend

BOUNDARIES

—··—··—··—	.... International Boundary
—··—··—··—	.... Internal Boundary
—··—··—··—··	.... National Park or Reserve
-------------	.... The Equator
....	.... The Tropics

SYMBOLS

◉ NEW DELHI	.... National Capital
● BOMBAY	.... Provincial or State Capital
● Pune	.... Major Town
● Barsi	.... Minor Town
■	.... Places to Stay
▼	.... Places to Eat
▲	.... Post Office
✈	.... Airport
ℹ	.... Tourist Information
◉	.... Bus Station or Terminal
66	.... Highway Route Number
☪ ✝ ⛪	...... Mosque, Church, Cathedral
∴	.... Temple or Ruin
✚	.... Hospital
☀	.... Lookout
Å	.... Camping Area
⌐	.... Picnic Area
⌂	.... Hut or Chalet
▲	.... Mountain or Hill
	.... Railway Station
	.... Road Bridge
	.... Railway Bridge
	.... Road Tunnel
	.... Railway Tunnel
	.... Escarpment or Cliff
	.... Pass
	.... Ancient or Historic Wall

ROUTES

——————	.... Major Road or Highway
-------------	.... Unsealed Major Road
———	.... Sealed Road
- - - - - - -	..... Unsealed Road or Track
═══════	.... City Street
+++++++	.... Railway
●═══◉═══●	.... Subway
....	.... Walking Track
- - - - - - -	.... Ferry Route
++++++++++	.... Cable Car or Chair Lift

HYDROGRAPHIC FEATURES

	.... River or Creek
	.... Intermittent Stream
	.... Lake, Intermittent Lake
	.... Coast Line
	.... Spring
	.... Waterfall
	.... Swamp
	.... Salt Lake or Reef
	.... Glacier

OTHER FEATURES

	Park, Garden or National Park
	.... Built Up Area
	... Market or Pedestrian Mall
	.... Plaza or Town Square
	.... Cemetery

Note: not all symbols displayed above appear in this book

Introduction

The Mayan lands of Yucatán, Guatemala and Belize were home to the western hemisphere's greatest ancient civilisation. Travellers who come to this region today want to see the huge pyramids and temples, the great stelae covered in hieroglyphic inscriptions, and the broad ball courts where mysterious athletic contests were held.

But Mayan lore is more than the forgotten culture of a long-dead empire. As you travel here, the Maya are all around you. Modern descendants of the ancient Maya drive your bus, catch the fish you dine upon, work in the bank where you change money, and greet you as you trudge up the side of a smoking volcano. The Mayan Empire may be dead, but the Maya – some two million of them – are very much alive in their ancient land.

The land is exceptionally varied, from the flat limestone shelf of Yucatán to the cool pine-clad mountains of Chiapas and Guatemala, from the steamy jungles of El Petén, rich with tropical birdlife, to the swamps and fens of northern Belize. It is also threatened. Pressured by rapid population growth, development and exploitation, it is in danger of overuse and consequent ecological destruction. The dense rainforest is disappearing at an alarming rate as farmers and ranchers, responding to personal need and world market conditions, slash and burn to carve out new fields for subsistence farming or pastureland for high-profit herds of beef cattle.

The rich heritage of Mayan civilisation and its environment has its defenders,

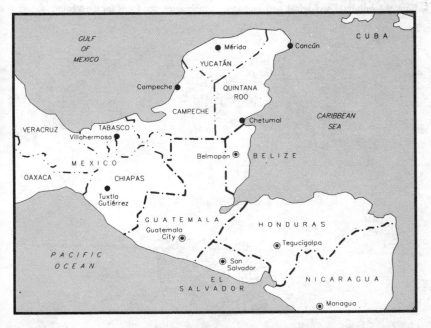

however. Governments and private organisations are instituting programmes to preserve and protect both the Mayan heritage and its natural setting. Tourism is one of the most important forces in these plans.

LA RUTA MAYA

La Ruta Maya (The Mayan Route) is a plan by the governments of Mexico, Guatemala, Belize and Honduras to make tourism work to the benefit of the Maya and their land. Conceived and championed by Wilbur E Garrett, former editor of the US *National Geographic* magazine, La Ruta Maya provides for carefully controlled touristic development with minimal adverse impact on the land, the people and the Maya's heritage. Income from increased tourism may be used to preserve and protect Mayan archaeological sites and jungle biosphere reserves; it may also offer an alternative source of income to those now destroying the forests.

The purpose of La Ruta Maya is to highlight the cultural, ecological and archaeological significance of the Maya's lands, to provide direction and resources for protection and conservation, and to help the Maya preserve their ancient culture while improving the conditions under which they live.

The plan envisions not one but many travel routes and circuits through the region, encompassing seaside resorts such as Cancún and Cozumel, jungle preserves in Chiapas, Quintana Roo, El Petén and Belize, Spanish colonial cities, and most archaeological sites, excavated and unexcavated.

This guidebook, while emphasising Mayan culture both ancient and modern, also gives complete information for those going to Mexico's Caribbean coast or to Belize's offshore islands for sun, sand, surf and snorkelling, and for those interested in Mérida's beautiful colonial architecture, Campeche's pirate history, and climbable volcanoes near Guatemala's Lake Atitlán. In short, it is a complete guide to the lands of the Maya, ancient and modern.

For more information and some suggested itineraries, see Facts for the Visitor.

Facts about the Region

HISTORY
Timeline

The history of the Maya and their predecessors stretches back 4000 years. The following timeline may help you to keep track of what was happening when and where. The division of historical periods for Mayan civilisation is that used by Professor Michael D Coe (author of *The Maya*). I've added notes in brackets on contemporary historical events in the Old World so you can compare developments.

13,000 to 2000 BC Archaic Period Hunting and gathering for food. After the end of the Ice Age (7500 BC), primitive agriculture begins.

2000 to 800 BC Early Preclassic Period In a few Mayan regions, formation of fishing and farming villages producing primitive crops. Early Olmec civilisation flourishes (1200 to 900 BC) at San Lorenzo, Veracruz; Teotihuacán culture flourishes in central Mexico. (Old Testament times of Abraham, Isaac and Jacob; Israel escapes from Egypt and crosses Jordan into the Promised Land; reigns of King David, King Solomon, Tutankhamen and Nefertiti. Invention of the alphabet.)

800 to 300 BC Middle Preclassic Period Larger towns; Olmec civilisation reaches its height at La Venta, Tabasco. Great increase in Mayan population. (Flowering of classical Hellenic culture and art around the Aegean Sea.)

300 BC to 250 AD Late Preclassic Period Mayan cities have large but simple temples and pyramids; pottery and decoration become elaborate. (Alexander the Great's conquests; Ptolemies in Egypt; Roman republic and early empire; life of Jesus.)

250 to 600 Early Classic Period Use of the Long Count calendar. In the highlands of Guatemala and Chiapas, great temples are built around spacious plazas; Mayan art is technically excellent. (Founding of Constantinople and building of Hagia Sophia; Huns invade Europe; Vandals sack Rome, beginning of Middle (or Dark) Ages in Europe; Saxons invade Britain.)

600 to 900 Late Classic Period High Mayan civilisation moves from the western highlands to the lowlands of Petén and Yucatán. Mayan art at its most sensitive and refined. (Life of Mohammed; rise of the Arab Empire; Dome of the Rock built in Jerusalem; Harun al-Rashid sends an ambassador to the court of Charlemagne.)

900 to 1200 Early Post-Classic Period Population growth, food shortages, decline in trade, military campaigns, revolutions and migrations cause the swift collapse of Classic Mayan culture. In central Mexico, Toltecs flourish at Tula, later abandon it and invade Yucatán, establishing their capital at Chichén Itzá. (Europe's Dark Ages continue; Norman invasion of Britain; Crusades.)

1200 to 1530 Late Post-Classic Period Toltec civilisation collapses mysteriously, and the Itzaes move from Campeche to El Petén, then to Belize, and finally dominate northern Yucatán. (Magna Carta; Mongol invasion of Eastern Europe under Genghis Khan; Gothic architecture; fall of Constantinople; reigns of Süleyman the Magnificent, Henry VIII, Charles V; European Renaissance; rise of the Inca Empire in Peru.)

1530 to 1821 Colonial Period Francisco de Montejo conquers Yucatán, and Pedro de Alvarado subdues Chiapas and Guatemala, but harsh colonial rule leads to frequent Mayan rebellions.

1821 to Present Independence Period Yucatán declares independence from Spain, and soon after joins the Mexican union. United Provinces of Central America proclaims independence, later divides into separate countries.

Archaic Period (13,000 to 2000 BC)

The great glaciers which blanketed northern Europe, Asia and North America in the Pleistocene Epoch robbed earth's oceans of a lot of water, lowering the sea level. The receding waters exposed enough land so that wandering bands of Asiatic men and women could find their way on dry land from Siberia to Alaska, and then southwards through the western hemisphere.

They made this journey some 13,000 years ago, and in the next 4000 years found their way to every part of North and South

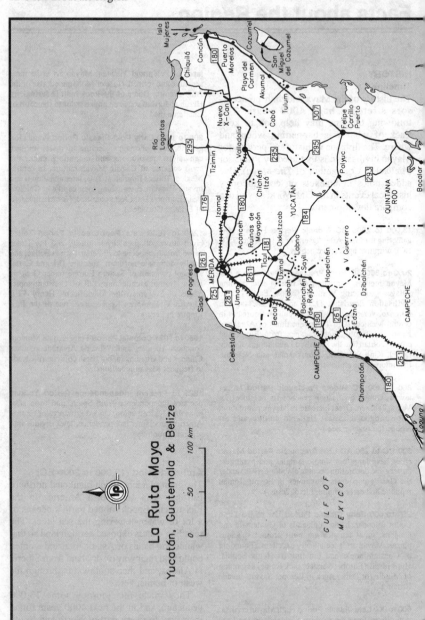

La Ruta Maya
Yucatán, Guatemala & Belize

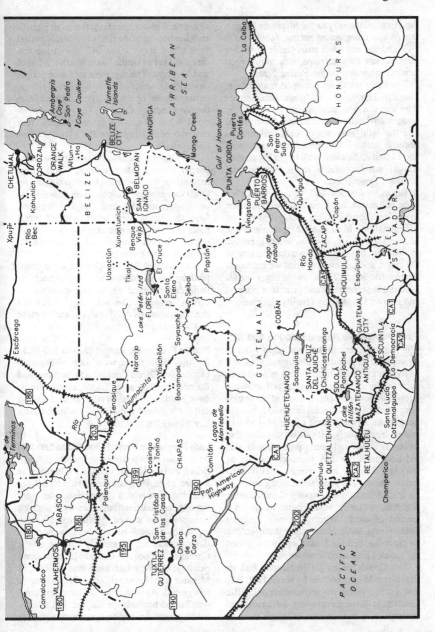

America, all the way to the Straits of Magellan. When the glaciers melted (about 7000 BC) and the sea level rose, the land bridge over which they crossed was submerged beneath what is now the Bering Strait.

The early inhabitants hunted mammoths, fished and gathered wild foods. After the Ice Age came a hot, dry period in which the mammoths' natural pastureland disappeared and the wild harvests of nuts and berries became scarce. The primitive inhabitants had to find some other way to get by, so they sought out favourable microclimates and invented agriculture.

Beans, tomatoes and squash (marrow) were cultivated, but these took second place to maize (corn), which was nurtured, by hybridisation, from a wild grass into the Mayan staff of life, a status which it enjoys to this day. Baskets were woven to carry in the crops, and turkeys and dogs were domesticated for food. These early homebodies used crude stone tools and primitive pottery, and shaped simple clay fertility figurines.

Early Preclassic Period (2000 to 800 BC)

The improvement in the food supply led to an increase in population, a higher standard of living, and more time to fool around with such things as decorating pots and growing ever-plumper ears of corn. Even at the beginning of the Early Preclassic period, people here spoke an early form of the Mayan language. These early Maya also decided that living in caves and under palm fronds was old-fashioned, so they invented the *na*, or thatched Mayan hut, which is still used today, some 4000 years later, along much of La Ruta Maya. Where spring floods were a problem, a family would build its na on a mound of earth. When a family member died, burial took place right there in the living room, and the Dear Departed attained the rank of honoured ancestor.

The Copán Valley (in Honduras) had its first proto-Mayan settlers by about 1100 BC, and a century later the settlements in Pacific Guatemala were developing a hierarchical society.

Olmecs

Without question, the most significant happening of the Early Preclassic period took place about 1000 BC, not in the traditional Mayan lands, but in nearby Tabasco and Veracruz. The mysterious Olmec people developed a writing system of hieroglyphics, perhaps based on knowledge borrowed from the Zapotecs of Oaxaca. They also developed what is known as the Vague Year calendar of 365 days (see The Mayan Calendar System).

The Olmecs' jaguar god art became widespread through Mesoamerica. Their huge, mysterious basalt-carved heads weighing up to 60 tonnes were sculpted with characteristic 'jaguar mouths' and Negroid features. How the heads were hewn without metal tools and moved some 100 km from basalt quarries to the Olmecs' capital city of La Venta remains a mystery to this day.

It's assumed that the Olmecs were trampled by waves of invaders, but aspects of their culture lived on among their neighbours, paving the way for the later accomplishments of Mayan art, architecture and science.

Middle Preclassic Period (800 to 300 BC)

By this time there were rich villages in Honduras' Copán Valley, and settlers had founded villages at Tikal. Trade routes developed, with coastal peoples exchanging salt for highland tribes' tool-grade obsidian. Everybody happily traded pots.

Late Preclassic Period (300 BC to 250 AD)

As the Maya got better at agriculture they got richer, and could then afford such luxuries as a class of scribes and nobility, and all the extravagances which these classes demand. Among the luxuries demanded were temples consisting of raised platforms of earth topped by a thatch-roofed shelter very much like a normal na. Pyramid E-VII-sub, of the Chicanel culture at Uaxactún, is a good example of this; others are found at Tikal, El Mirador and Lamanai, sites flourishing in this period. As with a na, the local potentate was buried beneath the shelter. In the lowlands, where limestone was abundant, they began to build platform temples from stone. As each succeeding local potentate had to have a bigger temple, more and larger platforms were put over other platforms, forming huge step pyramids with a na-style shelter on top, with the potentate buried deep within the stack of platforms. Sometimes the pyramids were decorated with huge stylised masks.

More and more pyramids were built around large plazas, much as the common people clustered their thatched houses in family compounds facing a common open space. The stage was set for the flourishing of classic Mayan civilisation.

Early Classic Period (250 to 600)
Armies from Teotihuacán (near Mexico City) invaded the Mayan highlands, conquered the Maya and imposed their rule and their culture for a time, but were finally absorbed into Mayan daily life. The so-called Esperanza culture, a blend of Mexican and Mayan elements, was born of this conquest. The great ceremonial centres of Copán, Tikal, Yaxchilán, Palenque and especially Kaminaljuyú (near Guatemala City) flourished during this time. Mayan astronomers used the elaborate Long Count calendar to date all of human history.

Late Classic Period (600 to 900)
At its height, the Mayan lands were ruled not as an empire but as a collection of independent but also interdependent city-states. Each city-state had its noble house, headed by a king who was the social, political and religious centre of the city's life. The king propitiated the gods by shedding his blood in ceremonies where he pierced his tongue and/or penis with a sharp instrument. He also led his city's soldiers into battle against rival cities, capturing prisoners for use in human sacrifices. Many a king perished in battles which he was too old to fight; but the king, as sacred head of the community, was required to lead in battle for religious as well as military reasons.

King Pacal ruled at Palenque and King Bird-Jaguar at Yaxchilán during the early part of this period, marking the height of civilisation and power in these two cities. Mayan civilisation in Tikal was also at its height during the Late Classic period. By the end of the period, however, the great Mayan cities of Tikal, Yaxchilán, Copán, Quiriguá, Piedras Negras and Caracol had reverted to little more than minor towns, or even villages. The focus of Mayan civilisation then shifted to northern Yucatán, where a new civilisation developed at Chichén Itzá, Uxmal and Labná, giving us the artistic styles known as Maya-Toltec, Puuc, Chenes and Río Bec.

Early Post-Classic Period (900 to 1200)
The collapse of classic Mayan civilisation is as surprising as it was sudden. It seems as though the upper classes demanded ever more servants, acolytes and labourers, and though the Mayan population was growing rapidly, it did not furnish enough farmers to feed everyone. Thus weakened, the Maya were prey to the next wave of invaders from central Mexico.

The Toltecs of Tula (near Mexico City) conquered Teotihuacán, then marched and sailed eastwards to Yucatán. They were an extremely warlike people and human sacrifice was a regular practice. The Toltecs were led by a fair-haired, bearded king named Quetzalcóatl (Plumed Serpent), who established himself in Yucatán at Uucil-abnal (Chichén Itzá). He left behind in Mexico, and then in Yucatán, a legend that he would one day return from the direction of the rising sun. The culture at Uucil-abnal flourished after the late 800s, when all of the great buildings were constructed, but by 1200 the city was abandoned.

Late Post-Classic Period (1200 to 1530)
Itzaes After the abandonment of Toltec Uucil-abnal, the site was occupied by a people called the Itzaes. Probably of Mayan race, the Itzaes had lived among the Putun Maya near Champoton in Tabasco until the early 1200s. They were forced to leave their traditional homeland by other invaders, and headed south-east into El Petén to the lake

which became known as Petén Itzá after their arrival. Some continued to Belize, later making their way north along the coast and into northern Yucatán, where they settled at Uucil-abnal. The Itzá leader styled himself Kukulcán, as had the city's Toltec founder, and recycled lots of other Toltec lore as well. But the Itzaes strengthened the belief in sacred cenotes, and even named their new home Chichén Itzá (At the Mouth of the Well of the Itzaes).

From Chichén Itzá, the ruling Itzaes travelled westwards and founded a new capital city at Mayapán (1263-83), which dominated the political life of northern Yucatán for several centuries. The Cocom lineage of the Itzaes ruled a fractious collection of Yucatecan city-states from Mayapán until the mid-1400s, when a subject people called the Xiú, from Uxmal, revolted and overthrew Cocom power. Mayapán was pillaged, ruined and never repopulated. For the next century, until the coming of the conquistadors, northern Yucatán was alive with battles and power struggles among its city-states.

The Coming of the Spanish The Spanish had been in the Caribbean since Christopher Columbus arrived in 1492, with their main bases on the islands of Cuba and Santo Domingo (modern Haiti and the Dominican Republic). Realising that they had not reached the East Indies, they began looking for a passage through the land mass to their west but were distracted by tales of gold, silver and a rich empire. Trading, slaving and exploring expeditions from Cuba were led by Francisco Hernández de Córdoba in 1517 and Juan de Grijalva in 1518 but didn't penetrate inland from Mexico's Gulf coast, where they were driven back by hostile natives.

In 1518 the governor of Cuba, Diego Velázquez, asked Hernán Cortés to lead a new expedition westward. As Cortés gathered ships and men, Velázquez became uneasy about the costs of the venture and about Cortés' questionable loyalty, so he cancelled the expedition. Cortés ignored the

Hernán Cortés 1485-1547

governor and set sail on 15 February 1519 with 11 ships, 550 men and 16 horses.

The story of the confrontation between Spanish and Aztecs is one of the most bizarre in history. A detailed first-hand account may be found in the *True History of the Conquest of New Spain* by one of Cortés' soldiers, Bernal Díaz del Castillo.

Landing first at Cozumel off the Yucatán, the Spanish were joined by Jerónimo de Aguilar, a Spaniard who had been shipwrecked there several years earlier. Moving west along the coast to Tabasco, they defeated some hostile Indians and Cortés delivered the first of many lectures to the Indians on the importance of Christianity and the greatness of King Carlos V of Spain. Cortés went on to conquer central Mexico, after which he turned his attentions – and his armies – to Yucatán.

The Cocoms and the Xiús were still battling when the conquistadors arrived. Yucatán's Maya could not present a united front to the invaders, and the invaders triumphed. In less than a century after the fall of Mayapán, the conquistadors conquered the Aztec capital of Tenochtitlán (1521; it's now Mexico City), founded Guatemala City (1527) and Mérida (1542), and controlled most of the formerly Mayan lands.

Colonial Period (1530 to 1821)
Yucatán Despite the political infighting of the Yucatecan Maya, conquest by the

Spanish was not easy. The Spanish monarch commissioned Francisco de Montejo (El Adelantado, the Pioneer) with the task, and he set out from Spain in 1527 accompanied by his son, also named Francisco de Montejo. Landing first at Cozumel on the Caribbean coast, then at Xel-ha on the mainland, the Montejos discovered (perhaps not to their surprise) that the local people wanted nothing to do with them. The Maya made it quite clear that they should go conquer somewhere else.

Montejo *père et fils* then sailed around the peninsula, conquered Tabasco (1530), and established their base near Campeche, which could be easily supplied with necessities, arms and new troops from New Spain (central Mexico). They pushed inland to conquer, but after four long, difficult years were forced to retreat and to return to Mexico City in defeat.

The younger Montejo (El Mozo, The Lad) took up the cause again, with his father's support, and in 1540 he returned to Campeche with his cousin named (guess what?) – Francisco de Montejo. The two Francisco de Montejos pressed inland with speed and success, allying themselves with the Xiús against the Cocoms, defeating the Cocoms and gaining the Xiús as converts to Christianity.

When the Xiú leader was baptised, he had to take a Christian name, and it must have seemed to him that there was only one choice, for he became – believe it or not – Francisco de Montejo Xiú.

The Montejos founded Mérida in 1542, and within four years had almost all of Yucatán subjugated to Spanish rule. The once proud and independent Maya became peons, working for Spanish masters without hope of deliverance except in heaven. The attitude of the conquerors toward the indigenous peoples is graphically depicted in the reliefs on the façade of the Montejo mansion in Mérida: in one scene, armour-clad conquistadors are shown with their feet holding down ugly, hairy, club-wielding savages.

Chiapas & Guatemala The conquest of Chiapas and Guatemala fell to Pedro de Alvarado (1485-1541), a clever but cruel soldier who had been Cortés' lieutenant at the conquest of Aztec Tenochtitlán. Several towns in highland Guatemala had sent embassies to Cortés, offering to submit to his control and protection. In response, Cortés dispatched Alvarado in 1523, and his armies roared through Chiapas and the highland kingdoms of the Quiché and Cakchiquel Maya, crushing them. The Mayan lands were divided into large estates or *encomiendas*, and the Maya living on the lands were mercilessly exploited by the landowning *encomenderos*.

With the coming of the Dominican Friar Bartolomé de las Casas, and groups of Franciscan and Augustinian friars, things got a bit better for the Maya. However, while in many cases the friars were able to protect the local people from the worst abuses, exploitation was still the rule.

The capital city of the Captaincy-General of Guatemala was founded as Santiago de los Caballeros de Guatemala at the site now called Ciudad Vieja, near Antigua (also known as Antigua Guatemala), in 1527. Destroyed by a mudslide less than two decades later, the capital was then moved to Antigua (1543). After a devastating earthquake (1773), the capital was moved to the present site of Guatemala City.

Friar Diego de Landa The Maya recorded lots of information about their history, customs and ceremonies in beautiful 'painted books' made of beaten-bark paper coated with fine lime. These 'codices' must have numbered in the hundreds when the conquistadors and missionary friars first arrived in the Mayan lands. But because the ancient rites of the Maya were seen as a threat to their adoption and retention of Christianity, the priceless books were destroyed upon the orders of the Franciscans. Only a handful of painted books survive, but these provide much insight into ancient Mayan life.

Among those Franciscans directly responsible for the burning of the Mayan books was Friar Diego de Landa who, in July of 1562 at Maní (near present-day Ticul in Yucatán), ordered the destruction of 27 'hieroglyphic rolls' and 5000 idols. Landa went on to become Bishop of Mérida from 1573 until his death in 1579.

Ironically, it was Friar Diego de Landa who wrote the most important book on Mayan customs and practices, the source for very much of what we know about the Maya. Landa's book, *Relacion de las Cosas de Yucatán*, was written in about 1565. It covers virtually every aspect of Mayan life as it was in the 1560s, from the climate, Mayan houses, food and drink, wedding and funeral customs, to the calendar and the counting system. In a way, Landa atoned for the cultural destruction for which he was responsible.

Landa's book is available in English as *Yucatán Before and After the Conquest*, translated by William Gates and first published in 1937; it was republished in 1978 by Dover Publications, 31 E 2nd St, Mineola, NY 11501-3582, USA. You can buy the book in a number of bookshops and shops at archaeological sites in Yucatán and Guatemala.

The Last Mayan Kingdom The last region of Mayan sovereignty was the city-state of Tayasal in Guatemala's department of El Petén. Making their way southwards after being driven out of Chichén Itzá, a group of Itzaes settled on an island in Lake Petén Itzá, at what is now the town of Flores. They founded a city named Tayasal, and enjoyed independence for over a century after the fall of Yucatán. The intrepid Cortés visited Tayasal in 1524 while on his way to conquer Honduras, but did not make war against King Canek, who greeted him peacefully. Only in the latter years of the 17th century did the Spanish decide that this last surviving Mayan state must be brought within the Spanish Empire, and in 1697 Tayasal fell to the latter-day conquistadors, some 2000 years after the founding of the first important Mayan city-states in the Late Preclassic period.

It's interesting to consider that the last independent Mayan king went down to defeat only a decade before the union of England and Scotland (1707), and at a time when Boston, New York and Philadelphia were small but thriving seaport towns.

Independence Period (1821 to Present)
During the colonial period, society in Spain's New World colonies was rigidly and precisely stratified, with Spanish natives at the very top; next were the creoles, people born in the New World of Spanish stock; below them were the *ladinos* or *mestizos*, people of mixed Spanish and Indian blood; and at the bottom were the Indians and Blacks of pure race. Only the native Spanish had real power, a fact deeply resented by the creoles.

The harshness of Spanish rule resulted in frequent revolts, none of them successful for very long. Mexico's Miguel Hidalgo y Costilla gave the Grita de Dolores, the 'Cry (of Independence) at Dolores', at his church near Guanajuato in 1810, inciting his parishioners to revolt. With his lieutenant, a mestizo priest named José María Morelos, he brought large areas of central Mexico under his control. But this rebellion, like earlier ones, failed. The power of Spain was too great.

Napoleon's conquests in Europe changed all that, and destabilised the Spanish Empire to its very foundations. When the French emperor deposed Spain's King Ferdinand VII and put his brother Joseph Bonaparte on the throne of Spain (1808), creoles in many New World colonies took the opportunity to rise in revolt. By 1821 both Mexico and Guatemala had proclaimed their independence. As with the American Revolution of 1776, the Latin American movements were conservative in nature, preserving control of politics, the economy and the military for the upper classes of Spanish blood.

Independent Mexico urged the peoples of Yucatán, Chiapas and Central America to join it in the formation of one large new state. At first Yucatán and Chiapas refused and Guatemala accepted, but all later changed their minds. Yucatán and Chiapas joined the

Mexican union, and Guatemala lead the formation of the United Provinces of Central America (1 July 1823), with El Salvador, Nicaragua, Honduras and Costa Rica. Their union, torn by civil strife from the beginning, lasted only until 1840 before breaking up into its constituent states.

Central American independence has been marred from the beginning by civil war and by conflicts among the various countries of the region, a condition which persists today.

Though independence brought new prosperity to the creoles, it worsened the lot of the Maya. The end of Spanish rule meant that the Crown's few liberal safeguards, which had afforded the Indians minimal protection from the most extreme forms of exploitation, were abandoned. Mayan claims to ancestral lands were largely ignored and huge plantations were created for the cultivation of tobacco, sugar cane and henequen. The Maya, though legally free, were enslaved by debt peonage to the great landowners.

Yucatán Geographically removed from the heart of Mexico, the colonists of the Yucatán Peninsula participated little in the War of Independence. Even though Yucatán joined newly liberated Mexico, its long isolation gave it a strong sense of independence, and the peninsula desired little subsequent interference from Mexico City.

Not long after independence, the Yucatecan ruling classes were again dreaming of independence, this time from Mexico, and perhaps union with the USA. With these goals in mind, the *hacendados* made the mistake of arming and training their Mayan peons as local militias in anticipation of an invasion from Mexico. Trained to use European weaponry, the Maya envisioned a release from their own misery and boldly rebelled against their Yucatecan masters.

The War of the Castes of 1847 began in Valladolid, a city known for its particularly strict and oppressive laws against the Maya; a Maya was not allowed to enjoy the main plaza or the prominent streets, but had to keep to the back streets and the outskirts. The Mayan rebels quickly gained control of the city in an orgy of killing, looting and vengeance. Supplied with arms and ammunition by the British through Belize, they spread relentlessly across Yucatán.

In little more than a year the Mayan revolutionaries had driven their oppressors from every part of Yucatán except Mérida and the walled city of Campeche. Seeing the Whites' cause as hopeless, Yucatán's governor was about to abandon the city when the rebels saw the annual appearance of the winged ant. In Mayan mythology, corn (the staff of life) must be planted at the first sighting of the winged ant. The sowing is not to be delayed, or Chac, the rain god, will be affronted and respond with a drought. The rebels abandoned the attack on Mérida and returned quickly to their farms to plant the corn.

This gave the Whites and mestizos time to regroup and to receive aid from their erstwhile enemy, the government in Mexico City. The counter-revolution against the Maya was without quarter and vicious in the extreme. Between 1848 and 1855, the Indian population of Yucatán was halved. Some Mayan combatants sought refuge in the jungles of southern Quintana Roo. There they were inspired to continue fighting by a religious leader working with a ventriloquist who, in 1850 at Chan Santa Cruz, made a sacred cross 'talk' (the cross was an important Mayan religious symbol long before the coming of Christianity). The talking cross convinced the Maya that their gods had made them invincible, and they continued to fight until 1866.

The governments in Mexico City and Mérida largely ignored the Mayan rebels of Chan Santa Cruz until the turn of the century, when Mexican troops with modern arms subdued the region. The shrine of the talking crosses at Chan Santa Cruz was destroyed, the town was renamed Felipe Carrillo Puerto in honour of a progressive Yucatecan governor, and the local Maya were allowed a good deal of autonomy. The region was only declared a Mexican 'territory' in 1936 and did not become a state until 1974. Today, if you visit Felipe Carrillo Puerto, you can visit the restored shrine of the talking cross above a cenote in what is now a city park.

Guatemala The history of the country since independence has been one of rivalry and struggle between the forces of left and right. The Liberals have historically wanted to turn backward Guatemala into an enlightened republic of political, social and economic progress. The Conservatives hoped to preserve the traditional verities of colonial rule, with a strong Church and a strong government. Their motto might have been 'power must be held by those with merit, virtue and property'. Historically, both movements have benefited the social and economic elites and disenfranchised the people of the countryside, mostly Maya.

Morazán & the Liberals The Liberals, the first to advocate independence, opposed the vested interests of the elite Conservatives, who had the Church and the large landowners on their side. Too often the rivalry has erupted from the political arena into armed conflict in the streets and the countryside.

During the short existence of the United Provinces of Central America, Liberal president Francisco Morazán (1830-39) instituted reforms aimed at correcting three persistent problems: the great economic, political and social power of the Church; the division of society into a Hispanic upper class and an Indian lower class; and the region's powerlessness in world markets. This Liberal programme was echoed by Guatemalan chief of state Mariano Gálvez (1831-38). But unpopular economic policies, heavy taxes and a cholera epidemic in 1837 led to an Indian uprising which brought a Conservative pig farmer, Rafael Carrera, to power.

Carrera held power until 1865, and undid much of what Morazán and Gálvez had achieved. The Carrera government allowed Great Britain to take control of Belize in exchange for construction of a road between Guatemala City and Belize City. The road called for in the treaty was never built, and Guatemala's claims for compensation were never resolved.

Liberal Reforms of Barrios The Liberals came to power again in the 1870s, first under Miguel García Granados, next under Justo Rufino Barrios, a rich young coffee *finca* (plantation) owner who held the title of president and ruled as a dictator (1873-79). With Barrios at its head the country made great strides toward modernisation with construction of roads, railways, schools, and a modern banking system. In order to boost the economy, everything possible was done to encourage coffee production. Peasants in good coffee-growing areas (up to 1400 metres altitude on the Pacific slope) were forced off their lands to make way for new coffee fincas, and those living above 1400 metres (mostly Indians), were forced to contribute seasonal labour on the fincas, as on plantations during colonial times. Idealistic Liberal policies, championed by the British and often meant to benefit the common people, ended up oppressing them. Most of the benefits of the Liberal reform movement benefited the finca owners and the traders in the cities.

Succeeding governments generally pursued the same policies. Economic control of the country was by a small group of land-owning and commercial families, foreign companies were given generous concessions, opponents of the government were censored, imprisoned or exiled by the extensive police force, and the government apparatus was subservient to economic interests despite a liberal constitution.

Cabrera & Minerva Manuel Estrada Cabrera ruled from 1898 to 1920, and his dictatorial style, while bringing progress in technical matters, placed a heavy burden on all but the ruling oligarchy. He was, in a way, the Guatemalan version of Mexico's reviled dictator Porfirio Díaz. He fancied himself a bringer of light and culture to a backward land, styling himself the 'Teacher and Protector of Guatemalan Youth'.

He sponsored Fiestas de Minerva (Festivals of Minerva) in the cities, inspired by the Roman goddess of wisdom, invention and technology, and ordered construction of temples to Minerva, some of which still exist (as in Quetzaltenango). Guatemala was to become a 'tropical Athens'. At the same time, however, he looted the treasury, ignored the schools, and spent millions on the armed forces.

Jorge Ubico When Estrada was overthrown, Guatemala entered a period of instability which ended in 1931 with the election of General Jorge Ubico as president. Ubico ruled as Cabrera had, but more efficiently. Though his word was law, he insisted on honesty in government, and he modernised the country's health and social welfare infrastructure. Debt peonage was outlawed, releasing the Indians from this servitude; but a new servitude of labour contributions to the government road-building programme was established in its place. Other public works projects included the construction of the vast presidential palace on the main plaza in Guatemala City, a fitting symbol of General Ubico's self-esteem.

In the 1940s Ubico dispossessed and exiled the great German coffee finca owners, and otherwise assumed a pro-Allied stance during the war, but at the same time he openly admired Spain's Generalissimo Francisco Franco. In 1944 he was forced to resign and go into exile.

Belize In the opinion of its Spanish conquerors, Belize was a backwater good only for cutting logwood to be used for dye. It had no obvious riches to exploit, and no great population to convert for the glory of God and the profit of the conquerors. Far from being profitable, it was dangerous because the barrier reef tended to tear the keels from Spanish ships which attempted to approach the shore.

Though Spain 'owned' Belize, it did little to rule it, as there was little to rule. The lack of effective government and the safety afforded by the barrier reef attracted English and Scottish pirates to Belizean waters

during the 1600s. They operated mostly without serious hindrance, capturing Spanish galleons heavily laden with the gold and other riches taken from Spain's American empire. In 1670, however, Spain convinced the British government to clamp down on the pirates' activities. The pirates, now unemployed, mostly went into the logwood business, becoming lumberjacks instead of buccaneers.

By today's standards the erstwhile pirates made bad timber managers, cutting logwood indiscriminately and doing damage to the jungle ecosystem.

During the 1700s the Spanish wanted the British loggers out of Belize, but with little control over the country and more important things to attend to in other parts of its empire, Spain mostly ignored Belize. The British did not, however. As British interests in the Caribbean countries increased, so did British involvement in Belize. In the 1780s, the British actively protected the former pirates' logging interests, assuring Spain at the same time that Belize was indeed a Spanish possession. This was a fiction. By this time Belize was already British by tradition and sympathy, and it was with relief and jubilation that Belizeans received the news, on 10 September 1798, that a British force had defeated the Spanish armada off St George's Caye. Belize had been delivered from Spanish rule, a fact that was ratified by treaty some 60 years later.

The country's new status did not bring prosperity, however. Belize was still essentially one large logging camp, not a balanced society of farmers, artisans, merchants, and traders. When the logwood trade collapsed, killed by the invention of synthetic dyes, the colony's economy crashed. It was revived by the trade in mahogany during the early 1800s, but this also collapsed when African sources of the wood brought fierce price competition.

Belize's next trade boom was in arms, ammunition and other supplies to sell to the Mayan rebels in Yucatán, who fought the War of the Castes during the mid-1800s. The war also brought a flood of refugees to

Belize. First it was the Whites and their mestizo lieutenants driven out by the wrath of the Maya; then it was the Maya themselves when the Whites regained control of Yucatán. These people brought farming skills that were to be of great value in expanding the horizons and economic viability of Belizean society. In 1862, while the USA was embroiled in its Civil War and unable to enforce the terms of the Monroe Doctrine, Great Britain declared Belize to be the colony of British Honduras. The declaration encouraged people from numerous parts of the British Empire to come and settle in Belize, which accounts in part for the country's present-day ethnic diversity.

The Mayan Lands Today

Yucatán Although the post-WW II development of synthetic fibres led to the decline of the henequen (rope) industry, it still employs about a third of the peninsula's workforce. The slack has been more than picked up by the oil boom in Tabasco, the fishing and canning industries of the peninsula, and the rapid growth of tourism in the past decade. Though the power elite is still largely of Spanish or mestizo parentage, Yucatán's Maya are better off today than they have been for centuries.

A good number of Maya till the soil as their ancestors have done for centuries, growing staples like corn and beans. Subsistence agriculture is little different from the way it was in the Classic period, with minimal mechanisation.

Guatemala Just when it appeared that Guatemalan politics was doomed to become a succession of well-intentioned but harsh dictators, the elections of 1945 brought a philosopher – Juan José Arévalo – to power. Arévalo, in power from 1945 to 1951, established the nation's social security system, a government bureau to look after Indian concerns, a modern public health system, and liberal labour laws. During his six years as president there were 25 coup attempts by conservative military forces – an average of one coup attempt every three months or less.

Arévalo was succeeded by Colonel Jacobo Arbenz Guzmán in 1951. Arbenz continued the policies of Arévalo, instituting an agrarian reform law that was meant to break up the large estates and foster high productivity on small individually owned farms. He also expropriated vast lands conceded to the United Fruit Company during the Estrada and Ubico years, but now held fallow. Compensation was paid, and the lands were to be distributed to peasants and put into cultivation for food. But the expropriation, supported by the Guatemalan Communist Party, set off alarms in Washington. The CIA organised an invasion from Honduras led by two exiled Guatemalan military officers, and Arbenz was forced to step down. The land reform never took place.

After Arbenz, the country had a succession of military presidents elected with the support of the officers' corps, business leaders, compliant political parties, and the Church. Violence became a staple of political life. Opponents of government power regularly turned up dead, not immediately, and not all at once, but eventually.

During the 1960s and 1970s, Guatemalan industry developed at a fast pace, and society felt the effects. Most profits from the boom flowed upwards, labour union organisation put more stresses on the political fabric, and migration from the countryside to the cities, especially the capital, produced urban sprawl and slums. As the pressures in society increased so did the violence of protest and repression, which led to the total politicisation of society. Everyone took sides, usually the poorer classes in the countryside versus the power elite in the cities.

In the early 1980s the military suppression of antigovernment elements in the countryside reached a peak. Alarming numbers of people, usually Indian men, were killed in the name of anti-insurgency, stabilisation and anticommunism. The bloodbath led to a cutoff of US military assistance to the Guatemalan government, which led in turn to the election in 1985 of a civilian president, Marco Vinicio Cerezo Arévalo, the candidate of the Christian Democratic Party.

Before turning over power to the civilians, the military ensured that its earlier activities would not be examined or prosecuted, and it established formal mechanisms for the military control of the countryside. There was hope that Cerezo's administration would temper the excesses of the power elite and the military and establish a basis for true democracy. When Cerezo's term ended in 1990, however, many people wondered if any real progress had been made.

Belize After WW II the Belizean economy worsened, which led to agitation for independence from the UK. Democratic institutions and political parties were formed over the years, self-government became a reality, and on 21 September 1981 the colony of British Honduras officially became the independent nation of Belize. Luckily, Belizeans did not follow the general pattern of political development in Central America, favouring verbal attacks on their political opponents rather than military ones. Despite its establishment by pirates, Belize's political life is surprisingly nonviolent.

Guatemala, which feared that independence would kill forever its hopes of reclaiming its 'lost department' of Belize, threatened war when independence was proclaimed, but British troops kept the dispute to a diplomatic squabble. In recent years Guatemala, the UK and Belize have come to terms on a *modus vivendi*, though Guatemala has not yet given up its claim to Belize; maps of Guatemala continue to show Belize as a part of the country.

Though the logwood and mahogany trade had brought some small measure of prosperity to Belize in the late 1700s and early 1800s, this was never a rich country. Its economic history in the 20th century has been one of getting by, benefiting from economic aid granted by the UK and the USA, and by money sent home from Belizeans living and working abroad. Tourism promises to be of great help in raising the Belizean standard of living and in providing funds for the protection and restoration of its many important Mayan archaeological sites.

GEOGRAPHY

The land of the Maya includes cool pine-clad volcanic mountain country, hot and dry tropical forest, dense jungle rainforest, broad grassy savannahs and sweltering coastal plains.

The Yucatán Peninsula

The Yucatán peninsula is one vast flat limestone shelf rising only a few metres above sea level. The shelf extends outward from the shoreline for several km under water. If you approach Yucatán or Belize by air, you should have no trouble seeing the barrier reef which marks the limit of the peninsular limestone shelf. On the landward side of the reef the water is shallow, usually no more than five or 10 metres deep; on the seaward side is deep water. The underwater shelf makes Yucatán's coastline wonderful for aquatic sports, keeping the waters warm and the marine life (fish, crabs, lobsters, tourists) abundant, but it makes life difficult for traders. At Progreso, north of Mérida, the *muelle* (wharf) extends from dry land for several km across the shallow water to reach water deep enough to receive ocean-going vessels.

The only anomaly on the flat shelf of Yucatán is the low range of the Puuc Hills near Uxmal, which attains heights of several hundred metres.

Because of their geology, northern and central Yucatán have no rivers and no lakes. The people on the land have traditionally drawn their fresh water from *cenotes*, limestone caverns with collapsed roofs, which serve as natural cisterns. Rainwater which falls between May and October collects in the cenotes for use during the dry season from October to May. South of the Puuc Hills there are few cenotes, and the inhabitants traditionally have resorted to drawing water from limestone pools deep within the earth. These wells *(chenes)* give the region its name.

Yucatán is covered in a blanket of dry thorny forest, which the Maya have traditionally slashed and burned to make space for planting crops or pasturing cattle. The soil is red and good for crops in some areas, poor in others, and cultivating it is hot, hard work.

Tabasco

West of the peninsula along the Gulf coast is the state of Tabasco, low, well-watered and humid country which is mostly covered in equatorial rainforest. Rainfall is abundant here – over 3½ metres annually – and the mighty Río Usumacinta provides another abundant source of water. The relative humidity at Palenque (just across the state border in Chiapas) averages 78%. The lush rainforest is endangered by farmers and cattle ranchers who slash and burn it to make way for more crops and cattle which, in this climate, are guaranteed to thrive.

Besides its agricultural wealth, Tabasco is one of Mexico's most important petroleum-producing regions. Villahermosa, the state capital, is an attractive city with an up-to-date infrastructure financed by the oil boom. Money abounds, which is good since everyone wants to buy air-conditioners to escape the sticky heat which blankets the region day and night, summer and winter.

Chiapas

Chiapas is a huge state comprising several distinct topographical areas. The northern part of the state is lowland and low hills similar to those of Tabasco, well watered, sparsely populated, and dotted with important Mayan cities such as Palenque, Toniná, Bonampak and Yaxchilán.

The central and south-central area is mountainous and volcanic, rising from several hundred metres in the west to more than 3900 metres in the south-east near the Guatemalan border. Rainfall varies from less than one metre at Tuxtla Gutiérrez, the state capital, to more than 5½ metres on the mountain slopes facing the Pacific Ocean. The high country around San Cristóbal de las Casas is known locally as the *tierra fría*, or cold country, because of the altitude and many cloudy days. The mountains here are covered in forests of oak and pine. The Con-

tinental Divide follows the ridge of the Sierra Madre, towering above the Pacific littoral.

South and west of the Sierra Madre is the Pacific slope of the mountains and the coastal plain, known as the Soconusco. Rainfall here is abundant as the weather arrives from the west and the clouds dump their wet loads as they ascend to vault the high mountains. Cotton is the choice crop on the plain, but on the mountain slopes (up to 1400 metres) it's cacao and coffee. Huge fincas were established here in the 19th century under German, US and British owners, and their descendants still administer them today.

Guatemala

In Guatemala, the western highlands linked by the Pan American Highway are the continuation of Chiapas' Sierra Madre, volcanic formations reaching heights of 3800 metres in the Cuchumatanes range north-west of Huehuetenango. Land that has not been cleared for Mayan *milpas* (cornfields) is covered in pine forests. Many of the volcanoes are active or dormant, and you should not be surprised to see, some dark night, the red glow of volcanic activity above a distant mountaintop. All this volcanic activity means that this is an earthquake area as well. Major quakes struck in 1773, 1917 and 1976, and there are more to come.

The Pacific slope of Guatemala is the continuation of Chiapas' Soconusco, with rich coffee, cacao, fruit and sugar plantations along the Pacific Highway (Carretera al Pacifico). Down along the shore the volcanic slope meets the sea, yielding vast beaches of black volcanic sand in a sweltering climate that is difficult to bear, even if you just sit and do nothing. It's great for growing grass, and rich grass is great for fattening cattle, which is what happens here.

South and east along the Pan American Highway the altitude decreases to about 1500 metres at Guatemala City.

North of Guatemala City the highlands of Alta Verapaz gradually decline to the lowland of El Petén, which is the continuation of southern Yucatán. Petén's climate and topography is like that of Yucatán, hot and humid or hot and dry, depending upon the season. To the south-east of Petén is the valley of the Río Motagua, dry in some areas, moist in others. The Motagua Valley is rich in dinosaur bones, and is wonderful for growing bananas, as you'll see when you visit Quiriguá.

Belize

Belize, like Yucatán, is tropical lowland, though in the western part of the country the Maya Mountains rise to almost 1000 metres. Even here the forest is lush and well watered, humid even in the dry season, but more pleasant than the lowlands.

Northern Belize is low tropical country, very swampy along the shore. The southern part of the country is similar, but even more rainy and humid.

Offshore, the water is only about five metres deep all the way out to the islands, called *cayes*. Just east of the cayes in the Caribbean is the barrier reef, a mecca for snorkellers and scuba divers.

Biosphere Reserves

Tropical forests have been called the 'lungs of the planet', converting carbon dioxide into oxygen, purifying and enriching the air we breathe. Besides acting as the planet's lungs, tropical forests are a storehouse of chemical and biological substances and gene materials which has yet to be extensively explored. The thousands of organisms in the forest may contain the materials needed to cure dreaded diseases and develop new forms of life. But if the forests disappear – and they are disappearing at an alarming rate worldwide – humankind will lose this great storehouse, and may not be able to breathe.

The bad news is that the destruction of tropical forests along La Ruta Maya is progressing at an alarming rate. One visit to the countryside around Palenque will confirm this. Huge tracts of cleared land are still smouldering from the fires that cleared the forest for the farmer's plough and the herder's cattle.

The good news is that preliminary steps have been taken to preserve vast tracts of tropical forest. *Biotopos*, or biosphere reserves, have been established in Mexico, Guatemala and Belize. The restrictions in these reserves vary, but in general the cutting or burning of forest and the hunting of animals is forbidden or controlled.

Of the many biosphere reserves, the most impressive is the vast multinational reserve formed by the juxtaposing of three large national reserves along the joint borders of Mexico, Guatemala and Belize. The large Calakmul Reserve in the southern part of the Yucatán peninsula adjoins the enormous Maya Biosphere Reserve which covers all of the northern Petén in Guatemala. Adjoining to the east is Belize's Río Bravo Conservation Area, over 1000 sq km of tropical forests, rivers, ponds and Mayan archaeological sites.

FLORA & FAUNA

As you might expect, the lush jungles of Chiapas, Guatemala and Belize are teeming with fascinating animals and plants. But the drier forests of Yucatán also provide habitats for a surprising number and variety of beasts.

The Maya call Yucatán 'The Land of the Pheasant and the Deer'. These two animals formed the basis for countless legends – and delicious meals – among the ancient Maya. The legends are still alive, and the animals are still on the menu today.

Birds

As you might imagine, birds are numerous and varied all along La Ruta Maya. In fact, bird-watching in itself is enough reason to plan an extended stay here.

Turkey The 'pheasant' of Mayan lore is actually the ocellated turkey, a beautiful bird which reminds one of a peacock. Originally, turkeys were native to New England and the Middle Atlantic states in the USA, and to Yucatán, not to Turkey. The birds got their odd Middle Eastern name when they were shipped from New England and Yucatán to the West Indies in the Triangle Trade, from where they then continued their journey to Europe. They were transshipped at Genoa onto English merchant ships returned from the Ottoman Empire; because they arrived in England aboard the 'Turkey boats' they were known as Turkey-birds. In Turkey, by the way, they're called *hindi* (Indian bird), because they came from the (West) Indies; the French name *dinde* (from India) derives from the same source.

Flamingo These long, lanky but graceful birds inhabit certain areas of northern Yucatán, principally the wetlands near the towns of Río Lagartos (north-east Yucatán) and Celestun (north-west Yucatán). Flamingoes can be white, pink or salmon-coloured. It's the pink and salmon ones which draw the oohs and ahhs. Look for them when the rainy season begins in late May.

In addition to the flamingo, other long-legged birds such as the heron, snowy egret and white ibis often visit Yucatán and Belize. The egrets are especially easy to see in cattle pastures.

Quetzal The gorgeous quetzal, its long, curving tailfeathers iridescent with blue and green (the colours associated with the Mayan world-tree), was highly valued by the ancient Maya for its incomparably beautiful plumage: quetzal feathers were important to the costumes of Mayan royalty. The quetzal is the national bird of Guatemala. It is also nearly extinct.

As the quetzal becomes scarcer, its value rises; and as the rainforests are slashed and burned, its habitat disappears. Still, there are quetzals to be seen, and you may be lucky enough

to see one if you work at it. The places to look are in the jungles of Chiapas, in the highlands of Guatemala, or at Tikal National Park. The Guatemalans have established a special quetzal forest reserve (Biotopo del Quetzal) on the road to Cobán, capital of the department of Alta Verapaz. But the bird is shy and elusive, and establishing a reserve does not guarantee that there will be birds in abundance for you to see.

Cats
Mayan culture, and that of the Olmecs which preceded it, could hardly get along without the jaguar, symbol of power, stealth, determination – and bloodletting. Jaguars still roam the forests along La Ruta Maya. You are unlikely to see one except in a cage (there's one in Villahermosa's Parque Museo La Venta), but that won't change your opinion of it. You'll realise at once that the jaguar is an animal worthy of respect.

The jaguar lives on deer, peccary and tapir, which may explain why the tapir, when attacked, runs blindly in any direction – anything to get away.

The ocelot and puma also live in the jungles here, but are just as rare as the jaguar these days.

Deer
Deer are plentiful enough in Yucatán for deer hunting to be still popular both as sport and

as a way of getting a cheap dinner. Venison appears on many restaurant menus in the tourist resorts (those that serve more than hamburgers or steak and lobster). Deer multiply rapidly, they love eating corn, and they don't seem to be in danger of depopulation.

Iguana
One animal you can see at any Yucatecan archaeological site is the iguana, a harmless lizard of fearsome appearance. There are many

Ocellated Turkey

different kinds of iguanas, but most are green with black bands encircling the body. Iguanas can grow to one metre in length, including their long, flat tails, though most of the ones you'll see will be shorter than 15 cm (about one foot). Iguanas love to bask in the sun on the warm rocks of old Mayan temples, but they'll shoot away from their comfy perches and hide if you approach them.

Sea Turtles

Giant sea turtles are found in the waters off Yucatán and Belize. They're protected by law, especially during mating and nesting seasons. Though there are legal methods for hunting small numbers of the turtles, most of the casualties come as the result of poaching and of egg-hunting, as sea turtle eggs are believed by the uninformed to be an aphrodisiac. You may see turtle on a menu. It may have been taken legally. Then again, who knows? My feeling is that it's best to discourage trade in any endangered species, even 'controlled' trade.

Other Reptiles

Yucatán is home to several varieties of snakes, including the very deadly coral snakes and tropical rattlesnakes. These beasts do not look for trouble, and will slither away from you if they can. It's unlikely that you'll meet one, and if you do, it's unlikely that you'll do something to anger it, and if you do it's unlikely that you'll get bitten. But if you do, you'll need help quickly as they are deadly poisonous. Watch where you step.

Another dangerous reptile is the cayman, a sort of crocodile, found mostly near the town of Río Lagartos on the northern coast of Yucatán. These beasts are fascinating to look at but unpleasant, even deadly, to meet up close. Keep your distance.

Armadillos & Anteaters

Armadillos are creatures about 25 to 30 cm long with prominent ears, snouts, tails, and hard bony coverings for protection. Though they look fearsome, they are dangerous only to insects, which is what they live on. Their sharp claws help them to dig for fat, tasty grubs, and also to hollow out underground burrows, which is where they live. You might see armadillos in northern Yucatán, most likely as road kill, unfortunately.

The anteater is a cousin of the armadillo, though it's difficult to see the resemblance. Anteaters have very long, flexible snouts and sharp-clawed shovel-like front paws, the two tools needed to seek out and enjoy ants and other insects. Unlike the armadillo, the anteater is covered in hair, with a long bushy tail.

Tapirs & Peccaries

Short of leg and tail, stout of build, small of eye, ear and intelligence, the tapir eats plants, bathes daily, and runs like mad when approached. If you're wandering the leafy paths of Tikal and you hear something crashing through the underbrush nearby, you've probably frightened a tapir. Or it could have been a peccary, a sort of wild pig that can grow to 30 kg (66 pounds) or more in weight. If the crashing has been particularly noisy, it's probably peccaries as they tend to travel in groups.

GOVERNMENT
Mexico

In theory, the United Mexican States (Estados Unidos Mexicanos) is a multiparty democracy with an elected president, a bicameral legislature, and an independent judiciary. The individual states of the union have similar governments, with state legislatures and elected governors.

In fact, Mexican political life has been dominated since the 1930s by one political party, the gigantic Partido Revolucionario Institucional, or PRI (el PREE). Presidential candidates are selected by the party's top leadership led by the current president, and they invariably win election as the party has complete control over the powerful government media apparatus and patronage system. A president serves one term of six years, *el sexenio*, and is not eligible for re-election.

During his or her term, Mexico's president is the worthy successor of Moctezuma or

Cortés, vested with enormous power and treated as royalty. The president's job is to guide the country with the huge PRI party apparatus, and assure the succession of his or her chosen PRI candidate at the end of the sexenio.

Corruption is traditional in politics, particularly in Latin America. But even some Mexican cynics, inured to stories of the disappearance of multibillions of pesos of their tax money, were shocked at the flagrant excesses of the López Portillo administration (1976-82), when breathtaking amounts of money disappeared and bureaucratic incompetence was the rule rather than the exception.

Bad government led to the rise of a true opposition – not just the tame opposition secretly supported by the PRI – in the form of the Partido de Acción Nacional, or PAN, which fielded candidates in the 1982 elections and got close to victory in some local contests despite massive fraud on the part of the PRI.

The sexenio of Miguel de la Madrid Hurtado (1982-88) was somewhat better, but the PRI was seen as becoming increasingly unfit to direct the country's destiny alone. Demands were made for fraud-free elections, and a faction from within the PRI split away from the main party, bent on reform. The faction, led by Cuauhtémoc Cárdenas, son of famed president Lázaro Cárdenas (1934-40), became the National Democratic Front.

In the elections of 1988, fraud was not quite so massive and the PRI candidate, Carlos Salinas de Gortari, won by the smallest margin in PRI history. His opponents claim that in fair elections he would have been defeated. Nevertheless, Salinas seems to have got the message that politics as usual was no longer possible. He has taken several bold steps to alleviate some of Mexico's most pressing problems and win back the popular support which had been lost to the PRI. Much of the electorate is hopeful that he will succeed, and everyone waits to see how truly democratic the elections of 1994 will be.

Guatemala

Government in Guatemala has traditionally been one of beautiful theory and brutal reality. Always a constitutional democracy in form, Guatemala has been ruled by a succession of military strongmen ever since Pedro de Alvarado came and conquered the Maya in the 1500s. With a few notable exceptions such as the administrations of Juan José Arévalo and Jacobo Arbenz Guzmán, Guatemala's government has been controlled by the commercial, military, landowning and bureaucratic classes of society, leaving little power to the large number of Indians in the countryside. While the niceties of democracy are often observed, real government takes place by means of intimidation and secret military activities.

With true democracies appearing in Latin America during the 1980s, the election of Vinicio Cerezo Arévalo as president in 1985 was taken as a sign that true democracy might have a chance in Guatemala. However, by the end of his term in 1990, Cerezo had been unable or unwilling to accomplish much in the way of strengthening civilian government. Abuses of power by military factions continued. Though the presidential elections of 1990 brought a spirited political debate, they also exhibited a wide disparity of views among powerful political factions with high passions and strong ideas. It appears that government will continue with a civilian face, but a military brain and heart, and a strong arm. The alternative to this gloomy prospect might well be an even gloomier one: a protracted civil war, as in neighbouring El Salvador.

Belize

British colonial rule left Belize with a tradition of representative democracy which continued after independence. The British monarch is Belize's head of state, represented on Belizean soil by the governor-general, who is appointed by the monarch with the advice of the Belizean prime minister. The Belizean legislature is bicameral, with a popularly elected House of Representatives and a nominated Senate similar in function to the British House of Lords.

The prime minister is the actual political head of Belize, and since independence the prime minister has usually been George Price, a founder of the People's United Party. The PUP was born in the 1950s during the early movement for independence from the UK. For the first decade of its existence, the PUP was seen as anti-British, and its leaders were harassed by the colonial authorities. But by 1961 the British government saw that Belizean independence was the wave of the future. Price went from being a thorn in the British side to being the prospective leader of a fledgling nation.

In 1964 Belize got a new constitution for self-government and the PUP, led by Price, won the elections in 1965, 1969, 1974 and 1979. The PUP was the leading force for full independence, achieved in 1981. Though it achieved its goal, the party did not fulfil the dreams of Belizeans for a more prosperous economy, partly due to world market conditions beyond its control. The party was also seen as having been in power too long; there were charges of complacency and corruption.

The PUP's main opposition, the multi-party coalition later named the United Democratic Party, won the elections of 1984 under the slogan 'It's time for a change', and Manuel Esquivel replaced George Price as prime minister. Priding itself on its handling of the economy, the UDP gained more ground in municipal elections held at the end of the decade. But the early national election of September 1989 held a surprise: PUP took 15 seats in the House of Representatives, while the UDP took only 13. The venerable George Price changed places with Manuel Esquivel, taking the prime minister's seat while Esquivel resumed his at the head of the opposition.

ECONOMY
Mexico

Yucatán, without plentiful water resources, has minimal agriculture, with some cattle ranches. The important exception to this rule is the cultivation of henequen, the plant from which sisal rope is made.

The export economy based on henequen thrived in the latter half of the 19th century. By WW I it was said that Mérida had more millionaires per capita than any other city in the world. The plantation owners were a de facto Yucatecan aristocracy and built opulent mansions along Mérida's Paseo de Montejo, many of which still stand. They decorated their homes with the artistic treasures of the world and sent their children off to the best schools of Europe.

With the invention of synthetic fibres such as nylon, henequen lost much of its importance, but it is still a significant part of Yucatán's agriculture.

Besides henequen, Yucatán has some pig and chicken farms, and light industry around Mérida and Chetumal. Tourism is very important in the states of Yucatán and neighbouring Quintana Roo.

Campeche is an important fishing port for fish, lobsters and shrimp, much of the catch being for export. Towns along the northern coast of the peninsula also depend on fishing.

By far the richest sector of the Mexican economy is petroleum. The deposits beneath Tabasco and Veracruz are among the richest in the world. Campeche has petroleum reserves as well.

Farming, mining, forestry and oil exploration are important in Chiapas, as is tourism. Tuxtla Gutiérrez, the Chiapan capital, is one of Mexico's coffee-production centres. The cattle ranches in Tabasco and Chiapas along the Gulf coast are expanding rapidly into the rainforest, threatening the ecosystem around Palenque.

Guatemala

The Guatemalan highlands are given over completely to agriculture, particularly corn, with some mining and light industry around the larger cities. The Pacific Slope has large coffee, citrus and sugar cane plantations worked by migrant labour from the highlands, and the Pacific coast has cattle ranches and some fishing villages.

Guatemala City is the industrial and commercial centre of the country, a copy in miniature of Mexico City, its great sister to the north. Like Mexico City, Guatemala City has problems of immigration, pollution and congestion arising from its near-monopoly on the commercial life of the country.

Guatemala's Motagua Valley has some mining, but agriculture is most important here, with vast banana plantations. In the hills of Alta Verapaz, dairy farming, agriculture and forestry are what people do for a living.

El Petén depends upon tourism and farming for its livelihood, and the two are not happy together. The rapid growth of agriculture and cattle farming is a serious threat to the ecology of Petén, a threat that will have to be controlled if the forests of this vast jungle province are to survive. Tourism, on the other hand, is a positive factor here, providing alternative sources of income in jobs which depend upon the preservation of the ecology for success.

Belize

Farming and ranching are important in the lands west and south of Belize City, and forestry in the Maya Mountains. In the north are large sugar cane plantations and processing plants. The cayes (islands) offshore depend on tourism and fishing for their income, and these two pursuits work together: the more fish and lobster you catch, the more tourists show up for dinner.

PEOPLE

Many of the Maya you meet today are the direct descendants of the people who built the marvellous temples and pyramids. To confirm this, all you need to do is compare their appearance with that of the ancient Maya shown in inscriptions and drawings.

Yucatán & Chiapas

Over millennia, the Maya of Yucatán and Chiapas have intermarried with neighbouring peoples, especially those of central Mexico with whom they had diplomatic and commercial relations and the occasional invasion and conquest. During the 20th

Farm boys from Todos Santos Cuchuman

century they have also intermarried, to some degree, with the descendants of the conquering Spanish. People of mixed Mayan and Spanish blood are called mestizos. Most of Mexico's population is mestizo, but the Yucatán Peninsula has an especially high proportion of pure-blooded Maya. In many areas of Yucatán and Chiapas, Mayan languages prevail over Spanish, or Spanish may not be spoken at all – only Mayan. In remote jungle villages, some modern cultural practices descend directly from those of ancient Mayan civilisation.

Thanks to the continuation of their unique cultural identity, the Maya of Yucatán are proud without being arrogant, confident without the *machismo* seen so frequently elsewhere in Mexico, and kind without being servile. And with the exception of those who have become jaded by the tourist hordes of Cancún, many Maya retain a sense of humour and a pleasant disposition.

Guatemala

In Guatemala's population of eight million people, the division between Mayan and Spanish descent is much stricter than in Mexico. Under Spanish rule, most of highland Guatemala was administered by the friars who came to convert the Maya. The friars did a great deal to protect the indigenous people from exploitation by the government authorities, and to preserve traditional Mayan society (though not Mayan religion). But the region around Guatemala City was directly administered by the colonial government without the softening effect of the friars' intervention, and the traditional life of the Maya was largely replaced by a hybrid culture that was neither Mayan nor strictly Hispanic. Interrelations produced a mestizo population known as ladinos, who had abandoned their Mayan traditions to adopt the Spanish ways, but who were not accepted into White Spanish society.

Today, Guatemala's Maya are proud of their Mayan heritage, and keep alive the ancient traditions and community practices which give meaning to their lives. Guatemalans of European blood are proud of their ancestry as well; they form the elite of the modern commercial, bureaucratic and military upper classes. Ladinos fill in the middle ground between the Old Guard White Hispanic, European and North American elite and the Mayan farmers and labourers. Ladinos are shopkeepers, merchants, traders, administrators, bureaucrats and especially politicians.

Belize

The peoples of Mexico and Guatemala, however diverse and interesting, are easily outdone by the fabulous, improbable ethnic diversity of little Belize, with a population of less than 200,000.

The Maya of Belize, located mostly in the northern and western parts of the country and on the cayes, are of three linguistic groups. In the north, bordering Yucatán, they speak Yucatec and also probably Spanish. Use of the Mayan language is decreasing, that of Spanish increasing, and English – the official language of Belize – is making inroads on both. The Mopan Maya live in Cayo district in western Belize, near the border town of Benque Viejo; the Kekchi live in far southern Belize. Pure-blooded Maya make up only about 10% of Belize's population, while fully one-third of Belize's people are mestizos, some of whom immigrated from Yucatán during the 19th century.

The largest segment of Belizeans is Creole, descendants of the African slaves and British pirates who first settled here to exploit the country's forest riches. Racially mixed and proud of it, Creoles speak a fascinating, unique dialect of English which, though it sounds familiar at first, is utterly unintelligible to a speaker of standard English. Most of the people you meet and deal with in Belize City and Belmopan are Creole.

Southern Belize is the home of the Garinagus (or Garifunas, also called Black Caribs), who account for less than 10% of the population. The Garinagus are of South American Indian and African descent. They look more African than Indian, but they speak a language that's much more Indian than African, and their unique culture combines aspects of both peoples.

Besides the Maya, the mestizos, the Creoles and the Garinagus, Belize has small populations of Chinese restaurateurs and merchants, Lebanese traders, German-Swiss Mennonite farmers, Indians from the subcontinent, Europeans and North Americans. A walk through Belize City is like a walk through the United Nations General Assembly on opening day.

Popular Attitudes

Machismo Among the mestizo (ladino) population along La Ruta Maya you may encounter instances of machismo (mah-CHEESS-moh), an exaggerated masculinity aimed at impressing other males rather than females. Its manifestations range from aggressive driving and the carrying of weapons to heavy drinking. Women, in turn, emphasise their femininity and don't question male authority. Machismo is often no more than a front, and at its extreme applies only to a minority. Nevertheless, feminism has a long way to go and only a small proportion of responsible jobs are held by women as it is difficult for macho men to take orders from a woman.

The macho image probably has its roots in the region's violent past, and seems to hinge on a curious network of family relationships: as several writers have pointed out, it's fairly common for husbands here to have mistresses. In response, wives lavish affection on their sons, who end up idolising their mothers and, unable to find similar perfection in a wife, take a mistress. And while the virtue of a man's daughters and sisters must be protected at all costs, other women are often seen as 'fair game'. This applies particularly to foreign women without male companions to offer similar protection.

Locals vs Gringos With only a few exceptions, the people you encounter along La Ruta Maya will be friendly, humorous and willing to help. Language difficulties can obscure this fact. Some people are shy or will ignore you because they haven't encountered foreigners before and don't imagine a conversation is possible. But just a few words of Spanish will often bring you smiles and warmth, not to mention lots of questions. Then someone who speaks a few words of English will pluck up the courage to try them out on you, and conversation is under way.

Some Indian peoples adopt a cool attitude to visitors; they have learned to mistrust outsiders after 4½ centuries of exploitation by Spanish and mestizos. They don't like being gaped at by crowds of tourists and can be sensitive about cameras, particularly in churches and at religious festivals.

If you have a white skin and speak a foreign language, you'll be referred to as a gringo or gringa, depending upon whether you're male or female, and you'll be assumed to be a citizen of the USA. Your presence may provoke any reaction from curiosity or wonder to reticence or, occasionally, hostility. If you're not a citizen of the USA and you make it known, you may get little reaction at all, or you may be treated as an even greater curiosity, perhaps even as a freak of nature.

The classic Mexican attitude to the USA is a combination of the envy and resentment that a poorer, weaker neighbour feels for a richer, more powerful one. While the USA is still seen by some as the land where everything you touch turns to dollars (or at least cars, cassette players and Disneyland T-shirts), enough Mexicans have worked as wetback labourers for it to be known that the gringos don't share their wealth too willingly. The *norteamericanos* have also committed the sin of sending their soldiers into Mexican territory three times.

Any hostility towards individual Americans usually evaporates as soon as you show that you're human too. And while 'gringo' isn't exactly a compliment – you may hear it in an annoying undertone after you've walked past someone – it can also be used with a brusque friendliness.

In Guatemala and Belize, however, it's Mexico that's the richer, more powerful 'neighbour to the north'. Guatemalan and Belizean attitudes towards North Americans are usually more intensely friendly when they're friendly, and more intensely hostile when they're hostile.

ARCHITECTURE

Mayan architecture is amazing for its achievements, but perhaps even more amazing because of what it did not achieve. Mayan architects never seem to have understood or to have used the true arch (a rounded arch with a keystone), and they never thought to put wheels on boxes and use them as wagons to move the thousands of tonnes of construction materials needed in their tasks. They had no metal tools – they were technically in a Stone Age culture – yet they could build breathtaking temple complexes and align them so precisely that windows and doors were used as celestial observatories of great accuracy.

The arch used in most Mayan buildings is the corbelled vault (or corbelled arch), which consisted of large flat stones on either side set at an angle inward and topped by capstones. This arch served the purpose, but limited severely the amount of open space beneath. In effect, Mayan architects were limited to long, narrow vaulted rooms. True (Roman) arches and Gothic-style vaulting would have allowed them to build stone roofs above far larger halls.

Another important element lacking to them was draught animals (horses, donkeys, mules, oxen). All the work had to be done by humans, on their feet, with their arms and with their backs, without wagons or even wheelbarrows.

The Celestial Plan

In Mayan architecture there was always a celestial plan. Temples were aligned in such a manner as to enhance celestial observation, whether of the sun, moon, or certain stars, especially Venus. The alignment might not be apparent except at certain conjunctions of the celestial bodies (ie at Venus Rising, or at an eclipse), but the Maya knew each building was properly 'placed', and that this enhanced its sacred character.

Temples usually had other features which linked them to the stars. The doors and windows might be aligned in order to sight a celestial body at a certain exact point in its course on a certain day of a certain year. This is the case with the Governor's Palace at Uxmal, which is aligned in such a way that, from the main doorway, Venus would have been visible exactly on top of a small mound some 3.5 km away, in the year 750 AD. You may notice when you visit Uxmal that all the buildings at the site are aligned on the same pattern except for the Governor's Palace. Venus is the reason why.

At Chichén Itzá the observatory building called El Caracol was aligned in order to sight Venus exactly in the year 1000 AD.

Furthermore, the main door to a temple might be decorated to resemble a huge mouth, signifying entry to Xibalba (the secret world or underworld). Other features might have significance in terms of the numbers of the Calendar Round, as at Chichén Itzá's El Castillo. This pyramid has 364 stairs to the top; with the top platform this makes 365, the number of days in the Mayan Vague Year. On the sides of the pyramid are 52 panels, signifying the 52-year cycle of the Calendar Round. The terraces on each side of each stairway total 18 (nine on either side), signifying the 18 'months' of the solar Vague Year. The alignment of El Castillo catches the sun and turns it into a sacred sky-serpent descending into the earth on the vernal equinox (21 March) each year. The serpent is formed perfectly only on that day, and descends during a short period of only 34 minutes.

As mentioned in the section on Religion, Mayan temples were often built on top of smaller, older temples. This increased their sacredness, and preserved the temple complex's alignment.

Mayan Architectural Styles

Mayan architecture's 1500-year history has seen a fascinating progression of styles. The style of architecture changed not just with the times, but with the particular geographic area of Mesoamerica in which the architects worked.

Late Preclassic Late Preclassic architecture is perhaps best exhibited at Uaxactún, north of Tikal in Guatemala's Petén department. At Uaxactún, Pyramid E-VII-sub is a fine example of how the architects of what is known as the Chicanel culture designed their pyramid-temples in the time from around 100 BC to 250 AD. E-VII-sub is a square stepped-platform pyramid with central stairways on each of the four sides, each stairway flanked by large jaguar masks. The entire platform was covered in fine white stucco. The top platform is flat, and probably bore a temple na made of wooden poles topped with palm thatch. This temple was well preserved because others had been built on top of it; these later structures were ruined by the ages, and were cleared away to reveal E-VII-sub. Chicanel-style temples similar to this one were built at Tikal, El Mirador and Lamanai (in Belize) as well.

By the end of the Late Preclassic period, simple temples such as E-VII-sub were being aligned and arranged around plazas, and all was prepared for the next phase of Mayan architecture.

Early Classic The Esperanza culture typifies this phase. In Esperanza-style temples, the king was buried in a wooden chamber beneath the main staircase of the temple; successive kings were buried in similar places in the pyramids built on top of the first one. Among the largest Early Classic Esperanza sites is Kaminaljuyú in Guatemala City; unfortunately, most of the site was destroyed by construction crews or covered by their buildings, and urban sprawl engulfed the site before archaeologists could complete their work.

Of the surviving Early Classic pyramids, perhaps the best example is the step-pyramid at Acanceh, a few km south of Mérida.

Late Classic The most important Classic sites flourished during the latter part of the period, the so-called Late Classic. By this time the Mayan temple-pyramid had a masonry building on top, replacing the na of wood poles and thatch. Numbers of pyramids were built close together, sometimes forming contiguous or even continuous structures. Near them, different structures now called palaces were built. These palaces sat on lower platforms and held many more rooms, perhaps a dozen or more.

In addition to pyramids and palaces, Classic sites have carved stelae and round 'altar-stones' set in the plaza in front of the pyramids. Another feature of the Classic and later periods is the ball court, with sloping playing surfaces of stone covered in stucco. Among the purest of the Classic sites is Copán in Honduras, which can be reached on a day's excursion from Guatemala's Motagua Valley. Along the eastern reaches of the Motagua is Quiriguá (Guatemala),

where the pyramids are unremarkable but the towering stelae and mysterious zoomorphs are unique.

Of all the Classic sites, however, Tikal is the grandest yet uncovered and restored. Here the pyramids reached their most impressive heights, and were topped by superstructures (called roofcombs by archaeologists) which made them even taller. As in earlier times, these monumental structures were used as the burial-places of kings.

If Tikal is the most impressive Classic Mayan city, Palenque (Chiapas) is certainly the most beautiful. Mansard roofs and large relief murals characterise the great palace, with its unique watchtower, and the harmonious Temple of the Inscriptions. Palenque exhibits the perfection of the elements of the Classic Mayan architectural style. The great stairways, the small sanctuaries on top of pyramids, the lofty roofcombs were all brought to their finest proportions here. The tomb of King Pacal in the Temple of the Inscriptions, reached by a buried staircase, is unique in its Egyptian-like qualities: a secret chamber accessible without dismantling the pyramid, and a great carved slab covering the sarcophagus.

Puuc, Chenes & Río Bec
Among the most distinctive of the Late Classic Mayan architectural styles are those which flourished in the western and southern regions of the Yucatán peninsula. These styles valued exuberant display and architectural bravado more than they did proportion and harmony.

The Puuc style, named for the low Puuc Hills near Uxmal, used facings of thin limestone 'tiles' to cover the rough stone walls of buildings. The tiles were worked into geometric designs and stylised figures of monsters and serpents. Minoan-style columns and rows of engaged columns (half-round cylinders) were also a prominent feature of the style, and were used to good effect on façades of buildings at Uxmal and at the Puuc Route sites of Kabah, Sayil, Xlapak and Labná. Puuc architects were crazy about Chac, the rain god, and stuck his grotesque face on every temple, many times. At Kabah, the façade of the Codz Poop temple is completely covered in Chac masks.

The Chenes style, prevalent in areas to the south of the Puuc Hills in Campeche, is very similar to the Puuc style, but Chenes architects seem to have enjoyed putting huge masks as well as smaller ones on their façades.

The Río Bec style, epitomised in the richly decorated temples at the Río Bec archaeological site on the highway between Escárcega and Chetumal, used lavish decoration as in the Puuc and Chenes styles, but added huge towers to the corners of its low buildings, just for show. Río Bec buildings look like a combination of the Governor's Palace of Uxmal and Temple I at Tikal.

Early Post-Classic The collapse of Classic Mayan civilisation created a power vacuum which was filled by the invasion of the Toltecs from central Mexico. The Toltecs brought with them their own architectural ideas, and in the process of conquest these ideas were assimilated and merged with those of the Puuc style.

The foremost example of what might be called the Toltec-Maya style is Chichén Itzá. Elements of Puuc style – the large masks and decorative friezes – coexist with Toltec Atlantean warriors and *chac-mools*, the odd reclining statues that are purely Toltec, and have nothing to do with Mayan art. Platform pyramids with very broad bases and spacious top platforms, such as the Temple of the Warriors, look as though they might have been imported from the ancient Toltec capital of Tula (near Mexico City), or by way of Teotihuacán, with its broad-based pyramids of the sun and moon. Because Quetzalcóatl (Kukulcán in Mayan) was so important to the Toltecs, feathered serpents are used everywhere as architectural decoration.

Late Post-Classic After the Toltecs came the Itzaes, who established their capital at Mayapán, south of Mérida, and ruled a confederation of Yucatecan states. After the Golden Age of Tikal and Palenque, even after the martial architecture of Chichén Itzá, the architecture of Mayapán is a disappointment. The pyramids and temples are small and crude compared to the glorious Classic structures. Mayapán's only architectural distinction comes from its vast defensive city wall, one of the few such walls ever discovered in a Mayan city. The fact that the wall exists testifies to the weakness of the Itzá rulers and the unhappiness of their subject peoples.

Tulum, another walled city, is also a product of this time. The columns of the Puuc style are used here, and the painted decoration on the temples must have been colourful, but there is nothing to rival the Classic age.

Cobá has the finest architecture of this otherwise decadent period. The stately pyramids here had new little temples built atop them in the style of Tulum, the walled seaport town on the coast east of Cobá.

In Guatemala, the finest and best preserved Late Post-Classic sites are: Mixco Viejo, north of Guatemala City; Utatlán (or K'umarcaaj), the old Quiché Maya capital on the outskirts of Santa Cruz del Quiché; and Iximché, the last Cakchiquel capital on the Pan American Highway near Tecpan. All of these sites show pronounced Central Mexican influences in their twin temple complexes, which probably descend from similar structures at Teotihuacán.

Colonial Architecture

The conquistadors, Franciscans and Dominicans brought with them the architecture of their native Spain, and adapted it to the conditions they met in the Mayan lands. Churches in the largest cities were decorated with baroque elements, but in general the churches are simple and fortress-like. The exploitation of the Maya by the Spanish led to frequent rebellions, and the strong, high stone walls of the churches worked well in protecting the upper classes from the wrath of the indigenous people.

As you travel La Ruta Maya, you'll be surprised to find so many very plain

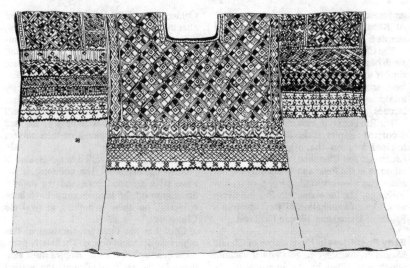

Huipil

churches – plain outside, and plain inside. The crude and simple borrowings from Spanish architecture are eclipsed by the richness of the religious pageantry taking place inside the buildings: the half Mayan-half Catholic processions, decorations and costumes in the churches of Yucatán; or the crowds of the faithful sitting among hundreds of lighted candles on the floor of the small church of Santo Tomás in Chichicastenango, Guatemala, inhaling the thick incense and scattering flower petals in offering to their ancestral spirits.

CULTURE
Traditional Dress

One of the most intriguing aspects of Indian life along La Ruta Maya is the colourful, usually handmade traditional clothing. This comes in infinite and exotic variety, often differing dramatically from village to village. Under the onslaught of modernity, such clothing is less common in everyday use than a few decades ago, but in some areas – notably around San Cristóbal in Chiapas – it's actually becoming more popular as Mayan pride reasserts itself and the commercial potential of handicrafts is developed. In general, Mayan women have kept to traditional dress longer than men.

Some styles still in common use go back to precolonial times. Among these (all worn by women) are the *huipil*, a long, sleeveless tunic; the *quechquémitl*, a shoulder cape; and the *enredo*, a wraparound skirt. Blouses are colonial innovations. Mayan men's garments owe more to Spanish influence; nudity was discouraged by the church, so shirts, hats and *calzones*, long baggy shorts, were introduced.

What's most eye-catching about these costumes is their colourful embroidery – often entire garments are covered in a multicoloured web of stylised animal, human, plant and mythical shapes which can take months to complete. Each garment identifies the group and village from which its wearer comes. *Fajas*, waist sashes, which bind the garments and also hold what we would put in pockets, are also important in this respect.

The designs often have multiple religious or magical meanings. In some cases the exact significance has been forgotten, but in others the traditional associations are still alive. To the Mayan weavers of Chiapas, diamond shapes represent the universe (the ancient Maya believed the earth was a cube), while wearing a garment with saint figures on it is a form of prayer.

Materials and techniques are changing but the pre-Hispanic back-strap loom is still widely used. The warp (long) threads are stretched between two horizontal bars, one of which is fixed to a post or tree, while the other is attached to a strap which goes round the weaver's lower back. The weft (cross) threads are then woven in.

Yarn is hand-spun in many villages. Vegetable dyes are not yet totally out of use, and natural indigo is employed in several areas. Red dye from cochineal insects and purple dye from sea snails are used by some groups. Modern luminescent dyes go down very well with the Maya, who are happily addicted to bright colours, as you will see.

The variety of techniques, materials, styles and designs is bewildering. (For more on clothing and other handicrafts, see Things to Buy in the Facts for the Visitor chapter.)

Music & Dance

Along La Ruta Maya you're likely to hear live music at any time on streets, plazas or even buses. The musicians are playing for their living and range from marimba teams (with big wooden 'xylophones') and mariachi bands (violinists, trumpeters, guitarists and a singer, all dressed in 'cowboy' costume) to ragged lone buskers with out-of-tune guitars and hoarse voices. Marimbas are particularly popular in Guatemala's highlands and on Mexico's Gulf coast.

Music and traditional dances are important parts of the many colourful festivals on the Mayan calendar. Performances honour Christian saints, but in many cases they have pre-Hispanic roots and retain traces of ancient ritual. There are hundreds of traditional dances: some are popular in many parts of the country, others can be seen only in a single town or village. Nearly all of them feature special costumes, often including masks.

Some dances tell stories of clear Spanish or colonial origin. Moros y Cristianos is a fairly widespread one which re-enacts the victory of Christians over Moors in medieval Spain.

The Bullfight

To gringo eyes, the bullfight is not very sporting or, for that matter, even much of a fight. Local people, however, see it as both and more. It's a traditional spectacle, more a ritualistic dance than a fight, that originated in Spain and readily lends itself to a variety of symbolic interpretations, mostly related to machismo. Symbolism aside, the importance of the bullfight to local society is underscored by the saying, often heard in Mexico, that Mexicans arrive on time for only two events – funerals and bullfights.

Traditionally, the *corrida de toros* or bullfight begins promptly on Sundays at 4 pm in the winter and 5 pm in the summer with the presentation of the matador and his assistants. Everyone leaves the ring except for the matador and his 'cape men', before the first of six bulls is released from its pen. The cape men try to tire the bull by working him around the ring.

After a few minutes, a trumpet sounds to mark the beginning of the first of three parts *(tercios)* of each 'fight'. Two men called *picadores* enter the ring on thickly padded horses carrying long lances and trot around until they are close enough to the bull to stick their lances into its shoulder muscles. Their main objective is to weaken the bull just enough to make him manageable, but not enough to kill him.

The second tercio begins after the picadores leave the ring. Men with *banderillas*, one-metre-long stilettos, then enter the ring on foot. Their objective is to jam three pairs of banderillas into the bull's shoulders without impaling themselves on the bull's horns.

With that done, the third tercio – the part everyone has been waiting for – begins. The matador has exactly 16 minutes to kill the bull by first tiring him with fancy cape-work. When he feels the time is right, the matador trades his large cape for a smaller one (the *muleta*) and takes up a sword. He baits the bull, lures it towards him and gives it what he hopes will be the death blow, the final *estocada* or lunge from the sword. If the matador succeeds, and he usually does, you can expect a quick and bloody end.

The bull collapses and an assistant dashes into the ring to slice its jugular and chop off an ear or two and sometimes the tail for the matador, if the spectators indicate that he deserves these honours.

Ancient Mayan Customs

Personal Beauty Friar Diego de Landa wrote that the Maya of the 16th century, just as in the Classic period, flattened the foreheads of their children by tying boards tightly to them, a flat forehead being a mark of beauty. Crossed eyes were another mark of beauty, and to encourage it parents would tie a bead of wax so as to dangle between the child's eyes. Young boys had scalding-hot cloths placed on their faces to discourage the growth of beards, which were considered ugly by the Maya. Both men and women made cuts in their skin so as to get much-desired scar markings, and both were enthusiastic about getting tattoos. Women sharpened their teeth to points, another mark of beauty which, for all we know, may have helped them to keep the men in line. And both men and women dyed their bodies red, though women refrained from dying their faces. Beauty was certainly a different thing among the ancient Maya.

Clothing As for clothing, in the old days the men wrapped long cloths around their loins, with the ends hanging in front and at the back; a square cape was worn on the shoulders, and leather sandals on the feet. Though this sort of clothing has long since disappeared, the men in many Guatemalan highland villages still wrap cloths around them to make a sort of skirt; they wear trousers underneath. Everybody still wears sandals, or goes barefoot.

The women wore huipiles, embroidered dresses that must have looked very much like the huipiles which are still worn by Mayan women in Yucatán, Chiapas and Guatemala today.

Food & Drink Landa tells us that the Maya loved to give banquets for one another, offering roast meat, stews with vegetables, corn cakes (perhaps tortillas or tamales), and cocoa, not to mention lots of alcoholic beverages. The lords got so drunk at these banquets that their wives had to come and drag them home, a condition which still exists. The 'banquets' today are cantinas, and the 'lords' are workmen, but the dragging remains the same. The attitude of the drinkers is aptly expressed in the name of a bar in Acanceh, south of Mérida: *Aqui me queda*, 'Here I stay'.

Sport The recreation most favoured by the Maya was hip-ball. Using a hard rubber ball on stone courts, players tried to stop the ball from hitting the ground, keeping it airborne by batting it with any part of their body other than their hands, head or feet. A wooden bat may have been used. In some regions, a team was victorious if one of its players hit the ball through stone rings with holes little larger than the ball itself.

The ball game was taken quite seriously and often used to settle disputes between tribes. On occasion, it is thought that the captain of the losing team was punished by the forfeiture of his life.

RELIGION
The World-Tree & Xibalba

For the Maya, the world, the heavens and the mysterious 'unseen world' or underworld called Xibalba (shee-bahl-BAH) were all one great unified structure which operated according to the laws of astrology and ancestor worship. The towering ceiba tree was considered sacred, for it symbolised the Wacah Chan, or world-tree which united the 13 heavens, the surface of the earth, and the nine levels of the underworld of Xibalba. The world-tree had a sort of cruciform shape, and was associated with the colour blue-green. In the 16th century, when the Franciscans friars came bearing a cross and required the Indians to venerate it, the symbolism meshed easily with established Maya beliefs.

Points of the Compass

In Mayan cosmology, each point of the compass had special religious significance. East was most important, as it was where the sun was reborn each day; its colour was red. West was black, because it was where the sun disappeared. North was white, and was the direction from which the all-important rains came, beginning in May. South was yellow because it was the 'sunniest' point of the compass.

Everything in the Mayan world was seen in relation to these cardinal points, with the world-tree at the centre; but the cardinal points were only the starting point for the all-important astronomical and astrological observations which determined fate. (See The Mayan Calendar below for more on Mayan astrology).

Bloodletting & Human Sacrifice

Humans had certain roles to play within this great system. Just as the great cosmic dragon shed its blood which fell as rain to the earth, so humans had to shed blood to link themselves with Xibalba. Bloodletting ceremonies were the most important religious ceremonies, and the blood of kings was seen as the most acceptable for these rituals. Thus when the friars said that the blood of Jesus, the King of the Jews, had been spilled for the common people, the Maya could easily understand the symbolism.

Sacred Places

Mayan ceremonies were performed in natural sacred places or their human-made equivalents. Mountains, caves, lakes, cenotes (natural limestone cavern pools), rivers and fields were all sacred, and had special importance in the scheme of things. Pyramids and temples were thought of as stylised mountains; sometimes these 'mountains' had secret chambers within them, which were like the caves in a mountain. A cave was the mouth of the creature which represented Xibalba, and to enter it was to enter the spirit of the secret world. This is why some Mayan temples have doorways surrounded by huge masks: as you enter the door of this 'cave' you are entering the mouth of Xibalba.

The plazas around which the pyramids were placed symbolised the open fields, or the flat land of the tropical forest. What we call stelae were to the Maya 'tree-stones', that is, sacred tree-effigies echoing the sacredness of the world-tree. These tree-stones were often carved with the figures of great Mayan kings, for the king was the world-tree of Mayan society.

As these places were sacred, it made sense for succeeding Mayan kings to build new and ever grander temples directly over older temples, as this enhanced the sacred character of the spot. The temple being covered over was not seen as mere rubble to be exploited as building material, but as a sacred artefact to be preserved. Certain features of these older temples, such as the large masks on the façade, were carefully padded and protected before the new construction was placed over them.

Ancestor worship and genealogy were very important to the Maya, and when they buried a king beneath a pyramid, or a commoner beneath the floor or courtyard of his na, the sacredness of the location was increased.

The Mayan 'Bible'

Of the painted books destroyed by Friar Landa and other Franciscans, no doubt some of them were books of sacred legends and stories similar to the Bible. Such sacred histories and legends provide a world-view to believers, and guidance in belief and daily action.

One such Mayan book, the Popol Vuh (or Wuh), survived not as a painted book but as a transcription into the Latin alphabet of a Mayan narrative text; that is, it was written in Quiché Maya, but in Latin characters, not hieroglyphs. The *Popol Vuh* was apparently written by Quiché Maya Indians of Guatemala who had learned Spanish and the Latin alphabet from the Dominican friars. The authors showed their book to Francisco Ximénez, a Dominican who lived and worked in Chichicastenango from 1701 to 1703. Friar Ximénez copied the Indians' book word for word, then translated it into Spanish. Both his copy and the Spanish translation survive, but the Indian original has been lost.

For a translation of the Spanish version into English, see *Popol Wuh: Ancient Stories of the Quiche Indians of Guatemala*, by Albertina Saravia E (Guatemala City: Editorial Piedra Santa, 1987), on sale in many bookshops in Guatemala for about US$4.

According to the Popol Vuh, the great god K'ucumatz created humankind first from earth (mud), but these 'earthlings' were weak and dissolved in water, so he/she tried again using wood. The wood people had no hearts or minds, and could not praise their Creator, so they were destroyed, all except the monkeys who live in the forest, who are the descendants of the wood people. The Creator tried once again, this time successfully, using substances recommended by four animals, the grey fox, the coyote, the parrot, and the crow. The substance was white and yellow corn, ground into meal to form the flesh, and stirred into water to make the blood.

After the devastating earthquake of 1976 in Guatemala, the government rebuilding programme included the printing and distribution of posters bearing a picture of an ear of corn and the words *Hombre de maís, levantate!* (Man of corn, arise!).

The Popol Vuh legends include some elements which made it easier for the Maya to understand certain aspects of Christian belief, including virgin birth and sacrificial death followed by a return to life.

Shamanism & Catholicism

The ceiba tree's cruciform shape was not the only correspondence the Maya found between their animist beliefs and Christianity. Both traditional Mayan animism and Catholicism have rites of baptism and confession, days of fasting and other forms of abstinence, religious partaking of alcoholic beverages, burning of incense and the use of altars. Today, the Mayan practice of Catholicism is a fascinating fusion of shamanist-animist and Christian ritual.

The traditional religious ways are so important that often a Maya will try to recover from a malady by seeking the advice of a religious shaman rather than a medical doctor. Use of folk remedies linked with animist tradition is widespread in Mayan areas.

THE MAYAN CALENDAR SYSTEM

In some ways, the ancient Mayan calendar is more accurate than the Gregorian calendar we use today. Without sophisticated technology, Mayan astronomers were able to ascertain the length of the solar year, the lunar month and the Venus year. Their calculations enabled them to pinpoint eclipses with uncanny accuracy; their lunar cycle was a mere seven minutes off today's sophisticated technological calculations, and their Venus cycle errs by only two hours for periods covering 500 years.

Time and the calendar, in fact, were the basis of the Mayan religion, which resembled modern astrology in some aspects. Astronomical observations played such a pivotal role in Mayan life that astronomy and religion were linked, and the sun and moon were worshipped. Most Mayan cities were constructed in strict accordance with celestial movements. One remarkable example of this is Chichén Itzá. During equinoxes, the sun illuminates a stairway of El Castillo, turning it into a sacred serpent which 'penetrates' the earth.

How the Calendar Worked

Perhaps the best analogue to the Mayan calendar is in the gears of a mechanical watch, where small wheels mesh with larger wheels which in turn mesh with other sets of wheels to record the passage of time.

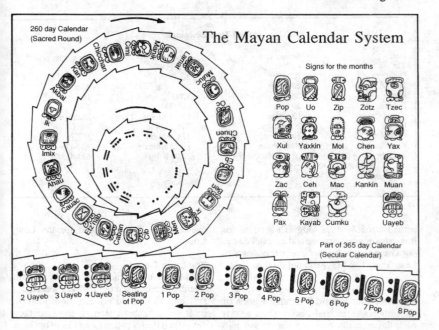

260 day Calendar
(Sacred Round)

The Mayan Calendar System

Signs for the months

Pop Uo Zip Zotz Tzec

Xul Yaxkin Mol Chen Yax

Zac Ceh Mac Kankin Muan

Pax Kayab Cumku Uayeb

Part of 365 day Calendar
(Secular Calendar)

2 Uayeb 3 Uayeb 4 Uayeb Seating of Pop 1 Pop 2 Pop 3 Pop 4 Pop 5 Pop 6 Pop 7 Pop 8 Pop

The Tonalamatl or Tzolkin The two smallest wheels in this Mayan calendar 'watch' were two cycles of 13 days and 20 days. Each of the 13 days bore a number from one to 13; each of the 20 days bore a name such as Imix, Ik, Akbal or Xan. As these two 'wheels' meshed, the passing days received unique names. For example, Day 1 of the 13-day cycle meshed with the day named Imix in the 20-day cycle to produce the day named 1 Imix. Next came 2 Ik, then 3 Akbal, 4 Xan, etc. After 13 days, the first cycle began again at one, even though the 20-day name cycle still had seven days to run, so the 14th day was 1 Ix, then 2 Men, 3 Cib, etc. When the 20-day name cycle was finished, it began again with 8 Imix, 9 Ik, 10 Akbal, 11 Xan, etc. The permutations continued for a total of 260 days, ending on 13 Ahau, before beginning again on 1 Imix.

The two small 'wheels' of 13 and 20 days thus created a larger 'wheel' of 260 days, called a *tonalamatl* or *tzolkin*. Let's leave the 13-day and 20-day 'wheels' and the larger 260-day wheel whirling as we look at another set of gears in the watch.

The Vague Year (Haab) Another set of wheels in the Mayan calendar watch were the 18 'months' of 20 days each, which formed the basis of the Mayan solar Vague Year calendar, or *haab*. Each month had a name – Pop, Uo, Zip, Zotz, Tzec, etc and each day had a number from zero (the first day or 'seating' of the month) to 19, much as our Gregorian solar calendar uses. There was 0 Pop (the 'seating' of the month Pop), 1 Pop, 2 Pop, etc to 19 Pop, then 0 Uo, 1 Uo, and so forth.

Eighteen months, each of 20 days, equals 360 days; the Maya added a special omen-filled five-day period called the *uayeb* at the end of this cycle in order to produce a solar calendar of 365 days. Anthropologists today call this the Vague Year, its vagueness coming from the fact that the solar year is

Mayan Time Divisions

Unit	Same as	Days	Gregorian Years*
Kin	-	1	-
Uinal	20 kins	20	-
Tun	20 uinals	360	0.99
Katun	20 tuns	7200	19.7
Baktun	20 katuns	144,000	394
(Great Cycle)	13 baktuns	1.872 million	5125
Pictun	20 baktuns	2.88 million	7885
Calabtun	20 pictuns	57.6 million	157,705
Kinchiltun	20 calabtuns	1.152 billion	3,154,091
Alautun	20 kinchiltuns	23.04 billion	63,081,809

*Approximate

actually 365.24 days long. To account for this extra quarter-day, we add an extra day to our Gregorian calendars every four years in Leap Year. The Maya did not do this.

The Calendar Round The huge wheels of the tzolkin and the haab also meshed, so that each day actually had two names and two numbers, a tzolkin name-number and a haab name-number, used together: 1 Imix 5 Pop, 2 Ik 6 Pop, 3 Akbal 7 Pop, and so on. By the time the huge 260-day wheel of the tzolkin and 365-day wheel of the Vague Year had meshed completely, exhausting all the 18,980 day-name permutations, a period of 52 solar years had passed.

This bewilderingly complex meshing of the tzolkin and the haab is called the Calendar Round, and it was the dating system used throughout Mesoamerica by the Olmecs, the Aztecs, the Zapotecs and the Maya. In fact, it is still in use in some traditional mountain villages of Chiapas and highland Guatemala.

Though fascinating in its complexity, the Calendar Round has its limitations, the greatest being that it only goes for 52 years. After that, it starts again, and it provides no way for Maya ceremony planners (or modern historians) to distinguish a day named 1 Imix 5 Pop in this 52-year Calendar Round cycle from the identically named day in the next cycle, or in the cycle after that, or a dozen cycles later. Thus the need for the Long Count.

The Long Count
As Mayan civilisation developed, Mayan scientists recognised the limits of a calendar system which could not run more than 52 solar years without starting over, so they developed the so-called Long Count or Great Cycle, a system of distinguishing the 52-year Calendar Round cycles from one another. The Long Count came into use during the Classic period of Mayan civilisation.

The Long Count system modified the Vague Year solar mechanism, then added yet another set of wheels to the already complex mechanism of Mayan time.

In place of the Vague Year of 365 days, the Long Count uses the *tun*, the 18 months of 20 days each, and ignores the final five-day period. In Long Count terminology, a day was a *kin* (meaning 'sun'). A 20-kin 'month' is called a *uinal*, and 18 uinals make a tun. Thus the 360-day tun replaced the Vague Year in the Long Count system.

The time wheels added by the Long Count were huge. The names of all the time divisions are shown in the table above.

In practice, the gigantic units above baktun (pictun, calabtun, etc) were not used except for grandiose effect, as when a very self-important king wanted to note exactly when his extremely important reign took place in the awesome expanse of time. The largest unit in use in monument inscriptions was usually the baktun. There were 13 baktuns (1,872,000 days, or 5125 Gregorian solar years) in a Great Cycle.

When a Great Cycle was completed a new one would begin, but for the Maya of the Classic period this was unimportant as Classic Mayan civilisation died out long before the end of the first Great Cycle. For them, the Great Cycle began on 11 August 3114 BC (some authorities say 13 August), and it will end on 23 December 2012 AD. The end of a Great Cycle was a time fraught with great significance – usually fearsome. Keep that date in mind, and let's see how this Great Cycle finishes up!

Even the awesome alautun was not the largest unit used in the Long Count. In order to date everything in proper cosmic style, one date found at Cobá is equivalent to 41,341,050,000,000,000,000,000,000,000 of our years! (In comparison, the Big Bang which formed our universe was a mere 15,000,000,000 years ago.)

It's important to remember that to the Maya time was not a continuum but a cycle, and even this incomprehensibly large cycle of years would be repeated, over and over, infinitely, in infinitely larger cycles. In effect, the Mayan 'watch' had an unlimited number of gear wheels, and they kept ticking around and around forever.

The Mayan Counting System

The Mayan counting system was elegantly simple: dots were used to count from one to four; a horizontal bar signified five; a bar with one dot above it was six, with two dots was seven, etc. Two bars signified 10, three bars 15. Nineteen, the highest common number, was three bars stacked up and topped by four dots.

To signify larger numbers the Maya used positional numbers, a fairly sophisticated system similar to the one we use today, and much more advanced than the crude additive numbers used in the Roman Empire.

In positional numbers, the position of a sign as well as the sign's value determine the number. For example, in our decimal system the number '23' is made up of two signs: a '2' in the 'tens' position and a '3' in the 'ones' position: two tens plus three ones equals 23.

The Maya used not a decimal system (base 10) but a vigesimal system, that is, a system with base 20; and positions of increasing value went not right to left (as ours do) but from bottom to top. So the bottom position showed values from one to 19, the next position up showed values from 20 to 380. The bottom and upper positions together could show up to 19 twenties plus 19 ones (ie 399). The third position up showed values from one 400 to 19 four hundreds (ie 7600). The three positions together could signify numbers up to 7999. By adding more positions one could count as high as needed.

Such positional numbers depend upon the concept of zero, a concept the Romans never developed, but which the Maya did. The zero in Mayan numbering was represented by a stylised picture of a shell or some other object – anything except a bar or a dot.

The Mayan counting system was used by merchants and others who had to tot up lots of things, but its most important use – and the one you will encounter during your travels – was in writing calendar dates.

Mayan Dates

A calendar date, to the Maya, was not just notation of a day. Each day had a particular significance, determined by its name and its astrology. Thus in writing a date to record a certain event, the Maya were also recording all the religious baggage which came with every date.

To write these all-important dates, the Maya modified their counting system. The first two positions remained unchanged from the everyday counting system; they signified the number of kins (days) as no ones to 19 ones, and the number of uinals ('months') as one 20 to 19 twenties, as before. But the third position signified tuns ('years', that is, periods of 360 days), the fourth position signified katuns (periods of 7200 days), the fifth baktuns (periods of 144,000 days). For most purposes, baktuns were as far as the system had to count.

A Mayan date (in our decimal notation) thus looks like this:

12.19.6.15.0

and translates as 12 baktuns, 19 katuns, six tuns, 15 uinals and zero kins (that is, 1,867,260 days) from the beginning of the current Great Cycle. This date, by the way, corresponds to 1 January 2000 in our Gregorian calendar, the beginning of our new millenium. The Mayan day-name is 9 Ahau 8 Kankin, and it is under the influence of the third Lord of the Night. (For more fascinating information on this important day, see *A Forest of Kings* by Linda Schele & David Freidel.)

Reading Mayan Date Inscriptions Date inscriptions were very important to Mayan religion, and any inscription may have within it numerous dates. But only one date is *the* date in the Long Count, known as the Initial Series date.

To read Mayan date inscriptions on stelae and other carved stones, you must be able to identify certain glyphs. First of all, there's the Initial Series Introductory Glyph, often an especially wide pictograph with three dots, ovals, bars, etc, at its bottom and three 'hats', waves, etc, on top, with a wide oval somewhere in the middle. After the Introductory Glyph come the counting symbols and glyphs for baktuns, katuns, tuns, uinals and kins, then the day-name. As the Classic period in Mayan culture occurred during Baktun 9, the first symbol after the Introductory Glyph is likely to be a bar and four dots, signifying 9, and the glyph for baktun, a stylised face with a hand holding the jaw.

Dates are usually written from top to bottom in two columns. The left column is read first, then the right, then the next row down, left and right, and so on. The Introductory Glyph either spans both columns at the top (with the baktun below-left and katun below-right), or is in the left-top position, with the baktun to its right.

There's a lot more to reading dates than this, as hard-to-read head glyphs representing numbers were sometimes substituted for the easy-to-read bar-and-dot symbols; and the positions of Venus and other celestial bodies were sometimes also mentioned within these Initial Series dates. For more on the reading of Mayan dates, try to find a copy of *The Mayan Calendar Made Easy*, by Sandy Huff, on sale in some bookshops in Yucatán for US$1.50, or available from the author, 10 Suncrest Drive, Safety Harbor, FL 33572 USA, for US$2.50 (shipping included). The classic work on reading glyphs is *An Introduction to the Study of the Maya Hieroglyphs*, by Sylvanus G Morley, originally published in 1915, but reprinted by Dover Publications in 1975, and on sale in bookshops along La Ruta Maya, or directly from Dover, 31 E 2nd St, Mineola, NY 11501-3582, USA.

LANGUAGE
Spanish is the most commonly spoken language of the countries of La Ruta Maya. English is the official language of Belize although both Spanish and a local Creole are widely spoken. For a thorough list of useful Spanish words and phrases try Lonely Planet's *Latin American Spanish Phrasebook*.

Ancient Mayan
During the Classic period the Mayan lands were divided into two linguistic areas. In the Yucatán Peninsula and Belize people spoke Yucatecan, and in the highlands and Motagua Valley of Guatemala they spoke a related language called Cholan. People in El Petén were likely to speak both languages, as this was where the linguistic regions overlapped. Yucatecan and Cholan were quite similar – about as similar as Spanish and Italian – a fact which facilitated trade and cultural exchange.

In addition, both Yucatecan and Cholan were written using the same hieroglyphic system, so a written document or inscription could be understood by literate members of either language group.

The written language of the Classic Maya was very complex: glyphs could signify a whole word, or just a syllable, and the same glyph could be drawn in a variety of ways. Sometimes extra symbols were appended to a glyph to help indicate pronunciation. To read ancient Mayan inscriptions and texts accurately takes a great deal of training and experience. In fact, many aspects of the written language are not fully understood even by the experts. In Classic Mayan times it was the same way, as only the nobility would have been able to understand the inscriptions and codices completely.

Modern Mayan

Since the Classic period, these two languages (Yucatecan and Cholan) have subdivided into 35 separate Mayan languages (Yucatec, Chol, Chorti, Tzeltal, Tzotzil, Lacandon, Mam, Quiché, Cakchiquel, etc), some of them unintelligible to speakers of others. Writing today is in the Latin alphabet brought by the conquistadors – what writing there is. Most literate Maya are literate in Spanish, the language of the government, the school, the church, the radio and TV, and the newspapers; they may not be literate in Mayan.

Pronouncing Mayan Words

There are several rules to remember when pronouncing Mayan words and place names. Mayan vowels are pretty straightforward; it's the consonants which give problems. Remember that:

'c' is always hard, like 'k'

'j' is always an aspirated 'h' sound. So *jipijapa* is pronounced HEE-pee-HAA-pah, and *abaj* is pronounced ah-BAHH; to get the 'HH' sound, take the 'h' sound from 'half' and put it at the end of ah-BAHH.

'u' is 'oo' except when it begins or ends a word, in which case it is like English 'w'. Thus 'baktun' is 'bahk-TOON', but 'Uaxactún' is 'wah-shak-TOON' and 'ahau' is ah-HAW.

'x' is like 'sh'

Mayan glottalised consonants, those followed by an apostrophe (b', ch', k', p', t') are similar to normal consonants, but pronounced more forcefully and 'explosively'. An apostrophe following a *vowel* signifies a glottal stop, *not* a more forceful vowel.

Another rule to remember is that in most Mayan words the stress falls on the last syllable. Sometimes this is indicated by an acute accent, sometimes not. Here are some pronunciation examples:

Abaj Takalik	ah-BAHH tah-kah-LEEK
Acanceh	ah-kahn-KEH
Ahau	ah-HAW
Dzibilchaltún	dzee-beel-chahl-TOON
Kaminaljuyú	k ah-mee-nahl-hoo-YOO
Oxcutzkab	ohsh-kootz-KAHB
Pacal	pah-KAHL
Pop	pope
Tikal	tee-KAHL
Uaxactún	wah-shahk-TOON
Xcaret	sh-kah-REHT
Yaxchilán	yahsh-chee-LAHN

Facts for the Visitor

PLANNING WHERE TO GO

People have been travelling La Ruta Maya for decades, zooming down the straight, flat highways of Yucatán, twisting up the serpentine roads into mountainous Chiapas, cruising along in Guatemala's Motagua Valley, and bashing over the ruinous roads in El Petén and Belize. In just the last few years, however, travel along La Ruta Maya has become considerably better. More archaeological sites have been opened to visitors, roads and bus services have been improved and expanded, and new air service has made it possible for those with time constraints to see all of the major sights efficiently. For the adventurous, new routes by bus and boat through the jungle provide both convenient shortcuts and low-budget trekking experiences. In the future, as regional cooperation develops, we can expect even more travel possibilities to open along La Ruta Maya.

One could easily spend months along La Ruta Maya climbing pyramids, lazing on beaches, admiring colonial buildings and browsing the Mayan markets. The lucky few who have a month or more to spend can see and do it all, but the rest of us must make the best use of the short time available to us.

Most travellers arrive at Cancún, as that resort city has the busiest airport and the most frequent and far-reaching air service. Other possible approaches are via Mexico City, Guatemala City or Belize City. For full information on travelling to the region, see the chapter called Getting There & Away.

The Top Sights in a Week

It is possible to see the top archaeological sites – Chichén Itzá, Uxmal and Tikal – on day trips or overnight excursions by air from Cancún. If you're addicted to the beaches, or if you've signed up for a package vacation which provides a hotel in Cancún, you may want to see them that way. If not, here's what to do:

Spend your first night in Cancún or Isla Mujeres, changing money, getting used to Mexico, and enjoying the beaches. Start for Chichén Itzá on the morning of the second day, visit the ancient city, and spend the night in the nearby town of Piste. On the third day return to the ruins in the relative cool of the morning, then drive to Mérida for the afternoon and overnight. On the fourth day visit Uxmal, south of Mérida, either staying overnight at the ruins or returning to Mérida. On the fifth day head back toward Cancún, either via Valladolid or via Felipe Carrillo Puerto and Tulum; spend the night in either of these cities, or in Cancún. On the sixth or seventh day, take a flight from Cancún to Tikal, Guatemala for a visit to the most magnificent of Mayan cities; stay overnight in nearby Flores, returning to Cancún the following day.

This itinerary is rushed, and you may want to go by rented car rather than by bus to make it more comfortable. The rented car and the flights make it quite expensive, but it does allow you to see the top sights – Cancún, Chichén Itzá, Mérida, Uxmal, Tulum, Tikal – and a good deal of the countryside in the shortest possible time.

Two Weeks

This itinerary gives you a good look at the Mayan sites in Mexico, the highlands of Guatemala, the fabulous ruins of Tikal, and a glimpse of Belize, all in 14 or 15 days. It includes one or two flights, but the rest can be done by bus. If you have 15 or 16 days, or if you move at a slightly faster pace, you can do it all by bus, which brings the cost down considerably.

Day 1 Cancún or Isla Mujeres, arrive and find your hotel

Day 2 Ride to Chichén Itzá, visit the ruins and stay overnight

Day 3 To Mérida and overnight

Day 4 Spend another day in Mérida if you like, or take a day trip to Dzibilchaltún and Progreso, or head south to Mayapán, Ticul and Uxmal

Day 5 Uxmal; overnight near the ruins

Day 6 Visit Kabah on the Puuc Route, and perhaps Sayil, then on to Campeche for the night; or, if you like, directly to Palenque

Day 7 To Palenque and overnight

Day 8 Visit the ruins at Palenque, then onward to San Cristóbal de las Casas

Day 9 From San Cristóbal, cross the border into Guatemala and get as far as Huehuetenango, or preferably Quetzaltenango

Day 10 If it's Wednesday or Saturday, go to Chichicastenango and find a hotel room in preparation for the market (Thursday and Sunday). If it's Tuesday or Friday go to Sololá and catch the market there before continuing to Panajachel on Lake Atitlán for the night.

Day 11 Depending upon market days, visit Chichicastenango, Sololá, or Antigua (markets every day, but especially Monday, Thursday and Saturday)

Day 12 Start early from Antigua to the airport at Guatemala City for a flight to Flores, then on to Tikal

Day 13 Visit Tikal. Return to Flores for the night, or to Guatemala City

Day 14 From Flores, fly to Guatemala City or to Belize City for a flight back to Cancún, or fly directly home

Day 15 If you have an extra day, go by bus from Flores to Belize City on Day 14, then from Belize City to Chetumal and back to Cancún on Day 15. This is a lot of bus time, but it saves the cost of a flight and gives you a look at Belize.

Three Weeks

An itinerary of three weeks would follow the same general course as the one for two weeks, but would include more time in several spots. You'd have time to see all the Puuc Route sites including Kabah, Sayil, Labná, Xlapak and the Grutas de Loltún, and you could take a detour to Villahermosa to visit the Parque Museo La Venta. You would also have time for visits to Quiriguá on Guatemala's Atlantic Highway, and to Copán, in Honduras, as well as more time in Belize. Three weeks also gives you an extra day or two at the beach, whether on the Belizean cayes, Mexico's Caribbean coast, Cozumel or Cancún.

Four Weeks

A month is enough time to delve deeply into the sights, people and settlements along La Ruta Maya. You'd have time to visit interesting but seldom-visited places such as Toniná, near Ocosingo in Chiapas; Cobá, inland from Tulum; Kohunlich near Chetumal; Lake Bacalar, the gorgeous and virtually untouristed lake just north of Chetumal; Mountain Pine Ridge in Belize, as well as the southern part of that country. You'd have lots of time for treks on horseback into the forests surrounding San Cristóbal de las Casas, time to look for pink flamingos at Río Lagartos in northern Yucatán, time to take a boat out to the bird sanctuary of Isla Holbox, and time to relax in a cabaña on the beach south of Tulum. In fact, one could easily spend up to five or six weeks travelling all of La Ruta Maya.

VISAS & EMBASSIES

In general, it's easy to get into Mexico, Guatemala and Belize if you have a valid passport and look respectable. In Mexico and Guatemala you must obtain a tourist card, but this is both easy and cheap to do. Mexican and Guatemalan tourist cards are available at the border and at arrival airports, from many travel agencies and airlines serving these countries, and from Mexican and Guatemalan diplomatic and touristic missions abroad.

Mexican Tourist Card

The Mexican tourist card is free of charge (if someone demands payment for it, you're paying a 'tip' or bribe). Normally the official who processes your card at the border or airport will write '90 days' in the space for length of stay. As you present your card (it's actually a multicopy paper form) to the official, ask for three months or you're liable to get less time.

Don't lose your tourist card, as obtaining another one from the Migración (Immigration) officials is a long, frustrating, time-consuming process.

When you leave Mexico, you're supposed to turn in your tourist card. You will certainly have to produce it and hand it over if you leave the country by air, or if you cross into Guatemala. You may not be asked for it if you travel to one of the Mexican cities along the US border and then cross over into the USA.

Parent & Child If you are an adult travelling with a child under 18 years of age, the Mexican immigration officer will require you to show a notarised affidavit from the child's other parent permitting you to take the child into Mexico. This is to prevent separated, divorcing or divorced parents from absconding to Mexico with a child against the wishes – or legal actions – of the other parent. If both parents are travelling together with the child or children, there's no problem and no affidavit is needed.

If you have any questions about this procedure, talk them over in advance of your trip with a Mexican diplomatic representative. Don't wait until you're at the border or airport without an affidavit and the immigration officer won't permit you and the child to enter the country!

Guatemalan Tourist Card
The Guatemalan tourist card is valid for three months from the date of entry to Guatemala. It carries a fee of US$5, payable when you receive the form; anything else is a bribe. You need only a tourist card, not a visa, if you are a citizen of Austria, Belgium, Canada, Denmark, Finland, France, Germany, Holland, Italy, Israel, Japan, Luxembourg, Norway, Spain, Sweden, Switzerland or the USA. If you are a citizen of Australia, the UK, New Zealand or another British Commonwealth country, you should obtain a visa from a Guatemalan consulate before you arrive at the Guatemalan border or airport. Note especially that you cannot obtain a Guatemalan visa in Belize as Guatemala has no diplomatic representatives there; the closest Guatemalan consulate is in Chetumal, Mexico. The Guatemalan Consulate may require you to furnish two or three photographs of yourself for use on the documents. This is all because of the dispute over Belize, which Guatemala claims is an 'unliberated' department of its territory.

You will be asked to turn in your Guatemalan tourist card when you leave the country by air, or at the border crossing into any other country. If you cross into Honduras on a day pass to visit Copán, the Guatemalan Migración official will stamp your tourist card 'Cancelado' as you leave, then cancel the cancellation when you return. For information on entering Honduras to visit Copán, refer to the section on Copán.

Minors Travelling Alone If you are under 18 years of age and travelling alone, technically you must have a letter of permission signed by both your parents and witnessed by a Guatemalan consular official in order to enter Guatemala. Call a Guatemalan Consulate if you have questions about this.

Belizean Visitor's Permit
British subjects and citizens of Commonwealth countries, citizens the USA, and citizens of Belgium, Denmark, Finland, Greece, Holland, Mexico, Norway, Panama, Sweden, Switzerland, Tunisia, Turkey and Uruguay who have a valid passport and an onward or return airline ticket from Belize do not need to obtain a Belizean visa in advance. The rubber stamp made in your passport by the Belizean immigration official at the border or at the airport is your visitor's permit. If you look young, or grotty, or poverty-stricken, the immigration officer may demand to see your airline ticket out, and/or a sizable quantity of money or travellers' cheques before you're admitted.

Embassies & Consulates Abroad
Some of the consulates mentioned here are actually honorary consuls or consular agencies. These posts can issue tourist cards and visas, but they refer more complicated matters to the nearest full consulate, or to the embassy's consular section.

Because Belize is a small country and far from rich, its diplomatic affairs overseas are usually handled by the British embassies and consulates.

Australia
Mexican Embassy, 14 Perth Avenue, Yarralumla, Canberra ACT 2600 (☎ (062) 73-39-05/47/63)
Mexican Consulate, 49 Bay Street, Double Bay, Sydney, NSW 2028 (☎ (02) 326-1292/1311)
Guatemala does not maintain an embassy in Australia; contact the Guatemalan Embassy in Tokyo.

Austria
Mexican Embassy, Renngasse 4, 1010 Wien (Vienna) (☎ (222) 535-1776 to 79)
Guatemalan Embassy, Opernring 1/R/4/407, A-1010 Wien (☎ (222) 56-91-01)

Belgium
Mexican Embassy, rue Paul-Emile Jansson 6, 1050 Brussels (☎ (2) 648-2671/2703)
Mexican Consulate, Quellinstraat 42, Bus 2, 2018 Antwerpen (☎ 234-1861, 231-7316/7)
Guatemalan Embassy, Boulevard General Wahis 53, 1030 Brussels (☎ (322) 736-0340; fax 736-1889)

Belize
Mexican Embassy, 20 North Park Street, Belize City (☎ 45367, 44301, 78742)

Canada
Mexican Embassy, 206-130 Albert Street, Ottawa, ON KIP 5G4 (☎ (613) 233-8988/9272)
Mexican Consulate, 1000 Sherbrooke West, Suite 2215, Montréal, QC H3A 3G4 (☎ (514) 288-2502/4816)
Mexican Consulate, 60 Bloor Street West, Suite 203, Toronto, ON M4W 3B8 (☎ (416) 922-2718/3196)
Mexican Consulate, 310-625 Howe Street, Vancouver, BC V6C 2T6 (☎ (604) 684-3547/5725)
Guatemalan Embassy, 100 Goulbourn St, Ottawa, ON (☎ (613) 237-3941/2; fax 237-0492)
Guatemalan Consulate, 1130 Boulevard de Maisonneuve Ouest, Montréal, QC (☎ (514) 288-7327)

Costa Rica
Mexican Embassy, 7a Avenida No 1371, San José (☎ 22-55-28, 22-54-85)
Guatemalan Embassy, Carretera a Pavas, 250 metros al oueste del Restaurante Reggio, San José (☎ 31-40-74, 31-56-54; fax 31-66-45)

El Salvador
Mexican Embassy, Paseo General Escalon No 3832, San Salvador (☎ 98-10-84, 98-11-76)
Guatemalan Embassy, 15 Avenida Norte 135, San Salvador (☎ 22-29-03, 71-22-25; fax 21-30-18)

France
Mexican Embassy, 9 rue de Longchamps, 75116 Paris (☎ 45-53-99-34, 45-53-76-43)
Mexican Consulate, 4, rue Notre-Dame des Victoires, 75002 Paris (☎ 40-20-07-32/33, 42-61-51-80)
Guatemalan Embassy, 73 rue de Courcelles, 75008 Paris (☎ 47-63-90-83, 42-27-78-63; fax 47-54-02-06)

Germany
Mexican Embassy, Oxfordstrasse 12-16, 5300 Bonn 1 (☎ (228) 63-12-26 to 28)
Mexican Consulate, Neue Mainzer Strasse 57, 6000 Frankfurt 1 (☎ (069) 23-6134, 23-5709)
Mexican Consulate, Hallerstrasse 70-1, 2000 Hamburg 13 (☎ (040) 45-8950, 44-8774)
Guatemalan Embassy, Ziethenstrasse 16, 5300 Bonn Bad Godesberg (☎ (228) 35-15-79; fax 35-48-18)

Guatemala
Mexican Embassy, 16 Calle 1-45, Zona 10, Guatemala City (☎ (02) 68-02-02, 68-28-27)
Mexican Consulate, 13 Calle 7-30, Zona 9, Guatemala City (☎ (02) 36-65-04, 36-35-73, 31-81-65)

Honduras
Mexican Embassy, Calle Republica del Brasil Suroeste 2028, Colonia Palmira, Tegucigalpa (☎ 32-64-71, 32-40-39)
Guatemalan Embassy, Avenida Francisco Morazán 1374, Colonia Tepeyac, Tegucigalpa (fax 31-15-43)
Guatemalan Consulate, Villa Don Clemente, Colonia Los Angeles, Comayaguela (☎ 33-57-02)

Israel
Mexican Embassy, 14 Hey I'yar, Kikar Ha-Medina, Tel Aviv (☎ (03) 210-266 to 268)
Guatemalan Embassy, 74 Hey I'yar Street, Apt 6, Kikar Ha-Medina, 62198 Tel Aviv (☎ (3) 546-7372; fax (3) 546-7317)

Italy
Mexican Embassy, Via Lazzaro Spallanzani No 16, 00161 Roma (☎ (6) 440-2319/2323)
Mexican Consulate, Via Cappuccini 4, Milano (☎ (2) 349-8782)
Guatemalan Embassy, Via Dei Colli Della Farnesina 128, 00194 Roma (☎ 327-2632; fax 329-1639)

Japan
Mexican Embassy, 2-15-1, Nagata-cho, Chiyoda-Ku, Tokyo 100 (☎ (3) 581-2150, 581-1131 to 35)
Guatemalan Embassy, KOWA 38 Bldg Room 905, 41224 Nishi Azabu, Minato-Ku, Tokyo 105 (☎ (03) 400-1830, 20)

Mexico
Guatemalan Embassy, Colonia Lomas de Virreyes II, Mexico, DF (☎ (5) 540-7520, 520-9249, 202-7951; fax 202-1142)
Guatemalan Consulate, 1 Calle Central Oriente No 10, Ciudad Hidalgo, Chiapas
Guatemalan Consulate, 1 Calle Sur Poniente No 42, Comitán, Chiapas
Guatemalan Consulate, 3 Avenida Norte No 1, Tapachula, Chiapas
Guatemalan Honorary Consulate, Paseo de Montejo No 495, Mérida, Yucatán

Netherlands
Mexican Embassy, Nassauplein 17, 2585 EB The Hague (☎ (70) 60-29-00, 60-68-57)
Mexican Consulate, Groothandelsgebow, Stationsplein 45, Rotterdam (☎ (010) 126-084)

Nicaragua

Mexican Embassy, Km 45, Carretera a Masaya, Colonia 25 Varas Arriba (Altamira), Managua (☎ (2) 75380, 75275 to 79)

Guatemalan Embassy, Carretera a Masaya Km 11½, Managua (☎ (2) 79478, 79697; fax 79478)

Panama

Mexican Embassy, Calle 50 at Calle San José, Bank of America Building, fifth floor, Panama City 7 (☎ 63- 50-21)

Guatemalan Embassy, Calle 55 y Eric Delvalle, Edificio ADIR sixth floor, Apto 6B, El Cangrejo (Apdo Postal 2352 Zona 9A) (☎69-34-06/75; fax 23-19-22)

Spain

Mexican Embassy, Avenida Paseo de la Castellana No 93, seventh floor, Madrid 28046 (☎ (1) 456-1349/1496)

Mexican Consulate, Avenida Diagonal No 626, fourth floor, Barcelona 08021 (☎ (343) 200-6265, 201-1822)

Sweden

Mexican Embassy, Grevgatan 3, 114 53 Stockholm (☎ (8) 661-6175, 660-3970)

Guatemalan Consulate, Pukslagargatan 18, S-123 Alvsjoel (☎ (468) 99-21-15; fax 99-21-32)

Switzerland

Mexican Embassy, Bernestrasse 57, 3005 Berne (☎ (31) 43-18-14, 43-18-75)

Guatemalan Embassy, Zimmerwaldstrasse 47, 3122 Kehrsatz Berne (☎ (031) 54-36-91)

UK

Mexican Embassy, 8 Halkin St, London SW1 (☎ (071) 235-6393, 235-6351, 245-9030)

Guatemalan Embassy, 13 Fawcett St, London SW 10 (☎ (071) 351-3042; fax 376-5708)

USA

Apart from the embassies in Washington DC there are consular offices in many other cities, particularly in the border states:

Arizona

Mexican Consulate, 515 10th St, Douglas, AZ 85607 (☎ (602) 364-2275)

Mexican Consulate, 135 Terrace Ave, Nogales, AZ 85621 (☎ (602) 287-2521)

Mexican Consulate, 700 East Jefferson, Suite 150, Phoenix, AZ 85034 (☎ (602) 242-7398/9)

California

Belizean Honorary Consul, Mr Ernesto Castillo, 1650 South Wilton Place, Los Angeles, CA 90019 (☎ (213) 385- 6499)

Mexican Consulate, 331 West Second Street, Calexico, CA 92231 (☎ (619) 357-3863/3880)

Mexican Consulate, 2839 Mariposa St, Fresno, CA 93721 (☎ (209) 233-3065/9770)

Mexican Consulate, 125 East Paseo de la Plaza, Suite 300, Los Angeles, CA 90012 (☎ (213) 624-9387/8)

Guatemalan Consulate, 548 South Spring St, Los Angeles, CA 90013 (☎ (213) 489-1891)

Mexican Consulate, 1506 South Street, Sacramento, CA 95814 (☎ (916) 446-4696/9024)

Mexican Consulate, 588 West 6th St, San Bernardino, CA 92401 (☎ (714) 888-2500/4700)

Mexican Consulate, 1333 Front Street, Suite 200, San Diego, CA 92101 (☎ (619) 231-8414/8427)

Mexican Consulate, 870 Market St, Suite 528, San Francisco, CA 94102 (☎ (415) 392-5554)

Guatemalan Consulate, 870 Market Street, Suite 528, San Francisco, CA 94102 (☎ (415) 392-5554 to 56, 392- 2897)

Mexican Consulate, 380 North First Street, Suite 102, San Jose, CA 95112 (☎ (408) 294-3414/5)

Colorado

Mexican Consulate, 707 Washington Street, Denver, CO 80203 (☎ (303) 830-0523/0704)

Guatemalan Honorary Consulate, 3109 East Warren Ave, Denver, CO 80210 (☎ (303) 756-2010)

Florida

Belizean Honorary Consul, Mr Theodore Gonzalez Fr, 8244 NW 68th Street, Miami, FL 33166 (☎ (305) 477-3636)

Mexican Consulate, 780 NW LeJeune Road, Suite 525, Miami, FL 33126 (☎ (305) 441-8780 to 83)

Guatemalan Consulate, 25 Southeast Second Ave, Miami, FL 33131 (☎ (305) 377-3190)

Georgia

Mexican Consulate, 410 South Tower, One CNN Center, Atlanta, GA 30303-2705 (☎ (404) 688-3258/3261)

Illinois

Mexican Consulate, 300 North Michigan Avenue, second floor, Chicago, IL 60601 (☎ (312) 855-1380 to 84)

Guatemalan Consulate, 333 North Michigan Ave, Chicago, IL 60601 (☎ (312) 332-1587)

Louisiana

Belizean Honorary Consul, Mr Salvador A Figueroa, 837 Gravier Street, Suite 310, New Orleans, LA 70112 (☎ (504) 523-7750)

Mexican Consulate, 1140 World Trade Center Building, 2 Canal St, New Orleans, LA 70130 (☎ (504) 522- 3596/7)

Guatemalan Consulate, International Trade Mart Suite 1601, New Orleans, LA 70130 (☎ (504) 525-0013)

Massachusetts

Mexican Consulate, 20 Park Plaza, Suite 321, Statler Building, Boston, MA 02116 (☎ (617) 426-4942/8782)

Michigan

Belizean Honorary Consul, Dr Lennox Pike, 27166 Selkirk, Southfield, MI 48706 (☎ (313) 559-7407)

Mexican Consulate, 1515 Book Building, Washington Boulevard at West Grand River, Detroit, MI 48226 (☎ (313) 965-1868/9)

Missouri

Mexican Consulate, 823 Walnut St, Kansas City, MO 64106 (☎ (816) 421-5956)

Mexican Consulate, 1015 Locust Street, Suite 922, St Louis, MO 63101 (☎ (314) 436-3233/3426)

New Mexico

Mexican Consulate, Western Bank Building, 401 Fifth Street, NW, Albuquerque, NM 87102 (☎ (505) 247- 2139/2147)

New York

Mexican Consulate, 8 East 41st St, New York, NY 10017 (☎ (212) 689-0456 to 60)

Pennsylvania

Mexican Consulate, Independence Mall East, 575 Philadelphia Bourse Building, Philadelphia, PA 19106 (☎ (215) 922-4262/3834)

Texas

Belizean Honorary Consul, Mr Al Dugan, 1415 Louisiana, Suite 3100, Houston, TX 77002 (☎ (713) 658-0207)

Mexican Consulate, 200 East Sixth Street, Suite 200, Hannig Row Building, Austin, TX 78701 (☎ (512) 478- 2300/2866/9031)

Mexican Consulate, Elizabeth & East Seventh Streets, Brownsville, TX 78520 (☎ (512) 542-4431/2051)

Mexican Consulate, 800 North Shoreline, One Shoreline Plaza, 410 North Tower, Corpus Christi, TX 78401 (☎ (512) 882-3375/5964)

Mexican Consulate, 1349 Empire Central, No 100, Dallas, TX 75247 (☎ (214) 630-7341/2024)

Mexican Consulate, 1010 South Main St, Del Rio, TX 78840 (☎ (512) 775-2352/9451)

Mexican Consulate, 140 Adams St, Eagle Pass, TX 78852 (☎ (512) 773-9255/6)

Mexican Consulate, 910 East San Antonio St, PO Box 812, El Paso, TX 79901 (☎ (915) 533-3644/5)

Mexican Consulate, 4200 Montrose Boulevard, Suite 120, Houston, TX 77006 (☎ (713) 524-4861/2300)

Mexican Consulate, 1612 Farragut St, Laredo, TX 78040 (☎ (512) 723-6360/1741)

Mexican Consulate, 1220 Broadway Avenue, Lubbock, TX 79401 (☎ (806) 765-8816)

Mexican Consulate, 1418 Beech Street, No 102-104, McAllen, TX 78501 (☎ (512) 686-0243/4)

Mexican Consulate, 730 O'Riety Street, Presidio, TX 79845 (☎ (915) 229-3745)

Mexican Consulate, 127 Navarro St, San Antonio, TX 78205 (☎ (512) 227-9145/6)

Utah

Mexican Consulate, 182 South 600 East, Suite 202, Salt Lake City, UT 84102 (☎ (801) 521-8502/3)

Washington State

Mexican Consulate, 1411 Fourth Avenue, Fourth Avenue Building, Suite 410, Seattle, WA 98101 (☎ (206) 343-3047, 682-8996)

Washington DC

Mexican Embassy, 2829 16th Street NW, Washington, DC 20009 (☎ (202) 234-6000 to 3)

Guatemalan Embassy, 2220 R St NW, Washington, DC (☎ (202) 745-4952)

Embassy of Belize, 3400 International Drive NW, Suite 2- J, Washington DC 20008-3098 (☎ (202) 363-4505; fax (202) 362-7468)

CUSTOMS

Customs officers only get angry and excited about a few things: drugs, weapons, large amounts of currency, automobiles and other expensive items which might be sold while you're in the country. Don't take illegal drugs or any sort of firearm across these borders. If you want to take a hunting rifle across a border, get a permit from the country's diplomatic mission in advance.

Importing Motor Vehicles

To take a motor vehicle (car, motorcycle, boat, etc) into Mexico, Guatemala or Belize you will need: the car's current valid registration; proof that you own it (if the registration is in a different name) or, if you don't own it, a notarised affidavit of authorisation from the car's owner stating that you are allowed to take the car out of the USA; your current valid driving licence; and a temporary import permit from the local authorities.

Temporary import permits are normally issued for free at the border when you enter, but the issuance of a permit may require prior purchase of liability insurance. (See the section on Motor Vehicle Insurance for details.) In Mexico the permits are normally valid for 90 days; in Guatemala it's 30 days, in Belize the same.

You must have a permit for each vehicle that you bring into Mexico. For example, if you have a motorcycle attached to your car, you must also have a permit for the motorcycle, but there is a catch: one person cannot have more than one permit even if that person owns both vehicles. Consequently, another person travelling with you must obtain the second permit. As with all rules of this sort, though, they are not written in stone. Changes, exceptions and neglect of the rule are not unheard of, especially if the official who might enforce the rule has somehow been induced to do otherwise in the past.

Another rule for drivers intending to travel in Mexico: you cannot leave the country without your vehicle even if it breaks down, unless you obtain permission from either the Registro Federal de Vehículos (Federal Registry of Vehicles) in Mexico City or a Hacienda (Treasury Department) office in another city or town. Similar rules apply for Guatemala and Belize.

Don't drive someone else's car across the border. The car will be registered on your tourist card or in your passport, and you will not be permitted to leave the country without taking the car or paying a huge customs import duty. If you drive into Mexico, officials will take your tourist card and issue you a single document which serves as both motor vehicle permit and tourist card; both you and the car must leave Mexico at the same time, surrendering the document as you leave.

Luggage Inspection

Normally the customs officer will not look seriously in your luggage, and may not look at all. At some border points the amount of search is inversely proportional to the amount of 'tip' you have provided; that is, big tip no search, no tip big search. As for expensive items, if you have an expensive camera, or electronic gizmo, or jewellery, there is a risk that they may be seen as leverage, or be deemed as liable for duty at Customs' discretion. Be prepared and be firm but flexible. (See the section on Crossing Borders for more information.) Whatever you do, keep it all formal and polite. Anger, surliness or impoliteness can get you thrown out of the country, or into jail, or worse.

CROSSING BORDERS

Most of the time and at most entry points, this is a breeze. If you fly into any of these countries you should have few, if any, hassles. If you cross at border points, you may run into other situations. There are a few things you ought to know.

La Mordida

Border officials in Latin American countries sometimes request small 'tips' or unofficial 'fees' from travellers at the border. Usually the *mordida*, the 'bite', is put on you in an official tone of voice: the officer will scribble something on your tourist card, or in a ledger, or stamp your passport, or do some other little action, then say, 'Too dallah'. When crossing from one Latin American country to another, the officials on both sides of the border may play this little game, causing you to part with a quantity of cash before you're finally through the formalities. There are several things you can do to avoid paying.

The first is to look very important by dressing in a suit and tie or other such intimidating clothing. If you are male, wearing dark sunglasses (a favourite expression of machismo, or manliness) can help.

The second is to scowl quietly and act worldly-wise. Scowl all you want, but whatever you do, keep everything formal. Never, *ever* raise your voice, mumble a curse, get angry, or verbally confront a Latin American official. This will get you nowhere – except into deep trouble. Act quietly superior and unruffled at all times.

The third thing is to ask for a receipt, *un recibo*. Some fees, such as charging for the disinfection of your car as you cross into Guatemala or Honduras, are official and legitimate. If the fee is legitimate, you'll be given an official-looking receipt; often the official will show you the receipt booklet when he makes the request, to prove to you that the fee is legitimate. If you don't get a receipt, you've succumbed to the mordida, a tip or bribe.

The fourth thing is to offer some weird currency such as Thai baht or even Norwegian kroner or Dutch guilders or Australian dollars – anything but US dollars or the currency of either of the countries at the border. Border officials are usually used to seeing only US dollars (and some Canadian ones), Mexican pesos, Belizean dollars,

Honduran lempiras and Guatemalan quetzals. At the sight of strange money the officer will probably drop the request. If he doesn't, or if the fee turns out to be legitimate, 'search' for several minutes in your belongings and come up with the dollars you need. In the unlikely event that the official will accept the unusual currency, inflate its value, declaring that a nearly worthless note is actually worth big bucks.

MOTOR VEHICLE INSURANCE

American, Canadian or any other 'foreign' motor vehicle liability insurance policies are not recognised as valid by the governments of Mexico, Guatemala or Belize. In each of these countries you must buy local insurance; thus if you drive your vehicle into all three countries, you will have to buy three separate policies.

Mexico

Though not strictly required in Mexico, it is foolish to travel without Mexican liability insurance because if there is an accident, and if you cannot show a valid insurance policy, you will be arrested and not permitted to leave the locale of the accident until all claims are settled, which could be weeks or months. Mexico's legal system follows the Napoleonic model in which all persons involved in an incident are assumed to be guilty until proven innocent; trial is by a court of three judges, not by a jury. Your embassy can do little to help you in such a situation, except to tell you how stupid you were to drive without local insurance.

Mexican insurance is sold in US, Guatemalan and Belizean towns near the Mexican border. Approaching the border from the USA you will see billboards advertising offices selling Mexican policies. At the busiest border-crossing points (Tijuana, Mexicali, Nogales, Agua Prieta, Ciudad Juárez, Nuevo Laredo and Matamoros), there are insurance offices open 24 hours a day.

Prices for Mexican policies are set by law in Mexico, so you can do little in the way of bargain-hunting. Instead of discounts (which cannot be offered), insurance offices offer incentives such as free guidebooks and/or maps, connections to automobile clubs (American Automobile Association, etc), and other treats.

Mexican motor vehicle insurance policies are priced so as to penalise the short-term buyer with extremely high rates. You may pay almost as much for a one-month policy (about US$200, average) as you would for a full year's policy (about US$215).

Guatemala

The situation in Guatemala is similar to that in Mexico. Liability insurance, available at insurance offices in the border towns, is a good buy because it saves you from a lot of red tape if you injure someone or their property. Rates are lower than in Mexico.

Belize

Liability insurance is required in Belize, and you must have it for the customs officer to approve the temporary importation of your car. It can usually be bought at booths just across the border in Belize for about US$1 per day. Note that the booths are generally closed on Sunday, meaning no insurance is sold that day, meaning no temporary import permits are issued.

MONEY

When travelling along La Ruta Maya, it's useful to carry your money in US dollars or US dollar travellers' cheques. Though you should be able to change other sorts of currency (especially Canadian dollars) in major banks in large cities, it can require some time-consuming hassles, and may be supremely difficult in smaller cities and towns. In many parts of the region (especially Mexico) it can take a lot of time just to change US dollars, let alone some currency that is, to a local bank teller, highly exotic.

Try to spend all of your local currency before you cross a border because the exchange rates between countries are often terrible. For example, if you exchange pesos for quetzals in Guatemala the rate will be very low; the same thing happens if you exchange quetzals for pesos in Mexico, and ditto for quetzals or pesos to Belizean dollars.

It is often difficult or impossible to exchange travellers' cheques on weekends. Friday should be one of your routine money-changing days so that you'll be supplied with cash for the weekend.

Mexican Peso

The Mexican unit of currency is the peso (MX$), further divided into 100 centavos, although centavos are now worth so little that they are not used. Mexican coins come in denominations of 20 and 50 centavos, and one, five, 10, 50, 100, 500 and 1000 pesos, and perhaps even larger denominations in the future. Bills (notes) are in denominations of 1000, 2000, 5000, 10,000, 20,000, 50,000 pesos and up, and as well-worn, rarely encountered notes of 50, 100 and 500 pesos.

The dollar sign ($) is used to indicate pesos in Mexico, so if you sit down to a plate of tacos and get a bill for $5000, don't panic – it's only pesos, and cheap at that. Since there is often confusion in tourist areas about whether a price is in pesos or dollars, with both currencies using the same sign, prices are often written as '$5000 mn', that is, '5000 pesos, *moneda nacional* (Mexican national currency); or as '$5 Dlls' ie, five US dollars.

Money exchange is at free market floating rates which may change daily. In the last decade or so, the value of the peso has fallen dramatically. Since 1980 it's gone from MX$22 = US$1 to more than MX$1300 =

US$1 in 1987 and MX$3000 = US$1 in 1990.

In such heavily touristed areas as Cancún and Cozumel you can often spend greenback dollars as easily as pesos (they go just as fast!) at hotels, restaurants and shops. Most of the time you won't get as good an exchange rate as if you changed your dollars for pesos at a bank; sometimes the rate in hotels, restaurants and shops will be downright outrageous. In other establishments, however, dollars are accepted at an exchange rate as good as or better than that of the banks as an inducement to get you to spend your money there.

Guatemalan Quetzal

The Guatemalan quetzal (Q), is named for the country's gorgeous but rare national bird; the quetzal is divided into 100 centavos. There are coins of one, five, 10 and 25 centavos, and bills (notes) of 50 centavos, one, five, 10, 20, 50 and 100 quetzals.

The quetzal and the US dollar were exactly equal in value for many years, but in the 1980s the quetzal slipped in value, and is now worth much less. As in Mexico, US dollars are the currency to take to Guatemala, as any other currency, even Canadian dollars, can cause delays and problems when being exchanged for quetzals.

Many establishments will accept cash dollars instead of quetzals, usually at the bank exchange rate, or even better, but sometimes worse. Even so, you'll find yourself exchanging your dollars for quetzals at banks because shopkeepers, restaurateurs and hotel desk clerks may not want to deplete their supplies of ready quetzals and take on dollars, which they must then take to the bank.

There's a healthy unofficial exchange market for dollars, paying slightly better than the bank rate. The national hotbed of this activity is around the main post office in Guatemala City. At most border crossing points you may find yourself buying quetzals unofficially as there are no banks; at the airport, the bank exchange desks are usually open only during banking hours, and you may find yourself buying your first quetzals (or your last, to pay the US$10-equivalent exit tax) at a shop in the terminal.

Belizean Dollar

The Belizean dollar (BZ$) bears the portrait of Queen Elizabeth II, and is divided into 100 cents. Coins are of one, five, 10, 25 and 50 cents; bills (notes) are of one, two, five, 10, 20, 50 and 100 dollars. You can exchange US and Canadian dollars and pounds sterling at any bank; other currencies are difficult to exchange. Cash US dollars are accepted virtually everywhere, and many establishments will also accept US dollar travellers' cheques.

Because US dollars are so widely accepted, there's a problem with quoting prices. People quote prices in dollars, and you must make sure that you know whether the dollars are US or Belizean, otherwise you might end up being surprised with a bill twice as high as you had anticipated. You may find yourself asking 'US or Belize?' dozens of times each day. Often people will quote prices as '20 dollars Belize, 10 dollars US' just to make it clear.

Credit Cards

Major credit cards such as VISA and Master-Card (Eurocard, Access) are accepted at all airline and car rental companies, and at the larger hotels and restaurants everywhere along La Ruta Maya; American Express cards are often accepted at the fancier and larger places, and at some smaller ones.

In Mexico, many smaller establishments will readily accept your card, even for charges as little as US$5 or US$10; Cancún, for example, lives on credit cards, and even has some telephones which accept these cards for long-distance (trunk) calls. In Belize, smaller establishments which accept credit cards may add a surcharge to your bill when doing so.

Exchange Rates

The rates for the Guatemalan and Belizean currencies are closely linked to the US dollar, and should remain fairly stable. The Mexican peso is subject to daily fluctuations and periodic large devaluations, and will no doubt be lower in value (ie, you'll get more pesos for your dollars, pounds, etc) by the time you arrive.

Foreign	Mexico	Guatemala	Belize
US$1	MX$3000	Q5.00	BZ$2.00
CN$1	MX$2580	Q4.25	BZ$1.72
UK£1	MX$5910	Q9.80	BZ$3.94
A$1	MX$231	Q3.85	BZ$1.54
NZ$1	MX$1800	Q3.00	BZ$1.20
DM1	MX$2040	Q3.50	BZ$1.36
L100	MX$2310	Q3.85	BZ$1.54

Costs

Bottom End For the very budget-conscious traveller, Guatemala offers the best bargains on accommodation, food, transportation and things to buy. Mexico is next, with low prices in the smaller towns but surprisingly higher prices in resorts such as Cancún and Cozumel. Belize, in general, is unusually expensive, especially considering what you get for your money. Though a middle-range traveller can do alright in Belize, the low-budget person may find money disappearing at an alarming rate.

Mexico Travel in Mexico can be quite cheap, but there are several factors to keep in mind. First is the peso, which is subject to high inflation and periodic large devaluations. Sometimes these devaluations are linked more to politics than to economics. When I was researching prices for this guide, it seemed to me that the peso was overvalued and that prices in Mexico were higher than they should be. This may be a sign that another large devaluation is about to occur. If you travel there before the devaluation occurs, you'll find Mexico to be expensive for what you get; after the devaluation, everything will seem marvellously cheap. I have no control over the value of the peso so the prices quoted in this guide, though completely accurate when I researched them, are subject to change, sometimes by a considerable amount.

The second factor which affects prices in Mexico is whether or not you are in a touristy area. Cancún and Cozumel are the two most expensive places in the country, far more expensive than Mexico City or even Acapulco. Small towns such as Tizimin and Izamal, not being heavily touristed, are much, much cheaper. Cities like Mérida and San Cristóbal de las Casas offer a good range of prices, with good value for money.

Taking both these factors into account, a single budget traveller staying in bottom-end or lower middle-range accommodation and eating two meals a day in restaurants may pay US$8 to US$15 per day, on average, for those basics. Add in the other costs of travel (roughly US$1 per hour on long-distance buses, snacks, purified water and soft drinks, admission to archaeological sites, etc), and you may spend more like US$12 to US$20 per day. If there are two or more of you sharing accommodation, costs per person come down considerably. Double rooms are often only a few dollars more than singles,

and triples or quadruples only a little more expensive than doubles.

Guatemala Prices here are a low-budget traveller's dream come true: beds in little pensions for US$3 per person in a double, camping places for much less, elaborate markets selling fruits and snacks for pennies, cheap eateries called *comedores* offering one-plate meals for US$2 or less, and bus trips at less than US$1 per hour. If you want a bit more comfort, you can readily move up to rooms with private showers and meals in nicer restaurants, and still pay only US$15 per day for room and two – or even three – meals.

Belize Though a poor country, Belize is surprisingly expensive. A small domestic economy and a large proportion of imports keeps prices high. That fried chicken dinner which cost US$3 in Guatemala costs US$5 in Belize, and is no better. That very basic waterless pension room, cheap in Guatemala and Mexico, costs US$7 to US$9 per person on Caye Caulker. You will find it difficult to live for less than US$15 per day for room and three meals in Belize; US$20 is a more realistic bottom-end figure, and US$25 makes life a lot easier.

Tipping
In general, staff in the smaller, cheaper places don't expect much in the way of tips, while those in the expensive resort establishments expect you to be lavish in your largesse. Tipping in Cancún and Cozumel is up to American standards of 15% to 20%; elsewhere, 10% is usually sufficient; in a small eatery you can get away without a tip.

Bargaining
Though you can attempt to haggle down the price of a hotel room, these rates are usually set and fairly firm, especially during the busy winter season. Off-season price reductions are sometimes negotiable.

For handicrafts and other souvenirs, and for anything in an open- air market, haggling is the rule, and you may pay many times the going price if you pay the first price quoted. The exception to this rule comes when you buy handicrafts from some Chiapan and Guatemalan artisans' cooperatives, which set their prices and won't budge from them.

Consumer Taxes

Mexico has a value-added tax called the Impuesto de Valor Agregado (IVA), usually referred to as *el IVA* (ehl EE-bah). By law the tax must be *included* in virtually any price quoted to you; it should not be added afterwards. Signs in shops and notices on restaurant menus usually reiterate this fact as *incluye el IVA* or *IVA incluido*. When asking prices, it's still not a bad idea to confirm that the tax will not be added to the price later.

Guatemala's IVA is 7%, and there's also a 10% tax on hotel rooms to pay for the activities of the Guatemala Tourist Commission (INGUAT), so a total tax of 17% will be added to your hotel bill. The very cheapest places usually ignore the tax and don't collect it from you.

In Belize, a tax of 5% is added to your bill for hotel room, meals and drinks, but there is no value-added tax.

A departure tax equivalent to approximately US$10 is levied in each of these countries for travellers departing by air to foreign destinations. Exit tax at Belizean land border crossing points is BZ$1 (US$0.50).

Student Discounts

Discounts for foreign students are virtually unknown along La Ruta Maya. A few places offer small discounts on admission fees to students under 26 who hold a card from either the Servicio Educativo de Turismo de los Estudiantes y la Juventud de México (SETEJ) or Consejo Nacional de Recursos para la Atención de la Juventud (CREA). These cards also entitle you to youth hostel membership. CREA cards can be obtained at most youth hostels in Mexico.

CLIMATE & WHEN TO GO

You can travel La Ruta Maya at any time of year; there is no off season. The Caribbean's pellucid waters are always invitingly warm, the beaches always good for sunning. But the topography of La Ruta Maya is varied, from low-lying Yucatán to the lofty volcanoes of Chiapas and Guatemala, so you will encounter a variety of climatic conditions whenever you go.

The height of the tourist season is in winter, from Christmas to the end of March. You should reserve middle and top-end hotel rooms in advance for Mérida, Uxmal, Cancún, Cozumel, Isla Mujeres, the resorts of Mexico's Caribbean coast, and Belize's cayes during this time. For bottom-end rooms, try to get to your destination as early in the day as possible so you can nail down a room at the price you want.

Hurricane season in the Caribbean, including Cancún, Cozumel, Isla Mujeres, Mexico's Caribbean coast, and all of the Belizean coast and its cayes, is from July to November, with most of the activity from mid-August to mid-September. Normally there are at least a few tropical storms in the area, which may or may not affect your travel plans. About once every decade, somebody gets clobbered, as Cancún was by Hurricane Gilbert in 1988. If there's a full-blown hurricane predicted for where you are, go somewhere else – fast! Sitting out a hurricane may look exciting in the movies, but hurricanes are always followed by lack of housing, transportation, electricity, water, food, medicine, etc, which can be very unpleasant – even unphotogenic – not to mention perilous.

Yucatán Peninsula

It is always hot in Yucatán, often reaching temperatures around 40° C (100° F) in the heat of the day. From May to October, the rainy season makes it hot and humid. From October to May it is hot and dry. There are occasional showers even in the dry season. The violent but brief storms called *nortes* can roll in any afternoon, their black clouds, high winds and torrents of rain followed within an hour by bright sun and utterly blue sky.

The dry season is generally preferred for travel in Yucatán because you needn't dodge the raindrops, the heat is not as muggy and, most importantly, it's winter in most of North America and Europe! November and early December are perhaps the best times as there are fewer tourists and prices are low. From mid-December to April is the busy winter tourism season when premium prices prevail, with surcharges around Christmas, New Year and Easter. May, the end of the dry season, and June, when the rains begin, are the hottest and muggiest months. If you have a choice of months, don't choose these. July and August are hot, not too rainy, and busy with the summer travel crowd. September and October are pretty good for travel as the traffic decreases, and so do the rains.

Tabasco & Chiapas
The low-lying state of Tabasco is always hot and muggy, but more pleasant in the dry season (October to May) than the rainy season. As in Yucatán, it's always hot here; unlike Yucatán, this area is not seasonally crowded with tourists.

Mountainous northern Chiapas can get lots of rain in summer, but at least it's cool at the higher altitudes. In winter the air is cool most of the time, warming up considerably on sunny days, though many days are overcast. In the *tierra fría* around San Cristóbal de las Casas, mornings and evenings are usually chilly (a thrill after the sticky heat of Palenque!), the nights downright cold (though frost is rare), especially if it's raining, which it often is from May to October.

The Soconusco, the Pacific Slope in Chiapas and Guatemala, is hot and humid all the time, and frequently rainy in summer.

Guatemala
In the Guatemalan highlands, temperatures can get down to freezing at night in the mountains, and days can be dank and chill during the rainy season, though warm and positively delightful in the dry season from October to May. Guatemala's Pacific coast is tropical, rainy, hot and humid, as is its Caribbean coast, with temperatures often reaching 32°C to 38°C (90°F to 100°F), and

almost constant high humidity, abating only a little in the dry season.

The vast jungle lowland of El Petén has a climate and topography like that of Yucatán, hot and humid or hot and dry, depending upon the season.

Belize
Belize, like Yucatán, is tropical lowland, though in the western part of the country the Maya Mountains rise to almost 1000 metres. Though it is comfortably warm during the day in the mountains, cooling off a bit at night, the rest of the country is hot and humid day and night most of the year. In the rainforests of southern Belize the humidity is very high because of the large amount of rainfall (almost four metres per year). Out on the cayes, tropical breezes waft through the shady palm trees constantly, providing natural air-conditioning; on the mainland, you swelter. As with the rest of the area, the dry season from October to May is the better time to travel, but prices are lower and lodgings on the cayes easier to find if you avoid the busy winter season from mid-December to April. Remember hurricane season, from July to November. Belize City was badly damaged by hurricanes, with heavy loss of life, in 1931, 1961 and 1978.

WHAT TO BRING
Clothing
Local people along La Ruta Maya tend to dress informally but conservatively. Most men of all classes, from taxi drivers to business executives, wear long trousers and sports shirts or *guayaberas*, the fancy shirts decorated with tucks and worn outside the belt, which substitute for jacket and tie in this warm climate. Women dress traditionally, in long white Mayan dresses with embroidered collars or bodices, or stylishly in dresses or blouses and skirts. The local people do not expect you to dress in the same manner. They allow for foreign ways, but know that shorts and T-shirts are the marks of the tourist.

In lowland areas such as Yucatán,

Tabasco, El Petén and Belize, both men and women should always have a hat, sunglasses and sunblock cream. If your complexion is particularly fair or if you burn easily, consider wearing light cotton shirts with long sleeves and light cotton slacks. Otherwise, men can wear light cotton trousers or shorts, tennis shoes or sandals and T-shirts, although more conservative wear is in order when visiting churches. Women can dress similarly except off the beaten track in villages unaccustomed to tourists. In general, it is better for women to dress somewhat more conservatively when in town – no shorts, tank tops, etc. Cancún is the exception; in Cancún, wear whatever you like. Bring a light sweater or jacket for evening boat rides. Blue jeans are often uncomfortably heavy in these warm, humid areas.

In the highlands of Chiapas and Guatemala you will need warmer clothing – a pair of slacks or jeans for sure – plus a sweater or jacket, perhaps both if you plan to be out for long periods in the evening or early morning. A light rain-jacket, preferably a loose-fitting poncho, is good to have from October to May, and is a necessity from May to October.

Other Items

Toiletries such as shampoo, shaving cream, razors, soap and toothpaste are readily available in all but the smallest villages. You should bring your own contact lens solution, tampons, contraceptives and deodorant.

Don't forget the all-important insect repellent containing DEET (see the Health section), which may be easier to find at home than along La Ruta Maya. Besides, if you buy it before you leave home, you'll have it when you need it.

Other items which you might find useful are: flashlight (torch) for exploring caves, pyramids, and your hotel room when the electricity fails, disposable lighter (for the same reasons), pocket knife, two to three metres of cord, diving or snorkelling equipment, fishing equipment, a small sewing kit, money belt or pouch, lip balm, and a small Spanish-English dictionary.

TOURIST OFFICES

Government tourist offices (federal, state and local) are a fair source of information. They have the latest information on the most visited areas and on official tourist matters such as tourist card requirements. They can also issue tourist cards and automobile permits. If they cannot issue what you need or answer your query, then they can usually direct you to someone who can. For Belize, write to the nearest Belizean Embassy or Consulate. If you write to the Belize Tourist Board, (☎ (2) 77213, 73255), PO Box 325, Belize City, Belize, allow several months for a reply.

Canada
Mexican Government Tourist Office, 1 Place Ville Marie, Suite 2409, Montréal, Québec H3B 3M9 (☎ (514) 871- 1052)
Mexican Government Tourist Office, 181 University Ave, Suite 1112, Toronto, Ontario M5H 3M7 (☎ (416) 364- 2455)
France
Mexican Government Tourist Office, 34 Ave George V, 75008 Paris (☎ (1) 47-20-69-07)
Germany
Mexican Government Tourist Office, Wiesenhüttenplatz 26, D600 Frankfurt Am Main 1 (☎ (69) 25-34-13)
Italy
Mexican Government Tourist Office, Via Barberini No 3, 00187 Rome (☎ (6) 474-2986)
Spain
Mexican Government Tourist Office, Calle de Velázquez No 126, Madrid 28006 (☎ (1) 261- 1827)
UK
Mexican Government Tourist Office, 7 Cork St, London W1X 1PB (☎ (071) 734-1058)
USA
Mexican Government Tourist Office, 10100 Santa Monica Blvd, Suite 2204, Los Angeles, CA 90067 (☎ (213) 203-8151)
Mexican Government Tourist Office, Two Illinois Center, 233 North Michigan Ave, Suite 1413, Chicago, IL 60601 (☎ (312) 565-2785)
Mexican Government Tourist Office, 405 Park Ave, Suite 1002, New York, NY 10022 (☎ (212) 755- 7261)
Mexican Government Tourist Office, 2707 North Loop West, Suite 450, Houston, TX 77008 (☎ (713) 880-5153)

BUSINESS HOURS

In Mexico, banks are open from 9 am to 1.30 pm, Monday to Friday. Businesses are generally open from 9 am to 2 pm and 4 to 7 pm, Monday to Friday; various sorts of shops are open on Saturday as well. Shops and offices close for siesta from roughly 1 or 2 to 4 or 5 pm, then open again until 7 or 8 pm.

In Guatemala, banks are generally open from 8.30 or 9 am to 2 pm Monday to Thursday, 8.30 am to 2.30 pm on Friday. A few banks in Guatemala City may have longer hours, till 3 pm, with a few walk- up teller windows open till 4.30 pm. Shops open about 9 am and close for lunch around 12.30 or 1 pm, reopening an hour or so later, and remaining open till about 6 pm, Monday to Friday; on Saturday many shops close for the day at 12.30 or 1 pm. Government office hours are officially 7.30 am to 3.30 pm, though there's some absenteeism around lunchtime.

In Belize, banking hours depend upon the individual bank, but most are open Monday to Friday from 8 am to noon or 1 pm; some are also open from 1 to 3 pm, and many have extra hours on Friday from 3 to 6 pm. Most banks and many businesses and shops are closed on Wednesday afternoon. Shops are usually open from 8 am to noon Monday to Saturday, and from 1 to 4 pm on Monday, Tuesday, Thursday and Friday. Some shops have evening hours from 7 to 9 pm on those days as well.

CULTURAL EVENTS
Holidays

You will notice that Sunday is indeed a day of rest along La Ruta Maya. Local people put on their best clothes, go to church, then spend the afternoon relaxing in the parks or strolling along the streets. Most businesses are closed, though some towns and villages have Sunday markets. Bus services may be curtailed. In the big resorts (Cancún, Cozumel, Isla Mujeres), Sundays are not observed so strictly.

The big national holidays are dictated by the Roman Catholic Church calendar. Christmas, and Holy Week (Semana Santa) leading up to Easter, are the most important, though the celebrations are often as much Mayan shamanist in spirit as Christian. Hotels and buses are very busy in Mexico and packed throughout Guatemala during Holy Week, especially in the towns which have particularly elaborate and colourful celebrations, such as Antigua.

January

Though the first two weeks of January see somewhat fewer hordes of tourists flocking to Cancún after the Christmas rush, the busy winter sun-and-fun season begins in earnest by mid- January. The weather is dry.

1 January – New Year's Day is a legal holiday in Mexico, Guatemala and Belize.
6 January – Día de los Reyes Magos, or Day of the Three Wisemen. Mexicans exchange Christmas presents on this day, in memory of the kings who brought gifts to baby Jesus.
Last Sunday in January – Día de la Inmaculada Concepción, or Festival of the Immaculate Conception. In Yucatán, nine days of devotions lead up to a secular festival including a dance which features a pig's head decorated with offerings of flowers, ribbons, bread, liquor and cigarettes. The traditional Yucatecan *jaranas* dances are usually performed as well.

February

Height of the tourist season, with most hotel rooms filled, most rental cars rented, and most other activities in full swing.

Religious Holidays – Late February or early March is when Carnival comes, preceding Lent, the start of which is determined by the date of Easter. Carnival festivities are important all along La Ruta Maya, and include parades with fantastic floats, folk dancing, athletic competitions and everybody dressing up in costumes. Carnival begins in earnest on the weekend preceding the beginning of Lent. The final day of Carnival is often called Mardi Gras (Fat Tuesday), the last day on which observant Catholics are allowed to eat meat. Fat Tuesday is followed by Ash Wednesday, first of the 40 days of Lent leading up to Easter. On Ash Wednesday the Carnival party is over; fasting and prayers are the rule. In 1994, Fat Tuesday is on 22 February. In 1992 and 1993, it falls in early March.
5 February – Constitution Day, a legal holiday in Mexico.

March

The tourist season continues at its height.

Religious Holidays – Carnival (see February) usually falls in early March. In 1992, Fat Tuesday is on 10 March; in 1993 it's on 2 March; in 1994 it falls in late February.

Holy Week, when things are especially busy along La Ruta Maya, and particularly in the towns of highland Guatemala, begins on 28 March in 1994, and runs to 3 April. The Friday before Easter Sunday (Good Friday), Holy Saturday and Easter Sunday are official holidays in all three countries. Holy Thursday is a holiday in Guatemala; Easter Monday is a holiday in Belize.

9 March – Baron Bliss Day, a legal holiday in Belize. It honours the English nobleman who dropped anchor in Belizean waters in the 1920s, fell in love with the place, and willed his considerable fortune (several million dollars) to the people of Belize. His bequest, held in trust and earning interest, has been funding worthwhile projects such as roads, schools, market halls, etc ever since.

21 March – Birthday of Benito Juárez, the plucky Indian president who fought off the French intervention headed by Emperor Maximilian of Hapsburg in the 1860s, a legal holiday in Mexico. Also on 20 or 21 March is the vernal equinox, celebrated at Chichén Itzá as the sun strikes the 'serpent' on the stairway of El Castillo (see the section on Chichén Itzá for details).

April

The rainy season may start by late April. The few weeks before it does are often the hottest of the year. Everyone and everything swelters in the lowlands, while up in the mountains the weather is delightful.

Religious Holidays – Holy Week begins on 13 April in 1992, and runs to 19 April (Easter Sunday); in 1993, Holy Week begins on 5 April and continues to 11 April (Easter Sunday). The Friday before Easter Sunday (Good Friday), Holy Saturday and Easter Sunday are official holidays in all three countries. Holy Thursday is a holiday in Guatemala; Easter Monday is a holiday in Belize.

21 April – Queen's Birthday, a legal holiday in Belize.

May

The rainy season begins in earnest, with heavy rains during the first few weeks after the season begins. No place escapes the rains, though they are heaviest to the west, in Chiapas and in Guatemala's highlands. In Yucatán the rains may be limited to an hour's downpour in the afternoon.

1 May – Labour Day, a legal holiday in Mexico, Guatemala and Belize.

Masked celebrant at the
Fiesta of San Sebastián

5 May – Cinco de Mayo, a legal holiday in Mexico commemorating the Battle of Puebla (1862), when Juárez's forces defeated French armies of Maximilian of Hapsburg decisively, ending the European-sponsored occupation of Mexico.

24 May – Commonwealth Day, a legal holiday in Belize.

June

Rains may continue to be heavy during June.

30 June – Army Day and commemoration of the revolution of 1871, a legal holiday in Guatemala.

July

Rains are less bothersome, and the summer tourist season is in full swing. The hurricane season officially begins in July, though historically there are few storms this month. Summer visitors are usually more interested in archaeology and local culture than the sun-and-sea crowd that comes in winter.

August
The summer tourist season continues. Hurricane season comes to the Caribbean; this is one of the most active months for tropical storms.

15 August – Festival of Guatemala in Guatemala City; offices and shops close for the day.
29 August – Postal Workers' Holiday; all post offices closed in Guatemala.

September
The summer crowd thins out, but it's still quite hot and humid. Hurricane season continues, another active month for tropical storms.

Religious Holidays – El Señor de las Ampollas, a festival in Mérida celebrating the 'Christ of the Blisters' in the cathedral, runs from the end of September into mid-October.
1 September – President's Message to Congress (Mexico).
10 September – Belize National Day, a legal holiday in Belize. It commemorates the Battle of St George's Caye fought in 1798 between British buccaneers and Spanish naval forces. The victory prize was Belize itself. The British won. Celebrations begin today, and continue until Independence Day on the 21st.
15 September – Independence Day, a legal holiday in Guatemala.
16 September – Independence Day, a legal holiday in Mexico.
21 September – Independence Day, a legal holiday in Belize. The colony of British Honduras gained its independence from the UK in 1981.

October
The rains cease sometime during October, as does most danger of hurricanes. The number of visitors drops off, facilities are less crowded, and there are many bargains to be had. It's a great time to travel here.

Religious Holidays – The festival of las Ampollas continues in Mérida (see September). In late October (18 to 28) Izamal (east of Mérida) is the place to be. The Día del Cristo de Sitilpech is celebrated as a venerated statue of Christ comes in procession from the village of Sitilpech to the great monastic church in Izamal. On the evenings of 25 and 28 October, jaranas (Yucatecan dances) are performed in the plazas.
12 October – 'Day of the Race' (Mexico); Columbus Day (Belize), a legal holiday.
20 October – Commemoration of the revolution of 1944 (Guatemala).

31 October – On the eve of Todos Santos (All Saints' Day) in Mexico, visitors place flowers on graves of the deceased, and light candles in their memory.

November
A low season for travel, it's wonderful for the person who wants uncrowded beaches, empty hotels, quiet restaurants, an unhurried pace and discount travel-service prices. Hurricane season officially comes to an end.

1 November – Todos Santos, or All Saints' Day (Guatemala). In Mexico, celebrations and observances continue until 8 November, the Day of the Dead.
19 November – Garifuna Settlement Day (Belize), when the Garinagus (Black Caribs) arrived to settle in Belize in 1823.
20 November – Anniversary of the Mexican Revolution (Mexico).

December
Until the Christmas rush to the resorts begins, December is an excellent month to visit, with little rain, good temperatures, low prices, and uncrowded facilities. The crowds begin to arrive – and prices rise substantially – after December 15.

8 December – Feast of the Immaculate Conception in many towns of Mexico and Guatemala. The festivities in Izamal, Yucatán, are particularly lively.
11-12 December – Day of the Virgin of Guadalupe, Mexico's patron saint, a legal holiday in Mexico.
24-25 December – Christmas Eve is a holiday in the afternoon in Mexico and Guatemala; Christmas Day is a holiday in all three countries.
26 December – Boxing Day, a legal holiday in Belize.
31 December – New Year's Eve afternoon is a holiday in Guatemala.

POST & TELECOMMUNICATIONS
Almost every city and town (but not villages) along La Ruta Maya has an Oficina de Correos (post office) where you can buy postage stamps and send or receive mail. Belize has the traditional red pillar boxes familiar to the British.

Sending Mail
If you are sending something by air mail from Mexico or Guatemala, be sure to clearly mark it with the words 'Por Avión'. An air-mail letter sent from La Ruta Maya to Canada or the USA may take anywhere from

four to 14 days. Air-mail letters to Europe can take anywhere from one to three weeks.

Receiving Mail

Receiving mail in Mexico can be tricky. You can send or receive letters and packages care of a post office if they're addressed as follows:

Jane SMITH (last name should be capitalised)
a/c Lista de Correos
Mérida, Yucatán
(numerical postal code if possible) MEXICO

When the letter arrives at the post office, the name of the addressee is placed on an alphabetical list called the Lista de Correos which is updated daily. If you can, check the list yourself because the letter might be listed under your first name instead of your last.

To claim your mail, present your passport or other identification; there's no charge. The snag is that many post offices only hold Lista mail for 10 days before returning it to the sender. If you think you're going to pick mail up more than 10 days after it has arrived, have it sent to you at Poste Restante, Correo Central, Town/City, State, Mexico. Poste restante usually holds mail for up to a month but no list of what has been received is posted. Again, there's no charge for collection.

If you can arrange for a private address to receive mail, do so. There's less chance of your mail getting put aside, lost or returned to the sender if you're late in picking it up.

Procedures are similar for Guatemala and Belize: have mail addressed to Poste Restante, and take your passport when you go to pick up mail.

Telephones

Local calls are cheap, international calls are generally very expensive. Don't go to the post office looking for telephones, as telephone companies in these countries are quasigovernmental corporations separate from the post office. Here are details on each country:

Mexico The Mexican government is undertaking to sell the government-controlled telephone company to private investors, which may result in better and cheaper service in future. For now, service is uncertain and can be very expensive.

Telephone numbers in Mexico have different numbers of digits for different cities and towns. You must dial seven digits in Mexico City, but only six in Mérida, and only five in Palenque, etc.

Local calls are laughably inexpensive and easy to place from public telephones (call boxes) and *casetas de teléfonos* (telephone call stations in shops). Sometimes hotels don't charge you for local calls. If you aren't placing the call from a caseta, be sure you have the often rare small-denomination coins (one, five, 10, 20 pesos, etc) accepted by public call-boxes. Sometimes call boxes don't work; other times they work and refuse to take any money, so you get your calls for free.

Long-Distance Calls from Mexico You may see the abbreviation Lada in connection with long distance calls; it's short for *larga distancia* (long distance). Domestic and international long-distance/trunk calls are exorbitantly taxed, laden with surcharges, and sometimes difficult to place. Be warned! If you make anything but the shortest possible call, you may be facing a bill of terrifying size. A 20-minute operator-assisted call to the USA can easily cost close to US$60, much more to Europe or Australia.

Tolls for calls placed from the USA or Canada to Mexico are much cheaper than for the same call placed from Mexico to Canada or the USA. Use a short call from Mexico to advise the call's recipient of your hotel telephone number in Mexico, and agree on a time for them to call you back (don't forget time zone differences!).

If you don't have a private or hotel line you have to find a *caseta de larga distancia*, or long-distance call station, of which there are usually several around the centres of larger towns and at least one in most other towns. These casetas are often in shops.

Reverse Charge Calls

To Call	Type of Call	Dial
Emergency assistance	Bilingual Spanish/English	07
Directory assistance	By operator	04
Another Mexican city	By operator	02
Another Mexican city	Direct station-to-station	91 + city code + local no
Another Mexican city	Direct person-to-person	92 + city code + local no
Another country	By operator/collect	09
USA or Canada	Direct station-to-station	95 + area code + local no
USA or Canada	Direct person-to-person	96 + area code + local no
Europe, Australia, etc	Direct station-to-station	98 + country code + city code + local no
Europe, Australia, etc	Direct person-to-person	99 + country code + city code + local no

From a caseta, an operator will connect your number and you speak from a booth. Calls may cost anywhere from US$1 to US$2 per minute within Mexico, or US$2 to US$5 per minute to the USA or Canada, or even more for countries farther away. Ask the agent in the caseta or at your hotel what the charge will be before you call!

If you can cajole someone into letting you use their private phone, and if you dial direct, you can save a bundle. Calls to Europe and the Middle East need cost only about US$14 for the first three minutes in peak times during the day, or US$10 off peak (Monday to Friday 7 pm to 7 am, all day Saturday, Sunday all day till 5 pm). However, most of the time you'll be forced to call from hotels and casetas.

A collect/reverse charge call *(llamada por cobrar)* is usually much cheaper than a normal operator-assisted call. It may go through without a hitch, or you may wait a long time to get through to the operator, or a hotel or caseta will either refuse to place a collect call or levy a fee for doing so, whether the call goes through or not. You may end up paying one or two dollars for the privilege of discovering that the party you're calling collect is not at home. See the table above.

Ladatel Phones Special Ladatel call stations are located at some airports and bus terminals in Mexico; keep an eye out for them as you travel, because they can make calling abroad much easier, quicker and cheaper. These phones have blue handsets and small liquid-crystal displays, and are clearly marked with the word Ladatel. Calling instructions are posted on Ladatel phones in Spanish, English, and French. From a Ladatel phone you can dial long-distance calls directly to any place in the world at much lower prices than operator connected calls.

You must be well supplied with peso coins or special Ladatel tokens. Find out the approximate rate per minute for your call by picking up the blue Ladatel handset – don't put any money in the phone yet! – and pressing the buttons for long-distance station-to-station service (91 for Mexico, 95 for the USA and Canada, 98 for the rest of the world), then the area code (for the USA and Canada), or the country and city codes (for other countries). The charge per minute in pesos will appear on the liquid-crystal display. Once you know the rate per minute, you can check your coin supply to be sure you have enough money to make the call.

Here's an example: if you pick up the handset and press 95-415, the liquid-crystal display will show the charge per minute for a call to San Francisco; 95-519 shows the charge for Toronto, 98-44-71 for London, 98-61-3 for Melbourne, etc. The charge for most calls from Mexico to cities in the USA and Canada is about US$1 per minute. Regular operator, caseta, and collect calls can cost 100% to 300% more, so the value of Ladatel phones is obvious.

All set? Press the buttons for your call and insert coins – the Ladatel phone will take 10 coins at a time, and the liquid-crystal display lets you know when to put in more coins. To call San Francisco, press 95 + 415 + the local number; for Toronto, 95 + 519 + the local number; for London press 98 + 44 + 71 + the local number; for Melbourne press 98 + 61 + 3 + the local number. Got it? If you don't know the country code of the place you're calling, refer to the list in this section.

Guatemala Local and domestic long-distance calls are quite cheap in Guatemala, and international direct calls much more expensive. The local phone company is called Guatel, and it has offices in all cities and many large towns such as Panajachel. The major problem is finding a public coin phone (call box), as these are not as plentiful as one would wish. Look near the Guatel office, in the lobbies of hotels, and in pharmacies/chemists' shops. If you can't find a coin phone, you may have to use a regular phone in a shop, at a higher charge.

Once you've found a coin phone, you'll no doubt wait in line for a while. After that, insert your five, 10 and 25-centavo coins and the phone will take them as you talk.

Guatemala is divided into eight calling zones. For five centavos you get 30 seconds for a call to another phone in the same zone, 20 seconds to an adjacent zone, or 15 seconds to a distant zone. Thus a local call costs about US$0.04 per minute, an adjacent-zone call about US$0.06 per minute, and a call all the way across the country about US$0.08 per minute. Rates are a bit lower between 7 pm and 7 am, and from noon on Saturday to 7 am Monday.

Most telephone numbers in Guatemala City have six digits, but some have only five. The shorter numbers work just as well. Don't think you've got the number wrong and are missing a digit. Dial it, and you'll get through.

International Calls from Guatemala International direct calls (called *discado internacional automática*, or DIA) can be made from coin phones if you have a heavy pocketful of Guatemalan 25-centavo pieces and don't mind feeding them fast. But your best bet, as in Mexico, is to make a short call, inform the other person of a time and telephone number at which you may be reached, then end the call.

Collect/reverse-charge calls may be made from Guatemala to the following countries only: Canada, Central America, Mexico, Italy, Spain, Switzerland, the USA (including Puerto Rico and the US Virgin Islands). More countries may be added in the future; ask the international operator for the latest information.

To place an international direct call, dial the international prefix '00' (that's zero zero), then the country code, area or city code, and local number. Here are some examples; rates apply to direct calls and also to semi-automatic (operator-assisted) calls:

To Call	Dial	Cost per Minute
Los Angeles	00 + 1 + 213 + local number	US$1 to US$2
Montréal	00 + 1 + 514 + local number	US$1 to US$2
Glasgow	00 + 44 + 41 + local number	US$3 to US$5
Sydney	00 + 61 + 2 + local number	US$3 to US$5

For semi-automatic (operator-assisted) calls, dial 171. The minimum call period is three minutes, and thus the minimum charge to the USA or Canada is about US$3 to US$6; to countries overseas (ie, outside the western hemisphere), the minimum charge is about US$8.

You may use the AT&T long-distance network to call the USA by dialling 190 from Guatemala; this connects you directly to an AT&T operator, who will complete your regular, collect or credit-card call; you must be a telephone subscriber in the USA, or have an AT&T credit card number, in order to use this 'USADirect' service, which is being provided on a trial basis at present, and may or may not be extended for the long term. Try it, and if it works you'll probably save money and hassles.

Belize The telephone system is operated by Belize Telecommunications Ltd, with offices (open 8 am to noon and 1 to 4 pm Monday to Friday, 8 am to noon on Saturday) in major towns. Rates for international calls from Belize are lower than from Mexico, though perhaps still more expensive than you may be used to at home.

Local calls cost BZ$0.25 (about US$0.13). To call from one part of Belize to another, dial 0 (zero), then the one or two-digit area code, then the four or five-digit local number.

Here are Belize's area codes:

Ambergris Caye	26
Belize City	2
Belmopan/Spanish Lookout	8
Benque Viejo	93
Burrell Boom	28
Caye Caulker	22
Corozal	4
Dangriga	5
Independence/Placencia	6
Ladyville	25
Orange Walk	3
Punta Gorda	7
San Ignacio	92

Telephone service has yet to be extended to all parts of Belize, and you may find that some remote ranches and island hotels are reachable only by radiotelephone. Dialling instructions given to you by these establishments may seem improbable, but they work. For instance, to call Banana Bank Ranch, in the bush off the Western Highway, from Belize City you press 08-23180, and after the first ring press *123 (that's asterisk-one-two-three) and say 'Calling Banana Bank'. It's odd, but it works.

The best plan for calling internationally from Belize is to dial your call direct from a telephone office; or you can call collect from your hotel. Be sure to ask before you call what the charges (and any hotel surcharges) may be. Here are some useful numbers:

Directory assistance	113
Local operator	112
Long-distance (trunk) operator	110
International operator	115
Time of day	121
Emergency service (Belize City)	90
Emergency service (Belmopan)	2222
Emergency service (elsewhere)	2022

To place a collect call, dial the international operator (115), give the number you want to call and the number you're calling from; the operator will place the call and ring you back when it goes through.

American callers who use AT&T can take advantage of special telephones in Belize which connect directly to an AT&T operator in the USA. Just pick up the handset and an AT&T operator will come on the line to help you with your collect or credit card call. These AT&T phones are located at the airport and at a few luxury hotels in Belize City.

Calling from Abroad Follow the international calling procedures for your home telephone company, which will include dialling an access code for international service, then the country code, area or city code, and local number. City codes are given for most telephone numbers in this guide. Country codes are (52) for Mexico, (502) for Guatemala, and (501) for Belize. For example, here's how it's done from the USA:

Calling from Abroad				
City	Access Code	Country Code	City	Local No
Mexico City	011 +	52 +	5 +	123-4567
Mérida	011 +	52 +	99 +	12-34-56
Guatemala City	011 +	502 +	2 +	12-34-56
Panajachel	011 +	502 +	62 +	1234
Belize City	011 +	501 +	2 +	12345
Caye Caulker	011 +	501 +	22 +	1234

Remember that in some parts of Mexico, Guatemala and Belize, telephone numbers may have fewer digits than in other parts. These numbers work just as well, even though they have fewer digits.

Country Codes Here are some useful country codes:

Country	Code	Country	Code
Australia	61	Israel	972
Austria	43	Italy	39
Belgium	32	Japan	81
Belize	501	Mexico	52
Canada	1	Netherlands	31
Costa Rica	506	New Zealand	64
Denmark	45	Nicaragua	505
Eire	353	Norway	47
El Salvador	503	Portugal	351
Finland	358	South Africa	27
France	33	Spain	34
Germany	49	Sweden	46
Guatemala	502	Switzerland	41
Honduras	504	UK	44
India	91	USA	1

Fax, Telex & Telegraph
Fax Many middle-range and most top-end hotels along La Ruta Maya have facsimile machines, as do airlines, car rental companies, tourist offices and other businesses. When making reservations or asking for information, a fax is often the cheapest and most efficient way of going about it. The recipient will get written instructions, which makes translations easier and minimises the chance for errors. Also, faxes usually take less time than voice calls, saving you money on telephone tolls. If you don't have access to a fax machine for free at a friend's office, contact one of the many businesses which will send your fax for a fee.

Telex In this age of the fax machine, telexes are used less often as they are slower, and the number of telex machines is fewer. However, you can send telexes to most top-end hotels along La Ruta Maya, and to many travel agencies. If your friends and family have access to a telex machine at home, you can send them messages from most larger tele-graph offices along La Ruta Maya, as these usually have telex machines.

Telegraph Most towns have *telégrafos*, offices from which you can send domestic and international telegrams – a simple but not always very quick means of communication (one from Mexico to Melbourne, Australia, took five days). From Mexico, a telegram to the USA costs about US$5 for the first 15 words, then US$0.15 for each extra word; words in the address go for free. To the UK or Australia you pay US$4 for the first seven words, then US$0.50 for each extra word, and you have to pay for the address.

TIME
North American Central Standard Time (Greenwich Mean Time minus six hours) is used in all parts of La Ruta Maya. Daylight-saving (or 'summer') time is not used. Here's the time in some other cities when it's noon in Cancún, Mérida, Belize City, Guatemala City, or any other place along La Ruta Maya:

City	Summer	Winter
Paris, Rome	8 pm	7 pm
London	7 pm	6 pm
GMT	6 pm	6 pm
New York, Toronto	2 pm	1 pm
Chicago, New Orleans	1 pm	noon
San Francisco, LA	11 am	10 am
Perth, Hong Kong	3 am*	2 am*
Sydney, Melbourne	5 am*	4 am*
Auckland	6 am*	7 am*
*next day		

ELECTRICITY
Electrical current, plugs and sockets (points) along La Ruta Maya are the same as in the USA and Canada: 110 to 120 volts, 60 cycles, with flat-pronged plugs.

LAUNDRY
The larger cities and towns along La Ruta Maya have modern laundries and dry-cleaning shops where you can leave your clothes to be cleaned. Often you can have your laundry back in a day; dry cleaning usually takes at least overnight. Addresses of conve-

nient laundries are given in this guidebook for each city which has them.

WEIGHTS & MEASURES

Mexico, Guatemala and Belize use the metric system. For conversion information, see the back of this book. Because of the great commercial influence of the USA, you may find that ounces *(onzas)*, pounds *(libras)*, feet *(pies)*, miles *(millas)* and US gallons *(galones)* are used informally, at village markets, for instance. Officially, however, everything's metric.

BOOKS & MAPS

Many aspects of Mayan life and culture remain shrouded in mystery. New discoveries are being made every year by Mayanists and released to the world in books and magazine articles. The books recommended here are among the most interesting ones available, and we can expect to see new ones appearing in the near future.

Although you can find books in English in most cities along La Ruta Maya, the choice is not extensive. Locally produced guides to pre-Hispanic sites are widely available, but are of dubious quality and accuracy. It is wise to find what you want before arriving in the country; exceptions are noted here.

Mayan Life & Culture

In preparation for your journey along La Ruta Maya, find a copy of *The Maya*, by Michael D Coe (New York and London: Thames and Hudson, 1987, 4th revised edition; paperback), the best general introduction to Mayan life and culture by an eminent scholar.

Another entertaining and academically accurate book is *A Forest of Kings: The Untold Story of the Ancient Maya*, by Linda Schele & David Freidel (New York: Morrow, 1990; hardback), a much more detailed look at Mayan history and beliefs.

Much of what we know about Mayan life and culture is derived from Friar Diego de Landa's book, translated as *Yucatan Before and After the Conquest* (Mineola, NY: Dover Publications, 1978; paperback). You can find

this in numerous bookshops along La Ruta Maya, or order it from your bookshop at home, or directly from the publisher, Dover Publications, 31 East Second St, Mineola, NY 11501-3582 USA.

If you have access to back issues of the *National Geographic Magazine* published in Washington, get hold of 'La Ruta Maya' and related articles, Volume 176, No 4 (October 1989), pp 424- 505, for the best short introduction to La Ruta Maya. Other *National Geographic* articles worth reading are 'Jade, Stone of Heaven' and 'Exploring a Vast Maya City, El Mirador', Volume 172, No 3 (September 1987), pp 282-339.

Guidebooks

Other guidebooks published by Lonely Planet cover areas adjacent to La Ruta Maya. The encyclopedic *Mexico – a travel survival kit* covers the entire country in great detail. *Central America on a shoestring* is the guide you want if you're travelling through the rest of the region on a tight budget. *Costa Rica – a travel survival kit* provides full information on that other top Central American destination.

The Complete Visitor's Guide to Mesoamerican Ruins by Joyce Kelly (University of Oklahoma Press, 1982; hardback) gives good directions on how to reach some of the remoter sites, but would be cumbersome to carry along on your trip.

Tikal: A Handbook of the Ancient Maya Ruins, by William R Coe (Philadelphia: The University Museum of the University of Pennsylvania, 1967; paperback) is available at Tikal for US$6, but may be cheaper if you buy it at home before you leave. If you expect to spend several days exploring Tikal, you'll want William Coe's excellent guide.

Backpacking in Mexico & Central America by Hilary Bradt & Rob Rachowiecki (Bradt Enterprises, Cambridge, Mass, and Chalfont St Peter, Bucks, England, 1982) covers only a few hikes in Mexico but has some useful general information plus details of hikes in all the other Central American countries.

Those who love old guidebooks should try

to find a copy of *Terry's Guide to Mexico*, which was produced from 1922 to 1947. It's highly detailed, though hopelessly out of date of course – but look at those wonderful old multicoloured fold-out maps. A copy of the 1935 edition at the Lonely Planet office reveals that the 1934 Mexican Customs regulations didn't have much to say about how many cigarettes or bottles of wine you could bring in with you, but did list exhaustively what clothes a female visitor was permitted to import duty-free:

Eighteen pieces of each kind of underwear, 12 night dresses or six pyjamas, 24 pairs of stockings, 24 handkerchiefs, six collars, two aprons, one pair of bath slippers, one bathing cap, one bathrobe, one bathing suit, one pair of slippers, 12 pairs of shoes, one pair of riding boots, one pair of rubber shoes, six house robes, one automobile robe, three overcoats or wraps, one mackintosh, three sweaters, four mufflers, six pairs of gloves, six belts, 12 street-dresses, two evening dresses, three sports gowns, one parasol, one umbrella and 10 hats.

Maps

One of the best overall maps of Mexico is published by Bartholomew in its World Travel Map series at a scale of 1:3 million – which means that it folds out to about 1.2 by 0.8 metres. It shows altitudes, rivers, cities and towns, roads, railways and state boundaries clearly and accurately. You can also get a good 1:3.5 million *Tourist Road Map* of the country, which includes good street plans of some cities, free from many tourist offices. For motorists in Mexico, the best road atlas is generally reckoned to be the *Pemex Atlas de Carreteras*, available from some Pemex petrol stations.

A letter to the Instituto Guatemalteco de Turismo (INGUAT, 7 Avenida 1-17, Zona 4, Guatemala City), sent well in advance of your departure, will yield a useful map of the country with city street plans, but the scale is fairly small. The same map, called the *Mapa Vial Turístico*, may be bought in Guatemala at shops or from street vendors for several dollars (you can bargain with vendors).

For Belize, the *Belize Facilities Map* issued by the Belize Tourist Board, PO Box 325, Belize City, has plans of all major towns in Belize, a road map, plans of the archaeological sites at Altun-ha and Xunantunich, and a list of facts about Belize. If you write to the Board in advance you may be able to get one for free; in Belizean shops the map is sold for US$4.

Travelogues

Most important of all are the delightful travel books written 1½ centuries ago by John L Stephens and beautifully illustrated by Frederick Catherwood. Stephens, a New York lawyer, sometime diplomat and amateur archaeologist, and Catherwood, a patient and skilled draughtsman, travelled extensively in the Mayan lands in the mid-19th century. The descriptions of their journeys, published soon after their return, were instant transatlantic best-sellers, entertaining readers throughout North America and Britain. More than just travelogues, their discoveries and painstaking explorations produced the first extensive and serious look at many Mayan archaeological sites. Their detailed descriptions and drawings are now the only evidence we have for some features of the sites which have been lost, destroyed or stolen.

The books, *Incidents of Travel in Central America, Chiapas and Yucatan*, in two volumes (1969 reprint of 1841 edition), and *Incidents of Travel in Yucatan*, in two volumes (1963 reprint of 1843 edition), by John L Stephens are available in paperback at some bookshops along La Ruta Maya, from many bookshops in the USA and elsewhere with good selections of travel literature, and also directly from the publisher, Dover Publications, 31 East Second St, Mineola, NY 11501-3582 USA.

Aldous Huxley travelled through Mexico too; *Beyond the Mexique Bay*, first published in 1934, has interesting observations on the Maya. Equally interesting is Graham Greene's *The Lawless Roads*, chronicling the writer's travels through Chiapas and Tabasco in 1938.

An engraving of one of Fredrick Catherwood's sketches of Uxmal, published in John L Stephens'
Incidents of Travel in Yucatán (1843).

UXMAL.
Front of the Casa de Las Tortugas

Contemporary writers have also found the countries of La Ruta Maya to be inspiring. *So Far from God: A Journey to Central America* by Patrick Marnham (New York: Viking, 1985 and now in a Penguin paperback) was the winner of the 1985 Thomas Cook Travel Book Award. It's an insightful and often amusing account of a leisurely meander from Texas down to Mexico City and on through Oaxaca and San Cristóbal de las Casas into Central America.

Time Among the Maya: Travels in Belize, Guatemala, and Mexico, by Ronald Wright (New York: Weidenfeld & Nicolson, 1989; hardback) is a thoughtful account of numerous journeys made in recent years among the descendants of the ancient Maya, and will certainly help you to 'feel' Mayan culture as you travel La Ruta Maya. Highly recommended.

Paul Theroux rides the rails through Mexico on *The Old Patagonian Express*, also available in paperback.

History

There are various worthwhile books on the pre-Hispanic period, on the Spanish conquest and its aftermath, and on recent events in Mexico. Starting at the beginning of the Mexican story there's Nigel Davies' *The Ancient Kingdoms of Mexico* (Allen Lane, London, 1982; also available in Pelican paperback). This is a succinct but scholarly study of four of Mexico's ancient civilisations: the Olmecs, the builders of Teotihuacán, the Toltecs and the Aztecs. Diagrams, illustrations, plans and maps complement the text.

Atlas of Ancient America by Michael Coe, Dean Snow & Elizabeth Benson (Facts on File, New York and Oxford, 1986) covers North, South and the rest of Central America as well as Mexico. It's too big to carry in a backpack but is a fascinating, superbly illustrated book. The whole course of ancient Mexico is charted and there are maps showing the areas controlled by the different

Mayan cities and the expansion of the Teotihuacán, Toltec and Aztec empires.

Ambivalent Conquests: Maya and Spaniard in Yucatan, 1517-1570 by Inga Clendinnen (Cambridge, New York, Melbourne, Sydney: Cambridge University Press, 1987; paperback) covers the formative years of the relationship between the Maya and their Spanish overlords, years which set the tone of Indian-Hispanic relations for the rest of Yucatecan history.

The multivolume *Handbook of Middle American Indians* (University of Texas Press, Austin, 1964-76) edited by Robert Wauchope, is an encyclopedic work which covers both the pre-Hispanic and more recent stages of Indian history and culture in great detail.

Culture, Art & Architecture

The basic text of Mayan religion is the Popol Vuh (or Popol Wuh), which recounts the Mayan creation myths. A version easily available in Guatemala is *Popol Wuh: Ancient Stories of the Quiche Indians of Guatemala*, by Albertina Saravia E (Guatemala City: Editorial Piedra Santa, 1987; paperback).

Mexico's post-1521 architectural heritage is documented in *Art & Time in Mexico* by Elizabeth Wilder Weismann & Judith Hancock Sandoval (Harper & Row), a good, fairly handy, recent book on colonial architecture, with many photos.

One of the most fascinating of all recent books on Mexico – but unfortunately too big for a backpack – is Chloë Sayer's *Mexican Costume* (London: British Museum Publications, 1985). This book is the fruit of immense research but very readable and not too long. It traces the designs, materials and techniques of the country's highly colourful and varied costumes from pre-Hispanic times to the present, and includes many photos and a great wealth of other intriguing detail about Mexican life past and present. The same author has also written *Crafts of Mexico* (Aldus Books). Another good book in English is *Mexican Folk Crafts* by Carlos Espejel (Barcelona: Editorial Blume, 1978).

The Blood of Kings: Dynasty & Ritual in Maya Art by Linda Schele & Mary Ellen Miller (New York: George Braziller, 1986) is a heavily illustrated guide to the art and culture of the Mayan period with particular emphasis on sacrifices, bloodletting, torture of captives, the ball game and other macabre aspects of Mayan culture. The illustrated analyses of Mayan art are fascinating.

To learn more about Mayan hieroglyphs, start with *An Introduction to the Study of the Maya Hieroglyphs* by Sylvanus Griswold Morley (Mineola, NY: Dover Publications, 1975 reprint of 1915 edition; paperback).

The incredibly complex and portentous Mayan calendrical system makes a fascinating study. Without understanding at least the basics of the system, one cannot hope to understand the Maya. *The Mayan Calendar Made Easy* by Sandy Huff (Safety Harbor, Florida: Sandy Huff, 1984) will start you off. For a scholarly work, get hold of *The Book of the Year: Middle American Calendrical Systems*, by Munro S Edmonson (Salt Lake City: University of Utah Press, 1988; hardback), an excellent but fairly expensive book.

Other Subjects

A Dream of Maya: Augustus and Alice Le Plongeon in Nineteenth-Century Yucatan, by Lawrence Gustave Desmond & Phyllis Mauch Messenger (Albuquerque, New Mexico: University of New Mexico Press, 1988; paperback) offers a look at a couple of passionate, wildly romantic archaeologists who regarded Mayan culture as one of the foundations of world civilisation.

MEDIA
Newspapers & Magazines

Some major American newspapers such as *USA Today*, the *Miami Herald* and the *Los Angeles Times* are on sale in luxury hotel newsstands and some big-city and airport bookshops along La Ruta Maya. *Newsweek* and *Time* magazines are also sometimes available, along with the *New York Times* and the *Wall Street Journal*. The better shops in Cancún have good selections of European newspapers and magazines in French, German, Italian and Spanish.

Mexico The English-language *Mexico City News* is distributed throughout Mexico wherever tourists gather. Price varies with sales point, but is usually about US$0.35. Mexico has a thriving local Spanish-language press as well as national newspapers. Even small cities often have two or three newspapers of their own. In Mérida it's El Diario de Yucatán. Chiapas has its own excellent independent magazine, *Perfil del Sureste*, which comes out every two months and covers many issues that the authorities would prefer to keep quiet.

For those interested in a nonestablishment view of events, *La Jornada* is a good national daily with a mainly left-wing viewpoint which covers a lot of stories that other papers don't. *Proceso* is a weekly news magazine with a similar approach. Both cover international and cultural events as well as domestic news. Another interesting opposition magazine is the weekly *Quehacer Político*. *Fem* is a national feminist magazine.

Guatemala The national daily newspapers are all in Spanish. Your best bet for English-language news is one of the US dailies mentioned above, which can be found at large newsstands in tourist centres.

Belize The English-language daily here is the *Belize Times*, publishing local news exclusively. It's a homey sheet, interesting mostly as a window into the daily life of the country. For international news, look for the US papers mentioned above.

Belize Currents is the local effort at a glossy magazine, published quarterly and priced at US$6 for about 30 pages. The articles are interesting, and, though the price is high, it's worth a look because printed sources of current information on Belize are so few. For a year's subscription (four issues), send a cheque for US$24 to Belize Currents, Box 42809-390, Houston, TX 77242 USA.

Radio & TV

Local radio broadcasting, both AM and FM, is all in Spanish except in Belize and for a few hours of English programming each day in Cancún. In the evening you may be able to pick up US stations on the AM (medium wave) band.

Many middle-range hotel rooms in Yucatán have TV sets, often with satellite hookups which can receive some US stations. Most popular are ESPN (the sports channel) and UNO, the Spanish-language US network. Local Spanish-language programming includes hours and hours of talk shows and soap operas, some sports, and reruns of old American movies dubbed in Spanish. The situation is similar in Guatemala.

In Belize, the local station is in English, so you can easily understand the news programmes, and you needn't read subtitles while watching the old movies.

FILM & PHOTOGRAPHY

According to customs laws in Mexico you are allowed to bring in no more than one camera and 12 rolls of film. I have never heard of this ever being enforced. Camera stores, pharmacies and hotels are the most common outlets for buying film. Be suspicious of film that is being sold at prices lower than what you might pay in North America – it is often outdated. You may not know this by glancing at the date on the back of the film carton because sometimes it's obscured by a sticker bearing the new lower price. Look under the sticker before you buy the film.

Print film, both B&W and colour, is easily found, though you may not find the brand you like without a search. Processing is not particularly expensive, and can be done in a day or two, even quicker in Cancún. Print film prices are US$1 or US$2 higher than in the USA.

Slide (transparency) film may be more difficult to find in Mexico, especially in smaller locales, and certain types are impossible to find in Guatemala and Belize. Kodachrome, for example, is not sold in these countries because they have no facilities to process it. Ektachrome slide film can be found, but it is very expensive.

Most people along La Ruta Maya do not mind having their photographs taken. Indeed, the children may joyously pester you to take theirs. I've taken photographs of military installations, shamans performing religious rites, country people at the weekly markets, and bathers at Fuentes Georginas near Quetzaltenango all quite publicly and I've never had a complaint. Of course one must use common sense and decency: ask permission before snapping away at anything military, religious, or close-up personal. And keep in mind that there are a few locations – the village of San Juan Chamula outside San Cristóbal de las Casas, other villages nearby, the church of Santo Tomás in Chichicastenango – where photography is strictly forbidden or frowned upon. If local people make any sign of being offended, you should put your camera away and apologise immediately, both out of decency and for your own safety.

HEALTH
Predeparture Preparations
Specific immunisations are not normally required for travel anywhere in these countries. All the same, it's a good idea to be up to date on your tetanus, typhoid-paratyphoid and polio immunisations; if you were born after 1957 you should also make sure that you're immune to measles (ask your doctor). If you plan to stay for more than a few weeks along La Ruta Maya, and you're adventurous in your eating, a gamma globulin shot is also recommended for protection against infectious hepatitis. You only need a yellow fever certificate to enter the country if, within the last six months, you have been to a country where yellow fever is present.

As La Ruta Maya runs through the tropics where food spoils easily, mosquitoes roam freely, and sanitation is not always the best, you must take special care to protect yourself from illness. The most important steps you can take are to be careful about what you eat and drink, to stay away from mosquitoes (or at least make them stay away from you), and

to practise safe sex. These measures are particularly important for adventurous travellers who enjoy getting off the beaten track, mingling with the locals, and trekking into remote areas.

Before I begin on this somewhat disturbing catalogue of potential illnesses, let me say that after dozens of journeys in every region of these countries in every season of the year, climbing pyramids in remote jungle sites, camping out, staying in cheap hotels and eating in all sorts of markets and restaurants, I have never got anything more serious than traveller's diarrhoea (but I've got that frequently!). I have rarely taken medicines to help get rid of diarrhoea, instead preferring to let my body heal itself. I have not taken malaria prevention medicine or gamma globulin, and I have not come down with malaria or hepatitis. Thus I believe that travel along La Ruta Maya is not a particularly perilous activity. But I have known people who have got dengue fever and typhoid fever, so I know that it can happen.

If you come down with a serious illness, be very careful to find a competent doctor, and don't be afraid to get second opinions. You may want to telephone your doctor at home for consultation as well. In some cases it may be best to end your trip and fly home for treatment, difficult as this may be. A friend of mine who contracted typhoid fever in Mexico went to the local hospital where a sympathetic doctor strongly recommended that she and her husband fly home to the USA and go to the hospital there, which she did. Medical practice along La Ruta Maya is not always the exact science it should be.

Medical Kit It is always a good idea to travel with a small first-aid kit. Some of the items that should be included are: Band-Aids, a sterilised gauze bandage, Elastoplast, cotton wool, a fever thermometer, tweezers, scissors, an antiseptic agent (Dettol or Betadine), burn cream (Caladryl is good for sunburn, minor burns and itchy bites), insect repellent containing DEET, and multivitamins.

Don't forget a full supply of any medication you're already taking; the prescription might be difficult to match abroad.

Basic Rules

Food & Water Food can be contaminated by bacteria, viruses and/or parasites when it is harvested, shipped, handled, washed (if the water is contaminated) or prepared. Cooking, peeling and/or washing food in pure water is the way to get rid of the germs. To avoid gastrointestinal diseases, avoid salads, uncooked vegetables, and unpasteurised milk or milk products (including cheese). Make sure the food you eat has been freshly cooked and is still hot. Do not eat raw or rare meat, fish or shellfish. Peel fruit yourself with clean hands and a clean knife.

As for beverages, don't trust any water except that which has been boiled for 20 minutes, or treated with purifiers, or comes in an unopened bottle labelled *agua purificada*. Most hotels have large bottles of purified water from which you can fill your carafe or canteen; some will put smaller capped bottles of purified water in your room. Local people may drink the water from the tap or from the well, and their systems may be used to it; or they may have chronic gastric diseases! Cancún supposedly has purified tap water safe to drink. All the same, I drink bottled water there, as I do everywhere else along La Ruta Maya. Purified water and ice are available from supermarkets, small grocery stores *(tiendas)* and liquor stores *(licorerías* or *vinos y licores)*.

Use only pure water for drinking, washing food, brushing your teeth, and ice. Tea, coffee, and other hot beverages should be made with boiled water. If the waiter swears that the ice in your drink is made from agua purificada, you may feel you can take a chance with it.

Canned or bottled carbonated beverages, including carbonated water, are usually safe, as are beer, wine and liquor.

If you plan to travel off the main roads and into the middle of nowhere, a water purification system is recommended as bottled water may not be readily available outside of touristed areas. Your water purification method might be one of these:

Tincture of iodine 2% *(yodo)* sold in chemist's shops/pharmacies; add about seven drops per litre of clear water; strain cloudy water through a clean cloth first, then add 14 drops of iodine per litre.

Water purification drops or tablets containing tetraglycine hydroperiodide or hydroclonazone, sold under brand names such as Globaline, Potable-Agua or Coughlan's in pharmacies and sporting goods stores in the USA. Along La Ruta Maya, ask for *gotas* (drops) or *pastillas* (tablets) *para purificar agua*, sold in pharmacies and supermarkets.

Boiled water; bringing it to a rolling boil will kill most germs, but you must boil it for at least 20 minutes to kill parasites.

A portable water filter which eliminates bacteria. Compact units are available from major camping supply stores in the USA such as Recreational Equipment, Inc (REI) (☎ (206) 431-5804), PO Box C-88126, Seattle, Washington 98188; and Mountain Equipment Inc (MEI) (☎ (800) 344-7422), 1636 South Second St, Fresno, California 93702, and through outfitters such as Eddie Bauer and L L Bean.

Protection against Mosquitos Many serious tropical diseases are spread by infected mosquitoes. If you protect yourself against mosquito bites, your travels will be both safer and more enjoyable.

Some mosquitoes feed during the day, others at night. In general, they're most bothersome when the sun is not too hot, in the evening and early morning, and on overcast days. There are many more mosquitoes in lowland and coastal regions and in the countryside than there are in cities or in highland areas, and many more during the rainy season (May to October) than during the dry (October to May). Avoid going to mosquito-infested places during these times and seasons if you can.

Mosquitos seem to be attracted more to dark colours than to light, so in mosquito-infested areas wear light-coloured long trousers, socks, a long-sleeved shirt and a hat. Clothing should be loose-fitting, as mosquitoes can drill right through the weave of a tight T-shirt. Mosquitos also seem to be attracted by scents such as those in perfume, cologne, lotions, hair spray etc, so avoid using these cosmetics if possible. Sleep in screened rooms or beneath mosquito netting after you have disposed of the little suckers who have somehow got in there with you. Check to make sure screens are intact, and that all openings to the outside are either screened or blocked.

Use insect repellent which has at least a 20% concentration of N,N diethylmetatoluamide (DEET) on any exposed skin. It's best to buy repellent before leaving home as repellents bought in Mexico, Guatemala or Belize may or may not have this most effective ingredient. To avoid reactions to the repellent, apply it sparingly only to exposed skin or to clothing, don't inhale the stuff or get it in your eyes or mouth or on broken or irritated skin, and wash it off after you enter a mosquito-free area. It's probably best not to use a repellent with an especially high – or low – concentration of DEET (concentrations reach 95%!) Be particularly careful with children: don't put it on hands which may be put in the mouth or eyes, use as little as possible, and wash it off afterwards.

In addition, you may want to use a pyrethrum-based flying insect spray in your sleeping room.

Medical Problems & Treatment
Traveller's Diarrhoea The food and water in a different country has different bacteria from what your digestive system is used to – germs that your immune system may not be prepared to combat. If you plunge right into the local culture and eat lots of food with high concentrations of these different bacteria, your body's natural defences will be overwhelmed and you may get sick.

Travellers to many less developed countries suffer from what is known medically as traveller's diarrhoea (TD) and informally as Montezuma's revenge, *turista*, or the trots, a condition defined as having twice as many (or more) unformed bowel movements as normal; typically one has four or five watery stools per day.

Symptoms In addition to frequent watery stools, other possible symptoms include abdominal cramps, nausea, fever, malaise, a bloated feeling, and urgency of bowel movements. The disease usually hits within the first week of travel, but may hit at any time, and may hit more than once during a trip. A bout of TD typically lasts three or four days, but may be shorter or longer. It seems to affect younger travellers more than older ones, which may be due to lack of caution among the young, or acquired immunity among the old.

Prevention Epidemiologists recommend that you *not* take medicines for TD prophylaxis, that is, don't take any medicine just in the hope that it will prevent a case of the disease. Taking prophylactic medicines such as antibiotics, bismuth subsalicylate (Pepto-Bismol), or difenoxine (Lomotil) can actually make it *easier* for you to get the disease later on by killing off the benign digestive bacteria which help to protect you from the 'foreign' bacteria. These strong drugs can also cause side effects (some of them serious) such as photosensitivity, a condition in which your skin is temporarily oversensitive to sunlight (in the sunny tropics!).

Instead, observe the rules of safe eating and drinking, and don't overdo it early in your trip. For the first week after arrival, be extremely careful and conservative in your eating habits, avoid overeating, or eating heavy or spicy food, don't get overtired, and don't drink lots of alcoholic beverages or coffee.

Treatment If you come down with a case of TD, take it easy, with no physical exertion; stay in bed if you can. Be especially careful to replace fluids and electrolytes (potassium, sodium, etc) by drinking caffeine-free soft drinks or glasses of fruit juice (high in potassium) with honey and a pinch of salt added, plus a glass of pure water with a quarter teaspoon of sodium bicarbonate (baking soda) added; weak tea, preferably unsweetened and without milk, is alright. Avoid dairy products. Eat only salted crackers or dry toast for a day or so. After that, eat easily digested foods that are not fatty or overly acid. Yoghurt with live cultures is particularly good as it helps to repopulate the bowel with benign digestive organisms. When you feel better, be particularly careful about what you eat and drink from then on.

As for medications, it's best if you cure yourself without them. If you must have some chemical help, go to a doctor, who may recommend one of the following treatments as described in the US Public Health Service's book, *Health Information for International Travel*. Treatments and dosages should be determined by a competent medical doctor who can tell you about side effects and contraindications; those noted here are the normal ones for otherwise healthy adults (*not* children), and are for information only:

Bismuth subsalicylate (Pepto-Bismol), one ounce of liquid or the equivalent in tablets every half-hour for four hours. This treatment is not recommended if symptoms last more than more than 48 hours, or if you have high fever, blood in the stool, kidney problems or are allergic to salicylates. Children under the age of two should not be given this medicine.

Diphenoxylate and loperamide (Lomotil, Imodium) are antimotility agents made from synthetic opiate derivatives. They temporarily slow down the diarrhoea but do not cure it, they increase the risk of getting TD again, and they can make you sluggish or sleepy. They should not be used if you have a high fever, or blood in the stool, or are driving a motor vehicle or operating machinery (your alertness is impaired). In any case, don't use them for longer than two full days.

Doxycycline (100 mg twice daily); or trimethoprim (200 mg twice daily); or trimethoprim (160 mg)/sulfamethoxazole (800 mg, once daily), known as TMP/SMX and sold in Mexico as Bactrim F (Roche), are antibiotics which may be indicated if there are three or more loose stools in an eight-hour period, especially with nausea, vomiting, abdominal cramps and fever.

It bears repeating: traveller's diarrhoea is self-limiting, and you're usually better off if you can get through it without taking strong drugs. If you feel that you need medicine, go to a doctor. Make sure that you have TD and not some other gastrointestinal ailment for which the treatment may be very different.

Medicines Not to Take You can walk into a chemist's/pharmacy in Mexico, Guatemala or Belize and buy medicines – often without a prescription – which might be banned for good reason in your home country. Well-meaning but incompetent doctors or chemists/pharmacists might recommend such medicines for gastrointestinal ailments, but such medicines may be worse than no medicine at all. Though they may bring some relief from the symptoms of TD, they may cause other sorts of harm such as neurological damage. Medicines called halogenated hydroxyquinoline derivatives are among these, and may bear the chemical names clioquinol or iodoquinol, or brand names Entero-Vioform, Mexaform or Intestopan, or something similar. It's best not to take these medicines without consulting a trusted physician, preferably your regular doctor at home.

Heatstroke Only slightly less common than traveller's diarrhoea are the illnesses caused by excessive heat and dehydration. These are more dangerous because they display fewer symptoms.

Symptoms If you exercise excessively in hot regions such as Yucatán, Belize and the low-lying regions of Guatemala, or if you fail to replace lost fluids and electrolytes (salt, potassium, etc), you can suffer from dizziness, weakness, headaches, nausea, and greater susceptibility to other illnesses such as traveller's diarrhoea. This is heat exhaustion, heat prostration or, in severe cases, heatstroke. In this last case, exposure to intense heat can cause convulsions and coma.

Prevention Protect yourself against heat-related diseases by taking special care to drink lots of fluids. If you urinate infrequently and in small amounts, you're not drinking enough fluids. If you feel tired and have a headache, you're not drinking enough fluids. Don't just drink when you're thirsty; make it a habit to drink frequently, whether you're thirsty or not. It's so easy to prevent dehydration that you should feel foolish if you succumb to it.

Alcohol, coffee and tea are diuretics – they make you urinate and lose fluids. They are not a cure for dehydration, they're part of the problem. Drink pure water, fruit juices and soft drinks instead; go easy on the beer. Salty food is good to eat as the salt helps your body to retain fluids.

Other measures to take against the heat: don't overdo it. Take it easy climbing pyramids and trekking through the jungle. Wear light cotton clothing that breathes and cools you; wear a hat and sunglasses. Allow yourself frequent rest breaks in the shade, and give your body a chance to balance itself. Use sunblock to prevent bad sunburn. Be doubly cautious if you spend time near or on the water, as the sun's glare from sand and water can double your exposure to the sun. You may want to swim or go boating wearing a T-shirt and hat.

Other Unpleasant Illnesses Mexico, Guatemala and Belize are in the tropics, and they have tropical diseases, some of which you may not know about. Though you're unlikely to contract anything more than an unpleasant bout of traveller's diarrhoea, you should be informed about the symptoms and treatments of these other diseases just in case.

Cholera After a recent outbreak in Peru, this serious disease is now spreading throughout South America, and threatens to spread northwards into Central America. Like dysentery, it is a disease of insanitation, and spreads quickly in areas, urban and rural, where sewerage and water supplies are rudimentary. It can also be spread in foods which are uncooked or parcooked, such as the popular *ceviche* which is made from marinaded raw fish, as well as salads and raw vegetables.

The disease is characterised by a sudden onset of acute diarrhoea with 'rice water' stools, vomiting, muscular cramps and extreme weakness. You need medical help – but first treat for dehydration, which can be extreme, and if there is an appreciable delay in getting to the hospital, then begin taking tetracycline (adults one 250 mg capsule four times a day, children half this dose, if they are under eight, one third.). Cholera vaccination is not all that effective, but the disease does respond to treatment if caught early.

Dengue Fever Symptoms include the fast onset of high fever, severe frontal headache, and pain in muscles and joints; there may be nausea and vomiting, and a skin rash may develop about three to five days after the first symptoms, spreading from the torso to arms, legs and face. It is possible to have subclinical dengue (that is, a 'mild' case of it), and also to contract dengue haemorraghic fever (DHF), a very serious and potentially fatal disease.

Dengue is spread by mosquitoes. Risk of contraction, though low for the average traveller, is highest during the summer (July to September), several hours after daybreak and before dusk, and on overcast days. There are four different dengue viruses, but no medicines to combat them.

There is no effective treatment for dengue. The disease is usually self-limited, which means that the body cures itself. If you are generally healthy and have a healthy immune system, the disease may be unpleasant but it is rarely serious. To prevent against getting dengue, see the section on Protection against Mosquitoes.

Dysentery There are two types of dysentery, both of which are characterised by diarrhoea containing blood and/or mucus. You require a stool test to determine which type you have.

Bacillary dysentery, the most common variety, is short, sharp and nasty but rarely persistent. It hits suddenly and lays you out with fever, nausea, cramps and diarrhoea, but it is self-limited. Treatment is the same as for traveller's diarrhoea; as it's caused by bacteria, the disease responds well to antibiotics if needed.

Amoebic dysentery is caused by amoebic parasites and is more dangerous. It builds up slowly, cannot be starved out and if untreated will get worse and can permanently damage your intestines. Do not have anyone other than a doctor diagnose your symptoms and administer treatment.

Giardiasis This is caused by a parasite named *Giardia lamblia*, contracted by eating faecally contaminated food or beverages or by contact with a surface which has been similarly contaminated. Symptoms usually last for more than five days (perhaps months!), may be mild or serious, and may include diarrhoea, abdominal cramps, fatigue, weight loss, flatulence, anorexia and/or nausea. If you have gastrointestinal gripes for a length of time, talk to a doctor and have a stool sample analysed for giardia. Medicine is available to rid you of this unpleasant little bug easily and safely.

Hepatitis This is a viral disease of the liver for which there are no medicines, and it can be very serious – even fatal – if not treated with bed rest. There are several types of hepatitis.

Though the risk is only moderate in Mexico, Guatemala and Belize, and is low for the average, careful traveller, the perfect scenario for getting viral hepatitis would be if you met someone on a remote, untouristed beach, had dinner in a beachfront cookshack with bad sanitation, then engaged in unprotected romantic activities; or if you handle lots of young children in areas with poor sanitation.

Symptoms appear 15 to 50 days after infection (generally around 25 days) and consist of fever, loss of appetite, nausea, depression, lack of energy and pains around the base of the rib cage. Skin turns yellow, the whites of the eyes yellow to orange, and urine deep orange or brown. Do *not* take antibiotics. There is no cure for hepatitis except complete rest and careful diet. The worst is over in about 10 days, but rest is still important.

The hepatitis A virus can be spread by contaminated food, beverages, cutlery or crockery, or by intimate contact with an infected person. You can protect yourself against hepatitis A by getting an immune globulin (IG) injection before you begin your travels, and by being careful of what you eat and how you have sex.

Hepatitis B is spread by direct contact with blood, secretions, or intimate sexual contact with an infected person. Risk is very low if you avoid these situations.

The mysterious hepatitis virus known as Non-A, Non-B is spread in the same way as Hepatitis A, by contaminated food and beverages.

Hepatitis may also be spread by use of contaminated, unsterilised needles for tattooing, acupuncture, drug abuse or medicinal injections. It can be avoided by making sure that needles are sterile.

If you get hepatitis, see a doctor immediately. The treatment is simple: go to bed and stay there for several weeks; eat only easily digestible low fat foods; drink no alcohol for at least six months. There is no medicine which helps cure hepatitis except B vitamins; on the contrary, many medicines such as antibiotics which must be detoxified by the already-weakened liver can cause hepatic (liver) failure which can be fatal. If a doctor prescribes anything but bed rest and B vitamins for hepatitis, go to another doctor.

Sexually Transmitted Diseases Sexual contact with an infected sexual partner spreads these diseases. While abstinence is the only 100% preventative, using condoms is also effective. Gonorrhoea and syphilis are the most common of these diseases; sores, blisters or rashes around the genitals, discharges or pain when urinating are common symptoms. Symptoms may be less marked or not observed at all in women. Syphilis symptoms eventually disappear completely but the disease continues and can cause severe problems in later years. The treatment of gonorrhoea and syphilis is by antibiotics.

There are numerous other sexually transmitted diseases, for most of which effective treatment is available. However, there is no cure for herpes and there is also currently no cure for AIDS. Using condoms is the most effective preventative.

AIDS can be spread through infected blood transfusions; most developing countries cannot afford to screen blood for transfusions. It can also be spread by dirty needles – vaccinations, acupuncture and tattooing can potentially be as dangerous as intravenous drug use if the equipment is not clean. If you do need an injection it may be a good idea to buy a new syringe from a pharmacy and ask the doctor to use it.

Malaria This is the one disease that everyone fears, and the one about which you must make an important decision.

Symptoms may include jaundice (a yellow cast to the skin and/or eyes), general malaise, headaches, fever and chills, bed sweats and anaemia. Symptoms of the disease may appear as early as eight days after infection, or as late as several months after you return from your trip. You can contract malaria even if you've taken medicines to protect yourself.

Malaria is spread by mosquitoes which bite mostly between dusk and dawn. Risk of infection is low in the major resort areas and in the highlands and lower in the dry season (October to May) than in the rainy season (May to October). But it is fair to say that somewhere along La Ruta Maya you will encounter mosquitoes. They may or may not carry infectious diseases. Mexico, Guatemala and Belize do not have chloroquine-resistant strains of *Anopheles* mosquitoes, so chloroquine medicines do help to prevent infection.

The best way to protect yourself against malaria is to protect yourself against mosquito bites (see that section). You can also take medicines to protect against malarial infection, usually chloroquine phosphate (Aralen) or hydroxychloroquine sulphate (Plaquenil), though other medicines may be indicated for specific individuals. You must consult a doctor on the use of these medicines, and get a prescription to buy them. Begin taking the medicine *one or two weeks before you arrive* in a malarial area, continue taking it while you're there, and also for a month after you leave the area, according to your doctor's instructions. Taking medicine does not absolutely guarantee that you will not contract malaria, though.

The choice you must make is whether or not to take preventive medicine. As an adventurous traveller, you are more at risk than a person who buys a package tour to Cancún. Although most visitors to Mexico, Guatemala and Belize do not take malaria medicine, and most do not get malaria, you must decide for yourself. Talk to your doctor. Call a hospital or clinic which specialises in tropical diseases (London Hospital for Tropical Diseases in the UK; in the USA, call the Centers for Disease Control's telephone information system toll-free on (800) 526-6367, or the CDC Malaria Hotline on (404) 332-4555). Whether or not you take medicine, do be careful to protect yourself against mosquito bites.

Rabies The rabies virus is spread through bites by infected animals, or (rarely) through broken skin (scratches, licks) or the mucous membranes (as from breathing rabid-bat-contaminated air in a cave, for instance). Typical signs of a rabid animal are mad or uncontrolled behaviour, inability to eat, biting at anything and everything and frothing at the mouth.

If any animal (but especially a dog) bites you, assume you have been exposed to rabies until you are certain this is not the case – there are no second chances. First, immediately wash the wound with lots of soap and water – this is very important! If it is possible, and safe to do so, try to capture the animal alive, and give it to local health officials who can determine whether or not it's rabid. Begin rabies immunisation shots as soon as possible; if you are taking antimalarial medicine, be sure to mention this to the doctor because antimalarial medicines can interfere with the effectiveness of rabies vaccine. Rabies is a potentially fatal disease, but it can be cured by prompt and proper treatment.

Schistosomiasis A parasitic worm makes its way into the bodies of certain tiny freshwater snails and then into humans swimming, wading or otherwise touching the infected fresh water in pools, ponds or cenotes. Two or three weeks after your dip you may experience fever, weakness, headache, loss of appetite, loss of weight, pain in the gut and/or pain in the joints and muscles. You may have nausea and/or coughing. Six to eight weeks after infection, evidence of the worm can be found in the stools.

After this very unpleasant month or two, diagnosis can correctly identify schistosomiasis as the culprit, and you can get rid of it quickly and effectively by taking an inexpensive medicine. To guard against the illness, don't swim in fresh water that may be infected by sewage or other pollution. If you accidentally expose your skin to schistosomiasis-infected water, rub the skin vigorously with a towel, and/or rub alcohol on it.

Typhoid Fever This serious disease is spread by contaminated food and beverages, and has symptoms similar to those of traveller's diarrhoea. If you get it, you should have close supervision by a competent doctor for a while, and perhaps a short time in the hospital. Inoculation can give you some protection, but is not 100% effective. If diagnosed and treated early, typhoid can be treated effectively.

Typhus If you go to a mountain town and get head lice, they can give you typhus; otherwise, risk is extremely low. Typhus is treated by taking antibiotics.

Hospitals & Clinics

Almost every town and city along La Ruta Maya now has either a hospital or medical clinic and Red Cross (Cruz Roja) emergency facilities, all of which are indicated by road signs which show a red cross. Hospitals are generally inexpensive for typical ailments (diarrhoea, dysentery) and minor surgery (stitches, sprains). Clinics are often too understaffed and overburdened with local problems to be of much help, but they are linked by a government radio network to emergency services.

If you must use these services, try to ascertain the competence of the staff treating you. Compare their diagnoses and prescriptions to the information in this section. If you have questions, call your embassy and get a referral for a doctor, or call home and have your doctor advise you.

By the way, Guatemalans and Belizeans with serious illnesses often go to Mexican cities (Chetumal, Mérida, Cancún, Villahermosa, or even Mexico City) for treatment in better medical facilities. People from all three countries look upon Miami, New Orleans and Houston as the medical centres of last resort.

Women's Health

Gynaecological problems, poor diet, lowered resistance due to the use of antibiotics for stomach upsets and even contraceptive pills can lead to vaginal infections when travelling in hot climates. Keeping the genital area clean, and wearing skirts or loose-fitting trousers and cotton underwear will help to prevent infections.

Yeast infections, characterised by a rash, itch and discharge, can be treated with a vinegar or even lemon-juice douche or with yoghurt. Nystatin suppositories are the usual medical prescription. Trichomonas is a more serious infection; symptoms are a discharge and a burning sensation when urinating. Male sexual partners must also be treated, and if a vinegar-water douche is not effective medical attention should be sought. Flagyl is the prescribed drug.

Pregnancy Most miscarriages occur during the first three months of pregnancy, so this is the most risky time to travel. The last three months should also be spent within reasonable distance of good medical care, as quite serious problems can develop at this time.

Pregnant women should avoid all unnecessary medication, but vaccinations and malarial prophylactics should still be taken where possible. Additional care should be taken to prevent illness and particular attention should be paid to diet and nutrition.

WOMEN TRAVELLERS

In general, the men along La Ruta Maya aren't great believers in the equality of the sexes (what would you expect from the home of machismo?), and women alone have to expect numerous attempts to chat them up. It's commonly believed that foreign women without male companions are easy game for local men.

This can get tiresome at times; the best discouragement is a cool, unsmiling but polite initial response and a consistent firm 'No'.

Avoid situations in which you might find yourself alone with one or more strange men, at remote archaeological sites, on empty city streets, or on secluded stretches of beach.

DANGERS & ANNOYANCES
Safety

Most places along La Ruta Maya are quite safe, but adventurous travellers especially should be aware that certain areas have been and may still be the scene of political and military conflict, and even attacks on foreign tourists. These incidents occur at random and are not predictable.

Don't let vague fears or rumours of trouble scare you off, as these areas offer exceptional travel experiences which you should not miss. Your best defences against trouble are up to date information and reasonable caution. You should take the trouble to contact your government and enquire about current conditions and trouble spots, and follow the advice offered. Up to date travel advisories are available from the US Department of State's Citizens Emergency Center (☎ (202) 647-5225), and the UK Foreign Office's Travel Advisory Service (☎ (071) 270-3000).

If you plan to travel by road in the Guatemalan Highlands or El Petén, you should also ask as many other travellers as possible about current conditions. Don't rely on local newspapers, governmental officials or business people as your sole sources of information, as they often cover up 'unpleasant' incidents which might result in the loss of tourist revenues. Your home country's government, on the other hand, has an interest in protecting the lives of its citizens.

Theft

All three countries have some reputation for violence thanks to Pancho Villa, foreign movies and machismo. Apart from the dangers mentioned above, however, there's really little to fear on the score of physical safety unless you insult someone's dignity (a grave offence in Latin lands), or get deeply involved in a quarrel. More at risk are your possessions, particularly those you carry around with you, as most crimes are those of stealth. Reports of theft from hotel rooms are infrequent but pickpockets are all too common, especially on transport and in cities.

Crowded buses, bus stops and markets are among the thieves' favourite haunts. They often work in small teams: one may grab your bag or camera, and while you're holding on to it for dear life another will pick your pocket. Or one may 'drop' a coin in a crowded bus and as he or she 'looks for it', a pocket will be picked in the jostling. Thieves also often carry razor blades with which they slit pockets, bags or straps.

The best precautions are to wear a money belt beneath your clothing and to carry as little as possible. Most hotels will lock things up for you, and some bus stations have *guarderías* (left-luggage offices).

On long-distance buses or trains keep your baggage with you if you can. If you let it disappear into a bus baggage compartment the chance of not seeing it again increases – or it may emerge considerably the worse for wear. Parked vehicles with goodies visible are also a prime target for thieves.

There's little point in going to the police after a robbery unless your loss is insured, in which case you'll need a statement from the police to present to your insurance company. You'll probably have to communicate with them in Spanish, so if your own is poor take a more fluent speaker along. Say *Yo quisiera poner una acta de un robo* (I'd like to report a robbery). This should make it clear that you merely want a piece of paper and aren't going to ask the police to do anything inconvenient like look for the thieves or attempt to recover your goods. With luck you should get the required piece of paper without too much trouble. You may have to write it up yourself, then present it for official stamp and signature.

Guerrillas

Guatemala has been the scene of antigovernment insurgent activity for a century or so. The guerrillas believe themselves to be fighting for the rights of the common people, and dream of overthrowing the government to establish a populist state. The government sees the guerrillas as a danger to public order and to its own legitimacy, and it attempts to suppress insurgent activity with great severity.

Whatever your beliefs, you should avoid clashes between government soldiers and guerrillas. Don't go wandering about the countryside at night. Chances are very small that you will have any serious encounter with either group. If you do, don't panic – chances are that you'll be on your way again in a few minutes with no harm done. In recent years the guerrillas who operate near Tikal have taken to stopping the occasional bus, lecturing its foreign occupants, pilfering stuff from the 'American imperialists' (but not from other nationalities), then sending everyone on their way unharmed.

WORK

According to law you must have a work permit to work in any of the countries along La Ruta Maya. In practice you may get paid under the table, or through some bureaucratic loophole, if you can find suitable work. The most plentiful work for native English speakers is of course teaching their language. Consult the classified advertisements in local newspapers (both English and Spanish-language), browse the bulletin boards in spots where gringos gather, and ask around. Big cities offer the best possibilities, of course. Pay may be very low, but it's better than a negative cash flow.

More lucrative teaching is to tutor business and bank executives. It takes a while to establish a network of contacts and referrals, so you should not plan to tutor for just a month or two. If you get a good reputation, however, it can pay quite well as your students are among the commercial élite.

ACTIVITIES

Mayan culture, art and archaeology are of prime interest along La Ruta Maya, and anyone visiting this area would want to spend some time exploring these. There are many other things to do as well. Some of them have a Mayan connection, some do not.

Water Sports

The Caribbean coast from Cancún and Isla Mujeres in the north to the Belizean cayes in the south is a paradise for water sports, including swimming, snorkelling, scuba diving, fishing, sailing and sailboarding. Cancún has the most water sports facilities, but Cozumel and the Belizean cayes have the barrier reef and thus the best diving to look at tropical fish, coral, and undersea flora. If you plan to dive, bring evidence of your certification to show the dive shop people, and check the rental equipment over carefully before you dive.

Guatemala's Pacific coast is relatively undeveloped, and water sports possibilities are not nearly as attractive as they are along the Caribbean. Likewise, the beaches and waters along Mexico's Gulf coast often leave something to be desired (usually cleanliness). The north coast of the Yucatán peninsula has some beaches, most notably at Progreso, but it also has mangrove swamps, shallow waters, and – in certain places – crocodile-like beasts called caymans.

Hiking & Climbing

Much of La Ruta Maya is flat, flat, flat, and tropical jungle to boot, not the most interesting trekking country. The exceptions are the highlands of Chiapas and Guatemala, which have excellent hiking possibilities and many picturesque volcanoes to climb. The best base for hikes into the forests and jungles of Chiapas is San Cristóbal de las Casas. Treks on horseback may be organised here as well. In Guatemala you can climb the volcanoes bordering Lake Atitlán, though caution is in order as rural areas hereabouts harbour guerrillas. The volcanoes near Antigua Guatemala (usually called Antigua) also offer excellent possibilities, but as this book goes to press it is not safe to climb them. See Dangers & Annoyances in this chapter for information on how to find out whether or not it is currently safe to climb.

Language Courses

Spanish-language courses are given in San Cristóbal de las Casas, Chiapas, and in Antigua, both of which are delightful cities in which to spend some time. I have not sampled the instruction in either place, and thus do not feel that I should recommend any particular school or course. Write in advance to the tourist offices in both cities, asking for brochures and information on the courses available. Two schools which readers have disliked in Antigua are Centro Linguistico and Centro Internacional Español, so you may do well to avoid them. If you discover a course or school which offers good value – or is to be avoided – please write and let me know so that I can advise other readers.

HIGHLIGHTS

The top sights along La Ruta Maya are among the most fascinating on the planet, and you will miss something if you don't see them. But keep in mind that some of the most enjoyable and memorable travel experiences happen in small towns and villages off the beaten track, places like Cobán, Guatemala, or San Ignacio, Belize, or Isla Mujeres, Quintana Roo. Just because these lesser known spots are not mentioned below does not mean they are unworthy of your time.

Cities & Towns

The first rank for charm, ambience and interesting things to do includes Mérida, San Cristóbal de las Casas and Antigua Guatemala. If you want to spend some time in cities along La Ruta Maya, these are the ones to spend it in. They are, however, all on the tourist track. Should you want to get off it, spend a few days in Campeche, an attractive, authentic, very untouristy place with a rich history, beautiful architecture, and low prices. Another good choice would be Valladolid, on the highway between Cancún and Chichén Itzá.

Pleasant small towns? First has to be Panajachel, on Guatemala's Lake Atitlán, in the highlands. It's very touristy, and for good reason: the lake is breathtakingly beautiful, and the villages on its shores offer fascinating possibilities for meeting and getting to know the modern Maya. In Belize, the most pleasant place to spend a few days – apart from the wonderful cayes – is San Ignacio, on the banks of a peaceful river in the forests of the Maya Mountains.

Mayan Archaeological Sites

Without a doubt the top three sites are Chichén Itzá and Uxmal in Yucatán, and Tikal in Guatemala. If I had to name a fourth it would be Palenque, Chiapas, near the city of Villahermosa. These sites have the tallest pyramids, the most buildings, the boldest architecture, and the best restoration. They are also the most visited.

If you enjoy having archaeological sites more or less to yourself, consider my favourites among the 'second rank': Kabah, Sayil and Xlapak on the Puuc Route south of Uxmal; Cobá, inland from Tulum; Edzná, near Campeche; Uaxactún, north of Tikal; and Quiriguá off Guatemala's Carretera al Atlantico (Atlantic Highway). Copán, just across the border from Guatemala in Honduras, is among the most important Mayan sites, and falls somewhere in between the first and second rank.

Museums

As for museums, the only top-class museums on La Ruta Maya are the ones in Villahermosa, Tabasco and in Guatemala City.

For Olmec lore – including the enormous basalt heads – the Parque Museo La Venta is worth the detour if you get as far as Palenque, only an hour or so east of Villahermosa by bus. And while you're in Villahermosa, take a tour through the good Museo Regional de Antropología Carlos Pellicer Cámara, which offers a competent introduction to Olmec and Mayan culture.

In Guatemala City, don't miss the Museo Popol Vuh, a superb private collection of pre-Columbian and colonial artefacts given to the university; also the Museo Ixchel, famous for its displays of exquisite traditional hand-woven textiles and other crafts still thriving in Guatemala.

ACCOMMODATION

Accommodation ranges from luxury resort hotels, tourist vacation hotels, budget hotels and motels to *casas de huéspedes* (guesthouses) and *albergues de la juventud* (youth hostels).

Hotels & Motels

The luxury resort hotels are mainly found in Cancún, though there are upper-class hostelries in Villahermosa, Guatemala City and Belize City as well. Some of the resorts on the Belizean cayes are positively sybaritic, with prices to match. They are all expensive but most offer excellent value for what you get compared to establishments of a similar class at home. Double-room rates start at about US$80 per night and go beyond US$250. Most of the guests at these palatial places do not pay these 'rack rates', however, but are booked on package tours which offer far better value.

In the middle range are comfortable hotels and motels, some with appealing colonial ambience, others quite modern with green lawns, tropical flowers and swimming pools shaded by palm trees; still others are urban high-rise buildings with many services and comforts. These range in price from US$25

to US$80 or so, the higher prices being charged in the major cities.

Budget lodgings, those costing US$6 to US$25 double, come in many varieties and degrees of comfort and cleanliness. Guatemala has the cheapest and simplest budget hotels and pensions, although as the country becomes more popular, hotels will no doubt raise prices as demand warrants; Belize has the most expensive ones, with quality not much higher than the Guatemalan ones. Mexico has a good range of options in all price ranges.

Casas de Huéspedes

The next cheapest option is the casa de huéspedes, or a home converted into simple guest lodgings. A double can cost anywhere from US$5 to US$10 with or without meals.

Youth Hostels

Mexico's albergues de la juventud or youth hostels are usually run by the Consejo Nacional de Recursos para la Atención de la Juventud (CREA), which is associated with the International Youth Hostel Association (IYHA). IYHA cards can be used or you can obtain a CREA card at the hostel. The charge is US$3 to US$4 per night for members, slightly more for nonmembers. Guatemala and Belize do not really have any usable official hostels.

Camping

You can camp for free on most beaches, though you must be careful to pick a safe place far from thieves. Wherever facilities are available for campers, though, expect to pay from US$1 to US$10 per night, depending upon the facilities and the choiceness of the location. Most equipped campgrounds are trailer parks designed for motor homes. If you plan to camp much, I highly recommend *Camping in Mexico* by Carl Franz (John Muir Publications, Santa Fe, New Mexico; paperback) as a resource for what to bring, how and where to camp, outdoor cooking and other camping topics.

Cabañas & Hammocks

These are the two cheapest forms of accommodation, usually found in low-key beach spots. Cabañas are palm huts, sometimes with a dirt floor and nothing inside but a bed, other times more solidly built with electric light, mosquito nets, fans, even a cooker. Prices range from US$1.50 up to US$10 or even more for the most luxurious in the choicest spots.

You can rent a hammock and a place to hang it for less than US$2 in some beach places – usually under a palm roof outside a small casa de huéspedes or a fishing family's hut. If you bring your own hammock the cost may be even less. It's easy enough to buy hammocks in Mexico; Mérida has many shops specialising in them, and they are widely available in other towns throughout Yucatán as well.

FOOD

There are similarities among the cuisines along La Ruta Maya, but there are also differences. Yucatecan cuisine is quite different from what is served in the rest of Mexico, with several distinctive ingredients such as turkey and venison. Guatemalan cooking, though derived from the same roots as Mexican, has regional specialities and variations. Belizean cooking tends to the rough and ready, reflecting its roots.

There are three meals a day: breakfast *(el desayuno)*, lunch *(la comida)* and supper *(la cena)*. Each includes one or more of three traditional staples:

Tortillas are thin round patties of pressed corn (maize) dough cooked on griddles. Tortillas may be wrapped around or topped with various foods. Fresh handmade tortillas are best, followed by fresh machine-made ones bought at a *tortillería*. Usually what one finds are fairly fresh ones kept warm in a hot, moist cloth. These are alright, but they take on a rubbery quality. Worst are old tortillas left to dry out; their edges curl and dry out while the centre could be used to patch a tyre. But don't confuse old tortillas with toasted, thoroughly dried, crisp tortillas, which are another thing altogether, and very good.

Frijoles are beans eaten boiled, fried, refried, in soups, spread on tortillas or with eggs. If you simply order frijoles they may come in a bowl swimming in their own dark sauce, as a runny mass on a plate, or as a thick and almost black paste. No matter how they come, they're usually delicious and very nutritious. The only bad ones are refried beans which have been fried using too much or low-quality oil.

Chillis (peppers) come in many varieties and are consumed in hundreds of ways. Some chillis such as the *habanero* and *serrano* are always spicy-hot while others such as the *poblano* vary in spiciness according to when they were picked. If you are unsure about your tolerance for hot chillis, ask if the chilli is *picante* (spicy-hot) or *muy picante* (very spicy-hot).

For full lists of menu items with translations, see the Language section at the back of this book.

Meals

Breakfast This can be either continental or American-style. A light, continental-style breakfast can be made of sweet rolls *(pan dulce)* or toast and coffee. Often a basket of pan dulce will be placed on your breakfast table when your coffee is served. When the time comes to pay, you tell the clerk how many you have eaten.

American-style breakfasts are always available: bacon or sausage and eggs, hot cakes (called just that: *hot cakes* in Mexico, *panqueques* in Guatemala), cold cereal such as corn flakes or hot cereal such as cream of wheat, fruit juice and coffee. You may order eggs in a variety of ways (see the Language section).

The Midday Meal This, the biggest meal of the day, is served about 1 or 2 pm. In restaurants which do not cater primarily to tourists, menus might change every day, every week or not at all. Meals might be ordered à la carte or table d'hôte. A fixed-price meal of several courses called a *comida corrida* (the bargain or daily special meal) is sometimes offered, and may include from one to five or six courses; choices and price are often displayed near the front door of the restaurant. Simple comidas corridas may consist of a plain soup or pasta, a garnished main course plate and coffee; more expensive versions may have a fancy soup or ceviche, a choice main course such as steak or fish, salad, dessert and coffee.

Supper La cena is a lighter version of lunch served about 7.30 pm. In beach resorts the evening meal tends to be the big one, as everyone is out at the beach during the day, and they hardly want to drag themselves inside for a big meal.

Yucatecan Food

It's tantalising to consider that some of the dishes prepared in Yucatán's kitchens today may be very similar to ones served in ancient times to Mayan royalty. Many traditional ingredients such as turkey (*pavo*), venison (*venado*) and fish (*pescado*) were available in ancient times, as they are today.

Yucatán's resident chilli is the habanero, and my own personal anthropological theory holds that in the old days the victims of human sacrifice were given a choice: munch a habanero or have your heart carved out. Most thought the heart option offered a less painful end. If you go after a habanero chilli, you had better be equipped with a steel tongue.

Despite its reputation as a fissionable material in vegetable form, the habanero is an important ingredient in *achiote*, the popular Yucatecan sauce which also includes chopped onions, the juice of sour Seville oranges, *cilantro* (fresh coriander leaf) and salt. You'll see a bowl of achiote on most restaurant tables in Yucatán. Put it on your food – or ignore it – as you like.

A local hearty breakfast favourite is *huevos motuleños*, or eggs in the style of the town of Motul, east of Mérida. Fresh tortillas are spread with refried beans, then topped with an egg or two, then garnished with chopped ham, green peas and shredded cheese, with a few slices of fried banana on the side. It can be slightly picante or muy picante, depending upon the cook.

An authentic Yucatecan lunch or supper might begin with *sopa de lima* (lime soup), a chicken stock containing shreds of chicken meat, bits of tortilla and lime juice. It's tangy and delicious if made well; made badly, it's greasy.

For a main course you might order *pollo pibil*, chicken marinated in achiote sauce, sour Seville orange juice, garlic, black pepper, cumin and salt, then wrapped in banana leaves and baked. There are no nuclear chillis to blow your head off. A variant is *cochinita pibil*, made with suckling pig instead of chicken.

The restaurant named Los Almendros in Ticul, Yucatán, claims to have created *pocchuc*, a dish that has spread throughout Yucatán, Quintana Roo and Campeche. Pocchuc is slices of tender pork marinated in sour orange juice, cooked and served with a tangy sauce and pickled onions. A more traditional pork dish is *frijol con puerco*, the Mayan version of pork-and-beans, with black beans, tomato sauce, and a serving of rice.

Another hearty dish is *puchero*, a stew made with chicken and pork, carrots, cabbage, squash (marrow) and sweet potato.

The turkey is native to Yucatán, and has been used as food for millenia. *Pavo relleno negro*, or dark stuffed turkey, is slices of turkey over a 'filling' made with pork and beef, all topped by a rich dark sauce.

Venison (venado), also native to Yucatán, is perhaps best as a *pipián de venado*, steamed in banana leaves a la pibil and topped with a sauce made with ground squash (marrow) seeds.

Lighter traditional dishes include *papadzules*, tortillas sprinkled with chopped hard-boiled eggs, rolled up and topped with a sauce made with squash or pumpkin seeds. *Salbutes* are the native tacos: fried corn tortillas topped with shredded turkey meat, avocado and pickled onions. *Panuchos* are similar, but made with refried beans.

As for seafood, the all-time favourite is *pescado frito*, simple fried fish, but there's also *langosta* (lobster). Usually only the tail of the lobster is used, fried in butter or grilled. The most interesting seafood concoctions are the ceviches, cocktails made of raw or parboiled seafood in a marinade of lime juice, tomato sauce, chopped onion and cilantro. Cheapest is the *ceviche de pescado* made with whatever fish is in season and cheap in the markets. More choices available include *ceviche de camarones* (with shrimp) and *ceviche de ostiones* (with oysters).

Besides the traditional Yucatecan and Mexican restaurants, other cuisines are represented in a few cities. Cancún has plenty of American-style food, numerous good Italian, French and Chinese restaurants, and a few places serving up even more exotic cuisines. Mérida has a few good French and Lebanese restaurants from the time when it was a rich and important trading city.

Guatemalan Food

When it comes to cuisine, Guatemala is the poorer cousin to the more elaborate cuisines of Mexico, the USA and Europe. You can find a few Mexican standards such as tortillas topped with beans, meat or cheese; enchiladas; *guacamole*, a salad of mashed or chopped avocados, onions and tomatoes; and *tamales*, steamed corn dough rolls, perhaps with a meat or other stuffing. But mostly you will encounter *bistec*, tough grilled or fried beef, *pollo asado*, grilled chicken, *chuletas de puerco*, pork chops, and lighter fare such as *hamburguesas*, hamburgers, and *salchichas*, sausages like hot dogs. Of the simpler food, *frijoles con arroz*, beans and rice, is cheapest and often best.

One of the unexpected and surprising things about Guatemala, however, is the omnipresence of Chinese restaurants. Virtually any city or town of any size has at least one Chinese eatery, usually small and not overly authentic, but cheap and good for a change of scene. If you come from a place with excellent Chinese restaurants, ratchet your taste buds down a few notches before plowing into the Guatemalan versions of sweet-and-sour pork or *chao mein*. And don't be surprised to find American-style white sandwich bread or even tortillas served with your Chinese meal.

Guatemala City and Antigua have several very good restaurants; Panajachel has a few interesting places as well. Out in the countryside, though, food is very basic.

Belizean Food

Cooking in Belize is mostly borrowed – from the UK, from the Caribbean, from Mexico, from the USA. Being a young, small, somewhat isolated and relatively poor country, Belize never developed its own elaborate native cuisine. Local dishes such as *boil-up* rarely appear on restaurant menus. Even so, there is some good food to be had.

Belizeans are justly proud of all the fresh fish and lobster (sometimes called 'crawfish') available from their coastal waters. Grilled or fried fish is always a good bet on the cayes and in coastal towns, though I'm not sure I'd trust it inland. By all means have lobster if it's in season when you're on the cayes or in Belize City.

Beef and chicken are the usual main courses, often served with fried potatoes, often greasy. But the traditional staple of the Belizean diet is certainly rice and beans. As a Belizean wag described it to me on my first visit years ago, 'We eat a lot of rice and beans in Belize, and when we get tired of that, we eat beans and rice'. What saves rice and beans from becoming boring by the third day are other ingredients – chicken, pork, beef, vegetables, even lobster – plus some spices and condiments like coconut milk.

More exotic traditional foods include *gibnut* or *paca*, a small brown-spotted rodent similar to a guinea pig, armadillo and venison, but their value is more as a curiosity than as a staple of the diet.

DRINKS

Because of the hot climate along La Ruta Maya, you will find yourself drinking lots of fluids. Indeed, you must remember to drink even if you don't feel particularly thirsty in order to prevent dehydration and heat exhaustion (see Health). In any case, drinking things is quite a pleasure along La Ruta Maya.

Water & Soft Drinks

Bottled or purified water is widely available in hotels and shops (see Food & Water in the Health section). You can also order safe-to-drink fizzy mineral water by saying 'soda'.

Besides the easily recognisable and internationally known brands of *refrescos* (soft drinks) such as Coca-Cola, Pepsi and Seven-Up, you will find interesting local flavours. Orange *(naranja)* flavoured soda is very popular, and grapefruit *(toronja)* is even better, though less readily available. Squirt (pronounced SKWEERT) is a Mexican brand of lemon-flavoured soda which is a bit drier than Seven-Up. Also in Mexico, try the two apple-flavoured drinks named Sidral and Manzanita.

Coffee, Tea & Cocoa

The Soconusco region along the Pacific slope of Chiapas and Guatemala has many large coffee plantations which produce excellent beans, including those typed as Guatemalan Antigua and Maragogipes. Some hotels in Antigua have coffee bushes growing right on their grounds. Coffee is available everywhere, strong and flavourful in Mexico, surprisingly weak and sugary in some parts of Guatemala.

Black tea *(té negro)*, usually made from bags (often locally produced Lipton), tends to be a disappointment to devoted tea drinkers. Best to bring your own supply of loose tea and a tea infuser, then just order *una taza de agua caliente* (a cup of hot water) and brew your own.

Herbal teas are much better. Camomile tea *(té de manzanilla)* is a common item on restaurant and café menus, and is a specific remedy for queasy stomach and gripy gut.

Hot chocolate or cocoa was the royal stimulant during the Classic period of Mayan civilisation, being drunk on ceremonial occasions by the kings and nobility. Their version was unsweetened, and dreadfully bitter. Today it's sweetened and, if not authentic, at least more palatable.

Fruit & Vegetable Juices

Fresh fruit and vegetable juices *(jugos)*, milkshakes *(licuados)* and flavoured waters *(aguas frescas)* are popular drinks along La Ruta Maya, but particularly in Mexico. Almost every town has a stand serving one or more of these, and Mérida seems to have one every few blocks. All of the fruits and a few of the squeezable vegetables mentioned are used either individually (as in jugos or aguas frescas) or in some combination (as in licuados).

The basic licuado is a blend of fruit or juice with water and sugar. Other items can be added or substituted: raw egg, milk, ice, flavourings such as vanilla or nutmeg. The delicious combinations are practically limitless.

Aguas frescas are made by mixing fruit juice or a syrup made from mashed grains or seeds with sugar and water. You will usually see them in big glass jars on the counters of juice stands. Try the *agua fresca de arroz* (literally rice water) which has a sweet nutty taste.

Alcohol

Supermarkets, grocery shops and liquor stores along La Ruta Maya stock both beer and wine, both imported and locally made. Some of the local stuff is quite good. You certainly won't go thirsty, and drinking won't bust your budget.

Beer Breweries were first established in Mexico and Guatemala by German immigrants in the late 19th century. European techniques and technology have been used ever since the beginning, which may explain why Mexico has so many delicious beers, both light and dark. Most beers along La Ruta Maya are light lagers, served cold from bottles or cans, but there are also a few flavourful dark beers such as Modelo Negro (Mexico) and Moza (Guatemala).

Mexico's breweries now produce more than 25 brands of beer including major labels such as Modelo, Superior, Corona, Bohemia and Carta Blanca. Local beers made in

Yucatán include the lagers Carta Clara and Montejo, and the dark León Negro.

Guatemala's two nationally distributed beers are Gallo (GAH-yoh, rooster) and Cabro (goat). The distribution prize goes to Gallo – you'll find it everywhere.

In Belize, Belikin beer is the cheapest, most popular local brew. Belikin Export, the premium version, comes in a larger bottle, is much tastier, costs more, and is worth it. When you get sick of Belikin you can readily find American and European beers (Heineken, Löwenbrau, etc), but they cost considerably more.

In restaurants and bars unaccustomed to tourists, beer is sometimes served at room temperature. If you want to be sure of getting a cold beer, ask for *una cerveza fría*. Sometimes the waiter or bartender will hand you the bottle or can and let you feel it for proper coldness. This usually means it's not very cold, and your choice is then the dismal one of 'this beer or no beer at all'.

Wine Wine is not the local drink of choice along La Ruta Maya. That distinction goes to beer and liquor made from sugar cane, by far. But as foreign wine lovers spread through the region, so does the availability of wine.

Mexico has three big wineries producing very drinkable vintages: Industrias Vinicolas Domecq, Formex-Ybarra and Bodegas de Santo Tomás.

Domecq is renowned in Mexico for its Los Reyes table wines. Formex has more than 800 acres of vineyards in the Valle de Guadalupe and is known for its Terrasola table wine. Santo Tomás hopes eventually to produce wines which can compete with California's, including varietal wines such as Pinot Noir, Chardonnay and Cabernet Sauvignon.

The situation in Guatemala and Belize is much worse. Local wines are no thrill to drink, and imported wines are fairly expensive, but at least they're available. In all but the best places you may have to specify that you want your red wine at room temperature and your white wine chilled.

Spirits The traditional Mayan ardent spirit in Yucatán is *xtabentún* (SHTAH-behn-TOON), an anise-flavoured brandy which, when authentic, is made by fermenting honey. The modern version has a goodly proportion of grain neutral spirits, however. It is made to be either dry *(seco)* or sweet *(crema)*. The seco tastes much like the Greek ouzo or French pastis; the crema is like the sweeter Italian Sambuca. It is served in some restaurants as an after dinner drink; you can find it readily in many liquor shops in Mérida, Cancún, and other Yucatecan towns.

Many other famous liquors, liqueurs and brandies are made in Mexico: Bacardi rum, Pedro Domecq brandy, Controy (orange liqueur, a knock-off Cointreau), Kahlua (coffee-flavoured liqueur) and Oso Negro vodka. All are of good quality and quite inexpensive.

Rum and *aguardiente* (sugar cane liquor) are the favourite strong drinks in Guatemala and Belize as well, and though most are of low price and matching quality, some local products are exceptionally fine. Zacapa Centenario is a very smooth Guatemalan rum made in Zacapa, off the Atlantic Highway. Aged 23 years, it should be sipped slowly, neat, like fine cognac. Cheaper rums and brandies are often mixed with soft drinks to make potent but cooling drinks like the *Cuba libre* of rum and Coke.

Other drinks include gin, mixed with tonic water, ice and lime juice to make what many consider the perfect drink for the hot tropics, and whisky, mostly American.

If this is your first visit to Mexico, you should know about the local national firewater, *tequila*, and its less sophisticated cousin, *mezcal*.

Tequila & Mezcal The most Mexican of spiritous drinks are these, made from the maguey plant. The maguey, sometimes called a century plant, is a relative of the aloe and the agave; it has long, wide, tough, fibrous leaves slightly curved, with sharp spikes at the tips.

Mezcal can be made from several species of maguey, but tequila is properly made from the *agave tequilana* which grows only in and around the Mexican town of Tequila, north-west of Guadalajara. The spikes of the maguey are stripped away to expose the plant's core or *piña*. The piña is chopped, roasted, shredded and then pressed to remove the juice. Sugar is added to the juice and, after the resulting mixture ferments for four days, it is put through a double distillation process.

After distillation the mezcal and tequila are aged in wooden casks for periods ranging from four months to seven years or longer. The final product is a clear liquid which is at its most potent as tequila. The longer the tequila has been aged, the higher its price.

The traditional steps in drinking mezcal or tequila are:

1. Lick the back of your hand and sprinkle salt on it
2. Lick the salt
3. Suck on a lime
4. Down the mezcal or tequila in one gulp
5. Lick more salt
6. Start over

When the bottle is empty, you are supposed to eat the worm *(gusano)* – preferably fried – which is traditionally added to each bottle before it's filled.

For foreigners not used to the potency of straight tequila, it is more popular as part of a mixed drink called a Margarita. The traditional Margarita is made with tequila (always), lime juice, orange liqueur (Controy is the Mexican brand) and a salt-rimmed glass. Fresh fruit such as strawberries and peaches can also be added.

If you are shopping for a bottle of tequila in Mexico, look on the label for the letters 'DGN' which stand for Dirección General de Normas (Bureau of Standards). The presence of the letters indicates government certification that the tequila is made using only the agave tequilana and not just any old garden-variety maguey.

ENTERTAINMENT

Cancún offers lots of nightclubs, bars, dancing places, spectacles, booze cruises and razzamatazz, all slickly packaged and marketed to the one-week tour crowd. Prices are high (for Mexico), but most people feel they get their money's worth, because the staff are certainly experienced at what they do. Some of the middle-range restaurants in Ciudad Cancún also provide entertainment – a pair of troubadours, a trio of mariachis, a lasso twirler – at no extra cost. The only other spot on La Ruta Maya with good nightclubs is Guatemala City. In smaller cities and towns it is not unusual to find a strolling guitarist or other musician(s) entertaining in the better restaurants.

The city government in Mérida sponsors weekly musical performances in several plazas. See the Mérida section for details.

Cinemas are located in the larger cities. Except in Belize, virtually all movies are in Spanish.

THINGS TO BUY

Most *artesanías* (handicrafts) originated in objects made for everyday use or for specific occasions such as festivals. Today many objects are made simply to sell as 'folk art' – some purely decorative, others with a useful function – but that doesn't necessarily reduce their quality. Although traditional materials, particularly textiles, are rarer than they used to be, some artisans have used the opportunity to develop their artistic talents to high levels.

The places where crafts are made aren't always the best places to buy them. There's wide trade in artesanías and you'll often find a better selection in shops and markets in towns and cities than in the original villages. Nor do prices necessarily get much higher in the bigger centres. Indeed, the artisans who make these crafts have learned that the real markets for their wares are in cities such as Mérida, San Cristóbal de las Casas, Panajachel and Antigua Guatemala where there are lots of appreciative tourists interested in buying.

You can get a good overview of the best that's available and an idea of prices by looking round some of the city stores devoted to these products. Buying in these places also saves the time and effort of seeking out the sometimes remote towns and villages where items are made. The government-run shops in several cities usually have good ranges of high-quality stock at decent prices.

Hammocks

Whether or not you plan to follow the Yucatecan custom of bedding down in a hammock, you should plan to take one home for lazy summer afternoons. Yucatecan hammocks are woven of fine cotton string, natural in tone or dyed in pale colours. With their hundreds of strings they are supremely comfortable and cool, and very cheap. For details, refer to the Mérida chapter, as that city is the centre of the hammock trade.

Textiles

Colourful hand-woven and embroidered Indian costumes come in a number of basic shapes and as many designs as there are weavers. Chiapas and the Guatemalan highland towns have the best work and the widest selection. Some of the finest huipiles are made in the villages around Lake Atitlán and in the villages near Antigua. Cheaper than the fairly pricey huipiles are the colourful waist sashes (fajas).

Other Woven Goods

Many goods are woven all over the country from palm, straw, reeds or sisal (rope made from the henequen plant). Mérida is a centre for sisal mats, hammocks, bags and hats.

Pottery

This comes in a huge variety of local forms. There are basically two types – unglazed earthenware and sturdier, Spanish-influenced, often highly decorated glazed ware. You can pick up attractive items for a couple of dollars or less in many places. The village of Amatenango del Valle turns out earthenware jugs, vases and animals, fired not in kilns but in open fires, and painted in pleasing 'natural' colours.

Wooden Masks

Ceremonial masks are fascinating, eye-catching, and still in regular use. You'll see them in the markets in San Cristóbal de Las Casas, Panajachel, Sololá, Chichicastenango and Antigua.

Getting There & Away

The easiest approach to La Ruta Maya, and the one most travellers use, is by air. The region's major international airports are at Cancún and Guatemala City, with a small but growing amount of international traffic heading for Belize City. Mexico City also receives a large number of flights from all parts of the world, with connecting flights to points along La Ruta Maya.

Approaches by road from Mexico and Central America (El Salvador and Honduras) are easy, with fairly good roads, and frequent service in comfortable (though not luxurious) buses.

Amtrak and Southern Railways trains approach the US-Mexican border along the Rio Grande, and there are some good Mexican trains from border towns southwards to Mexico City. But beyond the Isthmus of Tehuantepec train service is slow, unreliable, uncomfortable and often unsafe. There is no passenger train service connecting Guatemala with the rest of Central America.

There is no regular car or passenger ferry service between the countries of La Ruta Maya and the USA or Central America.

AIR
Routes
International air routes are structured so that virtually all flights into the region from the rest of the world pass through half a dozen 'hub' cities: Dallas/Fort Worth, Houston, Los Angeles, Miami, Mexico City or San Salvador. If you begin your trip in any other city you will probably find yourself stopping in one of these hub cities to change planes, and perhaps airlines, before continuing to your destination.

Discount Tickets
Buying airline tickets these days is like shopping for a car, a stereo or a camera – five different travel agents will quote you five different prices. Rule number one if you're looking for a cheap ticket is to go to an agent, not directly to the airline. The airline can only quote you the absolutely straight-up-and-down, by-the-rule-book regular fare. An agent, on the other hand, can offer all sorts of special deals, particularly on competitive routes.

Ideally an airline would like to fly all their flights with every seat in use and every passenger paying the highest fare possible. Fortunately life usually isn't like that and airlines would rather have a half-price passenger than an empty seat. Since the airline itself can't very well offer seats at two different prices, what they do when faced with the problem of too many seats is let agents sell them at cut prices.

Of course what's available and what it costs depends on what time of year it is, what route you're flying and who you're flying with. If you want to go to La Ruta Maya at the most popular time of year you'll probably have to pay more. If you're flying on a popular route or one where the choice of flights is very limited, then the fare is likely to be higher or there may be nothing available but the official fare.

Similarly, the dirt cheap fares are likely to be less conveniently scheduled, go by a less convenient route or with a less popular airline.

Round-the-World Tickets
Round-the-World (RTW) tickets have become very popular in the last few years and many of these will take you through Australia. The airline RTW tickets are often real bargains and since Australia is pretty much at the other side of the world from Europe or North America it can work out no more expensive or even cheaper to keep going in the same direction right round the world rather than U-turn when you return.

The official airline RTW tickets are usually put together by a combination of two airlines, and permit you to fly anywhere you want on their route systems so long as you do not backtrack. Other restrictions are that you (usually) must book the first sector in advance and cancellation penalties then apply. There may be restrictions on how many stops you are permitted and usually the tickets are valid from 90 days up to a year. Typical prices for these South Pacific RTW tickets are from £1400 to £1700 or US$2500 to US$3000. An alternative type of RTW ticket is one put together by a travel agent using a combination of discounted tickets. A UK agent like Trailfinders can put together interesting London to London RTW combinations including Australia for £850 to £1000.

To/From North America

American, Continental, Delta, Northwest, Pan Am and United are the US airlines with the most service to La Ruta Maya. Aeroméxico, Aeroquetzal, Aeronica, Aviateca, Belize Trans Air, COPA, LACSA, Mexicana and TACA are the Latin American airlines with flights to the USA. You can fly nonstop to Cancún from any of these North American cities: Baltimore, Chicago, Dallas/Fort Worth, Denver, Detroit, Houston, Los Angeles, Miami, New Orleans, New York, Philadelphia, San Francisco, Tampa/St Petersburg and Washington, DC.

Fares There are dozens of airfares which apply to any given air route. They vary with each company, class of service, season of the year, length of stay, dates of travel, date of purchase and reservation. Your ticket may cost more or less depending upon the flexibility in are allowed in changing your plans. The price of the ticket is even affected by how you buy it and from whom.

Travel agents are the first people to consult about fares and routes. Once you've discovered the basics of the airlines flying, the routes taken and the various discounted tickets available, you can consult your favourite bucket shop, consolidator or charter airline to see if their fares are better. Here are some sample fixed-date return fares

(sometimes called excursion fares) from various cities to Cancún:

Chicago	US$406
Dallas/Fort Worth	US$361
Los Angeles	US$509
Miami	US$235
New York	US$387
Toronto	US$589

Besides these excursion fares, there are many package tours from the USA which typically provide a round-trip (return) airfare, transfers and accommodation for a few days or a week. These are by far the most economical way to visit Cancún. Some of these tour packages allow you to extend your stay in order to tour the region on your own.

These package tours change in price and features as the seasons change. For a cheap flight to Cancún, read the advertisements in the travel section of your local newspaper and call a package tour operator, or a travel agent who sells such tours, and ask if you can buy 'air only' (just the round-trip air transportation, not the hotel or other features). Often this is possible, and usually it is cheaper than buying a discounted excursion ticket. Sometimes, though, the difference between air-only and a tour package with hotels is so small that it makes sense just to accept the hotel along with the flight.

Consolidators are organisations that buy bulk seats from airlines at considerable discounts and then resell them to the public, usually through travel agents. Though there are some shady dealers, most consolidators are quite legitimate. Consolidators in North America are similar to bucket shops in Europe. Ask your travel agent about buying a consolidator ticket, or look for the consolidator adverts in the travel section of the newspaper (they're the ones with tables of destinations and fares and a toll-free '800' number to call).

Cancún is easy to reach cheaply; it's a bit more difficult to find air-only fares to Guatemala City and Belize. Tour operators currently offering air-only fares to these cities are:

Solar Tours (☎ (202) 861-5864, (800) 554-5500), 1629 K Street, NW, Suite 502, Washington, DC 20006. Air-only round-trip tickets from Boston, New York and Washington to Belize City for US$400 and up; also from Los Angeles, New York and Washington to Guatemala City from US$350 to US$435.

Unique Tours (☎ (212) 689-5260, (201) 795-1416, (800) 852-5528; fax (212) 545-9793), 253 Fifth Avenue, Second Floor, New York, NY 10016. Air-only round-trip tickets from New York and Washington to Belize City for US$460 to US$550; also from Chicago, New York and Washington to Guatemala City from US$450 to US$500.

To/From Europe

Few European airlines fly directly to points along La Ruta Maya. Most take you to one of the US hub cities, where you change to a plane of a US, Mexican, Guatemalan or other Central American airline. Your flight then continues to Cancún, Chetumal, Cozumel, Guatemala City, Mérida, Tuxtla Gutiérrez or Villahermosa.

The most common types of ticket from Europe to La Ruta Maya are one ways, fixed-date returns, open returns, circle trips and ticketed surface sectors. Most of them are available at discount rates from cheap ticket agencies in Europe's bargain flight centres like London, Amsterdam, Paris and Frankfurt.

Fixed-date returns require you to decide dates of travel when you buy the ticket. Open tickets allow you to choose your dates later; they're usually valid for 180 days or a year and are a bit more expensive than fixed-date returns. Circle trips and surface sectors are useful if you want to travel from one part of La Ruta Maya to another, or between La Ruta Maya and elsewhere on the American continent, without backtracking. On both you usually depart from and return to the same city in Europe: circle trips give you flights between your different destinations along La Ruta Maya or Latin America en route, while with surface sectors you make your own way between your entry and exit points in Latin America. Some bargain fares are only open to students, teachers or people under 26.

Fares can also vary considerably between high and low seasons.

London For cheap tickets, pick up a copy of *Time Out*, *TNT* or any of the other magazines which advertise discount (bucket shop) flights, and check out a few of the advertisers. The magazine *Business Traveller* also has a great deal of good advice on air fare bargains. Most bucket shops are trustworthy and reliable but the occasional sharp operator appears – *Time Out* and *Business Traveller* give some useful advice on precautions to take. Agents which offer good-value fares to Mexico include Journey Latin America (☎ (081) 747-3108) at 16 Devonshire Rd, Chiswick, London W4 2HD (this company also has an information service for its customers and runs some small-group tours to Mexico); STA Travel (☎ (071) 581-1022) at 74 Old Brompton Rd, London W1 and 117 Euston Rd, London NW1; and London Student Travel (☎ (071) 730-3402) at 52 Grosvenor Gardens, London SW1.

An unusual and potentially interesting route to Mexico is via Paris and Havana with the Cuban airline Cubana. Journey Latin America quotes around US$650 one-way, US$1050 return for this.

Elsewhere in Europe Discount tickets are available at prices similar to London's in several European cities. Amsterdam, Paris and Frankfurt are among the main cheap flight centres. Air France, KLM, Iberia and the Colombian airline Avianca are some of the airlines whose tickets are handled by discount agents. KLM, Air France and Iberia all offer surface sector fares between Europe and numerous places in Latin America (Iberia's are particularly good value), and Avianca has some interesting round-trip options.

Here are some typical fixed-date return (excursion) fares to Cancún valid at the time of writing.

Amsterdam	US$2017
Frankfurt	US$2087
London	US$1690
Paris	US$1258

To/From Australasia

There are no direct flights from Australia to La Ruta Maya. The cheapest way of getting there is via the USA – often Los Angeles. Discount returns from Sydney to Los Angeles cost from A$1300. Cheap flights from the USA to La Ruta Maya are hard to find in Australia. Regular Los Angeles/Cancún fares are US$330 one way, US$440 return – but you may be able to pick up cheaper tickets if you are stopping a day or two in Los Angeles. There are also numerous flights between North American cities and several other destinations along La Ruta Maya (see To/From North America).

If you want to combine La Ruta Maya with South America, the cheapest return tickets from Sydney to Lima or Rio de Janeiro are about A$3100. Santiago and Buenos Aires are a little cheaper at about A$2600. If you want to fly into South America and out of the USA, or vice-versa, the best option is to get a return ticket to South America on an airline such as United, which flies to South America via the USA, and simply don't use one of the legs you have paid for. Fortunately, at the time of writing, United's fares for this route were much the same as those of airlines which go directly to South America – discount returns via the States from Sydney to Buenos Aires, Lima, Santiago or Rio de Janeiro were all available at around A$2750.

Round-the-world tickets with a Mexico/Guatemala option are sometimes available in Australia. STA Travel, with 40 offices around the country, is one of the most popular discount travel agents in Australia. It also has sales offices or agents all over the world.

Fixed-date return (excursion) fares to Cancún from Sydney, via Los Angeles, valid at the time of writing, are around A$1850. To Cancún via Los Angeles one way is A$1700.

A fixed date return (excursion) fare from

Auckland, New Zealand, to South America stopping in Los Angeles, Mexico, Buenos Aires, Lima and Santiago, are around NZ$2700.

To/From Canada

Japan Airlines' one-month excursion return fare between Vancouver and Mexico City is good value at US$340. Aeroméxico has non-stop flights between Acapulco and Montréal and Toronto.

To/From Central & South America & the Caribbean

Aeroméxico flies between Mexico City and Panama City, Caracas and Bogotá. Mexicana links Mexico City with Guatemala City, San Juan (Puerto Rico), Havana and San José (Costa Rica); it also has flights between San Juan and Cancún, and Havana and Mérida. Avianca, the Colombian airline, also links Mexico with South America. Cubana flies between Havana and Mexico City.

Departure Tax

A departure tax equivalent to approximately US$10 is levied in each of the La Ruta Maya countries for travellers departing by air for foreign destinations. Exit tax at Belizean land border crossing points is BZ$1 (US$0.50).

LAND

Mexico can be entered by land from the USA at 24 points: San Ysidro (Tijuana), Otay Mesa, Tecate, Calexico (Mexicali) and Algodones, San Luis Río Colorado, Sonoita, Sasabe, Nogales, Naco, Agua Prieta, Palomas, Ciudad Juárez, Guadalupe Bravos, Praxedis Guerrero, Ojinaga, Ciudad Acuña, Piedras Negras, Nuevo Laredo, Ciudad Alemán, Camargo, Reynosa, Nuevo Progreso and Matamoros.

Bus

It doesn't make sense to get to La Ruta Maya by bus unless you plan to stop and see the USA, Mexico or Central America along the way. The distances are great, and when you add up the cost of bus tickets, meals, hotel nights and incidentals, a bus trip can be more expensive than a flight. It's almost 6000 km from New York to Cancún, and more than 5000 km from Los Angeles to Cancún. At an average of 70 km/hour, these trips would take three or four days of constant travel, not counting border formalities or nights in hotels.

The Greyhound bus network does provide several services daily from within the USA to all the main towns on the USA side of the border. There are a few Mexican buses to destinations deep inside Mexico from the towns on the US side of the border, but these usually cost significantly more than buses from the towns on the Mexican side. To save money it's better to walk or take a local bus across the border and then get a long-distance bus from the Mexican side.

Once you've reached Mexico City, Oaxaca, San Salvador or Tegucigalpa (Honduras), taking the bus to La Ruta Maya makes sense. Refer to the various cities and sites along La Ruta Maya for details.

Train

As with bus travel, you must plan to tour the USA and Mexico to make it worthwhile. Plan to use trains in the USA and in Mexico west of the Isthmus of Tehuantepec if you like, but avoid trains in Yucatán and Guatemala. There are no trains in Belize.

TOURS

General and special-interest tours are an increasingly popular way to explore La Ruta Maya. Following are a few of the tour operators which offer these trips:

From the USA

Travel agents at most USA agencies can arrange package deals with a variety of operators.

Pacific Adventures (☎ (714) 684-1227), PO Box 5041, Riverside, California 92517, offers trips oriented to horseback riding, kayaking, scuba diving and sailing.

Mayan Adventure Tours (☎ (206) 523-5309), PO Box 15204 Wedgwood Station, Seattle, Washington 98115-15204, offers unique tours of obscure Mayan sites which are not easily accessible. Small groups of nine to 12 travel in private vehicles and stay in local hotels. Among the trips are Chichén Itzá during the equinox, the Yucatán coast to coast, the indigenous crafts centres of Oaxaca and Guatemala, and hidden beaches of the Yucatán.

Expeditions Inc (☎ (817) 861-9298), PO Box 13594, Arlington, Texas 76094-0594, can take you to about 16 archaeological or colonial destinations in two weeks (send for prices).

From the UK

Journey Latin America (☎ (071) 747-3108), 16 Devonshire Rd, Chiswick, London W4 2HD, runs a few small-group tours using local transport in Mexico. One two-week trip costing around US$1600 from London takes in Mexico City, Teotihuacán, Oaxaca and nearby sites, San Cristóbal de Las Casas, Palenque, Mérida and some Mayan sites in Yucatán.

Explore Worldwide does a 24-night small-group trip with 'expert leaders', which includes Mexico City, Oaxaca, San Cristóbal de Las Casas, Palenque, Tikal, Belize City, Ambergris Cay, Mérida, Uxmal, Chichén Itzá, Sayil and Labná. The company has offices in Aldershot, England (☎ (025) 231 9448); Sydney, Australia (☎ (02) 290 3222); Remuera, Auckland, New Zealand (☎ 545-118); Edmonton, Canada (☎ (403) 439-9118); Oakland, California (☎ (415) 654 1879); and Hong Kong (☎ 5-225181). From London the trip costs about US$2100.

WARNING

The information in this chapter is particularly vulnerable to change – prices for international travel are volatile, routes are introduced and cancelled, schedules change, rules are amended, special deals come and go, borders open and close. Airlines and governments seem to take a perverse pleasure in making price structures and regulations as complicated as possible and you should check directly with the airline or travel agent to make sure you understand how a fare (and ticket you may buy) works. In addition, the travel industry is highly competitive and there are many lurks and perks. The upshot of this is that you should get opinions, quotes and advice from as many airlines and travel agents as possible before you part with your hard-earned cash. The details given in this chapter should be regarded as pointers and are not a substitute for careful, up-to-date research.

Getting Around

In recent years the governments of Mexico, Guatemala and Belize have begun to cooperate in taking measures to facilitate travel along La Ruta Maya. Regional air service has improved dramatically, and you can now fly from Cancún directly to Belize City, Chichén Itzá, Tikal or Uxmal and return in a day. You can expect even more flights in years to come.

Bus travel has always been the most dependable means of travelling La Ruta Maya. Numerous private bus companies serve various segments of the region. Usually there are several companies serving the same route, giving you a choice of schedules, prices and comforts.

Unfortunately, car rental companies have yet to join this 'easy access' campaign. Rental cars are expensive in Yucatán, more expensive in Guatemala, and very expensive in Belize. In each case you may not drive a rental car outside the national territory of the country in which you rented it (that is, you cannot drive it across a border). Thus a plan to tour most of La Ruta Maya by rental car involves different rentals in three countries, and bus or plane in between.

AIR

To really explore La Ruta Maya in detail, most of your travel must be on the ground (by bus or car). But certain parts of the route are best done by air in order to avoid long, hot and fairly boring rides.

For example, Tikal is tedious to reach by road (bus or car), so it makes sense to fly there from Guatemala City, Belize City or Cancún. If you're not particularly interested in spending time on Yucatán's Caribbean coast but you want to see Belize, fly between Cancún and Belize City.

Another long, hot trip to avoid is the one between Campeche and Villahermosa; you may want to return from Campeche and Uxmal to Mérida and fly to Villahermosa (for Palenque).

To give you an idea of air travel possibilities along La Ruta Maya, here are details on regional flights.

Cancún

Cancún's international airport is unquestionably the busiest airport on La Ruta Maya, with the most flights (both regional and international).

Aero Cozumel and Aerocaribe (☎ (988) 4-81-03, 4-20-00, 4-12-31, 4-21-33 in Cancún), working together, cover destinations in the Yucatán peninsula and beyond, in small and medium-sized planes at these prices (one-way from Cancún):

Belize City	US$100
Chetumal	US$70
Ciudad del Carmen	US$120
Cozumel	US$32
Guatemala City	US$175
Mérida	US$60
Mexico City	US$155
Oaxaca	US$200
Tikal (Flores)	US$150-US$175
Veracruz	US$182
Villahermosa	US$130

Mérida

Most international flights to Mérida are connections through Mexico City or Cancún; there is no non-stop international service except for Aeroméxico's two daily flights from Miami.

Domestic service includes half a dozen Mexicana flights daily from Mexico City to Mérida, and one or two by Aeroméxico as well. Aero Cozumel and Aerocaribe are taking over most of the intermediate air traffic between Cancún, Mérida and Mexico City, meaning that if you want to fly to or from Cancún (US$60 one way, US$94 round-trip excursion), Chetumal, Villahermosa, or Tuxtla Gutiérrez (for San Cristóbal de las Casas), you should talk to those airlines.

Villahermosa

Because of its oil wealth, Villahermosa has good air services, with links to Mérida, Cancún, Tuxtla Gutiérrez and Mexico City.

Tuxtla Gutiérrez

Tuxtla has a few flights per week to other major cities, but air transport is mostly by small local airlines which fly small planes around the rugged Chiapan terrain. There are airstrips or airports at Tuxtla Gutiérrez, Ocosingo, Palenque, San Cristóbal de las Casas, Tapachula, and the ruins of Bonampak. The major airport for the region, however, is at the Tabascan capital of Villahermosa.

Guatemala City

Besides its international connections, Guatemala City has a good number of flights to Flores (Santa Elena) near Tikal. Aerocaribe, Aeroquetzal, Aerovías, Aviateca and TAPSA operate daily flights for US$55 one way. Four days a week, Aerovías flies between Flores and Belize City for US$50 one way. Aeroquetzal flies from Flores to Guatemala City, then on to Cancún on Tuesday and Saturday for US$175 one way. More regional flights will be operated in the near future.

Belize City

With few paved roads, Belize depends greatly on aeroplanes for fast, reliable transport within the country.

Four days a week, Aerovías flies between Flores and Belize City for US$50 one way. Tropic Air (☎ (02) 45671 in Belize City, or (026) 2012, 2117, 2029 in San Pedro, Ambergris Caye; fax (026) 2338), P O Box 20, San Pedro, Ambergris Caye, is the largest and most active of Belize's small airlines. Tropic Air has daily scheduled flights from Goldson Airport to San Pedro (Ambergris Caye, 10 flights), Big Creek/Placencia (one flight), Caye Chapel (10 flights), Corozal (via San Pedro, two flights), Punta Gorda (one flight), and to Cancún (one flight, 1½ hours, US$100 one way), using DeHavilland Twin Otter and Cessna aircraft. They also run

tours to Tikal in Guatemala (US$190 including round-trip flight, overnight in a Flores hotel, all meals and most taxes). For information in the USA call (800) 422-3435 or (713) 440-1867.

Maya Airways (☎ (02) 77215, 72313, 44032), 6 Fort St, (P O Box 458), Belize City, has a similar schedule of flights to points in Belize, and adds Dangriga (four flights daily) to the flight roster. For information in the USA call (800) 552-3419.

Island Air (☎ (02) 31140 in Belize City, (026) 2435 in San Pedro, Ambergris Caye) also flies between Belize City and San Pedro.

Aerovías (☎ (02) 75445; in the USA (305) 883-1345), the Guatemalan regional airline, operates several flights per week between Belize City's Goldson Airport and Flores (near Tikal) in Guatemala, with onward connections to Guatemala City. For details, see the El Petén chapter under Flores.

Fares for Tropic Air and Maya Airways flights depend upon the airport you use:

Fare to	From Goldson Int'l	From Municipal
Ambergris Caye (San Pedro)	US$30	US$24
Caye Chapel	US$24	US$15
Corozal	US$48	US$38
Dangriga	US$34	US$23
Punta Gorda	US$61	US$50

The fare between Corozal and Punta Gorda is US$87; between San Pedro and Punta Gorda, US$69.

BUS

The prevalent means of transport along La Ruta Maya is bus. You can travel on a bus to 95% of the sites described in this book (the other 5% can be reached by boat or on foot). Bus travel can be fairly comfortable or very uncomfortable, but it is usually cheap.

In general, bus traffic is most intense in the morning (beginning as early as 4 or 5 am), tapering off by mid or late afternoon. In many places along La Ruta Maya there are no buses in the late afternoon or evening.

Routes to remote towns and villages are run for the convenience of villagers going to

2nd-class bus travel along La Ruta Maya

market in larger market towns. This often means that the only bus departs from the village early in the morning, and returns from the larger market town by mid-afternoon. If you want to visit the village, you may find that you must take this late afternoon bus and stay the night in the village, catching the bus back to the market town the next morning. Remote villages rarely have hotels, so you should be prepared to camp.

Mexico
In Mexico the buses range from very comfortable air-conditioned cruisers to shabby but serviceable village buses. On most routes there is both 1st and 2nd-class service; 2nd class costs a little less than 1st class. The 1st-class equipment may or may not be more comfortable than 2nd class, but 1st-class routes are often faster than 2nd class because they make fewer stops.

Guatemala
Among Guatemala's many bus companies, by far the most popular sort of bus is the second-hand American schoolbus (usually a 'Blue Bird'), often with the original seats which allow room enough for school children but are very cramped for adults of European or North American stature. Fares

are very cheap and buses plentiful, but most bus activity dies down by late afternoon.

In addition to the school buses, several Guatemalan lines run more comfortable passenger buses on long-distance routes between Guatemala City and the Mexican and Salvadoran borders, and to Puerto Barrios on the Gulf of Honduras.

Belize
As in Guatemala, Belizean buses are usually used American schoolbuses running on marketeers' schedules. Fares are higher than in Mexico or Guatemala. Outside routes connecting the major towns, trucks willing to take on passengers connect some remote sites, travelling on rough roads.

Several bus lines operate direct buses from Chetumal, Mexico to Belize City. Other companies run between Belize City and Benque Viejo del Carmen on the Guatemalan border, connecting with Guatemalan buses headed for Flores (near Tikal). Some of these lines arrange connections so that you can travel between Flores and Chetumal directly, with only brief stops to change buses.

TRAIN
Trains connect Mérida with Campeche, Palenque, Veracruz and other points in Mexico. They also run from Veracruz to Juchitan and along the Soconusco (Pacific coast of Chiapas) to Tapachula. From Ciudad Tecún Umán, across the border from Tapachula in Guatemala, trains run to Guatemala City. There is sometimes service from Guatemala City to Puerto Barrios on the Gulf of Honduras as well.

All of these trains are very cheap, all are slow and unreliable, most are quite uncomfortable. Some are unsafe as sneak thieves and muggers work with train crew members to relieve foreign tourists of wallets and cameras. Trains along La Ruta Maya are more a means of adventure than a means of transport.

CAR
Private car, camper van or trailer/caravan is

perhaps the best way to travel La Ruta Maya. You can go at your own pace and easily reach many areas not served by frequent public transport. The major roads and many of the minor roads are easily passable by any sort of car, and border crossings are fairly easy.

The most apparent difficulty in driving is that most North American cars now have catalytic converters which require unleaded fuel. Unleaded fuel is available in many parts of Mexico, but not reliably so. In Guatemala and Belize it is unavailable. You can arrange to have your catalytic converter disconnected, and replaced with a straight piece of exhaust pipe soon after you cross into Mexico (it's illegal to have it done in the USA). Save the converter, and have it replaced before re-crossing the border into the USA.

Coming from overseas, you may want to buy a used car or van in the USA, where they're relatively cheap, drive through the USA to Mexico, and travel the entire Ruta Maya. One used to be able to sell a car at a profit in Belize, but now the procedures are more complicated and the duties much higher.

HITCHHIKING
Many people hitchhike along certain stretches of La Ruta Maya. Often it's necessary as bus service is infrequent or non-existent, particularly to the fairly remote Mayan archaeological sites. However, hitchhiking is not necessarily free transport. In most cases, if you are picked up by a truck, you will be expected to pay a fare similar to that charged on the bus (if there is one). In some areas, pickup and flatbed stake trucks *are* the 'buses' of the region, and every rider pays. Your best bet for free rides is with other foreign tourists who have their own vehicles.

BOAT
Though there is no long-distance sea transport along La Ruta Maya, boats are used for public transport in a surprising number of locations.

In Mexico, ferryboats and hydrofoils connect the island of Cozumel to the mainland, and ferries run to Isla Mujeres as well. Charter boats and hired fishing boats take you to Isla Holbox and other small uninhabited islands off Yucatán's coast. In Chiapas, you can take a boatride through the stupendous Cañon del Sumidero. Boats also transport adventurous travellers down rivers between Palenque (Mexico) and Flores (Guatemala).

Belize has the most transport by sea. Fast motor launches connect Belize City, Caye Chapel, Caye Caulker and Ambergris Caye several times daily. Other boats go to the many other cayes several times a week on scheduled services or by charter. There is a twice-weekly boat service connecting Punta Gorda, in southern Belize, with Lívingston and Puerto Barrios in Guatemala. In western Belize, boat, canoe or kayak trips along the rivers of Mountain Pine Ridge are mostly for fun, but also sometimes for transport when the rainy season has turned the unpaved roads to sloughs of mud.

Motor launches are the favoured means of transport on Guatemala's Lake Atitlán, and dugout canoes take you up the Río Dulce and El Golfete to Lake Izabal for a look at the wildlife. Dugouts are also used for excursions on Lake Petén Itzá around Flores (near Tikal).

LOCAL TRANSPORT
Bus
Except for Belize City, all major cities and towns along La Ruta Maya have public bus service. Buses are always the American schoolbus type of vehicle, usually rattly and uncomfortable, but always cheap, ranging from US$0.50 in Cancún to US$0.10 in Guatemala City. In most places the buses are insufficient to meet demand, and thus are packed solid at rush hours and perhaps at other times as well.

Jitney
Guatemala City has an extensive jitney cab network which becomes important at night after the city buses have ceased to run.

Taxi

Taxis are quite expensive all along La Ruta Maya, charging rates equal to or exceeding those in places like New York City. None have meters, so it's necessary to determine the price of the trip before setting out. Rates are set, but drivers will often try to rip you off by quoting a higher price. This means that you must usually resort to haggling, or asking several drivers.

Bicycle

Bicycling is not yet a popular way to travel La Ruta Maya. Roads are often not the smoothest, the sun can be relentless, and one may have to travel long distances between towns. Often there's not much to look at except the walls of jungle which hem in the road. Insects – both those that hit you in the face and those that eat you for lunch – are another disincentive.

This having been said, certain areas are beautiful for biking. The Guatemalan highlands are perfect, with light traffic, decent roads and manageable distances between towns. Highland Chiapas offers similar advantages. Unless you like pedalling in the rain, though, plan your trip for the dry season (from October to May).

Horseback

Horse riding is not so much a means of transport as a means of pleasure, though in the back country of western Belize it is also eminently practical. Treks on horseback are possible in many places, including San Cristóbal de las Casas, Lake Atitlán, Flores, and Mountain Pine Ridge.

MEXICO

Cancún & Isla Mujeres

Before Cancún, Mexico's premier resort for half a century was Acapulco, with its magnificent sheltered bay ringed by verdant mountains. Then in the 1970s Mexico's ambitious tourism planners decided to outdo Acapulco with a brand new world-class resort in Yucatán. The place they chose was a deserted sandspit offshore from the little fishing village of Puerto Juárez, on Yucatán's eastern shore. The island sandspit was shaped like a lucky '7'. The name of the place was Cancún.

As Cancún was discovered by the world, so was nearby Isla Mujeres. This tropical island had earlier been a haven for local mariners and adventurous young travellers in search of the simple life at low prices. Though Isla Mujeres retains some of its earlier allure, it is now also a day trip destination for boatloads of Cancúnites.

Although tropical Yucatán is warm year round, it is more comfortable to visit between September and April when there are some cooling breezes and the weather is relatively dry. The rainy season is from May to October, with high humidity and a cloying hot mugginess. July and August can be extremely sticky, with many days where the temperature hovers around 40°C and the humidity around 70% or 80%.

Whether you plan to visit Yucatán by limo or on the cheap, you must know something about Cancún because you will have to deal with it. Yucatán's major international airport is here, as are doctors, modern hospitals, consular representatives, rental car agencies and many other services.

CANCÚN
Population 250,000

In the last two decades, Cancún has grown from a tiny jungle village into one of the world's best-known holiday resorts. Dozens of mammoth hotels, each more lavish than the last, march along the island's shore as it extends from the mainland nine km east-ward, then 14 km southward, into the turquoise waters of the Caribbean. At the north the island is joined to the mainland by a bridge which leads to Ciudad Cancún; at the south a bridge joins a road leading inland to the international airport.

The Mexican government built Cancún as an investment in the tourism business. Vast sums were sunk into landscaping and infrastructure, so the roads are straight and well paved, the water potable (so they say) right from the tap. Cancún's reason-for-being is to shelter planeloads of tourists who fly in (usually on the weekend) to spend one or two weeks in a resort hotel before flying home again (usually on a weekend). During their stay they can get by with speaking only English, spending only dollars and eating only familiar food. During the day, group tourists enjoy the beaches, hire a car or board a bus for an excursion to Chichén Itzá or Tulum, or browse in an air-conditioned shopping mall straight out of Dallas. At night they dance and drink in clubs and discos to music that's the same all over the world. They have a good time. This is the business of tourism.

If you plan to visit Cancún for that sort of holiday, by all means sign up for a package tour. Cancún was designed for them and a tour is the cheapest way to get your flight, hotel, meals and excursions. But if you're an adventurer, you'll see Cancún another way; in fact, you'll experience an altogether different Cancún.

Orientation
Cancún is actually two places in one. On the mainland lies Ciudad Cancún, a planned community founded as the service centre of the resort. On the 23-km-long sandy island is the Zona Hoteles, or Zona Turística, with its towering, palatial hotels, landscaped grounds, huge theme restaurants, convention centre, shopping malls, golf course, water sports centres and so on.

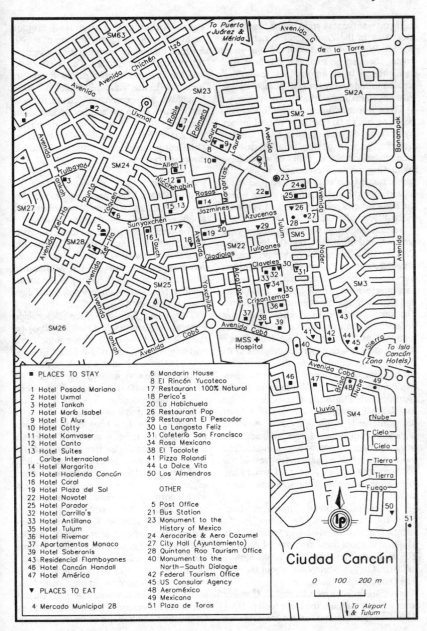

Ciudad Cancún

0   100   200 m

■ PLACES TO STAY

1 Hotel Posada Mariano
2 Hotel Uxmal
3 Hotel Tankah
7 Hotel María Isabel
9 Hotel El Alux
10 Hotel Cotty
11 Hotel Komvaser
12 Hotel Canto
13 Hotel Suites
   Caribe Internacional
14 Hotel Margarita
15 Hotel Hacienda Cancún
16 Hotel Coral
19 Hotel Plaza del Sol
22 Hotel Novotel
25 Hotel Parador
32 Hotel Carrillo's
33 Hotel Antillano
35 Hotel Tulum
36 Hotel Rivemar
37 Apartamentos Monaco
39 Hotel Soberanis
43 Residencial Flamboyanes
46 Hotel Cancún Handall
47 Hotel América

▼ PLACES TO EAT

4 Mercado Municipal 28

6 Mandarin House
8 El Rincón Yucateco
17 Restaurant 100% Natural
18 Perico's
20 La Habichuela
26 Restaurant Pop
29 Restaurant El Pescador
30 La Langosta Feliz
31 Cafetería San Francisco
34 Rosa Mexicano
38 El Tacolote
41 Pizza Rolandi
44 La Dolce Vita
50 Los Almendros

OTHER

5 Post Office
21 Bus Station
23 Monument to the
   History of Mexico
24 Aerocaribe & Aero Cozumel
27 City Hall (Ayuntamiento)
28 Quintana Roo Tourism Office
40 Monument to the
   North—South Dialogue
42 Federal Tourism Office
45 US Consular Agency
48 Aeroméxico
49 Mexicana
51 Plaza de Toros

To Airport
& Tulum

If you want to stay right on the beach, you must stay in the Zona Hoteles, out on the island. With the exception of the youth hostel, there are no budget hotels here. You can choose from among the few older, smaller, moderately priced hotels, or the many new, luxurious, pricey hotels.

Those who are content to trundle out to the beach by bus or taxi can save pots of money by staying on the mainland, in Ciudad Cancún, in one of the smaller, low to medium-priced hotels, many of which have swimming pools. Restaurants in the city centre range from ultra-Mexican taco joints to fairly smooth and expensive places where the Zona Hoteles people come to 'find someplace different for dinner'.

Several landmarks will help you find your way around this vast resort. In Ciudad Cancún, the main north-south thoroughfare is called Avenida Tulum; it's a one-km-long tree-shaded boulevard lined with banks, shopping centres, small hotels, restaurants and touts selling time-share condominiums. The central portion of Avenida Tulum is bounded on north and south with large traffic roundabouts. The northern roundabout has a soaring steeple-like concrete sculpture at its centre, the Monument to the History of Mexico; the southern one has an open ironwork construction, the Monument to the North-South Dialogue (!). Between the roundabouts, prominent on the east side of the boulevard, is the City Hall, marked 'Ayuntamiento Benito Juárez' and set back from the roadway across a wide plaza. The bus station is half a block north-west of the northern roundabout. The road out to the Zona Hoteles begins at the southern roundabout.

Cancún International Airport is about eight km south of Avenida Tulum. Puerto Juárez, the port for passenger ferries to Isla Mujeres, is about three km north of Avenida Tulum. Punta Sam, the dock for the slower car ferries to Isla Mujeres, is about five km north of Avenida Tulum.

Isla Cancún is shaped like a '7'. Coming from Ciudad Cancún, the main road is Blvd Kukulcán (sometimes called Avenida or Paseo Kukulcán), a four-lane divided highway going east along the top of the '7' for nine km before reaching the convention centre near Punta Cancún. The youth hostel and the few moderately priced hotels are located in the first few kms of Blvd Kukulcán. At the convention centre, the boulevard turns south for another 14 km before reaching Punta Nizuc and rejoining the mainland. The lower reaches of the island are still being developed, with construction crews everywhere.

Information

Tourist Office There are tourist kiosks dispensing maps and answers to questions daily at several points along Avenida Tulum.

For a real tourist office, go to the Quintana Roo State Tourism Office (Delegación Estatal de Turismo) (☎ (988) 4-80-73), 26 Avenida Tulum, next to the Multibanco Comermex, to the left (north) of the municipality. Hours are 9 am to 9 pm, seven days a week, or so they say.

The Federal Tourism Office (Delegación Federal de Turismo de Quintana Roo) (☎ (988) 4-32-38, 4-34-38) is in a stone-faced building at the corner of Avenida Cobá and Avenida Carlos J Nader, a block off Avenida Tulum on the way to the Zona Hoteles, on the left-hand side of the road. The federal office is open Monday to Friday from 8 am to 3.30 pm, closed weekends.

Cancún Tips is a booklet of advertisements and information published every six months and distributed free of charge at the airport and at many hotels. It contains some useful maps and telephone numbers as well as advertisements for hotels, restaurants, water sports shops, cruises and the like. It's worth having and the price is right.

In addition, *Cancún Tips* sponsors three information offices in the Zona Hoteles where you can get answers to your questions and look through their collections of restaurant menus. The most convenient office is in the Plaza Caracol Shopping Centre (next to Savio's), open every day from 10 am to 9 pm. Other offices are in El Parian (next to the Convention Centre) and at the Royal Yacht

Club next to Captain's Cove, open Monday to Friday from 8 am to 8 pm, Saturday from 9 am to 1 pm and Sunday from 10 am to 8 pm.

Money Banks on Avenida Tulum are open from 9 am to 1.30 pm, but many limit foreign exchange transactions to between 10 am and noon. Casas de cambio usually are open from 8 or 9 am to 1 pm and again from 4 or 5 pm till 7 or 8 pm; some casas are open seven days a week. There's a handy one next to the Dollar Rent-a-Car office near the Denny's restaurant at the north traffic roundabout on Avenida Tulum; it's half a block from the bus station.

Other casas are along Avenida Tulum. Travel agencies, hotels and the youth hostel will change money, but at rates less advantageous than the banks'.

Some restaurants along Avenida Tulum (usually the more expensive ones) will accept US dollars in payment at rates equal to or better than the banks'.

Post The main post office (Oficina de Correos, Cancún, Quintana Roo 77500) is at the western end of Avenida Sunyaxchén, which runs west from Avenida Yaxchilán; the post office is four or five short blocks from Avenida Yaxchilán. Hours for buying stamps and picking up Lista de Correos (poste restante) mail are from 8 am to 7 pm Monday to Friday, 9 am to 1 pm Saturday and holidays, closed Sunday. For international money orders and registered mail, hours are 8 am to 6 pm Monday to Friday, 9 am to noon Saturday and holidays, closed Sunday.

The Cancún office of the American Express Company (☎ (988) 4-19-99), c/o Hotel América, Suite A, Avenida Tulum, Cancún, Quintana Roo 77500, is in the Hotel América just south of Avenida Cobá and the southern traffic roundabout on Avenida Tulum. Hours are 9 am to 1 pm and 4 to 5 pm, Monday to Friday, 9 am to 1 pm Saturday, closed Sunday.

Telephone You'll find Ladatel telephones, those easy to use long-distance machines, in both the arrival and departure terminals of Cancún's airport, in the bus station off Avenida Tulum and in front of the post office at the western end of Avenida Sunyaxchén. There are also special Ladatel phones in the Plaza Caracol Shopping Centre which accept credit cards (VISA, Master-Card/Access/Eurocard) near the McDonald's restaurant and in the hall near the Gucci shop.

There are several TelMex long-distance telephone stations (casetas de larga distancia) in Ciudad Cancún. The one behind the restaurant El Tacolote on Calle Alcatraces off Avenida Cobá is open from 8 am to 10.30 pm daily and has a fax service.

Consulates The US Consular Agent (☎ (988) 4-24-11) is located at the offices of Intercaribe Real Estate, 86 Avenida Cobá, one block east off Avenida Tulum as you go towards the Zona Hoteles. Though the office is open from 9 am to 2 pm and 3 to 6 pm daily except Sunday, the consular agent is only on duty from 10 am to 2 pm Tuesday to Saturday. If the agent is not available, call the US Consulate General in Mérida (open 7.30 am to 3.30 pm weekdays) at (99) 25-50-11; in an emergency after hours or on holidays, call (99) 25-54-09. There is always a duty officer available to help in an emergency.

Other countries have consular agents reachable by telephone. If yours is not listed here, call your consulate in Mérida, or your embassy in Mexico City (see the Embassies & Consulates section in the Facts for the Visitor chapter).

Canada
    ☎ (988) 4-37-16
Costa Rica
    In the Omni Cancún Hotel (☎ (988) 5-02-26, 5-07-14); hours are 9 am to 1 pm, Monday to Friday
Germany
    In the Club Lagoon (☎ (988) 3-09-58, 3-28-58)
Italy
    ☎ (988) 3-21-13

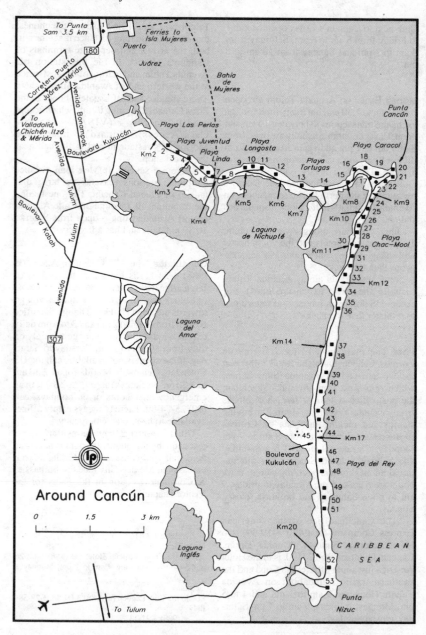

Around Cancún

0   1.5   3 km

■ PLACES TO STAY

2	Villa Deportiva Juvenil (Youth Hostel)
3	Club Verano Beat
4	Playa Blanca Hotel & Marina
5	Hotel Carrousel
6	Aquamarina Beach Hotel
8	Calinda Cancún Beach
9	Hotel Casa Maya Cancún
10	Hilton International Cancún
11	Villas Tacul
12	Hotel Maya Caribe
13	Hotel Dos Playas
14	Stouffer Presidente
15	Hotel Viva
16	Fiesta Americana Cancún
18	Hotel Camino Real Caribe
19	Fiesta Americana Coral Beach Cancún
20	Camino Real Cancún
21	Hyatt Regency Cancún
22	Krystal Cancún
24	Hotel Aristos Cancún
25	Miramar Misión
26	Hotel Inter-Continental
27	Hyatt Cancún Caribe
28	Fiesta Americana Plaza Cancún
29	Hotel Aston Flamingo
31	Hotel Brisas del Caribe
32	Hotel Baccara
33	Hotel Beach Club Cancún
34	Meliá Turquesa Hotel
35	Sheraton Cancún Resort & Towers
36	Paraíso Radisson Cancún
37	Hotel Tropical Oasis
38	Cancún Palace
39	Marriott's Cancún Resort
40	Meliá Cancún Hotel
41	Hotel Fiesta Americana Condesa Cancún
42	Hotel Oasis Cancún
43	Omni Cancún Hotel
46	Holiday Inn Crowne Plaza Cancún
47	Cancún Playa Hotel
48	Hotel Solymar
49	Ramada Renaissance Hotel Cancún
50	Aston Solaris Cancún
51	Hotel Casa Maya Caribe
52	Hotel Conrad Cancún
53	Club Méditerranée

OTHER

1	Ferry Service Office
7	Playa Linda Marine Terminal
17	Plaza Caracol Shopping Centre
23	Convention Centre
30	Plaza Flamingo
44	San Miguelito Archaeological Site
45	El Rey Archaeological Site

Spain
☎ (988) 4-18-95
Sweden
In the office of Rentautos Kankun in Ciudad Cancún (☎ (988) 4-72-71, 4-11-75)

Travel Agencies Any travel agent can book or change a flight for you. Most of the big hotels and many of the smaller, moderately priced hotels have travel agencies of their own.

Bookshops The best selection of English-language material (including *The Mexico City News, Wall Street Journal, USA Today,* etc) is at Librería Don Quijote on the Avenida Uxmal 18, corner of Margaritas, across Uxmal from the bus station. They have some Spanish, French and German publications and cassette tapes, snacks and medicines as well. Hours are 8 am to 10 pm, seven days a week.

Another store with periodicals and books in several languages is Fama, 105 Avenida Tulum, near the corner with Tulipanes, next to the Omega-Kodak Photo shop.

Laundry & Dry Cleaning There are several shops offering these services. The Lavandería Maria de Lourdes, near the hotel of the same name, is on Calle Orquideas off Avenida Yaxchilán. You might also try the Lavandería y Tintorería Cox-Boh, Avenida Tankah 26, Supermanzana 24. Walk toward the post office along Avenida Sunyaxchén; in front of the post office, bear right onto Avenida Tankah and Cox-Boh is on the right-hand side of the street.

Laundry costs US$1.50 per kg for bulk service. To have a pair of trousers washed and ironed costs US$1.70, or $3.50 for dry cleaning. Washing and ironing a shirt costs US$1.10. Cox-Boh is open every day except Sunday.

Mayan Ruins

There are Mayan ruins in Cancún and while they are not that impressive they are worth a look if you have lots of time. Most extensive are the ruins in the Zona Arqueológica El Rey, south of the Sheraton and Conrad hotels. Heading south along Blvd Kukulcán from Punta Cancún, watch for the marker for Km 17. Just past the marker there's an unpaved road on the right which leads to the ruins, open from 8 am to 5 pm every day; admission costs US$0.35. El Rey consists of a small temple and several ceremonial platforms.

If you've seen larger ruins, you may want to take just a quick glimpse at El Rey. To do this, continue on Blvd Kukulcán 700 metres past the Km 17 marker and up the hill. At the top of the hill, just past the restaurant La Prosperidad de Cancún, you can survey the ruins without hiking in or paying the admission charge.

The tiny Mayan structure and chac-mool statue set in the beautifully kept grounds of the Sheraton Hotel are actually authentic ruins found on the spot.

Archaeological Museum

The Museo de Antropología y Historia, next to the Convention Centre in the Zona Hoteles, has a limited collection of Mayan artefacts. Although most of the items are from the Post-Classic period (1200-1500 AD), including jewellery, masks and skull deformers, there is a Classic period hieroglyphic staircase inscribed with dates from the 6th century as well as the stucco head which gave the local archaeological zone its name of El Rey (The King).

The museum was badly damaged by Hurricane Gilbert in 1988 and has not reopened at the time of writing. There are plans to expand the Cancún Convention Centre considerably and it's possible that the museum will be moved to another site before being reopened.

Blue-crowned mot-mot

Aviary

Since Cancún is home to over 200 species of birds, you might enjoy seeing some of them close at hand at the Mauna Loa restaurant complex across Blvd Kukulcán from the Convention Centre. There are some beautiful long-tailed *mot-mot* (known to some as the 'clock bird' due to its pendulum-like tail), pretty parrots, frigate birds, ospreys and herons.

Beaches

The dazzling white sand of Cancún's beaches is light in weight and cool underfoot even in the blazing sun. That's because it is composed not of silica but rather of microscopic plankton fossils called disco-aster (a tiny star-shaped creature). The coolness of the sand has not been lost on Cancún's ingenious promoters, who have dubbed it 'air-conditioned'. Combined with the crystalline azure waters of the Caribbean, it makes for beaches that are pure delight.

All of these delightful beaches are open to you because all Mexican beaches are public property. Several of Cancún's beaches are set aside for easy public access, but you should know that you have the right to walk and swim on any beach at all. In practice it may be difficult to approach certain stretches of beach without going through a hotel's property, but few hotels will notice you walking through to the beach in any case.

Starting at Ciudad Cancún and heading out to Isla Cancún all the beaches are on the left-hand side of the road as you go; the lagoon is on your right. They are: Playa Las Perlas, Playa Linda, Playa Langosta, Playa Tortugas, Playa Caracol, and then Punta Cancún, the point of the '7'. South from Punta Cancún are the long stretches of Playa Chac-Mool and Playa del Rey, reaching all the way to Punta Nizuc at the base of the '7'. The beach at the Club Méditerranée, near Punta Nizuc, is noted for its nude bathing.

Beach Safety As any experienced swimmer knows, a beach fronting on open sea can be deadly dangerous and Cancún's eastern beaches are no exception. Though the surf is usually gentle, undertow is a possibility and sudden storms (called *nortes*) can blacken the sky and sweep in at any time without warning. The local authorities have devised a system of coloured pennants to warn beachgoers of potential dangers. Look for the coloured pennants on the beaches where you swim:

Blue Normal, safe conditions
Yellow Use caution, changeable conditions
Red Unsafe conditions: use a swimming pool instead

Getting There & Away To reach the beaches, catch any bus marked 'Hoteles', or 'Zona Hoteles' going south along Avenida Tulum or east along Avenida Cobá. The cost of a taxi depends upon how far you travel. For details, see Getting Around at the end of the Cancún section.

Snorkelling
Most snorkellers who wish to explore reefs pay a visit to nearby Isla Mujeres – see that section for information. If you just want to see the sparser aquatic life off Cancún's beaches, you can rent snorkelling equipment for about US$4 from most luxury hotels.

The bigger hotels and travel agencies can also book you on day-cruise boats which take snorkellers to La Bandera, Los Manchones, Cuevones and Chital reefs.

Scuba Diving
This expensive sport is all the pricier in equipment rental and boat transport from Cancún. Veteran divers might prefer nearby Cozumel's justly famous Palancar Reef. Nonetheless, agencies and hotels rent gear and provide passage to some fine reefs in the vicinity. Los Manchones and Cuevones reefs, situated between Cancún and Isla Mujeres, afford diving depths of 10 to 15 metres.

Fishing
Deep-sea fishing excursions can be booked through a travel agent or one of the large hotels.

Other Water Sports
Numerous dive shops and water sports marinas offer rentals of waterskis, sailboats, sailboards, jet-skis, scuba and snorkelling gear. Many of the larger hotels have water sports shops with similar rentals.

Places to Stay – bottom end
Though there are more than 20,000 hotel rooms in Cancún, this resort offers the low-budget traveller the worst selection of cheap accommodation at the highest prices of any place in Mexico. You must adjust to the fact that you will pay more here, for less, than anywhere else during your journey. Indeed, for a longer stay I suggest you settle down on nearby Isla Mujeres. It is no longer the 'backpacker's Cancún' that it used to be, but it is still cheaper than Cancún. But if you are about to catch a plane, or if you simply must try out Cancún's air-conditioned beaches, be advised that a night in Cancún need not bankrupt you and you need not stay in a hovel.

To make your room search as easy as possible, I've arranged my hotel recommendations on walking itineraries starting from the bus station. All you need do is get off the bus and follow the itinerary until you come to a hotel which has a vacant room that suits your budget. If you arrive by air and take a minibus into town (see below under Getting Around), your minibus driver will drop you at your chosen hotel at no extra charge.

In general, bottom-end rooms range from US$15 to US$35 a double, tax included, in the busy winter season. Prices drop 15% to 20% in the less busy summer months. In most of the rest of Mexico, including Mexico City, a room costing US$35 would be moderate or even deluxe. In expensive Cancún it's at the high end of the budget price range. For this amount of money you'll get a room with private bathroom, fan and probably air-conditioning and the hotel might even have a small swimming pool.

Youth Hostel The IYH youth hostel is the only low-budget lodging on Isla Cancún, in the Zona Hoteles four km from the bus station. Officially called the *Villa Deportiva Juvenil* (☎ (988) 3-13-37), it's at Blvd Kukulcán Km 3.2, on the left-hand (north) side of the road just past the Km 3 marker as you come from Ciudad Cancún. Look for the sign which reads 'Deportiva Juvenil'.

Single-sex dorm beds (there are over 600 of them) go for US$6.50, with a US$7.25 deposit. Camping costs US$3.25 on the hostel's grounds; for that price you get a locker and the right to use the hostel's facilities as there are none for the camping area itself. Meals are available in the hostel's cafeteria; breakfast is US$2.25, lunch or dinner costs US$2.75. Coming from the airport by minibus, the driver will drop you here at no extra charge. From the bus station, walk out to Avenida Tulum and catch a local bus (Ruta 1, 'Hoteles') heading south.

Avenida Uxmal Except for the youth hostel, all of Cancún's cheap hotels are in Ciudad Cancún and many are within a few blocks of the bus station. Turn left as you leave the bus station waiting rooms and walk a few dozen metres to Avenida Uxmal. Turn right on Uxmal and you'll come to the following cheap lodgings:

Hotel El Alux (☎ (988) 4-06-62, 4-05-56, 4-66-13), Avenida Uxmal 21, is a tidy little place only a block from the bus station on the right-hand side of the road. Air-conditioned doubles with shower go for US$28. They'll rent you a moped here, as well. An *alux*, by the way, is the Mayan version of a leprechaun.

Across Uxmal on the south side is the *Hotel Cotty* (☎ (988) 4-13-19, 4-05-50), Avenida Uxmal 44, a motel-style place with rooms behind the lobby and at right angles to the street, so it's more or less quiet. Doubles with shower and air-con cost US$21, or US$22 if you want a room with two double beds and a TV. If you're driving, they offer off-street parking.

A few steps farther along Uxmal is Calle Palmera, one of Cancún's loop streets: you'll cross Palmera and then the next street you come to will be the other end of Palmera. Look down the street and you'll see the *Hotel María Isabel* (☎ (988) 4-90-15), Calle Palmera, S M 23, a tiny place with window screens, a minuscule upper-floor patio with umbrella-shaded table and a quieter location a third of a block off busy Uxmal. Doubles with private shower and air-con cost US$22.

One long block farther along Uxmal, on the left-hand side just before the corner with Avenida Chichén Itzá, stands the *Hotel Uxmal* (☎ (988) 4-22-66, 4-23-55), Uxmal 111, a clean, family-run hostelry where US$22 will buy you a double room with fan and/or air-con, TV and off-street parking.

Rock-bottom lodgings are available just a bit farther along at the *Hotel Posada Mariano* (☎ (988) 4-39-73), Avenida Chichén Itzá near Uxmal, S M 62, 100 metres to the right of the big Coca-Cola bottling plant. The lobby door has iron bars and basic double rooms go for US$11 with fan, private shower and hot water.

Avenida Yaxchilán If you've not found what you want, backtrack on Uxmal to Avenida Yaxchilán. Turning onto Avenida Yaxchilán you enter one of the richest concentrations of cheap and moderately priced hotels in Cancún.

The *Hotel Komvaser* (☎ (988) 4-16-50) at Yaxchilán 15 offers a swimming pool and well-kept air-conditioned rooms with hot plates to heat stuff up and refrigerators to keep stuff cold. Singles/doubles/triples with bath cost US$20/22/25. The hotel has no sign, so look for the largeish building on the right-hand (west) side which has lots of rooms with glass doors and beach towels hanging out on the balconies.

A short distance along Yaxchilán past the Komvaser near Avenida Sunyaxchén is the *Hotel Canto* (☎ (988) 4-12-67), on Calle Tanchactalpen (Manzana 22, Retorno 5), behind Pizza Bambino's. Being on a side street, it's fairly quiet, especially since you can close your windows and use your room's air-con. Rooms with private shower cost US$22. There's a caseta de larga distancia adjoining the lobby.

Avenidas Sunyaxchén & Tankah Staying here puts you close to the post office and Mercado 28 with its good, cheap eateries. You're still only a few blocks from Avenida Tulum and the centre of the action.

Just off Avenida Yaxchilán stands the *Hotel Hacienda Cancún* (☎ (988) 4-12-08, 4-36-72), Sunyaxchén No 39-40, on the right-hand (north) side. One of the Amigotels chain, this place is hardly budget, but it offers exceptional value for what you pay. For US$30 (single or double) you get an air-conditioned room with colour TV and private bath, use of the hotel's pretty swimming pool and patio and a good location.

A few steps farther along Sunyaxchén on the opposite (left) side of the street, about halfway to the post office, is the *Hotel Coral* (☎ (988) 4-05-86), Sunyaxchén 30 (Supermanzana 25, Manzana 3), at Calle Grosella. There's a tiny swimming pool, but the attraction is the air-conditioned rooms with shower going for US$15/18/25/30 a single/double/triple/quad. This is good value, as Cancún goes.

Continue along Sunyaxchén to the post office and bear right onto Avenida Tankah. Watch on the right-hand side of the street for the *Hotel Tankah* (☎ (988) 4-44-46, 4-48-44), Tankah No 69, an undiscovered place charging only US$14 for a double with fan,

US$1 more for a similar room with air-con. One short block past the hotel, on the same side of the road, is the Lavandería Cox-Boh.

Avenida Cobá From the intersection of Avenidas Yaxchilán and Sunyaxchén, continue south and bear left onto Avenida Cobá. Soon, on the left-hand side, you'll come to *Apartamentos Monaco* (☎ (988) 4-52-19), Cobá 31 (Supermanzana 22), next to the Clinica Cobá and near the back of the IMSS hospital. Here you can rent a complete little apartment with two beds, fridge, cooker and air-con for US$30 per day or US$200 per week.

Continue along Avenida Cobá to reach Avenida Tulum and bear left.

Avenida Tulum Hotels along the main street tend to be noisy and not particularly well kept, but the location is certainly central.

As you come from Avenida Cobá heading north on Avenida Tulum, the *Hotel Rivemar* (☎ (988) 4-11-99, 4-13-72, 4-17-08), Avenida Tulum near Calle Crisantemas, will be on the left-hand side. The air-conditioned rooms with bath, favoured mostly by men rather than couples, cost US$22 for one or two people, US$32 for three.

A bit farther along on the same side, the *Hotel Tulum* (☎ (988) 4-13-55), Avenida Tulum, charges US$25/30/34/40 for a single/double/triple/quad for somewhat nicer rooms, right in the middle of town.

Places to Stay – middle
Middle-range hotel rooms cost from US$36 to US$85 in the busy winter season, somewhat less during the summer. During the very slow times (late May to early June, October to mid-December), prices may be only half of those quoted here, particularly if you haggle a bit. These hotels offer air-conditioned rooms with private bath, a swimming pool, restaurant and perhaps some other amenities such as a bar, lifts (elevators) and shuttle vans from the hotel to the beach. Much of the clientele of these places is small tour groups.

A walk around the loop formed by

Avenidas Tulum, Cobá, Yaxchilán and Uxmal takes you past virtually all of Ciudad Cancún's moderately priced hotels. Starting from the northern traffic roundabout near the bus station, walk south along Avenida Tulum looking for moderately priced rooms.

Avenida Tulum Just south of the roundabout on the left-hand (east) side of the road is the *Hotel Parador* (☎ (988) 4-13-10, 4-10-43, 4-19-22), Avenida Tulum 26, a modern building with 66 air-conditioned rooms, all with two double beds, TV and tiled private shower. Long, narrow interior courts filled with tropical plants lead back to a pretty swimming pool with bar. The small restaurant off the lobby was closed during my last visit, but other eating-places are nearby. The hotel has its own small parking lot and charges US$44 single/double.

Directly across Avenida Tulum from the Parador, on the west side, is the *Hotel Novotel* (☎ (988) 4-29-99), Avenida Tulum 75 (Apdo Postal 70); despite its name, it is not a member of the French hotel chain. The 40 rooms here all have private baths, air-conditioning and colour TV and some have tiny balconies. Though the building is modern stucco, the decor is colonial in theme, with wrought iron, tiles and Mexican crafts. One advantage here is the selection of rooms. With fan, they go for US$30 a single/double, US$33 a triple; with air-conditioning the price is US$38 a single/double, US$43 a triple, US$47 a quad.

Walk south along Avenida Tulum from the Novotel and look for Calle Claveles, the fifth little street. The *Hotel Carrillo's* (☎ (988) 4-12-27), Calle Claveles (Supermanzana 22, Retorno 3), is behind the restaurant of the same name. Rooms here are usable, though nothing special, but quieter than those right on the avenue. Prices are US$36 a single/double, US$41 a triple.

Perhaps my favourite city hotel from the standpoint of friendliness, value for money, comfort and quiet is the *Hotel Antillano* (☎ (988) 4-15-32, 4-11-32), Calle Claveles, a block farther along Avenida Tulum from Carrillo's. The Antillano's 48 guestrooms are all air-conditioned, with private shower and colour cable TV; there's a small pool, a disco and a bar. Rates are a reasonable US$36 a single, US$40 a double, US$43 a triple.

Several long blocks down Tulum, cross over Avenida Cobá and continue until you see the *Hotel Cancún Handall* (☎ (988) 4-11-22, 4-14-12; fax 4-63-52), on the west side of the street. The Handall is modern, simple, comfortable and specialises in tour groups. But just so you'll know, rooms go for US$48 a single/double.

Across Tulum from the Handall, down here south of Avenida Cobá, stands the large *Hotel América* (☎ (988) 4-15-00, 4-79-45, 4-16-12), Tulum at Calle Brisa (Apdo Postal 600). Perhaps the most luxurious and expensive hotel in Ciudad Cancún, it charges US$84 for a room, single or double, but that includes central air-conditioning, particularly nice decor and facilities such as a large pool with swim-up bar, a restaurant and a shuttle bus to the hotel's own beach club out on Isla Cancún.

Avenida Cobá Backtrack a bit to Avenida Cobá, turn west and you'll see *Hotel Soberanis* (☎ (988) 4-18-58; fax 4-34-00), Avenida Cobá 5-7 (Apdo Postal 421), a recently refurbished place with the standard mid-range comforts going for US$41, single or double.

Continue along Cobá and bear right onto Avenida Yaxchilán.

Avenida Yaxchilán Yaxchilán has many small inexpensive or moderately priced lodging places and restaurants. Five short blocks along is the intersection with Avenida Sunyaxchén and three good middle range lodging choices. The large *Hotel Plaza del Sol* (☎ (988) 4-38-88), Avenida Yaxchilán 31, corner of Jazmines, has 87 centrally air-conditioned rooms with bath, two double beds, carpeting and colour TV, priced at US$58/69 a single/double. Services here include a pretty swimming pool with swim-up bar and lounge chairs, a restaurant and coffee shop, lobby bar, lifts and private car park.

A block farther along Yaxchilán at the other end of the loop formed by Calle Jazmines stands the new (1990) *Hotel Margarita* (☎ (988) 4-93-33; fax 4-92-09), with services similar to the Plaza del Sol. The price for a room is US$54 a single/double. You can call toll-free for reservations in the US and Canada: (800) 223-9815; in New York (212) 545-8469.

Directly across Yaxchilán from the Margarita is the huge *Hotel Suites Caribe Internacional* (☎ (988) 4-30-87; fax 4-19-93), Avenidas Yaxchilán con Sunyaxchén 36. The 80 rooms here include double rooms with two beds, cable colour TV and private bath; and junior suites with two beds, a sofa, colour cable TV, private bath, kitchenette with cooker and refrigerator and a living room. Prices (tax included) are US$70 a single/double, US$82 a triple for a room and US$92 a double for a junior suite, US$12 for an extra person.

Avenida Nader A city centre lodging offering exceptionally good value is the *Residencial Flamboyanes* (☎ (988) 4-15-03, 4-74-14), Avenida Carlos J Nader 101; Nader is parallel to and one block east of Avenida Tulum. From Tulum, walk east along Avenida Cobá from the southern traffic roundabout and turn left around the stone Federal Tourism Office (SECTUR) onto Nader and the Flamboyanes is half a block down on the right-hand side.

The 25 spacious, airy suites here are set in 4000 sq metres of well-kept grounds of emerald lawns, shady palms and *flamboyanes* trees, with a fine swimming pool as a centrepiece. It's quiet here. Each suite can sleep four and comes with fully equipped kitchenette, including refrigerator, a dining area and cool terrace. A small shelf of used English-language novels awaits guests' use in the lobby.

Rates are a reasonable US$33 a single/double and US$4 for each extra person. Once you've found the Flamboyanes, you can take the short cut through the flea market across the street to reach Avenida Tulum.

Zona Hoteles A few of the older, smaller or simpler hotels on Isla Cancún charge rates under US$100 for a double room during the high winter season. In summer, many more bargains are to be had. Driving out along Blvd Kulkulcán from Ciudad Cancún, you will come to these moderately priced hotels in the following order; all are on the left-hand (north or east) side of the road.

The *Playa Blanca Hotel & Marina* (☎ (988) 3-03-44; in the USA (800) 221-4726), Apdo Postal 107, is at Km 3.5; it's a 161-room hotel with lush gardens, comfortable air-conditioned rooms, several bars and three restaurants. There's a pool and a nice stretch of beach. Clientele is mostly young adults who come on package excursions. Rooms cost US$60 to US$80 in winter, depending upon the month.

Not far past the Playa Blanca is the newer *Aquamarina Beach Hotel* (☎ (988) 3-14-25, 3-13-44, 3-19-37; fax 3-17-51; in the USA (800) 446-8976), Blvd Kulkulcán Km 5 (Apdo Postal 751), built with tour groups of young adult sunlovers in mind. The rooms are comfortable and serviceable though not fancy, with the requisite colour cable TV, private bath and air-conditioning. Some have kitchenette and refrigerator, but cost no more – ask for one of these when you reserve your room. The price is US$75 a double in winter. The Aquamarina Beach is connected to the Best Western hotel chain.

The next moderately priced place is the *Hotel Maya Caribe* (☎ (988) 3-20-00), Blvd Kukulcán Km 6.5 (Apdo Postal 447), with 64 rooms, each with two double beds, minibar, balcony, hammock and a view of either the ocean or the lagoon. Three swimming pools, two restaurants, a bar and water sports equipment round out the services. This one is a favourite of Mexican and Mexican-American vacationers. Rooms go for US$72 in winter.

Just before coming to Punta Cancún, about Km 8.5, you'll see the great white block of the *Hotel Viva* (☎ (988) 3-01-08 or 3-08-00), right next to the Fiesta Americana Cancún. Though the Viva is cheek-by-jowl with several far more luxurious hotels, its rooms and services are in the middle range, as are its prices. In winter you can get a nice room with a view of the sea, two double beds, a refrigerator and other comforts for US$106, perhaps a bit less if you haggle.

Following Blvd Kukulcán around past Punta Cancún and southward brings you to the *Hotel Aristos Cancún* (☎ (988) 3-00-11), Blvd Kukulcán Km 10 (Apdo Postal 450), with 250 comfortable air-conditioned rooms, restaurant, bar, pool, and access to the beach. Prices in winter can be US$90 or US$45, depending upon how full the hotel is – they're sensitive to supply and demand and adjust prices accordingly. If your timing is right, you can stay in the midst of the luxury hotels for little more than the price of a budget room.

Places to Stay – top end

Cancún's top places range from comfortable but boring to luxurious full-service hostelries of an international standard. Prices range from US$130 to US$250 and more for a double room in winter. All the top places are located on the beach, many have vast grounds with rolling lawns of manicured grass, tropical gardens, swimming pools (virtually all with swim-up bars – a Cancún necessity) and facilities for sports such as tennis, handball, waterskiing and sailboarding. Some are constructed in whimsical fantasy styles with turrets, bulbous domes, minarets, dramatic glass canopies and other architectural megalomania. Guestrooms are air-conditioned, equipped with minibar and TV linked to satellite receivers for US programmes.

Room prices given below include the 15% IVA tax and are for the winter high season; off-season rates in summer will be considerably lower – perhaps 30% to 40%. No meals are included in these rates unless specifically mentioned below. The charge for an extra person in a room is typically about US$23. The best room prices are offered to those who sign up for package tours or multinight stays. Be sure to ask about special packages when you call for reservations.

When you arrive in Cancún, your taxi or minibus will take you from the airport to Isla Cancún via Punta Nizuc, coming up from the south. Once you settle in at your hotel, you'll be travelling to and from Ciudad Cancún, so I'll describe the hotels as you'll see them coming from the city centre, from west to east and north to south. All are on the eastern (left) side of Blvd Kukulcán as you travel east and south. Addresses along Blvd Kukulcán are usually given in km from the centre.

Km 6 *Calinda Cancún Beach* (☎ (988) 3-16-00; in the the USA (800) 221-2222) faces the Playa Linda Marine Terminal across the channel connecting Bahía de Mujeres with Laguna de Nichupte. Decor here is of red tiles, white stucco and modern muted colours, all with a light, airy feel. Though it has most of the luxury services – pool with swim-up bar, satellite-dish TV, minibar – prices for the 280 rooms are at the lower end of the luxury range: US$133 to US$150 a single, US$138 to US$156 a double.

Hotel Casa Maya Cancún (☎ (988) 3-05-55; fax 3-11-88), Blvd Kukulcán, is an enormous building, obviously a high-rise hotel, but with some ancient Mayan architectural features. Each of the 250 rooms has a balcony with ocean view and all the conveniences. Besides the requisite swimming pools and beach, there are two tennis courts. Rates are US$144 to US$167 single or double.

Hilton International Cancún is under construction at the time of writing, but should be open by the time you plan your trip. For current information on the hotel call Hilton Reservation Service (in the USA (800) 445-8667).

Km 8 *Stouffer Presidente* (☎ (988) 3-02-00; fax 3-25-15; in the USA (800) 468-3571), Blvd Kukulcán Km 7.5, has recently been renovated – almost rebuilt – from top to bottom. All rooms face the Caribbean, some are specially equipped for the handicapped, others are set aside for nonsmokers. If you ask for a wake-up call, they deliver a free cup of coffee at the same time. The beach is among the best and safest and one of the swimming pools is equipped with five whirlpool baths. The 294 guestrooms rent for US$196 to US$288 a single/double.

Fiesta Americana Cancún (☎ (988) 3-14-00; in the USA (800) 343-7821) is an oddity among Cancún hotels. While all its neighbours boast sleek, space-age architecture, the Fiesta Americana resembles nothing so much as an old-city streetscape, an appealing jumble of windows, balconies, roofs and other features. The interior is anything but quaint, however, as this luxury place has all the amenities. The 281 rooms are priced at US$202 to US$219, single or double.

Punta Cancún (Km 9) *Fiesta Americana Coral Beach Cancún* (☎ (988) 3-29-00; fax 3-25-02; in the USA (800) 343-7821), Blvd Kukulcán at Punta Cancún (Apdo Postal 14), is a brand-new hostelry and one of the most luxurious. Many of the 602 rooms are actually large junior suites, most with balcony, marble floors and all the luxuries; master suites even have their own private whirlpool baths. There are three indoor tennis courts, 13 restaurants and bars and a 600 metre serpentine swimming pool. Rates are US$213 to US$242 for a single/double.

Camino Real Cancún (☎ (988) 3-01-00, 3-12-00; fax 3-17-30; in the USA (800) 228-3000), Apdo Postal 14, was one of Cancún's first luxury hotels and thus had the best pick of locations. Situated at the very tip of Punta Cancún, the Camino Real enjoys panoramic sea views, a lavish country club layout, lots of restaurants and bars and full luxury service. The Convention Centre, museum and shopping centres are all within walking distance. The price for a room, single or double, is US$225 to US$288.

Hyatt Regency Cancún (☎ (988) 3-09-66; fax 3-13-49; in the USA (800) 228-9000), Apdo Postal 1201, shares Punta Cancún with the Camino Real and several other hotels. The Hyatt is actually a gigantic cylinder, with a lofty open court at its core and the 300 guestrooms arranged round it. For all the luxury services, plus this prime location, you pay US$184 to US$207 for a single/double; the Regency Club rooms on the top three floors are priced at US$242 a single/double, continental breakfast included.

Krystal Cancún (☎ (988) 3-11-33; fax 3-17-90; in the USA (800) 231-9860), Punta Cancún, is also in that excellent location near the Convention Centre. Creamy marble abounds in the decor and the 330 guestrooms feature tropical bamboo accents. The swimming pool complex overlooking the beach is among Cancún's most striking, with its Ionic columns. Prices are US$196 to US$242 a single/double, the higher price being on the special-service 'club' floor.

Km 10 *Miramar Misión* (☎ (988) 3-17-55; in the USA (800) 648-7818), Blvd Kukulcán, is the Cancún branch of the Mexican Misión hotels chain. Among the better features here are the lanai terraces, one on each of the 225 rooms, all with views of both the Caribbean and the Nichupte Lagoon. The beach faces the open sea and one must swim with caution (this applies to all hotels on the north-south part of Isla Cancún).

Hyatt Cancún Caribe (☎ (988) 3-00-44; fax 3-15-14; in the USA (800) 228-9000), Blvd Kukulcán, has recently been fully modernised; its 180 rooms are more comfortable than ever. This is now the more luxurious of the two Hyatt hotels in Cancún, charging US$207 to US$260 for its rooms, single or double.

Km 11 & 12 *Fiesta Americana Plaza Cancún* (☎ (988) 3-10-22; fax 3-22-70, 5-14-03; in the USA (800) 343-7821), Blvd Kukulcán Km 11, is a gigantic hotel designed as an interconnected mass of Spanish-style villas. As you move about it, the hotel seems to be on a pleasantly human scale, even though it holds some 638 guestrooms, two lighted tennis courts and a squash court, a racquetball court, three swimming pools and seven restaurants. Prices are US$161 to US$201, single or double.

Hotel Beach Club Cancún (☎ (988) 4-16-43; in the USA (800) 346-8225), Blvd Kukulcán, is smaller than neighbouring mega-hotels and has more of a club's atmosphere. Of the 160 rooms, 117 are suites. If you favour a smaller establishment with larger rooms, this one's for you. Prices are US$127 for a guestroom, US$157 for a junior suite, US$248 to US$322 for a penthouse suite or apartment.

Meliá Turquesa Hotel (☎ (988) 3-25-44; fax 5-12-41; in the USA (800) 336-3542), Blvd Kukulcán Km 12, is one of two Cancún hotels operated by the Spanish hotel chain which prides itself on its European-style service. The Turquesa has 408 guestrooms, 36 junior suites and two master suites, each with balcony and water view of sunrise on the Gulf or sunset on Nichupte lagoon. Local elements are incorporated in the design, which has hints of a step-pyramid and a huge palapa out by the pools, overlooking the beach.

Km 12 & 13 *Sheraton Cancún Resort & Towers* (☎ (988) 3-19-88; fax 5-00-83, 3-14-50; in the USA (800) 325-3535), Blvd Kukulcán (Apdo Postal 834), is a complex of three large Mayan step-pyramid buildings and the V-shaped Towers section set in lush tropical gardens right on the beach. The 748 guestrooms and suites are plush and attractive, with the usual Cancún luxuries: satellite TV with movie channels, minibar and piped music. Suites in the Towers building have balconies with sea views.

Besides its six lighted tennis courts, fitness centre with sauna, steam bath and whirlpool, basketball court and minigolf links, the Sheraton has an ambitious daily schedule of activities such as aerobics and swimnastics classes, arts and crafts lessons, Spanish-language courses and theme parties. There's a children's playground as well. Room prices are quite reasonable (for Cancún) at US$161 to $US184, single or double; suites go for US$242.

Paraíso Radisson Cancún (☎ (988) 5-01-12, 5-02-33; fax 5-09-99; in the USA (800) 333-3333), Blvd Kukulcán, is a moderate-size full luxury hotel right on the beach, offering 300 very comfortable rooms at prices surprisingly lower than its neighbours. In the winter season, rates for a room, single or double, are US$138 to US$173. The Radisson is more traditional in layout, eschewing the bold design for which Cancún hotels are famous (or infamous).

Km 15 *Cancún Palace* (☎ (988) 5-05-33; fax 5-15-93; in the USA (800) 346-8225), Blvd Kukulcán (Apdo Postal 1730), is one of three Cancún hotels owned by Cancún Hoteles Corporativos. As the hotel is not part of a big international chain, it works extra hard to offer good value to guests. The 421 rooms and suites have all the amenities you'd expect, including balconies with water views and all the services, from shopping arcade to swimming pools and tennis courts. Babysitting and special kids' programmes attract families. Besides the standard rates of US$167 to US$196 for a single/double, the Palace frequently offers special lower priced package plans. Ask about these when you call for reservations.

Marriott's Cancún Resort (☎ (988) 5-20-00; fax 5-17-31; in the USA (800) 228-9290), Blvd Kukulcán, is a six-storey luxury hotel with 450 rooms, all with private balconies, in-room safe deposit boxes, hair dryers, plus all the usual luxuries. Rooms are decorated in a modern Mexican style with ceiling fans (there's air-conditioning as well, of course), Mexican tile floors and soft rose, mauve and earth-tone colour schemes. Swimming pools, tennis courts, health club – the Marriott has them all, plus a Japanese steakhouse and 1960s-theme nightclub. Rates are reasonable at US$167 a single/double; package plans and special rates often bring the price down even further – ask about them.

Meliá Cancún Hotel (☎ (988) 5-11-60; fax 5-10-85; in the USA (800) 336-3542), Blvd Kukulcán Km 15, will startle you with its dramatic geometry: cascades of stepped facades topped by glass pyramids. The 447 guestrooms and suites have all the comforts that US$60 million in construction can provide.

Ruinas El Rey (Km 16) *Fiesta Americana Condesa* (☎ (988) 5-10-00, 5-12-66; fax 5-18-00; in the USA (800) 343-7821), Blvd Kukulcán (Apdo Postal 5478), has 500 luxury rooms in three buildings around a large swimming pool. Besides all the five-star services you'd expect, you'll find a fully equipped health club, three indoor tennis courts and a variety of restaurants and bars. Rates are US$202 to US$219 for a single/double.

Hotel Oasis Cancún (☎ (988) 5-08-67; fax 5-01-31; in the USA (800) 446-2747) lives up to its name as a huge (960-room) self-contained resort boasting a pyramidal central building and four accommodation buildings arranged around a marvellous system of interconnected swimming pools almost half a km long. The hotel grounds range along 800 metres of beautiful beach. Rates are US$161 to US$184 for a single/double. All the rooms are equally luxurious, with private lanai-style balconies, but they differ according to view: cheapest are rooms with a view of the lagoon, next are those with garden or partial ocean views; most expensive rooms have full oceanfront views.

Omni Cancún Hotel (☎ (988) 5-01-74; fax 5-00-59; in the USA (800) 843-6664), Blvd Kukulcán (Apdo Postal 127), has 320 guestrooms with pink marble floors, regional wood furnishings and private balconies. Other services include three swimming pools (some with waterfalls), tennis courts, health club with steam bath and sauna, seven restaurants and the usual assortment of swim-up bars. Rates are US$170 to US$190 single or double, the difference, as always, being one of view: oceanfront rooms cost more.

At Punta Nizuc *Holiday Inn Crowne Plaza Cancún* (☎ (988) 5-10-50, 5-10-22; fax 5-17-07 extension 6100; in the USA (800) 465-4329), Blvd Kukulcán Km 18.5 (Apdo Postal 5-477), is a dramatic glass-fronted building with 366 fully equipped luxury guestrooms, all of the expected luxury hotel services, including an Olympic-size swimming pool, another swimming pool beneath the glass canopy, two tennis and two racquet ball courts. Rooms cost US$184 a single/double in winter.

Cancún Playa Hotel (☎ (988) 5-11-11/15; fax 5-11-51, 5-10-76; in the USA (800) 683-4482), Blvd Kukulcán (Apdo Postal 203), looks like a cross between a modern luxury hotel and several Mayan step-pyramids. Between the hotel and the beach is a complex system of swimming pools, bars, sundecks, shady sitting areas, restaurants and other services. There are 388 luxury rooms, all services and rates of US$184 for a single/ double in winter.

Ramada Renaissance Hotel Cancún (☎ (988) 5-01-00; fax 5-03-54; in the USA (800) 228-9898), Blvd Kukulcán Km 23, features updated Mayan architecture in its eight-storey building. Though offering all luxury services, the Ramada is smaller and more congenial than many Cancún mega-hotels. There are 226 very comfortable rooms here priced at US$173 for a single/double; rooms on the top two 'Renaissance Club' floors have several additional amenities.

Aston Solaris Cancún (☎ (988) 5-06-00; fax 5-09-75; in the USA (800) 922-7866), Blvd Kukulcán Km 20, bills itself as 'Mexico's Mediterranean village on the Caribbean', and indeed the sugar-cube architecture of white stucco does make one think of some futuristic Greek isle with Moorish overtones. Less lavish in its layout than many of its neighbours to the north, the Solaris makes up the difference with 'character' and decent prices. Rooms go for US$144 to US$167 for a single/double in winter; ask for a 'studio' and you'll get a room half as big again and equipped with a kitchenette, at the same price.

Hotel Conrad Cancún (☎ (988) 5-00-86, 5-05-37; fax 5-00-74; in the USA (800) 445-8667), Blvd Kukulcán Km 20 (Apdo Postal 1808), is a brand-new luxury hotel very near Punta Nizuc with all the luxuries and most up-to-date features. All 391 rooms have water views and are priced from US$173 to US$242 single or double in winter. Conrad Hotels is the international subsidiary of Hilton USA.

Club Méditerranée (☎ (988) 4-29-00; fax 4-24-09; in the USA (800) 258-22633), Punta Nizuc, has a different layout, as you might expect. The central building houses the dining room, cocktail lounge, theatre, pool, boutique and dance floor. Accommodation is in two and three-storey beachfront buildings. There are eight tennis courts (four are lighted), volleyball and basketball courts, table tennis and bocce ball, as well as virtually all water sports. Rates include three meals and vary from US$120 to US$180 per person per day, depending upon when you stay here.

Places to Eat

I have eaten meals in Mexico, on and off, for more than 20 years. Nowhere have I found more mediocre food at higher prices than in Cancún. It appears to me that Cancún's restaurateurs are far more interested in theme decors, strolling guitarists, jokey menus, sassy bilingual waiters and raking in the pesos than they are in serving tasty food. The good restaurants (and there are a few) are not all expensive or all fancy. They just care about what they serve.

Don't expect too much from Cancún's restaurants and when you get a memorable meal (and you will have at least a few) you'll be pleasantly surprised.

Places to Eat – bottom end

As with hotels, so with eating places: Cancún is much more expensive than the rest of Mexico. But the local people, who live on Mexican workers' incomes, have to eat and they eat good meals at low prices. You can, too. Bottom-end meals cost between US$2.50 and US$6 or so.

Ciudad Cancún As usual, market eateries provide the biggest portions at the lowest prices. Ciudad Cancún's market, near the post office, is more modern than most. To find it, walk up Avenida Sunyaxchén to the post office (Correos) and bear left. A hundred metres along on the right is a building set back from the street and emblazoned with the name Mercado Municipal Artículo 115 Constitucional. Called simply Mercado 28 (that's 'mercado veinte y ocho') by the locals because it is in Supermanzana 28, this large, spacious, modern maze of buildings extends

well back from the street in a series of courtyards. Shops selling fresh food, prepared meals, plastic sandals, watches, apparel and a thousand other things, surround the courtyards.

In the second courtyard in from the street are the eateries: *Restaurant Margely*, *Cocina Familiar Económica Chulum*, *Cocina La Chaya*, etc. Six more loncherías are lined up along the opposite side of the courtyard. These are not the dives often found in some countries, but pleasant, simple eateries with tables beneath awnings and industrious señoras cooking away behind the counter. Most are open for breakfast, lunch and dinner and all offer full meals (comidas corridas) for as little as US$2.50, and individual sandwiches and platters for even less.

While you're here at the market, stock up on any snacks, fruit, vegetables, fish, or meat you might need; or thread, plastic basins, pipe fittings, audio cassettes, shoes, washing machines, etc.

El Rincón Yucateco, Avenida Uxmal 24, across from the Hotel Cotty, to the left of the Hotel El Alux and only about a block west of the bus station, serves good Yucatecan *típico* food at decent prices during long hours. The dining area is open to the noisy street, cooled by ceiling fans and ready to serve you from 7 am to 10 pm every day. The Mayan classics such as cochinita pibil, poc-chuc and papadzules are offered, as are fish dishes and tacos de cochinita. Main courses cost US$2 to US$3.

El Tacolote, on Avenida Cobá across from the big red IMSS hospital, is brightly lit and attractive with dark wood benches, stuccoed arches in ochre paint, ceiling fans and lots of Mexican families in attendance. Tacos are the draw, with a dozen types priced from US$0.75 to US$3 per portion. El Tacolote (the name is a pun on taco and *tecolote*, owl) is open from 7 to 11.30 am for breakfast, then till 10 pm for tacos.

Between the Hotel Parador and the Ayuntamiento, just off the northern roundabout on Avenida Tulum, is the *Restaurant Pop* (☎ 4-19-91), Avenida Tulum 26, a bright, simple, modern place with an air-conditioned dining room and shaded patio tables out the front. The food is not exciting, but the selection of dishes is interesting, with yogurt, fresh fruit salads, hamburgers and other sandwiches, soups, spaghetti, cakes and desserts. Prices are at the high end of the budget range. Expect to spend about US$4 or $5 for a good, filling meal, more if you're very hungry and drink several cervezas. Pop (the name is that of the first month of the 18-month Mayan calendar) is open from 8 am to 10.30 pm (closed Sunday).

The *Cafetería San Francisco*, in the big San Francisco de Assis department store on the east side of Avenida Tulum in the centre of town, used to be a cheap place for local shoppers to grab a bite. Progress has brought a new aquamarine decor, waiters in black-and-white and welcome air-conditioning and prices have risen. But the food is pretty good, as is the value for money. A huge club sandwich plate goes for US$4.50, hamburgers, chicken tacos, or enchiladas suizas for even less. You can spend as much as US$12 for a full, heavy meal with dessert and drink, but most people keep their bill below US$6. The cafetería is open from 7 am to 11 pm daily.

Isla Cancún As you might imagine, there is little in the way of cheap eateries out here in the Zona Hoteles. Workers bring their own lunches or eat in service cafeterias. Tourists are expected to spend. I'd advise you to make and bring your own sandwiches if you head out here for a day at the beach.

For inexpensive fare, seek out *Mr Papa's*, which specialises in big, filling baked potatoes topped with all sorts of things: mushrooms, cheese, bacon, creamed spinach or broccoli and more, for US$3 to US$6. Burritos and burgers are in the same range. Look for the modern upbeat decor in the Terramar Plaza shopping centre (☎ 3-14-11), Flamingo Plaza (☎ 3-31-06) opposite the Hotel Aston Flamingo and downtown on Avenida Tulum (☎ 4-06-91). They're open for lunch and dinner every day.

Otherwise, there's *Otto's*, Blvd Kukulcán Km 9, on the lagoon side of the road just west of the Convention Centre and just past the big Mauna Loa restaurant complex. Pizzas, burgers, sandwiches and drinks fill the menu, mostly costing US$6 or US$7 (pizzas go as high as US$9). An all-you-can-eat breakfast costs less than US$5. Otto's is open from 7 am to midnight every day.

Places to Eat – middle
If you're willing to spend between US$10 and US$20 for dinner you can eat fairly well in Cancún. Most of these restaurants concentrate more on their food than do the elaborately decorated expensive places.

Ciudad Cancún Most of the moderately priced restaurants are located in the city centre. The *Restaurant El Pescador* (☎ 4-26-73), Tulipanes 28, has been serving dependably good meals since the early days of Cancún – and is one of the very few restaurants which can make that claim. The streetside dining terrace is small, but is the best place to sit, though the interior and upper-floor rooms are alright. Cooling is by ceiling fans, service is by experienced staff and the menu lists lime soup and fish ceviche for starters, charcoal-grilled fish, red snapper in garlic sauce and beef shish kebab for main courses, among many others. If you have simple quesadillas and a beverage you can get away with spending US$11 per person. For a full meal, expect to pay almost US$20. El Pescador is open for lunch and dinner (closed Monday). Most nights it's full by 7 pm; by 7.30 pm there's a long waiting line.

Pizza Rolandi (☎ 4-40-47), Avenida Cobá 12, between Tulum and Nader just off the southern roundabout, is an attractive Italian eatery open every day. It serves elaborate, tasty one-person pizzas (US$4 to US$6), spaghetti plates and more substantial dishes of veal and chicken. Ceiling fans circulate the air. Watch out for drink prices, which can swell your bill surprisingly. Hours are 1 pm to midnight (Sunday, 4 pm to midnight).

Every visitor to Cancún makes the pilgrimage to *Los Almendros* (☎ 4-08-07), Avenida Bonampak at Calle Sayil, the local incarnation of Yucatán's most famous restaurant chain. Started in Ticul in 1962, Los

Almendros set out to serve *platillos campesinos para los dzules* (country food for the bourgeoisie, or townfolk). The chefs at Los Almendros (The Almond Trees) claim to have created poc-chuc, a dish of succulent pork cooked with onion and served in a tangy sauce of sour orange or lime. The modern dining room is bright and almost bare, but not unpleasant with its gaily painted ranch chairs. Waiters scurry about bearing *papadzules* (tortillas wrapped around chopped egg and marrow seeds, topped with tomato sauce), rice soup with fried bananas, tangy lime soup with rafts of floating tortillas, cochinita pibil (suckling pig flavoured with achiote sauce, wrapped in banana leaves and baked in a pit oven, or pib) and other Yucatecan specialities such as turkey in a dark sauce. If you don't know what to order, try the *combinado yucateco*, or Yucatecan combination plate.

A full meal here costs about US$10 per person, all included. Come any day for lunch or dinner. The restaurant is at the southern end of Avenida Bonampak directly across from the bullring, more than a km from the centre of town.

Restaurant-Jazz Club 100% Natural (☎ 4-36-17), Avenida Sunyaxchén at Yaxchilán, is a pleasant, airy café decorated in light pastel colours and patronised by a chic sun-oriented crowd. Though the menu lists several natural food items such as fruit salads and juices, green salads and milkshakes with granola or yogurt or vegetables, they also serve hamburgers, fish fillets, enchiladas and burritos, not to mention wine and beer. Drop in to peer at the gilded youth, both Mexican and gringo, order a glass of orange juice, a plate of burritos and a serving of apple pie and you'll pay about US$7.

Perico's (☎ 4-31-52), Avenida Yaxchilán 71 at Calle Marañón, is quintessential Cancún, a huge thatched structure stuffed with stereotypical Mexican icons: saddles, enormous sombreros, baskets, bullwhips, etc. An army of señors and señoritas dressed in exaggerated Mexican costumes doesn't serve so much as 'dramatise your dining experience'. Oh, well. But if you're in the

mood for dinner a la Disney, Perico's is not a bad place to have it. The food is decent, the menu heavy with the macho fare most popular with group tourists: filet mignon, jumbo shrimp, lobster, barbecued spareribs. 'Pancho Villa's Plate' will get you an assortment. After the show, fork over US$20 to US$25 per person to pay your bill. It's supposedly open from noon to 2 am, but may in fact serve only dinner.

You can get Chinese food at *Mandarin House* (☎ 4-71-83), Avenida Sunyaxchén at Avenida Tankah, across from the post office. The Cantonese classics are on the menu for lunch and dinner every day but Wednesday (closed) and a full meal need cost only US$10, or less.

La Langosta Feliz (The Happy Lobster), Avenida Tulum 33C, in the centre of town on the west side of the street, is typical of the restaurants fronting on the busy avenue. Open for breakfast, lunch and dinner (7 am to 10.30 pm), it features a varied menu including cheaper fare such as tacos, enchiladas and tostadas and fancier dishes like *huachinango* (red snapper), lobster tail and steaks. Ceiling fans provide cooling, waiters in white do the honours and the clientele includes both locals and tourists. Lunch or dinner costs about US$6 to US$10, more for lobster.

Just off the northern roundabout, at the corner of Avenidas Tulum and Uxmal just a few steps to the right of the Novotel, stands a branch of *Denny's*, the American restaurant chain. True to form it is clean and attractive, with welcome air-conditioning, decent service and a menu of popular dishes moderately priced. The food was less than exciting, the soft drinks (US$1!) and orange juice diluted when I ate there, but perhaps this will change with experience. It has the advantage of being right near the bus station and open 24 hours a day. Popular Mexican dishes and various burgers cost about US$4, steaks and fish up to US$8.

Isla Cancún You can dine well without blowing your moderate budget at *Casa Rolandi* (☎ 3-18-17), in the posh Plaza

Caracol shopping centre at Km 8 near Punta Cancún. Northern Italian, Mexican and international dishes fill the menu, things like carpaccio of salmon and *cabrito al horno de leña* (wood-roasted kid). The catch of the day comes as a fillet or as a whole fish. Decor and clients are mod, food is good. A full dinner goes for US$15 to US$25 per person; lunch costs less. It's open from 1.30 to 11.30 pm daily and from 6 to 11.30 pm Sunday.

Los Rancheros (☎ 3-27-13), in the Plaza Flamingo across from the Aston Flamingo hotel Blvd Kukulcán Km 11) specialises in Mexican favourites interpreted for visiting gringos and gringas: nachos, *caldo tlalpeño* (spicy chicken soup), beef tenderloin *filete tampiqueña* (in savoury tomato sauce) and red snapper fillet. There's even a 'make-a-taco' plate of beef, chicken, pork, guacamole and beans – you roll your own. Hand-painted ranch chairs and *norteño* music get you in the mood. Full dinners cost US$15 to US$25 per person, all inclusive. Hours are 8 am to 11 pm every day.

Places to Eat – top end

Traditionally, Mexican restaurants have followed the European scheme of simple decor and elaborate food. Cancún, however, caters mostly to the sort of sun-baked North Americans who seem to prefer simple food served in elaborate surroundings. Half the menus in town are composed of such grill-me items as steak, jumbo shrimp, fish fillet and lobster tail. Thus Cancún's expensive restaurants are elaborate, with rhapsodic menu prose, lots of tropical gardens, mirrors, waterfalls, paraphernalia, even fishtanks and aviaries of exotic birds. The food can be good, forgettable or execrable. If the last, at least you'll have pleasant music and something to look at as you gnaw and gag.

Here are the exceptional places:

Ciudad Cancún A long-standing favourite is *Rosa Mexicano* (☎ 4-63-13), Calle Claveles 4, the place to go for unusual Mexican dishes in a pleasant hacienda decor. No tacos here, but rather delicious traditional recipes such as *memela pellizcada* (a tortilla topped with refried beans, beef, chorizo, fried banana, avocado and egg), or tender nopal cactus leaves cooked with corn, onion, peppers and cilantro, topped with vinaigrette and crumbled white cheese. There are some concessions to Cancún such as tortilla soup (good, though) and filete tampiqueña, but also squid sautéed with three chillis, garlic and scallions and shrimp in a *piptan* sauce (ground pumpkin seeds and spices). For dessert, have the *dulce de camote*, a Puebla delicacy of yams baked in brown sugar and cinnamon, served with mild yellow cheese. Dinner, served daily from 5 to 11 pm, goes for about US$20.

Another dependable favourite, since 1977, is *La Habichuela* (☎ 4-31-58), Margaritas 25, just off Parque Las Palapas in a residential neighbourhood. Enter through a Mayan garden complete with fountain to several small, cosy dining rooms of dark wood, gleaming glass, low music and lights. The menu tends to dishes easily comprehended and easily perceived as elegant: shish kebab flambé, lobster in champagne sauce, jumbo shrimp and beef tampiqueña. But the food is good, the service experienced, the prices not bad: US$22 to US$32 per person for dinner. Hours are 1 pm to about 11 pm, every day of the year. La Habichuela (LAH-b'CHWEH-lah) means The Stringbean.

La Dolce Vita (☎ 4-13-84), Avenida Cobá 87, just east of Avenida Nader, is a nice little place that's been serving good food for years. The small terrace, sunk a few steps below sidewalk level, may be too noisy for you, but the pastel dining rooms won't be. Though the menu includes Italian favourites (lots of veal and pasta), there's also sea conch and calamari sautéed in garlic, herbs and soy sauce and tournedos of beef. Full dinners, served from 5 pm to midnight daily, cost US$18 to US$40 per person.

On Isla Cancún Visiting gringos flock to *Carlos 'n' Charlie's* (☎ 3-13-04), Blvd Kukulcán Km 5.5, opposite the Casa Maya, because they enjoy the who-cares atmosphere, jokey waiters, purple menu prose, decent food and they don't mind paying

US$20 to US$35 for dinner. Trendy Mexican dishes (guacamole, fajitas, ceviche) join the requisite steaks, shrimp and lobster on the menu. You pay US$2 for a beer, US$3 for anything stronger. There's dancing by the water after dinner.

The same upbeat theme is carried over into the other Carlos restaurants in Cancún: the adjoining *Señor Frog's*, which serves lunch and dinner with live reggae music for clapping and dancing; and *La Mamá de Tarzan*, a cafeteria on Blvd Kukulcán at Km 9.5, just south of Punta Cancún.

For German food, try *Karl's Keller* (☎ 3-11-04), in the Plaza Caracol shopping centre, Blvd Kukulcán Km 8. The original menu has been diluted by much 'international' fare, but you can still get hot Bavarian salad with sausage, *wienerschnitzel, rinds rouladen* (meat roll filled with bacon, onions and pickles) and *apfelstrudel* for dessert. The bill might be US$15 to US$20. Hours are 8 am to 11 pm (11 am to 11 pm on Sunday).

Once you've exhausted the aforementioned dining possibilities, drop by the Cancún Tips Information Office in the Plaza Caracol shopping centre and look through their collection of restaurant menus for other places.

Entertainment
There are discos at most of the luxury hotels in the Zona Hoteles, but the action depends very much upon the clientele in residence. A convention of Golden Agers will leave the disco sleepy, but busloads of body types will make it thunder.

Most of the nightlife is loud and bibulous as befits a supercharged beach resort. If the theme restaurants don't do it for you, take a dinner cruise on a mock pirate ship.

The local Ballet Folklorico performs some evenings at various halls for about US$25 per person, which includes dinner. The dancers come on at 8.30 pm. Don't expect the finesse and precision of the one in Mexico City.

Bullfights (four bulls) are held each Wednesday afternoon at 3.30 pm in the Plaza de Toros at the southern end of Avenida Bonampak, across the street from the Restaurant Los Almendros, about one km from the centre of town. Tickets cost about US$15 and can be purchased from any travel agency.

Things to Buy
There are gift shops and touts everywhere in Cancún, with crafts from all over Mexico at sometimes exorbitant prices. Save your shopping for other Mexican destinations. If you hanker for a hammock, buy it in Mérida. Still, window-shopping in Cancún's air-conditioned and often extremely luxurious shopping centres is good fun. The Plaza Caracol near Punta Cancún is very posh, with arctic air-conditioning. Also, have a wander around the Plaza Nautilus with its art galleries and boutiques. Don't miss the amazing 'sculptures' of Sergio Bustamante.

Getting There & Away
Air The offices of Aeroméxico (☎ (988) 4-35-71, 4-10-97, 4-11-86) are at Avenida Cobá 80 between Avenida Tulum and Avenida Bonampak, on the south side of the road. Take a customer number from the dispenser by the door or you'll end up waiting half an hour for nothing.

Aerocaribe (☎ (988) 4-21-33/11, 4-13-64), the important regional carrier with flights to Chichén Itzá, Mérida, Uxmal, Cozumel and other points in Yucatán, is in a complex at the intersection of Avenida Tulum and Avenida Uxmal, east of the traffic roundabout not far from the Hotel Parador.

Mexicana's office (☎ (988) 4-12-65, 4-14-32/44) is at Avenida Cobá 13, not far from the Aeroméxico office.

The office of Lacsa (☎ (988) 4-12-76), the Costa Rican airline with flights to Guatemala, is at Avenida Yaxchilán 5.

Other companies have only desks at the airport. These include American (☎ (988) 4-29-47, 4-26-51), Continental (☎ (988) 4-25-40, 4-27-06), Northwest (☎ (988) 4-09-46, 4-50-44) and United (☎ (988) 4-28-58, 4-25-28).

Cancún's international airport is very busy

with scheduled flights and also lots of charter traffic. Be sure to ask your travel agent about charter and group flights, which can be quite cheap, especially in summer.

Of the scheduled flights from North America, most are by Aeroméxico, American, Mexicana, Continental, Delta, Pan Am, Northwest and United from Baltimore, Chicago, Dallas/Fort Worth, Denver, Detroit, Houston, Los Angeles, Miami, New Orleans, New York, Philadelphia, San Francisco, Tampa/St Petersburg and Washington, DC.

Aero Cozumel and Aerocaribe (☎ (988) 4-81-03, 4-20-00, 4-12-31, 4-21-33 in Cancún), working together, cover destinations in the Yucatán Peninsula and somewhat beyond, in small and medium-sized planes at these prices (one-way): Chetumal US$70, Ciudad del Carmen US$120, Cozumel US$32, Mérida US$60, Mexico City US$155, Oaxaca US$200, Veracruz US$182 and VillahermosaUS$130.

They are also presently running flights on an experimental basis between Cancún and Belize City and Cancún and Flores (for Tikal) in Guatemala. Aerocaribe is a regional airline owned by Mexicana; it offers a special fare deal called the Mayapass, good for a series of flights at reduced prices. For terms and conditions, contact Aerocaribe or Mexicana.

A special excursion fare from Cancún to Mérida and return is US$94. You can also book a flight to Chichén Itzá and return for US$69.

Aeroméxico and Mexicana also handle some domestic flights from Cancún to Villahermosa and Mexico City, at similar fares.

Bus Several companies share the traffic to and from Cancún. The bus station on Avenida Uxmal just west of Avenida Tulum and the northern traffic roundabout, serves them all. The station has a cafeteria, snack shops and a newsstand, but no left luggage lockers.

Autotransportes de Oriente Mérida-Puerto Juárez SA, in the right-hand portion

of the bus station, runs 29 1st-class buses daily along the route to Mérida via Valladolid and Chichén Itzá. First-class buses depart at least every hour between 6 am and midnight for:

Chichén Itzá – 205 km, three to 3½ hours, US$3.25
Mérida – 320 km, 5½ to six hours, US$5.50
Valladolid – 161 km, two hours, US$3

There is 2nd-class service to these cities as well and also to Tizimin (US$3), at fares slightly lower than 1st class.

Oriente buses to Playa del Carmen (1½ hours, US$1.50) and Tulum (two hours, US$3) are *de paso*, meaning that you'll get a seat only if there's one seat free after the bus pulls in.

Autotransportes del Caribe, in the left-hand portion of the bus station, runs eight 1st-class and nine 2nd-class buses daily south along the coast to Puerto Morelos, Playa del Carmen, Akumal, Xel-ha, Tulum, Felipe Carrillo Puerto, Limones, Bacalar and Chetumal.

Local buses (Ruta 8) take about 20 minutes from stops on Avenida Tulum to the Puerto Juárez and Punta Sam ferry docks if you're going to Isla Mujeres. For more information on getting from Cancún to Isla Mujeres, see the Isla Mujeres section.

Car Rental cars are astoundingly expensive in Mexico in general and in Cancún in particular. A Volkswagen Beetle or similarly sized Nissan without air-conditioning, radio, or other comforts can cost over US$70 per day with unlimited kilometrage. Compare this to US$40 per day with unlimited mileage for a brand-new, very comfortable air-conditioned mid-sized rental car in the USA. When you talk to the rental agent, keep in mind that distances in Yucatán are great and that the kilometrage will end up being your biggest cost, far more than the daily rental charge. When estimating costs, be sure to take into consideration the high collision damage waiver costs and the 15% IVA (value-added tax) as well.

If you must rent a car in Cancún, share the

cost with others if you can. The rental agency desks at the airport are as good a place as any to haggle over rates (and haggling does help), but don't expect to get a cheap car, no matter how much you haggle.

In fact, if your plans allow it, I strongly recommend that you take the bus (or even fly) to Mérida and rent a car there, where costs are considerably lower (though still quite high by world standards). See the Mérida chapter for details and recommendations.

Getting Around
To/From the Airport To get to Ciudad Cancún or Isla Cancún from the airport, you must take an airport van or a taxi. The airport vans (Transporte Terrestre) are orange-and-beige Volkswagen Combi minibuses. You buy your ticket (US$2.50) inside the arrivals terminal just to the right of the exit door. Hand your luggage to the driver, tell him the name of your hotel, climb in the van and when it's full it will start off.

The route is invariably via Punta Nizuc and north up Isla Cancún along Blvd Kukulcán, passing all of the luxury beachfront hotels before reaching the youth hostel and Ciudad Cancún. If your hotel is in Ciudad Cancún, the ride to your hotel may take as long as 45 minutes. At the end of the ride, many passengers tip the driver.

The alternative to the van is to take a taxi, or hire a van for a private trip, straight to your hotel. This costs US$20. If you walk out of the airport and follow the access road, you may be able to flag down a taxi which will take you for less because the driver is no longer subject to the expensive regulated airport fares.

To return to the airport you must take a taxi; you cannot call or wave down one of the airport vans. The taxi drivers have seen to it that this is the rule. A taxi to the airport costs far less than a taxi from the airport, though. The fare to the airport is US$7.50 from anywhere in Ciudad Cancún or Isla Cancún.

Bus Although you can walk everywhere in

Ciudad Cancún, to get to the Zona Hoteles, catch a 'Ruta 1, Zona Hoteles' local bus heading southward along Avenida Tulum. They proceed down Avenida Tulum to Avenida Cobá, turn left and continue along Blvd Kukulcán almost to Punta Nizuc. The bus fare is US$0.20. There are never enough buses and they are always packed and frequently impossible to squeeze yourself into.

To reach Puerto Juárez and/or Punta Sam for the ferries bound for Isla Mujeres, take a Ruta 8 bus ('Pto Juárez' or 'Punta Sam'); the fare is US$0.20 to US$0.35. Returning from Isla Mujeres to Punta Sam, note that the bus drivers seem to have been pressured by the *taxistas* to depart *just before the ferry arrives*, thereby forcing arriving ferry passengers to take taxis back to Ciudad Cancún. If you're willing to wait, another Ruta 8 bus will come. The bus waits on the road outside the gate to the ferry area.

Taxi Cancún's taxis do not have meters so you must haggle over fares. Some of the large hotels have fares to various points posted on signs near their front entrances. Generally, the fare between Ciudad Cancún and Punta Cancún (Hyatt, Camino Real and Krystal hotels and the Convention Centre) is US$1 or US$1.50, the same or slightly less to shuttle between two of the big hotels on Isla Cancún.

To go from Ciudad Cancún all the way down to the Club Med at Punta Nizuc might cost US$5 or US$6. To the airport costs US$7.50, a flat rate from any point in the city or on the island. To Puerto Juárez you'll pay about US$2.50, to Punta Sam about US$3 or US$3.50.

Because there are never enough buses, at peak travel times (late morning, before dinner in the evening) there are also never enough taxis. You will find transport difficult at these times, no matter how you wish to travel or what you're willing to spend.

Ferry There are frequent passenger ferries to Isla Mujeres from Puerto Juárez, about three km north of Avenida Tulum. Car ferries, which also carry passengers, depart from

Punta Sam, about five km north of Avenida Tulum. There are also three daily ferries to Isla Mujeres from the Playa Linda Marine Terminal, Blvd Kukulcán Km 5 on Isla Cancún, just west of the bridge, between the Aquamarina Beach and Calinda Cancún hotels.

ISLA MUJERES
Population 13,500

Isla Mujeres (Island of Women), has a reputation as a 'backpackers' Cancún', a place where one can escape the high-energy, high-priced mega-resort for the laid-back life of a tropical isle – at bargain prices. Though this was true for many years, it is less true today. Cancún has been so successful that its version of the good life has spilled over onto its neighbour island. Prices are higher now than before: some once-simple cookshops have become trendy restaurants and basic hotels have upgraded their prices along with their facilities.

This does not mean that Isla Mujeres is stacked with high-rise hotels and condos. Rather it plays Greenwich Village to Cancún's Manhattan, a community built more on a human scale, with signs of an authentic Caribbean past.

The chief attribute of Isla Mujeres is its relaxed social life in a tropical setting with surrounding waters that are turquoise blue and bathtub warm. If you have been doing some hard travelling through Mexico, you will find many travellers you met along the way taking it easy here. Others make it the site of their one to two-week holiday. Many visitors have a hard time tearing themselves away.

But the island is changing. The town can become crowded to capacity on many days, its streets, hotels and restaurants packed. By day there's the noise of jackhammers and by night the blare of radio rock and roll. Moreover, the principal beach is rather small and the island as a whole not all that attractive. Most of the palm trees were killed by a blight, the rest swept away by Hurricane Gilbert in 1988 and the part of the island not built up consists of Yucatán scrub bush. The

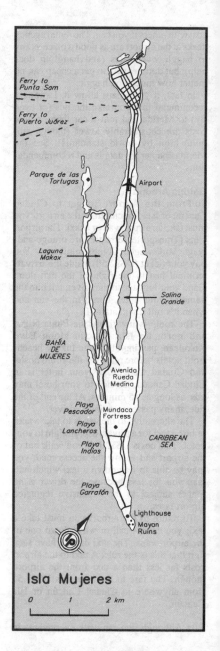

Isla Mujeres

0   1   2 km

ballyhooed snorkelling at Garrafón National Park is overrated because of crowding. Prices, while not outrageous like Cancún's, are higher than you will find in most of Mexico. And Cancún makes itself felt each morning as boatload after boatload of package tourists arrive on Isla Mujeres for a day's excursion.

History

Although it is said by some that The Island of Women got its name because Spanish buccaneers kept their lovers here while they plundered galleons and pillaged ports, a less romantic but still intriguing explanation is probably more accurate. In 1519, a chronicler sailing with Hernández de Córdoba's expedition wrote that when the conquistadors' ships were forced by high winds into the island's harbour, the crew reconnoitred. What they found onshore was a Mayan ceremonial site filled with clay figurines of females. Today, some archaeologists believe that the island was a stopover for the Maya en route to worship their goddess of fertility, Ixchel, on the island of Cozumel. The clay idols are thought to represent the goddess.

Orientation

The island is about eight km long and anywhere from 300 to 800 metres wide. There is a small mid-island airstrip. The good snorkelling and some of the better swimming beaches are on the southern part of the island along the western shore; the eastern shore is washed by the open sea and the surf is dangerous. The ferry docks, the town and the most popular sand beach (Playa Cocoteros) are at the northern tip of the island. The small grid of narrow streets in the town is easily comprehensible, particularly as there is little vehicular traffic except along the main coastal road, Avenida Rueda Medina. The grid streets are named after the usual Mexican revolutionary heroes, but there are few street signs.

After 20 minutes of wandering, you'll know your way around. There is a main plaza which also serves as a basketball court just inland from the ferry docks, a municipal market (Mercado Municipal) with a number of cheap eateries, a post office and a largeish cemetery. For locations, refer to the map.

Information

Tourist Office Located on Guerrero one block west of Hotel Isleño and just past Hotel Carmelina, at the end of a narrow passage, is the island's tourist office (☎ (988) 2-01-73, 2-01-88). They have crude map handouts and will change money at a not-so-great rate after banking hours as well as make international collect calls for a fee. Hours are theoretically 9 am to 2 pm and 5 to 7 pm from Monday to Saturday, although the office is sometimes closed during these hours. The clerk is one of the few islanders who speaks little English!

Money The island's Banco del Atlantico at Juárez 5 and Banco Serfin at Juárez 3, are so packed during the two hours a day (10 am to noon, Monday to Friday) when foreign currency may be exchanged that many travellers change money at a lower rate at a grocery store, their hotel or at the tourist office. Travellers who want the bank rate justify the wait in line as an opportunity to meet interesting people.

Laundry The family that runs the Posada San Jorge has opened a laundromat *(lavandería)* (☎ 2-01-55) at Avenida Juárez 29, just in front of the posada. Come any day between 6 am and 8 pm, drop off three kg of laundry and your choice of detergent and you'll pay US$2.75 to have it washed, US$1 to have it dried, or US$3.50 for wash and dry. You can go to the beach and drop by later to pick up your clean clothes.

Garrafón National Park

Although the waters are translucent and the fish abundant, Garrafón is perhaps a bit overrated. Hordes of day trippers from Cancún fill the water during the middle of the day, so you are more often ogling fellow snorkellers than aquatic life. Furthermore, the reef is virtually dead, which makes it less likely to

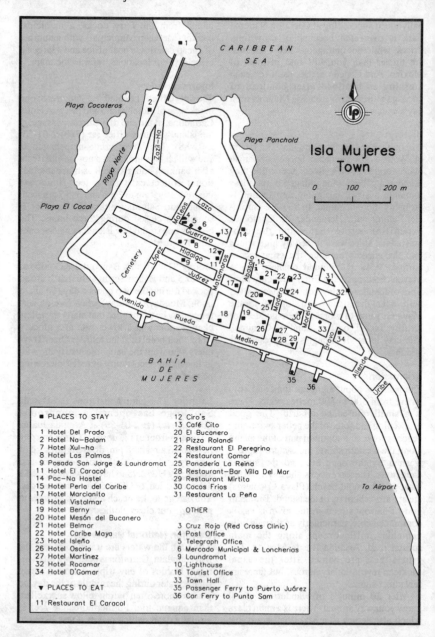

Isla Mujeres Town

CARIBBEAN SEA

Playa Cocoteros
Playa Norte
Playa Panchold
Playa El Cocal
Cemetery
BAHÍA DE MUJERES
To Airport

0   100   200 m

■ PLACES TO STAY

1 Hotel Del Prado
2 Hotel Na-Balam
7 Hotel Xul-ha
8 Hotel Las Palmas
9 Posada San Jorge & Laundromat
11 Hotel El Caracol
14 Poc-Na Hostel
15 Hotel Perla del Caribe
17 Hotel Marcianito
18 Hotel Vistalmar
19 Hotel Berny
20 Hotel Mesón del Bucanero
21 Hotel Belmar
22 Hotel Caribe Maya
23 Hotel Isleño
26 Hotel Osorio
27 Hotel Martínez
32 Hotel Rocamar
34 Hotel D'Gomar

▼ PLACES TO EAT

11 Restaurant El Caracol

12 Ciro's
13 Café Cito
20 El Bucanero
21 Pizza Rolandi
22 Restaurant El Peregrino
24 Restaurant Gomar
25 Panadería La Reina
28 Restaurant-Bar Villa Del Mar
29 Restaurant Mirtita
30 Cocos Fríos
31 Restaurant La Peña

OTHER

3 Cruz Roja (Red Cross Clinic)
4 Post Office
5 Telegraph Office
6 Mercado Municipal & Loncherías
9 Laundromat
10 Lighthouse
16 Tourist Office
33 Town Hall
35 Passenger Ferry to Puerto Juárez
36 Car Ferry to Punta Sam

Top: Cancún, the mega-resort (TB)
Left: Flying over the Zona Hoteles, Cancún (TW)
Right: Isla Mujeres ferry (TW)

Top: Convento de San Antonio de Padua, Izamal (TB)
Bottom: Pyramid of Kukulcán, Chichén Itzá (TW)

inflict cuts but reduces its colour and the intricacy of its formations.

The water can be extremely choppy, sweeping you into jagged areas. When the water is running fast here – not an unusual occurrence – snorkelling is a hassle and can even be dangerous. Those without strong swimming skills should be advised that the bottom falls off steeply quite close to shore; if you are having trouble, you might not be noticed amidst all those bobbing heads.

Garrafón is open daily from 8 am to 5 pm and the earlier you get here (see the Getting Around section at the end of this chapter), the more time you will have free of the milling mobs from Cancún. Admission to the park costs US$1. There are lockers for your valuables – recommended as a safeguard – for about US$1. Snorkelling equipment can be rented for the day at US$3. Garrafón also has a small aquarium and museum.

Playa Cocoteros

Walk north along Calle Hidalgo or Guerrero to reach Playa Cocoteros, sometimes called Playa Los Cocos, the town's principal beach. The slope of the beach is very gradual and the transparent and calm waters are only chest-high far from the shore. However, the beach is relatively small for the number of sunseekers and while there are some palapa-thatched huts for shelter from direct rays, the coconut palms for which the beach was named have long since been swept away by hurricanes and development. Try to come early in the morning or later in the day – at midday Playa Cocoteros can be crowded and hot. If you can't tear yourself away from the beach, there are a couple of restaurant palapas selling food, beer and soft drinks at beach prices.

Along the northern edge of Playa Cocoteros at the pier adjacent to Hotel del Prado, the clear water and colourful aquatic life make for good snorkelling and it's infinitely less crowded than Garrafón. There is no admission charge for these waters and you can also rent snorkelling gear in town cheaper than at Garrafón.

Ixchel, old moon goddess and goddess of fertility

Playa Lancheros

Four km south of the town and 1.5 km north of Garrafón is Playa Lancheros, the southernmost point served by local buses. The beach is less attractive than Cocoteros, but there are free festivities on Sundays and you might want to come to enjoy the music.

Mayan Ruins

Just past Garrafón National Park, at the southern tip of the island, are the badly ruined remains of a temple to Ixchel, Mayan goddess of the moon, fertility and other worthy causes. Observed by Hernández de Córdoba when his ships were forced by high winds into the island's coastal waters in 1519, the temple has been crumbling ever since. Hurricane Gilbert almost finished it off in 1988.

There's really little left to see here other than a fine sea view and, in the distance, Cancún. The clay female figurines were pilfered long ago and a couple of the walls were washed into the Caribbean.

You can walk to the ruins, beyond the lighthouse at the south end of the island, from Garrafón.

Mundaca Fortress

The story behind the ruins of this house and

fort are more intriguing than what remains of them. A slave-trading pirate, Fermín Antonio Mundaca de Marechaja, fell in love with a visiting Spanish beauty. To win her, the rogue built a two-storey mansion complete with gardens and graceful archways as well as a small fortress to defend it. While Mundaca built the house, the object of his affection's ardour cooled and she married another islander. Brokenhearted, Mundaca died and his house, fortress and garden fell into disrepair.

The Mundaca Fortress is east of the main road near Playa Lancheros, about four km south of the town. Watch for signs.

Scuba Diving

Diving to see sunken ships and beautiful reefs in the crystalline waters of the Caribbean is a memorable way to pass time on Isla Mujeres. If you're a qualified diver, you'll need a licence, rental equipment and a boat to take you to the good spots. All of these are available from Mexico Divers (Buzos de México, ☎ (988) 2-01-31), Avenida Rueda Medina at Madero. Costs range from US$40 to US$70 depending upon how many tanks you use up.

A regular stop on the dive-boat's route is the Sleeping Shark Caves, about five km north of the island and at 23 metres' depth, where the otherwise dangerous creatures are alleged to be lethargically nonlethal due to the low oxygen content of the caves' waters. Veteran divers say it's foolish to test the theory: you could become shark bait. It's far better to explore the fine reefs off the island like Los Manchones, La Bandera, Cuevones or Chital.

Isla Contoy Bird Sanctuary

You can take an excursion by boat to tiny Isla Contoy, a national bird sanctuary, about 25 km north of Isla Mujeres. It's a treasure trove for birdwatchers, with an abundance of brown pelicans, olive cormorants and red-pouched frigates, as well as frequent visits by flamingoes and herons. There is good snorkelling both en route and just off Contoy.

Getting There & Away For a private trip, contact Ricardo Gaitan and he will take you to Contoy in his 10-metre sailboat, *Providencia*. Gaitan will supply food and snorkelling equipment for the two-day venture at roughly US$30 per person. You will need suntan lotion, insect repellent and a sleeping bag. If you just want a one-day excursion, for about US$20, ask at the Sociedad Cooperativa Transporte Turística 'Isla Mujeres' (☎ (988) 2-02-74) on Avenida Rueda Medina to the north of the ferry docks.

Places to Stay

During the busy seasons (late December to March and midsummer), many island hotels are booked solid by midday; at these times prices are also highest. From May to mid-December prices are lower and you may even be able to haggle them still lower if business is slack. If you're travelling alone, you may have to haggle a bit, as there are few single rooms on the island. Double rooms will usually be rented as singles at a slightly lower price if demand for rooms is not high.

Places to Stay – bottom end

Poc-Na (☎ (988) 2-00-90), on Matamoros at Carlos Lazo, is a privately run youth hostel and an international travellers' hangout built in a style that might be termed 'modern Maya'. The fan-cooled dormitories, which take both men and women together, are clean, as are the communal toilets. Poc-Na is close to both the beach and the town, yet the location is fairly quiet. The cafeteria serves decent food at inexpensive prices; the patio dining room is a meeting place for travellers and a great place to get up-to-date info on other parts of Mexico.

The charge for bunk and bedding is US$4; you must put down a deposit of US$7.25 on the bedding. To get to Poc-Na from the ferry, walk to the left three blocks and then to the right four blocks.

Hotel El Caracol (☎ (988) 2-01-50), Matamoros 5, between Hidalgo and Guerrero, is run by a smiling and efficient señora and her family who keep everything clean and neat. The tidy restaurant off the lobby serves meals at decent prices. Rooms have insect screens, ceiling fans, clean tiled bathrooms and many have two double beds. You pay US$18 a double if you stay only one night, US$15 per night if you stay two or more.

The *Hotel Martínez* (☎ (988) 2-01-54), Madero 14, is an older hotel that's been fairly well maintained by the same family for more than 20 years. Some rooms have sea views, all have ceiling fans, private baths and well-used furnishings. Doubles go for US$13. When the aging proprietors retire it might go upscale, but for now it's dependable for cheap, clean accommodation.

Almost across the street, a few steps farther inland, is the *Hotel Osorio* (☎ (988) 2-00-18), Madero at Juárez. The older hotel on the opposite side of the street from the Martinez (the building with the odd façade of rounded stones) has huge, clean rooms with fan and bath; the newer building facing it across Madero has more up-to-date rooms. The rate for a double is US$13 to US$16, depending upon the room, the season and your bargaining abilities.

Cheaper still is *Posada San Jorge* (☎ (988) 2-01-55), Juárez 29A, behind the laundromat of the same name. Its bare, basic rooms are acceptably clean and quite inexpensive for Isla Mujeres. Singles with fan and bath cost US$9, doubles US$11. The enterprising family which operates the hotel also runs the laundromat in front.

Hotel Las Palmas (☎ (988) 2-04-16), Guerrero 20, across from the Mercado Municipal, offers nice clean new rooms with fan and bath for US$11/13 a single/double. Staying here, you're near the market's cheap eateries and the post office and closer to the beach than most hotels in town.

Hotel Caribe Maya (☎ (988) 2-01-90), Madero 9, between Guerrero and Hidalgo, charges $US13 a double, but offers good value for money at that price. Rooms are the familiar simple but clean ones, with fan and private shower.

Hotel Marcianito (☎ (988) 2-01-11), Abasolo 10, between Juárez and Hidalgo, is a place to try if everything else is full. Rooms here are serviceable, but a bit more closed-in and older than those in nearby hotels; and the price here is a bit higher, at US$15 a double with fan and shower.

Hotel Isleño (☎ (988) 0-03-02), Madero 8 at the corner of Guerrero, has rooms with ceiling fans and good cross-ventilation, but without running water, for US$11 a double, the lowest price this side of Poc-Na. There's a shared bathroom for each three guestrooms, so the facilities aren't really overcrowded. Get a room on the upper floor if you can, as it'll be quieter.

Hotel Vistalmar (☎ (988) 2-00-96), Avenida Rueda Medina between Abasolo and Matamoros, is a final place to look if all else is full. True to its name, the Vistalmar has nice sea views from its front porch, but rooms are as simple and functional as any in town, yet cost a bit more than most: US$15 a double.

Places to Stay – middle

Moderately priced hotel rooms cost anywhere from US$22 to US$60 a double. For this you usually (but not always) get air-conditioning, more in the way of decor, perhaps a balcony and/or a nice sea view and sometimes other services such as restaurant, bar and swimming pool. Rooms may be pretty small or fairly large, depending upon the hotel; all have private bathrooms.

Hotel Perla del Caribe (☎ (988) 2-04-44, 2-03-02), Madero just east of Guerrero, right on the eastern beach, has 63 rooms on three floors, most with balconies, many with wonderful sea views and good cross-ventilation. There's a cafeteria and snack bar, a TV lounge, a swimming pool and a sunning deck. Rooms are in four categories (all doubles): for US$33, you can have a room facing the town with fan or air-con; for US$46, your room has a sea view, but is on a lower floor; for US$51 you get a similar room with sea view on an upper floor; and for US$58 you can have one of the newest, most luxurious rooms opening onto the swimming pool.

Hotel Belmar (☎ (988) 2-04-29, 2-04-30; fax 2-04-29), Hidalgo between Abasolo and Madero, is right above the Pizza Rolandi restaurant and run by the same family. Though it doesn't look like much from its entrance, the hotel's rooms are very nicely decorated and well kept, with fan, air-con, TV and lots of colourful Mexican tiles. The price, US$25 a double, is good for what you get. Don't just pass this one by. Take a look at a room.

The new *Hotel D'Gomar* (☎ (988) 2-01-42), Hidalgo 5, is easily visible from the ferryboats as you dock here. The guestrooms on the four floors above a boutique are tastefully decorated by the boutique owners, who have a vested interest in style and rent for a reasonable US$25 a double. Each has a fan and two double beds.

The *Hotel Rocamar* (☎ (988) 2-01-01) is on the opposite side of the town from the ferry above the main square where Guerrero meets Bravo. This was the first real hotel to be built in town many years ago and though it now shows its age a bit, maintenance is excellent and it still has the advantages of an excellent hilltop site, wonderful sea views and very good cross-ventilation (in the old days before air-conditioning, they designed hotels to stay cool naturally). Nautical decor is everywhere, from the thick rope balustrades to the transparent plastic vanities with embedded seashells. The hotel's restaurant, El Limbo, shares the fine sea view. Singles/doubles/triples with fan and bath cost US$32/35/40.

The 40 rooms at the *Hotel Berny* (☎ (988) 2-00-25, 2-00-26), on Abasolo at the corner of Juárez, are built around a central court with a small swimming pool. Burnished red tile floors set off the extensive use of white stucco. The rooms are comfortable and modernish though not fancy; with ceiling fan and private bath, they cost US$22 a double.

The brand-new *Hotel Xul-ha*, on Hidalgo not far from López Mateos, is a stucco structure with up-to-date rooms, all with balconies and air-con, renting for US$30 a double.

Hotel Mesón del Bucanero (☎ (988) 2-02-36), Hidalgo 11, between Abasolo and Madero, is above the restaurant of the same name and directly across the street from Pizza Rolandi and the Hotel Belmar. Rooms at the Bucanero are nice enough and they come with ceiling fans, but the prices are upscale at US$35 to US$40 a double.

Places to Stay – top end
The island's poshest place to stay is the *Hotel Del Prado* (☎ (988) 2-00-29/43, 2-01-22), Islote del Yunque, once called El Presidente Caribe and before that the Zazil-Ha. The dramatic inclined façade faces north across the water from its perch on a tiny islet at Isla Mujeres' northernmost point, just 100 metres north of Playa Cocoteros. As you approach Isla Mujeres from the mainland, you can't help but see the hotel. The 100 rooms here have all the conveniences and most of the luxuries; there's a restaurant and bar, a pool and a tiny beach, though most of the islet is jagged rock (but Playa Cocoteros is just across a narrow channel). On one side of the hotel there's a shallow lagoon ideal for kids to swim in, while the sea beats the rocky shore on the other side. At the end of the islet there's a pier and some good snorkelling. Singles/doubles cost US$78/87, tax included. Call toll-free for reservations in Mexico at (800) 9-04-44, or in the USA at (800) 782-9639.

Hotel Na-Balam (☎ (988) 2-04-46; same for fax), Calle Zazil-Ha 118, faces Playa Cocoteros at the northern tip of the island just a few hundred metres from the Hotel Del Prado. A new two-storey structure, it holds 12 spacious junior suites, most with fabulous sea view, ceiling fan, refrigerator, two double beds and, of course, private bath. There are numerous nice touches, such as the bathroom vanities made of colourful travertine.

Prices for suites with balcony are US$55 a double in season, US$35 off season; without a balcony, prices are US$5 lower. Though it does not have the big-hotel services, the rooms here are perhaps even more comfortable than those at the Del Prado. More hotels similar to the Na-Balam (the name means House of the Jaguar) are being built facing the beach here; some may be available by the time you arrive.

Places to Eat

Few Cancún-style dinner-as-entertainment restaurants crowd Isla Mujeres' narrow streets. Dining here is more sedate and prices are lower, but not as low as in the rest of Mexico. Service is universally inexperienced, slow and inattentive, at least in my experience. The waiters are the last and greatest repository of the island's old laid-back 'What? Me worry?' lifestyle.

Places to Eat – bottom end

Walk from the main plaza north-west along Guerrero and, just before the intersection with López Mateos, you'll pass the Mercado Municipal on the right-hand side, across Guerrero from the Hotel Las Palmas. Beside the market are several *cocinas económicas* (economical kitchens) serving simple but tasty and filling meals at the best prices on the island. Sit in the shade by the *Lonchería Ciovanni*, the *Lonchería San Martin*, the *Lonchería Carolina* or *Tacostumbras* and have a big plate with fried chicken, chips and salad for US$2.50, or various Mexican antojitos for US$1.75. Tacos are even cheaper. Prices are not marked, so ask before you order. These market eateries are nicer than those in most Mexican towns and only a bit more expensive. Hours are usually (and approximately) 7 am to 6 pm.

Fresh baked goods are available at *Panadería La Reina*, on Madero between Juárez and Hidalgo, a good place to stop for breakfast or picnic supplies.

Café Cito, a tiny place on Guerrero near the corner with Matamoros, has a New Age menu which includes 10 varieties of crepes, ingenious sandwiches, huge salad plates and tempting daily special platters. The menu is in English and German. Expect to spend US$2.50 to US$5 for a meal here. Hours are 9 am to noon and 6 to 10 pm, closed Monday.

Few places on the island even approach the market eateries in terms of low price and value for money, but for variety you might try the simple meals at Poc-Na or the Hotel El Caracol. If you'd like to eat in other island restaurants, which tend to be more expensive, avoid the expensive dishes (shrimp, lobster, whole fish, steaks) and stick with the traditional foods (filete de pescado, enchiladas, tacos).

Self-Catering To buy your own supplies, there's the municipal market (see map) and also the Supermercado Mirtita, Juárez 14, corner of Nicolas Bravo, one block inland from the ferry docks and the Super Betino, on the main plaza.

Place to Eat – middle Most of the island's restaurants fall into the middle category. Depending upon what you order, breakfast goes for US$2.50 to US$4, lunch or dinner for US$5 to US$15 per person, unless you order lobster.

El Bucanero (☎ 2-02-36), Avenida Hidalgo 11 between Abasolo and Madero in the Mesón del Bucanero, has a long and interesting menu: breakfast omelettes of ham and cheese (US$2.50), fried chicken or fish (US$3.50) and Mexican traditional foods (enchiladas, tacos, etc) for about the same. Besides the usual, they serve offbeat things like asparagus au gratin with wholemeal bread. Turned wood, stone and lots of plants make this an attractive place with a tropical feel to it. It's open every day for all three meals.

Pizza Rolandi (☎ 2-04-30), directly across Hidalgo from El Bucanero, serves pizzas and calzones cooked in a wood-fired oven and pastas with various sauces, for US$4 to US$7 per person. The menu has expanded to include fresh salads, fish and lobster as well as some Italian specialities. Hours are 1 pm to midnight daily, 6 pm to midnight on Sunday.

Restaurant El Peregrino (☎ 2-01-90), Madero 8, adjoining the Hotel Caribe Maya, has a small streetside dining area and several interior rooms that are pleasantly decorated. Though the menu is similar to those at the aforementioned places, the prices here are lower and the food is as good.

Restaurant La Peña (no phone), Guerrero 5, behind the bandstand on the main square, used to be fairly laid-back with low prices. Now it serves platters designed for the tourist trade: fish or beef brochettes with salad, chips and a glass of beer or wine for US$5.50. Colour photographs by the entrance show you what you're supposed to get. The modular-menu approach keeps the price fairly reasonable, but sometimes portions on the real-world platters don't quite live up to the photographs. All the same, there are people who come here just to enjoy the sea view from the terrace at the back, ordering one of the many complicated and expensive drinks. La Peña is open daily from 8 am to midnight.

Another place favoured mostly for ambience is *Cocos Frios*, Hidalgo 4, with a nice portico on two sides set with dining tables and a spacious interior dining room. Specials here are not chilled coconuts so much as fried chicken, chicken tacos, fried fish and beef served in various ways. Breakfast here is a favourite – again, more for the mood than the food.

Somewhat more expensive, *Restaurant Gomar* (☎ 2-01-42), on Hidalgo at the corner with Madero, serves excellent seafood and chicken dishes in the island's thickest neocolonial decor. The huge noncolonial VCR shows movies while you dine. There are tables outside on the verandah as well. Expect to spend about US$7 to US$9 for a decent seafood dinner here. Hours are supposedly from 8 am to 11 pm.

Ciro's, on Matamoros at Guerrero, serves a varied menu of sandwiches, soups, chicken, meats, fish and lobster at moderate prices, but the real draw here is the air-conditioned dining room. It's open from 2 to 10 pm daily. A large club sandwich with chips costs US$2.50 and most meat, chicken and fish plates are about US$3.75.

You'll see the *Restaurant Mirtita* (☎ 2-01-57), facing the ferry dock on Avenida Rueda Medina, as you disembark from your ferry. Its location at a busy traffic point keeps it full of tourists most of the day. The menu is in English as was the sports news issuing from the big TV when I was there. Though the dining room has air-conditioning, most of the time they use the ceiling fans instead. Portions are a bit on the small side and prices

on the big, but it's convenient to the ferry. Another choice is the nearby *Restaurant Tropicana*, also on Rueda Medina, at the corner of Nicolas Bravo, which is more favoured by *isleños*.

Also facing the ferry docks is the *Restaurant-Bar Villa Del Mar* (☎ 2-00-31), Avenida Rueda Medina 1 Sur, which is fancier in decor and ambience but not all that much higher in price.

Places to Eat – top end
Big spenders from Cancún and well-heeled visitors to Isla Mujeres often head for *María's Kan-Kin Restaurant Française* (☎ 3-14-20, 2-00-15), several km down the coast near Garrafón and open daily from 8 am to 9 pm. The lobsters are live, the prices for the continental-inspired cuisine are high, but the food is said to be good.

Entertainment
The first place to go is the main plaza, where there's always something to watch (a football match, a basketball or volleyball game, an impromptu concert or serenade) and lots of somebodies watching it.

The island's only cinema, the Cine Blanquita, on Morelos, is on the north-west side of the square. It sometimes has foreign films in English with subtitles in Spanish, but ask – don't assume.

As for discos, there's Buho's (☎ 2-00-86), which is also a restaurant and bar, in the Hotel Cabañas María del Mar, Avenida Carlos Lazo 1, at Playa Cocoteros. It's been here a while and is usually satisfactory. Nearby is the Bad Bones Café, next to the north lighthouse, for a change of pace. Tequila Video Bar (☎ 2-00-19), at the corner of Matamoros and Hidalgo, is a favourite with locals (who don't feel they must be near the beach), but draws a respectable number of foreigners as well. Hours are 9 pm to 3 am every day except Monday.

Getting There & Away
Bus Most people travelling to Isla Mujeres take a Ruta 8 bus heading north on Avenida Tulum (US$0.30) or a taxi (US$2.50) to

Puerto Juárez, about three km north of Ciudad Cancún's Avenida Tulum; a Cancún airport minibus will take you to Puerto Juárez on a private trip for about US$20, but it'd be cheaper to ride the minibus with others into Ciudad Cancún (US$2.50 per person) and then take a taxi (US$2.50) from there. There are also direct buses to Puerto Juárez from Mérida, Chichén Itzá and Valladolid.

To get to Punta Sam, take the Ruta 8 bus (US$0.30, 25 minutes) heading north from Avenida Tulum, or a taxi (US$3 or US$3.50, 15 minutes).

Ferry There are three points of embarkation from the mainland by ferry to Isla Mujeres, 11 km off the coast. Two are north of Ciudad Cancún, the other is on Isla Cancún.

To/From Puerto Juárez From Puerto Juárez, the official schedule says that passenger ferries depart every hour on the half-hour from 8.30 am to 8.30 pm, with extra boats at 6 and 10 am. In practice, the schedule depends upon demand and if few people show up for a particular voyage, it'll be cancelled. One-way fare is US$1.75, or US$3 if you take the fancier and more comfortable *Caribbean Queen*. The voyage takes about 30 minutes. Return schedules from Isla Mujeres are equally frequent; most hotels on the island have schedules posted.

The smaller Puerto Juárez boats can be seasick-machines in rough weather and you can get drenched by spray from the bow if you're not careful. If the sea is choppy, consider taking the slower but more stable (and cheaper) car ferry from Punta Sam.

To/From Punta Sam The dock at Punta Sam, about five km north of Avenida Tulum and 3.5 km north of Puerto Juárez, is the departure point for car ferries to Isla Mujeres. These offer greater stability than the Puerto Juárez passenger ferries, but the car ferries are slower, taking 45 minutes to an hour to reach the island.

Ferries leave Punta Sam at 7.15 and 9.45 am, at noon and at 2.30, 5.15, 7.45 and 10 pm. Departures from Isla Mujeres are at 6, 8.30 and 11 am and at 1.15, 4, 6.30 and 9 pm. Passengers pay US$1.50; a car costs US$6.50. If you're taking a car, be sure to get to the dock an hour or so before departure time. Put your car in line and buy your ticket early or you may have to wait for the next voyage.

To/From Playa Linda Marine Terminal Three times daily, *The Shuttle* (☎ (988) 4-63-33 or 4-66-56) departs from Playa Linda on Isla Cancún for Isla Mujeres. Voyages are at 8 and 11 am and 2 pm from Playa Linda; return voyages depart Isla Mujeres at 9.30 am and 12.30 and 5 pm. The round-trip fare is US$12, but this includes free beer and soft drinks on board.

Show up at the Playa Linda Marine Terminal, Blvd Kukulcán Km 5 on Isla Cancún, just west of the bridge, between the Aquamarina Beach and Calinda Cancún hotels, at least 30 minutes before departure so you'll have time to buy your ticket and get a good seat on the boat.

Taxi Returning from the island to Puerto Juárez or Punta Sam, there will be swarms of taxis awaiting your command and much as they try to shoo away the buses, you can catch a Ruta 8 bus back into town. Another tactic is to chat up fellow passengers during the voyage and offer to share a cab into Ciudad Cancún, or wherever you're headed. Even better, convince one of the people shipping a car to drop you in town for free.

Getting Around
The town of Isla Mujeres is small and everything's within walking distance. If you arrive with heavy luggage, little boys will wheel it on push-bikes to your hotel.

Bus By local bus from the market or dock, you can get within 1.5 km of Garrafón; the terminus is Playa Lancheros. The personnel at Poc-Na Youth Hostel can give you an idea of the bus's erratic schedule. (Locals in league with taxi drivers may tell you the bus doesn't exist.)

If you walk to Garrafón, bring some water – it's a hot two-hour, six-km walk. By taxi, it costs about US$2 to Garrafón, just over US$1 to Playa Lancheros. Rates are set by the municipal government and are posted at the ferry dock, though the sign is frequently defaced by the taxi drivers.

Bicycle & Moped Bicycles can be rented from a number of shops on the island including Sport Bike, on the corner of Juárez and Morelos, a block from the ferry docks. Before you rent, compare prices and the condition of the bikes in a few shops, then arrive early in the day to get one of the better bikes. Costs are US$3 to US$5 for four hours, only a bit more for a full day; you'll be asked to plunk down a deposit of US$8 or so.

Everybody and their grandmother are prepared to rent you a motorbike on Isla Mujeres. It must be a lucrative business! Shop around, compare prices and look for these things: new or newer machines in good condition, full gas tanks and reasonable deposits. Cost per hour is usually US$3 or US$4 with a two-hour minimum, US$18 all day, or even cheaper by the week. Shops away from the busiest streets tend to have better prices, but not necessarily better equipment.

When driving, remember that far more people are seriously injured on motorbikes than in cars. Your enemies are inexperience, speed, sand, wet or oily roads and other people on motorbikes. Don't forget to slather yourself with sunblock before you take off. Be sure to do your hands, feet, face and neck thoroughly, as these will get the most sun.

If a motorbike is not for you, go to the Hotel Perla del Caribe, which rents little motorised buggies similar to golf carts.

Valladolid & Chichén Itzá

Coming from ultramodern Cancún, Valladolid will take you by surprise, for if Cancún is the Yucatán of today and tomorrow, Valladolid is the Yucatán of history. Small and manageable with an easy pace of life, graced with many handsome colonial buildings and provided with a decent-enough array of hotels and restaurants, Valladolid is a delightful place to stop, spend the night and get to know the real Yucatán.

VALLADOLID
Population 80,000
Valladolid is only 160 km (about two hours) west of Cancún and 40 km (half an hour) east of Chichén Itzá but as it has no sights of stop-the-car immediacy, few tourists do stop here; most prefer to hurtle on through to the next major site. It's just as well, for this preserves Valladolid for the rest of us who want to enjoy it.

History
The Mayan ceremonial centre of Zací was here long before the Spanish arrived to lay out a new city on the classic Spanish colonial plan. The initial attempt at conquest in 1543 by the conquistador Francisco de Montejo, nephew of Montejo El Adelantado, was thwarted by fierce Mayan resistance, but El Adelantado's son Montejo El Mozo ultimately conquered the Indians and took the town.

During much of the succeeding colonial era, Valladolid's distance from Mérida, its humidity and surrounding rainforests kept it isolated and thus relatively autonomous of royal rule. With the French and American revolutions as a catalyst, in 1809 local Mayan leaders plotted a rebellion which was discovered and quashed. Nonetheless, the seeds of future unrest were sown and Valladolid would play an important role in the next uprising.

Brutally exploited and banned along with the mestizos from even entering this town of pure-blooded Spanish, the Maya rebelled and in the War of the Castes of 1847 they made Valladolid their first point of attack. Besieged for two months, Valladolid's Spanish defenders were finally overcome; many of the citizens fled to the safety of Mérida and the rest were slaughtered by the Mayan forces.

Today, Valladolid is a marketing centre for agricultural products and crafts, with some light industry as well. Although it may appear sleepy, Valladolid is a prosperous seat of agrarian commerce and is the principal city of the peninsula's midsection.

Orientation
Because this compact town has streets on a numbered grid, it's easy to find your way around Valladolid. Odd-numbered streets run east-west, even-numbered streets north-south. Recommended hotels are on the main plaza, called the Parque Francisco Cantón Rosado, or just a block or two away from it. The plaza is bounded by Calles 39 and 41 (east-west) and 40 and 42 (north-south).

The main highway goes right through the centre of town. Eastbound, you travel on Calle 41; westbound, on Calle 39 or 35.

The bus station is at the corner of Calles 39 and 46. Exit the station to Calle 39, turn left, walk two blocks and you're at the main plaza.

The post office is on the east side of the main plaza at Calle 40 195A. Hours are Monday to Friday from 8 am to 6 pm, Saturday 9 am to 1 pm.

Church of San Bernardino de Siena & Convent of Sisal
Although Valladolid has a number of interesting colonial churches, the Church of San Bernardino de Siena and the Convent of Sisal, three blocks south-west of the plaza on Calle 41A at the corners of Calles 41 and 46, are said to be the oldest Christian structures in Yucatán. Constructed in 1552, the

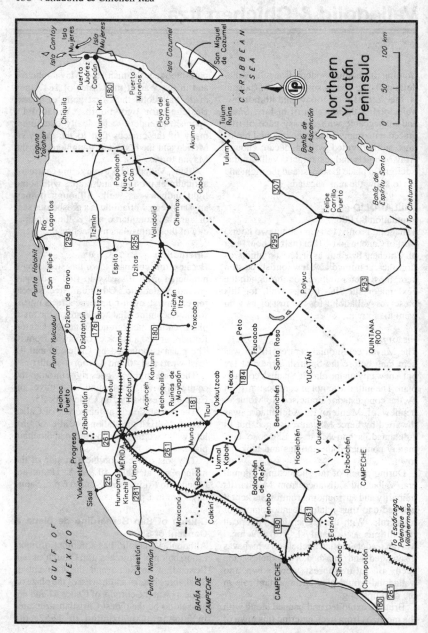

Northern Yucatán Peninsula

complex was designed to serve as a dual function as fortress and church, given the enmity of the Indians toward the Spanish.

If you venture inside, apart from the miracle-working Virgin of Guadalupe on the altar, the church is relatively bare of ornamentation. During the uprisings of 1847 and 1910, angry Indians responded to the clergy's links with landowners by stripping the church of its decoration.

Other Churches

Other churches of note are the Cathedral of San Gervasio, which sits with its pretty garden on the plaza San Roque at the corner of Calles 41 and 38 with its exhibition hall of Mayan artefact photographs, Santa Ana at the corner of Calles 41 and 34, La Candelaria at Calles 44 and 35, San Juan Iglesia at the corner of Calles 49 and 40 and Santa Lucía at the corner of Calles 40 and 27.

Cenotes

Cenotes, those vast underground wells formed of limestone, were the Maya's most dependable source of water. The Spanish depended upon them also and the Spanish town of Valladolid benefited in its early years from several cenotes in the area. The Cenote Zací, Calle 36 between Calles 39 and 37, a three-block walk from the plaza, is perhaps the most famous.

It's set in a pretty park which also holds the town's museum exhibits, an open-air amphitheatre and traditional stone-walled thatched houses. The cenote itself, at the end of a flight of slippery stairs, is vast, dark, impressive and covered with a layer of scum. If this is your first cenote, you'll be impressed; if you don't think you'll get the chance to see another, by all means make the short walk to this one. It's open daily from 8 am to 8 pm; admission costs US$0.35 for adults, half-price for children.

More impressive and beautiful, but less easily accessible, is Cenote Dzitnup, seven km west of Valladolid's main plaza. Follow the main highway west towards Mérida for five km; you'll pass a Coca-Cola bottling plant on the right-hand side. Turn left (south)

at the sign for Dzitnup and go just under two km to the site, on the left. A taxi from Valladolid's main plaza charges US$6 for the excursion there and back, with half an hour's wait.

Another way to reach the cenote is on a bicycle rented from the Refaccionaría de Bicicletas de Paulino Silva on Calle 44 between Calles 39 and 41, facing Hotel María Guadalupe; look for 'Alquiler y Venta de Bicicletas'. Rental costs US$0.60 per hour. The first five km are not particularly pleasant because of the traffic, but the last two km are on a quiet country road. It should take you only 20 minutes to pedal to the cenote.

Another way to get there is to hop aboard a westbound bus, ask the driver to let you off at the Dzitnup turning, then walk the final two km (20 minutes) to the site.

Cenote Dzitnup is open from 7 am to 6 pm daily. Admission costs US$0.35.

As you approach, a horde of village children will surround you, each wanting to be your 'guide' to the cenote, 10 metres away. Even if you don't appoint one to be your guide, the children will accompany you down into the cave, warning you to watch your head on the low overhang, telling you how beautiful the cenote is, clambering up on the stalagmites behind the viewing area to show you the 'shiny stone' with its brilliant crystals. As you leave, they will wait hopefully for tips.

If you've brought a bathing suit and towel you can go for a swim here. The electric pump on the rim shows that the water is used by local people, though probably not for drinking. One problem with swimming in unfamiliar fresh water is schistosomiasis, a parasitic worm that can penetrate unbroken skin. Swimming in stagnant cenotes is an excellent way to contract the disease; whether Cenote Dzitnup has the snail larvae which carry the worm eggs I can't say, so you're on your own.

Places to Stay – bottom end

The best budget choice in town is the *Hotel María Guadalupe* (☎ (985) 6-20-68), Calle

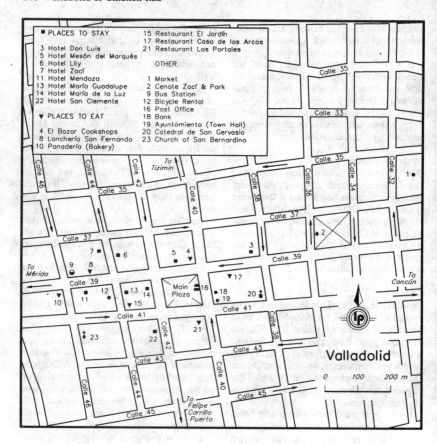

PLACES TO STAY

3 Hotel Don Luis
5 Hotel Mesón del Marqués
6 Hotel Lily
7 Hotel Zací
11 Hotel Mendoza
13 Hotel María Guadalupe
14 Hotel María de la Luz
22 Hotel San Clemente

▼ PLACES TO EAT

4 El Bazar Cookshops
8 Lonchería San Fernando
10 Panadería (Bakery)

15 Restaurant El Jardín
17 Restaurant Casa de los Arcos
21 Restaurant Los Portales

OTHER

1 Market
2 Cenote Zací & Park
9 Bus Station
12 Bicycle Rental
16 Post Office
18 Bank
19 Ayuntamiento (Town Hall)
20 Catedral de San Gervasio
23 Church of San Bernardino

Valladolid

0   100   200 m

44 No 188, between Calles 39 and 41, only a block and a half from the bus station and the same distance from the plaza. Get ready for fluorescent light, because the María Guadalupe is a study in modernity in the midst of this colonial town. Kept clean and in fresh paint, the simple rooms here go for US\$9/11/15 a single/double/triple with private shower and fan. Because it's clean, presentable and cheap, it's also usually full. Arrive early in the day to get a room here.

You can't go wrong at the excellent *Hotel Zací* (☎ (985) 6-21-67), Calle 44 No 191, between Calles 37 and 39, two blocks from

the plaza and even closer to the bus station. The Zací's rooms are built around a quiet, pleasant, long-and-narrow grassy garden courtyard complete with swimming pool. Though the hotel has obviously been completely renovated, it preserves a bit of the colonial ambience. Choose from rooms with fan (US\$10/12.50/14 a single/double/triple) or with air-conditioning (US\$12.50/15/16 a single/double/triple). The Zací is just up the street from the María Guadalupe. Head north on Calle 44, cross Calle 39, walk half a block and look for the Zací on the left-hand side.

Across the street and down a few doors is

the *Hotel Lily* (☎ (985) 6-21-63), Calle 44 No 190, between Calles 37 and 39. Rooms are cheaper here, as they should be for what you get: US$9 a double in one bed, US$9.50 for a double in two beds, with private bath and fan. The housekeeping could be better. If the Zací is full, or if you're really hard up for cash, the Lily's for you.

In the unlikely event that all of the aforementioned hotels are full, I'll mention the *Hotel Mendoza* (☎ (985) 6-20-02), Calle 39 No 204, only a few metres from the bus station. Modern in construction, its guestrooms are bare and basic, but they do have private baths and ceiling fans and prices of US$11 a double. The management was utterly immobilised by TV enthralment when I last visited.

Places to Stay – middle

If you're willing to spend more money, the rest of the town's hotel choices are open to you. All have secure parking facilities.

The best hotel in town is *El Mesón del Marqués* (☎ (985) 6-20-73), Calle 39 No 203, on the north side of the main plaza. There are two beautiful colonial courtyards here, the first with a talkative macaw, the second with a beautiful, clean swimming pool; both are decorated with flowers. Looking onto the courtyards from several levels are the modernised guestrooms. There's a dining room and several other good eateries within a block's walk. All rooms have air-con, some have fans; but as there are screens only on the bathroom windows and mosquitoes are a problem hereabouts, you're more or less forced to use the air-con even if you'd prefer a fan.

There are three categories of rooms here, regular, junior suite and deluxe, priced from US$22 to US$32 for a single, US$24 to US$35 for a double and US$27.50 to US$39 for a triple.

Next best choice is the *Hotel San Clemente* (☎ (985) 6-22-08), Calle 42 No 206 at the corner of Calle 41, at the south-west corner of the main plaza. Colonial decoration abounds here, but the 64 rooms have private baths and either air-con or fans. The hotel has

a swimming pool and a decent little restaurant named Los Cupules. Large families or small groups should ask about renting adjoining rooms; some rooms sleep up to five people. With ceiling fan/air-con, rooms cost US$13/16 a single, US$15/18 a double, US$19/22 a triple.

The *Hotel Don Luis* (☎ (985) 6-20-08), Calle 39 No 191, at the corner of Calle 38, is a modern motel-style structure a block from the main plaza with a palm-shaded patio and swimming pool as well as acceptable rooms. Singles with fan and bath cost US$15, doubles US$16. If you want air-conditioning, the price goes up US$1 or US$2.

The cheapest air-conditioned rooms on the plaza are in the *Hotel María de la Luz* (☎ (985) 6-20-70) on Calle 42 near Calle 39, at the north-west corner of the plaza. Rooms surround a tiny court with trees and a much-used (and perhaps a bit murky) swimming pool. Rooms are also much used and simple, but priced at only US$15/18 a single/double with private bath and air-con. Rooms with fan are a dollar or two cheaper.

Places to Eat – bottom end

The bus station has itinerant snack sellers, but the offerings are pretty unappetising. A few steps east of the bus station on Calle 39 is the *Lonchería San Fernando*, which has the standard Mexican antojitos at low prices.

The food is much better and the surroundings more pleasant at *El Bazar*, a collection of little open-air market-style cookshops at the corner of Calles 39 and 40 (north-east corner of the plaza) near the Hotel El Mesón del Marqués. This is my favourite place for breakfast: a huge glass of freshly squeezed orange juice costs only US$0.75, eggs with ham, beans and bread only US$1.50. At lunch and dinnertime, comidas corridas of soup, main course and drink cost just over US$2. There are a dozen eateries here – Doña Mary, El Amigo Panfilo, Sergio's Pizza, La Rancherita, El Amigo Casiano, etc – open from 6.30 am to 2 pm and from 6 pm to about 9 or 10 pm.

You'll need to know some Spanish to read the menus: *higado encebollado* is liver and onions, *longaniza* is a spicy sausage, *pollo asado o frito* is roasted or fried chicken, *bistec de res/puerco* is a beef or pork steak, *puerco empanizado* is a crumbed pork chop, *bistec a la Mexicana* is bits of beef sautéed with chopped tomatoes and hot peppers.

For a bit more you can dine at the breezy tables in the *Hotel María de la Luz*, overlooking the plaza. Substantial sandwiches sell for US$1.50 to US$1.75, main course platters of meat or chicken for about twice as much.

Places to Eat – middle

For those willing to spend a bit more, *Restaurant Casa de los Arcos* (☎ (985) 6-24-67), on Calle 39 between Calles 38 and 40, half a block east of the plaza, serves Yucatecan cuisine in a series of simple but pleasant, cavernous dining rooms separated by arcades and cooled by ceiling fans. The menu is in English and Spanish. You might start with sopa de lima, lime soup made with chicken, tomatoes, onions, bits of fried tortilla and tangy lime juice. Continue with pork loin Valladolid-style (in a tomato sauce), or grilled pork steak with achiote sauce and finish up with guava paste and cheese. With drink, tax and tip, the bill would be US$9 to US$11 per person. If you're confused by Yucatecan cooking, order the combination plate (US$3.75). The restaurant is open every day from 7 or 8 am to 10 pm.

The other good middle-range restaurant in town is the dining room of *Hotel El Mesón del Marqués*, Calle 39 No 203 on the north side of the main plaza.

Getting There & Away

Bus Autotransportes de Oriente Mérida-Puerto Juárez handles most of the buses between Cancún and Mérida via Valladolid from their terminal at the corner of Calles 39 and 46. Virtually all buses from here are de paso, meaning that they've originated their journeys somewhere else; there may or may not be seats free. Often, you won't know until half an hour or less before departure time.

There are 24 buses daily to Mérida, either 1st class (160 km, three hours, US$2.75) or 2nd class (3½ hours, US$2.50); most of these will stop at Chichén Itzá if you remind the driver (42 km, 30 to 45 minutes, US$0.50). The same number of buses run daily to Cancún/Puerto Juárez (161 km, two to 2½ hours, US$2.75), but early-morning buses may be jam-packed with commuters.

Direct buses from Valladolid run to Playa del Carmen (230 km, 3½ hours, US$3.75) at 2 am, noon and 1 pm; to Tulum (360 km, six hours, US$7), there are buses at 1.30, 5 and 8 am and 2 pm.

Autobuses del Noreste en Yucatán operates daily buses to Tizimín (51 km, one hour, US$0.75) at 6.30 and 10.30 am and 1.30 and 3.30 pm; the 10.30 am bus goes on to Río Lagartos (103 km, two hours, US$1.50); if you miss this one, you must change buses in Tizimín.

If you are going to Isla Holbox (155 km, 2½ hours, US$1.40), there is at least one Chiquila-bound bus daily.

Taxis A quicker, more comfortable but more expensive way to Cancún is by taking one of the shared taxis parked outside the bus station, which leave as soon as all seats are filled. The trip costs about twice the bus fare.

TIZIMÍN

Many travellers bound for Río Lagartos will change buses in Tizimín (Place of Many Horses), the second largest city in the state of Yucatán and a farming centre of note (cattle ranches, beehives and citrus groves make the wealth here). There is little to warrant an overnight stay, so Tizimín is relatively free of tourists.

The main plaza is pleasant. Two great colonial structures, the Convento de los Tres Reyes Magos (Monastery of the Three Wise Kings) and the Convento de San Francisco de Assis (Monastery of Saint Francis of Assisi) are worth a look. Five lengthy blocks from the plaza, north-west on Calle 51, is a modest zoo, the Parque Zoológico de la Reina.

The Banco del Atlantico, next to the Hotel San Jorge on the south-west side of the plaza,

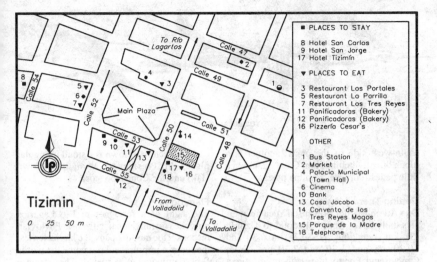

PLACES TO STAY

8 Hotel San Carlos
9 Hotel San Jorge
17 Hotel Tizimín

PLACES TO EAT

3 Restaurant Los Portales
5 Restaurant La Parrilla
7 Restaurant Los Tres Reyes
11 Panificadoras (Bakery)
12 Panificadoras (Bakery)
16 Pizzería Cesar's

OTHER

1 Bus Station
2 Market
4 Palacio Municipal (Town Hall)
6 Cinema
10 Bank
13 Casa Jacobo
14 Convento de los Tres Reyes Magos
15 Parque de la Madre
18 Telephone

Tizimín

0   25   50 m

will change money for you between 10 am and noon from Monday to Friday.

Places to Stay

The *Hotel San Jorge* (☎ (986) 3-20-37), Calle 53 No 411, near Calle 52, on the south-west side of the plaza, is perhaps the town's best and boasts a swimming pool the size of a hot tub. Basic but serviceable rooms with private bath and fan cost US$13/15 for a single/double; for air-conditioning, add US$5 to the room price.

Next best is the *Hotel San Carlos* (☎ (986) 3-20-94), Calle 54 No 407, 1½ long blocks from the plaza. A modern place built like a motel, it charges almost identical prices for similar rooms. Its small pool was dry at my recent visit. You can ask about room prices and availability for the San Carlos at the Casa Jacobo shop, south-east corner of the plaza.

The *Hotel Tizimín* (☎ (986) 3-21-52), Calle 50 at the corner of Calle 53, is on the south-east corner of the plaza on the 2nd floor. It's much cheaper and much less comfortable, with rooms for US$7/9 for a single/double with fan and private shower, another dollar or so with air-con.

Places to Eat

The market, a block north-west of the bus station, has the usual cheap eateries. Perhaps the best dining in town is at *Restaurant Los Tres Reyes* (☎ 3-21-06), on the corner of Calles 52 and 53. It opens early for breakfast and is a favourite with town notables and hangers-on who take their second cup of coffee around 9 am. You can eat lunch or dinner here for US$2 to US$3.

Otherwise, there's *Pizzería Cesar's*, in the same building as the Hotel Tizimín at the corner of Calles 50 and 53; Cesar's faces the Parque de la Madre. Pizza and pasta are the attractions here, in the evening (5.30 to 11 pm) only. You can eat in air-conditioned comfort for US$1.50 to US$3.50 or so.

Restaurant Los Portales is near the august portals of the Palacio Municipal (Town Hall) on the north-east side of the plaza. It's a simple place, good for a quick sandwich or burger and a cold drink. *Restaurant La Parrilla*, on the north-west side of the plaza, is another simple place open for lunch and dinner only.

For snacks, make-your-own breakfasts and bus food, drop by either branch of the *Panificadora La Especial*; one is on the

Yucatecan flamingos

south-west side of the plaza, another is a block directly behind it on Calle 55, down a little pedestrian lane from the plaza.

Getting There & Away

Bus Autobuses del Noreste en Yucatán operates daily buses from Valladolid to Tizimin (51 km, one hour, US$0.75) at 6.30 and 10.30 am and 1.30 and 3.30 pm. From Cancún and Puerto Juárez, there are direct buses to Tizimin at 7.30 am and 1.30 and 6.30 pm (215 km, four hours, US$3.25). There are several daily 1st and 2nd-class buses between Tizimin and Mérida via Valladolid. For Río Lagartos there are three 1st-class departures and five daily 2nd-class buses which continue to San Felipe.

RÍO LAGARTOS

For those interested in the most spectacular flamingo colony in Mexico, it is worth going out of your way to this little fishing village 103 km north of Valladolid and 52 km north of Tizimin. In addition to thousands of flamingos, the estuaries are home to snowy egrets, red egrets, great white herons and snowy white ibis. Although Río Lagartos (Alligator River) was named after the once substantial alligator population, don't expect to see any of the reptiles as hunting has virtually wiped them out.

The town of Río Lagartos itself, with its narrow streets and multihued houses, has little charm, though the panorama of the boats and the bay is pleasant. Were it not for the flamingos, you would have little reason to come here. Although the state government has been making noises about developing the area for tourism, this has not happened yet.

At the centre of town is a small triangular plaza, the Presidencia Municipal (Town Hall) and the Conasupo store.

Flamingos

The sight of a foreigner in Río Lagartos provokes in any local citizen a Pavlovian response: the mouth opens, the larynx tenses, the lungs compress and out come the words 'Los flamingos! A la playa!' The response from the foreigner is equally automatic: 'Sí!'

Your first encounter with a Lagartan thus highlights your first duty here; to find a reliable boat-owner and a good price for the trip to see the flamingos or to swim at the beach nearby. The Spanish word *flamenco*, which means 'flaming', makes sense in terms of the bird's name as you approach a horizon of hundreds of brilliantly hued, flaming red-pink birds. When the flock takes flight, the sight of the suddenly fiery horizon makes the long hours on the bus to get here all worthwhile. However, in the interests of the flamingos' well-being, convince your local guide not to frighten the birds into flight. Being frightened away from their habitat several times a day can't be good for them, however good it may be for the guide's business.

Birdwatching by Boat Everybody in town will offer to set you up with a boat. Haggling over price is essential. In general, a short trip (two to three hours) to see a few nearby local flamingos and to have a swim at the beach costs US$15 to US$18 for a five-seat boat. The much longer voyage (four to six hours) to the flamingos' favourite haunts costs US$52 or so for the boat, or about US$10 per person for a full load. If you can't put together a suitable itinerary by yourself, you might inquire at the Hotel Nefertiti.

Birdwatching on Foot If you walk some of the 14 km along the beach from the lagoon out to Punta Holohit on the sea, you will most likely see colourful bird life. Among the species common here are egrets, herons, flamingos, ibis, cormorants, stilts, pelicans and plovers. Wear some decent footwear that you can get wet as well as clothes that you can go in the water with. You might be able to arrange to have a boat pick you up at Punta Holohit for your return if you walk all the way.

Places to Stay & Eat
The *Hotel Nefertiti* (☎ 14-15), Calle 14 No 123, is the only hostelry in town. Rooms in this large, unfinished, already crumbling, dusty hulk of a place cost US$15 a double. All rooms along its maze of hallways have private baths, ceiling fans, insect screens and good cross-ventilation driven by the constant sea breezes. I believe that ghosts inhabit many of the rooms for lack of other tenants.

The cavernous palapa-shaded *Restaurant Los Flamingos* at the back is equally empty most of the time. To find the hotel, walk from the triangular plaza keeping the Presidencia Municipal on your left. Pass Conasupo on your right and at the next corner turn left and walk 100 metres to the hotel.

It is sometimes possible to rent a bed or a pair of hammock hooks in a local house, which brings down considerably the cost of sleeping.

If the hotel's restaurant is empty, you might do better by grabbing a bite at the *Restaurant La Económica* directly across the street from it. There's also the *Restaurant Los Negritos* facing a little park with a statue of Benito Juárez, two blocks inland from the main square.

Getting There & Away
Bus Autobuses del Noreste en Yucatán operates daily buses from Valladolid to Tizimin (51 km, one hour, US$0.75) at 6.30 and

10.30 am and 1.30 and 3.30 pm. The 10.30 am bus goes on to Río Lagartos (103 km, two hours, US$1.50); if you miss this one, you must change buses in Tizimin. There is also one direct bus daily between Tizimin and Mérida.

SAN FELIPE
Population 400
This tiny fishing village of painted wooden houses on narrow streets, 12 km west of Río Lagartos, makes a nice day trip from Río Lagartos. While the waters are not Caribbean turquoise and there's little shade, in spring and summer scores of visitors come here to camp. Other than lying on the beach, birdwatching is the main attraction, as just across the estuary at Punta Holohit there is abundant bird life.

Places to Stay & Eat
There are no hotels in San Felipe, but the proprietor of La Herradura grocery store near the pier will tell you about inexpensive house rentals. Spartan rooms are sometimes available for rent above the Cinema Marrufo. Campers are ferried across the estuary to islands where they pitch tents or set up hammocks.

The town's sole eatery, *Restaurant El Payaso*, is cheap and quite good for seafood.

Getting There & Away
Bus Some buses from Tizimin to Río Lagartos continue to San Felipe and return. The 12-km ride takes about 20 minutes.

ISLA HOLBOX
Fed up with the tourist hordes of Cancún, Isla Mujeres and Cozumel? Want to find a beach site virtually devoid of gringos? In that case Isla Holbox (pronounced HOHL-bosh) might appeal to you, but before you make haste for the island note that the most basic facilities are in short supply and the beaches are not Cancún-perfect strips of clean, air-conditioned sand. To enjoy Isla Holbox, you must be very willing to rough it.

The 25-km by three-km island has sands that run on and on, as well as tranquil waters where you can wade out quite a distance before the sea reaches shoulder level. Moreover, Isla Holbox is magic for shell collectors, with a galaxy of shapes and colours. The fishing families of the island are friendly – unjaded by encounters with exotic tourists or the frenetic pace of the urban mainland.

As to drawbacks, the seas are not the translucent turquoise of the Quintana Roo beach sites, because here the Caribbean waters mingle with those of the darker Gulf. Seaweed can create silty waters near shore at some parts of the beach. While there are big plans to develop Isla Holbox one day, at the time of writing there is only one modest hotel, the aptly named *Hotel Flamingo* (with doubles for US$6) and a few snack shops. Most travellers camp or stay in spartan rooms rented from locals.

Getting There & Away
Bus If you are going from Isla Mujeres or Cancún to Isla Holbox, catch a direct bus from Puerto Juárez or Cancún.

Ferry To reach Isla Holbox, you take the ferry from the unappealing port village of Chiquila. Buses make the 2½-hour trip three times a day from Valladolid to Chiquila and in theory the ferry is supposed to wait for them. However, it may not wait for a delayed bus or may even leave early (!) should the captain feel so inclined.

It is therefore recommended that you reach Chiquila as early as possible. The ferry is supposed to depart for the island at 8 am and 3 pm and make the trip in about an hour. Ferries return to Chiquila at 2 and 5 pm. The cost is US$1.

Try not to get stuck in Chiquila, as it is a tiny hole of a port with no hotels, no decent camping and very disappointing food service.

CHICHÉN ITZÁ
The most famous and best restored of Yucatán's Mayan sites, Chichén Itzá will awe the most jaded of ruins visitors. Many

mysteries of the Mayan astronomical calendar are made clear when one understands the design of the 'time temples' here. But one astronomical mystery remains: why do most people come here from Mérida and Cancún on day trips, arriving at 11 am, when the blazing sun is getting to its hottest point and departing around 3 pm when the heat finally begins to abate? Climbing El Castillo at midday in the awful heat and humidity is my idea of torture.

To appreciate this ancient ceremonial centre better, I strongly recommend that you stay the night nearby and do your exploration of the site either early in the morning or late in the afternoon, or both. By staying in the vicinity, you can get to the ruins at 8 am, explore the site for four hours, have lunch and perhaps a swim and take a siesta while the tour bus-borne unfortunates are staring groggily into the face of heat prostration. Return at 3 pm if you like and stay until the 5 pm closing. Or arrive at midday, check into your hotel, have some lunch and head out to the ruins in the afternoon, then finish off the next morning before climbing on an air-conditioned bus for the next leg of your journey.

Should you have the good fortune to visit Chichén Itzá on the vernal equinox (20 to 21 March) or autumnal equinox (21 to 22 September), you can witness the light-and-shadow illusion of the serpent ascending or descending the side of the staircase of El Castillo. The illusion is almost as good in the week preceding and the week following the equinox.

History
Chichén Itzá (The Mouth of the Well of the Itzaes) had two periods of greatness and was abandoned between those epochs. Still the subject of much debate is the question of who was responsible for the superior civilisation that flourished here.

Most archaeologists agree that Chichén Itzá's first major settlement, during the Late Classic period between 550 and 900 AD, was pure Mayan. At Uxmal you can see the Puuc-style architectural similarities between that

Valladolid & Chichén Itzá 147

site and the older buildings of Chichén, particularly La Casa Colorada (The Red House). In about the 10th century, the city was largely abandoned for unknown reasons.

The city was resettled about 1100 AD. Shortly thereafter, according to what archaeologists at one point believed almost unanimously, Chichén was invaded by the Toltecs, who had moved down from their central highlands capital of Tula, north of Mexico City. The Toltecs fused their culture with that of the Maya, incorporating the cult of Quetzalcóatl (Kukulcán in Mayan).

Quetzalcóatl, the plumed serpent, was a blonde king with great powers who was supposedly cast out of his kingdom and exiled from the central highlands to Mexico's south-east. Legend had it that he would reappear and bring a great era with him. This legend would ultimately help pave the way for Cortés in his conquest of Mexico.

You will see images of both Chac, the Mayan rain god 'and Quetzalcóatl, the plumed serpent, throughout the city. However, because there appears to be evidence of Toltec influence long before the supposed Toltec invasion, there is speculation that Tula had once been a colony of Chichén and that Toltec influence filtered back to the Yucatán.

Who conquered and influenced whom remains the subject of much debate. Whatever its origin, the substantial fusion of highland central Mexican and Puuc architectural styles make Chichén unique among Yucatán's ruins. The fabulous El Castillo, the Temple of Panels and the Platform of Venus are all outstanding architectural works built during the height of the Toltec cultural input.

The warlike Toltecs contributed more than their architectural skills. They elevated human sacrifice to a near obsession, for there are numerous carvings of the bloody ritual in Chichén. After a Toltec leader moved his political capital to Mayapán while keeping Chichén as his religious capital, Chichén Itzá fell into decline. Why it was subsequently abandoned in the 14th century is a mystery, but the once-great city remained the site of Mayan pilgrimages for years to come.

Orientation

The highway bypasses the archaeological site to the north; the old highway used to go right through the middle of the site. This old road now serves as the access road from the highway to the ruins. Coming from Cancún, it's 1.5 km from the highway along the access road to the eastern entrance to the ruins. On the way you pass the Villa Arqueológica, Hacienda Chichén and Mayaland luxury hotels. The moderately priced Hotel Dolores Alba is 3.1 km east of the eastern entrance to the ruins, on the highway to Cancún.

Except for these hotels, Chichén's lodgings, restaurants and services are ranged along one km of highway in the village of Piste (PEESS-teh), to the west (Mérida) side of the ruins. It's 1.5 km from the western entrance of the ruins to the first hotel (Pyramide Inn) in Piste, or 2.5 km from the ruins to the village square (actually a triangle), shaded by a huge tree. Buses generally stop at the square; you can make the hot walk to or from the ruins in 20 to 30 minutes.

Chichén's little airstrip is north of the ruins, on the north side of the highway.

Information

Money There's a Banamex branch just west of the main square (near the Restaurant Poxil) in Piste for changing money, or you can change it in the Unidad de Servicios at the western entrance to the ruins.

Telephone For long-distance telephone calls you must go to the Teléfonos de México caseta de larga distancia in Piste. Look for the Restaurant Xaybe, across the highway from the Hotel Misión Chichén; the caseta is in the same group of buildings, open from 8 am to 9 pm.

The Archaeological Zone

Chichén Itzá is open every day from 8 am to 5 pm; the interior passageway in El Castillo is open only from 11 am to 1 pm and from 4 to 5 pm. Admission to the site costs US$5, US$9 extra for your video camera and US$5.50 extra if you use a tripod with your

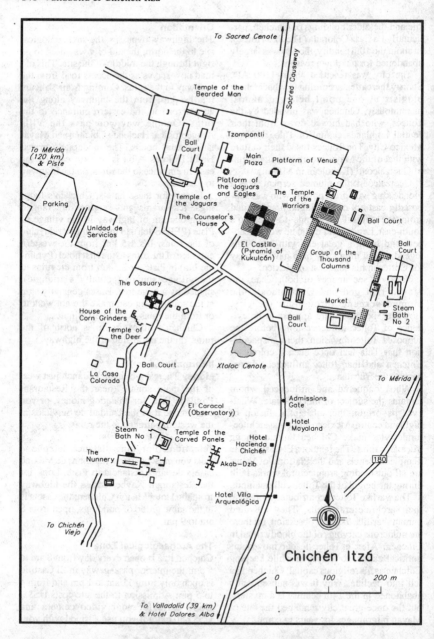

Chichén Itzá

0   100   200 m

camera. Admission is free to children under 12 years of age.

The main entrance to the ruins is the western one, with a large car park (US$0.35) and a big, modern entrance building called the Unidad de Servicios, open 8 am to 10 pm. The Unidad has a small but worthwhile museum (open 8 am to 5 pm) with sculptures, reliefs, artefacts and explanations of these in Spanish, English and French. The Chilam Balam Auditorio next to the museum has audio-visual shows about Chichén in English at noon and 4 pm. In the central space of the Unidad stands a scale model of the archaeological site and off towards the toilets is an exhibit on Thompson's excavations of the sacred cenote in 1923. There's also a souvenir and book shop, currency exchange desk (open 9 am to 1 pm) and a *guardarropa* at the main ticket desk where you can leave your belongings (US$0.35) while you explore the site.

Sound-and-light shows are held each evening in Spanish from 7 to 7.35 pm for US$0.75 and in English from 9 to 9.35 pm for US$1.

El Castillo As you pass through the turnstiles from the Unidad de Servicios into the archaeological zone, El Castillo rises before you in all its grandeur. Standing nearly 25 metres tall, El Castillo (The Castle) was originally built before 800 AD, prior to the Toltec invasion. Nonetheless, the plumed serpent was sculpted along the stairways and Toltec warriors are represented in the doorway carvings of the temple at the top.

Climb to the top for a view of the entire site. This is best done early in the morning or late in the afternoon, both to beat the heat and to see Chichén before the crowds arrive.

The pyramid is actually the Mayan calendar formed in stone. Each of El Castillo's nine levels is divided in two by a staircase, making 18 separate terraces which commemorate the 18 20-day months of the Vague Year. The four stairways have 91 steps each; add the top platform and the total is 365, the number of days in the year. On each façade of the pyramid are 52 flat panels,

reminders of the 52 years in the Calendar Round.

Most amazing of all, during the spring and autumn equinoxes (around 21 March and 21 September), light and shadow form a series of triangles on the side of the north staircase which mimic the creep of a serpent (note the serpent's head at the bottom of the staircase). The serpent appears to ascend in March and descend in September. This incredible illusion lasts three hours and 22 minutes and was all arranged by the brilliant Mayan architects and astronomers who designed El Castillo.

This pyramid holds more surprises: there's another pyramid *inside* El Castillo. When archaeologists opened it, they found a brilliant red jaguar throne with inlaid eyes and spots of shimmering jade. The inner sanctum also holds a Toltec chac-mool figure, even though it was built before the Toltec intrusion. Did the Toltecs place the figure there? Or does it support the newer theory that it was the Maya who initially colonised the Toltecs at Tula?

The inner pyramid is only open from 11 am to 1 pm and 4 to 5 pm. The dank air inside can make climbing the stairs a sweltering experience.

Principal Ball Court Just after you enter Chichén, walk to your left (or north-west of El Castillo) and you will see the best preserved and largest ball court in all of Mexico. This principal ball field is only one of the city's eight courts, indicative of the importance the games held here. The field is flanked by temples at either end and bounded by towering parallel walls with stone rings cemented up high.

There is evidence that the ball game may have changed over the years. Some carvings show players with padding on their elbows and knees and it is thought that they played a soccer-like game with a hard rubber ball, forbidding the use of hands. Other carvings show players wielding bats; it appears that if a player hit the ball through one of the stone hoops, his team was declared the winner. It may be that during the Toltec period the losing captain, and perhaps his team-mates as well, were sacrificed.

Along the walls of the ball court are some fine stone reliefs, including scenes of decapitations of losing players. Acoustically the court is amazing – a conversation at one end can be heard 135 metres away at the other end, and if you clap, you hear a resounding echo.

Temple of the Bearded Man & Temple of the Jaguars The structure at the northern end of the ball court, known as the Temple of the Bearded Man and named for a carving inside it, has some finely sculpted pillars and reliefs of flowers, birds and trees. See also the temple at the end of the court facing out on El Castillo. This Temple of the Jaguars (the south-eastern corner of the ball court) has some rattlesnake-carved columns and jaguar-etched tablets. Inside are faded mural fragments depicting a battle, possibly between the Toltecs and the Maya.

Tzompantli The Tzompantli, a Toltec term for Temple of Skulls, is between the Temple of the Jaguars and El Castillo. You can't mistake it because the T-shaped platform is festooned with carved skulls and eagles tearing open the chests of men to eat their hearts. In ancient days this platform held the heads of sacrificial victims.

Platform of the Jaguars & Eagles Adjacent to the Temple of Skulls, this platform's carvings depict jaguars and eagles gruesomely grabbing human hearts in their claws. It is thought that this platform was part of a temple dedicated to the military legions responsible for capturing sacrificial victims.

Platform of Venus Near the path to the Sacred Cenote, looking north from El Castillo and east from Tzompantli, you will find the Platform of Venus. Rather than a beautiful woman, the Toltec Venus is a feathered serpent bearing a human head between its jaws. The platform is decked with feathered snake figures. Some maps refer to this

Carving of a jaguar eating a human heart,
Platform of the Jaguars & Eagles, Chichén Itzá

as the Tomb of Chac-Mool because a figure of the reclining god was found within the structure.

Sacred Cenote Near the Platform of Venus, you will see a 300-metre dirt path running north to the huge sunken well that gave this city its name. The Sacred Cenote is an awesome natural well, some 60 metres in diameter and 35 metres deep. The walls between the summit and the water's surface are ensnared in tangled vines and other vegetation.

Although some of the guides enjoy telling visitors that female virgins were sacrificed by being thrown into the cenote to drown, divers in 1923 brought up the remains of men, women and children. Whether they were drowned here for religious or other reasons is not known.

Skeletons were not all that was found in the Sacred Cenote. Around the turn of the century, Edward Thompson, a Harvard professor and US Consul to the Yucatán, bought a hacienda which included Chichén for US$75. It was his decision to have the cenote dredged. Artefacts as well as valuable gold and jade jewellery from all parts of Mexico were recovered; these objects were given to Harvard's Peabody Museum, which later returned many of them. Some of Thompson's excavation equipment is on view in the building at the western entrance to the site.

The artefacts' origins show the far-flung contact the Maya had (there are some items from as far away as Colombia). It is believed that offerings of all kinds, human and otherwise, were thrown into the Sacred Cenote to please the gods.

Subsequent diving expeditions sponsored by the National Geographic Society in the 1960s turned up hundreds more of the valuable artefacts.

Group of the Thousand Columns Comprising the Temple of the Warriors, Temple of Chac-Mool and Sweat House or Steam Bath, this group takes its collective name from the copious number of pillars in front. The platformed temple greets you with a statue of the reclining god, Chac, as well as stucco and stone-carved animal deities. The temple's roof caved in long ago; columns entwined with serpents once served as roof supports. If you have been to Tula, you will see some similarities between its Toltec temple and this one.

A 1926 restoration revealed an edifice inside the Temple of the Warriors, constructed prior to it – the Temple of Chac-Mool. You may enter via a stairway on the north side. The temple walls have largely deteriorated murals of what is thought to be the Toltecs' defeat of the Mayan defenders here.

Just east of the Temple of the Warriors sits the rubble of a Mayan sweat house, with an underground oven and drains for the water. The sweat houses were regularly used for ritual purification.

Market If you walk south from the Temple of the Warriors, you will come to some colonnaded chambers once thought to house Chichén's elite. Nearby is a remnant of what may have been an area of walled market stalls. None of these structures are in good condition.

Ossuary The Ossuary, otherwise known as the Bonehouse or High Priest's Grave, is a deteriorated pyramid, the first building you come to as you take the dirt path south from El Castillo. As with most of the buildings in this southern section, the architecture is more Puuc than Toltec, adding to the belief that when the Toltecs took control they moved the focus of the city north. During excavation of the Ossuary, the remains of a man believed to be a high priest were found in a natural grotto over which the pyramid was built. This structure may be restored soon.

La Casa Colorada La Casa Colorada or The Red House, on the right fork leading from the Ossuary, was named by the Spanish, who saw the red paint of the deteriorating mural on its doorway. This building has little Toltec influence and its design shows largely a pure Puuc-Mayan style. Referring to the stone latticework at the roof façade, the Maya named this building Chichén-Chob, or House of Small Holes. What was thought to be a Toltec ball court to its rear has now been carbon dated to three centuries prior to the Toltec invasion, adding to the debate over who originally conquered whom.

Temple of the Deer Until it deteriorated in the 1920s, the mural of a deer gave this classical little Mayan structure its name. The only reason to see this edifice is to go to the back of the building and climb to the top for a nice view of the surrounding ruins.

El Caracol Take the path to the left from the Ossuary to reach Chichén's observatory. Called El Caracol (The Giant Conch Snail) by the Spanish due to its interior spiral staircase, the observatory is one of the most fascinating and important of all of Chichén Itzá's buildings. Its circular design resembles some central highlands structures, although, surprisingly, not those of Toltec Tula. In a fusion of architectural styles and religious imagery, there are Mayan Chac rain god masks over four external doors facing the cardinal directions.

The windows in the observatory's dome are aligned with the appearance of certain stars at specific dates. From the dome the priests decreed the appropriate times for rituals, celebrations, corn-planting and harvests. The observatory was built over several centuries and is a product of Toltec times, though its base was undertaken earlier.

Nunnery & Annexe Thought by archaeologists to have been a palace for Mayan royalty, the Nunnery, with its myriad rooms, resembled a European convent to the conquistadors, hence their name for the building. The Nunnery's dimensions are imposing: its base is 60 metres long, 30 metres wide and 20 metres high. The construction is Mayan rather than Toltec, although a Toltec sacrificial stone stands in front. A small building added onto the west side is known as the Annexe. These buildings are in the Puuc-Chenes style, particularly evident in the lower jaw of the Chac mask at the opening of the Annexe. There are several other Chac statues on the façade of the Nunnery.

The Church Near the Annexe sits a relatively small building, notable only for upper façade masks alternating Chac with animal gods called *bacabs* – crab, turtle, snail and armadillo – which Mayan mythology claims hold up the sky.

Akab-Dzib On the rough path east of the Nunnery, the Akab-Dzib is thought by some archaeologists to be the most ancient structure excavated here. The central chambers date all the way back to the 2nd century. Akab-Dzib means Obscure Writing in Mayan, referring to the south-side Annexe door whose lintel depicts a priest with a vase etched with hieroglyphics. The writing has never been translated, hence the name. Note the red fingerprints on the ceiling, thought to symbolise the deity Zamna, a sun god from whom the Maya sought wisdom.

Chichén Viejo Chichén Viejo, or Old Chichén, comprises largely unrestored, basically Mayan ruins (some have Toltec additions). Here you'll see a pristine part of Chichén without much archaeological restoration.

Although visiting Old Chichén is best done with a guide, if you wish to go there yourself take the path which runs from the south-west corner of the Nunnery. Follow this for about 20 minutes until you come to some thatched huts. Take the trail behind the smallest hut and you will first reach a group of ruins labelled by archaeologists 'the Date Group'. A date lintel here (879 AD) explains the name; it's set over two columns of a former temple which is now largely rubble. Nearby, the House of the Phalli is well preserved and named for the phalli set in the edifice's chambers.

Beyond the House of the Phalli, take the trail another 20 minutes to the Lintel Group. Of these, all are poorly preserved except for the restored Temple of the Three Lintels. Built in traditional Puuc-Chenes style with rain god masks adorning the building's corners, the temple is named for its three dated lintels. There are other ruins in the vicinity, best located with the help of a guide.

Grutas de Balankanché

Maya residing near Chichén Itzá had long believed that there was something sacred from the past buried in the region. This was borne out in 1959 when a guide to the ruins was exploring a cave on his day off. Pushing against one of the cavern's walls, he is said to have broken through into a larger subterranean opening. Archaeological exploration revealed a path that runs some 300 metres past carved stalactites and stalagmites, terminating at an underground pool.

The Grutas de Balankanché (Balankanché Caves) are six km east of the ruins of Chichén Itzá, two km east of the Hotel Dolores Alba on the highway to Cancún. Second-class buses heading east from Piste toward Valladolid and Cancún will drop you at the Balankanché road; the entrance to the caves is 350 metres north of the highway.

As you approach the caves, you enter a pretty botanical garden displaying many of Yucatán's native flora, including many species of cactus. In the entrance building is a little museum, a shop selling cold drinks and souvenirs and a ticket booth. Plan your visit for an hour when the compulsory tour and Light & Colour Show will be given in a language you understand: the 40-minute show (minimum six persons, maximum 30) is given in the cave at 11 am, 1 and 3 pm in English, at 9 am, noon and 2 and 4 pm in Spanish and at 10 am in French. Tickets are sold from 9 am to 4 pm (last show) daily. Admission costs US$2.50

Discovered in the caves and now on exhibition are offerings to Tlaloc, the Toltec central Mexican rain god (similar to the Mayan Chac). Among the offerings were incense burners carved with the image of Tlaloc and some miniature metates used for grinding corn. These are found principally in two places: a large domed cavern called The Throne where you'll find a fused pillar of stalactites and stalagmites (Balankanché means Hidden Throne in Mayan), and the subterranean pool area.

Places to Stay

Most of the lodgings convenient to Chichén are in the middle and top-end price brackets. No matter what you plan to spend on a bed, be prepared to haggle off season (May to October). Prices should be lower at every hotel during these months.

Places to Stay – bottom end

Unfortunately, there's not much. Your best bet is the *Posada Chac-Mool*, just east of the Hotel Misión Chichén on the opposite (south) side of the highway. The proprietor here keeps the rooms quite tidy and so far there's no musty smell. Showers are tiled, but there are no toilet seats to speak of. Ceiling fans move the air and insect screens keep the bugs out. Doubles are priced at US$15; single travellers might pay a bit less.

The other low-end place in town is the similar *Posada El Paso*, a few dozen metres west of the Stardust Inn. An L-shaped motel-style building, it has the blessings of insect screens on the windows, ceiling fans and private showers. Ground-floor rooms are musty, so get one on the upper floor if possible (arrive by lunchtime). Rooms are overpriced at US$15 a double, but there's little else at the low end since the old Posada Novelo closed down.

Camping There's camping at the *Piramide Inn & Trailer Park* on the eastern edge of town (closest to the ruins). For under US$3 per person, you can pitch a tent, enjoy the Piramide Inn's pool and watch satellite TV in the lobby. There are hot showers and clean, shared toilet facilities. Those in vehicles pay US$7.50 for two for full hook-ups.

Places to Stay – middle

Hotel Dolores Alba (☎ in Mérida (99) 21-37-45), Carretera Km 122, is just over three km east of the eastern entrance to the ruins and two km west of the road to Balankanché, on the highway to Cancún. There are more than a dozen rooms here, some recently renovated, all well kept, surrounding a small, clean swimming pool. The dining room is good and prices moderate, which is important since you're pretty much at their mercy here, with no other eating facility nearby. The Sanchez family, which owns the hotel, has been running a good hostelry here (and two more in Mérida) for almost 20 years. They will transport you to the ruins, but you must take a taxi, bus or walk back.

Single/double rooms with fan and shower cost US$12.50/18. There are a few air-conditioned rooms for about US$3 extra. If you're coming here by bus, remind the driver to drop you off shortly after the Balankanché road and before you reach the eastern access road to the ruins.

In Piste proper, to telephone any of the hotels you must dial (985) 6-25-13, which gets you the long-distance telephone exchange, and leave a message.

The newest hotel is the *Stardust Inn*, next to the Pirámide Inn and less than two km from the ruins. It's an attractive place with two tiers of rooms surrounding a little, palm-shaded swimming pool. Each room has an air-conditioning unit, TV and private bath and a price of US$33 single or double. There's a good little restaurant, too. Watch out for noise from the disco, unless you're a late-night type.

The *Pirámide Inn* next door has been here for years. Its grounds are very pretty, having had years to mature, and its swimming pool is a blessing on a hot day. There's a selection of different rooms, some older, some newer (look before you buy), all air-conditioned and priced at US$29/30/33/35 a single/double/triple/quad. Here, you're as close as you can get to the archaeological zone's western entrance.

Places to Stay – top end

All of these hotels have beautiful swimming pools, restaurants, bars, well-kept tropical gardens, very comfortable guest rooms and tour groups coming and going. Several of the top-end hotels have the great advantage of being very close to the ruins. You can leave the ruins any time the crowds or the heat get too much and zip back to your hotel in minutes for a swim in the pool or a drink from the bar. In fact if you are going to splurge on just one expensive hotel in Mexico, this is a good place to do it.

Hotel Mayaland has the advantage of being a mere 200 metres from the eastern entrance to the archaeological zone. It's the oldest and most gracious of the hotels at Chichén, having been built in 1923. Standing in the lobby of the hotel, you look through the main portal to see El Caracol framed as in a photograph. Extensive renovations in 1989 added air-conditioning, telephones and satellite TV to the rooms; the hotel has a gymnasium, beauty parlour, tennis courts and riding stables. Here you have the ambience of a hacienda, but the services of a Gran Turismo hotel. The Mayaland is always busy with tour groups coming and going. Rooms are priced at US$83 a double. For reservations, call the Mérida office of Mayaland Tours at (99) 25-23-42, 25-22-46; fax (99) 25-70-22.

Sister hotel to the Mayaland is the *Hotel Hacienda Chichén*, just a few hundred metres farther from the ruins on the same eastern access road. This was the hacienda where the archaeologists lived when excavating Chichén. Their bungalows have been refurbished and new ones built; a swimming pool has been added and the gardens landscaped. It's a very pleasant, quiet place, the choice of the discerning traveller who wants to avoid the noise and crowds of the tour buses yet have some of the comforts. The favourite evening activity here is to sit in a rocking chair on the verandah, sip a drink and trade stories with other travellers.

Rooms in the garden bungalows have ceiling fans and private baths, but no TVs or phones and rent for US$69 a double. The dining room serves good, simple meals at moderate prices. Unfortunately, there is not enough demand in summer to keep both the Mayaland and the Hacienda Chichén open, so the Hacienda Chichén closes from May to October. For reservations, call as for the Mayaland.

The *Hotel Villa Arqueológica* (☎ (985) 6-28-30), Apdo Postal 495, Mérida, is a few hundred metres east of the Mayaland and Hacienda Chichén on the eastern access road to the ruins. Run by Club Med, it's a modern layout with a good restaurant, tennis courts and swimming pool. Rooms are fairly small but comfortable and air-conditioned and priced at US$49/51 a single/double; there are also pleasant two-bedroom suites at US$65, ideal for families.

Apart from being architecturally attractive with its lush garden courtyard and pool, the hotel is decorated with showcases holding Mayan sculpture and pottery; the French take their Mayan culture seriously. If you want to try out the French-inspired Mexican-Mayan restaurant, it'll cost you about US$15 per person for a table d'hôte lunch or dinner, and almost twice that much if you order à la carte – but the food is good. For the price, this is the best deal in luxury digs at Chichén.

On the western side of Chichén in the village of Piste, the *Hotel Misión Chichén* (☎ in USA (800) 648-7818) is two km from the ruins entrance on the north side of the highway. Two tiers of rooms are arranged around a nice swimming pool; the huge restaurant and bar are off the lobby. It's comfortable without being distinguished. Air-conditioned singles/doubles cost US$44/50.

Places to Eat

The cafeteria in the *Unidad de Servicios* at the western entrance to the archaeological zone serves mediocre food at high prices (ham and cheese sandwich and chips for US$3.75) in pleasant surroundings. It's not air-conditioned.

The highway through Piste is lined with little restaurants, most of them fairly well tarted up in a Mayan villager's conception of what foreign tourists expect to see. Prices are fairly high for what you get and most of these places serve only table d'hôte meals at lunch, which means you must pay one set price for a full-course meal; you can't pick and choose from a menu or just order something light as one might want to do in the heat.

Of the Piste restaurants, the *Restaurant Sayil*, facing the Hotel Misión Chichén, is probably the cheapest, a plain little *restaurante económico* serving cochinita or pollo pibil for US$2.25, rice with garnish for US$0.75 and egg dishes for US$1.50.

Another simple little eatery is the *Restaurant Parador*, where meat and chicken platters cost less than US$5 and egg dishes even less, tacos less than US$2.

Prices are only slightly higher at the attractive, family-run *Restaurant Carrousel*, where you can order a platter of pollo pibil or cochinita pibil for under US$5, eggs and a few antojito choices for even less. The big palapa-covered dining room is pleasant and open from 10.30 am to 6.30 pm.

If you are willing to spend the money, the *Restaurant Xaybe* opposite the Hotel Misión Chichén has excellent cuisine, usually served buffet style in a surprisingly formal, air-conditioned dining room for the tour bus clientele. Figure on paying US$7.50 for lunch, and just slightly more for dinner, for all you can eat. Customers of the restaurant

get to use its swimming pool for free, but even if you don't eat here, you can still swim for about US$1.

Most tarted up of the resturants in Piste is the fantastical *Restaurant Fiesta*, which is worth a look if not a meal. The luncheon table d'hôte goes for US$7.50, but you can order from the menu in the evening, when substantial portions of meat cost US$4.75, of tacos US$2.50 to US$3.75

The luxury hotels all have restaurants, with the Club Med-run *Villa Arqueológica* serving particularly distinguished cuisine. Count on around US$35 to US$50 for dinner for two at the Villa, including a bottle of wine and the tip. Light meals like hamburgers are around US$6. At the Hotel Misión in Piste, the five-course comida corrida at lunch costs US$8.

Getting There & Away

Air Aerocaribe runs excursions by air from Cancún to Chichén Itzá in little planes, charging US$69 for the flight. If you want to get to Chichén, see a lot and return to Cancún the same day, this is your best bet.

Bus All the considerable bus traffic between Mérida, Valladolid and Cancún, both 1st and 2nd-class (at least two dozen buses daily), passes by Chichén Itzá and many buses stop in the neighbouring village of Piste. Ask about stopping in Piste or Chichén when buying your ticket and also when boarding your bus. Here are some bus routes from Piste:

Cancún – 205 km, three to 3½ hours, US$3.25
Izamal – 95 km, two hours, US$2.50, change buses at Hóctun
Mérida – 116 km, 2½ to three hours, US$2.50
Valladolid – 42 km, 30 to 45 minutes, US$0.50

These are 1st-class times; 2nd-class buses can be a bit slower.

Getting Around

Be prepared for walking at Chichén Itzá: walking from your hotel to the ruins, walking and climbing around the ruins and walking back to your hotel, all in the very hot sun. The air can be breathlessly muggy in summer as well. For the Grutas de Balankanché, you can set out to walk early in the morning when it's cooler (it's eight km from Piste, less if you're staying on the eastern side of the ruins) and then hope to hitch a ride or catch a bus for the return.

A few taxis are available in Piste and sometimes at the Unidad de Servicios car park at Chichén Itzá, but you cannot depend upon finding one unless you've made arrangements in advance.

IZAMAL
Population 40,000
In ancient times, Izamal was a centre for the worship of the supreme Mayan god Itzamná and the sun god Kinich Kakmó. A dozen temple pyramids in the town were devoted to these or other gods. Perhaps this Mayan religiosity is why the Spanish colonists chose Izamal as the site for an enormous and very impressive Franciscan monastery. As a site for the monastery's main church, the planners selected the platform of one of the major Mayan temples.

Today Izamal is a small, quiet provincial town with the atmosphere of life in another century. The occasional horse-drawn carriage clip-clopping through town reinforces this feeling. Its two principal squares are surrounded by impressive arcades and dominated by the gargantuan bulk of the Convento de San Antonio de Padua. There is very little evidence of the 20th century's main contribution to Yucatán – tourism.

Convento de San Antonio de Padua
When the Spanish conquered Izamal, they destroyed the major Mayan temple, the Popul-Chac pyramid and in 1533 they began to build from its stones one of the first monasteries in the hemisphere. The work was finished in 1561.

As you enter the centre of town, you can't miss the monastery, which dominates everything. The arcade, an architectural feature both useful and beautiful, was fully and abundantly used by Izamal's colonial

designers. First used in the monastery, it was echoed later in the Palacio Municipal, the small market and many other town buildings. The traditional yellow you see everywhere gives the town its nickname of Ciudad Amarilla.

The monastery's principal church is the Santuario de la Virgen de Izamal, approached by a ramp from the main square. Walk up the ramp and through an arcaded gallery to the Atrium, a spacious arcaded courtyard in which the fiesta of the Virgin of Izamal takes place each 15 August. Across the Atrium is the 12-metre-high church, which is very simple in design, without much decoration. A miraculous portrait of the Virgin hangs in the church; the Virgin of Izamal is patron saint of Yucatán. The original of the portrait was brought here from Guatemala in 1558, but was destroyed by fire in 1829 and replaced with a copy.

Entry to the church is free. The best time to visit is in the morning, as it may be closed during the afternoon siesta.

If you wander around town, you may come across remnants of the other 11 Mayan pyramids. The largest is the temple of Kinich Kakmó; all are unrestored piles of rubble.

To get fully into the spirit of the town, hire a carriage from the *sitio* on the main square for a short tour of the squares and main streets.

Henequen
En route from Chichén Itzá to Mérida, you pass through the henequen fields that gave

rise to Yucatán's affluence in the 19th century. Prosperity in these parts reached its high point during WW I when the demand for rope was staggering and synthetic fibres had not yet been invented.

Sometimes you can smell the greyish spikey-leafed henequen plants before you see them, as they emit a putrid, excremental odour. Once planted, henequen can grow virtually untended for seven years. Thereafter, the plants are annually stripped for fibre. A plant may be productive for upwards of two decades.

Although growing henequen for rope is still economically viable, synthetic fibres have significantly diminished profits. This decline has not been all that devastating for Mayan peasants, as the crop never employed that many labourers to begin with. Those who worked during its heyday on the haciendas were badly exploited.

Places to Stay & Eat

Few travellers stay the night in Izamal. The small *Hotel Kabul* (☎ (995) 4-00-08), on Calle 31, facing the main plaza near the horse-drawn carriage stand, will put you up in simple but fairly clean rooms without private bath for US$9 in one bed (one or two persons), or US$11 in two beds. Next door to the hotel is the *Cocina Económica La Reina Itzalana*, where the food is cheap and filling. Directly across the square from it are more cheap little loncherías and also the small market area.

Getting There & Away

There are direct buses several times daily from Mérida (72 km, 1½ hours, US$1.75). Coming from the east (Cancún, Valladolid and Chichén Itzá) you must change buses at Hóctun. If you're driving from the east, turn north at Kantunil.

Mérida

Population 600,000

The capital of the state of Yucatán is a charming city of narrow streets, colonial buildings, shady parks and Mayan pride. It has been the centre of Mayan culture in Yucatán since before the conquistadors arrived; today it is the peninsula's centre of commerce as well. If Cancún is Yucatán's cash register, Mérida is Yucatán's heart and soul.

Though it is the largest city in southeastern Mexico, the commercial Mérida of furniture factories, breweries, flour mills, auto dealerships and warehouses filled with sisal products, fruit, timber, tobacco and beef, is mostly on the outskirts. At the city's heart is a colonial street grid dotted with beautiful old mansions and churches. There are lots of hotels and restaurants of every class and price range and good transportation services to any part of the peninsula and the country. Mérida can be your base for numerous excursions into the Mayan countryside which surrounds it.

Mérida used to be the peninsula's transportation hub, its bus station and airport the busiest in the region, but the growth of Cancún has changed all that. Now most of Mérida's international flights are via Cancún and a proportion of the long-distance bus traffic bypasses the city on its way to the beaches.

If Mérida has drawbacks, they are traffic pollution and heat. The city's narrow colonial streets do not lend themselves to modern urban transportation. Noisy buses pump clouds of noxious fumes into the air; it's unpleasant but bearable. And Yucatán's high temperatures, bad enough in spacious city centre archaeological zones and on Cancún's beaches, seem even higher in this city. Many buildings catch the heat and hold it well into the evening. Even these sensory assaults will do little to dampen your enjoyment of this interesting city, however.

Mérida seems busiest with tourists in high summer (July and August), which is the worst time to visit because of the humidity. In winter there are fewer visitors and there's plenty of room for everybody.

HISTORY

The Spanish had to work hard to conquer Yucatán. Mayan forces put up such fierce resistance to the advance of Francisco de Montejo's conquistadors in the early 1530s that Montejo returned to his base in central Mexico utterly discouraged. But his son, also named Francisco de Montejo, took up the struggle and returned to found a Spanish colony at Campeche in 1540. From this base he and his army were able to take advantage of political dissension among the Maya, conquering Tihó (now Mérida) in 1542. By the end of the decade, Yucatán was mostly under Spanish colonial rule.

When Montejo's conquistadors entered defeated Tihó, they found a major Mayan settlement of lime-mortared stone which reminded them of Roman architectural legacies in Mérida, Spain. They promptly renamed the city after its Spanish likeness and proceeded to build it into the colonial capital and centre of control. Mérida took its colonial orders directly from Spain, not from Mexico City, and Yucatán has had a distinct cultural and political identity ever since.

With the conquest of Yucatán, the indigenous people became little more than slaves. With religious redemption as their rationale, the colonial governors and church leaders built their own little empires on the backs of the Indians. Harsh rule engendered resentments that would later explode.

When the Mexican War of Independence ended in 1821, the Spanish colonial governor of Yucatán resigned his post and the peninsula enjoyed a brief two years as an independent nation before it finally threw in its lot with Mexico, joining the union of Mexican states in 1823.

Spanish control, harsh as it was, had prevented certain abuses of power from becoming too much of a problem in Yucatán. With colonial rule removed, local potentates were free to build vast estates, or haciendas, based on the newly introduced cultivation of sugar cane and henequen. The lot of the indigenous peoples got even worse. Though the Indians were nominally free citizens in a new republic, their hacienda bosses kept them in debt peonage.

As the hacendados grew in power and wealth, they began to fear that outside forces (the government in central Mexico, or the USA) might covet their prosperity. The government in Mérida organised armed forces and issued weapons to the soldiers, who were the same Indians being oppressed on the haciendas. Given the power to achieve their freedom, the Indians rebelled in 1847, beginning the War of the Castes.

Only Mérida and Campeche were able to hold out against the rebel forces; the rest of Yucatán came under Indian control. On the brink of surrender, the ruling class in Mérida was saved by reinforcements sent from central Mexico in exchange for Mérida's agreeing to take orders from Mexico City. Though Yucatán is certainly part of Mexico, there is still a strong feeling of local pride in Mérida, a feeling that the Mayab (Mayan lands) are a special realm set apart from the rest of the country.

ORIENTATION

Mérida's street grid makes it relatively easy to find your way around. Odd-numbered streets run east to west, with higher numbered streets always to the south; even-numbered streets run north to south, with higher numbered streets always to the west. The main plaza, or Plaza Mayor, is bounded by Calles 60, 62, 61 and 63. Be advised that house numbers may progress very slowly; you cannot know whether Calle 57 No 481 and Calle 56 No 544 are one block or ten blocks apart. Perhaps for this reason, addresses are usually given in this form: Calle 57 No 481 X 56 y 58 (between Calles 56 and 58). Most of the hotels and restaurants recommended in this guide are within a five-block walk of the main plaza.

Though the centre of Mérida is around the Plaza Mayor, many important buildings and services (the Anthropology Museum, luxury hotels, banks, consulates) are along the grand Paseo de Montejo, a wide boulevard which begins nine blocks north of the plaza and extends northwards to the outskirts of the city.

INFORMATION
Tourist Office

There are information booths of minimal usefulness at the airport and the 1st-class bus station. Your best bet for information is the Tourist Information Centre (☎ (99) 24-92-90, 24-93-89), at the corner of Calles 60 and 57, in the south-west corner of the huge Teatro Peón Contreras, less than two blocks north of the Plaza Mayor.

Money

Banamex operates a casa de cambio in the Palacio Montejo on the main plaza. In addition, there are lots of banks along Calle 65 between Calles 60 and 62, the street one block behind Banamex/Palacio Montejo (that is, one block south of the Plaza Mayor). Banking hours are generally 9.30 am to 1.30 pm, Monday to Friday.

Post

The main post office (Correos) (☎ (99) 21-25-61) is in the market area on Calle 65 between Calles 56 and 56A, open Monday to Friday from 8 am to 7 pm and Saturday from 9 am to 1 pm. There are postal service booths at the airport and the 1st-class bus station, open on weekdays. There is an American Express office which holds mail for clients at the Hotel Los Aluxes, Calle 60 No 444, at the corner of Calle 49.

Telephone

To make long-distance telephone calls, go to the casetas at the airport, the bus station, at the corner of Calles 59 and 62 or Calles 64 and 57, or on Calle 60 between Calles 53 and 55.

Foreign Consulates

A number of countries have consulates in Mérida:

Belgium
    Calle 25 No 159, between Calles 28 & 30 (☎ (99) 25-29-39)
Denmark
    Calle 32 No 198 at Calle 17, Colonia Garcia Ginerés
France
    Avenida Itzaes 242 (☎ (99) 25-46-06)
Spain
    Km 6, Carretera Mérida-Uman (☎ (99) 29-15-20)
UK
    Calle 53 No 489, at Calle 58 (☎ (99) 21-67-99). You can get information about travel in Belize at the British Vice-Consulate, weekday mornings from 9.30 am to noon.
USA
    Paseo de Montejo 453, at Avenida Colón (☎ (99) 25-50-11)

Bookshops

Librería Dante Peón (☎ 24-95-22), in the Teatro Peón Contreras, at the corner of Calles 60 and 57, two blocks north of the main plaza, has some English, French and German books as well as Spanish ones. It's open seven days a week. At the south-west corner of Parque Hidalgo, half a block north of the Plaza Mayor, is Hollywood (☎ 21-36-19), Calle 60 No 496, which has a selection of international newspapers, magazines and some novels and travel guides.

Laundry

There's a good laundry on Calle 59 between Calles 72 and 74. A full load done within hours of delivery costs about US$1.60. Another place is the Tintorería El Danubio, Calle 62 No 426, between Calles 49 and 51, open (so they say) from 8 am to 6.30 pm, Monday to Friday.

PLAZA MAYOR

The most logical place to start a tour of Mérida is in the main plaza, or Plaza Mayor. This was the religious and social centre of ancient Tihó; under the Spanish it was the Plaza de Armas, or parade ground, laid out by Francisco de Montejo the Younger. Sur-rounded by harmonious colonial buildings, its carefully pruned laurel trees provide welcome shade for those who come here to relax or socialise. On Sunday, the main plaza's adjoining roadways are off limits to traffic and hundreds of Méridans take their paseo in this municipal park. If you speak Spanish, this is a good place to meet locals.

The Plaza Mayor is bounded by the city's most impressive buildings: to the east there is the cathedral and the former archbishop's palace; to the north the Palacio de Gobierno, seat of the state government of Yucatán; to the west the Palacio Municipal, Mérida's Town Hall; and to the south the Casa de Montejo, or Montejo mansion.

Cathedral

On the east side of the plaza, on the site of a Mayan temple, is Mérida's huge, hulking, severe cathedral, begun in 1561 and completed in 1598. Some of the stone from the Mayan temple was used in the cathedral's construction.

Walk through one of the three doors in the Baroque façade and into the sanctuary. To your right after you enter is a painting of Tutul Xiú, *cacique* (local ruler) of the town of Maní, paying his respects to his ally Francisco de Montejo at Tihó (Montejo and Xiú jointly defeated the Cocoms; Xiú converted to Christianity and his descendants still live in Mérida).

Look in the small chapel to the left of the principal altar for Mérida's most famous religious artefact, a statue of Jesus called Cristo de las Ampollas, or the Christ of the Blisters. Local legend has it that this statue was carved from a tree in the town of Ichmul. The tree, hit by lightning, supposedly burned for an entire night yet showed no sign of fire. The statue carved from the tree was placed in the local church where it alone is said to have survived the fiery destruction of the church, though it was blackened and blistered from the heat. It was moved to the Mérida cathedral in 1645. The faithful still make pilgrimages here.

The rest of the church's interior is very plain, its rich decoration having been

Top: Swimming in the Cenote Xlacah, Dzibilchaltún archaeological site (TB)
Left: Palacio de Montejo, Mérida (TW)
Right: Tiano's Restaurant on the Parque Hidalgo, Mérida (TB)

Top: Pyramid of the Magician, Uxmal (JL)
Bottom: Temple of Five Levels, Edzná, Campeche (TB)

stripped by angry peasants at the height of anticlerical feeling during the Mexican Revolution.

Palace of the Archbishop

The former Palace of the Archbishop to the south of the cathedral became a military post when much of the church's property was secularised during the Mexican revolution. Today it remains an army headquarters.

Palacio de Gobierno

On the north side of the plaza, the Palacio de Gobierno houses the State of Yucatán's executive government offices; it was built in 1892 on the site of the palace of the colonial governors. Make your way past the armed guards (every self-respecting Palacio de Gobierno has them) to see the historical murals painted by local artist Fernando Castro Pacheco. After 25 years of work, the murals were completed in 1978.

In vivid colours, the murals portray a symbolic history of the Maya and their interaction with the Spanish. Over the stairwell is a painting of Mayan sacred corn, the 'ray of sun from the gods'. Overall, the murals suggest that despite the oppressive intrusion of the Europeans, the spirit of Mayan culture lives on. The palace is open every day from 8 am to 8 pm.

On Sunday at 11 am, there's usually a concert (jazz, classical pops, traditional Yucatecan) in the Salón de la Historia of the Palacio de Gobierno.

Palacio Municipal

Facing the cathedral across the square, the Palacio Municipal (Town Hall) is topped by a clock tower. Originally built in 1542, it has twice been refurbished, in the 1730s and the 1850s.

Today the building also serves as the venue for performances of Yucatecan dances (especially the jarana) and music at the weekly Vaquería Regional, a regional festival held to celebrate the branding of the cattle on haciendas. Performances are on Monday evenings at 9 pm.

Every Sunday at 1 pm, the city sponsors a re-enactment of a colourful mestizo wedding at the Palacio Municipal. The performance is by the city's ballet folklorico and the police orchestra.

Casa de Montejo

From its construction in 1549 until the 1970s, the mansion on the south side of the plaza was occupied by the Montejo family. Sometimes called the Palacio de Montejo, it was built at the command of the conqueror of Mérida, Francisco de Montejo the Younger. These days the great house shelters a branch of Banamex and you can look around inside whenever the bank is open (usually from 9 am to 1.30 pm, Monday to Friday). If the bank is closed, content yourself with a close look at the Plateresque façade, where triumphant conquistadors with halberds hold their feet on the necks of generic barbarians (who are not Maya, but the association is inescapable). Also gazing across the plaza from the façade are busts of Montejo the Elder, his wife and his daughter. The armorial shields are those of the Montejo family.

WALKING TOUR

A walk north from the Plaza Mayor along Calle 60 takes you past many of Mérida's churches, parks, hotels and restaurants and brings you finally to the beginning of Paseo de Montejo.

A block north of the main plaza is the shady refuge of the **Parque Hidalgo** (sometimes called the Parque Cepeda Peraza after a 19th-century general who collected a significant library). The park's benches always hold a variety of conversationalists, lovers, taxi drivers, hammock pedlars and tourists staying at the two hotels (the Gran and the Caribe) which open onto the park.

At the far end of the park, several restaurants, including Café El Mesón and Tiano's, offer alfresco sipping and dining. Tiano's often has a marimba band in the evening, enjoyable whether you eat there or just sit nearby. The city sponsors free marimba concerts here on Sunday mornings at 11.30 am as well.

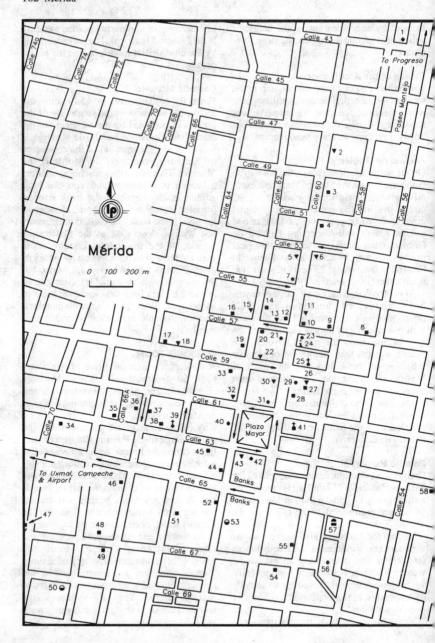

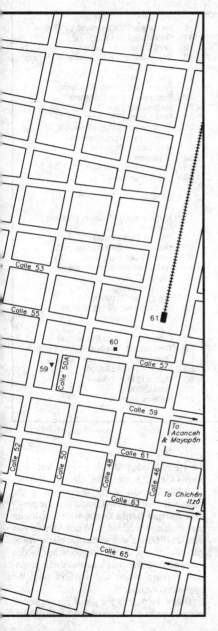

Calle 53

Calle 55

61

60

59

Calle 50A

Calle 57

Calle 59

To
Acanceh
& Mayapán

Calle 52

Calle 50

Calle 48

Calle 46

Calle 61

To Chichén
Itzá

Calle 63

Calle 65

Just to the north of the parque rises the 17th-century **Iglesia de Jesús**, also called the Iglesia El Tercer Orden. Built by the Jesuits in 1618, it is the surviving edifice in a complex of Jesuit buildings which once filled the entire city block. Always interested in education, the Jesuits founded schools which later gave birth to the **Universidad de Yucatán**, just a few steps farther to the north. General Cepeda Peraza's library of 15,000 volumes is housed in a building behind the church.

Directly in front of the church is the little **Parque de la Madre**, sometimes called the Parque Morelos. The modern madonna and child statue, which is a common fixture of town squares in this nation of high birth rates, is a copy of a statue by Lenoir which stands in the Jardin du Luxembourg in Paris.

Just north of the Parque de la Madre you confront the enormous bulk of the great **Teatro Peón Contreras**, built from 1900 to 1908 during Mérida's henequen heyday. Designed by Italian architect Enrico Deserti, it boasts a main staircase of Carrara marble, a dome with frescos by Italian artists imported for the purpose and, in its southwest corner, the **Tourist Information Centre**.

The main entrance to the theatre is at the corner of Calles 60 and 57. A gallery inside the entrance often holds exhibits by local painters and photographers; hours are usually 9 am to 2 pm and 5 to 9 pm Monday to Friday, 9 am to 2 pm Saturday and Sunday. To see the grand theatre itself, you'll have to attend a performance. Perhaps the best and most interesting performance to attend is Yucatán y sus Raices (Yucatán & its Roots), a ballet folklorico show sponsored by the university and held each evening at 9 pm in the Teatro Peón Contreras. Admission costs US$3.75.

Across Calle 60 from the Teatro Peón Contreras is the entrance to the main building of the **Universidad de Yucatán**. Though the Jesuits provided education to Yucatán's youth for centuries, the modern university was not established until the 19th century,

	PLACES TO STAY		6	Restaurant Vegetariano La Guaya
			11	Restaurant El Tucho
3	Hotel Los Aluxes		12	Wini Cafeteria
4	Hotel Trinidad Galería		13	Pop Cafetería & Restaurante Portico
8	Hotel Mucuy			del Peregrino
9	Posada Toledo		15	Las Mil Tortas
10	Hotel Casa del Balam		18	Restaurant Cedro del Libano
12	Hotel Mérida Misión		22	Pizzeria de Vito Corleone
14	Hotel Trinidad		26	Restaurant Tiano's
16	Hotel El Castellano		27	Restaurant El Mesón
17	Hotel del Gobernador		28	Restaurant El Patio Español
19	Hotel del Parque		30	Café-Restaurant Express
20	Hotel Colonial		31	Restaurant Nicte-Ha
27	Hotel Caribe		32	El Louvre
28	Gran Hotel		43	Panificadora Montejo
33	Hotel Reforma		59	Los Almendros
34	Hotel María del Carmen			
35	Hotel Las Monjas			OTHER
36	Hotel Latino			
37	Hotel Margarita		1	Anthropology Museum (Palacio
38	Casa de los Artesanías			Cantón)
44	Hotel Sevilla		7	Parque Santa Lucia
45	Hotel Lord		21	Universidad de Yucatán
46	Casa Bowen		23	Teatro Peón Contreras
47	Hotel D'Champs		24	Tourist Information Centre
48	Posada del Angel		25	Iglesia El Tercer Orden
49	Casa Becil		29	Parque Hildalgo
51	Hotel María Teresa		31	Palacio de Gobierno
52	Hotel Oviedo		39	Ex-Convento de las Monjas
54	Hotel América		40	Palacio Municipal
55	Hotel Peninsular		41	Cathedral
58	Hotel Dolores Alba		42	Casa de Montejo (Banamex)
60	Hotel Janeiro		50	Terminal de Autobuses (Main Bus
				Terminal)
	PLACES TO EAT		53	Progreso Bus Station
			56	Mercado Municipal
2	Restaurant La Casona		57	Post Office
5	Patio de las Fajitas		61	Railway Station

when the job was done by Governor Felipe Carrillo Puerto and General Manuel Cepeda Peraza. The story of the university's founding is rendered graphically in a mural done in 1961 by Manuel Lizama. Walk in and ask for directions to the mural.

The central courtyard of the university building is the scene of concerts and folk performances every Tuesday or Friday evening at 9 pm (check with the Tourist Information Centre for performance dates and times).

Continue your walk north on Calle 60 past

the Hotel Mérida Misión (on the left) and, across the street, the Hotel Casa del Balam.

A block north of the university, at the intersection of Calles 60 and 55, is the pretty little **Parque Santa Lucia**, with arcades on the north and west sides. When Mérida was a lot smaller, this was where travellers would get into or out of the stagecoaches which bumped over the rough roads of the peninsula, linking towns and villages with the provincial capital.

Today the park is the venue for orchestral performances of Yucatecan music on Thursday evenings at 9 pm and Sunday mornings at 11 am. Also here on Sunday at 11 am is the Bazar de Artesanías, the local handicrafts market.

To reach the Paseo de Montejo, walk 3½ blocks north along Calle 60 from the Parque Santa Lucia to Calle 47. Turn right on Calle 47 and walk two blocks to the paseo, on your left.

PASEO DE MONTEJO

The Paseo de Montejo was an attempt by Mérida's 19th-century city planners to create a wide European-style grand boulevard, similar to Mexico City's Paseo de la Reforma or Paris's Avenue des Champs-Elysées. Since this is Mérida, not Paris, the boulevard is more modest. But it is still a beautiful swath of green and open space in an urban conglomeration of stone and concrete.

As Yucatán has always looked upon itself as distinct from the rest of Mexico, the peninsula's powerful hacendados and commercial barons maintained good business and social contacts with Europe, concentrating on these to balance the necessary relations with Mexico City. Europe's architectural and social influence can be seen along the paseo in the surviving fine mansions built by wealthy families around the turn of the century. Many other mansions have been torn down to make way for the banks, hotels and other high visibility establishments which always want prime places on the grand boulevards of the world. Most of the remaining mansions are north of Calle 37, which is three blocks north of the Anthropology Museum. Sidewalk cafés and restaurants south of Calle 39 can provide sustenance during your stroll along the avenue.

Two and a half blocks north along the paseo from Calle 47 brings you to the splendid white Palacio Cantón, home of Mérida's Anthropology Museum.

Anthropology Museum

The great white palace at the corner of Paseo de Montejo and Calle 43 is the Museo Regional de Antropología de Yucatán,

housed in the Palacio Cantón. The great mansion was designed by Enrico Deserti, also responsible for the Teatro Peón Contreras. Construction took place from 1909 to 1911. When it was completed, the mansion's owner, General Francisco Cantón Rosado (1833-1917) moved in and lived here for a brief six years before he headed off to that great mansion in the sky.

After General Cantón's death his palace served as a school, as the official residence of the governors of the state of Yucatán and now as the Anthropology Museum. No building in Mérida exceeds it in splendour or pretension. It's a fitting symbol of the grand aspirations of Mérida's elite during the last years of the Porfiriato.

Admission to the museum costs US\$0.35; it's open Tuesday to Saturday from 8 am to 8 pm, Sunday from 8 am to 2 pm, closed Monday. The museum shop is open from 8 am to 3 pm (2 pm on Sunday). Labels on the museum's exhibits are in Spanish only, but if you know a bit about Yucatán's history and culture you'll be able to learn a lot here.

The first room on your right is a gallery for temporary exhibits. After that, museum rooms take you through the peninsula's history from the very beginning, when mastodons roamed here. Exhibits on Mayan culture include explanations of the forehead-flattening which was done to beautify babies and other practices such as sharpening teeth and implanting them with tiny jewels. If you plan to visit archaeological sites near Mérida, you can study the many exhibits here – lavishly illustrated with plans and photographs – which cover the great Mayan cities of Mayapán, Uxmal and Chichén Itzá, as well as lesser sites.

Monumento a la Patria

Walking north along Paseo de Montejo from the Palacio Cantón, you pass several high-class hotels, big banks and, after six long blocks, the US Consulate General, on the left at the intersection with Avenida Colón. The luxury Holiday Inn hotel is just beyond the Consulate on Colón. At this same intersection is the Parque de las Américas, which boasts trees and shrubs collected from many countries of the western hemisphere.

Walking north two more blocks from the Avenida Colón intersection brings you to the Monument to the Fatherland, an elaborate sculpture in neo-Mayan style executed in 1956 by Rómulo Rozo. The fatherland, here, takes on a distinctly Mayan appearance.

PARQUE CENTENARIO

On the western edge of the city, 12 blocks from the Plaza Mayor, lies the large, verdant Parque Centenario, bordered by Avenida de los Itzaes, the highway to the airport and Campeche. There's a zoo in the park which specialises in exhibiting the fauna of Yucatán. To get there, take a bus westwards along Calle 61 or 65.

FESTIVALS

Prior to Lent in February or March, Carnival features colourful costumes and nonstop festivities. It is celebrated with greater vigour in Mérida than anywhere else in Yucatán. During the first two weeks in October, the Christ of the Blisters (Cristo de las Ampollas) statue in the cathedral is venerated with processions.

PLACES TO STAY

Mérida has an excellent array of lodgings in all price ranges, from the basic but very cheap to international luxury class. Most of the cheap and middle-range hotels are within about six blocks of the plaza; the largest concentration of luxury hotels is along the Paseo de Montejo, 12 to 16 long blocks from the plaza.

PLACES TO STAY – BOTTOM END

Prices for basic but suitable double rooms in Mérida range from about US$10 to US$20. This price can get you a small but clean room with fan and private shower only a short walk from the plaza. All hotels should provide purified drinking water at no extra charge. (Sometimes the water bottles are not readily evident, so ask for agua purificada.) Here they are, listed in order of price, from cheapest to more expensive.

Hotel Las Monjas (☎ (99) 21-98-62), Calle 66A No 509 at the corner of Calle 63, is one of the best deals in town. All 20 rooms in this little place have ceiling fans and running water (sinks or private baths with hot and cold water). Rooms are tiny and most are dark, but they are clean. Room No 12 is the best, quiet because it's at the back, light and cool because its windows provide good cross-ventilation. The price is US$9 a double.

Hotel Margarita (☎ (99) 21-32-13), Calle 66 No 506, between Calles 61 and 63, is a favourite with foreigners because of its low price, convenient location 1½ blocks west of the plaza and clean (if very small) rooms with fan and running water for US$8.75 a single, US$10 a double (in one bed) or US$11.50 (in two beds), US$13 a triple, US$15 a quad. Air-conditioning is available in some rooms for a few dollars more.

Hotel Latino (☎ (99) 21-48-31), Calle 66 No 505, between Calles 61 and 63, right across the street from the Hotel Margarita, takes the overflow. The Latino lacks something of the Margarita's convivial spirit and prices are a bit higher at US$10/12/14 a single/double/triple with fan, but it's still pretty good value.

Hotel Mucuy (☎ (99) 21-10-37), Calle 57 No 481, between Calles 56 and 58, has been serving thrifty travellers for more than a decade. It's a family-run place with 26 tidy rooms on two floors facing a long, narrow garden courtyard. Sra Ofelia Comin and her daughter Ofelia speak English; Sr Alfredo Comin understands it and all do their best to help and make your stay pleasant. Rooms with ceiling fan and private shower cost US$11.50/14/16 a single/double/triple. The location is fairly convenient, the welcome exceptionally warm.

Hotel María Teresa (☎ (99) 21-10-39), Calle 64 No 529, between Calles 65 and 67, could be a bit tidier but most of the rooms are acceptable. If you don't like the first room they show you, ask to see others. With fan and private bath, doubles cost US$11; with air-con, US$16.

Casa Bowen (☎ (99) 21-81-12), Calle 66

No 521B, near Calle 65, is a longtime favourite with budget travellers. A large old Mérida house has been converted to a hotel and the building next door has been joined to it, renovated and equipped with guest rooms. The narrow courtyard at the Bowen has a welcome swath of green grass and comfortable chairs for talking and relaxing. Rooms are very simple, even bare, and some are quite dark, but all have the necessary fans and showers. Rates are US$11.50 a double with fan, US$18 a double with air-con.

There are very few suitable hostelries near Mérida's central bus station. The ones facing the station are unbearably noisy and hot, others on nearby streets are overpriced. The Casa Becil (☎ (99) 21-29-57), Calle 67 No 550C, between Calles 66 and 68, is a converted town house with a pleasant high-ceilinged sitting room/lobby with a traditional tile floor and small guest rooms at the back. With private shower and fan, the price is US$12.50 a double. The family management tries hard to please.

Hotel Sevilla (☎ (99) 23-83-60, 28-24-81), Calle 62 No 511, at the corner of Calle 65, offers good news and bad news. The good news is the whisper of faded elegance in the black-and-white tiled terraces, the coloured faience wall panels, the high ceilings, gracious spaces and convenient location. The bad news is that most rooms are musty and dark, but they might well have been so a century ago when the house was elegant, so at least it's authentic. The price is not too bad: US$12/13/15 for a single/double/triple.

Another of Mérida's faded glory hostelries is the *Hotel Oviedo* (☎ (99) 21-36-09), Calle 62 No 515 between Calles 65 and 67, a 33-room former town house with a nice courtyard. There are fewer bits of battered elegance here, but the rooms – small, with ceiling fans and private showers – are marginally better than those of the nearby Hotel Sevilla and they cost the same: US$12/13/15 a single/double/triple.

Hotel América (☎ (99) 21-51-33), Calle 67 No 500, between Calles 58 and 60, is, like the Hotel Oviedo, a member of the Amigotels group. Unlike the Oviedo, though, this place is modern. Rooms at the front are quite noisy; all have fans and showers, but are not such good value: a double costs US$14.50.

Hotel Trinidad (☎ (99) 21-30-29, 23-20-33), Calle 62 No 464 between Calles 55 and 57, has been a budget favourite for several years. Owner and artist Manolo Riviera, who speaks some English, has decorated the hotel with modern Mexican paintings and the tiny courtyard is filled with plants. Though the hotel has charm, it could also use some paint. The guest rooms are all different, as are their facilities; they range in price from US$12.50 for a small double with sink to US$27 a double for a large room with private bath and air-conditioning. Discounts of US$1 to US$4 are granted if you pay cash.

The Trinidad's sister hotel, the *Hotel Trinidad Galería* (☎ (99) 23-24-63), Calle 60 No 456, at the corner of Calle 51, was once a gracious residence, then an appliance showroom and is now an unlikely hotel. The showroom space serves as the lobby, its vast emptiness (now that all the appliances are gone) filled with big plants. There's a small swimming pool, a bar, art gallery and antique shop as well as presentable rooms with fans and private showers renting for US$11/15/18 a single/double/triple.

Hotel Lord (☎ (99) 23-93-71, 23-96-77), Calle 63 No 516, between Calles 62 and 64, is only half a block from the plaza. It's clean, bright and barracks-like with a long central courtyard used as a car park and yellow tiles everywhere. Though perilously short on charm, it is reasonably well run. An adjoining café can provide breakfast and light meals. Rooms cost US$16 a double with a fan, US$20 a double with air-con.

Hotel Peninsular (☎ (99) 23-69-96), Calle 58 No 519 between Calles 65 and 67, is in the midst of Mérida's market district. You enter down a long corridor from the street to find a neat little restaurant (three-course comida corrida for US$3.25) and a maze of rooms, some large, some small, most with windows opening onto the interior spaces. Maintenance is pretty good here and prices represent decent value for money:

US$13.50/16/19 a single/double/triple with private bath and fan; add a few dollars for air-conditioning.

Hotel del Parque (☎ (99) 24-78-44), Calle 60 No 497 at Calle 59, is only steps from the Parque Hidalgo and Parque de la Madre, in the midst of the action. Though the entrance is colonial in style, the rooms are actually in the adjoining modern structure. Rooms are small but clean and bright, with fans and private showers. Those at the front are very noisy. Singles/doubles/triples cost US$16/17.25/19.

Posada del Angel (☎ (99) 23-27-54), Calle 67 No 535 between Calles 66 and 68, is two blocks north-east of the bus station and is quieter than most other hotels in this neighbourhood. It's a small brick and wrought-iron place meant to evoke thoughts of colonial Mérida, although the structure is obviously modern. It's tidy and convenient, with its own little restaurant, but a bit expensive for what you get: clean rooms with fan and bath cost US$18 a double, or US$23.50 a double with air-conditioning.

PLACES TO STAY – MIDDLE

Mérida's middle-range places provide surprising levels of comfort for what you pay. Most charge US$20 to US$40 for a double room with air-conditioning, ceiling fan and private shower; most of these hotels have restaurants and bars and little swimming pools.

Hotel Dolores Alba (☎ (99) 21-37-45), Calle 63 No 464, between Calles 52 and 54, is one of the top choices in Mérida because of its obliging manager, Sr Angel Sánchez, because of its pleasant courtyard and beautiful swimming pool and because of its clean, comfortable rooms priced at US$18 a double (slightly more for air-conditioning). There's room for a few small cars in the courtyard. The one slight drawback is the hotel's location 3½ blocks east of the main plaza.

(By the way, the Sánchez family also owns the Hotel Dolores Alba at Chichén Itzá. You can make reservations for a room there by talking to the people at the hotel here.)

Another hotel owned by the Sánchez

family is the *Hotel Janeiro* (☎ (99) 23-36-02), Calle 57 No 435, between Calles 48 and 50, seven blocks north-east of the plaza. Rooms and facilities are similar to those at the Dolores Alba and the price for a room is identical.

Hotel Caribe (☎ (99) 24-90-22), Calle 59 No 500, at the corner of Calle 60, is actually at the back corner of the Parque Hidalgo. It's a perennial favourite with visiting foreigners because of its central location, its nice little rooftop swimming pool, its three tiers of rooms surrounding a central courtyard and its two restaurants. Most rooms have air-conditioning and cost US$23.50/27/30.50 for a single/double/triple, but there are also a number of rooms with just ceiling fans, not quite as well kept but still serviceable, for US$3.75 per room less. Air-conditioned suites cost US$34 a double. All rooms have private showers, of course. The Caribe is often booked solid, so reserve in advance, or arrive early in the day to claim a room.

Also next to the Parque Hidalgo is the *Gran Hotel* (☎ (99) 24-76-22, 24-77-30), Calle 60 No 496, between Calles 59 and 61, on the southern side of the park. True to its name, this was Mérida's grand hotel about a century ago. Corinthian columns support terraces on three levels around the verdant central courtyard and fancy wrought-iron and carved wood decoration evoke a past age. Several years ago the management undertook to repaint both the turn-of-the-century murals and the guest rooms; upkeep is fairly good, though not perfect. Rooms with private shower and ceiling fan cost US$21.50/25/29for a single/double/triple and a suite is US$50. The hotel's good little Restaurant Español (open 7 am to 11 pm) serves enchiladas for US$2.50 to US$3.25 and many other plates at similar prices. If you're looking for Old Mérida, you'll find it here.

Perhaps even more evocative of 19th-century Mérida is the *Posada Toledo* (☎ (99) 23-22-56, 23-16-90), at Calle 58 No 487, right at the corner of Calle 57, three blocks north-east of the main plaza. This grand city residence has a courtyard where a viney jungle runs rampant, a dining room straight out of the 19th century and small, modernised rooms with private shower and either fan or air-con for US$18/21.50/25 a single/double/triple. The staff are very friendly and helpful. A breakfast buffet is served in the dining room each morning (US$3). This is one of my favourite places in all of Yucatán.

Hotel Colonial (☎ (99) 24-21-20, 24-81-08), Calle 62 No 476, at the corner of Calle 57, is anything but colonial. Rather, it's a modern structure with neocolonial touches and more than 50 modern air-conditioned rooms, each with TV and telephone, priced at US$27/30.50 for a single/double. There's a small swimming pool. Here you're only two blocks north of the plaza and right next door to the university.

Hotel Reforma (☎ (99) 24-79-22), Calle 59 No 508, corner of Calle 62, is an old hotel that preserves a little of its 19th-century elegance – very little, but at least there's something: a bit of coloured faience, a twisty wrought-iron stairway, a spacious lobby. The old-fashioned rooms have high ceilings, fans, bathrooms and are priced at US$21.50 a double. If you'd like a TV set, you pay about US$1 more per day. The hotel has a small swimming pool which may or may not have water in it.

Hotel del Gobernador (☎ (99) 23-71-33), Calle 59 No 535, at the corner of Calle 66, is an attractive, modern hotel favoured by Mexican business executives because of its efficient service, arctic air-conditioning and pleasant, comfortable rooms. Off the lobby is a cheerful, bright restaurant. The price is good for what you get: US$33 a double.

PLACES TO STAY – TOP END

Mérida's list of top-rank hostelries includes one well-known name and several good local establishments. Top-end hotels charge between US$40 and US$100 for a double room. All rooms in this class are air-conditioned and each hotel has a restaurant, bar, swimming pool and probably other services like a travel agency, newsstand, hairdresser and nightclub.

Holiday Inn Mérida (☎ (99) 25-68-77; in the USA (800) 465-4329), Avenida Colón 498 at the corner of Calle 60, half a block off the Paseo de Montejo behind the American Consulate General, is Mérida's most luxurious establishment, complete with US satellite TV, swimming pool and tennis courts. Its 213 air-con rooms all have minibars and purified water and cost US$91, tax included. The Holiday Inn is often full, so reserve a room in advance.

Perhaps the best choice for all-round quality, convenience and price is the *Hotel Los Aluxes* (☎ (99) 24-21-99; fax 23-38-58), Calle 60 No 444, at the corner of Calle 49. This relatively new 109-room hotel is an easy walk from the city centre and from the Paseo de Montejo. It has all of the top-end services, plus attractive modern architecture and an intriguing name: *aluxes* (ah-LOO-shess) are the Mayan equivalent of leprechauns or wee folk, benevolent but usually invisible fairies. Rates are moderate: US$57.50 for a single/double, US$66 for a triple, US$74 for a suite.

Hotel Mérida Misión (☎ (99) 39-51-00; in the USA (800) 648-7818), Calle 60 No 491, at the corner of Calle 57, is centrally located on the same corner as the university and the Teatro Peón Contreras. Half modern and half colonial in decor, the hotel is very comfortable and convenient without being particularly charming. Rates for the 150 air-conditioned rooms, all with colour satellite TV and phone, are US$47/50/54 for a single/double/triple and US$57 for a suite. There's a nice little swimming pool, dining room and a branch of the modern Wini Cafetería chain right in the same building.

Hotel Casa del Balam (☎ (99) 24-88-44; fax 24-50-11), Calle 60 No 488 at Calle 57, directly across the street from the aforementioned Mérida Misión, has a nice neocolonial atmosphere, swimming pool, restaurant, bar and travel agency. The central courtyard with fountain and wicker rockers under the arcade is very pleasant. It's popular with groups, which may account for the brusque and hurried service. Air-conditioned rooms with TV are priced fairly high at US$66 a double, but the location – just across the street from the Teatro Peón Contreras – is excellent.

Hotel El Castellano (☎ (99) 23-01-00), Calle 57 No 513, between Calles 62 and 64, 2½ blocks north-west of the main plaza, is a favourite with Mexican business travellers and some foreign tourists as well. Its well-maintained facilities include 170 air-conditioned rooms, swimming pool, solarium, restaurant, bar and coffee shop. Rates are US$50 for a single/double, US$66 for a triple/suite.

Hotel María del Carmen (☎ (99) 23-91-33), Apdo Postal 411 (Calle 63 No 550, between 68 and 70), is the first choice for many repeat visitors to Mérida and also some groups. Recently completely renovated and modernised, it is now fairly posh, with marble everywhere, a lovely big swimming pool and all the other upscale hotel services. Rates at last check were US$50 a double, but these may go up as the 'new' María del Carmen catches on with travellers. It's almost four blocks west of the plaza.

Hotel D'Champs (☎ (99) 24-86-55; fax 23-60-24), Calle 70 No 543, between Calles 65 and 67, was once the Hotel Cayré. But major renovations have turned this once dowdy hostelry into a fairly luxurious place to stay. You enter through a gracious old Mérida mansion to find a spacious courtyard complete with lawn, trees, swimming pool and shady pergola. The 92 guest rooms surrounding the court are done in an undated classic decor of white and gold, with marble vanities, sparkling showers, air-conditioning, colour TV and two double beds. Mexican business executives are happy to pay US$41 a double to stay here and you will be too. There's free parking. The Hotel D'Champs is five fairly long blocks south-west of the plaza.

Besides the Holiday Inn, the Paseo de Montejo has three other comfortable hotels, all about ten or twelve blocks north of the main plaza.

Hotel El Conquistador (☎ (99) 26-21-55; fax 26-88-29), Paseo de Montejo No 458, at Calle 35, has 90 air-conditioned rooms and suites in a modern nine-storey structure; rooms have two double beds, colour TV and all the other expected comforts. A small enclosed pool on the second floor is yours for a refreshing dip and a restaurant, coffee shop and lobby bar with live entertainment provide sustenance. Rates are US$54 for a single/double, US$62 a triple and US$68 for a junior suite.

Hotel Montejo Palace (☎ (99) 24-76-44), Paseo de Montejo 483-C and *Hotel Paseo de Montejo* (☎ (99) 23-90-33), Paseo de Montejo 482, face one another across the Paseo at Calle 41. Both hotels are under the same management. The Montejo Palace, with 90 rooms on the west side of the Paseo, is slightly fancier, charging US$47 a single/double for rooms with two double beds, colour TV, mini-bar and woody neocolonial decor.

The Hotel Paseo de Montejo's rooms are simpler and older, but still comfortable and well priced at US$30 double. Between the two establishments you have your choice of six restaurants and bars. The swimming pool at the Montejo Palace is open to guests staying at the Paseo de Montejo as well.

PLACES TO EAT

Mérida's restaurants are less numerous than Cancún's, but they are also less hyped, less expensive and more varied in cuisine. In Cancún it's expected that you want expensive lobster and shrimp at every meal; in Mérida you can order Yucatecan, Mexican, American, Italian, French, even Lebanese. The best restaurants are only moderately priced and the market eateries are cheap and good.

PLACES TO EAT – BOTTOM END

The cheapest full meals are, as usual, in and around the market. Walk two blocks south from the main plaza to Calle 67, turn left (east) and walk another two or three blocks to the market. Continue straight up the ramping flight of steps at the end of Calle 67. As you ascend, you'll pass the touristy Mercado de Artesanías on your left. At the top of the ramp, turn left and you'll see a row of market eateries with names like *El*

Chimecito, La Temaxeña, Saby, Mimi, Saby y El Palon, La Socorrito, Reina Beatriz and so forth. Comidas corridas here are priced from US$1.75 to US$2.25, big main-course platters of beef, fish or chicken with vegetables and rice or potatoes go for US$1.50 to US$2.25 and specialities such as frijol con puerco (Yucatán-style pork and beans) for US$1.50. Bistec (beefsteak) and chuletas (chops, veal or pork) cost only a bit more. Though no place in Mérida can be called cool, it's at least shady and breezy here. The market eateries are open from early morning until late afternoon every day.

For cheap food right in the city centre, seek out *El Louvre* (☎ 21-32-71), Calle 62 No 499, corner of Calle 61 at the north-west corner of the Plaza Mayor. This bright, bare, well-used place has a loyal local clientele, efficient waiters and low prices. Sandwiches go for US$0.75 to US$1.75, full breakfasts for US$2 and the daily comida corrida for about US$2.50. The first room you enter suffers from street noise, but the back rooms are quieter. Once you've tried El Louvre, you might want to try the other places north along Calle 62, including *Cafetería Erik's* right next door.

For cheap sandwiches, try *Las Mil Tortas*, Calle 62 between Calles 57 and 55. Though they don't really offer a thousand different sandwiches, the ones they do offer are cheap, ranging in price from US$0.60 to US$1.25. It's a tiny hole-in-the-wall, short on atmosphere, but often full of students, with many more customers dropping by to pick up takeaway orders. Breakfast is served here for US$1.50 to US$2.25.

Another place for takeaway food is the *Pizzería de Vito Corleone* (☎ 23-68-46), Calle 59 No 508, at the corner of 62, near the Hotel Reforma. This tiny eatery suffers from street noise, so many customers take their pizzas to the Parque Hidalgo instead. Small one-person pizzas go for US$2.25 to US$2.75 depending upon ingredients; larger pizzas to feed two or three cost US$5.60 to US$6.50. If you decide to eat here, head for the upstairs dining room.

For fairly cheap food in clean, modern

surroundings and air-conditioned comfort, try the soups, sandwiches, tortas, salads and desserts at the *Wini Cafetería*, Calle 60 No 491, just north of Calle 57 in the Hotel Mérida Misión building and also at Paseo de Montejo 466. Though a huge club sandwich costs US$4.50, those with ham, cheese, pork or chicken go for US$2.50 to US$3; tortas are about the same. They serve several good Mexican dishes such as burritas, enfrijoladas and enchiladas as well. Desserts are a specialty, from pies and cakes to banana splits and sweet crepes.

The best cheap breakfasts can be had by picking up a selection of pan dulces (sweet rolls and breads) from one of Mérida's several *panificadoras* (bakeries). A convenient one is the *Panificadora Montejo* at the corner of Calles 62 and 63, at the south-west corner of the main plaza. Pick up a metal tray and tongs, select the pastries you want and hand the tray to a clerk who will bag them and quote a price, usually US$1 or so for a full bag.

PLACES TO EAT – MIDDLE

Those willing to spend a bit more money can enjoy the pleasant restaurants of the Parque Hidalgo at the corner of Calles 59 and 60.

The least expensive, yet one of the most pleasant restaurants here, is the *Cafetería El Mesón* (☎ 21-92-32) in the Hotel Caribe. Its white wrought-iron chairs and tables shaded by umbrellas are set out on the Parque Hidalgo and they're usually busy with gringos sipping cool beers, munching sandwiches and fending off the hammock pedlars; local patrons often choose the inside dining room. Meat, fish and chicken dishes are priced from US$3.25 to US$7, but sandwiches and burgers are only US$1.75 to US$2.50. They often have Montejo beer here, which is not easily found elsewhere. El Mesón is open for breakfast, lunch and dinner daily.

Right next to El Mesón in the Parque Hidalgo, crowding its tables upon it, is *Tiano's* (☎ 23-71-18), Calle 59 No 498, at the corner of Calle 60, a fancier version of El Mesón. In the evening the restaurant often hires a marimba group to entertain its patrons as well as the dozens of hangers-on in the square. There's a dining area in the courtyard behind the plaza tables, as well. Have sopa de lima, puntas de filete, dessert and a drink and your bill might be US$13. If you're satisfied with just a main course of red snapper or chicken you'd pay US$6 and a sandwich costs less than half that much. The menu is long and varied, with steaks, seafood and a few Yucatecan dishes. Tiano's is supposedly open 24 hours a day, though you'll see it locked up tight from about midnight to 7 am. Breakfast, lunch and dinner are served.

In the Gran Hotel, facing the Parque Hidalgo, is *El Patio Español*, the hotel's restaurant, serving good Mexican and Yucatecan food at moderate prices. Filling enchilada dishes go for US$2.50 to US$3.25 and many other main courses are about US$3. You can get breakfast here, as the restaurant is open from 7 am to 11 pm every day.

Across Calle 60, facing the Parque Hidalgo, is an old Mérida standard, the *Café-Restaurant Express* (☎ 21-37-38), Calle 60 No 502, south of Calle 59. Busy with a loyal crowd of regulars and foreigners, Express is a bustling and noisy meeting place, but the food is good, service is fast and prices are fair. The daily comida corrida goes for US$4 and most main-course plates cost US$3.50 to US$5.25. Breakfast is good as well. Hours are 7 am to midnight daily.

A block and a half north-west of the Parque Hidalgo stands *Pop Cafetería* (☎ 21-68-44), Calle 57 between 60 and 62, on the north side of the street. Plain, modern, bright and air-conditioned, Pop provides breakfast, lunch, afternoon pie and coffee and dinner to locals who like to linger in the cool air. The menu is limited but adequate, with hamburgers for US$1.50 to US$1.75, big plates of spaghetti for US$2.50 and main-course platters such as chicken in mole sauce for US$3. Breakfasts cost from US$1.80 for pan dulce and coffee to US$3 for bacon, eggs and the works. The first month of the 18-month Mayan calendar is named Pop, which is how the restaurant got its name.

For food or snacks on the Plaza Mayor try the *Restaurant Nicte-Ha* (☎ 23-07-84), Calle 61 No 500, on the north side of the square beneath the arcade of the Palacio de Gobierno. It's not much for decor or atmosphere, but tables set out under the arcade provide good views of the action in the square. Selection is varied, from tacos and enchiladas to sandwiches and full-course lunches and dinners. Prices are low: you can fill up for US$2 to US$5.

Also on the north side of the main plaza is the *Dulcería y Sorbetería Colón*, a good place to unwind with a pastry (US$0.40), ice cream (US$1.10) or soft drink (US$0.20) as you survey the activity in the Plaza Mayor.

Restaurant Cedro del Libano (☎ 23-7531), Calle 59 No 529 between Calles 64 and 66, is simple and clean, with one of the most interesting menus in Mérida – it's Lebanese. Why is there a Lebanese restaurant in Mérida? Because Lebanese traders made up a significant minority in the population during the 19th century and their descendants remain loyal citizens of Mérida to this day. *Berenjena con tijini* (eggplant with tahini), *labne* (yogurt), *tabule*, *kibi* and *alambre de kafta* (ground meat mixed with spices and grilled on skewers) are a few of the choices you'll have. For a full meal, expect to pay US$7 or US$8. Hours are 11.30 am to 11.30 pm every day.

For vegetarian fare (dinner only), there's the *Restaurant Vegetariano La Guaya* (☎ 23-21-44), Calle 60 No 472, between Calles 55 and 53, a short distance north of the Parque Santa Lucia. La Guaya advocates a whole way of life, not just healthy eating. Within the restaurant's courtyard are a bookstore and art gallery concentrating on things good for mind, soul and body. As for the food, it's heavy on salads, grains, vegetables and fruits. Portions are big and prices moderate, with dinner and a drink costing about US$5 to US$7. Hours are 5 to 11 pm Monday to Saturday, closed Sunday.

PLACES TO EAT – TOP END

Mérida's better restaurants are surprisingly good and inexpensive when compared to eateries of similar rank in Europe or North America. You can have an excellent three-course repast, either continental or Yucatecan, for US$10 to US$15 per person, wine, tax and tip included.

Among the city's most dependable dining-places is the *Restaurante Portico del Peregrino* (☎ 21-68-44), Calle 57 No 501, between Calles 60 and 62, right next to Pop. This 'Pilgrim's Refuge' consists of several pleasant, almost elegant traditional dining rooms (some are air-conditioned) around a small courtyard replete with colonial artefacts. Yucatecan dishes are the forte, but you'll find many continental dishes as well: come for brochettes of beef or pavo relleno and you'll be satisfied either way. Lunch (noon to 3 pm) and dinner (6 to 11 pm) are served every day and your bill for a full meal might be US$12 to US$16 per person.

La Casona (☎ 23-83-48), Calle 60 No 434 between Calles 47 and 49, is a fine old city house now serving as a nice restaurant, just one block north of the Hotel Los Aluxes. Dining tables are set out on a portico next to a small but lush garden; dim lighting lends an air of romance. Italian dishes crowd the menu, with a few Yucatecan plates to top it off. Besides the inevitable pollo pibil, there are lots of steak, fish and pasta platters. Plan to spend anywhere from US$8 to US$16 per person, everything included; the highest prices are reserved for those who order shrimp and lobster dishes. La Casona is open every evening for dinner; on weekends, you might want to make reservations.

Los Almendros (☎ 21-28-51), Calle 50A No 493 between Calles 57 and 59, facing the Plaza de Mejorada about five blocks west of the Plaza Mayor, is Mérida's branch of the Yucatecan culinary effort which began in the town of Ticul, south of Mérida, in 1962 and now has a branch in Cancún as well. The speciality is authentic Yucatecan country cuisine such as pavo relleno negro (grilled turkey with hot peppered pork stuffing), papadzul (tacos filled with egg smothered in a fiery sauce), sopa de lima (chicken broth with lime and tortillas) or Los Almendros' most famous dish, the zingy onion-and-

tomato pork dish poc-chuc. All meals are served with hot handmade tortillas. For those who don't read Spanish, there is a photo-menu of each dish.

Some people are disappointed at Los Almendros because they go expecting delicacies; this is hearty food, not subtle, though it is tasty. If you have sopa de lima, poc-chuc, dessert and a bottle of beer, the bill will be US$9 or US$10; you can dine for somewhat less, but not much more.

Want entertainment as you dine Yucatán-style? *Restaurant El Tucho* (☎ 24-23-23), Calle 60 No 482 between 57 and 55), features a menu of Yucatecan specialties (cochinita pibil, pavo en escabeche, poc-chuc, pan de cazón, etc). You enter from the street, pass down a long hallway and emerge in a dining room fashioned to look like an enormous na, with thatched roof and bamboo walls. It's not fancy, but rather a place where the locals come for eating, drinking and singing, from 6 pm to midnight, seven days a week. Most main courses cost US$5 and a full meal can be yours for US$10 or US$12. Beware of the high prices for drinks; a beer costs US$1.75 here, a mere soft drink US$1.25.

Mérida's most famous French restaurant is the *Yannig Restaurante* (☎ 27-03-39), some distance from the centre at Avenida Perez-Ponce No 105, near the Iglesia de Itzimná. Chef Yannig Oliviero is from France and his menu has classic French dishes as well as those which might be termed *nouvelle Yucatán*. If you like onion soup, freshly made paté, coq au vin, poisson amandine and peche Melba, you'll like Yannig. Dinner is the only meal served Monday to Saturday from 5 to 11.30 pm; on Sunday there's lunch and dinner from 1 to 10.30 pm. A full meal might cost US$10 to US$15 with wine.

Patio de las Fajitas (☎ 28-37-82), Calle 60 No 467 at the corner of Calle 53, is a fine old colonial mansion with many period furnishings, lots of plants and dining tables with lots of space around them. Fajitas (beef, chicken, pork, etc) are the speciality, of course, priced from US$6.50 to US$7.50.

Come for lunch or dinner fajitas from 1 to 11 pm daily (closed Monday).

ENTERTAINMENT

Though many visitors choose to enjoy a long dinner with drinks and conversation, or just to relax in the Plaza Mayor, others like to spend the evening at concerts or the cinema. There's plenty to do.

Concerts & Folklore

Proud of its cultural legacy and attuned to the benefits of tourism, the city of Mérida offers nightly folkloric events put on by local performers of considerable skill. Admission is free to city-sponsored events.

Monday
A regional Vaquería features the city's ballet folklorico accompanied by the local Jarana Orchestra; it is staged behind the Municipal Palace in the Garden of the Composers at 9 pm
Tuesday
Yucatán y sus Raices (Yucatán & its Roots), a ballet folklorico show sponsored by the university, is held at 9 pm in the Teatro Peón Contreras, at the corner of Calles 60 and 57. Admission costs US$3.75
A city band plays music from the past and present. Performances are in Santiago Park, at the intersection of Calles 59 and 72
Some Tuesdays there are concerts in the university courtyard; check with the Tourist Office
Wednesday
Mérida's string ensemble plays light classical and popular music in Santa Ana Park at the corner of Calles 60 and 47
Thursday
Traditional Yucatecan folkloric dancers and troubadours entertain in the Parque Santa Lucia at Calles 60 and 55 at 9 pm
Friday
Local theatre is presented in the Garden of the Composers at the back of the Palacio Municipal. Also, in the university's patio in a building at the intersection of Calle 60 and 57, entertaining folkloric dances and music are performed
Saturday
Musical performances (jazz, classical pops and traditional Yucatecan) at 11 am in the Salón de la Historia of the Palacio de Gobierno on the Plaza Mayor
City sponsored marimba concerts take place in Parque Hidalgo, Calles 60 and 59, at 11.30 am

At 1 pm, the city sponsors a re-enactment of a colourful mestiza wedding by the city's ballet folklorico and police orchestra at the Palacio Municipal
The weekly Bazar de Artesanías is held from 11 am to 3 pm in Parque San Lucia. As the bazaar begins, there's a performance of traditional folk dancing and music
A number of travel agencies promote the Mayan Spectacular presented at Tulipanes Restaurant at Calle 42 462A. In my estimation, the show is melodramatic – more Hollywood than Mérida – and the food doesn't make up for what the show lacks. But you should judge for yourself. Admission charge for the show is US$6, not including dinner. For a more contemporary Mayan experience, go for dinner to the Restaurant El Tucho, described above

Cinemas

Many English films, some of fairly recent release, are screened in Mérida with Spanish subtitles. Buy your tickets (usually about US$0.75) before showtime and well in advance on weekends. The popular Cine Cantarell, Calle 60 No 488, next door to the Restaurant Express, and Cine Fantasio, facing the Parque Hidalgo between the Gran Hotel and Hotel Caribe, are convenient. There's also the Cine Olimpia Vistarama, Calle 60 between Calles 57 and 55, next to the Hotel Mérida Misión, the Cine Premier, at the corner of Calles 57 and 62 and the Cinema 59, Calle 59 between Calles 68 and 70.

THINGS TO BUY

From standard shirts and blouses to Mayan exotica, Mérida is *the* place on the peninsula to shop. Purchases you might want to consider include traditional Mayan clothing such as the colourful women's embroidered blouse called a huipil, a Panama hat woven from palm fibres, local craft items and of course the wonderfully comfortable Yucatecan hammock which holds you gently in a comfortable cotton web.

Mérida's main market, the Mercado Municipal Lucas do Gálvez, is bounded by Calles 56 and 56A at Calle 67, four blocks south-east of the Plaza Mayor. The market building is more or less next door to the city's main post office (Correos) and telegraph office, at the corner of Calles 65 and 56. The surrounding streets are all part of the large market district, lined with shops selling everything one might need.

The Bazar de Artesanías, Calle 67 at the corner of Calle 56A, is set up to attract tourists and their dollars. You should have a look at the stuff here, then compare the goods and prices with independent shops outside the Bazar.

Handicrafts

The place to go for high-quality craft and art items is the Casa de los Artesanías, Estado de Yucatán on Calle 63 between 64 and 66; look for the doorway marked 'Dirección de Desarrollo Artesanal DIF Yucatán'. It's open Monday to Friday from 8 am to 8 pm, Saturday from 8 am to 6 pm, closed Sunday. This is a government-supported marketing effort for local artisans. The selection of crafts is very good, quality usually high and prices reasonable.

You can also check out locally made crafts at the Museo Regional de Artesanías on Calle 59 between Calles 50 and 48. The work on display is superlative, but the items for sale are not as good. Admission is free and it's open from Tuesday to Saturday from 8 am to 8 pm and Sunday 9 am to 2 pm, closed Monday.

Guayaberas

Kary's on Calle 64 between Calles 65 and 67 sells a good selection of traditional Yucatecan guayaberas (fancy dress shirts) at reasonable prices. Check the cut, fit and stitching carefully before you buy any guayabera.

Panama Hats

Panama hats are woven from jipijapa palm leaves in caves and workshops in which the temperature and humidity are carefully controlled, as humid conditions keep the fibres pliable when the hat is being made. Once blocked and exposed to the relatively drier air outside, the hat is surprisingly resilient and resistant to crushing. The Campeche

town of Becal is the centre of the hat-weaving trade, but you can buy good examples of the hatmaker's art here in Mérida.

The best quality hats have a very fine, close weave of slender fibres. The coarser the weave, the lower the price should be. Prices range from a few dollars for a hat of basic quality to US$25 or more for top quality.

A store famous for its Panama hats is appropriately named Becal and is located at Calle 56 No 522. Another is El Becaleño, Calle 65 No 483, at the corner of Calle 56A, very near the post office. A third is La Casa de los Jipis, Calle 56 No 526, near Calle 65.

Hammocks

The fine strings of Yucatecan hammocks make them supremely comfortable. In the sticky heat of a Yucatán summer, most locals prefer sleeping in a hammock, where the air can circulate around them, rather than in a bed. Many inexpensive hotels used to have hammock hooks in the walls of all guest rooms, though the hooks are not so much in evidence today.

Yucatecan hammocks are normally woven from strong nylon or cotton string and dyed in various colours; there are also natural, undyed versions. In the old days, the finest, strongest, most expensive hammocks were woven from silk.

Hammocks come in several widths. From smallest to largest, the names generally used are *sencillo* (about 50 pairs of end strings, US$8), *doble* (100 pairs, US$10 to US$15), *matrimonial* (150 pairs, US$15 to US$20) and *matrimonial especial* or *quatro cajas* (175 pairs or more, US$20 and up). You must check to be sure that you're really getting the width that you are paying for. Because hammocks fold up small and the larger hammocks are more comfortable (though more expensive), consider the bigger sizes.

During your first few hours in Mérida you will be approached by pedlars on the street wanting to sell you hammocks and you will be approached every hour or so thereafter, as long as you stay. Pedlars may quote very low prices, but a price is only as good as the quality is high and the quality of street-sold hammocks is mediocre at best. If you want to buy from a vendor, check the particular hammock very carefully.

Here's what to look for in buying a hammock. Look closely at the string. It should be sturdy and tightly and evenly spun. Check the end loops, which should be fairly large and tightly wrapped in string. Many hammocks are made for sleepers of Mayan stature (ie, very short). To make sure you get a hammock long enough for you, hold the hammock at the point where the end strings join the main body of the hammock; raise your hand as high as your head; the other end of the body of the hammock should extend at least to the ground. In other words, the body of the hammock (not counting the end strings) should be as long as you are tall. In many cases, the hammocks sold by street vendors will be too short for you.

Open the hammock and look at the weave, which should be even, with few mistakes. Watch out for dirty patches and stains. Check the width. Any hammock looks very wide at first glance, but a matrimonial especial should be truly enormous, at least as wide as it is long and probably wider.

You can save yourself a lot of trouble by shopping at a hammock store with a good reputation. I first recommended La Poblana (☎ 21-65-03), at Calle 65 No 492 between Calles 58 and 60, a dozen years ago and I've never had a complaint about cheating or shoddy goods. Here you are welcome to ask questions and are not rushed into a purchase. In theory, prices are set, but some travellers report a small measure of success with bargaining. La Poblana will safely mail your purchase home for you, saving you the typical post office hassle. Some travellers report slightly cheaper prices for good quality at El Aguacate, Calle 58 No 604 at the corner of Calle 73. El Campesino at Calle 58 No 548 between Calles 69 and 71 is cheaper but provides less guidance – so you should really know what you are looking for and check quality.

You may be able to save a little money on your hammock purchase if you bus out to the nearby village of Tixcocob to watch them being woven. The bus runs regularly from the Progreso bus station south of the main plaza at Calle 62 No 524 between Calles 65 and 67. But if you don't want to expend the effort to go out there, you'll do fine in Mérida.

GETTING THERE & AWAY
Air
Most international flights to Mérida are connections through Mexico City or Cancún; the only nonstop international services are Aeroméxico's two daily flights from Miami.

Domestic service includes half a dozen Mexicana flights daily from Mexico City to Mérida and one or two by Aeroméxico as well. Aero Cozumel and Aerocaribe are taking over most of the intermediate air traffic between Cancún, Mérida and Mexico City, meaning that if you want to fly to or from Cancún (US$60 one way, US$94 round-trip excursion), Chetumal, Villahermosa, or Tuxtla Gutiérrez (for San Cristóbal de las Casas), you should talk to those airlines.

Mérida's modern airport is several km south-west of the centre off Highway 180 (Avenida de los Itzaes). There are car rental desks for Avis, Budget, Dollar, Hertz, Max, National and VW Rent. A Tourism Information booth can help with questions and hotel reservations. Note that there are no currency exchange facilities at Mérida's airport.

Bus
The Terminal de Autobuses operated by the Unión de Camioneros de Yucatán is on Calle 69 between 68 and 70, about six blocks south-west of the main plaza. This is the main – though not the only – bus station in the city. (If you're arriving from points east such as Cancún, Valladolid or Chichén Itzá, your Autobuses de Oriente Mérida-Puerto Juárez bus might make a stop, or even terminate the journey, at its garage on Calle 50 between Calles 65 and 67. The garage is six blocks east of the Plaza Mayor and about 12 blocks east of the Terminal de Autobuses.)

At the Terminal de Autobuses, you'll find a bank, telegraph office, travel agency, Yucatán state tourism booth, an instant B&W photo booth and a bank of Ladatel coin-operated long-distance telephones (next to the ticket window of the Autotransportes de Oriente Mérida-Puerto Juárez company).

Half a dozen different companies use the Terminal de Autobuses. Each company specialises in services to a certain part of the region or the country, but some companies' territories overlap. Shop around a bit before you buy your ticket, as fares, travel times and comfort can vary from one company to the next. Here's a quick rundown on the companies (their abbreviated name appears after the company name):

Autobuses de Oriente (ADO) – long-haul 1st-class routes to Campeche, Palenque, Villahermosa, Veracruz and Mexico City

Autotransportes Peninsulares (A Peninsulares) – frequent 1st-class buses to Chetumal

Autotransportes de Oriente Mérida-Puerto Juárez (A de O M-PJ) – frequent buses between Mérida and Cancún stopping at Chichén Itzá, Valladolid and Puerto Juárez (for Isla Mujeres boats); they also run buses to Tizimín and to Playa del Carmen (for Cozumel boats)

Autotransportes del Sur (A del Sur) – frequent buses to Uxmal, Kabah and Campeche and one bus a day to Villahermosa

Autotransportes del Caribe (A del Caribe) – nine buses daily to Ticul; also 1st and 2nd-class buses to Felipe Carrillo Puerto, Bacalar, Chetumal, Tulum and Akumal

Autotransportes del Sureste en Yucatán (A del Sureste) – one bus daily to Palenque and one to Tuxtla Gutiérrez

Here's information on trips to and from Mérida; all buses are daily and all times are by 1st-class bus (2nd class may be slower):

Akumal – 350 km, six or seven hours; three 2nd-class buses daily by A de O M-PJ and three by A del Caribe

Bacalar – 420 km, 8½ hours; four 1st-class buses (US$6.65), four 2nd-class buses (US$6.10) by A del Caribe

Campeche – 195 km (short route via Becal), three hours; 250 km (long route via Uxmal), four hours; 26 1st-class buses (US$3.15) by ADO; 13 2nd-class buses (US$2.90) by A del Sur

Cancún – 320 km, 5½ to six hours; almost every 30 minutes 1st class (US$5.50) by A de O M-PJ; 2nd-class buses (US$4.75) on the hour from 5 am to midnight (except no buses at 4, 7, 8, 9 and 10 pm) by A de O M-PJ

Chetumal – 456 km, eight to nine hours; seven 1st-class buses (US$8) by A Peninsulares and six 1st-class buses (US$8) by A del Caribe; four 2nd-class buses (US$7.25) by A del Caribe

Chichén Itzá – 116 km, 2½ to three hours; many 1st-class (US$2.50) and 2nd-class buses (US$2) by A de O M-PJ heading for Valladolid, Cancún, Playa del Carmen, etc. A special round-trip excursion bus by A de O M-PJ departs from Mérida at 8.45 am and returns from Chichén Itzá at 3 pm.

Felipe Carrillo Puerto – 310 km, 5½ to six hours; two 1st-class buses (US$5) by A del Caribe; others of this line may stop there as well. One 2nd-class bus (US$4.50) by A de O M-PJ.

Kabah – 101 km, two hours; six 1st-class buses (US$1.10) by A del Sur

Mexico City – 1550 km, 28 hours; six 1st-class buses (US$25.50) by ADO

Palenque – 556 km, 10 or 11 hours; one 1st-class bus (US$7.25) by A del Sureste directly to Palenque; some 1st-class ADO buses stop at Palenque as well. Many more will drop you at Catazaja, the main highway junction 27 km to the north of the town, from which you can hitchhike to the town.

Playa del Carmen – 385 km, seven hours; six 1st-class buses (US$6.50) and six 2nd-class buses (US$5.75) by A de O M-PJ

Progreso (leaves from another terminal – see below)

Ticul – 85 km, 1½ hours; nine 2nd-class buses (US$1.25) by A del Caribe

Tizimín – 210 km, four hours; three 1st-class buses (US$3.25) by A de O M-PJ; or take a bus to Valladolid and change there for Tizimín

Tulum – 320 km, six hours; three 2nd-class buses (US$6) via Cobá by A del Caribe; three 2nd-class buses (US$6.75) via Cancún by A de O M-PJ take two hours longer

Tuxtla Gutiérrez – 1296 km, 20 hours; one 1st-class bus (US$14) by A del Sureste, or take a bus to Villahermosa and change there for Tuxtla

Uxmal – 80 km, 1½ hours; eight 2nd-class buses (US$1.10) by A del Sur, or take a bus bound for Campeche or beyond by the inland (longer) route and get off at Uxmal

Veracruz – 1180 km, 18 hours; two 1st-class buses (US$18.25) by ADO

Villahermosa – 700 km, 10 hours; 13 1st-class buses (US$10.50) by ADO; one 2nd-class bus (US$9.50) by A del Sur

If you take an all-night bus, don't put anything valuable in the overhead racks, as there have been several reports of gear being stolen at night.

For buses to Progreso and the ruins at Dzibilchaltún, go to the Progreso bus station 1½ blocks south of the main plaza at Calle 62 No 524 between Calles 65 and 67. Buses depart every 15 minutes on the run to the Dzibilchaltún access road (15 km, 30 minutes, US$0.60) and Progreso (33 km, 45 minutes, US$0.75).

Those heading to the Celestún flamingo region can choose from several departures a day from the Autotransportes del Sur station at Calle 50 No 531 at the corner of Calle 67.

To Río Lagartos or San Felipe you will find Autotransportes del Noroeste buses departing three times daily from Calle 52 between Calles 63 and 65.

Train

In the Yucatán Peninsula, buses are preferable to trains in that they are considerably faster and infinitely safer. Rail robberies in some areas (between Mérida, Campeche and Palenque in particular) have reached epidemic proportions. There are no *dormitorios* to lock on trains travelling the peninsula – just vulnerable 1st and 2nd-class seating.

If you still want to get between Mérida and other points by rail, a train with no diner departs at midnight for Campeche, Palenque and ultimately Mexico City (two days journey). The station is at Calle 55 between Calles 46 and 48, about nine blocks northeast of the main plaza. Tickets should be bought several hours in advance.

Car

There are three ways to visit the old Mayan capital of Mayapán and the fascinating Puuc Route archaeological sites of Kabah, Sayil, Labná, Xlapak and Loltún: you can take a tour, take a bus to Kabah and walk many km (with the occasional hitchhike) in the hot sun, or you can rent a car.

Rental cars are expensive in Mexico, but cheaper in Mérida than in Cancún. Assume you will pay about US$60 per day for the cheapest car offered, usually a bottom-of-the-line Volkswagen or Nissan. If you can

find others to share the cost, car rental is the best way to see the Puuc Route sites. The longer the rental, the less you'll spend per day for the car.

I can strongly recommend a small local car rental company, Mexico Rent a Car (☎ (99) 27-49-16, 23-36-37), Calle 62 No 483E between Calles 59 and 57, owned and operated by Alvaro and Teresa Alonzo. Several friends of mine have used them for years with no complaints.

The big international car rental companies all have agencies in Mérida, the most active of which is Budget Rent-a-Car (☎ (99) 27-87-55), Paseo de Montejo Prolongación 497.

GETTING AROUND
To/From the Airport

Bus 79 ('Aviación') travels infrequently between the airport and city centre for US$0.17. Most arriving travellers use the Transporte Terrestre minibuses (US$1.75) to go from the airport to the centre; to return to the airport you must take a taxi (US$4).

Bus

Most parts of Mérida that you'll want to visit are within five or six blocks of the Plaza Mayor and are thus accessible on foot. Given the slow speed of city traffic, particularly in the market areas, travel on foot is also the fastest way to get around.

The city's bus system is confusing at best, with routes meandering through the city, finally terminating in a distant suburban neighbourhood. For exact route information, ask at the tourist office.

The bus system is supplemented by minibus jitneys, which are easier to use as they run shorter and more comprehensible routes. The minibus (colectivo) you're liable to find most useful is the Ruta 10 (US$0.20) which departs the corner of Calles 58 and 59, half a block east of the Parque Hidalgo and travels along the Paseo de Montejo to Itzamná.

To walk from the Terminal de Autobuses on Calle 69 between Calles 68 and 70 to the Plaza Mayor, exit the terminal to the street in front (Calle 69), turn right and walk three blocks, passing the Church of San Juan de Dios and a park, to Calle 62. Turn left on Calle 62 and walk the remaining three blocks north to the plaza.

Around Mérida

The region around Mérida is the heartland of late Mayan civilisation, abounding in ancient ruins, colonial towns, traditional crafts and even some beaches. Using Mérida as your base you can see many of the wonders of Yucatán on day trips, or you can stay the night in most of the sites worth visiting.

Mérida's heat can be oppressive, even in the winter. When it gets too hot and especially on hot weekends, Mérida's citizens flock to the beaches at Progreso, a mere 33 km north of the city. Along the way, you might want to stop at the ruined city of Dzibilchaltún. Besides an interesting ruin or two, the site boasts a cool, clear cenote dedicated to swimming.

DZIBILCHALTÚN

This was the longest continuously utilised Mayan administrative and ceremonial city, serving the Maya from 1500 BC or earlier until the European conquest in the 1540s. At the height of its greatness, Dzibilchaltún covered 80 sq km. Archaeological research in the 1960s mapped 31 sq km of the city, revealing some 8500 structures. Today there is little for the casual visitor to see except a few ruined pyramids, a sacbé (ceremonial road) or two, the interesting little Temple of the Seven Dolls and the cenote swimming pool.

Dzibilchaltún (Place of Inscribed Flat Stones) is a large site, open from 8 am to 5 pm every day; admission costs US$2.50.

As you enter past the museum, the cenote is 100 metres directly ahead; the Temple of the Seven Dolls is almost 1000 metres to the left .

Walking to the temple along the ancient ceremonial way, the scrubby, dry tropical vegetation and jagged limestone rubble crunching underfoot reminds one more of an archaeological site in the Middle East than a rainforest site like Guatemala's Tikal. This is indeed *la tropica seca*, the dry tropics, and the pyramids, while ruined, are not overgrown by the luxuriant verdure of a rainforest.

You can probe the mysteries of the Temple of the Seven Dolls much better from a distance than from close up. While still a good distance away from the temple, note that you can see right through the building's doors and windows on the east-west axis. But when you approach, this view is lost. The temple's construction is such that you can't see through from north to south at all. I suspect that the rising and setting sun of the equinoxes 'lit up' the temple's windows and doors, making them blaze like beacons and signalling this important turning-point in the year. Thus the temple is impressive not for its size or beauty, but for its precise astronomical orientation and its function in the Great Mayan Time Machine.

The Temple of the Seven Dolls got its name from seven grotesque dolls discovered here during excavations; they may have been used in some healing rite. A few are on display in the museum. Once you reach the temple, sit in its doorway, enjoy the view and also the breeze that wafts through. It's cool here!

On the walk back, note the Sendero Ecológico (Ecology Trail) which starts on the south side of the sacbé and winds through the scrub to rejoin the sacbé near the cenote. It'll take you about 15 or 20 minutes to walk the trail.

The Cenote Xlacah, now a public swimming pool, is over 40 metres deep. In 1958, an expedition sponsored by the National Geographic Society sent divers down and recovered some 30,000 Mayan artefacts, many of ritual significance. The most interesting of these are now on display in the site's small but good museum. But enough history – plunge in and cool off!

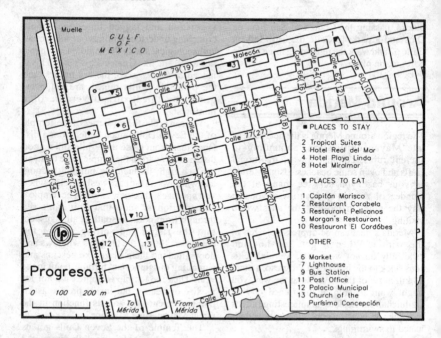

PLACES TO STAY

2 Tropical Suites
3 Hotel Real del Mar
4 Hotel Playa Linda
8 Hotel Miralmar

PLACES TO EAT

1 Capitán Marisco
2 Restaurant Carabela
3 Restaurant Pelicanos
5 Morgan's Restaurant
10 Restaurant El Cordóbes

OTHER

6 Market
7 Lighthouse
9 Bus Station
11 Post Office
12 Palacio Municipal
13 Church of the
   Purísima Concepción

Getting There & Away

Bus Buses depart every 15 minutes on the run to the Dzibilchaltún access road (15 km, 30 minutes, US$0.60) on the right (east) side of the highway. It's five km from the highway to the entrance of the ruins along a sleepy country road and through a little village; the best time to hitch a ride is in the morning. From the site entrance, it's another 700 metres to the building housing the museum, admission ticket window and soft drinks stand.

PROGRESO

Population 30,000

This is a seafarers' town, the port for Mérida and north-western Yucatán. The Yucatecan limestone shelf declines so gradually into the sea that a marvellously long *muelle* (pier) had to be built to reach the deep water. The arches of Progreso's famous *muelle* extended one km into the sea for years, but recent construction has taken the *muelle* a full 6.5 km into the water so that cruise ships can use Progreso as a port of call.

This same gradual slope of land into water is what makes Progreso's long beach so inviting. The waters are shallow, warm and safe from such dangers as riptide and undertow. Hurricane Gilbert wreaked its fury on Progreso's waterfront in the autumn of 1988. The destruction spurred efforts for urban renewal and the government has now tidied up the seafront with lots of palm trees, a seaside boulevard and promenade and nice facilities for beachgoers.

Progreso is normally a sleepy little town, but on weekends, especially in summer, it seems as if all of Mérida is here. If it's crowded, walk six km east along the palm-fringed beach to the tiny village of Chicxulub, a pleasant escape from the crowds. Alternatively, five km west of Progreso is Yucalpetén, whose new harbour is stealing some of the thunder from Progreso's business. For true solitude, walk a few km west of Yucalpetén to the tranquil sands of Chelem and Chuburná.

History

After the founding of Mérida, the conquistador Francisco de Montejo advised his son that a road should be built to the coast, facilitating the export of goods. The port of Sisal, south-west of Progreso, served that function until the middle of the 19th century, when its shallow harbour and distance from Mérida proved inadequate for the needs of the growing henequen industry. In 1840, local leaders suggested the site of Progreso, but the War of the Castes delayed the project until 1872 when it was established as a village. During the heyday of the henequen boom, Progreso prospered as Yucatán's most prominent port. A new harbour is scheduled for construction in the hope that cruise ships will dock here and Progreso will once again prosper.

Orientation

Progreso is long and narrow, stretched out along the seashore. If you want to move around the town and you don't have your own vehicle, you'll find yourself fighting the distances.

Though Progreso has an apparently logical street grid, it illogically is subject to two numbering systems fifty numbers apart. One system has the city centre's streets numbered in the 60s, 70s and 80s, another has them in the 10s, 20s and 30s. Thus you might see a street sign on Calle 30 calling it Calle 80 or on a map Calle 10 might also be referred to as Calle 60. I've included both systems on my map.

What anyone coming to Progreso wants to find first are the beach and the muelle. The highway into town becomes Calle 78 (one-way northbound) which leads past the main square directly to the muelle. To the right (east) of the muelle is the Malecón, or seaside promenade and beach, stretching for one km eastward. The Malecón, extending from Calle 60 (also called Calle 10) in the east to Calle 78 (or Calle 28) and the muelle in the west, is one way westbound for motor vehicles.

The bus stations are near the main square. It's six short blocks from the main square to the Malecón and the muelle.

Places to Stay

Progreso is looked upon as a resort, if a modest one, so rooms here tend to be a bit more expensive than in other Yucatecan towns. On Sundays in July and August, even the cheapest hotels fill up.

The best of Progreso's budget inns is the *Hotel Miralmar* (☎ (993) 5-05-52), Calle 27 No 124 at the corner of Calle 76, offering rooms with private shower, fan and one double bed for US$10.50, with two beds for US$12.50. Rooms on the upper floor are preferable – they're not as dungeon-like as the ground-floor rooms.

Several good lodging places are located right on the Malecón facing the sea. *Hotel Playa Linda* (☎ (993) 5-11-57), Malecón at Calle 76, is a simple little two-storey place with rooms renting for US$12.50 double with two beds. You get a private shower, a fan, lounge chairs on the front terrace, a small shop selling souvenirs, snacks and cold drinks and a moped rental agency. The beach is just on the other side of the Malecón.

Three blocks east at the corner of Malecón and Calle 70 are two more hotels. *Tropical Suites* (☎ (993) 5-12-63) is the nicest I've mentioned so far, with tidy rooms with showers and fans going for US$14.50 a double. Some rooms have sea views.

Hotel Real del Mar (☎ (993) 5-05-23), behind the Restaurant Pelicanos, is an older hostelry which looks its age sometimes, but is still a good deal as it's right on the Malecón. Rooms with shower and fan cost US$12.50 a single/double in one bed, US$16 a double/triple in two beds, or US$18 for a suite.

Places to Eat

Seafood is the strong point on the menus of Progreso's restaurants, of course. Note that if you come on a day trip to Progreso, you can often change clothes at the *vestidores* (changing cubicles) attached to most beachfront restaurants.

An all-purpose inexpensive eatery on the north side of the main square is *Restaurant El Cordóbes*, at the corner of Calles 81 and 80, open from early morning until late at night. Standard fare – tacos, enchiladas, sandwiches, chicken, etc – is served at good prices ranging from US$1.25 to US$3; fish, at US$3 to US$5 is the strong suit. It's a plain, simple place with good food and low prices.

About the best prices you can find at an eatery on the Malecón are at *Morgan's*, Malecón between Calles 80 and 78, a Mexican beach restaurant where you can get a full fish dinner for about US$7.50, everything included.

As you move eastward along the Malecón, restaurant prices rise. *Restaurant Carabela*, Malecón between Calles 70 and 72, is the spot for the young and hip beach crowd who come for the high-volume soft rock music (the bass notes shake the tables). Shady tables here have views of the Malecón and the sea and the menu offers seafood cocktails and ceviches for US$3.25 to US$4.25, fish for US$4.50 to US$5.75; hamburgers and other sandwiches are under US$3.

At the eastern end of the Malecón between Calles 62 and 60, almost one km from the muelle, stands *Capitán Marisco* (☎ 5-06-39), perhaps Progreso's fanciest seafood restaurant and certainly one of its most pleasant. The attractive nautical decor of the breezy, high-ceilinged dining room spills over to the shaded terrace from which there are fine panoramas of the beach and the sea. Clientele here is drawn from the well-to-do vacationers who rent or own the villas near this part of the Malecón. Begin a meal with shrimp cocktail or octopus ceviche, order the mixed seafood plate, add a glass or two of wine and your bill might be US$15 per person, all inclusive. A bonus here is the restaurant's own vestidores where you can change into your bathing suit for a dip in the sea before lunch or dinner.

Getting There & Away

Both Dzibilchaltún and Progreso are due north of Mérida along a fast four-lane highway that's basically a continuation of the Paseo de Montejo. If you're driving, head north on the Paseo and follow signs for Progreso. Those travelling by bus must go to the special Progreso bus station 1½ blocks south of the main plaza at Calle 62 No 524 between Calles 65 and 67.

Progreso is 18 km (20 minutes) beyond the Dzibilchaltún turn-off. A bus from Mérida to Progreso costs US$0.75 one way.

WEST TO CELESTÚN

Famed as a bird sanctuary, Celestún makes a good beach-and-bird day trip from Mérida. Although this region abounds in anhingas and egrets, most birdwatchers come here to see the flamingos.

The town is located at the southern tip of a spit of land between the Río Esperanza and the Gulf of Mexico. The beach here is not the peninsula's most appealing and on some days fierce afternoon winds swirl clouds of choking dust through the town. The dust makes the sea silty and therefore unpleasant for swimming in the afternoon.

Given the winds, the best time to see birds is in the morning. Hire a boat from the bridge where launches are docked about one km from the town. The rental should run to about US$10 for a 1½ hour tour of the flamingo-inhabited areas.

Places to Stay

The *Hotel Gutiérrez*, Calle 12 No 22, is the top budget choice, with well-kept rooms with fan and bath costing US$10. Cheaper and not as nice is the *Hotel San Julio* (☎ 1-85-89) at Calle 12 No 92, where singles with fan and bath cost US$7 and doubles US$9.

Places to Eat

For good food and variety, dine at *La Playita* on the shore. *Restaurant Celestún* also serves reasonably good seafood.

Getting There & Away

Buses run from Mérida's Autotransportes del Sur station on Calle 50 No 531 at Calle 67. They depart hourly until 2 pm and every two hours thereafter until 10 pm. The 92-km trip takes about 1½ to two hours and costs US$1.20.

Uxmal & the Puuc Route

La Ruta Maya continues southwards from Mérida, penetrating a region rich in ancient Mayan sites which have been restored and made accessible to the public. The towns of this region, Acanceh, Ticul and Oxkutzcab, provide views of how the Maya live today.

You cannot possibly visit all of these towns and ruins in a day trip from Mérida. Uxmal alone deserves most of a day, the Puuc Route sites another day. If time is short, go to Uxmal and Kabah. Otherwise, plan to stay overnight for at least one or two nights along the way. Lodgings at Uxmal are expensive; those in Ticul are cheap.

Ticul is also well known as the place to get excellent local handicrafts as well as being a good stopover on the way to Campeche.

After exploring the archaeological wealth of this area, head south past Bolonchén de Rejón and Hopelchén to Cayal and the turn-off for the ruins of Edzná and finally to Campeche. If your goal is the Caribbean coast, go south-east from Ticul and Oxkutzcab to Felipe Carrillo Puerto, then north to the coast or south to Chetumal and Belize.

GETTING AROUND

Bus Let's face it, the best way to see all there is to see in the area south of Mérida is by private car. Bus services to some points (Uxmal, Kabah, Ticul, Oxkutzcab) are frequent, but most of the Puuc Route sites are virtually impossible to reach by public transport, and to sites such as Mayapán, transport is fairly inconvenient – you'll spend a good deal of time waiting on country roads in the hot sun. If you decide to go by bus, plan to walk from one Puuc Route site to the next (say, between Kabah and Labná), with the occasional hitchhike. I've included exact distances between sites so that you'll know what you're in for.

Car If you rent a car, plan on at least two days and preferably three, to see all there is to see

here. Spend the first day driving from Mérida to Uxmal, with a stop along the way at the hacienda of Yaxcopoil. Spend the night at Uxmal and continue to Kabah and the Puuc Route sites the next day. You can return to Mérida for the night, or to Uxmal, or go to Ticul. If you return via Yucatán state highway No 18, you can stop for a visit to the ruins of Mayapán and a look at the pyramid in Acanceh.

Those going directly to Campeche should take the shorter, faster route via Highway 180.

There are actually three major routes between Mérida and Campeche. The westernmost route – the fastest route to Campeche – leaves Mérida by Avenida de los Itzaes, passes the airport and travels through the towns of Uman, Chochola, Kopoma and Maxcaná on its way to Campeche.

The more interesting route to Campeche heads south-east at Uman to Uxmal and Kabah; after Kabah you can make a detour east to see the Puuc Route archaeological sites at Sayil, Labná, and Xlapak as well as the Grutas de Loltún.

It's 78 km from Mérida to Uxmal via Highway 180 south-west to Uman, then Highway 261 to Muna and Uxmal. Highway 261 continues south to Kabah and the junction with the road to the Puuc Route sites of Sayil, Xlapak and Labná. After the junction, Highway 261 continues south to the Grutas de Xtacumbilxunaan, the town of Bolonchén de Rejón and Hopelchén, where you turn to reach the ruins of Dzibalchén. From Hopelchén the highway heads west towards the turning for Edzná and beyond the turning, Campeche. This is a fairly well-travelled bus route and if you don't have your own car, this is probably the way you'll come. The urban conglomeration of Mérida extends almost to the suburb of Uman, 17 km from the centre. At Uman you turn left and head south towards Muna. After 16 km

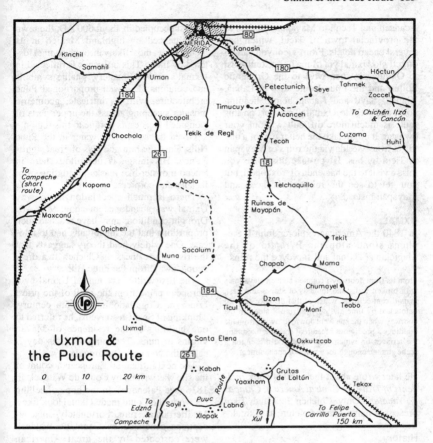

Uxmal & the Puuc Route

0   10   20 km

---

there's a bend in the road and, on the right-hand (west) side of the road, the hacienda of Yaxcopoil.

The hacienda's French Renaissance-style buildings have been restored and turned into a Museum of the 17th Century. This vast estate specialised in the growing and processing of henequen and here you can see how it was all done.

Twenty-nine km south of Yaxcopoil is Muna, an old town with several interesting colonial churches, including the former Convento de la Asunción and the churches of Santa María, San Mateo and San Andrés.

Another 16 km south of Muna is Uxmal; the highway passes the Hotel Misión Uxmal on the right and comes to the Hotel Hacienda Uxmal. Just across the highway from the hotel is the short entrance road (400 metres) to the ruins.

The third, easternmost route south goes via Acanceh and the ruins of the old Mayan capital city of Mayapán before reaching Ticul, from which you can head north-west and south to Uxmal, or south-east to Oxkutzcab, Loltún and the Puuc Route sites, ending up at Uxmal. Take Yucatán state highway No 18 south-east via Kanasin,

Acanceh and Tecoh to Mayapán, then on to' the provincial town of Ticul, which has several cheap hotels. From Ticul you can go directly to Uxmal via Muna or go south-east to Oxkutzcab, then west to the Grutas de Loltún and the Puuc Route sites of Labná, Xlapak, Sayil and Kabah before heading north and west to Uxmal. Transport on this route is much more difficult without your own car. It might take the better part of a day to get from Mérida via the ruins of Mayapán to Ticul by bus. If you take this route you miss a visit to the hacienda of Yaxcopoil, but you get to see the ruins at Acanceh and Mayapán instead.

UXMAL

In 1840 the American explorer John L Stephens stood atop the Pyramid of the Magician at Uxmal and surveyed the ruins:

From its front doorway I counted sixteen elevations, with broken walls and mounds of stones and vast, magnificent edifices, which at that distance seemed untouched by time and defying ruin. I stood in the doorway when the sun went down, throwing from the buildings a prodigious breadth of shadow, darkening the terraces on which they stood and presenting a scene strange enough for a work of enchantment.

He later wrote about them in his book *Incidents of Travel in Central America, Chiapas & Yucatan*. Only Chichén Itzá and Tikal present as magnificent a picture as Uxmal.

History

Set in the Puuc Hills, which lent their name to the architectural patterns in this region, Uxmal was an important city during the Late Classic period (600-900 AD) of a region which encompassed the satellite towns of Sayil, Kabah, Xlapak and Labná. Although Uxmal means Thrice Built in Mayan, it was actually reconstructed five times.

That a sizable population flourished at all in this area is a mystery, as there is precious little water in the region. The Maya built a series of lime-lined reservoirs and cisterns *(chultunes)* to catch and hold water during the dry season which must have been adequate.

First occupied in about 600 AD, the town is influenced by highland Mexico in its architecture, most likely through contact fostered by trade. This influence is reflected in Uxmal's serpent imagery, phallic symbols and columns. The well-proportioned Puuc architecture, with its intricate, geometric mosaics sweeping across the upper parts of elongated façades, is unique to this region.

Given the scarcity of water in the Puuc Hills, Chac the rain god was of great significance. His image is ubiquitous here in stucco monster-like masks protruding from façades and cornices.

There is much speculation as to why Uxmal was abandoned in about 900 AD. Drought conditions may have reached such proportions that the inhabitants had to relocate. One widely held theory suggests that the rise to greatness of Chichén Itzá drew people away from the Puuc Hills.

The first written account of Uxmal by a European came from the quill of the priest López de Cogullado in the 16th century. Thinking of Spanish convents, he referred to one building as the residence of Mayan virgins or nuns. The temple to this day is called the Nunnery Quadrangle.

The next influential European account of the site was written by Count de Waldeck in 1836 (see Palenque). In the hope of selling his work, the Count made Uxmal look like a Mediterranean ruin. Fortunately, misconceptions generated by Count de Waldeck were corrected by the great American archaeologist John L Stephens and his British illustrator Frederick Catherwood, who wrote about and drew the site with accuracy.

Uxmal was excavated in 1929 by Frans Blom. His was the first modern excavation and paved the way for others. Although much has been restored, there is still a good deal to discover.

Orientation & Information

As you come into the site from the highway, you'll enter a car park (US$0.40 per car); the Hotel Villa Arqueológica is to the left at the end of a short entrance road. You enter the

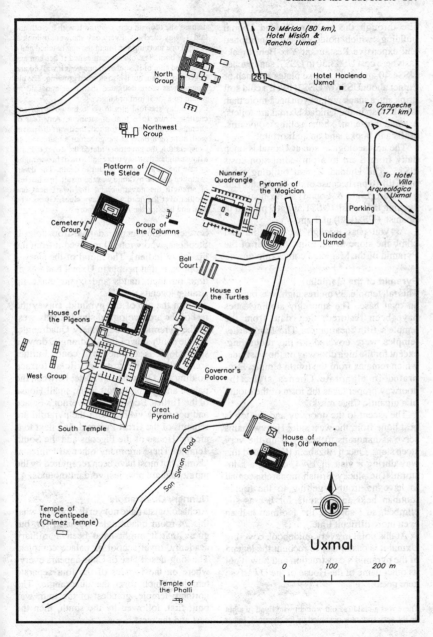

To Mérida (80 km),
Hotel Misión &
Rancho Uxmal

Hotel Hacienda
Uxmal

To Campeche
(171 km)

North
Group

Northwest
Group

To Hotel
Villa
Arqueológica
Uxmal

Platform of
the Stelae

Nunnery
Quadrangle

Pyramid of
the Magician

Parking

Cemetery
Group

Group of
the Columns

Unidad
Uxmal

Ball
Court

House of
the Turtles

House of
the Pigeons

West Group

Governor's
Palace

Great
Pyramid

House of
the Old Woman

South Temple

San Simon Road

Temple of
the Centipede
(Chimez Temple)

Temple of
the Phalli

Uxmal

0   100   200 m

site through the modern Unidad Uxmal building, which holds the air-conditioned and expensive Restaurant Yax-Beh; breakfasts here cost US$3.50 to US$7, sandwiches US$4.40 and main course plates at lunch or dinner about US$6 or US$7. Even a cold soft drink and a snack will set you back more than US$1. Also in the Unidad Uxmal are toilets, a small museum, shops selling souvenirs, crafts and books, and an auditorium.

The archaeological site at Uxmal is open daily from 8 am to 5 pm; admission costs US$5. The Unidad Uxmal building stays open till 10 pm because of the 45-minute Luz y Sonido (Light & Sound) show, held each evening in English (US$1.50) at 9 pm and in Spanish (US$0.80) at 7 pm.

As you pass through the turnstile and climb the slope to the ruins, the rear of the Pyramid of the Magician comes into view.

Pyramid of the Magician

This tall temple, 39 metres high, was built on an oval base. The smoothly sloping sides have been restored; they date from the temple's fifth incarnation. The four earlier temples were covered in the rebuilding, except for the high doorway on the west side, which remains from the fourth temple. Decorated in elaborate Chenes style, the doorway proper takes the form of the mouth of a gigantic Chac mask.

The ascent to the doorway and the top is best done from the west side. Heavy chains serve as handrails to help you up the very steep steps. Queen Elizabeth II ascended this way during a visit in 1974, during a rainstorm. The plucky British monarch seemed to have no trouble getting to the top; a footman held an umbrella for her as she climbed, so I suppose the footman had an even more difficult time.

At this point in every guidebook covering Uxmal it is customary to recount the legend of the pyramid's construction and how it got its other name of the House of the Dwarf, so here goes:

There was a childless old woman who lived in a hut on the very spot now occupied by the pyramid. In her distress she took an egg, covered it with a cloth and laid it away carefully. Every day she went to look at it, until one morning she found the egg hatched and a creature born. The old woman called it her son and took good care of it, so that in one year it walked and talked like a man, but it also stopped growing. The old woman was more delighted than ever and said he would be a great lord or king.

One day she told him to go to the governor and challenge him to a trial of strength. Any feat of strength the governor performed, the dwarf did just as well, striking a blow at the governor's manhood. In exasperation, the governor ordered the dwarf to build a house higher than any other and to do it in one night, or else the dwarf would be put to death. The dwarf complied and the pyramid was the result. In a last test of strength the governor and the dwarf beat one another over the head with heavy clubs. Guess who won and became the new governor?

So there's the legend, adapted from John L Stephens, who wrote, 'I received it from the lips of an Indian'. The moral of the story, I suppose, is that people in Uxmal had lots of time on their hands and could make up strange legends.

From the top of the pyramid, survey the rest of the archaeological site. Directly west of the pyramid is the Nunnery Quadrangle. On the south side of the quadrangle, down a short slope, is a ruined ball court. Further south stands the great artificial terrace holding the Governor's Palace; between the palace and the ball court is the small House of the Turtles. Beyond the Governor's Palace and not really visible from the pyramid are remains of the Great Pyramid, and next to it are the House of the Pigeons and the South Temple. There are many other structures at Uxmal, but most have been recaptured by the jungle and are now just verdant mounds.

Nunnery Quadrangle

Archaeologists have not yet deciphered what this 74-room quadrangle was used for, but guess that it might have been a military academy, royal school or palace complex. The long-nosed face of Chac appears everywhere on the façades of the four separate temples which form the quadrangle. The northern temple, grandest of the four, was built first, followed by the south, then the east and the west.

Several decorative elements on the façades show signs of Mexican, perhaps Totonac, influence. The feathered serpent (Quetzalcóatl) motif along the top of the west temple's façade is one of these. Note also the stylised depictions of the na, or Mayan thatched hut, over some of the doorways in the northern building. The na motif alternates with stacks of Chac masks over the doors. Similar na depictions are over the doors of the southern building as well.

Ball Court

Pass through the corbelled arch in the middle of the south building of the quadrangle and continue down the slope to the ball court, which is much less impressive than the great ball court at Chichén Itzá.

House of the Turtles

Climb the steep slope up to the artificial terrace on which stands the Governor's Palace. At the top of the climb, on the right, is the House of the Turtles, which takes its name from the turtles carved on the cornice. The frieze of short columns or 'rolled mats' which runs around the top of the temple is characteristic of the Puuc style. Turtles were associated by the Maya with the rain god Chac. According to Mayan myth, when the people suffered from drought so did the turtles and both prayed to Chac to send rain.

Governor's Palace

When Stephens laid eyes on the Governor's Palace, he wrote:

There is no rudeness or barbarity in the design or proportions; on the contrary, the whole wears an air of architectural symmetry and grandeur; and as the stranger ascends the steps and casts a bewildered eye along its open and desolate doors, it is hard to believe that he sees before him the work of a race in whose epitaph, as written by historians, they are called ignorant of art... If it stood...in Hyde Park or the Garden of the Tuileries, it would form a new order...not unworthy to stand side by side with the remains of Egyptian, Grecian and Roman art.

The magnificent façade of the palace, nearly 100 metres long, has been called 'the finest

Chac mask on corner of building, Uxmal

structure at Uxmal and the culmination of the Puuc style' by Mayanist Michael D Coe. The style is named for the Puuc Hills, the low range of hills to be seen around Uxmal, the highest of which rises to barely over 100 metres. Buildings in Puuc style have walls filled with rubble, faced with cement and then covered in a thin veneer of limestone squares; the lower part of the façade is plain, the upper part festooned with stylised Chac faces and geometric designs, often lattice-like or fretted. Other elements of Puuc style are decorated cornices, rows of half-columns as in the House of the Turtles and round columns in doorways as in the palace at Sayil. The stones forming the corbelled vaults in Puuc style are shaped like boots.

When Stephens visited Uxmal in 1840, the façade of the palace was virtually intact except for the collapse of several wooden lintels. These had been cut from a very hard wood found near Lake Petén in Guatemala; they had been in place, but showed signs of worms, rot and other destruction. One of the lintels still in place was beautifully carved. To preserve it, Stephens and his local workers painstakingly removed it, wrapped it in 10 cm of grass padding covered by burlap and shipped it to New York along with many other valuable artefacts carefully collected during his expeditions. The museum holding Stephens' collection, including the lintel from the Governor's Palace, was completely destroyed by fire a short time afterwards.

Great Pyramid
Adjacent to the Governor's Palace, this 32-metre mound has been restored only on the northern side. There is a quadrangle at the top which archaeologists theorise was largely destroyed in order to construct another pyramid above it. This work, for reasons unknown, was never completed. At the top are some stucco carvings of Chac, birds and flowers.

House of the Pigeons
West of the great pyramid sits a structure whose roofcomb is latticed with a pigeonhole pattern – hence the building's name. The nine honeycombed triangular belfries sit on top of a building which was once part of a quadrangle. The base is so eroded that it is difficult for archaeologists to guess its function.

House of the Old Woman & Temple of the Phalli
Both sites are located between the main highway and the San Simon road, south of the Governor's Palace. The House of the Old Woman, largely rubble, was, according to Mayan mythology, the home of the dwarf magician's mother, a sorceress. Just to the south sits the Temple of the Phalli, festooned with phallic sculptures. Some of these served as spouts to drain water from the roof. Some archaeologists think the temple was constructed by later invaders, as the Maya are not believed to have had any phallic cult.

Cemetery Group
Lying on the path west of the ball court, these stone altars have skull-and-crossbone sculptures, but there is no real evidence that this was a cemetery.

Places to Stay & Eat – bottom end
As there is no town, not even a village, at Uxmal, only the archaeological site and several top-end hotels, you cannot depend upon finding cheap food or lodging. Campers can pitch their tents five km north of the ruins on Highway 261, the road to Mérida, at *Rancho Uxmal*. The rate is US$2 per person. Several serviceable guestrooms with shower and fan go for US$16 a double, a bit expensive for what you get, but cheap for Uxmal. You can have a filling lunch or dinner platter in the thatch-roofed restaurant for about US$4 or US$5. It may take you 45 to 55 minutes to walk here – in the hot sun – from the ruins; there's some possibility of hitching a ride.

Other than the Rancho Uxmal, there's no cheap lodging in the area. If you don't want to return to Mérida for the night, make your way to Ticul.

As for food, the best thing to do is to bring your own food with you from Mérida. If you haven't done that, try the aforementioned *Restaurant Yax-Beh* in the Unidad Uxmal. It's not cheap, but it is air-conditioned and if you linger over your sandwich long enough you might get your money's worth out of the cool air.

Otherwise, try the *Posada Uxmal Restaurant Nicté-Ha*, just across the highway from the road to the ruins, on the grounds of the Hotel Hacienda Uxmal. This simple eatery is open from 12.30 to 7 pm daily and offers sandwiches, fruit salads and similar fare at prices slightly lower than those at the Yax-Beh. Often they'll allow you to use the hotel's swimming pool after you've bought a meal, which is a wonderful bonus.

Places to Stay & Eat – top end
The *Hotel Hacienda Uxmal* (☎ 4-71-42), 500 metres from the ruins across the

highway, originally housed the archaeologists who explored and restored Uxmal. High ceilings with fans, good cross-ventilation and wide, tiled verandahs set with rocking-chairs make this an exceptionally pleasant and comfortable place to stay and the beautiful swimming pool is a dream come true on a sweltering hot day. Many rooms have both bathtub and shower; several triples serve families and small groups.

Meals in the dining room are good, though not exceptionally so – and they are a bit pricey at US$7 for breakfast and US$16 for lunch or dinner. Rooms cost US$50 a single or double, but with breakfast and dinner included the price rises to almost US$100 a double. You can supposedly make reservations in Mérida at the Mérida Travel Service in the Hotel Casa del Balam (☎ (99) 24-88-44), at the corner of Calles 60 and 57, but they seem not to know the correct room prices and have always told me the hotel is full, even if it isn't.

Hotel Villa Arqueológica Uxmal (In Mérida, Apdo Postal 449, ☎ (99) 24-70-53) is the closest lodging to the ruins. Run by Club Med, this attractive modern hotel offers a swimming pool, tennis courts, a good French-inspired restaurant and air-conditioned guestrooms for US$40/44 a single/double. Spacious two-bedroom family rooms cost US$55. In the restaurant, you can have a very good dinner for US$18 to US$30 per person. A cold beer by the pool costs US$1.50.

The *Hotel Misión Inn Uxmal* (in Mérida ☎ (99) 24-73-08) is the newest of the hotels, set on a hilltop 2 km north of the turn-off to the ruins. Many rooms have balcony views of Uxmal and all are air-conditioned. Facilities include a swimming pool, restaurant and bar. Rooms are priced at US$38/40 a single/double.

If you tour the ruins in the morning, then want lunch before returning to the ruins, your best bet is the *Restaurant Yax-Beh* in the Unidad Uxmal. For a more elaborate and delicious lunch, make the five-minute walk to the *Hotel Villa Arqueológica Uxmal*. After lunch they won't mind if you use their swimming pool for a cooling dip. The same goes for the *Hotel Hacienda Uxmal*.

Getting There & Away

Air An airstrip is under construction near Uxmal. When it is finished routes from Cancún will be developed, making it possible for Cancúnites to visit Uxmal on a day excursion.

Bus From Mérida's Terminal de Autobuses it's 80 km (1½ hours) to Uxmal. Eight 2nd-class (US$1.10) buses of the Autobuses del Sur line make the trip daily and there are other buses as well. They'll drop you right at the turn-off to the ruins, only 400 metres away. For the return trip to Mérida, wait by the Hotel Hacienda Uxmal and flag down a bus as it approaches. In late afternoon there may be standing room only.

If you're going to Ticul, hop on a bus heading north, get off at Muna and get another bus eastwards to Ticul.

For buses to Kabah, the Puuc Route turn-off and points on the road to Campeche, flag down a bus at the turn-off to the ruins.

THE PUUC ROUTE

Uxmal is undoubtedly the finest of the Puuc sites, but the ruins at Kabah, Sayil, Xlapak, Labná and the Grutas de Loltún offer a deeper acquaintance with the Puuc Mayan civilisation. The Palace of Masks at Kabah and El Palacio at Sayil are really worth seeing and if you're not prepared to make the rounds of all the Puuc sites I'd suggest that you visit at least these two. The Grutas de Loltún (Loltún Caves) are also impressive, especially if you enjoy visiting cool caves. You can then continue to Oxkutzcab and Ticul if you like. The easiest and fastest but most expensive way to visit these sites is by private car; next best is an organised tour from Mérida. But you can get around by bus and hitchhiking if you allow enough time.

Kabah

Heading south-east from Uxmal, 15 km brings you to the village of Santa Elena, where the highway turns south. Another 3.5

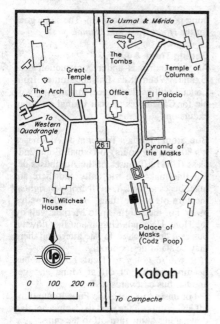

Kabah

Each of these mosaic masks consists of more than two dozen carved stones. The temple is unusual in having several series of rooms, with both front and back chambers.

The temple's Mayan name, Codz Poop (Rolled Mat) is explained in various ways by archaeologists and travel writers, none of them convincing. John L Stephens wrote:

> To many of these structures the Indians have given names stupid, senseless and unmeaning, having no reference to history or tradition. This one they call Xcocpoop, which means in Spanish petato doblado, or a straw hat doubled up; the name having reference to the crushed and flattened condition of the façade and the prostration of the rear wall of the building.

Other Kabah Ruins To the north of the Palace of Masks is a small pyramid. Behind and to the left of the Palace of Masks is El Palacio, with a broad façade having several doorways; in the centre of each doorway is a column, a characteristic of the Puuc architectural style. El Palacio at Sayil is somewhat similar in design, but much larger and grander.

Walk around the left side of El Palacio and follow a path into the jungle for several hundred metres to the Temple of Columns, called by John L Stephens the Tercera Casa, famous for the rows of semi-columns on the upper part of its façade. The effect is similar to that on the House of the Turtles at Uxmal, but this temple is much larger and grander, with lots more columns.

Cross the highway, walk up the slope and on your right you'll pass a high mound of stones that was once the Gran Teocalli, or Great Temple. Continue straight on to the sacbé, or cobbled elevated ceremonial road, and look to the right to see a monumental arch with the Mayan corbelled vault (two straight stone surfaces leaned against one another, meeting at the top). This arch is ruined; the one at Labná is in much better condition. It is said that the sacbé here runs past the arch and through the jungle all the way to Uxmal, terminating at a smaller arch; in the other direction it went to Labná. Once all of Yucatán was connected by these marvellous 'white roads' of rough limestone.

km brings you to the Zona Arqueológica Puuc and the ruins of Kabah. The highway passes right through the middle of the site, which is open from 8 am to 5 pm; admission costs US$4.

The guard shack and souvenir shop are on the east side of the highway as you approach. The day I was there a hawk wheeled overhead in the superheated air as scratchy mariachi music entertained the guards and shopkeeper. Cold drinks and junky snacks are available.

Palace of Masks The Palace of Masks, set on its own high terrace, is truly an amazing sight, its façade covered in nearly 300 masks of Chac, the rain god or sky serpent. Unlike other Puuc buildings, the lower part of this façade is not severely plain; the decoration of masks extends from the base of the building all the way to the top. So Chacified is the façade that you enter some of the rooms by stepping on a Chac mask's hooked nose!

Beyond the sacbé, about 600 metres farther from the road, are several other complexes of buildings, none as impressive as what you've already seen. The Western Quadrangle (Cuadrángulo del Oeste) has some decoration of columns and masks. North of the quadrangle are the Temple of the Key Patterns and the Temple of Lintels; the latter had intricately carved lintels of tough sapodilla wood similar to those that used to be in the Governor's Palace at Uxmal. And, like the ones at Uxmal, John L Stephens had them removed and shipped to New York for 'safekeeping', where they were destroyed in a fire shortly after their arrival. Luckily, Stephens' assistant Frederick Catherwood had made detailed drawings of the lintels before they were shipped.

Getting There & Away Kabah is 101 km from Mérida, a ride of about two hours, or just over 18 km south of Uxmal. Six 1st-class buses of the Autobuses del Sur line make the run daily, continuing to Campeche and returning along the same route; a one-way ticket costs US$1.10. To return to Mérida, stand on the east side of the road at the entrance to the ruins and flag down a bus. Try hitchhiking as well, because the buses are often full and thus won't stop. You may have the same problem of full buses if you stand on the west side of the highway and flag down a bus to take you to the Puuc Route turn-off, five km south of Kabah, or to other sites along Highway 261 farther south.

Many visitors come to Kabah by private car and may be willing to give you a lift southwards on the Puuc Route. You should offer to share fuel expenses as a courtesy. Those with cars would make this writer very happy if they offered rides to others, as transport along the Puuc Route is so difficult – and the sun on the road so hot.

Sayil
Five km south of Kabah a road turns east: this is the Puuc Route. Despite the interesting archaeological sites along this route, there is not much traffic and hitchhiking can be difficult. The ruins of Sayil are 4.5 km from the

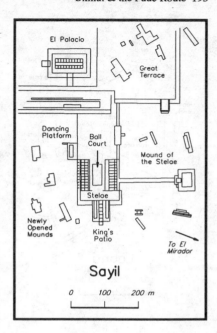

Sayil

junction with Highway 261, on the south side of the road. Sayil is open from 8 am to 5 pm daily; admission costs US$1.

El Palacio Sayil is best known for El Palacio, the huge three-tiered building with a façade some 85 metres long that makes one think of the Minoan palaces on Crete. The distinctive columns of Puuc architecture are used here over and over, as supports for the lintels, as decoration between doorways and as a frieze above the doorways, alternating with huge stylised Chac masks and 'descending gods'.

Climb to the top level of the Palacio and look to the north to see several chultunes, or stone-lined cisterns, in which precious rainwater was collected and stored for use during the dry season. Some of these chultunes can hold more than 30,000 litres.

Should you visit the Palacio just before Easter, you can test a local superstition. John L Stephens, after his visit to Sayil (which he

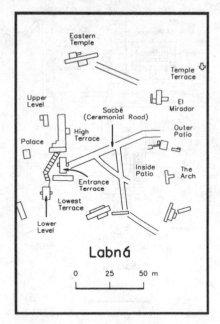

Labná

0   25   50 m

called Zayi), wrote that the Indians 'believed that the ancient buildings were haunted and, as in the remote region of Santa Cruz del Quiché, they said that on Good Friday of every year music was heard sounding among the ruins.'

El Mirador If you take the path southwards from the palace for about 400 metres you come to the temple named El Mirador, with its interesting rooster-like roofcomb once painted a bright red. About 100 metres beyond El Mirador by the path to the left is a stela beneath a protective palapa which bears a relief of a phallic god, now badly weathered.

Xlapak

From the entrance gate at Sayil, it's six km to the entrance gate at Xlapak (shla-PAK). The name means Old Walls in Mayan and was a general term among local people for ancient ruins, about which they knew little.

The site is open from 8 am to 5 pm; admission is US$1.

The ornate palace at Xlapak is smaller than those at Kabah and Sayil, measuring only about 20 metres in length. It's decorated with the inevitable Chac masks, columns and colonnettes and fretted geometric latticework of the Puuc style. To the right is the rubble of what were once two smaller buildings.

If you trek along the remnant of an old 4WD road behind the palace, you may be rewarded with the sight of some brilliantly coloured tropical birds. The long-tailed mocmoc, or clock bird, is here in good number.

Labná

From the entrance gate at Xlapak, it's 3.5 km to the gate at Labná. The site here is open from 8 am to 5 pm; admission costs US$1.

The Arch Labná is best known for its magnificent arch, once part of a building which separated two quadrangular courtyards. It now appears to be a gate joining two small plazas. The corbelled structure, three metres wide and six metres high, is well preserved and stands close to the entrance of Labná. The mosaic reliefs decorating the upper façade are exuberantly Puuc in style.

If you look at the ornate work on the north-eastern side of the arch, you will make out mosaics of Mayan huts. At the base of either side of the arch are rooms of the adjoining building, now ruined, including upper lattice patterns constructed atop a serpentine design. Archaeologists believe a high roofcomb once sat over the fine arch and its flanking rooms.

El Mirador Standing on the opposite side of the arch and separated from it by the limestone-paved sacbé, is a pyramid with a temple atop it called El Mirador. The pyramid itself is poorly preserved, largely stone rubble. The temple, with its five-metre-high roofcomb, true to its name, looks like a watchtower. When John L Stephens saw El Mirador in 1840, it had a row of death's heads along the top and two lines of human figures beneath; over the centre doorway was a colossal seated figure in high relief.

Palace & Chultún Archaeologists believe that at one point in the 9th century, some 3000 Maya lived at Labná. To support such numbers in these arid hills, water was collected in chultunes. At Labná's peak there were some 60 chultunes in and around the city. Today you can spot one of these cisterns on the 2nd storey of the palace which sits near the entrance to Labná. This one is particularly well preserved but you will see others in various degrees of deterioration around the site.

The palace, the first edifice you come to at Labná, is connected by a sacbé to El Mirador and the arch. One of the longest buildings in the Puuc Hills, its design is not as impressive as its counterpart at Sayil. There's a ghoulish sculpture on the eastern corner on the upper level of a serpent gripping a human head between its jaws. According to Mayan mythology, crocodile jaws symbolised the entrance to the underworld. Close to this carving is a well-preserved Chac mask.

Grutas de Loltún (Loltún Caves)

From Labná it's 15 km eastward to the village of Yaaxhom, surrounded by lush orchards and palm groves which are surprising in this generally dry region. From Yaaxhom a road goes another four km to Loltún.

Loltún Caves are the most interesting *grutas* in Yucatán. More than just a fine subterranean realm for spelunkers, Loltún provided a treasure trove of data for archaeologists studying the Maya as well as some impressive artefacts. Carbon dating has provided evidence that the caves were first used by humans some 2500 years ago, perhaps seeking shelter or looking for water. The caves contain spectacular stalactite and stalagmite formations.

There is no sign on the road to tell you that you've arrived at the grutas, so you must look for a park-like enclosure entered by a gravel road. To explore the 1.5-km labyrinth,

you must take a scheduled tour with a guide. Tours supposedly depart at 9.30 and 11 am and at 12.30, 2 and 3.30 pm, but may depart early if enough people are waiting. The guides may be willing to take you through at other hours if you offer a substantial tip (a few dollars). Occasionally there is a guide on the premises who speaks English – check to see if the tour will be in a language you understand.

Admission to the caves costs US$2.50 (children under 12 years of age go free); the guides, who are not paid by the government, expect a tip at the end of the hour-long tour.

For refreshments there's the *Restaurant El Guerrero* near the exit of the caves, a walk of eight to 10 minutes (600 metres) in the wilting heat along a marked path from the far side of the parking lot near the cave entrance. Once you get to the restaurant you'll find that their comida corrida costs about US$6. They serve icy-cold drinks, but a simple soft drink costs US$0.75.

Touring the Caves Within these awesome caverns (distractingly illuminated by coloured lights) you will see both spectacular natural formations and those carved over the years by the Maya. In a chamber where soot on the walls indicates that Indians cooked there, you will see ancient Mayan stone *metates* or corn grinders. The caverns were used as recently as the War of the Castes (1847-1901) by Indian fighters seeking refuge from their Spanish-speaking enemies.

During my explorations here, I came upon a pure white centipede, which lacked all colour as a result of living in total darkness.

In the Gallery of the Five Chultunes, a carved eagle and a monster overlook the startlingly realistic, naturally formed head of a dolphin (the product of erosion) dropping water into cisterns. The Maya believed water in this cave was sacred and used it in their religious rituals.

As you walk through the various underground caverns, it takes little imagination to see other formations resembling animals and humans which were carved by the forces of erosion. Among the more obvious are camels, jaguars and, towards the tour's end, the carved petals which made the Maya name the cave Flower of the Rock.

Among the highlights of this subterranean world is a grand cavern appropriately called The Cathedral. The Maya held major religious ceremonies in this immense grotto, where stalagmites and stalactites create the sense of a stone forest.

In another chamber, erosion has opened its roof to the sun, permitting a huge tree and other vegetation to grow. Tropical birds link the underworld with the heavens.

In the last cave you come to is the ladder that takes you back to the sunlight. A smaller ladder takes you to a site where a mastodon's fossils were found; the bones are in the National Museum of Anthropology in Mexico City.

Getting There & Away Loltún is on a country road leading to Oxkutzcab (8 km) and there is usually some transport along the road. Try hitching, or catch a paying ride in one of the colectivos – often a pickup truck or *camión* – which ply this route charging about US$0.20 for the ride. A taxi from Oxkutzcab may charge US$4 or so, one way, for the eight-km ride.

Buses run frequently every day between Mérida and Oxkutzcab via Ticul.

If you're driving from Loltún to the Puuc Route site of Labná, drive out of the Loltún car park, turn right and take the next road on the right, which passes the access road to the restaurant. Do not take the road marked for Xul. After four km you'll come to the village of Yaaxhom, where you turn right to join the Puuc Route westwards.

UXMAL TO CAMPECHE

South of Uxmal and Kabah, Highway 261 leaves the Puuc Hills and heads straight for the border with the neighbouring state of Campeche. There is little except jungle until, 31 km south of Uxmal, you pass beneath the great arch over the roadway which marks the border between the two Mexican states.

Three km north of Bolonchén, just off the highway, is the archaeological zone of Itzimté, with its many unrestored buildings in the Puuc style. This is the southernmost limit of the style; south of this point the ancient Mayan buildings are more elaborately decorated in a style called Chenes, named for the many natural wells in the region. The suffix '-chén' is often found at the end of town names hereabouts.

Bolonchén de Rejón & Xtacumbilxunaan

Another 25 km brings you to the town of Bolonchén de Rejón. John L Stephens visited in 1840 and wrote:

Bolonchen derives its name from two Maya words: *Bolon*, which signifies nine and *chen*, wells and it means the nine wells. From time immemorial, nine wells formed at this place the centre of a population and these nine wells are now in the plaza of the village.

Since that time the name has been stretched to honour Manuel Crescencio Rejón, a famous lawyer and author of the provision in Mexico's constitution which guarantees a citizen's civil rights. Sr Rejón was born here. The local festival of the Santa Cruz is held each year on May 3rd.

Today, as in John L Stephens' time, Bolonchén is noted mostly as the town near the Grutas de Xtacumbilxunaan (or Xtacumbinxuna, as it's sometimes spelled), located about three km south of town. Follow Highway 261 south and watch on the right (west) for a small sign indicating the caves, which are 800 metres off the highway.

These Caves of the Hidden Girl get their unpronounceable Mayan name from a legend (of course): a girl was stolen from her mother by her lover and hidden in the cave. If this is true, the lovers left no trace of their tryst. Stephens writes that the Nine Wells of Bolonchén would fail each year during the dry season and the local inhabitants would make their way to this cave and go down several hundred metres into the earth through a narrow, claustrophobic system of tunnels to fill their small water jars. A system of ladders allowed the descent. A huge, broad, crude ladder permitted access to the main chamber; Stephens' friend and artist Frederick Catherwood made a famous drawing of the ladder and reproductions are still on sale in Yucatán.

Today you can visit the cavern by taking a 30 to 45-minute tour with the guide/caretaker for the price of a tip. The cave is 'open' whenever the caretaker is around, which is most of the time during daylight hours. If you've seen – or plan to see – Loltún, you can skip Xtacumbilxunaan, though it is an interesting cave.

Hochob & Dzibilnocac

South of the caves, the next 33 km of highway penetrate more scrubby jungle without relief. Facing the plaza in Hopelchén is a scruffy cantina, Ladies Bar. 'Are there any ladies in there?' I asked the men sitting in the plaza. 'What do you think?' they responded. 'If you were a lady, would you go in there?'

Hopelchén is nevertheless the jumping-off place for a visit to some secondary ruins, mostly unexcavated and with no services, that have examples of Chenes-style architecture. The main sites are called Hochob and Dzibilnocac.

Hochob rewards the off-the-beaten-track traveller with ruins in the purest Chenes style. Hochob's central ceremonial plaza, where the only real excavation has been done to date, sits on a hill overlooking the jungle.

The building on the right of the plaza is festooned with some fine Mayan stucco carvings of geometric designs. Most impressive, although you will have to use your imagination a bit, is the façade of the structure which was constructed in the image of a gigantic mask of Chac, with the sizable door serving as an angry mouth. Though eroded (there's a full reconstruction of the building at the National Museum of Anthropology in Mexico City), the face of Chac in this isolated jungle setting is spooky enough to let the viewer imagine secret Mayan ceremonial rites.

Opposite Hochob's entrance, you will see another edifice bearing Chac's image. To the right is a steep pyramid which is the site's tallest building. Although Hochob has a dirt track running to other mounds, they are yet to be excavated and the path is worth pursuing to get a sense of the enormousness of the site. Who knows what splendid ruins wait to be unearthed from the jungles here?

At Dzibilnocac, the first two temples you encounter may make you wonder why you have ventured off the beaten track to come here. The third temple will reward you. With its rounded base and delicately narrow design, it is unique. Climb the edifice and see primitive cave paintings on the way up. On the upper level, you will see in full detail a stunning if frightening carving of Chac. Looking down, you'll see how little has been excavated around here.

Getting There & Away The central point for visiting these two sites is the village of Dzibalchén, 41 km south of Hopelchén. If you are trying to get here by bus, be prepared to spend at least one night in Dzibalchén – in other words, bring a hammock, food, water and insect repellent.

Take a 2nd-class bus to Dzibalchén from Campeche (with a transfer at Hopelchén if there is no direct bus). From Dzibalchén, walk back (north) about one km on the road to Campeche and where you see the Chencoh sign, start hitching the nine km south-west to that village. You will probably have to walk the four km to Hochob from Chencoh. Once you're at the ruins, there is nothing or no-one to stop you from camping here. Just bring food, water and plenty of insect repellent.

Dzibilnocac is north-west of Dzibalchén near the village of Iturbide (renamed Vicente Guerrero in recent times). From Dzibalchén village, there might be a bus to Iturbide/Guerrero; they don't run every day. You can walk to the site of Dzibilnocac from Iturbide.

To drive to the Dzibilnocac ruins, take Highway 261 to the town of Hopelchén, then take the road south to Dzibalchén. Turn left at the plaza and follow the road to the village of Iturbide/Vicente Guerrero. Bear to the right past Iturbide's plaza on a rugged dirt track (make sure your car has fairly high clearance) to the ruins.

To reach these sites by car, start out early from Campeche (if you don't want to camp), take food and water and attempt it only if your car has high clearance and, in the rainy season, good traction or 4WD.

Edzná

Continuing west on Highway 261 from Hopelchén brings you, after 40 km, to the village of San Antonio Cayal and the junction with the road south to Edzná (20 km).

Edzná, meaning House of Grimaces or House of Echoes, may well have been host to both, as there has been a settlement here since about 800 BC. Most of the carvings are of a much later date: 550 to 810 AD. Though a long way from the Puuc Hills, some of the architecture here is similar to Puuc style, but with local variations in design.

The refreshments stand to the left as you enter has icy-cold bottled drinks, which you will probably want in the intense heat. The site is open from 8 am to 5 pm daily, for US$4 admission.

Though the archaeological zone covers two sq km, the thing to see here is the main plaza, 160 metres long and 100 metres wide, surrounded by temples. Every Mayan site has huge masses of stone, but at Edzná there are cascades of it, terrace upon terrace of bleached limestone.

The major temple here, the 30-metre-high Temple of Five Levels, is to the left as you enter the plaza from the ticket kiosk. Built on a vast platform, it rises five levels from base to roofcomb, with rooms and some weathered decoration of masks, serpents and jaguars' heads on each level. A great central staircase of 65 steps goes right to the top. On the opposite (right) side of the plaza as you enter is a monumental staircase 100 metres wide, which once led up to the Temple of the Moon. At the far end of the plaza is a ruined temple that may have been the priests' quarters.

Getting There & Away From Campeche's market at the eastern end of Calle 53 across Avenida Circuito Baluartes Este, catch a 2nd-class village bus early in the morning headed for Edzná (66 km), which may mean a bus going to the village of Pich, some 15 km south-east of Edzná, or to Hool, about 25 km south-west. Either bus will drop you at the access road to the site. A sign just north of the junction says 'Edzná 2 km', but don't let it fool you. The ruins are just 500 metres beyond the sign, only about 400 metres off the highway. Coming from the north and east, get off at San Antonio Cayal and hitch or catch a bus 20 km south to Edzná.

When you leave you'll have to depend on hitching or buses to get you to San Antonio Cayal, from which you can hitch or catch a bus west back to Campeche or east and north to Hopelchén, Bolonchén and ultimately Uxmal.

Alternatively, guided tours (US$17 per person) are set up by the larger hotels in Campeche if they have enough people.

If you're coming from the north (Uxmal) in your own car and you don't plan to visit Campeche, you can leave Edzná and head west toward the village of Hool. This road bypasses Campeche completely, turning south at the coast for Champotón, Escárcega, Palenque and Villahermosa. However, most people will want to spend the night in Campeche before making the long drive to Palenque as the selection of hotels available along the way is not as good as what Campeche has to offer.

TICUL

Ticul is a centre for fine huipil weaving – the embroidery on these dresses is extraordinary. For both quality and price, Ticul is a good place to buy the traditional Mayan garment. While you are here, you can pay homage to the best Yucatecan cooking by dining at the original Restaurant Los Almendros, which has branches in Mérida and Cancún.

Ticul's main street is Calle 23, sometimes called the Calle Principal, going from the highway north-east past the market and the town's best restaurants to the main plaza.

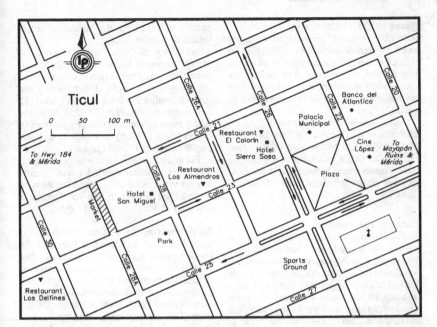

Ticul

0   50   100 m

To Hwy 184
& Mérida

To Mayapán
Ruins &
Mérida

Places to Stay – bottom end

Hotel Sierra Sosa (☎ (997) 2-00-08/53), Calle 26 No 199A, half a block north-west of the plaza, has very basic rooms for US$4/5.50 a single/double. A few rooms at the back have windows, but most are dark and dungeon-like; all are fairly beat-up. Before you move in, check to be sure the ceiling fan works. If no one seems to be around at the hotel, check next door in the electronics shop.

Similarly basic but more expensive is the *Hotel San Miguel* (☎ (997) 2-03-82), Calle 28 No 195, near Calle 23 and the market. Singles at the San Miguel cost US$5.50 with fan and bath, doubles US$7.25 to US$9, triples US$9 to US$11 and rooms for four cost US$12.50 to US$14.50.

Places to Stay – middle

Ticul's better hotels don't really offer too much more in the way of comfort and both are on the highway on the outskirts of town, an inconvenient two-km walk from the centre, but fine if you have a car.

Best in town is the new *Hotel Bougambillias* (☎ (997) 2-01-39), near the junction of the western end of Calle 25 and the highway to Muna and Mérida. Fake chac-mools and ceramic frogs greet you as you enter the tidy grounds. The darkish rooms are simple but newer and cleaner than the competition's. Orange and white tiles abound. Prices are US$11 for two in one bed, US$22 for two in two beds, but you can often haggle the price down.

A hundred metres north-west of the Bougambillias on the opposite side of the highway is the older *Hotel-Motel Cerro Inn* (no phone). Set in more spacious, shady grounds, the Cerro Inn has nine well-used rooms with private shower and ceiling fan going for US$9 to US$11 a double. A palapa restaurant, usually empty, can provide drinks and snacks.

Places to Eat – bottom end

Ticul's lively market provides all the ingredients for picnics and snacks. It also has lots of those wonderful market eateries where the food is good, the portions generous and the prices low. For variety, try out some of the loncherías along Calle 23 between Calles 26 and 30.

Should you want a sit-down meal, there's the *Restaurant El Colorín* (☎ 2-03-14), Calle 26 No 199B, just to the right of the Hotel Sierra Sosa half a block north-west of the plaza. Sandwiches, burgers and traditional Mexican dishes are priced from US$0.50 to US$1.25.

Places to Eat – middle

By this time you've probably been to Cancún and Mérida. If you haven't had a meal at the *Restaurant Los Almendros* in those cities, you can try the original one (☎ 2-00-21) here in Ticul at Calle 23 No 207, between Calles 26A and 28. Set up in a fortress-like town house with a large courtyard and portico, the restaurant is fairly plain, but the food is authentic. The *combinado yucateco*, or Yucatecan combination plate, with a soft drink or beer, will cost less than US$6.50 and that's the most expensive item on the menu.

Fancier, perhaps Ticul's fanciest dining-place, is the *Restaurant Los Delfines*, Calle 23 No 218, at the corner of Calle 30, with pretensions to decor and a menu which – surprisingly – lists numerous seafood dishes, especially shrimp. Hours are from 8 am to 1 pm and from 5 to 11 pm daily. Expect to spend about the same here as at Los Almendros, or perhaps a bit more.

Getting There & Away

It's 85 km between Mérida and Ticul, a 1.5-hour journey. Nine 2nd-class buses of the Autobuses del Caribe line run daily, charging US$1.25 one way.

You can catch a minibus (combi) from the intersection of Calles 23 and 28 in Ticul to Oxkutzcab (that's osh-kootz-KAHB), 16 km away and from Oxkutzcab a minibus or pickup truck to Loltún (eight km); ask for the camión to Xul (SHOOL), but get off at Las Grutas de Loltùn.

Minibuses to Santa Elena (15 km), the village between Uxmal and Kabah, also depart from the intersection of Calles 23 and 28, taking a back road and then leaving you to catch another bus north-west to Uxmal (15 km) or south to Kabah (3.5 km). You may find it more convenient to take a minibus or bus to Muna (22 km) on Highway 261 and another south to Uxmal (16 km).

For getting around Ticul, the local method is to hire a three-wheeled cycle, Ticul's answer to the rickshaw – you'll see them on Calle 23 just up from the market. The fare is less than US$0.35 for a short trip.

To Felipe Carrillo Puerto Those headed eastwards back to Quintana Roo and the Caribbean coast can go via Highway 184 from Muna and Ticul via Oxkutzcab to Tekax, Tzucacab and Peto. At Polguc, 130 km from Ticul, a road turns left (east), ending after 80 km in Felipe Carrillo Puerto, 210 km from Ticul, where there are hotels, restaurants, fuel stations, banks and other services. The right fork of the road goes south to the region of Lake Bacalar.

From Oxkutzcab to Felipe Carrillo Puerto or Bacalar there are few services: very few places to eat (those that exist are rock-bottom basic), no hotels and few fuel stations. Mostly you see small typical Yucatecan villages with their *topes* (speed bumps), traditional Mayan na thatched houses and agricultural activity.

MÉRIDA TO TICUL VIA ACANCEH & MAYAPÁN

The route south from Mérida via Acanceh and the ruins of Mayapán to Ticul and Oxkutzcab reveals a landscape of small Mayan villages, crumbling haciendas surrounded by henequen fields, a ruined Mayan capital city and of course the expected expanses of limitless scrubby jungle.

Those taking this route, whether by car or bus, should be careful to distinguish between Ruinas de Mayapán, the ruins of the ancient city and Mayapán, a Mayan village some 40 km south-east of the ruins past the town of Teabo. The Ruinas de Mayapán are right on the main road (Yucatán state highway 18) between Telchaquillo and Tekit.

Getting Around

Buses and colectivos run fitfully along this route, but you should plan the better part of a day, with stops in Acanceh and Ruinas de Mayapán, to travel the route by public transport.

If you're driving, follow these directions carefully:

Leave Mérida on Calle 59, which is one-way eastward. When you come to a four-lane boulevard with railway tracks running in its centre, you've reached Circuito Colonias. Turn right onto this boulevard and go south until you reach a traffic roundabout with a fountain. Go three-quarters of the way around (you enter at 6 o'clock and exit at 9 o'clock) and head due east on the road marked for Kanasin, Acanceh and Tecoh.

Kanasin is virtually a suburb of Mérida. If you neglected to fill your fuel tank in Mérida, you can do it here. Beyond Kanasin, the road passes through the hamlets of San Antonio and Tepich. At Petectunich, about 22 km south-east of Mérida, there's a Centro Porcino Ejidal or Collective Pig Farm. The village has a graceful little church, several old houses with fancy doors and windows going to ruin and, of course, many traditional Mayan na houses of sticks or wattle and daub with thatched roofs.

Acanceh

The road enters Acanceh and goes to the main plaza flanked by a shady park and the church. To the left of the church is a partially restored pyramid and to the right of the church are market loncherías if you're in need of a snack. In the park, note the statue of the smiling deer; the name Acanceh means Pond of the Deer. Another local sight of interest is the cantina Aqui Me Queda (I'm Staying Here), a ready-made answer for wives who come to the cantina to urge their husbands homeward.

Trundling through the henequen fields,

past more pig farms and piles of litter by the roadside, there are only occasional glimpses of the local people in the day's heat – you may see two boys coax an iron hoop along the road with sticks while a mother hangs out the family washing.

Tecoh

Tecoh, 35 km from Mérida, has a church and well-kept Palacio Municipal separated by a green football pitch. The municipal market is to the right of the palacio. In 1840, as John L Stephens came through Tecoh on his way to Mayapán, he noted that the road south to Telchaquillo was brand new, having been cut through the jungle by the citizens of Telchaquillo so that the *cura* (priest) of Tecoh could visit their town.

Telchaquillo

This village, 11 km south of Tecoh, has a cenote beneath its plaza. Stephens wrote:

At a distance the square seemed level and unbroken; but women walking across it with *cantaros* or water-jars suddenly disappeared and others seemed to rise out of the earth. On a nearer approach, we found a great orifice or opening in the rocky surface, like the mouth of a cave. The descent was by irregular steps cut and worn in the rocks. Overhead was an immense rocky roof and at a distance of perhaps five hundred feet from the mouth was a large basin or reservoir of water... Women, with their water-jars, were constantly ascending and descending; swallows were darting through the cave in every direction and the whole formed a wild, picturesque and romantic scene.

Ruinas de Mayapán

One or two km past Telchaquillo (about 48 km from Mérida), look for a sign on the right-hand (west) side of the road indicating the Ruinas de Mayapán.

At the caretaker's hut 100 metres in from the road, pay the admission fee of US$2.50 and enter the site any day between 8 am and 5 pm. If you have camping equipment, the caretaker may grant you permission to camp near his hut. Facilities consist of a latrine and a well with a bucket.

History Mayapán was supposedly founded by Kukulcán (Quetzalcóatl) in 1007, shortly after the former ruler of Tula arrived in Yucatán. His dynasty, the Cocom, organised a confederation of city-states which included Uxmal, Chichén Itzá and many other notable cities. Despite their alliance, animosity arose between the Cocoms of Mayapán and the Itzaes of Chichén Itzá during the late 1100s and the Cocoms stormed Chichén Itzá, forcing the Itzá rulers into exile. The Cocom dynasty under Hunac Ceel Canuch emerged supreme in all of northern Yucatán and obliged the other rulers to pay tribute in cotton clothing, fowl, cacao and incense resin.

Cocom supremacy lasted for almost 2½ centuries, until the ruler of Uxmal, Ah Xupán Xiú, led a rebellion of the oppressed city-states and overthrew Cocom hegemony. Every member of the Cocom dynasty was massacred, except for one prince who had the good fortune to be away on business in Honduras. The great capital of Mayapán was utterly destroyed and was uninhabited ever after.

The Xiú victors founded a new capital at Maní, which remained the strongest Mayan city until the arrival of the conquistadors. But there was no peace in Yucatán after the Xiú victory. The Cocom dynasty recovered and marshalled its forces and frequent struggles for power erupted until 1542, when Francisco de Montejo the Younger founded Mérida. At that point the current lord of Maní and ruler of the Xiú people, Ah Kukum Xiú, offered to submit his forces to Montejo's control in exchange for a military alliance against the Cocoms, his ancient rivals. Montejo willingly agreed and Ah Kukum Xiú was baptised as a Christian, taking the unoriginal name of Francisco de Montejo Xiú. The Cocoms were defeated and – too late – the Xiú rulers realised that they had willingly signed the death warrant of Mayan independence.

Orientation The city of Mayapán was huge, with a population estimated at around 12,000; its ruins cover several sq km, all surrounded by a great defensive wall. Over 3500 buildings, 20 cenotes and traces of the city wall were mapped by archaeologists working in the 1950s and in 1962. The workmanship was inferior to the great age of Mayan art; though the Cocom rulers of Mayapán tried to revive the past glories of Mayan civilisation, they succeeded only in part.

Jungle has returned to cover many of the buildings, though you can visit several cenotes (including Itzmal Chen, a main Mayan religious sanctuary) and make out the large piles of stones which were once the Temple of Kukulcán and the circular Caracol. When John L Stephens visited in 1840, the ground here was covered with carved stones which had apparently fallen from the façades of the many temples. Though the ruins today are far less impressive than those at other sites, Mayapán has a stillness and a loneliness (usually undisturbed by other tourists) that seems to fit its melancholy later history.

Getting There & Away After visiting the ruins, head south again to Tekit, about eight km from the ruins (67 km from Mérida). Turn right and go through the town square to find the road marked for Oxkutzcab. Another seven km brings you to Mama, with its particularly fortress-like church. At Mama, the road forks: straight on to Oxkutzcab (27 km), right to Chapab and Ticul (25 km).

MÉRIDA TO CAMPECHE – SHORT ROUTE (HIGHWAY 180)

The short route from Mérida to Campeche is the fast way to go and if you simply buy a bus ticket from Mérida to Campeche, this is the route your bus will follow. If you'd prefer to go the long way via Uxmal and Kabah, you must ask for a seat on one of the less frequent long route buses. If you'd like to stop at one of the towns along the short route, catch a 2nd-class bus.

Becal, Calkini & Hecelchakan

Becal, 85km south-west of Mérida and just across the boundary in the state of Campeche, is a centre of Yucatán's Panama hat trade. The soft, pliable hats, called Jipi Japa by the locals, have been woven by townfolk from the fibres of the huano palm tree in humid limestone caves since the mid-19th century. The caves provide just the right atmosphere for shaping the fibres, keeping them pliable and minimising breakage. So devoted to hatmaking is Becal that the sculpture in the main square is composed of several enormous concrete hats tipped up against one another. As soon as you descend from your bus, someone is sure to approach you and ask if you want to see the hats being made; the guide expects a tip of course.

Jipi hats are of three general quality grades, judged by the pliability and fineness of the fibres and closeness of the weave. The coarse, open weave of large fibres is the cheapest grade, and should cost only a few dollars. Middle-grade hats have a finer, closer weave of good fibres and cost about

$US10. Truly beautiful hats of the finest, closest weave may cost twice that amount.

Eight km south of Becal you pass through Calkini, site of the 17th-century Church of San Luis de Tolosa, with a Plateresque portal and lots of baroque decoration. Each year the Festival of San Luis is celebrated on 19 August.

Another 24 km brings you to Hecelchakan, home of the Museo Arqueologíco del Camino Real, where you will find some burial artefacts from the island of Jaina, as well as ceramics and jewellery from other sites. The museum is open from Monday to Saturday from 9 am to 6 pm, closed Sunday. The Church of San Francisco is the centre of festivities on the saint's day, 4 October. From 9 to 18 August, a popular festival called the Novenario is held, with bullfights, dancing and refreshments.

From Hecelchakan it's another 77 easy km to the city of Campeche.

Campeche

Campeche is the least visited state on the Yucatán peninsula. This is a blessing for the traveller who wants to get away from the Caribbean tourist mobs and explore a richly historical region. The impressive walled city of Campeche with its ancient fortresses or *baluartes* propels the visitor back to the days of the buccaneers. Those who explore the region's ancient Mayan Chenes-style ruins of Edzná, Dzibilnocac and Hochob may find they have the sites all to themselves.

CAMPECHE

Population 170,000

For a real respite from the touristy Caribbean coast, Campeche is the place. Tranquil, cheap and filled with historic buildings, Campeche is a worthwhile stopover between Mérida and Villahermosa. Worthwhile, yes, for its picturesque buildings, streets and baluartes, but not for its beaches. They are few, small and generally not of any interest.

History

Once a Mayan trading village called Ah Kim Pech (Lord Sun Sheep-Tick – a delightful name), Campeche was invaded by the conquistadors in 1517. The Maya resisted and for nearly a quarter of a century the Spanish were unable to fully conquer the region. Campeche was founded in 1531, but later abandoned due to Mayan hostility. Finally, by 1540 the conquistadors had gained sufficient control, under the leadership of Francisco de Montejo the Younger, to found a settlement here which survived. They named it the Villa de San Francisco de Campeche.

The settlement soon flourished as the major port of Yucatán under the careful planning of Viceroy Hernández de Córdoba. Locally grown timber, chicle and dyewoods were major exports to Europe, as were gold and silver mined from other regions and shipped from Campeche. Such wealth did not escape the notice of pirates, who began

their attacks only six years after the town was founded.

For two centuries, the depredations of pirates terrorised Campeche. Not only were ships attacked, but the port itself was invaded, its citizens robbed, its women raped and its buildings burned. In the buccaneers' Hall of Fame were the infamous John Hawkins, Diego the Mulatto, Lorencillo Graff, Barbillas and the notorious 'Pegleg' himself, Pato de Palo. In their most gruesome of assaults, in early 1663, the various pirate hordes set aside their jealousies to converge upon the city as a single flotilla, massacring many of Campeche's citizens in the process.

It took this tragedy to make the Spanish monarchy take preventive action, but not until five years later. Starting in 1668, 3.5-metre-thick ramparts were built. After 18 years of construction, a 2.5-km hexagon incorporating eight strategically placed baluartes surrounded the city. A segment of the ramparts extended out to sea so that ships literally had to sail into a fortress, easily defended, to gain access to the city.

With Campeche nearly impregnable, the pirates turned their attention to ships at sea and other ports. In response, in 1717, the brilliant naval strategist Felipe de Aranda started attacking the buccaneers and in time made the Gulf safe from piracy.

Originally part of the state of Yucatán, Campeche became an autonomous state of Mexico in 1863. In the 19th century it fell into an economic decline brought on by the demise of mineral shipments to Spain. Independence, the freeing of Indians from plantation slavery, the devastation wrought by the War of the Castes and overall isolation put the port into a protracted decline.

Without highways to link Campeche to the rest of the country, the state's economy languished until the 1950s, when road and communication networks were finally built. Today, the hardwood timber and fishing industries are thriving and the discovery of offshore oil has led to a mini-boom in the city of Campeche. Tourism remains at a modest level here, something which travellers with a yen to avoid the gringo trail will appreciate.

Orientation

The old part of Campeche, enclosed by fragments of the sturdy walls, is where you'll spend most of your time. Though the baluartes stand, the walls themselves have been razed and replaced by streets which ring the city centre just as the walls once did. This is the Avenida Circuito Baluartes, or Circular Avenue of the Bulwarks.

The centre of the old city is the unsuccessfully futuristic main plaza, called Plaza Moch-Cuouh, on the western side of the old city near the waterfront. On the southern side of the plaza are the Palacio de Gobierno (sometimes called the Edificio Poderes), the Government Headquarters for the state of Campeche and the Casa de Congreso, or state legislature's chamber, home of the Camara de Diputados (Chamber of Deputies). The Casa de Congreso looks like a huge squared-off clam.

Along the waterfront on the western edge of the city is a boulevard called Avenida Ruiz Cortines. The top hotels are located between Plaza Moch-Cuouh and this Avenida; cheaper hotels and restaurants overlook the plaza from its eastern side, or are located a block or two off the plaza in the grid of streets to the east.

Besides the modern Plaza Moch-Cuouh, Campeche also has its Parque Principal, also called the Plaza de la Independencia, the standard Spanish colonial park with the cathedral on one side and former Palacio de Gobierno on another. This plaza is about three blocks north-east of the Plaza Moch-Cuouh.

According to the compass, Campeche is oriented with its waterfront to the north-west, but tradition and convenience hold that the water is to the west, inland is east. The street grid is numbered so that streets running north-south have even numbers, while east-west streets have odd numbers; street

numbers ascend towards the south and the west.

The ADO bus terminal is 1.7 km north-east of Plaza Moch-Cuouh along Avenida Gobernadores (Highway 180).

The railway station is three km north-east of the centre, south of Avenida Gobernadores on Avenida Héroes de Nacozari in the district called Colonia Cuatro Caminos.

The airport is east of the railway station at the northern end of Avenida López Portillo. To reach the air terminal you must go east to Avenida López Portillo, then north to the terminal, 3.5 km from Plaza Moch-Cuouh.

The central market, Mercado Pedro Saiz de Baranda, is at the junction of Calle 53 and Avenida Circuito Baluartes Este, just inland from the old city.

Information

Tourist Office Campeche's penchant for oddly dysfunctional modern architecture reaches its apex in the State Tourism Office (☎ (981) 6-60-68, 6-67-67), a fortress-like partly subterranean structure located near the southern end of the Plaza Moch-Cuouh, on Calle 61 between Avenidas 16 de Septiembre and Ruiz Cortines. The entrance, facing the sea, is not visible until you're at it, as though most tourists were going to arrive by boat.

To find the office, look for the shaft rising from the roof of the low building with the word 'Turismo'(with a letter or two missing) on it. Walk to the sea side of the building to find the entrance. The staff are very friendly once you get there and available Monday to Saturday from 8 am to 2.30 pm and 4 to 8.30 pm; closed Sunday.

Money For currency exchange, there are several banks, all open Monday to Friday from 9 am to 1 pm: Bancomer across from Baluarte de la Soledad at Calle 59 No 2A, at Avenida 16 de Septiembre, Banco del Atlantico at Calle 50 No 406 and Banamex at Calle 10 No 15.

Post The central post office (☎ (981) 6-21-34), at the corner of Avenida 16 de Septiembre and Calle 53, is in the Edificio

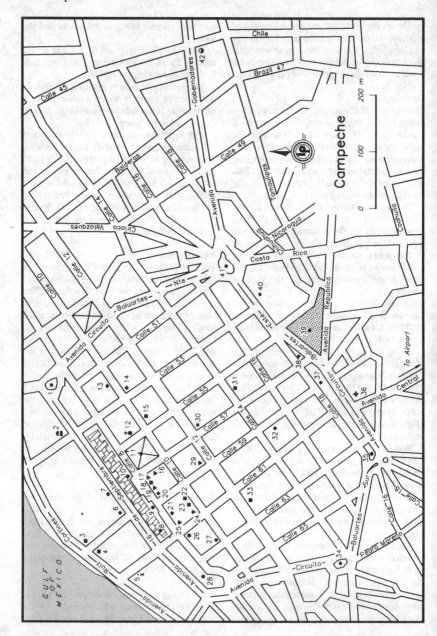

■ PLACES TO STAY

3 Ramada Inn Campeche
4 Hotel Baluartes
15 Posada del Angel
18 Hotel Reforma
22 Hotel América
23 Hotel Roma
26 Hotel Castelmar
31 Hotel Colonial
33 Hotel López

▼ PLACES TO EAT

16 Café & Restaurant Campeche
17 Restaurant del Parque
18 Restaurant Marganzo
19 Restaurant-Bar Familiar La Parroquía
24 Panificadora Nueva España
25 Restaurant Miramar
26 Cafetería y Nevería Continental
29 Restaurant Vegetariana Natura 2000

OTHER

1 Baluarte de Santiago & Jardín Botánico

2 Post Office (Edificio Federal)
5 Tourist Office
6 Bank
7 Bank
8 Plaza Moch-Cuouh
9 Puerta del Mar
10 Baluarte de la Soledad
11 Parque Principal
12 Catedral de la Concepción
13 Mansión Carvajal
14 Bank
20 Bank
21 Bank
27 Bank
28 Baluarte de San Carlos
30 Cine Selem
32 Museo Regional de Campeche
34 Baluarte de Santa Rosa
35 Baluarte de San Juan
36 IMSS Hospital
37 Puerta de Tierra
38 Baluarte de San Francsico
39 Alameda
40 Market
41 Baluarte de San Pedro
42 ADO (1st-Class) Bus Terminal

Federal near the Baluarte de Santiago at the north-western corner of the old town. Hours are Monday to Friday 8 am to 7 pm, Saturday 8 am to 1 pm and Sunday 8 am to 2 pm.

Walking Tour

Campeche, the first city in the New World completely encircled by walls to prevent pirate plundering, began to modernise by tearing down some of its impressive baluartes. Fortunately, in homage to its heritage (and also to lure tourists), seven bulwarks still stand; four of them are of great interest. You can see them all by following the Avenida Circuito Baluartes around the city on a two-km walk.

Because of traffic, some of the walk is not all that pleasant, so you might want to limit your excursion to the first three or four baluartes described below, which house museums and gardens. If you'd rather have a guided tour, you can sign up for a city tour at either the Ramada Inn or Hotel Baluartes

for US$13. We'll start at the south-western end of the Plaza Moch-Cuouh.

Close to the modern Palacio de Gobierno, at Circuito Baluartes and Avenida Justo Sierra, near the intersection of Calles 8 and 65 and a ziggurat fountain, is the **Baluarte de San Carlos**. The interior of the bulwark is now arranged as the **Sala de las Fortificaciones**, or Chamber of Fortifications, with some interesting scale models of the city's fortifications in the 18th century. You can also visit the dungeon, and look out over the sea from the roof. Baluarte de San Carlos is open from 9 am to 1 pm and 5 to 7.30 pm daily; there is no charge for admission.

From the Baluarte de San Carlos, head north along Calle 8. At the intersection with Calle 59, notice the **Puerta del Mar**, or Sea Gate, which provided access to the city from the sea before the area to the north-west was filled in. The gate was demolished in 1893 but rebuilt in 1957 when its historical value was realised.

The **Baluarte de la Soledad**, on the north side of the Plaza Moch-Cuouh close to the intersection of Calles 8 and 57, is the setting for the **Museo de Estelas Maya**. Many of the Mayan artefacts here are badly weathered, but the precise line drawing next to each stone shows you what the designs once looked like. The bulwark also has an interesting exhibition of colonial Campeche. Among the antiquities are 17th and 18th-century seafaring equipment and armaments used to battle pirate invaders. The museum is open 9 am to 2 pm and 3 to 8 pm Tuesday to Saturday, 9 am to 1 pm on Sunday, closed Monday. Admission is free.

Just across the street from the baluarte is the **Parque Principal**, Campeche's favourite park. Whereas the sterile, modernistic, shadeless Plaza Moch-Cuouh was built to glorify its government builders, the Parque Principal (Plaza de la Independencia) is the pleasant place where locals go to sit and think, chat, smooch, plot, snooze, stroll and cool off after the heat of the day, or have their shoes shined. (If you have your shoes shined, the shiner will be sure to make the cloth squeak across the leather near the end of his work, to show that the shine is really hard and good.)

Construction was begun on the **Catedral de la Concepción**, on the north side of the plaza, shortly after the conquistadors established the town, but it wasn't finished for centuries. One of the church's towers is called the **Spanish Tower** because it was completed during Spanish rule. The other, the **Tower of Campeche**, was completed after independence. The cathedral is usually open in the morning and evening. The attractive, arcaded former **Palacio de Gobierno** (or Palacio Municipal) dates only from the 19th century.

Continue north along Calle 8 several blocks to the **Baluarte de Santiago**, at the intersection of Calles 8 and 51. It houses a minuscule yet lovely tropical garden, the **Jardín Botánico Xmuch Haltun**, within its walls. Here you can ease your mind from the rigours of your travels amidst the shade and perfume of 250 species of tropical plants set around a lovely courtyard of fountains. Tours of the garden are given in Spanish every hour or so in the morning and evening, and in English at noon and 4 pm. The garden is open Tuesday to Saturday from 9 am to 8 pm and Sunday 9 am to 1 pm. Admission is free.

From the **Baluarte de Santiago**, walk east (inland) along Calle 51 to Calle 18, where you'll come to the Baluarte de San Pedro, in the middle of a complex traffic intersection which marks the beginning of the Avenida Gobernadores. Within the bulwark is the **Exposición Permanente de Artesanías**, a regional exhibition of crafts, open Monday to Friday from 9 am to 1 pm and 5 to 8 pm. Admission is free.

If the heat and traffic haven't got to you, make the entire circuit of where the old city walls once stood by heading south from the Baluarte de San Pedro along the Avenida Circuito Baluartes to the **Baluarte de San Francisco** at Calle 57 and, a block farther along at Calle 59, the **Puerta de Tierra**, or Land Gate. The **Baluarte de San Juan**, at Calles 18 and 65, marks the south-western-most point of the old city walls. From here you bear right (south-west) along Calle 67 (Avenida Circuito Baluartes) to the intersection of Calles 14 and 67 and the **Baluarte de Santa Rosa**, now a municipal library. Walk north-west three blocks to end your circuit at the starting point, the Baluarte de San Carlos.

Museo Regional de Campeche

The Regional Museum (☎ 6-91-11) is set up in the former mansion of the Teniente del Rey, or King's Lieutenant, at Calle 59 No 36, between Calles 14 and 16. As in the Regional Museum of Anthropology in Mérida, displays here are well done: Mayan artefacts are accompanied by explanatory text, photographs and diagrams. You can learn, for instance, how the Maya deformed their babies' skulls as a mark of beauty and nobility – and you can see the deformed skulls, too. Architecture, hydrology, commerce, art, religion and Mayan science are all dealt with in interesting and revealing displays.

Hours are 8 am to 2 pm and 2.30 to 8 pm

Mansión Carvajal, Campeche

Tuesday to Saturday, 9 am to 1 pm Sunday, closed Monday. Admission costs US$0.35.

Mansión Carvajal

Campeche's commercial success as a port town is evident in its stately houses and mansions. Perhaps the most striking of these is the Mansión Carvajal, on Calle 10 between Calles 51 and 53, mid-block on the left (west) side of the street as you come from the Plaza de la Independencia.

When I first came to Campeche years ago, the mansion had been used as a hotel; it later served as a dance hall, a residence for oilfield foremen during the oil boomlet and as a federal office building. It now holds state offices and handicrafts shops. It started its eventful history as the city residence of Don Fernando Carvajal Estrada and his wife Sra María Iavalle de Carvajal. Don Fernando was among Campeche's richest hacendados, or hacienda-owners. The monogram you see throughout the building, 'RCY', is that of Rafael Carvajal Ytorralde, Don Fernando's father and founder of the fortune.

The mansion is open every day except Sunday from early morning until late in the evening, when the craft shops close; you can walk around and have a look for free. As you enter from the street your eye is immediately gratified with a vision of marble floors, a forest of columns and Arabic ogee arches.

After you've seen the Mansión Carvajal, wander through Campeche's streets – especially Calles 55, 57 and 59 – looking for more beautiful houses. The walk is best done in the evening when the sun is not blasting down and when the lights from inside illuminate courtyards, salons and alleys.

Forts

Four km south of the Plaza Moch-Cuouh along the coast road stands the Fuerte de San Luis, an 18th-century fortress of which only a few battlements remain. Near the fort, a road off to the left (south-east) climbs the hill one km to the Fuerte de San Miguel, a restored fortress once housing the archaeological museum but now closed to the public. The view of the city and the sea is beautiful, but the walk uphill is a killer.

Getting There & Away To reach the Fuerte de San Luis, take a 'Lerma' or 'Playa Bonita' bus south-west along the coastal highway (toward Villahermosa); the youth hostel is out this way as well (see below).

Beaches

Campeche's beaches are not particularly inviting. The Balneario Popular, four km south of the Plaza Moch-Cuouh along the coastal road just past the Fuerte de San Luis, should be avoided. A few km farther along is Playa Bonita with some facilities (restaurant, lockers, toilets) but water of questionable cleanliness and, at the weekends, wall-to-wall local flesh.

If you're really hard up for a swim, head south-west to the town of Seybaplaya, 33 km from Plaza Moch-Cuouh. The highway skirts narrow, pure-white beaches dotted with fishing smacks, the water is much cleaner, but there are no facilities. The best beach here is called Payucan.

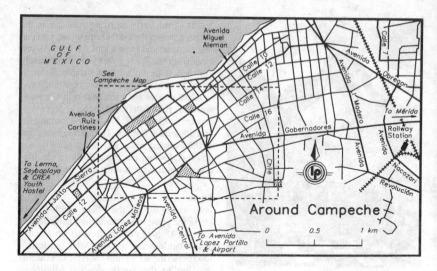

Edzná Ruins

Should you want to visit the ruins at Edzná from Campeche, you can sign up for a tour at one of the larger hotels (about US$17), or you can do it on your own by bus. See the Uxmal to Campeche section in the previous chapter for details.

Places to Stay – bottom end

Youth Hostel Campeche's *CREA Youth Hostel* (☎ (981) 6-18-02), on Avenida Agustín Melgar, is 3.5 km south-west of the Plaza Moch-Cuouh off the shore road; the shore road is Avenida Ruiz Cortines in town, but changes its name to Avenida Resurgimiento as it heads out of town toward Villahermosa. Buses marked 'Lerma' or 'Playa Bonita' will take you there. Ask the driver to let you off at the Albergue de la Juventud and you'll cross some railway tracks and pass a Coca-Cola/Cristal bottling plant before coming to the intersection with Avenida Agustín Melgar, near which the bus will drop you. Melgar is unmarked, of course. Look for the street going left (inland) between a Pemex fuel station and a VW dealership – that's Melgar. The hostel is 150 metres up on the right-hand side.

This is actually a university youth-and-sports facilities complex. To find the hostel section, walk into the compound entrance and out to the large courtyard with swimming pool, turn left and walk 25 metres to the dormitory building. The rate is less than US$2 per person per night. There is a cafeteria which serves inexpensive meals.

Hotels Central Campeche has a number of good hotels with low prices. Because it gets relatively few tourists, its hotel prices are authentically Mexican and after Cancún and Mérida, you'll find Campeche's prices a dream come true.

The well-located *Hotel Castelmar* (☎ (981) 6-51-86) at Calle 61 No 2, between Calles 8 and 10, is an old house surrounding an interior courtyard set with a few plants. The rooms are fairly clean, have fans and hammock hooks and the rooms at the front of the building are large and airy. You get a room with hot shower and (in some rooms) balcony for only US$6/7.50 a single/double. The hotel's name is in huge letters on the façade, visible from the Plaza Moch-Cuouh – you can't miss it.

Second choice is the *Hotel Roma* (☎ (981)

6-38-97), Calle 10 No 254, between Calles 59 and 61. Less presentable but still serviceable, and undeniably cheap, rooms with fan and shower go for US$4.50/6.50 a single/double.

Hotel Reforma (☎ (981) 6-44-64), Calle 8 No 257, between Calles 57 and 59, facing the Baluarte de la Soledad, has a prominent location, low price (US$5.50 a double) and very grungy rooms and showers. If all else fails, or if you're desperate to save a dollar, take a look here.

Moving up the price scale, the *Hotel Colonial* (☎ (981) 6-22-22), Calle 14 No 122, between Calles 55 and 57, offers a great deal more comfort for just a bit more money. The hotel was once the mansion of Doña Gretrudis Eulalia Torostieta y Zagasti, former Spanish governor of Tabasco and Yucatán. It's quiet and well kept, with a little crystal chandelier in the lobby and pretty coloured tiles all round. There's a tidy courtyard and the well-furnished rooms have good showers with hot water. Price is US$7.50 a single, US$9 a double, a few dollars more for a room with air-conditioning.

Hotel América (☎ (981) 6-45-88/76), Calle 10 No 252 (Apdo Postal 94), is perhaps the best choice for the money, a fine colonial house with broad stairs, courtyard, large rooms overlooking the interior court, nicely furnished and equipped with good bathrooms. The management is used to dealing with foreigners, who often fill the hotel by mid-afternoon. Rooms go for US$12.50 a single/double with fan; an extra person in a room pays US$3.75 more.

Similarly good value is the *Posada del Angel* (☎ (981) 6-77-18), Calle 10 No 309, between Calles 55 and 53, just off the Parque Principal on the east side of the church. The rooms remind one of a cell block somewhat, but they're modern and clean, with air-conditioning, for US$14/16.50 a single/double.

Hotel López (☎ 6-33-44), Calle 12 No 189, between Calles 61 and 63, offers similarly clean rooms with showers at US$12.50 a double with a fan, US$16.50 a double with air-conditioning. The decor here is vaguely

Art Deco, not colonial, with long slot-like corridors, but it's tidy and quiet.

Places to Stay – middle

The best hotel in town is the 119-room *Ramada Inn Campeche* (☎ (981) 6-22-33), Avenida Ruiz Cortines No 51, 24000 Campeche, just west of Plaza Moch-Cuouh on the waterfront boulevard. Built some years ago as part of the El Presidente chain, it has been completely refurbished with all the standard comforts: nice air-conditioned rooms with balconies overlooking the sea, a swimming pool and lawns, a restaurant, bar, nightclub, coffee shop and fenced parking area. Prices are reasonable for what you get: US$36/50/55 for a single/double/triple; suites cost US$60 to US$72.

Just south of the Ramada is its competition, the older but still comfortable *Hotel Baluartes* (☎ (981) 6-39-11), Avenida Ruiz Cortines s/n, 24000 Campeche. Though without the polish of the Ramada, the Baluartes' well-used rooms are still air-conditioned, comfortable, with sea views and cheaper at US$32/36 for a single/double. The hotel has a pool, a nice dining room, an air-conditioned garden café, a nightclub and a vast open car park in front of it.

Places to Eat

Campeche has some good, reasonably priced seafood – particularly its shrimp *(camarones)*, as this is a major shrimping port.

Places to Eat – bottom end

Cheapest eats, as always, are near the market, in this case the Mercado Pedro Saiz de Baranda, at the eastern end of Calle 53 across the Avenida Circuito Baluartes Este. You can buy your own food and prepare it, or take it ready-made from the market cookshops.

As for restaurants, Campeche has too few, but there are at least enough to satisfy your needs during the short time you'll be here. Among the cheapest eateries is the *Restaurant Marganzo* (☎ 6-23-28), Calle 8 No 265, between Calles 57 and 59, facing the sea and the Baluarte de la Soledad. It's very simple and very cheap, with seafood plates for US$5 or so, traditional Mexican plates for much less.

Also quite cheap is the *Cafetería y Nevería Continental* (☎ 6-22-66), Calle 61 No 2, at the corner of Calle 8, beside the entrance to the Hotel Castelmar. The main theme here is ice cream, cakes, desserts and drinks, but they have a few items from which to make a good, cheap lunch. Filete de pescado goes for US$2.25. You might also try the hearty soup *caldo xochitl* for only half that much.

If you'd just like to pick up some sweet rolls, biscuits, bread or cakes, head for the *Panificadora Nueva España*, Calle 10 at the corner of Calle 61, which has a large assortment of fresh baked goods at very low prices.

The *Café y Restaurant Campeche* (☎ 6-21-28), Calle 57 No 2, at Calle 55, is beneath the very beat-up Hotel Campeche facing the Parque Principal, next door to the Restaurant del Parque. The building was the birthplace of Sr Justo Sierra, founder of Mexico's national university, but the restaurant is very simple, bright with fluorescent light bulbs, loud with a blaring TV set. Prices are refreshingly low, however; the daily special *platillo del día* usually costs only US$2. Fish and meat dishes cost up to US$3. The Campeche is open early for breakfast.

To the right of the Campeche, in the same block facing the plaza is the *Restaurant del Parque* (☎ 6-02-40), Calle 57 No 8, a cheerful little place serving fish various ways for about US$3.75, meat and shrimp for up to US$6. Fruit drinks, alcoholic beverages and desserts are served and the restaurant opens early for breakfast.

To the left of the Restaurant Campeche is the aptly named *Café Literario El Murmullo* (The Murmur), where the clientele (mostly men) sit, talk, sip, murmur and ponder literature. Some evenings a strolling guitarist entertains.

Restaurant Vegetariano Natura 2000, corner of Calles 12 and 59, is plain and simple and pure, with white chairs and tablecloths. Appropriately, it's right next to a fitness centre. Fruit, granola, tofu, yoghurt and similar good, healthy stuff is combined in imaginative ways and served at reasonable prices, usually not exceeding US$2 per item. It's open every day for breakfast, brunch, lunch and tea, but closes at 4.30 pm – no dinner. You can still get good health food, however, by dropping by the *Natura 2000* health food shop on Calle 12 between 55 and 57.

Places to Eat – middle
Campeche's most famous traditional seafood place is the *Restaurant Miramar* (☎ 6-28-83), corner of Calles 8 and 61 a block south of the Puerta del Mar. A high-ceilinged room here is decorated in pseudo-colonial style, with arches, dark wood and wrought iron. It's cooled by sea breezes and ceiling fans, and efficient waiters glide around serving oyster cocktails (US$3), and chicken, shrimp and beef dishes for US$5.50 to US$6.50. If you're on a strict budget, have the rice with seafood platter for US$3.75. Miramar is open 8 am to midnight Monday to Friday, till 1 am Saturday, and 11 am to 7 pm Sunday.

Perhaps the best known restaurant in town is the *Restaurant-Bar Familiar La Parroquía* (☎ 6-18-29), now in a new location at Calle 8 No 267, between 57 and 59, facing the Puerta del Mar. The complete family restaurant-café-hangout, La Parroquía serves breakfasts priced at US$1.25 to US$2.50 from 7 to 10 am Monday to Friday and substantial lunch and dinner fare like chuleta de cerdo (pork chop), filete a la tampiqueña, shrimp cocktail or shrimp salad and even fresh pampano, for US$2.75 to US$7.50. You can have a full meal here for US$5 to US$12 – it's up to you.

The air-conditioned restaurants in the two top hotels also offer good food at decent prices. The *Restaurante La Almena* in the Hotel Baluartes has tablecloths, waiters in livery and a *long* menu listing everything from enchiladas and tacos to fish and shrimp to chicken; there are 20 meat dishes. Expect to spend US$7.50 to US$18 per person for a full meal here.

Entertainment

On Friday evenings at 8 pm (weather permitting) from September to May, the state tourism authorities sponsor Estampas Turísticas, performances of folk music and dancing, in the Plaza Moch-Cuouh. Other performances, sponsored by the city government, take place in the Parque Principal on Thursday, Friday and Saturday evenings at about 7 pm. Be sure to confirm these times and places with the tourist office.

Campeche's most popular discos are at the Ramada Inn and Hotel Baluartes. Local cinemas sometimes have English-language films with Spanish subtitles.

Getting There & Away

Most travellers arrive by bus and have about a 25-minute, 1.5-km walk to the centre of town. City buses marked 'Gobernadores' or 'Centro' run past the bus station on Avenida Gobernadores. As you leave the bus station, turn left and you'll be looking down Gobernadores in the direction of the centre of town. If you're up to the walk, head down Gobernadores until you see your first baluarte, the Baluarte de San Pedro. Cross the mad intersection as best you can and find Calle 51 heading west to the sea. As you walk along Calle 51 you'll come to Calles 16, 14, 12, etc and you can choose the best route to your hotel. From the bus station the taxi fare is about US$1.50 to any hotel, more to the youth hostel.

Air The airport is west of the railway station at the end of Avenida López Portillo (Avenida Central), across the tracks about 800 metres away, or 3.5 km from Plaza Moch-Cuouh. You must take a taxi (US$3) to the city centre.

Bus Campeche's ADO bus terminal is on Avenida Gobernadores, 1.7 km from Plaza Moch-Cuouh, or about 1.5 km from most hotels. For village buses to Cayal, Pich and Hool (for Edzná), go to the market at the eastern end of Calle 53 across Avenida Circuito Baluartes Este.

Here's information on daily buses from Campeche. Prices and times are 1st class; 2nd class is slightly cheaper and may be slower.

Acayucan – 690 km, 10 hours (US$11.10), three evening buses

Cancún – 512 km, 9 hours; change at Mérida

Chetumal – 422 km, 7 hours (US$7), two buses

Edzná – 66 km, 1½ hours; or take a faster bus to San Antonio Cayal (45 km) and hitch south from there

Escárcega – 150 km, 2½ hours (US$3), eleven 1st-class buses

Mérida – 195 km (short route via Becal), three hours; 250 km (long route via Uxmal), four hours; 33 1st-class buses (US$3.15), by ADO round the clock; 13 2nd-class buses, US$2.90, by Autobuses del Sur

Mexico City – 1360 km, 21 hours (US$22.25), eight buses

Palenque – 362 km, 5½ hours (US$6), one direct bus at 6.30 pm; many other buses drop you at Catazaja (Palenque turnoff), 27 km north of Palenque village

San Cristóbal de las Casas – 820 km, 14 hours; change at Villahermosa

Tuxtla Gutiérrez – 736 km, 12 hours; change at Villahermosa

Villahermosa – 450 km (US$7.50), 15 buses; they'll drop you at Catazaja (Palenque junction) if you like

Train The railway station is three km northeast of the centre, south of Avenida Gobernadores on Avenida Héroes de Nacozari in the district called Colonia Cuatro Caminos. Buses departing from a stop to the right (west) as you leave the station will take you to the centre.

CAMPECHE TO ESCÁRCEGA

The highway south-west from Campeche (Highways 180 & 261) skirts the seacoast for a short time, then enters a range of low hills. This winding portion of road is tedious as overtaking is difficult and heavy vehicles must climb slowly. When the road descends from the hills and straightens out at Seybaplaya, 33 km from Campeche, you're ready for it.

South of Seybaplaya the highway skirts the shore again, lined with narrow but welcome sand beaches in between fishing villages. Champotón, 65 km south of Cam-

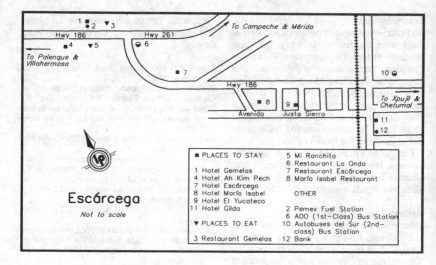

peche, is a fairly attractive fishing town with a nice harbour, some serviceable hotels and some decent restaurants. Highway 261 turns inland here and you won't see the sea again for some time. The ride to Escárcega is straight and fast.

ESCÁRCEGA
Population 18,000

Most buses passing through Escárcega stop here to give passengers a refreshments break, but there is no other reason to stop in this town at the junction of highways 186 and 261, 150 km south of Campeche and 301 km from Villahermosa. Dust, pigs, noise, heat – that's Escárcega. A few travellers are exhausted enough to spend the night, or have to change buses to head eastwards to Chetumal via the Mayan archaeological sites of Becan and Xpujil.

Orientation & Information

Coming into Escárcega from Campeche or Villahermosa/Palenque, you'll think it's just a crossroads with a fuel station, a few scruffy restaurants and hotels and the ADO bus station. But most of the town is spread out along two km of Highway 186 toward

Chetumal. If you plan to spend the night or change bus companies here, you may find yourself walking a km or two in the blazing heat.

It's 1.7 km between the ADO and Autobuses del Sur bus stations. Most hotels are nearer to the Autobuses del Sur bus station than to the ADO; most of the better restaurants are near the ADO bus station.

Places to Stay

You pay more than you should for what you get here. Among the better places is the *Hotel El Yucateco* (☎ (981) 4-00-65), Calle 50 No 42-A, only a few hundred yards from Autobuses del Sur, a neat and tidy place charging US$10 a double for a room with fan and private shower, or US$11.25 for a double with air-conditioning.

The *Hotel María Isabel* (☎ (981) 4-00-45), Avenida Justo Sierra No 127 is among the better places in town. Comfortable (for Escárcega) double rooms with private bath and fan go for US$12.50, or US$18 with air-con. It's 450 metres from Autobuses del Sur, 1200 metres from ADO. The hotel backs onto Highway 186, so avoid the noisy rooms at the back if you can.

In the centre of the commercial section, not far from Autobuses del Sur, the *Hotel Gilda* charges US$7.50/11 a single/double for bearable but noisy rooms with shower. Try for a room at the back to cut the noise. The *Hotel Gemelas*, behind the big Pemex fuel station, near ADO at the junction of Highways 186 and 261, charges about the lowest price in town, US$7.50 a double, but is in bad disrepair and is not worth even that price.

Hotel Ah Kim Pech, on Highway 186 across from the Pemex fuel station near ADO, is a bit noisy but serviceable. Cleanish rooms with showers go for US$12.50 a double with fan, US$16.50 with air-con.

Hotel Escárcega (☎ (981) 4-01-86/7/8), Also on Hwy 186, is the best place in town, set on the main street but at right angles to it so noise is minimised; all the same, get a room as far from the street as possible, near the little garden. Rooms cost US$8/11/14 a single/double/triple with private shower and fan, about twice as much with air-conditioning. The restaurant here is fairly tidy as well. The hotel is one km from Autobuses del Sur, 550 metres from ADO.

Places to Eat

Perhaps the most popular place in town, where the food's always fresh, is the *Restaurant La Onda* in the ADO bus station at the junction of highways 261 and 186. The selection is good, prices are low and there's lots of activity to keep you entertained. The main problem may be finding a table.

Hotel Escárcega has a tidy dining room with decent prices, as does the *Hotel María Isabel* and at the latter there's air-conditioning.

Across from the Pemex fuel station near ADO is *Mi Ranchito*, a popular place for grilled meat and chicken. Just south of it, in the Hotel Ah Kim Pech, is the *Restaurant Juanita*. The *Restaurant Gemelas* next to Pemex is good for a cold drink and that's about it.

Getting There & Away

Escárcega lives by and for buses. There are lots of them to everywhere, but very few originate here. Most buses are de paso, meaning that there may or may not be seats available.

The two major companies with bus stations here are Autobuses de Oriente (ADO) and Autobuses del Sur (A del Sur). All buses below are daily:

Acayucan – 540 km, seven hours; one evening and two night 1st-class buses (US$11.50) by ADO

Campeche – 150 km, 2½ hours; eight 1st-class buses (US$3.50) by ADO, 19 2nd-class buses (US$3) by A del Sur

Cancún – 615 km, eight hours; six 1st-class buses (US$8) by ADO

Chetumal – 275 km, four hours; four 1st-class (US$4.75) by ADO, morning, afternoon and midnight; three 2nd-class night buses (US$4) by A del Sur

Mérida – 345 km, 5½ hours; seven 1st-class buses (US$5) by ADO, nine 2nd-class buses (US$4) by A del Sur

Palenque – 212 km, three hours; one 1st-class evening bus (US$4.25) by ADO, three 2nd-class night buses (US$3.50) by A del Sur

San Cristóbal de las Casas (via Palenque) – 400 km, eight hours; two 2nd-class buses, lunchtime and midnight (US$7.25) by A del Sur

Tuxtla Gutiérrez (via Palenque) – 485 km, 10 hours; two 2nd class early evening (US$9) by A del Sur

Villahermosa – 301 km, four hours; four 1st-class buses (US$5.75) by ADO, six 2nd-class buses (US$5) by A del Sur

Xpujil – 155 km, 2½ hours; five 2nd-class buses (US$2.50) by A del Sur

ESCÁRCEGA TO CHETUMAL

Highway 186 heads due east from Escárcega through the scrubby jungle to Chetumal. Right on the border between the states of Campeche and Quintana Roo near the village of Xpujil, 153 km east of Escárcega and 120 km west of Chetumal, are several important Mayan archaeological sites: Xpujil, Becan, Chicanna and Río Bec. Exploring these sites remains a pleasure reserved for the very adventurous with camping gear and lots of insect repellent, or those with their own cars, as Xpujil has no services.

Xpujil, Becan & Chicanna Ruins

These pristine unrestored sites, largely free

of tourists, will fascinate true ruins buffs, but be forewarned that those expecting park-like sites such as Uxmal and Chichén Itzá will be disappointed. Most of what you see here is jungle and rubble.

Orientation The village of Xpujil is the landmark, where the buses stop. The Xpujil ruins are visible from the highway; those of Becan are eight km west of Xpujil and 200 metres north of the highway. Chicanna, 2.5 km to the west of Becan, is only about 500 metres south of the highway. If you want to do all these ruins in a day, hop on an early bus from Escárcega, cajole the driver to drop you at Chicanna, go on to Becan, then Xpujil and wait in the village at Xpujil for a bus to take you onward to Chetumal, or return to Escárcega. If the driver won't stop (as is usual), you'll have to start your explorations in the village of Xpujil.

Xpujil The latticed towers of Xpujil's pyramid greet you as you explore the village. This temple is the only truly excavated building on the site. It is built in the Río Bec style (see below). There are two sculpted masks carved into the rear of the temple. Nothing else has been excavated here. The site flourished from 400 to 900 AD, though there was a settlement here much earlier.

Becan Becan means Path of the Snake in Mayan. It is well named, as a two-km moat snakes its way around the entire city to protect it from attack. Seven bridges used to provide access to the city. Becan was occupied from 550 BC until 1000 AD.

Still to be excavated from Becan's profuse jungle cover are subterranean rooms and passages linked to religious ritual. Archaeologists have dug up some artefacts from Teotihuacán here, but still must determine whether they got here through trade or conquest. There's little to thrill the eye, though a few of the monumental staircases stimulate the imagination.

Chicanna Buildings at Chicanna are in a mixture of Chenes and Río Bec styles. The city flourished about 660 to 680 AD, when the eight-room 'palace' here was probably occupied by nobles. The palace's monster-mask façade symbolises Itzamná, the Mouth of the Serpent. Each inner room in the palace has a raised bench of stone; the other rooms show signs of having had curtains draped across their doorways for privacy.

Río Bec This site actually includes about 10 groups of buildings placed here and there in a site of 50 sq km. The sites are difficult to reach; a 4WD and guide are recommended.

Río Bec gave its name to the prevalent architectural style of the region characterised by long, low buildings that look as though they're divided into sections, each with a huge serpent-mouth for a door. The façades are decorated with smaller masks, geometric designs and columns. At the corners of the buildings are tall, solid towers with extremely small, steep steps, topped by small temples. Many of these towers have roofcombs as well.

ESCÁRCEGA TO PALENQUE
Approaching Tabasco and Chiapas from Yucatán by road, you pass through the uninspiring highway junction town of Escárcega. The 212-km ride from Escárcega to Palenque is uneventful, but very hot. Upon leaving Escárcega and heading south-west, the fast, straight Highway 186 passes through regions aptly known as El Tormento (Torment) and Sal Si Puedes (Save Yourself if You Can).

The jungle forest cover has been burnt off in this part of the country to provide grazing land for big white Brahma cattle. The Brahmas are attended by flocks of egrets. Signs along the roadside advertise cattle stud services.

By the time you reach Río Champon (or Chumpan), the traditional Mayan na with thatched roof and walls of sticks, wattle-and-daub or stone, has disappeared, giving way to board shacks with roofs of corrugated iron. As you enter the region of the Río Usumacinta the landscape becomes lush, the rich greenery a pleasant surprise after the semi arid, riverless limestone shelf of Yucatán. But along with the lushness comes high humidity and no coolness.

About 184 km south-west of Escárcega you come to Catazaya, the junction with the road to Palenque, Ocosingo and San Cristóbal de las Casas. Turn left (south) for Palenque, 27 km south of the highway junction. If your goal is Villahermosa, continue straight on along Highway 186. The greenery persists, but the hills fade in the distance as the highway skirts the flood plain and delta of the Usumacinta. At the turn-off for Palenque, huge signs over the highway announce that the road to Palenque is your 'access' to the mountainous state of Chiapas. After the flatness of Yucatán, the green hills of Chiapas, covered with a thick mantle of tropical rainforest, come as a surprise. The bulk of this huge and mountainous state is situated in the mountains and along the Pacific coast. But the state border runs along the Usumacinta almost to its delta, enclosing a short portion of the highway and the region around Palenque.

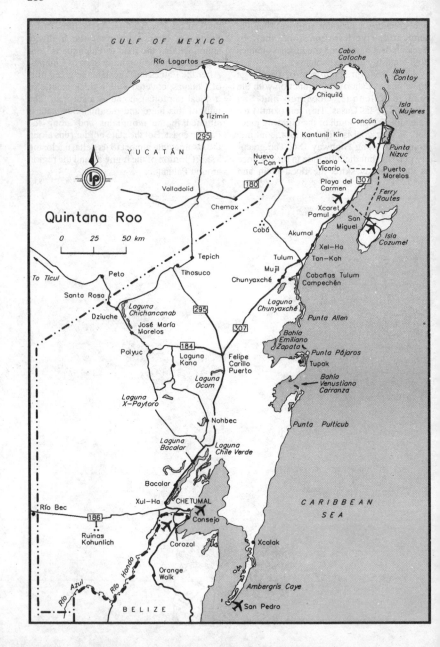

Yucatán's Caribbean Coast

CHETUMAL
Population 110,000
Laid out on a grand plan with many wide, divided boulevards, Chetumal has yet to grow into its obvious destiny as the important capital city of the state of Quintana Roo. In times BC (Before Cancún), the sparsely populated territory of Quintana Roo received special tax relief from the Mexican federal government to encourage immigration from other parts of the country. Quintana Roo was upgraded from a territory to a state in 1974, but Chetumal still enjoys lower taxes than other parts of the country (6% tax on imports, instead of the 15% elsewhere). You'll see many shops selling fancy imported goods at the low-tax prices in this town.

Before the conquest, Chetumal was a Mayan port for shipping gold, feathers, cacao and copper from this region and Guatemala to northern Yucatán. After the conquest, the town was not actually settled until 1898 when it was founded to put a stop to the illegal trade in arms and lumber carried on by the descendants of the War of the Castes rebels. Dubbed Payo Obispo, the town's name was changed to Chetumal in 1936.

Many of the older houses on the outskirts are built of the mahogany or rosewood abundant in the area (the Maya called the settlement Place of Hard Wood); as in Belize, many are built in the Caribbean style. Chetumal was virtually obliterated by Hurricane Janet in 1955, which is why the centre of the city is modern.

Besides its special tax status, Chetumal is the gateway to and from Belize, and you may encounter groups of Belizeans coming to the 'big city' on shopping sprees. Prices are generally much lower in Mexico than in Belize. The shoppers add an exotic note to this odd town which is a strange mixture of the cosmopolitan and the provincial.

Though the city has nothing special to hold you for long, the surrounding area has several significant attractions. The beautiful Laguna Bacalar, sometimes called the Laguna de Siete Colores (Lake of Seven Colours) and the nearby Cenote Azul are 39 km north-west of the city, easily reached by minibus. The significant Mayan archaeological site of Kohunlich is about 67 km due west of Chetumal.

Chetumal is hot all year, with the sticky humidity worst during the summer months. In winter and early spring, the humidity abates somewhat, but it's still uncomfortable.

Orientation
Despite its sprawling street grid layout, the centre of this small city is easily manageable on foot. Once you find the all-important intersection of Avenida de los Héroes and Avenida Alvaro Obregón, you're within 50 metres of three cheap hotels and four cheap restaurants. The best hotels in town are only four or five blocks from this intersection, the best independent restaurant a mere half a block away. Be careful when walking in isolated areas at night, as thieves from Belize City have been known to take advantage of gringos passing through Chetumal.

The market is on Héroes ten blocks north of the Bay of Chetumal, five blocks north of the intersection of Héroes and Obregón. Many local and regional buses and minibuses depart from the market area. Several hospitals are only a block from the market.

The city's new bus station is two km north of the centre of town at the intersection of Avenida de los Insurgentes and Avenida Belice.

For currency exchange, most banks are located along Héroes in the centre of town. For instance, there's a Bancomer (☎ (983) 2-02-05) at Héroes 6 and a Banamex (☎ (983) 2-27-10) at the intersection of Obregón and Juárez. Banking hours are 9.30 am to 1 pm, Monday to Friday.

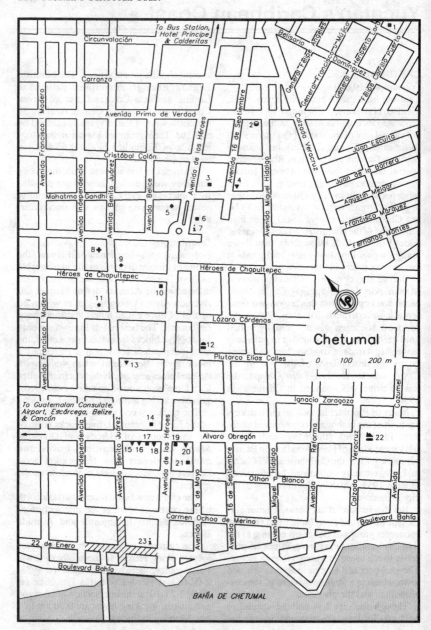

■ PLACES TO STAY

1	Posada Pantoja
3	Hotel Ucum
6	Hotel Continental Caribe
10	Hotel Del Prado
14	Hotel Jacaranda
17	Hotel María Dolores
19	Hotel Baroudi
21	Hotel El Dorado
22	Albergue CREA (Youth Hostel)

▼ PLACES TO EAT

3	Restaurant Ucum
4	Restaurant Pantoja
13	Restaurant Típico El Taquito
14	Restaurant Jacaranda
15	Restaurant Pollo Brujo
16	Restaurant Señorial
17	Restaurant Sosilmar
18	Panadería La Muralla
18	Restaurant Campeche
20	Sergio's Pizzas

OTHER

2	Combi Corner (Minibus Stops)
5	Mercado (Market)
7	Tourist Information Kiosk
8	Hospital Morelos
9	Centro de Salud (Clinic)
11	Teléfonos de México
12	Correos (Post Office)
23	Palacio de Gobierno & Tourist Office

The post office (☎ (983) 2-00-57) is three blocks south and two blocks east of the bus station at Plutarco Elias Calles 2A. The postal code for Chetumal is 77000.

Information

The tourist office (☎ (983) 2-02-66) is in the Palacio de Gobierno, located at the southern end of Héroes, on the bay. It's open Monday to Friday from 8 am to 2.30 pm and 6 to 10 pm but closed on the weekend. The personnel here are helpful and some speak English. There is also a tourist information kiosk on Héroes at the eastern end of Aguilar, across from the market. Hours here are 8 am to 1 pm and 5 to 8 pm.

As for consulates, there used to be a Belizean Consulate here, but it was closed on my last visit. There is a Guatemalan Consulate at Obregón 342 (☎ (983) 2-13-65), corner of Rafael Melgar, one km from the intersection of Héroes and Obregón, on the left just past a big park and school which are on the right as you come from the intersection. It's open from 9 am to 2 pm Monday to Friday and offers quick visa service.

Things to See

No one comes to Chetumal for sightseeing. Most of what's worthwhile in the area is outside of Chetumal (see Around Chetumal), but you might check out the market if you have the time.

Places to Stay – bottom end

Try to find a room early, as budget lodging tends to fill up with people plying the duty-free trade. The *Albergue CREA* (☎ (983) 2-05-25), the youth hostel also called the Casa de la Juventud, Calzada Veracruz at the corner with Obregón, is the cheapest place in town. It has a few drawbacks: single-sex dorms, 11 pm curfew, and a location five blocks east of the intersection of Héroes and Obregón. The cost is US$3 for a bunk in a room with four or six beds and shared bath. Breakfasts are US$1.75 and dinners US$2 in the hostel's cafeteria.

Hotel Baroudi (☎ (983) 2-09-92), Obregón 39, east of Héroes, is stark, bare, central and cheap. Cleanish rooms with fan and private bath cost US$8 a single, US$11 for two people sharing a bed, and – surprisingly – only US$10 for two beds. Some rooms are better than others, so look at several before choosing.

Hotel María Dolores (☎ (983) 2-05-08), Obregón 206 west of Héroes has tiny, stuffy rooms but they are reasonably clean and cheap at US$7.50 a single and US$9 to US$10 a double with fans and private bath. Being at right angles to the busy street, rooms here are fairly quiet. You can spot the building easily by looking for the Restaurant Sosilmar on the ground floor.

Hotel Ucum (☎ (983) 2-07-11), M Gandhi 167, is a large, rambling old place near the market with lots of rooms around a bare central courtyard and a good cheap little restaurant of the same name facing the street. Plain but cheap rooms equipped with fan and private bath cost US$6 a single, US$8 a double, US$9 a triple. To find the hotel, walk from the market east along Gandhi, cross Héroes, and look for the hotel on the left-hand side.

Hotel Jacaranda (☎ (983) 2-14-55), on Obregón just west of Héroes, is plain and bright with fluorescent lights, but the rooms are clean and you have the choice of either fan or air-con. Rates are US$7.50 to US$8.75 a single, US$10 to US$12.50 a double, US$13 to US$16 a triple; the higher prices get you the air-con. Note that this hotel has many noisy rooms; choose carefully. The Restaurant Jacaranda is next to the hotel lobby.

Want a very clean, quiet room with good cross-ventilation, fan, TV and private bath for only US$11 a single, US$12 a double? Then find your way to the *Posada Pantoja* (☎ (983) 2-39-57), Lucio Blanco 95, one km north-east of the market in a peaceful residential area. This tidy, modern establishment is run by the same family responsible for the popular Restaurant Pantoja (see Places to Eat). To find it, walk five blocks north from the market along Héroes to Camelias, turn right, walk two blocks to Calzada Veracruz, cross over this main street and walk a short distance north-east on it to Lucio Blanco, on the right. The Posada is 4½ short blocks along Lucio Blanco, between Heriberto Jara and Felipe Carrillo Puerto.

At Obregón 193 (slightly east of Héroes) is the *Hotel Quintana Roo*. Pleasant rooms with fan and bath at this well-managed hotel cost US$9.

Camping There's a camping area at Laguna Bacalar and a trailer park with hook-ups at Calderitas; the trailer park is the closest camping area to the city.

Places to Stay – middle
Hotel El Dorado (☎ 2-03-15), Avenida 5 de Mayo 42 (Apdo Postal 30), a block east of

Héroes between Obregón and O Blanco, is perhaps the best of the mid-range places. Here you will find large, tidy rooms with fan or air-conditioning for US$16 to US$25 a single, US$20 to US$32 a double, US$25 to US$37 a triple, US$29 to US$43 a quadruple, the higher prices being for rooms with air-conditioning.

Places to Stay – top end
Hotel Del Prado (☎ (983) 2-05-42), Avenida Héroes at Chapultepec, 1½ blocks south of the market, is generally regarded as the best hostelry in town, with a nice swimming pool set in grassy lawns, a children's pool, guarded car park and decent restaurant. Air-conditioned rooms with TV, rich in nubbly white stucco, cost US$63 a single or double. (This used to be called the Hotel El Presidente.)

Two blocks north of the Del Prado along Héroes, on the right-hand side near the tourist information kiosk, is the *Hotel Continental Caribe* (☎ (983) 2-10-50, 2-13-71), Héroes 171 (Apdo Postal 1); its comfortable rooms overlook several swimming pools, restaurant and bar, and there is also a nightclub featuring (on my last visit) the Acapulco Transvestite Show. Air-conditioned rooms cost US$37 a single, US$45 a double; junior suites are US$56 a single, US$67 a double.

Hotel Principe (☎ (983) 2-51-67, 2-47-99), Prolongación Héroes 326, is on the northern extension of Avenida Héroes, about 1.5 km from the centre and also 1.5 km from the bus station, making it a good choice if you have your own wheels. This new, modern building set back from the street holds five floors of rooms with all the comforts: TV, air-con, private bath. Rates are unbeatable value: US$25 a single or double, US$29 for a suite.

Places to Eat
As with inexpensive hotels, so with restaurants: the first place to look is near the intersection of Obregón and Héroes. On the south side of Obregón just west of Héroes are no fewer than five eateries all in a row, with another one on the northern side of the street.

Nearest to Héroes is the quaint old *Restaurant Campeche*, in a Caribbean-style wooden building which may give way to the bulldozers and rampant modernisation at any moment. Until it does, you can enjoy cheap food in an old Chetumal atmosphere.

Next door is the *Panadería La Muralla*, providing fresh baked goods for bus trips, picnics, and make-your-own breakfasts.

Restaurant Sosilmar, next along Obregón west of Héroes, is perhaps the cleanest, tidiest and brightest of the eateries in this area. Prices are listed prominently; filling platters of fish or meat go for US$3 to US$3.50.

To the right of the Sosilmar is the *Restaurant Señorial*, and to the right of that is *Pollo Brujo*, a roast chicken place where you can roll your own burritos. The roast chicken goes for US$3.25 for half a chicken, US$6.50 for a whole one; wheat tortillas *(tortillas de harina)* are US$0.40, and soft drinks US$0.25.

Facing these establishments on the north side of Obregón is a serviceable hotel eatery, the *Restaurant Jacaranda*, in the Hotel Jacaranda, on Obregón just west of Héroes, where you can get a plate of four tostadas, panuchos or salbutes for US$2.50, or six chicken tacos for US$2.75.

The family-owned and operated *Restaurant Pantoja*, on the corner at M Gandhi 164 and 16 de Septiembre 181, just east of the Hotel Ucum, not far from the market and Combi Corner, is a neighbourhood favourite serving decent, inexpensive Mexican fare. A bright, newish place decorated in pink and white with fluorescent lights, it opens for breakfast early, and later provides a comida corrida for US$2.50, enchiladas for US$1.75, and meat plates such as bistec or liver and onions (higado encebollado) for US$3. Recommended. The nearby *Restaurant Ucum*, in the Hotel Ucum, also provides good cheap meals.

To sample the typical traditional food of Quintana Roo, head for the *Restaurant Típico El Taquito*, Avenida P E Calles 220 at Juárez. You enter past the cooks, hard at work, to an airy, simple dining room where

good, cheap food is served: beef tacos for US$0.45 each, hamburgers for US$1.50, and *frijoles refritos*, the speciality of the house, for US$0.75. It's straightforward, good value, and always busy.

Chetumal doesn't have many places for an upscale meal. The hotel restaurants are serviceable without being inspiring. The *Restaurant El Grill* at the Hotel Del Prado serves a comida corrida for US$8 plus drink and tip, and, at dinner, such dishes as a cheeseburger for US$5, *puntas de filete a la Mexicana* for US$9, or shrimp in garlic sauce for US$13. The restaurant at the Continental Caribe is similar, if a bit cheaper. But my favourite place to dine in Chetumal is, believe it or not, *Sergio's Pizzas* (☎ 2-23-55), Obregón 182, a block east of Héroes. Look for the stained glass windows, enter the delightfully air-conditioned dining room, order a cold beer in a frosted mug or one of the many wines offered, and select a pizza priced from US$3.50 (small, plain) to US$16 (large, fancy). The pleasant wood-panelled dining room has classical paintings and soft classical music, red and white checked tablecloths, and attentive service. A small ham and pineapple pizza (US$3.50) is plenty for one person, enough for two with heat-shrunk appetites at lunch. Sergio's is open from 1 pm to midnight every day.

Getting There & Away

Air Chetumal's small airport is less than two km north-west of the city centre along Avenida Obregón and Avenida Revolución. You can walk the distance from the intersection of Héroes and Obregón in less than half an hour; otherwise take a taxi.

Aerocaribe (☎ (983) 2-66-75 at the airport) operates flights between Chetumal and Mérida, Cozumel and Cancún. For flights to Belize City (and on to Tikal) or to Belize's cayes, cross the border into Belize and fly from Corozal; see the Belize section for details.

Bus Chetumal's large new bus station, two km north of the city centre, handles convenient buses running west to Escárcega, then on to Campeche or Palenque, Villahermosa and beyond; north to Mérida, to Valladolid, and along the coast to Cancún; and south to Corozal and Belize City.

The dominant company for buses to points in Mexico is Autobuses del Caribe, with 1st and 2nd-class services, some run in conjunction with Autobuses de Oriente (ADO). All buses listed below run daily by Autobuses del Caribe unless otherwise specified. For Belize there are two lines, Venus Bus Line and Batty's Bus Service, with ticket offices right in the Chetumal bus station and very frequent services.

Akumal – 275 km, five hours; seven 2nd class (US$4.25) by A del Caribe, and five 1st class (US$4.75) by A del Caribe

Bacalar – 39 km, 45 minutes; nine 2nd class (US$0.75)

Belize City – 160 km, four hours (express 3¼ hours); Venus has buses every hour on the hour from 4 am to 10 am for US$3.50; Batty's has buses every two hours on the hour from 4 am to 6 pm for the same price. The one express bus departs Chetumal at 2 pm

Campeche – 422 km, 1st-class buses (US$7) at 12.30 and 7 pm

Cancún – 382 km, seven hours; five 1st class (US$7.50) and seven 2nd class (US$6.50)

Corozal (Belize) – 30 km, one hour with border formalities; see Belize City schedule, or catch a minibus for the 12 km ride to the border at Subteniente López (see Minibus).

Escárcega – 275 km, four hours; 10 1st-class buses (US$4.75)

Felipe Carrillo Puerto – 155 km, three hours; five 1st class (US$2.75) and nine 2nd class (US$2.25)

Kohunlich – 67 km, 1¼ hours; take a bus heading west to Xpujil or Escárcega and get off just before village of Francisco Villa and walk nine km (1¾ hours) to site.

Mérida – 456 km, eight to nine hours; seven 1st class (US$8) by A Peninsulares, and eight 1st class (US$8) by A del Caribe; nine 2nd class (US$7.25) by A del Caribe

Muna – 375 km, seven hours; nine 2nd class (US$6.25)

Playa del Carmen – 315 km, 5½ hours; five 1st class (US$5.25), and seven 2nd class (US$4.75)

Puerto Morelos – 350 km, 6¼ hours; seven 2nd class (US$5.25)

Ticul – 352 km, 6½ hours; nine 2nd class (US$5.75)

Tizimin – 352 km, 6½ hours; two 2nd class (US$5.50) at 8.30 am and 4.50 pm

Tulum – 251 km, four hours; five 1st class (US$4.25) and seven 2nd class (US$4)

Tuxtla Gutiérrez – 762 km, 16 hours; one 2nd class (US$10) at 1.15 pm

Valladolid – 305 km, five hours; two 2nd class (US$4.75) at 8 am and 4 pm

Villahermosa – 575 km, 10 hours; two 1st class (US$9.75) and one 2nd class (US$6.25) at 1.15 pm

Xpujil – 120 km, two hours; three 2nd class (US$2) at 6.30 am, noon and 7.30 pm

Minibus Not far from the market are several minibus departure and arrival points. Volkswagen combi minibuses run from here to points in the vicinity of Chetumal such as Laguna Bacalar and the Belizean border at Subteniente López. Combi Corner, as I call it, is the intersection of Primo de Verdad and Hidalgo, two blocks east of Héroes (four blocks north-east of the market).

AROUND CHETUMAL
Calderitas
If you want to go out to a beach, catch a Calderitas bus on Avenida Belice between Colón and Gandhi, just by the market, for a 15 to 20-minute, six-km ride to Calderitas Bay and its rocky beach. Palapas (thatched roofs) here shelter you from the sun; refreshment stands provide snacks and drinks. If you wish to pitch a tent, there's a campsite. Note that on Sundays the beach is packed with locals and their families on their day off.

Laguna Bacalar
Minibuses depart from Combi Corner in Chetumal about every 20 minutes from 5 am to 7 pm for the 39-km (40 minutes, US$1.50) run to the town of Bacalar, on the lake of the same name; some buses (US$0.75) departing from the bus station will drop you near the town of Bacalar. Along the way they pass Laguna Milagros (14 km), Xul-ha (22 km) and the Cenote Azul (33 km), and all four of these places afford chances to swim in fresh water. The lakes are gorgeous, framed by palm trees, with crystal clear water and soft white limestone-sand bottoms.

Heading west out of Chetumal, you turn

north onto Highway 307; 15.5 km north of this highway junction is a turn on the right marked for the Cenote Azul and Costera Bacalar.

Cenote Azul & Costera Bacalar The Cenote Azul is a 90-metre-deep natural pool on the south-western shore of Laguna Bacalar, 200 metres east of Highway 307. (If you're approaching from the north by bus, get the driver to stop and let you off here.) Being a cenote there's no beach, just a few steps leading down to the water from the vast palapa which shelters the restaurant. A small sign purveys the traditional wisdom: 'Don't go in the cenote if you can't swim'.

The restaurant has its own little aviary with colourful peacocks and macaws; main course dishes of fish or meat are US$3.75 to US$9.50; you might pay US$7.50 to US$10 for the average meal here.

The road which leaves Highway 307 at Cenote Azul is called the Costera Bacalar. It winds its way along the hilly country by the lakeshore past a few lodging and camping places to the town of Bacalar. Only 1.5 km past Cenote Azul along the Costera is a nameless little camping area on the shore run by a family who live in a shack on the premises. You can camp in the dense shade of the palm trees, enjoy the view of the lake from the palapas, swim from the grassy banks, all for US$4 per couple. Bring your own food and drinking water, as the nearest supplier is the restaurant at Cenote Azul.

Hotel Laguna (☎ (983) 2-35-17 in Chetumal, (99) 27-13-04 in Mérida), 2.2 km from Cenote Azul along the Costera, is only 150 metres east of Highway 307, so you can ask a bus driver to stop here for you. Twenty years ago this place was a dump, but it's now been fixed up to become a hidden paradise: clean, cool and hospitable, with a wonderful view of the lake, a nice swimming pool, breezy terrace and restaurant, and the Bar AA (which usually stands for Alcohólicos Anónimos, but here means Alcohólicos Activos). Three toilets in a row are labelled M to one side, F to the other, and Indeterminato in between. Rooms at the

Laguna cost US$30 a single or double with fan, good cross-ventilation and private bath. In the restaurant, sandwiches go for US$2, and fried chicken, fish or beef for US$3.75 to US$4.50.

Continuing along the Costera, just over three km from Cenote Azul is the *Meson Nueva Salamanca*, Costera 51, with tidy little motel-type rooms for US$19 a double. There's no restaurant, but a little shop sells cold drinks and snacks.

The town of Bacalar, with its old fortress and its swimming facilities, is 5.5 km north of Cenote Azul along the Costera Bacalar.

The fortress was built over the lagoon to protect citizens from raids by pirates and Indians. It served as an important outpost for the Whites in the War of the Castes. In 1859, it was seized by Mayan rebels who held the fort until Quintana Roo was finally conquered by Mexican troops in 1901. Today, with formidable cannon still on its ramparts, the fortress remains an imposing sight. It houses a museum exhibiting colonial armaments and uniforms from the 17th and 18th centuries. The museum is open daily from 8 am to 1 pm and has a small admission charge of US$0.25.

A divided avenue runs between the fortress and the lakeshore northward a few hundred metres to the balneario, or bathing facilities. Small restaurants line the avenue and surround the balneario, which is very busy on weekends.

Should you approach the town of Bacalar by combi, it will stop on the main plaza just above the fortress. A place called Baca Burger is just across the road from the minibus stop, providing sandwiches, drinks and snacks; other small restaurants are located around the plaza.

Kohunlich Ruins
West of Chetumal along Highway 186 is rich sugar cane and cattle country; logging is still important here as it was during the 1700s and 1800s. The archaeological site of Kohunlich is only partly excavated, with many of its nearly 200 mounds still covered with vegetation. The surrounding rainforest is thick,

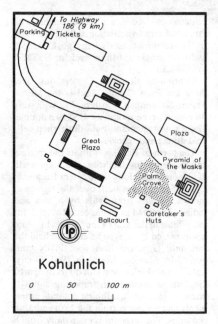

To Highway
186 (9 km)
Parking / Tickets

Great
Plaza

Plaza

Pyramid of
the Masks

Palm
Grove

Ballcourt   Caretaker's
Huts

Kohunlich

0   50   100 m

but the archaeological site itself has been cleared selectively and is now a delightful forest park. Kohunlich's caretaker, Señor Ignacio Ek, may offer you a tour, after which a tip is in order. Otherwise, admission to the site costs US$1, and is open from 8 am to 5 pm daily. Drinks are sold at the site, but nothing else.

These ruins, dating from the late Preclassic (100-200 AD) and Early Classic (250-600 AD) periods, are famous for the impressive Pyramid of the Masks: a central stairway is flanked by huge, three-metre-high stucco masks of the sun god. The thick lips and prominent features are reminiscent of Olmec sculpture. Though there were once eight masks, only two remain after the ravages of archaeology looters. The masks themselves are impressive, but the large thatch coverings which have been erected to protect them from further weathering also obscure the view; you can see the masks only from close up. Try to imagine what the

pyramid and its masks must have looked like in the old days as the Maya approached it across the sunken courtyard at the front.

The hydraulic engineering used at the site was a great achievement; nine of the site's 21 hectares were cut to channel rainwater into Kohunlich's once enormous reservoir.

Getting There & Away At the time of writing, there is no public transport running directly to Kohunlich. To visit the ruins without your own vehicle, start early in the morning, and take a bus heading west from Chetumal to Xpujil or Escárcega, then watch for the village of Nachi-Cocom some 50 km from Chetumal. About 9.5 km past Nachi-Cocom, just before the village of Francisco Villa, is a road on the left (south) which covers the nine km to the archaeological site. Have the bus driver stop and let you off here, and plan to walk and hope to hitch a ride from tourists in a car; hold up this guidebook for the driver to see. (If you're the ones in the car, please pick up tourists on foot carrying a copy of this guide!).

To return to Chetumal or head westward to Xpujil or Escárcega you must hope to flag down a bus on the highway.

FELIPE CARRILLO PUERTO
Population 17,000
Heading north, 155 km from Chetumal is the dusty town of Felipe Carrillo Puerto , once called Chan Santa Cruz. During and after the War of the Castes, Chan Santa Cruz was a centre of rebel activities. As you enter the town from the south you see a monument to *Martires de la Guerra de Castes*. After the suppression of the Mayan rebels, the town was renamed in honour of a progressive governor who was assassinated.

Because of its location at the intersection of several important highways, the town is a way-station for travellers in need of food, fuel or a bed.

History
In 1849 the War of the Castes went against the Maya of northern Yucatán, who made their way to this town seeking refuge.

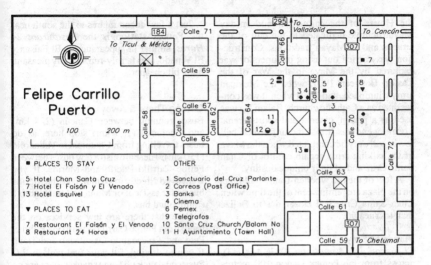

Felipe Carrillo Puerto

0   100   200 m

■ PLACES TO STAY

5 Hotel Chan Santa Cruz
7 Hotel El Faisán y El Venado
13 Hotel Esquivel

▼ PLACES TO EAT

7 Restaurant El Faisón y El Venado
8 Restaurant 24 Horas

OTHER

1 Sanctuario del Cruz Parlante
2 Correos (Post Office)
3 Banks
4 Cinema
6 Pemex
7 Telegrafos
10 Santa Cruz Church/Balam Na
11 H Ayuntamiento (Town Hall)

Regrouping their forces, they were ready to sally forth again in 1850, just when a 'miracle' occurred. A wooden cross erected at a cenote on the western edge of the town began to 'talk', telling the Maya they were the chosen people, exhorting them to continue the struggle against the Whites, and promising the Maya forces victory. The talking was done by a ventriloquist who used sound chambers, but the people nonetheless looked upon it as the authentic voice of their aspirations.

The oracular cross guided the Maya in battle for eight years, until their great victory in conquering the fortress at Bacalar. For the latter part of the 1800s, the Maya in and around Chan Santa Cruz were virtually independent of governments in Mexico City and Mérida; the British in Belize even recognised Mayan sovereignty by dealing with them on the diplomatic level.

In 1893 the Mexican government negotiated a border treaty with the British, who were thus forced to give up their support for the Maya of Chan Santa Cruz, and in 1901 the Mexican army conquered the region, but retreated in 1915, leaving it to the Maya again. In the 1920s a boom in the chicle

market brought prosperity to the region and the Maya decided to come to terms with Mexico City, which they did in 1929. Some of the Maya, unwilling to give up the cult of the talking cross, left Chan Santa Cruz to take up residence at small villages deep in the jungle, where they still revere the talking cross to this day. You may see some of them visiting the site where the cross spoke in its little park, especially on 3 May, the day of the Holy Cross.

Things to See

You can visit the **Sanctuario del Cruz Parlante** five blocks west of the Pemex fuel station on the main street (Highway 307) in the commercial centre of town. Besides the cenote and a stone shelter, there's little to see in the park, though the place reverberates with history.

On the town's main plaza, the Palacio Municipal (H Ayuntamiento) now stands where the rebel Maya built Chikin Ik, the Palace of the West Wind, to house the militant priests of the talking cross who governed the rebel armies and state.

Across the plaza is the church, now quite Catholic, but originally built as Balam Na, the House of the Jaguar, a modern-day Mayan temple dedicated to the cult of the crosses and to Mayan traditions. Construction was carried out using prisoners of war captured by the Maya in the War of the Castes. Between 1901, when the Mexican army triumphed, and 1950 when it was consecrated as a Catholic church, Balam Na was used as a prison, cinema and sports arena. Local legend has it that the unfinished bell tower will only be completed when the Maya of the talking cross regain control of Chan Santa Cruz and of their unique destiny.

A few of the old wooden-frame buildings on the plaza are reminiscent of the time when Chan Santa Cruz had closer ties to Belize than to Yucatán.

Places to Stay

El Faisan y El Venado (☎ (983) 4-00-43), across from the Pemex station 100 metres south of the traffic roundabout, has 13 clean rooms with private showers and either ceiling fans or air-con. Prices are US$6.50 to US$12 a single, US$8.75 to US$13 a double, US$10.50 to US$15 a triple, the higher prices being for those with air-con, of course.

Just off the main plaza is the *Hotel Chan Santa Cruz* (☎ (983) 4-01-70), with acceptable if plain rooms around a courtyard priced similarly to that at El Faisan y El Venado.

Last time I visited Felipe Carrillo Puerto, the management at the *Hotel Esquivel*, just off the plaza more or less across from the church, didn't seem at all interested in renting me a room. They quoted a price of US$15 a double with fan and private bath. Maybe you'll have better luck than I did.

Places to Eat

The two dependable restaurants of long standing in this town are the *Restaurant El Faisan y El Venado*, in the same building as the hotel of that name, on the main street (Highway 307). The big, pleasant, shady palapa-covered dining room is cooled by fans, and the menu offers main dishes for about US$3.75. I had a large fruit cocktail, a club sandwich and a bottle of mineral water for US$4.

Just a few dozen metres to the south near the Pemex station is the *Restaurant 24 Horas*, similar in appearance to El Faisan y El Venado, also family-run, equally pleasant, but a bit cheaper.

Getting There & Away

Buses running between Cancún (224 km) and Chetumal (155 km) stop here, as do buses travelling from Chetumal to Valladolid (150 km). There are also a few buses between Felipe Carrillo Puerto and Mérida. If you want to go directly to Uxmal, take the Mérida bus as far as Ticul or Muna and transfer to a southbound bus.

Note that there are few services on the route from Felipe Carrillo Puerto via Polyuc, Peto and Tzucacab to Oxkutzcab and Ticul. If you're driving, fill your fuel tank in F C Puerto and pick up some snacks; there are no real restaurants. Cold drinks are all you can depend upon finding.

TULUM

The ruins of Tulum, though well preserved, would hardly merit rave notices if it weren't for their setting. And what a setting! Here the grey-black buildings of the past sit on a palm-fringed beach, lapped by the turquoise waters of the Caribbean.

While Tulum literally means City of the Dawn in Mayan, a looser translation is City of Renewal. For those travellers who are 'ruined out', the dramatic environs of Tulum will renew their desire to explore antiquities.

Like Chichén Itzá, Tulum's proximity to the tourist centres of Cancún and Isla Mujeres make it a prime target of tour buses. To best enjoy the ruins, visit them either early in the morning or late in the day. The ruins are open from 8 am to 5 pm and there is a US$4 admission charge. Around midday, when Tulum's fortress city is besieged by busloads of tourists, it is best to make use of either the ruin's beaches or the sands south of here. After a siesta, you'll be refreshed enough to return to the more lightly populated ruins in the late afternoon.

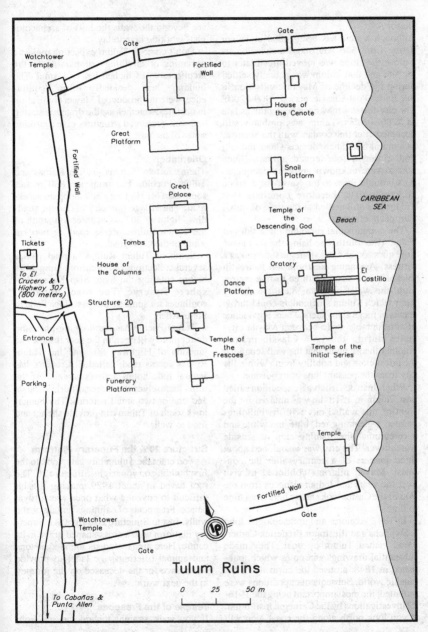

Tulum Ruins

Watchtower Temple

Gate

Gate

Fortified Wall

Fortified Wall

House of the Cenote

Great Platform

Snail Platform

Great Palace

Tombs

House of the Columns

Structure 20

CARIBBEAN SEA

Beach

Temple of the Descending God

Oratory

El Castillo

Dance Platform

Temple of the Initial Series

Temple of the Frescoes

Tickets

To El Crucero & Highway 307 (800 meters)

Entrance

Parking

Funerary Platform

Temple

Watchtower Temple

Gate

Fortified Wall

Gate

Temple

To Cabañas & Punta Allen

0   25   50 m

History

Although a stela has been found at Tulum dating from 546 AD, most archaeologists believe the stone was moved much later to the site and that Tulum was actually settled during the decline of Mayan civilisation in the Early Post-Classic period (900-1200). The city-fortress may have been built as late as 1200. In fact, Tulum was probably still occupied after first contact with the Spanish, as a mural found here depicts Chac, the rain god, riding a four-legged animal. Since horses were unknown until the conquistadors brought them to the New World, some archaeologists therefore conclude that Tulum was still settled at the time of initial European intrusion.

The ramparts that surround three sides of Tulum (the fourth side being the sea) leave little question as to its strategic function as a fortress. Averaging nearly seven metres in thickness and standing three to five metres high, the walls have an interior walkway from which Tulum's defenders could throw spears or rocks at invaders. There is evidence of considerable strife between Mayan city-states during the Late Classic period. Another theory holds that the wall separated the priest class and nobility living within the city from the peasant huts built outside.

When Juan de Grijalva's expedition sailed past Tulum in 1518, he was amazed by the sight of this walled city with its buildings painted a gleaming red, blue and white and a ceremonial fire flaming atop its seaside watchtower. The city was abandoned about three-quarters of a century after the conquest. Mayan pilgrims continued to visit over the years and Indian refugees from the War of the Castes took shelter here from time to time.

In 1842, explorer and archaeologist John L Stephens and illustrator Frederick Catherwood visited Tulum by boat. They made substantial drawings and notes which, published in 1848, aroused the curiosity of the outside world. Subsequent expeditions were mounted, the most important being the 1916-22 investigations by the Carnegie Institution. If you look north along the coast, you will see beyond the walls the huts of archaeologists working here today.

Don't come to Tulum expecting majestic pyramids or anything comparable to the architecture of Chichén Itzá or Uxmal. The buildings here, decidedly Toltec in influence, were the product of Mayan civilisation in decline. Nonetheless, the dramatic setting and well-preserved structures give a striking sense of the past.

Orientation

There are two Tulums, Tulum Ruinas and Tulum Pueblo. The ruins are 800 metres south-east off Highway 307 along an access road. The village *(pueblo)* of Tulum straddles Highway 307 about three km south of the Tulum Ruinas access road, or two km south of the Cobá road.

South of Tulum Ruinas, a road passes several collections of beachfront bungalows before entering the huge Sian Ka'an Biosphere Reserve. The road, unpaved, continues for some 50 km past Boca Paila to Punta Allen.

Tulum Pueblo has one lodging-place; no doubt more will open in the near future. The junction of Highway 307 and the Tulum Ruinas access road, called El Crucero, has several little hotels and restaurants. At the ruins themselves there are soft drink stands and one or two small eateries. The bungalows south of Tulum can provide shelter and food as well.

Structure 20 & the Funerary Platform

As you enter the Tulum city gate, look to the first building on your right, Structure 20. The roof caved in about 1929, making it a bit difficult to envision what once was a royal palace. Fragments of paintings remain on the walls. Just to Structure 20's right is a Funerary Platform with a cross-shaped grave in its centre. Here archaeologists found skeletons and animal offerings, the latter to provide sustenance for the deceased on the journey to the next world.

Temple of the Frescoes

If you walk straight toward the sea from

Fresco from the Temple of the Frescoes, Tulum

Structure 20, you will come to the relatively well-preserved Temple of the Frescoes. Thought initially to have been built about 1450, the temple has been added to on several occasions. Here you will see a carved figure very much in evidence at Tulum, the diving god. Equipped with wings and a bird's tail, this fascinating deity has been linked by some archaeologists with the Venus morning-star symbol of Quetzalcóatl. Others believe it bears some relation to the Mayan god of the bee, honey being a valued sweetener and a major Yucatecan trade product. On the western façade are stucco masks thought to symbolise Quetzalcóatl in another form.

Inside the temple the best preserved of the greenish-blue on black murals may be seen through protective bars. The mural is painted in three levels demarcating the three realms of the Mayan universe: the dark underworld of the deceased, the middle order of the living and the heavenly home of the creator and rain gods. Look closely at the middle level and you will see a god astride a four-legged beast – an image probably indicating knowledge of the conquistadors' horses.

The Great Palace

To the left of the Temple of the Frescoes, as you face the sea, is the Great Palace. Smaller than El Castillo, this largely deteriorated site contains a fine stucco carving of a diving god.

El Castillo

Look straight toward the sea from the Temple of the Frescoes and you can't miss Tulum's tallest building, a watchtower fortress overlooking the Caribbean, appropriately named El Castillo by the Spanish. Over the years, El Castillo was built as a series of additions. It started as a palace-like base, upon which a staircase and a crowning temple were constructed.

Note the serpent columns of the temple's entrance, with rattlers' tails supporting the roof and their heads adjoining the floor. Chichén Itzá's Temple of the Warriors has a similar columnar design influenced by the Toltec plumed serpent. On top of the entrance columns of El Castillo's temple is a fine carving of the diving god.

Take the pyramid-like staircase to the summit's temple for the view. On one side you'll see the luminous Caribbean shimmering in the tropical sun and on the other the antiquities of Tulum. This watchtower guarded the city against sea invasion. Imagine how surprised the Maya of Tulum must have been to spy the sails of the first Spanish ships along this coast.

Look down to the north from El Castillo and you will see a good small beach, great for sunning and a refreshing dip. There's a bit of an undertow here, so swim with caution.

Temple of the Descending God

Facing north (left as you face the sea) from the front of El Castillo, you will see the Temple of the Descending God. True to its name, there is a good stucco carving of a diving god on top of the door. If you ascend the inner staircase, you will see paint fragments of a religious mural.

Temple of the Initial Series

At the south flank of El Castillo stands a restored temple named for a stela now in the British Museum, which was inscribed with the Mayan date corresponding to 564 AD. At first this confused archaeologists, who had evidence that Tulum was not settled until some time later. Today, scholars believe that the stela was moved here from a city founded much earlier. This temple has a handsome arch and windows on three sides.

Places to Stay

There are no very cheap lodgings near Tulum, but if you're willing to spend a bit more you can find places at El Crucero, Tulum Pueblo, and along the road south to Punta Allen.

El Crucero Right at the junction of Highway 307 and the Tulum access road are several hotels and restaurants, including the *Motel El Crucero* (no phone). Older rooms with fan and private shower rent for US$15 a double. There's a restaurant and a shop selling ice, pastries, snacks and souvenirs.

Facing the Motel El Crucero across the access road is the *Hotel El Faisan y El Venado* (no phone), which is slightly fancier with better rooms, but also a bit more expensive at US$17 a double for a room with fan, private bath and TV with a satellite hook-up. There's a small swimming pool out the back and a decent restaurant as well.

Tulum Pueblo The *Hotel Maya Tulum* is on the west side of Highway 307 as it passes through the village, right near the village bus stop. Opened in 1990, this simple hotel charges US$15 for a double room with ceiling fan and private bathroom. The problem is that here you're four km (almost an hour's walk) from the ruins. For reservations, call the caseta (village telephone office) at (987) 2-16-33 and leave a message for Irma Cruz, manager of the hotel.

Along the Boca Paila/Punta Allen Road

South of the archaeological zone is a paradise of palm-shaded white beach dotted with collections of cabañas, little thatched huts of greater or lesser comfort, and simple wooden or concrete bungalows. Most of these places have little eateries at which you can take your meals, and some have electric generators which provide electric light for several hours each evening. There are no phones.

The cheapest way to sleep here is to have your own hammock, preferably with one of those tube-like mosquito nets to cover it; if you don't carry your own, several of the cheaper places will rent you what you need. If you have candles or a torch, it'll come in handy here. In the cheapest places you'll have to supply your own towel and soap.

Rumour has it that the Mexican government plans to do away with these hostelries because of drug use by visitors, and out of concern for the Sian Ka'an Biosphere Reserve, in which some of these places are located. Until the government acts, you can enjoy this ideal location.

Unfortunately, these lodgings are located some distance south of the ruins and there is no public transport along the road. Though you may occasionally be able to hitch a ride, you can depend only upon your own two feet to get you from your bungalow to the ruins, which may be up to seven km away.

I'll start by describing the places closest to Tulum ruins, then head south to describe the places farther and farther away.

Closest to the ruins are *Cabañas El Mirador* and *Cabañas Santa Fe*, on the beach about 600 metres south of the Tulum ruins parking lot. Of the two, the Santa Fe is preferable, though a bit more expensive, charging US$2 per person for a campsite, US$5 to hang your hammocks in a cabin, single or double.

One km south of the parking lot is *Cabañas Don Armando*, another step up the price and quality scale. For US$8 (single or double) you get one of 17 cabins built on concrete slabs, with lockable doors, hammocks or beds (you pay a deposit for sheets and pillows), mosquito netting, good showers, and a good, cheap restaurant. Lighting is by candles. This place is fun, right on the beach, and still only a 10-minute walk to the ruins.

Next to the south is the *Hotel El Paraíso*, 1.5 km south of the ruins, which approaches a conventional hotel in its services. Some of the rooms are in older bungalow units, others in newer motel-style structures up on the hill; all benefit from the constant cooling onshore breezes. The newer rooms, with two double beds and private bath, cost US$25. There's a nice little restaurant with a good sea view.

South of El Paraíso it's over three km to the next lodgings, *Cabañas Familia Canché*, 4.5 km south of the ruins. Just south of the Canché is *La Perla Restaurant*, and after that the paved road ends, giving way to a good sand track.

Cabañas Chac-Mool are just north of the Sian Ka'an Biosphere Reserve entrance, about 5.7 km south of the ruins. You can camp here or rent one of the comparatively expensive cabañas, and dine in the cosy vegetarian restaurant.

As you go south the cabañas get a bit more expensive, comfortable and scuba-diver-oriented, charging between US$20 and US$30 for a double room. *Los Arrecifes*, seven km south of the ruins, is just this way, with large, fairly luxurious (for Tulum) bungalows on the beach for US$50, or much cheaper, simpler ones back from the beach (no view) for US$20. Despite the lofty prices, there's no electricity.

Restaurant y Cabañas de Anna y José is next door to the south, with simple lodgings but a decent if plain restaurant.

The last set of cabañas in this group is *Cabañas Tulum*, over seven km south of the ruins, where little concrete bungalows look out through the palm shade to the sea and the beach – a perfect hideaway from the world. Each has two double beds, light bulb, window screens, cold-water private shower, a table, and a porch perfect for hammock-hanging; the rate is US$20 per night, single or double. The electric generator runs (if it's working) from dusk to 10 pm each evening.

Places to Eat
There are no truly expensive meals to be had near Tulum, only cheap ones, but value for money is best at the camping and cabaña places south of the ruins.

El Crucero The *Motel El Crucero* has a popular, very simple but somewhat expensive restaurant. Go the American route with a cheeseburger plate for US$3.50, or have Yucatecan cochinita pibil for the same price. Tacos and enchiladas go for US$3.25, and it's a good idea to stick to these simple items rather than to hazard money on the fancier dishes costing several times as much. The seafood, for instance, would be of questionable freshness.

At the *Restaurant El Faisan y El Venado* across the street the surroundings are a bit more attractive, the food similar, the prices just a bit higher.

Tulum Ruinas The car park at the ruins is surrounded by little stalls selling souvenirs. Most of these used to be tiny eateries, but the profits are in cheap souvenirs so the eateries got driven out. A few survive, however, including the *Restaurant México*, on the left as you come into the car park from the highway. It serves decent sandwiches of cheese, ham or chicken for US$3, and fried chicken for US$3.75. Sometimes they have spaghetti or fish, and they always have cold beer and soft drinks.

The little restaurant right next door to the left of the Restaurant México is similar but not quite so nice. At the far end of the parking lot near the road to Punta Allen is the *Restaurant Garibaldi*.

Getting There & Away
Getting to Tulum from Cancún, Playa del Carmen, Chetumal or Felipe Carrillo Puerto is no problem: you simply buy a ticket for a seat on the bus and get off at El Crucero near Tulum Ruinas. But getting away from Tulum may be difficult as you must depend upon passing buses to pick you up, and these are often full. Sometimes a sympathetic tourist in a rented car will give you a lift if you hitchhike. In any case, plan to wait a while for a bus, and don't expect to find a seat on the first one that stops.

During the day, northbound and southbound buses stop at El Crucero about every two hours. If you are venturing between Tulum and points north along the Caribbean coast, try hitchhiking while you are waiting for the bus as there are many gringos going to or from the ruins in rental cars. Note that 1st-class buses, if full, may not take you aboard and are reluctant to drop you between Tulum and Akumal. With 2nd class, you will have to stand if all seats are taken. There are shared long-distance taxis, but fares between Tulum and Cancún are several times those of the bus.

TULUM TO BOCA PAILA & PUNTA ALLEN

If you think you might find a tourist-free paradise by taking the unpaved road to land's-end some 50 km south of Tulum past Boca Paila, forget it. The scenery en route is the typically monotonous flat Yucatecan terrain. Furthermore, the beaches are far from spectacular, though there's no doubt you will find plenty of privacy.

You ultimately meet land's-end at the lobster-fishing village of Punta Allen. While not without some charm, its beaches are less attractive than, say, the sands around Cabañas Los Arrecifes just a short drive from Tulum.

It's important to have plenty of fuel before heading south from Tulum as there is no fuel available on the Tulum-Punta Allen road.

Places to Stay

One of the two hotels on the road to Punta Allen is *La Villa de Boca Paila*, where luxury cabañas complete with kitchens cost about US$90 per double, including two meals. The clientele is predominantly affluent American sport fishers. For reservations write to Apdo Postal 159, Mérida, Yucatán, Mexico. Boca Paila is 25 km south of the ruins.

Ten km south of Boca Paila you cross a rickety wooden bridge. Beyond it is *El Retiro Cabañas* where you can hang hammocks or camp for a few dollars.

Punta Allen does have some rustic lodgings. The *Curzan Guest House* has cabañas with hammocks for about US$20 a double. The couple who run it prepare breakfast and lunch at a cost of US$5 per person and charge US$10 for dinner. They can arrange snorkelling and fishing expeditions, or visits to the offshore island of Cayo Colibri, known for its bird life. To write for reservations, the address is Curzan Guest House, c/o Sonia Lillvik, Apdo Postal 703, Cancún, Quintana Roo 77500.

If you wish to camp on Punta Allen's beach, simply ask the Maya in front of whose house you would be sleeping for permission.

COBÁ

Fifty km north-west of Tulum lies a more impressive, yet less frequently visited, ruined Mayan site. Perhaps the largest of all Mayan cities, Cobá – whose ruins extend at least 50 sq km – offers the chance to explore mostly unrestored antiquities set deep in tropical jungles. Prepare to do some walking on jungle paths and dress for humidity, wear decent footgear and cover yourself with repellent because the forest here can be thick with mosquitoes. It's also a good idea to bring a canteen of water because it's hot and the refreshment stands are outside the main gate. Avoid the midday heat.

Don't let all this put you off; no other site in the Yucatán Peninsula offers such an opportunity to play at being an archaeologist. The estimated 5% of Cobá that has been unearthed will reward you by letting you walk the streets of one of the Maya's greatest cities.

Cobá is worth visiting for other reasons. On jungle walks, you are likely to see tropical birds, butterflies, reptiles and insects.

History

Cobá was settled earlier than Chichén or Tulum, its heyday dating from 600 AD until the site was abandoned about 900 AD. Cobá's architecture is a mystery; its towering pyramids and stelae resemble the architecture of Tikal, several hundred km away, rather than that of Chichén Itzá and other sites of northern Yucatán a quarter of that distance.

While there is not yet a definitive explanation, some archaeologists theorise that an alliance with Tikal was made through marriage to facilitate trade between the Guatemalan and Yucatecan Maya. Stelae appear to depict female rulers from Tikal holding ceremonial bars and flaunting their power by standing on captives. These Tikal royal females, when married to Cobá's royalty, may have brought architects and artisans from Guatemala with them.

Archaeologists are also baffled by the network of extensive stone-paved avenues or *sacbeob* in this region, with Cobá as the hub. The longest runs nearly 100 km from the base of Cobá's great pyramid Nohoch Mul to the Mayan settlement of Yaxuna. In all, some 40 sacbeob passed through Cobá. Why did the Maya build such an extensive road network if they had no pack animals to traverse the wide (some measuring 10 metres across) straight roads? The best guess is that the sacbés' function was mostly ceremonial, perhaps allowing Mayan astronomers to get an early fix on a rising celestial body. In effect, the sacbeob may have been parts of the huge astronomical 'time machine' that was evident in every Mayan city.

Archaeologists believe that this vast city once held 40,000 Maya. They don't know why it was abandoned. The small populace presently inhabiting the region raises the question of what happened to all the people.

The first excavation was by the Austrian archaeologist Teobert Maler. Hearing rumours of a fabled lost city, he came to Cobá alone in 1891. There was little subsequent investigation until 1926 when the Carnegie Institute financed the first of two expeditions led by J Eric S Thompson and Harry Pollock. After their 1930 expedition not much happened until 1973, when the Mexican government slowly began to finance excavation. Archaeologists now estimate that Cobá contains some 6500 structures of which just a small percentage have been excavated and restored.

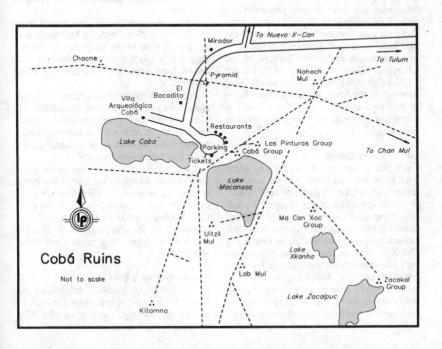

Cobá Ruins

Not to scale

Orientation

About 650 metres after you bear left at a fork in the road to approach Cobá village, notice a sign marked 'Mirador'. At my last visit there was nothing to see from this 'viewpoint' except jungle, but several years ago the jungle had been cut back to reveal part of the sacbé which went from Cobá to Yaxuna. Perhaps when you visit the jungle will have been attacked again (but ultimately it always wins).

The small village of Cobá, 1.5 km past the Mirador, is what you see first as you approach the archaeological site. Just past the village is the lake; turn left for the ruins, right for the Villa Arqueológica Cobá hotel.

The village has several small, simple and cheap lodging and eating places. There are also four small cookshops by the entrance to the archaeological site. The site is open from 8 am to 5 pm; admission costs US$4.

Cobá Group

Soon after you enter the site, you will see a right fork designated 'Cobá Group'. Take this path past unexcavated mounds and the rubble of ruins until you come to the enormous pyramid called the Temple of the Churches. Climb to the top of this steep edifice for a view of the Nohoch Mul pyramid to the north and shimmering lakes to the east and south-west. If you continue along this path you will ultimately come to Lake Cobá.

Las Pinturas Group

From the Temple of the Churches, come back to the main path and follow it until you see the sign for the Conjunto de las Pinturas, or the Temple of Paintings, located on a trail branching off from the main path. En route to the temple, you can take a one-km circular subtrail past some stelae dubbed Grupo Ma Can Xoc. Some of the stelae on this trail are very fine, others badly deteriorated. It is from one of these that archaeologists theorised that the carved woman with the ceremonial bar as well as the woman standing arrogantly on a captive were royal females from Tikal.

Returning to the trail to the Temple of the Paintings, you will find disappointingly bare walls upon reaching the temple. Today there remain mere fragments of the murals which once gave this edifice its name. Take the trail from the temple entrance to a break in the bush and you will see a huge stela. Here, a regal-looking man stands over two figures, one of them kneeling with his hands bound behind him. Sacrificial captives lie beneath the feet of a ruler at the base of the deteriorating stela.

Nohoch Mul – The Great Pyramid

Return to the main trail and follow the signs to Nohoch Mul. It's a 1.5-km walk through lush, humid jungle and though you may be hot and tired at this point, the trek is well worth the effort. At a splendid 42 metres high, the Great Pyramid is the tallest of all Mayan structures in the Yucatán Peninsula. Climb the 120 steps for a panoramic view of the surrounding jungle, observing that the Maya carved shell-like forms where you put your feet.

There are some diving gods carved over the doorway of the Nohoch Mul temple at the top, similar to the sculptures at Tulum. Apparently this temple at the summit was added long after the pyramid was constructed.

From the Great Pyramid's face, look to the right in the plaza and you will see Temple 10. The building itself is not particularly noteworthy, but in front of it is the exquisitely carved Stela 20, with a ruler standing over two kneeling captive slaves.

There are unexcavated ruins as far from the entrance as Ixtil, 19 km distant. For those seeking the unusual, there is a three-storeyed pyramid near Kucilan (eight km south of Cobá's centre) which, unlike other Mayan structures of its kind, has lower storeys, which were never filled in, to support the added level.

Places to Stay & Eat

In the village of Cobá is the *Restaurant Isabel*, which also offers rooms for rent. In fact on my last visit lodging was the only business being done as the restaurant bore a sign reading 'No Functione'. The spartan but basically acceptable rooms with fans and shared bath here cost US$5 a single and US$7 a double.

Fifty metres from Hotel Isabel, *Restaurant Bocadito* has clean doubles with bath for US$7 a single, US$10 a double; some minor fixing up would make all the difference! Still, the manager is very helpful and will do his best to make you comfortable. As for the restaurant, it's your best bet for a cheap meal in these parts. More pleasant and lower in price than the eateries facing the parking lot at the entrance to the archaeological site, *Bocadito* (Little Mouthful) offers ham and cheese sandwiches for US$2, guacamole for just a bit more, and main course platters such as beef, pork or chicken for US$5.

Next door to the Bocadito is *Cabañas Económicas*, which was not open at my last visit, but these places have a way of opening and closing without warning, so have a look in any case.

As for camping, there's no organised spot, though you can try finding a place along the shore of the lake.

For upscale lodging and dining the choice is easy: there's only the *Villa Arqueológica Cobá* (☎ in Cancún (988) 4-25-74). This pleasant hotel is a gathering spot for archaeologists and those interested in antiquities. There is a library here with the focus on Mayan culture and history, and a study of Mexican, Guatemalan and Honduran archaeological sites. The very pleasant hotel has a swimming pool and good restaurant. Air-conditioned rooms cost US$45 a single, US$48 a double, US$54 a triple. Lunch or dinner in the good restaurant might cost US$15 to US$22, depending partly upon what and how much you drink.

For reservations if you are based in the USA, phone (800) 528-3100; or when in Mexico City call 203-38-86. You can supposedly make bookings through the travel agent at the Hotel Antillano lobby in Cancún. He's a helpful guy but there's no guarantee that you'll actually find a room reserved for you when you arrive in Cobá! If there's no

room available in Cobá they may let you sleep in the library or fix you up with a room in the employees' quarters.

Getting There & Away

Buses veer onto the Cobá road from Highway 307, north of Tulum Pueblo, for Cobá at 6 and 11 am on their way to Valladolid via Nuevo X-Can. The 50-km trip to Cobá takes about an hour and costs US$2. From Valladolid, buses leave for Cobá at 4 am and noon, arriving about two hours later. Be sure to mention to the driver that you want to get out at Cobá, because the road does not pass directly through the village of Cobá and thus you might miss it. If the driver drops you at the junction with the dead-end road to the village and the ruins, you'll have a 2-km walk to the village, a 2.5-km walk to the ruins.

A more comfortable, dependable but expensive way to reach Cobá is by taxi from the parking lot at the Tulum ruins. Find some other travellers interested in the trip and split the cost, about US$15 or US$20 round-trip, including two hours at the site.

If you start out early enough from Tulum and are willing to be patient, you may have some luck hitching a ride with tourists in rented cars. Hold up your copy of this book, and hope that another reader of it in a car will help you out.

Coming from Chichén Itzá or Valladolid, simply catch one of the two daily buses which depart from Valladolid, at 4 am or noon. From Cancún you must take a bus to Nuevo X-Can and wait at the junction with the Cobá road for the bus from Valladolid.

By the way, many maps show a road from Cobá to Chemax, but this road is not practicable and should not really be shown. The only passable road north from Cobá is the one to Nuevo X-Can.

BEACHES ALONG THE COAST

Some of the world's most beautiful beaches lie between Cancún and Tulum. If you want a beach of your own, away from the tourist throngs of Cancún and Isla Mujeres, this

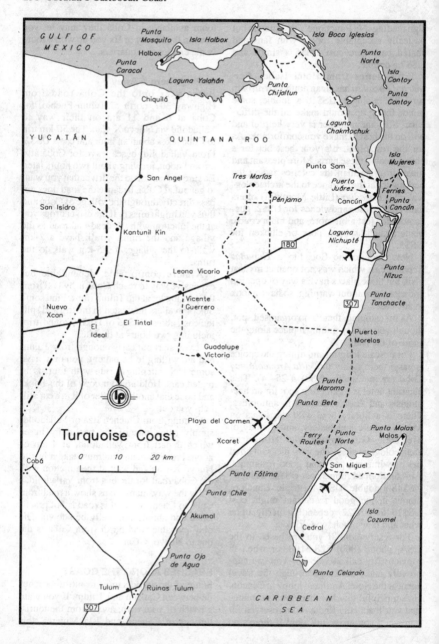

stretch of Caribbean coast may make your dreams come true.

Privacy does come at a cost. Several of the beaches are difficult to reach, others have no lodging or only expensive hotels. If you have a tent, hammock and mosquito netting, you will be rewarded for roughing it.

Although buses run sporadically between Cancún and Tulum during the day, 1st class is often full and may not stop to pick you up. Even if 2nd class is not full, all of the seats may be; you may be lucky to get standing room, and you'll have to stand with your baggage because time is rarely taken to put it underneath in the luggage compartment. During the day, Caribbean coastal buses tend to run at roughly two-hour intervals.

While you are waiting for the bus to get you between beaches, try hitchhiking. Every day, scores of tourists who have rented cars in Cancún go day-tripping down the coast. Beachcombers find it relatively easy to catch a ride if they start out early enough. The bus fare between beaches is generally less than US$1 so don't bother hitching just to save money. The highway itself is straight and dull; dense vegetation spills back from the road on both sides and there's little sign of habitation. Access roads to the beaches are not always well marked; you may see only a narrow unpaved road heading eastwards one or two km to the beach. But the less well marked it is, the emptier it may be.

Xel-Ha Lagoon (Km 245)

Once a pristine natural lagoon brimming with iridescent tropical fish, Xel-Ha (SHELL-hah) is now a Mexican national park with landscaped grounds, changing rooms, restaurant and bar. The fish are regularly driven off by the dozens of busloads of day-trippers who come to enjoy the beautiful site and to swim in the pretty lagoon. The activity and suntan lotion of the swimmers guarantees that the fish will mostly stay outside the designated swimming and snorkelling area.

Should you visit Xel-Ha? Sure, so long as you come off-season (in summer), or in winter either very early or very late in the day

to avoid the tour buses. Bring your own lunch as the little restaurant here is overpriced. Entry to the lagoon area costs US$3; it's open from 8 am to 6 pm daily.

If you're lucky enough to swim at Xel-Ha when there are few other swimmers around, you'll enjoy a feast for the eyes. Brightly coloured, improbably shaped parrot, angel and butterfly fish are among the nearly 50 species here. You can rent snorkelling equipment; the price is a high US$5, and you may get a mask that's been worn to the point of no longer being watertight. If a rented mask is not suitable for you, ask for another no matter how much the vendor tells you that the mask is fine and you are to blame for not snorkelling correctly.

Museum & Ruins The small maritime museum contains artefacts from the wreckage of the Spanish galleon *Mantancero*. The galleon sank in 1741 just north of Akumal and in 1958 Mexican divers started their salvage operation. On display are guns, cannons, coins and other items. There are also items from some more recent wrecks as well as Mayan artefacts. Admission costs US$0.30.

There is a small archaeological site on the west side of the highway 500 metres south of the lagoon entry road, open from 8 am to 5 pm for US$1. The ruins, which are not all that impressive, date from Classic and Post-Classic periods, and include El Palacio and the Templo de los Pajaros.

Xcacel (Km 247)

Xcacel (shkah-CELL) has no lodging other than camping (US$2 per person), no electricity and only a small restaurant stall. This is actually fortunate, because if Xcacel was more developed, this magnificent Caribbean beach would be overrun. As it stands, you can enjoy this patch of paradise in relative privacy for a day-use charge of only US$1.

For fine fishing and snorkelling, try the waters north of the campground. The rocky point leads to seas for snorkelling, and the sandy outcropping is said to be a good place to fish from. The waters directly in front of the campground are not the best to swim in as there is no reef to break the waves. Swimming, like snorkelling, is best from the rocky point to the north end of the beach.

Xcacel offers good pickings for shell collectors, including that aquatic collector, the hermit crab. There are also some colourful and intricate coral pieces to be found. When beachcombing here, wear footgear.

Take the old dirt track which runs two km north to Chemuyil and three km south to Xel-Ha, and you may spy parrots, finches or the well-named clockbird (mot-mot) with its long tail.

Chemuyil (Km 248)

This is a beautiful alabaster sand beach shaded by coconut palms. There is good snorkelling in the calm waters with exceptional visibility, and fishing from the shore is said to be good.

Chemuyil is just starting to be developed, with some condos already built. During winter's high season there are a fair number of campers here.

If you camp toward the south end of the shoreline, you will avoid those who have come just for the day and enjoy the isolation and tranquillity.

The only accommodation is spartan screened shade huts with hammock hooks. Enquire about availability at the bar; they cost US$10, and showers and toilets are communal.

Unless you have the equipment and goods to cook for yourself, the only option is the local fare prepared at the bar, including some seafood.

Las Aventuras (Km 250)

Developers got the first chance at Las Aventuras, which now has a planned community of condominiums, villas, and the beautiful *Aventuras Akumal Hotel*, which has double rooms for about US$85. All rooms face the sea and each has a balcony looking out on the fine stretch of beach. There's some coral just offshore and the resort also has a pool and bar. The resort's *Los Tucanas* restaurant is pleasant, and

dinner for two with beer, dessert and coffee will cost about US$25.

Akumal (Km 255)

Famed for its beautiful beach shaded by graceful palm trees (often photographed for travel brochures), Akumal suffered some damage from Hurricane Gilbert. Many of its palms were swept away by the storm, but enough remain to keep this a beautiful place. Akumal (Place of the Turtles in Mayan), does indeed see giant turtles come ashore to lay their eggs during the summer.

Akumal Bay was once a coconut plantation which went out of business in 1925. The following year Akumal became briefly known to the world when the *New York Times*-sponsored Mason-Spinden expedition along Quintana Roo's coast noted how picturesque the bay was. Thereafter, Akumal lay forgotten by the outside world until 1958 when a Mexican diving organisation investigating the wreck of a Spanish galleon publicised the beauty of this bay. At the time, the only way to get here other than on foot was by boat from Cozumel. In 1964 a road was built and developers' pesos financed the resort hotels and bungalows in evidence today.

The beach is large enough to give you a measure of privacy. An offshore reef teeming with multicoloured fish breaks the waves, keeping the beach waters relatively calm.

Beach Activities There are two dive shops here where you can rent snorkelling gear. The best snorkelling is at the north end of the bay; or try Yal-Ku Lagoon, 1.5 km north of Akumal.

World-class divers come here to explore the Spanish galleon *Mantancero* which sank in 1741. You can see artefacts from the galleon at the museum at nearby Xel-Ha. The dive shops will arrange all your scuba excursion needs. Beginners' scuba instruction can be provided for less than US$100; if you want certification, the dive shops offer three-day courses. They will also arrange deep-sea fishing excursions.

Places to Stay Accommodation here is in the top end category, and favours vacationers spending a week or more. The least expensive of this resort's three hotels is the *Hotel-Club Akumal Caribe Villas Maya*, where basic two-person air-conditioned cabañas with bath and the amenities of tennis and basketball courts cost US$75 to US$105 a double. Make reservations through Akutrame, ☎ (915) 584-3552, or toll-free outside Texas (800) 351-1622), PO Box 13326, El Paso, Texas 79913, USA.

The *Hotel Ina Yana Kin Akumal Caribe* on the south end of the beach is an attractive two-storey modern lodge with swimming pool, boat rental and night tennis. Spacious air-conditioned rooms equipped with refrigerators cost US$90. These can sleep six people.

On the north side of the beach you will find the cabañas of *Las Casitas Akumal* (☎ (987) 2-25-54) consisting of a living room, kitchen, two bedrooms and two bathrooms. Bungalows cost US$135 in the busy winter season, US$110 in summer. For reservations write to Las Casitas (☎ (201) 489-6614; fax (201) 489-5070), 270 River St, Box 522, Hackensack, NJ 07602, USA,

Places to Eat Even the shade-huts near the beach are expensive for light lunches and snacks, considering what you get. Just outside the walled entrance of Akumal is a grocery store patronised largely by the resort workers; if you are day-tripping here, this is your sole inexpensive source of food. The store also sells tacos and other típico food.

For those willing to splurge, both the *Zasil Restaurant* next to Las Casitas on the north side of the shore and the *Lol Ha* (ask for the specials) next to the dive shop on the beach have a reputation for fine cuisine. Somewhat cheaper is the restaurant owned by the *Hotel Ina Yana Kin*.

Yal-Ku Lagoon (Km 256.5) One of the secrets of snorkelling aficionados, Yal-Ku Lagoon is not even signposted. Its dirt road turn-off is across from a stone-walled house with a windmill. The tiny lagoon is a good place to snorkel, filled with a delightful array of aquatic life. Best of all, you may have the lagoon to yourself.

Yal-Ku is basically for day trips, as there is little shade and not much in the way of decent places to pitch a tent. Bring your own refreshments and snorkelling gear.

Puerto Aventuras (Km 269.5)
The Cancún lifestyle spreads inexorably southward, dotting this recently pristine coast with yet more sybaritic resort hideaways. One such is the *Puerto Aventuras Resort* (☎ (987) 2-22-11), PO Box 186, Playa del Carmen, Quintana Roo, a modern luxury complex of hotel rooms, swimming pools, beach facilities and other costly comforts.

Pamul (Km 274) Although Pamul's small rocky beach does not have long stretches of white sand like some of its Caribbean cousins, the palm-fringed surroundings are inviting. If you walk only about two km north of Pamul's little hotel, you will find an alabaster sand beach to call your own. If you're collecting coral, try the shores just south of Pamul. The least rocky section is the southern end, but watch out for spiked sea urchins in the shallows offshore.

Giant sea turtles come ashore here at night in July and August to lay their eggs. Why they return to the same beach every year is a mystery not understood by zoologists. If you run across a turtle during your evening stroll along the beach, keep a good distance from it and don't use a light, as this will scare it. Do your part to contribute to the survival of the turtles, which are endangered: let them lay their eggs in peace.

Places to Stay & Eat *Hotel Pamul* offers basic but acceptable rooms with fan and bath for US$12 a single and US$20 a double. There is electricity in the evenings until 10 pm. The friendly family that runs this somewhat scruffy hotel and campsite also serves breakfasts and seafood at their little restaurant for reasonable prices.

The fee for camping is US$5 for two

people per site. There are showers and toilets.

Xcaret (Km 290)

Look for the Restaurant Xcaret on the east side of the highway; this marks the access road to this beautiful spot. The road cuts through the Rancho Xcaret turkey farm, to which you must pay an admission fee of US$1, before reaching several small tumble-down Mayan ruins, and then a beautiful inlet, or *caleta*, filled with tropical marine life. Bring your snorkelling gear. A small restaurant provides refreshments at resort prices. Inland a few metres from the coast is Xcaret cenote, a limpid pool in a limestone cave, which is also an excellent place for a swim.

PLAYA DEL CARMEN

For decades Playa (as it's called) was just a simple fishing village on the coast opposite Cozumel. With the construction of Cancún, however, the number of travellers roaming this part of Yucatán increased by an order of magnitude. Playa, as the jumping-off point for Cozumel, got plenty of new traffic.

Playa is still something of a 'raw' beach town, with unpaved sand streets and an 'instant' infrastructure of cheaply con-structed buildings, few telephones, and even fewer services. Most of the hotels are owned and run by foreigners for foreigners, at prices higher than in Mexican-run establishments. Sometimes it seems as though the locals and tourists could be living on different planets. The beach resort parts of Playa are like a poor person's Cozumel pasted onto a subsistence Yucatecan fishing town. Even so, Playa is pleasant, with good beaches, snorkelling and scuba diving and a more authentically Yucatecan ambience than either Cancún or Cozumel.

Few people come to Playa del Carmen for just one or two nights. Most travellers don't stay here at all, but head straight through on their way to or from Cozumel. Of the ones who do stay, many come for the diving and snorkelling, planning to stay a week or more. Others settle in for a month. If you plan to

spend some time in Playa during the hectic winter season, it's a good idea to write early for reservations.

One thing is certain: Playa del Carmen is changing at lightning speed. I expect that most of what I write here will be out of date within a year as new buildings go up, old buildings are razed, and ever more hotels and restaurants open for business. Still, the infor-mation below will help you to get your bearings.

Orientation

It's just over one km from Highway 307 along Avenida Principal, the town's only wide, divided street, to Playa's main square and the docks for the ferries to Cozumel. Avenida Quinta, the street a block inland from the beach, is the main commercial thor-oughfare. Town blocks are about 100 metres square. In half an hour's strolling you can see the entire settlement.

The Beach

The beach runs on and on, with palms shading the sands and bathtub-warm waters. You can walk out quite a distance in the quiet seas before the water reaches to your shoul-ders.

Playa has one of the few nude beaches in Mexico. Go north from the Blue Parrot Inn around the point and you will see the beach. It's long enough to let you stake out some isolated sands.

If you want to snorkel, walk to the north-ern end of the nude beach where there's a small reef. Or take a day trip to Cozumel for snorkelling and scuba. Since Playa has beaches superior to Cozumel's and is cheaper, many travellers prefer to stay in Playa and make occasional day trips to Cozumel.

Places to Stay – bottom end

Many of Playa's budget lodging places, busy all the time in winter, are fairly empty in summer. Several even close down for the summer months.

Villa Deportiva Juvenil (youth hostel; no phone), 1.2 km from the ferry docks, is a

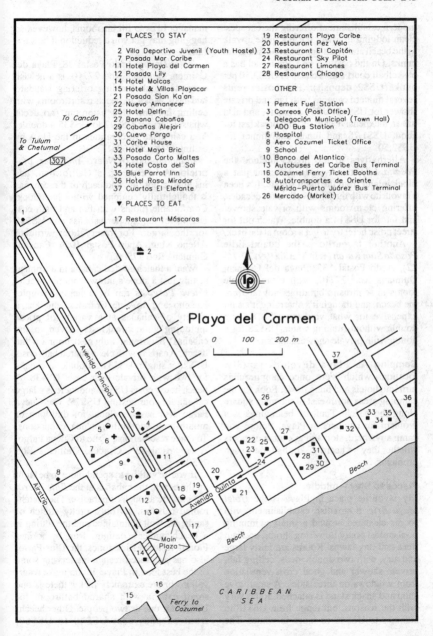

■ PLACES TO STAY

2 Villa Deportiva Juvenil (Youth Hostel)
7 Posada Mar Caribe
11 Hotel Playa del Carmen
12 Posada Lily
14 Hotel Molcas
15 Hotel & Villas Playacar
21 Posada Sian Ka'an
22 Nuevo Amanecer
25 Hotel Delfin
27 Banana Cabañas
29 Cabañas Alejari
30 Cuevo Parga
31 Caribe House
32 Hotel Maya Bric
33 Posada Corto Maltes
34 Hotel Costa del Sol
35 Blue Parrot Inn
36 Hotel Rosa Mirador
37 Cuartos El Elefante

▼ PLACES TO EAT

17 Restaurant Máscaras

19 Restaurant Playa Caribe
20 Restaurant Pez Vela
23 Restaurant El Capitán
24 Restaurant Sky Pilot
27 Restaurant Limones
28 Restaurant Chicago

OTHER

1 Pemex Fuel Station
3 Correos (Post Office)
4 Delegación Municipal (Town Hall)
5 ADO Bus Station
6 Hospital
8 Aero Cozumel Ticket Office
9 School
10 Banco del Atlantico
13 Autobuses del Caribe Bus Terminal
16 Cozumel Ferry Ticket Booths
18 Autotransportes de Oriente
   Mérida–Puerto Juárez Bus Terminal
26 Mercado (Market)

To Cancún

To Tulum
& Chetumal

307

Playa del Carmen

0   100   200 m

Avenida Principal

Airstrip

Avenida Quinta

Main
Plaza

Beach

Beach

CARIBBEAN
SEA

Ferry to
Cozumel

modern establishment offering the cheapest clean lodging in town, but it's quite a walk to the beach and you sleep in single-sex dorm bunks. On the positive side, the hostel has a basketball court and is cheap at US$3.50 per bunk (US$2 deposit). The hostel rents several modern cabañas with fan and private shower for US$12 (US$4 deposit), and also has an inexpensive café serving breakfast for about US$1.75 and lunch and dinner for US$2.50.

Alternatives to the hostel include the *Posada Lily*, on Avenida Principal just a block inland from the main square. It's been a favourite with thrifty travellers for decades, offering clean rooms with private shower and fan for US$14 a double. Watch out for street noise here; try to get a room at the back.

Another favourite is the quaint little *Posada Sian Ka'an* (☎ in Mérida (99) 29-74-22), Apdo Postal 135, Playa del Carmen, Quintana Roo 77710, with clean, simple rooms in semirustic buildings not far from the beach, and though it's charming it's a bit expensive for what you get: US$18 for a double without running water, US$28 for a double with private shower and fan.

Camping As Playa develops rapidly, locations which were once campgrounds turn into hotels and bungalows. Look for the camping areas north-east of the main square along the beach. Theft of belongings is a problem for campers in Playa. Before you camp anywhere, stop and ask other campers whether they've heard of – or had – any such problems.

Places to Stay – middle
My favourite place in Playa is the *Hotel Maya Bric*, a smallish establishment with rooms clustered around a small swimming pool amidst pretty flowering shrubs, coconut trees and tiny lawns. Rooms are fairly large and airy, with two double beds, ceiling fan, private shower and good cross-ventilation from windows on three sides. A small dive shop and snack stand is attached. Rates vary with the seasons, but range from US$18 in summer to US$40 or more in winter. The

manager likes to fill his rooms, however, so haggling may get you a reduction if he's not full.

Hotel Delfín, Apdo Postal 38, Playa del Carmen, Quintana Roo 77710, is a newish concrete block building offering standard laid-back Mexican beach resort rooms with ceiling fan and tiled bathroom (no decor whatsoever) for US$22 to US$35 a double. You can make reservations in the USA by calling (718) 297-6851.

In the grounds of *Nuevo Amanecer*, proprietor Arlene King, a Californian, has installed a hot tub, and each of the cabañas is thoughtfully equipped with a hammock. Comfortable rooms with fan and bath cost US$40 for the smaller cabañas and US$45 for the larger. For reservations write to Arlene King, Apdo Postal 1056, Cancún, Quintana Roo 77500.

Want a thatch-roofed cabaña in a tropical setting just a stone's throw from the beach? *Cueva Pargo* is run by a helpful couple, Huacho and JoAnne Corrales, and has a variety of cabañas at a variety of prices including good breakfasts served in the cabañas' Sailorman Pub next door on the beach. A cabaña with clean shared bath costs US$28 a single, US$31 a double; a cabaña for two with private bath costs US$38. A beach house costs US$70 and there is a large cabaña for four costing US$75. The Cueva Pargo also has a sailboat for day-long or month-long snorkelling/scuba excursions. To make reservations, write to Cueva Pargo, Apdo Postal 838, Cancún, Quintana Roo 77500.

If you're willing to spend more to be right on the beach, the cabañas at the *Blue Parrot Inn* provide a touch of paradise. The thatch-roofed cabañas, set on a pretty stretch of sands, are well maintained and the setting is a beachcomber's delight. Run by former Florida resident Rick Jones, the Blue Parrot also has a terraced restaurant serving some of the best food in Playa. If you make reservations or are extremely lucky, there is one small cabaña with shared bathroom for US$35 for one or two people. Other beachfront cabañas cost US$40 to US$60, depending upon facilities. For reservations, write to the Blue Parrot Inn, PO Box 652737, Miami, Florida 33265, USA.

Next to a tropical garden is the popular *Banana Cabañas*. Run by the friendly Sam and Martha Beard, the cabañas are reasonably priced at US$25 for one or two people. Larger cabañas sleeping up to four cost from US$28 to US$35. A cabaña with a kitchenette costs US$30.

Places to Stay – top end

Those seeking luxury lodging in town will find the *Hotel & Villas Playacar* to their liking. Cabañas have kitchens, and tennis, waterskiing and scuba trips are offered. During the high season, prices range from US$110 to US$250; during the low season (summer) they range from US$70 to US$150.

Built above the ferry dock with pretty seaside views, the *Hotel Molcas* charges US$60 to US$90 (depending upon the season) for its comfortable air-conditioned double rooms. For reservations, write to Apdo Postal 79, Playa del Carmen, Quintana Roo 77710 (☎ in Mérida (99) 25-69-90, in Cancún (988) 4-64-33, in Cozumel (987) 2-04-77, in Miami (305) 534-3716; fax (305) 534-0541).

Places to Eat

Playa's collection of restaurants changes annually as new ones open and others close. Eating establishments can be divided into two categories: those run by Mexicans for Mexicans, and those run by foreigners for foreigners. The former are cheap and basic, the latter are more atmospheric and expensive, with fancier food that may not taste much better. Many of the 'foreign' restaurants operate only during the winter season.

A favourite for any meal, especially an early breakfast, is the simple *Restaurant Playa Caribe*, which seems to be a bit cheaper than the other local places. Hotcakes go for US$2, full breakfasts for less than US$3.

Of the more expensive places, the *Res-taurant Máscaras*, on the main plaza, is the most famous and long-lived. Each evening the large palapa roof shelters a diverse collection of Playa's foreign visitors and residents who come for the convivial atmosphere, listen to American music from the 1950s and '60s, have a drink at the bar decorated with wooden masks, and dine on fish for US$6, pizza for US$4 to US$10 or pasta for about the same. The pizza is the best choice; my fish was very uninspiring. Drinks are fairly expensive.

A better choice as far as the food is concerned is the *Restaurant Limones*, next to Banana Cabañas, where the atmosphere is more sedate than jolly, and the food is a bit more expensive but well worth the extra money.

Friends of mine recommend the *Restaurant La Terraya*, around the corner from the Hotel Maya Bric and down on the beach, filled each evening with divers, fishing buffs and nautical wannabes. Fish is served many ways: *a la plancha* (roasted on a board), *al mojo de ajo* (in garlic sauce), *a la mantequilla* (in butter), and *a la Veracruzana* (in a tomato sauce), just to name a few. Prices for fish range from US$3.50 to US$6.

Entertainment

Playa's restaurants are the main venues for evening entertainment, which consists of eating, drinking, conversation, seeing and being seen. The *Restaurant Sky Pilot* on Avenida Quinta had the hippest music and people last time I was in Playa.

Getting There & Away

Air Aero Cozumel (☎ in Cozumel (987) 2-05-03, 2-09-28), with an office next to Playa's airstrip, runs little aircraft across the water from Cozumel to Playa and return every two hours from 8 am to 6 pm during the winter season. In summer there are usually four flights per day in each direction, departing from Cozumel at 9 and 11 am, and 3 and 5 pm, returning from Playa del Carmen 20 minutes later. The flight costs US$10 one way.

Bus Three companies serve Playa del Carmen, and each has its own terminal (see map). By far the most useful line is Autotransportes de Oriente Mérida-Puerto Juárez SA, with 1st and 2nd-class buses to major destinations throughout Yucatán. Autotransportes del Caribe is the line to take if you're going south to Felipe Carrillo Puerto or Chetumal, or west to Oxkutzcab, Ticul or Uxmal. ADO (Autobuses de Oriente) has only a few long-distance buses passing through Playa.

Cancún – 65 km, one hour; six 1st class (US$1.50), seven 2nd-class (US$1.25) by Autotransportes de Oriente; Autotransportes del Caribe also has eight buses daily.

Chetumal – 315 km, 5½ hours; five 1st class (US$5.25), and five 2nd class (US$4.75) by Autotransportes del Caribe, stopping at Felipe Carrillo Puerto and Bacalar

Cobá – 113 km, two hours; Autotransportes de Oriente has three 1st-class (US$1.25) and two 2nd-class (US$1) buses daily on the route Tulum, Cobá, Valladolid.

Mérida – 378 km, eight hours; seven 1st class (US$7), seven 2nd class (US$6) by Autotransportes de Oriente; these buses stop at Valladolid and Chichén Itzá. A del Caribe buses to Mérida go via Oxkutzcab, Ticul and Muna.

Tulum – 63 km, one hour; Autotransportes de Oriente's Cobá buses stop at Tulum (US$1), but Autotransportes del Caribe has the most traffic, with 10 buses daily heading south via Tulum to Chetumal.

Valladolid – 213 km, four hours; the many Autotransportes de Oriente buses to Mérida stop at Valladolid (US$4 1st class, US$3.60 2nd class), but it's faster to go on the *ruta corta* (short route) via Tulum and Cobá; (see Cobá).

Boats to Cozumel A variety of watercraft ply the seas between Playa del Carmen and Cozumel, taking between 30 and 75 minutes to make the voyage and charging US$2.25 to US$4.25 one way. Schedules, particularly in summer, are highly mutable, and I advise that you buy one-way tickets only. That way, if your chosen boat doesn't materialise for a scheduled return trip, you can buy a ticket on another line and lose neither money nor time.

Fastest boats are the waterjets *México*, *México 2*, and *Cozumeleño*, charging the top price, but whisking you across the water in the shortest time. You sit in an aircraft-type seat in air-conditioned comfort as cartoons and rock videos play on TV monitors to entertain you. The catamaran hull gives a smooth ride. Soft drinks, beer and snacks are sold on board. The waterjets are scheduled to run about every two hours from dawn to dusk, but voyages may be cancelled at the last moment if the boat breaks down or if there aren't enough passengers. Note also that 'fast boat' emblazoned on ticket offices and billboards may not mean 'waterjet', and the 'fast boat' may actually be slower than the waterjet.

The next best boat is the *Playa del Carmen*, offering only slightly less in the way of comfort, speed and price.

The slowest, oldest, least comfortable but cheapest boat is the *Xel-Ha*, which is best avoided by those prone to seasickness.

Ticket Problems Buying a ticket for a boat can be a confusing experience. Ticket sellers, who often sell tickets for more than one company, may announce that Boat X will be the next to leave, sell you a ticket (all tickets are nonrefundable), then later declare that Boat X will not be running after all, and that Boat Y will be next – but Boat Y is operated by a different company, so you must buy a different ticket for it. Boat X then may, in fact, run on schedule, or it may never appear. Boat Y may run on time or it may not. Sometimes this is just normal Mexican confusion, sometimes it's a scam to get you to buy tickets on more than one boat.

If you wait until the last minute to buy your ticket (so you can actually see Boat X ready to depart), you may not be able to buy a ticket because of the chaotic last rush of ticket-buyers at the kiosk. The ticket-sellers usually do not have enough change, and may spend all their time until the boat departs arguing with prospective passengers over paying with exact change. By the time you get to the seller, the tickets for that sailing may be sold out. *Buen viaje!*

Puerto Morelos (Km 328)

Puerto Morelos, 32 km south of Cancún, is

a sleepy fishing village known principally for its car ferry to Cozumel. There is a good budget hotel and travellers who have reason to spend the night here find it refreshingly free of tourists.

Snorkelling & Diving A splendid reef lies 600 metres offshore from Puerto Morelos but you'll need a boat to reach it. The reef and the wreck of a Spanish galleon seven km off the coast to the north-east make Puerto Morelos a popular destination for scuba divers. The infamous Sleeping Shark Caves are eight km to the east. You may book a trip and rent snorkelling or diving equipment from the Hotel Playa Ojo de Agua's dive shop one block north of the main plaza.

Places to Stay & Eat For good basic budget lodging, stay at the *Posada Amor* (no phone). Family run, the Posada is a wood and white stucco place with lots of plants and a happy atmosphere. The name comes from Dios es Amor (God is Love), but there are no religious overtones except those of goodwill. Rooms with fan and a clean shared bathroom cost US$20, single or double. Good breakfasts in the cosy dining room go for US$3 to US$4, lunches and dinners for US$6 to US$7.50.

On the main square (parque) in the centre of the village is the *Hotel Plaza Morelos* (no phone), with uninspired but serviceable rooms with private bath for US$28 a double.

In the unlikely event that you fall in love with Puerto Morelos and want to stay for a while, try the *Reef Inn*, on the waterfront street half a block from the car ferry dock, which rents rooms in a converted house by the day, week or month.

The *Hotel Playa Ojo de Agua*, a block north of the main square, has a swimming pool, restaurant and bar. Divers receive a special rate if they make use of the hotel's dive-shop excursions and equipment rental. Rooms and three meals cost US$95. For reservations and information write to Nery Vada, Apdo Postal 299, Cancún, Quintana Roo 77500.

La Ceiba Beach Hotel, on the beach north

of Puerto Morelos, has a restaurant, small swimming pool and dive shop which runs scuba excursions. Rooms come with refrigerators and have balconies overlooking the beach. Singles or doubles cost about US$80, with a discount for divers. For reservations, write to the hotel, Apdo Postal 1252, Cancún, Quintana Roo 77500.

Getting There & Away All 2nd-class and many 1st-class buses stop at Puerto Morelos coming from, or en route to, Cancún, 34 km (45 minutes) away. Buses generally come by every few hours during the day.

Hitchhiking south from Puerto Morelos is generally pretty good if you start out early in the day. If you are driving, the Pemex station here is the last fuel you will find until Tulum.

The car ferry *(transbordador;* ☎ in Cozumel (987) 2-08-27, 2-09-50) to Cozumel leaves Puerto Morelos daily early in the morning, returning at midday. Departure times vary from season to season. Unless you plan to stay for awhile on Cozumel, it's hardly worth shipping your vehicle. You must get in line two or three hours before departure time and hope there's enough space on the ferry for you. Fare for the 2½ to four-hour voyage is US$20 per car, US$3 per person; you needn't have a car in order to steam over to Cozumel on this boat, of course. Note that rough seas often prevent the ferry from sailing. At times, it has remained in port for up to a week until the weather cleared.

Departure from Cozumel is from the dock in front of the Hotel Sol Caribe, south of town along the shore road. Be there several hours ahead of departure time in order to get in line.

COZUMEL
Population 175,000
This resort island is 71 km south of Cancún in the midst of the Caribbean's crystalline waters. Its legendary Palancar Reef was made famous by Jacques Cousteau and is a lure for divers from all over the world. Scuba diving is not an inexpensive sport and visitors to Cozumel tend to be better heeled than

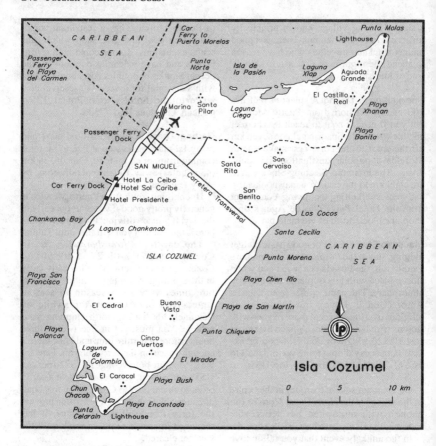

CARIBBEAN SEA

Car Ferry to Puerto Morelos

Punta Molas
Lighthouse

Passenger Ferry to Playa del Carmen

Punta Norte

Isla de la Pasión

Laguna Xlap

Aguada Grande

El Castillo Real

Playa Xhanan

Marina

Santa Pilar

Laguna Ciega

Passenger Ferry Dock

SAN MIGUEL

Playa Bonita

Santa Rita

San Gervaiso

Carretera Transversal

Car Ferry Dock

Hotel La Ceiba
Hotel Sol Caribe

Hotel Presidente

San Benito

Los Cocos

Chankanab Bay

Laguna Chankanab

Santa Cecilia

CARIBBEAN SEA

ISLA COZUMEL

Punta Morena

Playa San Francisco

Playa Chen Río

El Cedral

Buena Vista

Playa de San Martín

Playa Palancar

Cinco Puertos

Punta Chiquero

Laguna de Colombia

El Mirador

Isla Cozumel

Chun Chacab

El Caracol

Playa Bush

0   5   10 km

Punta Celarain

Playa Encantada

Lighthouse

those staying at Isla Mujeres or Playa del Carmen. Prices are not cheap by Mexican standards, but you can stay and eat at Cozumel on a moderate budget. If you're looking for a low-budget room, plan to take an early boat from Playa del Carmen and pin down your chosen room by midmorning. In the busy winter season it may be well to spend a bit more and fly over, thereby beating the hordes of budget room shoppers which will disembark from the ferries soon after your flight lands.

Though it has that beautiful offshore reef, Cozumel does not have many good swim-

ming beaches. The western shore is mostly sharp, weathered limestone and coral, and the eastern beaches are too often pounded by dangerous surf. If you're looking for diving, Cozumel is the place; if you prefer good beaches, spend your time in Cancún, Isla Mujeres or Playa del Carmen.

History

Measuring 53 km long and 14 km wide, Cozumel is the largest of Mexico's islands. Mayan settlement here has been traced by archaeologists back to 300 AD. During the Post-Classic period, Cozumel flourished both as a commercial centre and as a major ceremonial site. Maya sailed here on pilgrimages to shrines dedicated to Ixchel, the goddess of fertility and the moon.

Cozumel's Mayan name was Cutzmil or Cuzamil, (Place of Wild Turkeys or Place of Swallows). The island's civilisation reached its height after the eclipse of the great mainland Mayan cities, but its commercial prominence is believed to have given the island's inhabitants a high standard of living.

Although the first Spanish contact with Cozumel in 1518 by Juan de Grijalva was peaceful, it was followed by the Cortés expedition in 1519. Cortés, en route to his conquest of the mainland, laid waste to Cozumel's Mayan shrines. The Maya offered staunch military resistance until they were conquered in 1545. The coming of the Spanish brought smallpox to this otherwise surprisingly disease-free place. Within a generation after the conquest, the island's population had dwindled to only 300 souls, Mayan and Spanish.

While the island remained virtually deserted into the late 17th century, its coves provided sanctuary and headquarters for several notorious pirates including Jean Lafitte and Henry Morgan. Pirate brutality led the remaining populace to move to the mainland and it wasn't until 1848 that Cozumel began to be resettled by Indians fleeing the violence of the War of the Castes.

At the turn of the century, the island's population – which was now largely mestizo – grew thanks to the craze for chewing gum. Cozumel was a port of call on the chicle export route and locals harvested chicle on the island. Although chicle was later replaced by synthetic gum, Cozumel's economic base expanded with the building of a US air force base here during WW II.

When the US military departed, the island fell into an economic slump and many of its people left. Those who stayed fished for a livelihood until 1961, when underwater scientist Jacques Cousteau arrived, explored the reef, and told the world about Cozumel's beauties. A resort destination was born.

Cozumel was pretty laid-back, with diving enthusiasts coming for a week or two, until the development of Cancún. Now there are one-day diving tours by air from the mega-resort, and Cozumel is a busier, more upscale resort than it was before.

Orientation

It's easy to make your way on foot around the island's only town, San Miguel de Cozumel, where most of the budget lodgings are. Some of the middle-range places are here as well. For top end hotels, you'll probably have to take a taxi up or down the coast. The airport, two km north of town, is accessible only by taxi or on foot.

The all-important waterfront boulevard is Avenida Rafael Melgar; on the west side of Melgar south of the ferry docks is a narrow but usable sand beach. Just opposite the ferry docks (officially called the Muelle Fiscal) on Melgar in the centre of town is the main plaza. Running inland (eastward) from the main plaza is Avenida Benito Juárez, the main east-west thoroughfare. Juárez divides the town into norte (north) and sur (south). North-south streets (parallel to Avenida Melgar) are called avenidas, east-west streets (parallel to Avenida Juárez) are calles. Calles north of Juárez have even numbers, those south of Juárez have odd numbers.

Information

Tourist Office The local tourist office (☎ (987) 2-09-72) is in a building facing the main square to the left of the Bancomer, on the 2nd floor; hours are Monday to Friday from 9 am to 3 pm and 6 to 8 pm. There's also a little booth in the main plaza, open (in theory) from 8 am to 1.30 pm and 5.30 to 8 pm, but the hours are really at the caprice of the clerk. If the booth is closed you're not missing much as they're not particularly well informed. For the federal (SECTUR) tourism headquarters, head south on Avenida Melgar past the post office and look for SECTUR on the right. This is not an information office, but they might help with special problems.

Money For currency exchange, Bancomer

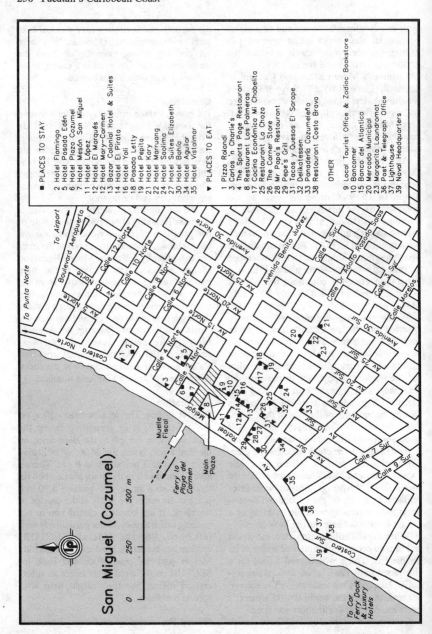

San Miguel (Cozumel)

■ PLACES TO STAY

2 Hotel Flamingo
6 Hotel Posada Edén
6 Hotel Plaza Cozumel
7 Hotel Mesón San Miguel
11 Hotel López
12 Hotel El Marqués
12 Hotel Mary-Carmen
13 Bazor Colonial Hotel & Suites
14 Hotel El Pirata
16 Hotel Yoli
18 Posada Letty
19 Hotel Pepita
21 Hotel Kary
22 Hotel Marruang
24 Hotel Saolima
27 Hotel Suites Elizabeth
30 Hotel Bahío
34 Hotel Aguilar
35 Hotel Vistolmar

▼ PLACES TO EAT

1 Pizza Rolandi
3 Carlos 'n Charlie's
4 The Sports Page Restaurant
8 Restaurant Las Palmeras
17 Cocina Económica Mi Chabelita
25 Restaurant La Choza
26 The Corner Store
28 Mr Pepo's Restaurant
29 Pepe's Grill
31 Tacos y Quesos El Sarape
32 Delikatessen
33 Panadería Cozumeleño
38 Restaurant Costa Brava

OTHER

9 Local Tourist Office & Zodiac Bookstore
10 Bancomer
15 Banco del Atlantico
20 Mercado Municipal
23 Margarita Laundromat
36 Post & Telegraph Office
37 Lighthouse
39 Navol Headquarters

and Banco del Atlantico off the main plaza change money only from 10 am to 12.30 pm, Monday to Friday. Banpaís facing the ferry docks will change your travellers' cheques from 9 am to 1.30 pm Monday to Friday for a 1% commission. Most of the major hotels, restaurants and stores will change money at a less advantageous rate when the banks are closed.

Post The post and telegraph office (☎ (987) 2-01-06) is south of Calle 7 Sur on the waterfront just off Avenida Melgar. Hours are Monday to Friday from 9 am to 1 pm and 3 to 6 pm, and Saturday from 9 am to noon. Cozumel's postal code is 77600.

Laundry The clean and tidy *Margarita Laundromat*, Avenida 20 Sur 285, between Calle Salas and Calle 3 Sur, is open Monday to Saturday from 7 am to 9 pm, Sunday from 10 am to 6 pm, and charges US$1.50 to wash a load (US$0.25 extra if you don't bring your own detergent), US$0.90 for 10 minutes in the dryer, or US$1.70 for 20 minutes. Ironing and folding services are available at an extra charge. Look for the sign reading Lavandería de Autoservicio.

Bookshop The Zodiac Bookstore, on the south-east side of the plaza 40 metres from the clock tower, next to Bancomer, is open seven days a week selling English, French, German and Spanish books, and English and Spanish magazines and newspapers.

Around the Island

In order to see most of the island (except for Chankanab Bay) you will have to rent a moped or bicycle, or take a taxi (see Getting Around). The following route will take you south from the town of San Miguel, then anticlockwise around the island.

Chankanab Bay Beach This bay of clear water and fabulously coloured fish is the most popular on the island. It is nine km south of the town.

You used to be able to swim in the adjoining lagoon, but so many tourists were fouling the water and damaging the coral that Chankanab Lagoon was made a National Park and put off limits to swimmers. Don't despair – you can still snorkel in the sea here and the lagoon has been saved from destruction.

Snorkelling equipment can be rented for US$6 per day. Divers will be interested in a reef offshore; there is a dive shop, and scuba instruction is offered.

If you get hungry, there is a restaurant and snack shop on the premises. The beach has dressing rooms, lockers and showers, which are included in the US$2 admission price to the National Park, open 9 am to 5 pm daily. The park also has a botanical garden with 400 species of tropical plants.

Getting There & Away There's one daily local beach bus which leaves San Miguel at 11 am, returns at 5 pm and costs US$1. The taxi fare from San Miguel to Chankanab Bay is about US$5.

San Francisco & Palancar Beaches San Francisco Beach, 14 km from San Miguel, and Palancar Beach, a few km to the south, are the nicest of the island's beaches. San Francisco's white sands run for more than three km, and rather expensive food is served at its restaurant. If you want to scuba or snorkel at Palancar Reef you will have to sign on for a day cruise or charter a boat.

El Cedral To see these small Mayan ruins, the oldest on the island, go 3.5 km down a paved road a short distance south of San Francisco Beach. Although El Cedral was thought to be an important ceremonial site, its minor remnants are not well preserved. The surrounding area is the agricultural heart of Cozumel.

Punta Celarain The southern tip of the island has a picturesque lighthouse, accessible via a dirt track, four km from the highway. To enjoy truly isolated beaches en route, climb over the sand dunes. There's a fine view of the island from the top of the lighthouse. Fried fish and beer are served here on Sunday.

East Coast Drive The wildest part of the island, the eastern shoreline, is highly recommended for beautiful seascapes of rocky coast. Unfortunately, except for Punta Chiquiero, Chen Río and Punta Morena, swimming is dangerous on Cozumel's east coast due to potentially lethal rip tides and undertow. Be careful! Swim only in coves protected from the open surf by headlands or breakwaters. There are small eateries at both Punta Morena and Punta Chiquiero and a hotel at Punta Morena. Some travellers camp at Chen Río.

El Castillo Real & San Gervasio Ruins Beyond where the east coast highway meets the Carretera Transversal (cross-island road) that runs to town, intrepid travellers may take the sand track about 17 km from the junction to the Mayan ruins known as El Castillo. They are not very well preserved and you need luck or a 4WD vehicle to navigate the sandy road.

If you are a real ruins buff, there is an equally unimpressive ruin called San Gervasio on a bad road from the airport. 4WD vehicles can reach San Gervasio from a track originating on the east coast, but most rental car insurance policies do not cover unpaved roads such as this. The jungle en route is more interesting than the ruins.

Punta Molas Lighthouse There are some fairly good beaches and minor Mayan ruins in the vicinity of the north-east point, accessible only by 4WD vehicle or foot.

Activities

Scuba Diving For equipment rental, instruction and/or boat reservations, there are numerous dive shops on Avenida Melgar along San Miguel's waterfront. Generally, a two-tank, full-day scuba trip will cost US$45 to US$60 and an introductory scuba course in the neighbourhood of US$70.

The most prominent scuba destinations are: the five-km-long Palancar Reef, where stunning coral formations and a 'horseshoe' of coral heads in 70-metre visibility offer some of the world's finest diving; Maracaibo Reef, for experienced divers only, which offers a challenge due to its current and aquatic life; Paraiso Reef, famous for its coral formations, especially brain and star coral; and Yocab Reef, shallow yet vibrantly alive and great for beginners.

For a map complete with depth chart of Cozumel's reefs, find a copy of the *Chart of the Reefs of Cozumel Mexico* prepared by Ric Hajovsky, which is sold in many of the dive shops.

Snorkelling You can go out on a boat tour for US$15 to US$20 or, far cheaper, rent gear for about US$6 and snorkel at the following places: Chankanab Bay, San Francisco Beach, La Ceiba Beach near the car ferry dock (where a plane was purposely sunk for the film *Survive)*, Presidente Hotel and Palancar.

Glass-Bottom Boat If you don't want to snorkel, in fact if you don't want even to go in the water, you can enjoy the coral formations and aquatic life by taking a tour by glass-bottom boat. The craft are supposed to leave the car ferry dock area every day at 10 am, noon and 2 pm, but generally wait until they are filled. They cost US$8 to US$12, but if you don't come to Cozumel at the height of the tourist season you might try to bargain for a lower price.

Fishing There's great fishing off the coast of Cozumel, with marlin, tuna, bonito, tarpon, red snapper, barracuda and – most prized of all – sailfish. Game fish supposedly run at their height in these waters from late February to late June. Chartering a deep-sea fishing craft costs at least US$125 per day for the smallest of seagoing boats.

Places to Stay – bottom end
You will have to pay more for a room – any room – on Cozumel than on the mainland.

Indeed, you had better think less of cost and more about availability, as the cheapest lodgings fill up early and often.

Hotel Flamingo (☎ (987) 2-12-64), Calle 6 Norte 81 between Avenida Melgar and Avenida 5 Norte, three blocks north of the plaza, is not the cheapest place in town, but it's undoubtedly the best value for money. Run by an efficient señora, this fairly new but still simple place is all gleaming white. The 21 rooms on three floors go for US$20 to US$25 a double, depending upon the season.

Hotel Marruang (☎ (987) 2-16-78, 2-02-08), Calle Adolfo Rosado Salas 440, five blocks east of the plaza and facing the municipal market, is proud of its newness, its Simmons box-spring mattresses and its ceiling fans. A clean room cared for by a vigilant señora, with one double and one single bed, costs US$18 to US$24, depending upon the season. The entrance to the hotel is down a passageway opposite the market. If there's no one in evidence, ask at the juice bar *(fuente de sodas)* on the right at the beginning of the passageway.

Hotel Posada Edén (☎ (987) 2-11-66, 2-15-82), Calle 2 Norte 12, between Avenidas 5 and 10 Norte, also called the Edem, is a simple, uninspiring but fairly cheap and quiet place charging US$13 a single and US$18 a double for a room with private shower and ceiling fan.

Posada Letty (☎ (987) 2-02-57), Calle 1 Sur at Avenida 15 Sur is among the cheapest lodgings in town, a small, plain place marked only by a minuscule sign. Ask for rooms at the small shop on the left on the corner. Well-used rooms with ceiling fan, decent cross-ventilation and private tiled shower go for US$14 in summer, US$18 in winter. Just around the corner from the Letty is the Hotel Pepita, described below in the middle-range lodgings.

Hotel Yoli (☎ (987) 2-00-24), Calle 1 Sur 164, a block east of the main plaza between Avenidas 5 and 10 Sur, is family run and though the rooms are a bit dingy, they are fairly clean. Because of its convenient location the Yoli (or Yoly) fills up fast. The

very plain rooms with fan and bath cost US$12 a single or double.

Hotel Saolima (☎ (987) 2-08-86), Calle Adolfo Salas 268, between Avenidas 10 and 15 Sur, is among the best deals in town. The Saolima has clean, pleasant rooms in a quiet locale, with ceiling fans and private showers, for US$13 a single, US$15 a double.

Hotel López (☎ (987) 2-01-08), Calle 1 Sur (Apdo Postal 44), on the south side of the plaza, used to be a divers' hangout but now caters to budget travellers with air-conditioning on their minds. The simple rooms with good private baths – some have views of the water or the plaza – go for US$18 a single (with fan), US$28 a double (with air-con) in summer, somewhat higher in winter. If the hotel is not full, haggle with the owner, Sr Miguel López Vivas, for a discount.

Camping To camp anywhere on the island you'll need a permit from the island's naval authorities, obtainable 24 hours a day, for free, from the naval headquarters south of the post office on Avenida Rafael Melgar. Best camping places are along the relatively unpopulated eastern shore of the island.

Places to Stay – middle
Middle-range hostelries, though still simple, offer welcome amenities such as air-conditioning and swimming pools. Prices are not too much higher than at bottom-end places. All of the rooms in these hotels have private bathrooms.

Hotel Vista del Mar (☎ (987) 2-05-45; fax 2-04-45), Avenida Rafael Melgar 45, at Calle 5 Sur, has it all: rooms with private bath and air-conditioning, a small swimming pool, restaurant, liquor store, rental car and travel agency. Some rooms have balconies with sea views. The price in summer is US$40 a double, rising to US$55 in winter.

Tried and true, clean, comfortable lodgings are yours at the *Hotel Mary-Carmen* (☎ (987) 2-05-81), Avenida 5 Sur 4, half a block south of the plaza. Enter the courtyard to find a small reception desk and shop, behind which is a large mamey tree and 27 tidy air-con rooms with carpeting, a few pieces of decoration, private baths, and prices of US$30 a double in summer. A bevy of serious-minded ladies keeps everything shipshape. Rooms here provide excellent value for money.

Equally pleasant is the accommodation at *Hotel Suites Elizabeth* (☎ (987) 2-03-30), Calle Adolfo Salas 44 (Apdo Postal 70), half a block east of Avenida Rafael Melgar. These clean and well-kept suites only 30 metres from the town beach offer air-con bedrooms with kitchenettes (cooker, refrigerator and utensils) for US$25 to US$30 a double in summer, US$40 to US$45 in winter.

Yet another good value is the *Hotel Pepita* (☎ (987) 2-00-98), Avenida 15 Sur 2, corner of Calle 1 Sur, three blocks from the town beach. Well-maintained air-con rooms around a delightful garden in a tranquil part of town go for US$25 to US$30 in summer, US$35 to US$40 in winter. Most rooms have two double beds, insect screens, fans and little refrigerators as well as the air-con. The hotel runs scuba diving tours as well.

Bazar Colonial Hotel & Suites (☎ (987) 2-05-06; fax 3-03-09, 2-13-87), Avenida 5 Sur 9, half a block south of the plaza, across the street from the Hotel Mary-Carmen, has the distinction of being one of the few hotels in town with a lift. The modern, attractive rooms here are actually studio or one-bedroom suites (some of which can sleep up to four people) with kitchenette (cooker, refrigerator, utensils), air-con and pretensions to decor. Rates are a reasonable US$35 to US$40 a double in summer, US$45 to US$50 in winter.

Hotel Bahía (☎ (987) 2-02-09), Avenida Rafael Melgar at Calle 3 Sur, operated by the same people as the Bazar Colonial, has pleasant modern suites, some with sea views, all with air-con, satellite TVs with US stations, telephones and kitchenettes for US$45 to US$50 a double in summer, US$50 to US$60 in winter. Good location, decent value here, especially for small groups or families.

Hotel El Pirata (☎ (987) 2-00-51, 2-15-28), Avenida 5 Sur 3-A, a few steps south of the plaza, offers decent air-con rooms for US$28 a double in summer, US$40 in winter.

Hotel Aguilar (☎ (987) 2-03-07), Avenida 5 Sur at Calle 3 Sur, a block east of Avenida Melgar, has rooms in white cement-block bungalows grouped around a small swimming pool amidst pleasant if ill-kept gardens. All rooms are air-conditioned, and go for US$25 a single and US$30 a double in summer, US$40 to US$45 a double in winter. The management often seems mentally remote, interested more in the moped rental business, but it's a serviceable place for all that. The hotel has touts working the docks. Don't believe their rates; they get a commission if they bring you here and you pay extra for it. Simply find the Aguilar on your own and the rates will be cheaper.

Hotel Costa Brava (☎ (987) 2-14-53), Avenida Rafael Melgar 601, south of the post office and inland from the naval base, is set well back from the street behind the Restaurant Costa Brava, and is therefore fairly quiet. The modern rooms are comfy if simple, with good cross-ventilation and ceiling fans (air-con in some). Rates are US$25 a double in summer, US$35 in winter.

Hotel Kary (☎ (987) 2-20-11), Calle Adolfo Rosado Salas at Avenida 25 Sur, is five blocks from the water and seven blocks from the plaza, just east of the municipal market. The location is a bit out of the way, but the hotel offers something in return: nice double rooms grouped around a swimming pool priced at US$18 to US$26 a double with fan, US$24 to US$32 with air-con; the higher prices apply during the busy winter season.

Hotel Plaza Cozumel (☎ & fax (987) 2-00-66), Calle 2 Norte 3, just off Avenida Melgar a block north of the plaza, is a new, modern, comfortable hotel – one of the few in town – with many nice extras. The rooftop swimming pool and thatched-roof bar are the most obvious, but there's also a lift to whisk you to your room, which is air-conditioned and equipped with two large beds, colour TV with satellite hook-up, as well as an up-to-date bathroom. The price? A moderate US$48 in summer, US$72 in winter.

Hotel Mesón San Miguel (☎ (987) 2-02-33, 2-03-23), Avenida Juárez 2-B, on the north side of the plaza, has a supremely convenient location, a welcome little swimming pool, blissful air-con, a restaurant, and 97 air-con rooms with balconies. There's also a separate beach club with water sports facilities seven blocks from the hotel on the water. Rates are low in summer, at US$35 a double, and higher in winter at US$55 a double.

Hotel El Marqués (☎ (987) 2-05-37, 2-06-77), Avenida 5 Sur 12, half a block south of the plaza, has what seemed to me to be lackadaisical and inept management. It also has a good location and fairly cheap, presentable air-conditioned rooms for US$28 a double in summer, US$40 in winter.

Places to Stay – top end

Several km south of town are the big luxury resort hotels of an international standard. North of town along the western shore of the island are numerous smaller, more modest resort hotels, usually cheaper than the big places, but catering mostly to package tour groups.

South of town, the *Stouffer Presidente Cozumel* (☎ (987) 2-03-22; fax 2-13-60), Carretera a Chankanab Km 6.5, is hard to miss with its 259 rooms, many with sea views, set amidst tropical gardens. The water sports facilities are particularly good, and there are numerous restaurants and bars. Other recreational facilities include two swimming pools, five jacuzzis, a lighted tennis court and a marina with boats for rent. Price for double rooms in the high winter season range from US$161 to US$253 a double, tax included. You can expect substantial discounts in summertime.

Fiesta Americana Sol Caribe Cozumel (☎ (987) 2-70-00; fax 2-13-01), Playa Paraíso Km 3.5 (Apdo Postal 259), Cozumel, Quintana Roo 77600, has 321 luxurious rooms and a lavish layout with tropical swimming pool complete with a large 'island', three tennis courts, moped and bicycle rental, lots of water sports facilities and its own scuba diving facilities. There are six restaurants

and bars. Winter season prices are US$135 to US$170 a double, with hefty reductions available in summer. Fiesta Americana has a slightly cheaper hotel, the *Fiesta Inn*, not far away from the Sol Caribe. For reservations at either hotel, call (800) 343-7821 in the USA.

Meliá Mayan Cozumel (☎ (987) 2-02-72; fax 2-15-99), Playa Santa Pilar, is a 200-room resort with a full list of water sport equipment, numerous seafood restaurants and bars and opportunities for parasailing. Another Meliá hotel, the *Sol Cabañas del Caribe* (☎ (987) 2-01-61, 2-00-17; fax 2-15-99) caters mostly to divers, who stay in the comfortable hotel rooms or garden villas. For reservations, call (800) 336-3542 in the USA.

Places to Eat

Food on Cozumel tends to suffer from Resort Syndrome: it is often mediocre and overpriced. But some of it is good, and some restaurants have settings and views that almost justify the prices, so grin and bear it, this is Cozumel.

Places to Eat – bottom end

Cheapest of all eating places, with fairly tasty food to boot, are the market loncherías, seven in all, located next to the Mercado Municipal on Calle Adolfo Rosado Salas between Avenidas 20 and 25 Sur. All of these little señora-run eateries offer soup and a main course plate for about US$2.25, with a large selection of dishes available. Latin music issuing from multiple boom boxes is provided for your dining pleasure. Hours are 6.30 am to 6.30 pm daily.

Restaurant Costa Brava (no phone), on Avenida Rafael Melgar just south of the post office, is among the more interesting – read funky – places to dine on the island. The charming Mexican nautical decor used to be augmented by a partial view of the sea, but the construction of the big naval headquarters building across the street blocked that view forever. Besides good ambience, the Costa Brava provides cheap breakfasts

(US$1.50 to US$2.50), and such filling dishes as chicken tacos, grilled steak and fried fish or chicken for US$2.75 to US$6. Hours are 6.30 am to 11.30 pm daily.

The Corner Store, at the corner of Calle Adolfo Rosado Salas and Avenida 5 Sur, is an excellent place to have a healthy breakfast, light lunch or vitamin-filled snack. Fresh fruit juices are priced at US$0.75 to US$1.50, sandwiches from US$1.25 to US$2; the house speciality, a fruit salad with granola and yoghurt – just the thing to beat the heat – goes for US$2 to US$2.75.

Restaurant La Choza, Calle Adolfo Rosado Salas 198, at the corner of Avenida 10 Sur, specialises in *cocina típica Mexicana*, authentic Mexican traditional cuisine, which is not all tacos and enchiladas. An open-air place shaded by a palapa, it provides eggs served in a multitude of ways, brochettes of beef or chicken, and numerous other dishes. Among my favourites is the *pozole*, a spicy meat-and-hominy stew. You get a huge bowl of it crowded with hominy and laced with shredded pork, accompanied by sliced onion, radish and cabbage, limes for squeezing, and tortilla chips for dipping; it's definitely a full meal. With a soft drink, you pay US$6.

Tacos y Quesos El Sarape, Avenida 5 Sur between Calles 1 and 3 Sur, is a tiny and tidy glass-fronted place selling simple meals for low prices. It's closed Sunday.

Cocina Económica Mi Chabelita, Avenida 10 Sur between Calle 1 Sur and Calle Adolfo Rosado Salas, 1½ blocks from the plaza, is a tiny, fairly cheap eatery run by a señora who serves up decent portions of decent food at decent prices. It's not the cheapest in town, but good for the money. You can fill up for US$4 or less here. It opens for breakfast at 7 am; don't linger over dinner as it closes at 7 pm.

For do-it-yourself breakfast or snack supplies seek out the *Panadería Cozumeleño*, at the corner of Calle 3 Sur and Avenida 10 Sur, four blocks south-east of the plaza. Bread for sandwiches and pan dulce (sweet rolls) for breakfast or snacks are fresh every morning, and cheap all day long.

Places to Eat – middle

You can't help noticing *Restaurant Las Palmeras* (☎ 2-05-32). It's the one right at the edge of the main plaza by the ferry docks with lots of shaded terraces with leafy plants and wood accents where the air is kept moving by sea breezes, ceiling fans and the bustle of white-jacketed waiters. Food can be fairly mediocre, but the location is so good for people watching, and so convenient to everything, that it's usually full. Try it, you might get lucky and find something tasty. A bowl of sopa de lima is a good bet at US$3 as is a big fruit plate for US$6. Most Mexican traditional dishes go for US$5 to US$7, fish and squid for US$7.50 to US$11.

A longtime favourite in Cozumel – not because of the location but because of the food – is *Pizza Rolandi*, Avenida Rafael Melgar between Calles 6 and 8 Norte, four blocks north of the plaza. One-person (20-cm diameter) pizzas range in price from the Margherita with tomato, cheese, basil and olive oil (US$6.25) to the Four Seasons with ham, asparagus, mushrooms and olives for US$8. Wine is sold by the quarter and half-litre; beer and other drinks are served as well. Come to Rolandi from 11.30 am to 11.30 pm; closed Sunday.

Among the restaurant chains spawned by Cancún's development, *Mr. Papa's* is among the better ones. The name is a pun on *papas* (potatoes), and indeed potatoes, filling, healthy and delicious, are the main course here. They come topped with sauces laden with meats, vegetables and spices, and cost between US$5 and US$6.

Cozumel is so Americanised that it has its own sports buffs' watering hole, *The Sports Page* (☎ 2-11-99), a block north of the plaza at the corner of Calle 2 Norte and Avenida 5 Norte. A loudspeaker carries current broadcast sports action to the world outside; inside, a noticeboard bears schedules of future sports broadcasts to be monitored on the restaurant's radio and TV. Food is hearty and prices are moderate. For a full meal beginning with guacamole or stuffed potato skins followed by a bacon cheeseburger, along with a drink, you'd pay US$9, which

Top: Baluarte de San Carlos, and the modern 'clamshell' Casa de Congreso, Campeche (TB)
Bottom: T-shirts on sale at Tulum (TW)

Top: Tulum ruins and beach (JL)
Bottom: Mayan petroglyphs, Tulum (JL)

is also the price for a plate of fajitas. Steak, lobster and shrimp cost US$12 to US$20; fruit plates and omelettes are only a few dollars.

For picnic supplies, head for the *Delikatessen*, Avenida 10 Sur 264, between Calle Adolfo Rosado Salas and Calle 3 Sur. Open from 9 am to 9 pm (closed Sunday), the Deli sells delicacies: smoked salmon, provolone, camembert, brie, imported biscuits and meats, etc. It's not cheap, but if your picnic demands brie, this is the place to find it.

Places to Eat – top end
Cozumel's traditional place to dine well and richly is *Pepe's Grill* (☎ 2-02-13), on Avenida Rafael Melgar at Calle Adolfo Rosado Salas. Flaming shrimps, grilled lobster, caesar salad and other top-end items can take your bill to the lofty heights of US$30 or US$40 per person, but the food is good and the atmosphere rich and nautical. Call for reservations in season.

Entertainment
Cinemas Far cheaper than live entertainment are the town's two cinemas which sometimes screen English-language films with Spanish subtitles. Cine Borgues is on Avenida Juárez at Avenida 35, Cine Cozumel is on Avenida Rafael Melgar at Calle 4 Norte, two blocks north of the plaza.

Discos Nightlife in Cozumel is pricey, but if you want to dance, the most popular disco is Disco Neptuno, five blocks south of the post office on Avenida Rafael Melgar. Cover charge is US$4, with drinks (even Mexican beer) for US$2.50 and up. Another hot spot, similarly priced, is Disco Scaramouche at the intersection of Avenida Melgar and Calle Adolfo Rosado Salas. For Latin *salsa* music, try Los Quetzales, Avenida 10 Sur at Calle 1 Sur, a block from the plaza. It's open every evening from 6 pm.

A block and a half north of the plaza on Avenida Rafael Melgar is the local incarnation of the Carlos'n Charlie's chain. Unlike the other restaurants, which combine hip menus, sassy waiters and decent food with moderately high prices, this one is more like a rowdy bar.

The luxury hotels (Stouffer Presidente, Fiesta Americana Sol Caribe and La Ceiba) have discos with similarly lofty cover charges and drink prices.

Things to Buy
Near the plaza and along Avenida Rafael Melgar are numerous boutiques selling the favourite local souvenir, jewellery made with black coral. Legitimate shops will probably not try to cheat you on quality, but beware the cut-price merchants who substitute black plastic for the real thing. True black coral is 'weathered', with gold-coloured streaks in it. It is very light – lighter than the plastic fakes – and true coral will not burn, as does plastic.

Getting There & Away
Air Cozumel has a surprisingly busy international airport, with numerous direct flights from other parts of Mexico and the USA. Flights from Europe are usually routed via the USA or Mexico City. There are nonstop flights on Continental (☎ (987) 2-02-51) and American (☎ (987) 2-08-99) from their hubs at Dallas, Houston, and Raleigh-Durham, with many direct flights from other US cities via these hubs. Mexicana (☎ (987) 2-02-63) has nonstops from Miami and direct flights from Mérida and Mexico City.

Aero Cozumel (☎ (987) 2-09-28, 2-05-03), with offices at Cozumel airport, operates flights between Cancún and Cozumel about every two hours throughout the day for US$30 one way. Reserve your seat in advance, as many of these little planes are filled by groups of divers coming for a day's plunge. Aero Cozumel also runs those convenient and inexpensive flights to and from Playa del Carmen. In summer there are usually four flights per day in each direction, departing from Cozumel at 9 and 11 am and 3 and 5 pm, and returning from Playa del Carmen 20 minutes later. The flight costs US$10 one way.

Ferry For details on taking the fast waterjet

passenger ferries from Playa del Carmen, see that section. If you must bring your car to Cozumel, you'll have to take a car ferry from Puerto Morelos. Details are in that section.

Getting Around

To/From the Airport The airport is about two km north of town. You can take a minibus from the airport into town for less than US$1, slightly more to the hotels south of town, but you'll have to take a taxi (US$3 or US$4) to return to the airport.

Bus & Taxi Cozumel's taxi drivers have a lock on the local transport market, defeating any proposal for a convenient bus service. A single bus leaves daily from the tourist booth on the plaza in town (near the ferry) at 11 am, heading south toward Chankanab Bay, returning at 5 pm. Fare is US$1. The walk from the Stouffer Presidente Hotel south to Chankanab is about one km.

For other points on the island you will have to take a taxi. Fares average US$3 or US$4 for every 15 minutes of travel, or roughly US$18 per hour.

Rental Vehicles The alternative to taxis is to rent a vehicle. Rates for rental cars correspond to those charged throughout the tourist belt of Mexico's Caribbean – upwards of US$60 to $70 per day, all inclusive. You could probably haggle with a taxi driver to take you on a tour of the island, drop you at a beach, come back and pick you up, and still save money; keep this shocking fact in mind when you consider renting a car.

With rental car prices so high, it's not surprising that rented mopeds are extremely popular with those who want to tour the island on their own. It seems that every citizen and business in San Miguel – hotels, restaurants, gift shops, morticians – rents mopeds, generally for US$25 to US$30 per day (24 hours), though some rent from 8 am to 5 pm for US$15. Insurance and tax are included in these prices. It's amusing that a 24-hour rental of two mopeds (for two people) almost equals the cost of renting a car (for up to four people) for the same period of time.

You must have a valid driving licence, and you must use a credit card to rent, or put down a hefty deposit (around US$50).

The best time to rent is first thing in the morning, when all the machines are there. Pick a good one, with a working horn, brakes, lights, starter, rear-view mirrors, and a full tank of fuel; remember that the price asked will be the same whether you rent the newest, pristine machine or the oldest, most beat-up rattletrap. (If you want to trust yourself with a second-rate moped, at least haggle the price down significantly.) You should get a helmet and a lock and chain with the moped.

When riding, keep in mind that you will be as exposed to sunshine on a moped as if you were roasting on a beach. Slather yourself with sunblock (especially the backs of your hands, feet and neck, and your face), or cover up, or suffer the consequences. Also, be aware of the dangers involved. Of all motor vehicle operators, the inexperienced moped driver on unfamiliar roads in a foreign country has the highest statistical chance of having an accident, especially when faced by lots of other inexperienced moped drivers. Drive carefully.

Tabasco & Lowland Chiapas

Coming from Yucatán, you enter the state of Tabasco before you enter Chiapas. Tabasco is a low-lying coastal area to the north of Chiapas, kept fertile by the huge rivers – Usumacinta, San Pedro, Grijalva, Tonalá – which slice through the state on their way to the Gulf of Mexico. Unlike Chiapas with its varied topography and climate, Tabasco is mostly hot and humid. It was in this unlikely country that the Olmecs developed Mesoamerica's first great civilisation. Besides its cultural wealth, Tabasco is noted for its mineral riches, particularly petroleum, which in recent years has brought great prosperity to the state capital, Villahermosa.

The state of Chiapas has enormous variety, from the tropical lowland jungles of Palenque to the cool, foggy mountains of San Cristóbal de las Casas. For most of its long history Chiapas has been more intimately connected with Guatemala, culturally and politically, than with Mexico. Pre-Hispanic civilisations in the area spread across the modern international border, and for most of the colonial era Chiapas was governed from Guatemala.

PALENQUE & ENVIRONS

Surrounded by emerald jungle, Palenque is unique among ancient Mayan sites. Although not as expansive or massive as Chichén Itzá and Uxmal, Palenque's setting is superb and its architecture and decoration exquisite.

From Palenque you can trek into the Lacandón jungle, one of Mexico's largest areas of tropical forest, to visit the Mayan ruins at Yaxchilán and Bonampak. San Cristóbal de las Casas is a tranquil hill-country colonial town surrounded by a number of traditional Indian villages. Between Palenque and San Cristóbal are the Agua Azul waterfalls. Using Palenque town as a base you can take a quick trip to Nututun for swimming, a longer excursion to the beautiful waterfall and chilly jungle pool at Misol-Ha, or an even longer one to the cascades at Agua Azul. For full information on these sites, see below in the section covering the road from Palenque to San Cristóbal de las Casas.

History

The name Palenque means Palisade in Spanish and has no relation to the ancient city, the real name of which is still uncertain or unknown. It could be Nachan, (City of Snakes), or Chocan, (Sculptured Snake), or Culhuacán, Huehuetlapalla, Xhembobel Moyos, Ototium... No one knows for sure.

Evidence from pottery fragments indicates that Palenque was first occupied more than 1500 years ago. It flourished from 600 to 800 AD, and what a glorious two centuries they were! The city first rose to prominence under Pakal, a club-footed king who reigned from 615 to 683 AD. Archaeologists have determined that Pakal is represented by hieroglyphics of sun and shield. He lived to a ripe old age, possibly 80 to 100 years.

During Pakal's reign, many plazas and buildings, including the superlative Temple of Inscriptions, were constructed within the 20 sq km of the city. The structures were characterised by mansard roofs and very fine stucco bas-reliefs. Hieroglyphic texts at Palenque state that Pakal's reign was predicted thousands of years prior to his ascension and would be celebrated far into the future.

Pakal was succeeded by his son Chan-Balum, symbolised in hieroglyphics by the jaguar and the serpent. Chan-Balum continued Palenque's political and economic expansion as well as the development of its art and architecture. He completed his father's crypt in the Temple of the Inscriptions and presided over the construction of the Plaza of the Sun temples, placing sizable narrative stone stelae within each. One can

see the influence of Palenque's architecture in the ruins of the Mayan city of Tikal in Guatemala's Petén region and in the pyramids of Comalcalco near Villahermosa.

Not long after Chan-Balum's death, Palenque started on a precipitous decline. Whether this was due to ecological catastrophe, civil strife or invasion has been disputed, but after the 10th century Palenque was largely abandoned. Situated in an area receiving the heaviest rainfall in Mexico, the ruins were overgrown with vegetation and lay undiscovered until the latter half of the 18th century.

Rediscovery of Palenque

It is said that Hernán Cortés came within 40 km of the ruins without any awareness of them. In 1773, Mayan hunters told a Spanish priest that stone palaces lay in the jungle. Father Ordoñez y Aguilar led an expedition to Palenque and wrote a book claiming that the city was the capital of an Atlantis-like civilisation.

An expedition led by Captain Antonio del Río set out in 1787 to explore Palenque. Although his report was then locked up in the Guatemalan archives, a translation of it was made by a British resident of Guatemala who was sufficiently intrigued to have it published in England in 1822. This led a host of adventurers to brave malaria in their search for the hidden city.

Among the most colourful of these adventurers was the eccentric Count de Waldeck who, in his 60s, lived atop one of the pyramids for two years (1831-33). He wrote a book complete with fraudulent drawings which made the city resemble great Mediterranean civilisations, causing all the more interest in Palenque. In Europe, Palenque's fame grew and it was mythologised as a lost Atlantis or an extension of ancient Egypt.

Finally, in 1837, John L Stephens reached Palenque with artist Frederick Catherwood. Stephens wrote insightfully about the six pyramids he started to excavate and the city's aqueduct system. His was the first truly scientific investigation and paved the way for research by other serious scholars.

Orientation

There are two Palenques: the town and the archaeological zone, 6.5 km apart. Coming south from Highway 186, you'll go about 20 km before passing through the settlement at the Palenque railway station; the main part of town is several km farther on. If you arrive by train, try hitching into town, or take a taxi for US$3.

Several more km brings you past the airstrip on the left (east), and then to a fork in the road. You'll know the fork by the huge, bombastic statue of a Mayan chieftain's head. Bear left at the statue for Palenque town (one km) or bear right for the ruins (5.5 km) within the national park. The road to the right toward the ruins also leads to the turnoff (left) for Nututun, Misol-Ha, Agua Azul and San Cristóbal de las Casas.

Though most hotels and restaurants are in the town centre, the camping areas and several middle and top-end hotels and restaurants are located along the road to the ruins. There are also a few good hotels and restaurants just to the left of the Mayan statue as you come in from the highway.

Though relatively small, the town is spread out. From the Mayan statue at its

western limit to the Hotel Misión Palenque at the eastern end is about two km. But most of the bus offices are clustered a few hundred metres east of the Mayan statue past the Pemex fuel station on the way into town, and the walk to most hotels is 800 metres or less.

The main road from the Mayan statue into town is Avenida Juárez, which ends at the town's plaza. Juárez is also the centre of the commercial district.

This town takes its statistics seriously. To the left of the Mayan statue on the road to Hotel La Cañada is a sign proclaiming that Palenque has 60,000 residents, 80 metres altitude, and an average humidity of 78%. Considering that it's always hot here, that last statistic is the one which will have true meaning for you as you make your way around town and struggle to sleep at night. It's always sweltering in Palenque, and there's rarely any breeze.

Information

Tourist Office Located just off the main plaza in part of the Palacio Municipal (H Ayuntamiento), the tourist office has English-speaking staff but no adequate map of either the ruins or the town. The office is open Monday to Saturday 8 am to 2 pm and 5 to 8 pm, Sunday 9 am to noon.

Money Bancomer, three blocks west of the plaza on Juárez, changes money between 10 and 11.30 am Monday to Friday. Banamex, four blocks west of the plaza, changes money from 10.30 am to noon Monday to Friday. Hotels and better restaurants will also change money, though at less favourable rates.

Post The post office is just off the plaza on the left side of the Palacio Municipal. It's open Monday to Friday 8 am to 1.30 pm and 4 to 6 pm, Saturday 8 am to noon.

Medical Services Palenque has a pharmacy open 24 hours a day, named appropriately the Farmacia 24 Horas, on 20 de Noviembre near Abasolo. Don't expect to see the lights

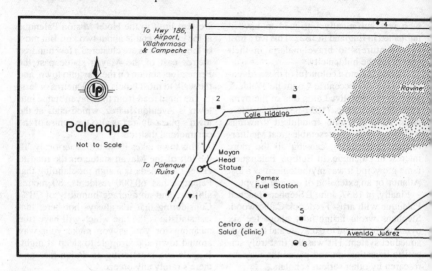

Palenque
Not to Scale

To Hwy 186,
Airport,
Villahermosa
& Campeche

To Palenque
Ruins

Calle Hidalgo

Mayan
Head
Statue

Pemex
Fuel Station

Centro de
Salud (clinic)

Avenida Juárez

Ravine

■ PLACES TO STAY		19	Restaurant Chan-Kah
2	Hotel Maya Tulipanes	20	Restaurant Maya
3	Hotel La Cañada	23	Restaurant Arsemio's
5	Hotel Avenida	25	Taquerías
9	Hotel Kashlan	28	Restaurant Las Tinajas
13	Hotel Regional	31	Restaurant Yunuen
17	Hotel Misol-Ha		
18	Hotel Casa de Pakal		OTHER
24	Hotel La Croix	4	Market
26	Hotel Palenque	6	2nd Class Bus Station
29	Posada Charito	7	ADO (1st Class) Bus Station
31	Hotel Vaca Vieja	8	Lavandería Automática
32	Hotel Misión Palenque	10	Colectivos Chambalu
		12	Banamex
▼ PLACES TO EAT		15	Bancomer
		16	Mercado de Artesanías (Crafts
1	Restaurant-Bar Hardy's (La Selva)		Market)
3	Restaurant Cañada	21	Post Office
11	Piccolini's Pizza	22	Palacio Municipal & Tourist Office
14	Expendio de Pan Virginia	27	Casa de la Cultura
18	Restaurant Castellano	30	Farmacia 24 Horas

on day and night, but feel free to wake the family up in an emergency.

The Palenque Ruins

The archaeological zone of Palenque is situated in a much larger reserve, the Parque

Nacional Palenque. You pass through a thatched gateway into the national park a km or so before coming to the ruins.

Only 34 of Palenque's nearly 500 buildings have been excavated. As you explore the ruins, try to picture the grey edifices as bright

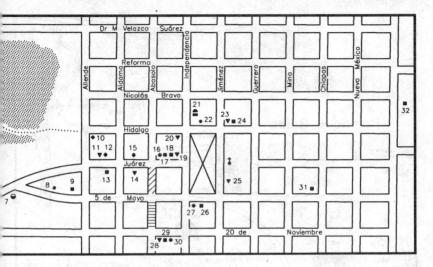

red; at the peak of Palenque's power, the entire city was painted vermilion. Everything you see here was achieved without metal tools, pack animals or the wheel.

One of the prime times to visit the site is just after it opens, when a humid haze rises and wraps the ancient temples in a mysterious mist. The effect is best in the winter when the days are shorter.

The archaeological site is open from 8 am to 5 pm; the crypt in the Temple of Inscriptions – not to be missed – is only open from 10 am to 4 pm; the small museum is open from 10 am to 5 pm. Admission to the site costs US$5; parking in the car park by the gate costs US$0.20. There is no additional charge for entry to the crypt or the museum. Drinks, snacks and souvenirs are for sale in stands facing the car park.

Temple of Inscriptions After you enter the enclosure and walk along the path, look for a small stone structure on the left-hand side. This is the tomb of Alberto Ruz Lhuillier, the tireless archaeologist who revealed many of Palenque's mysteries.

The magnificent pyramid on the right is the tallest and most prominent of Palenque's buildings. Constructed on eight levels, it has a central staircase rising some 23 metres to a temple which crowns the structure; it once had a tall roofcomb as well. Between the doorways are stucco panels with reliefs of noble figures. On the temple's rear wall are three panels with a long inscription in Mayan hieroglyphs which gives the temple its name. The inscription, dedicated in 692 AD, recounts the history of Palenque and of the temple.

Ascend the 69 steep steps to the top, both for a magnificent vista of Palenque and surrounding jungle and for access to stairs down to the tomb of Pakal (open 10 am to 4 pm). This crypt lay undiscovered until 1952 when Alberto Ruz Lhuillier, who had been excavating the staircase, found a sealed stone passageway in which were seated several skeletons. These victims of religious sacrifice were intended to serve Pakal in death and were buried with clay pots, jewellery and tools for his journey to the next world.

Although Pakal's jewel-bedecked skeleton and jade mosaic death mask were taken to Mexico City and the tomb recreated in the Museo Nacional de Antropología, the stone sarcophagus lid remains here. (The priceless

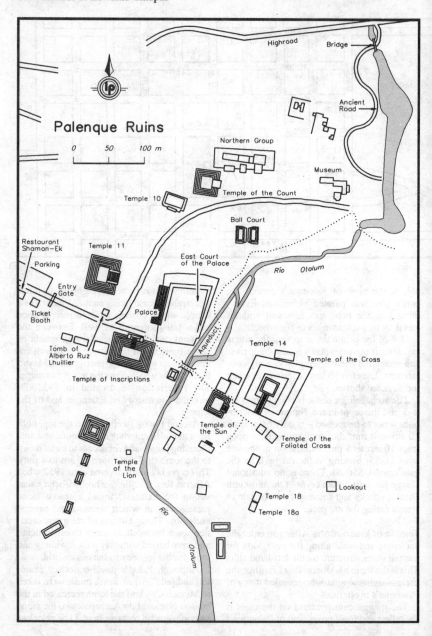

Palenque Ruins

0   50   100 m

Highroad

Bridge

Ancient Road

Northern Group

Museum

Temple 10

Temple of the Count

Ball Court

Restaurant Shaman-Ek

Parking

Temple 11

East Court of the Palace

Río Otolum

Entry Gate

Ticket Booth

Palace

Tomb of Alberto Ruz Lhuillier

Temple of Inscriptions

Aqueduct

Temple 14

Temple of the Cross

Temple of the Sun

Temple of the Foliated Cross

Temple of the Lion

Lookout

Temple 18

Temple 18a

Río Otolum

death mask was stolen from the site museum in 1985.) The carved stone slab protecting the sarcophagus includes the image of Pakal encircled by serpents, mythical monsters, the sun god and glyphs recounting Pakal's reign. Carved on the wall are the nine lords of the underworld. Between the crypt and the staircase, a snake-like hollow ventilation tube connected Pakal to the realm of the living.

This was the first crypt found in Mayan pyramids, and it gave rise to wild speculation linking the Maya with Egypt. Evidence of a few other pyramid crypts has been found, but nothing as elaborate as this.

The Palace Diagonally opposite the Temple of Inscriptions, lying in the centre of Palenque's plaza, is the Palace, an unusual and significant structure harbouring a maze of courtyards, corridors and rooms. If you walk up to the tower (restored in 1955), you will see fine stucco reliefs on the walls. Palenque's stucco figures of royalty and prominent priests are superb. Using a mixture derived from clay and tree bark to make the stucco dry more slowly, Mayan sculptors were able to create intricate details. Archaeologists and artists alike say that the carved stonework of Palenque's ruins stands unparalleled among Mayan sites in Mexico.

On the northern interior wall are imposing monster masks. Archaeologists and astronomers believe that the tower was constructed so that Mayan royalty and the priest class could observe the sun falling directly into the Temple of the Inscriptions during the 22 December winter solstice. Some archaeologists believe that like the sun, Pakal was deified and that the Maya thought he would also rise again.

Within the tower's courtyard, you will see a singular well-preserved stone known as the Oval Tablet. Engraved on it is the image of Zac-Kuk, Pakal's mother, handing her son the ruler's ceremonial headdress. She ruled as regent for three years until Pakal was sufficiently mature (aged 12½ years) to rule on his own.

In the northern section of the palace are some interesting carved stucco figures, on

Stucco head found in the tomb in the Temple of Inscriptions, Palenque

the piers facing the stairs. They apparently depict war; one warrior brandishes an axe over the head of his victim. Within the courtyard, nine substantial stone figures are shown kneeling, possibly awaiting sacrifice or rendering tribute. Another theory suggests that they represent the nine gods of the night.

There is much to explore in the subterranean passageways and courtyards of the palace. In the eastern patio stand three-metre-tall statues of warriors thought to be worshipping a god. At the base of the tower are thought to have been steam baths and toilet drains. The subterranean tunnels harbour stucco carvings best appreciated if you bring a torch.

Temples of the Cross Although Pakal had only the Temple of Inscriptions dedicated to him during his 68-year reign, Chan-Balum had three buildings dedicated to him, known today as the Temples of the Cross. Follow the path leading between the Palace and the Temple of Inscriptions, cross the Río Otolum (a mere stream; the name means Place of Fallen Stones) and climb the slope to the Temple of the Sun, on the right. The temple's decoration includes narrative inscriptions dating from 642, replete with scenes of offerings to Pakal, the sun-shield king. The Temple of the Sun has the best preserved roofcomb of all the buildings at Palenque.

The smaller, less well-preserved Temple XIV next door also has tablets showing ritual offerings – a common scene in Palenque. Here a woman makes an offering to a 'dancing man' believed to be Chan-Balum.

Follow the path a few more metres to the largest of the buildings in this group, the Temple of the Cross, restored in 1990. Inside are sculpted narrative stones; some tablets have been taken from this relatively poorly preserved temple to the National Museum of Anthropology in Mexico City. One archaeologist suggests that Chan-Balum may be buried under this temple, as the symbolism of its decoration is similar to that on the sarcophagus lid of Pakal. One particularly fine stucco carving shows a priest smoking a sacred pipe.

To the right of the Temple of the Sun, seemingly cut out from the jungle hillside, stands the Temple of the Foliated Cross. Here, the deterioration of the façade lets you appreciate the architectural composition, with the arches fully exposed. A well-preserved tablet carving shows a king with a sun-shield (most likely Pakal) emblazoned on his chest, corn growing from his shoulder blades and the sacred quetzal bird atop his head. One interpretation of this tablet is that it depicts the Mayan reverence for the life force of the god of maize. The symbol of the sacred ceiba tree's branched cross reflects the Mayan sense of the intersection of the heavens and the underworld to produce life as they knew it.

Other Ruins & Museum Cross the plaza, heading away (north) from the Temple of Inscriptions, and follow the road around to the north side of the Palace. On your left is the Northern Group of buildings, unrestored; on your right, just north of the Palace, the ruins of a ball court. Crazy Count de Waldeck lived in one of the temples of the Northern Group – hence its name, Temple of the Count. Constructed in 647 AD under Pakal, it is one of Palenque's oldest mansard-roofed buildings.

Continue on the road keeping the Palace on your right, then through a clearing to the museum, on the left by the river, open from 10 am to 5 pm. Among the small museum's most interesting exhibits are stone tablets covered with finely wrought calendar glyphs, votive figurines, statues and a chart of Mayan history.

Jungle Walks You can hike on jungle paths just outside the ruins; perhaps you'll encounter the howler monkeys often heard roaring in trees overhead. It's best to bring mosquito repellent for any jungle trek, particularly in the rainy season (May to October). You can continue on the path past the museum and across the river. Another path is outside the enclosure, back along the road to Palenque Town about 250 metres on the left. Hidden in the jungle is the Cascada Motiepa, a scenic waterfall and pool which give off cooling zephyrs.

Places to Stay
Palenque is a cow town, and the quality of its hospitality services reflects this fact. Hotels are not all that well maintained, service is lackadaisical, but as this is a tourist mecca, prices are high. Add the heat and humidity and you've got an altogether delightful place to stay! But the magnificent ruins are worth it, so the crowds continue to arrive and to seek beds here.

Places to Stay – bottom end
Hotels in town are cheaper than those on the road to the ruins, with the notable exception of the camping grounds.

Hotel La Croix (☎ (934) 5-00-14), Hidalgo No 10 is the cheapest and most popular place to stay, but it's usually full by mid-afternoon at the latest. Conveniently situated on the north side of the plaza opposite the church, La Croix has ground-floor rooms facing the plaza. It can be a bit noisy but with its pretty interior courtyard, potted tropical plants and adequate rooms with fan and bath, La Croix's prices are right. Singles and doubles are a mere US$9.

Posada Charito (☎ (934) 5-01-21), 20 de Noviembre No 15, two blocks west of the plaza, has numerous advantages. It's quiet here, the rooms are kept in fairly good shape by its family owners and prices are a bit lower: US$7.50 a double for a room with private shower, clean sheets, new ceiling fan, and Gideon Bible (in Spanish) on your pillow.

Between the centre of town and the Mayan statue, not far from the Pemex fuel station and opposite the 2nd-class bus station, the *Hotel Avenida* (☎ (934) 5-01-16), at Juárez No 183, lets you hear every thunderous unmuffled bus. In addition to lack of sleep, you may have to contend with broken bathroom fixtures, but the price is right and the camaraderie is infectious. A single/double with bath costs US$7/9.

Hotel Vaca Vieja (☎ (934) 5-03-77), Avenida 5 de Mayo No 42 at Chiapas, located three blocks east of the plaza, is well maintained and has pleasant rooms with fan and tiled bathrooms priced at US$10/12.50 for a single/double. The proprietor used the proceeds from the sale of his cattle herd to fund the construction of the hotel, hence its name (Old Cow) and the sign.

On Avenida Juárez half a block west of the plaza is the basic but clean *Hotel Misol-Ha* (☎ (934) 5-00-92), with serviceable if bare rooms going for US$11.25/14/17 a single/double/triple, private shower and fan included. Try haggling if business is slack as these prices are a bit high.

The *Hotel Regional* (☎ (934) 5-01-83), Juárez at Aldama, has white stucco walls and black steel windows around a small plant-filled courtyard. The rooms, nothing to write home about but adequate, are on two levels; each has private shower and fan. The

problem here is the price, which is too high for what you get. Haggle them down from the standard US$15 a double and you'll do alright.

Camping Campers can string a hammock or pitch a tent at the *Camping Mayabell*, on the southern side of the road to the ruins, within the national park boundaries. The Mayabell charges US$1.50 per person and the same for a car. It offers toilets and showers, some shade, full hook-ups, snacks and drinks for sale, and is only two km from the ruins, though the walk is all uphill.

Camping María del Mar, three km from the ruins on the opposite side of the road, is similar but with less shade, at the same price.

You can also camp on the grounds of the *Hotel Nututum Viva*, 3.5 km along the road from Palenque to San Cristóbal de las Casas, on the banks of the Río Usumacinta. You use the hotel's facilities. The fee is US$1.50 per person, and US$2.25 per vehicle.

Places to Stay – middle
The top moderate choice is just out of town near the Mayan statue, a 10 to 15-minute walk from the plaza. *Hotel La Cañada* (☎ (934) 5-01-02), Calle Hidalgo s/n (also called Calle Merle Green or Calle Cañada), is a group of cottages in a quiet spot surrounded by jungle. Most of the cottages are air-conditioned and all come with baths; many have huge ceramic tubs. This was a favourite with archaeologists working at the ruins, and still maintains its legendary attraction for many visitors. Cottages cost US$18/23.50 for a single/double with fan, slightly more for air-conditioning.

La Cañada has a good thatch-roofed restaurant and the attractive Restaurant La Selva is close by. The hotel is worth the walk, and is actually as close to the bus and colectivo stations as are the hotels in the centre. If you don't mind a bit of adventure, ask the manager to show you the shortcut path to town that snakes down into the ravine, past squatters' houses, and up to the Avenida Hidalgo.

Sharing some of La Cañada's advantages is the nearby *Hotel Maya Tulipanes* (☎ (934) 5-02-01), Calle Cañada No 6, only 100 metres from the Mayan statue and the highway. Rooms are on two levels; the upstairs ones tend to catch more of the breeze and thus are a bit cooler. Bright, cheerful, cool blue-and-white flowered sheets are the rule here, on either single or double beds. With ceiling fans, rooms go for US$20/21.50 a double; add US$2 per person to get the price of a room with air-con. There may be some new rooms by the time you arrive as there was construction under way in the hotel's former camping area next door.

In the centre of town, your best bet is the relatively new *Hotel Kashlan* (☎ (934) 5-02-97, 5-03-09), Avenida 5 de Mayo No 105 at Allende, quite near the ADO bus station. Clean, bright and modern, the Kashlan offers its rooms with ceiling fan and shower for decent prices of US$14.50 a single, US$18 a double.

Hotel Palenque (☎ (934) 5-01-88), Avenida 5 de Mayo No 15, at Independencia, is one of the oldest hotels here. It was once the most comfortable place to stay, but is now only moderately so due to ageing. Look at your room before you sign in. Bonuses here are the convenient location, very pretty gardens in the interior court, a small and often presentably clean swimming pool, and rooms with either ceiling fan (US$14.50 a double) or air-conditioning (US$18 a double).

The *Hotel Casa de Pakal*, on Juárez near the plaza, has 14 small rooms with air-conditioning, TV and private bath, and prices are not unreasonable if you must have coolness: US$22.50 a double.

Readers with their own cars might want to consider staying at the new *Hotel El Paraíso* (☎ (934) 5-00-33/45), Carretera a las Ruinas Km 2.5, which, as the address indicates, is 2.5 km along the road to the ruins, on the right-hand side. Large, airy, clean rooms here with two double beds, gleaming tiled bathrooms and individual air-conditioning units cost US$27 a double. Most rooms are at the back of the Restaurant El Paraíso and

thus farther from the road, although there is little noise but that of the jungle out here.

Places to Stay – top end
Palenque's top accommodation in terms of comfort is at the *Hotel Misión Palenque* (☎ (934) 5-02-41, 5-01-10), Rancho San Martín de Porres, Palenque, Chiapas 29960, at the far eastern end of town along Avenida Hidalgo. A member of a Mexican hotel chain with properties at Chichén Itzá, Uxmal, Cancún and many other locations, the Misión Palenque is large (160 rooms) and attractive with well-kept gardens and a decor of wood, stone and stucco; it also has air-conditioned rooms, swimming pool, restaurant and bar. The rate is US$54 a double. The hotel's minibus shuttles guests to the ruins and back every two hours (four trips per day).

The most attractive and interesting lodgings at Palenque are at *Chan-Kah* (☎ (934) 5-03-18), three km from town on the road to the ruins. Individual cottages here are made of dark wood and stone in a handsome modern style with Mayan accents. The vast palapa-topped restaurant and enormous stone-bound swimming pool, the lush jungle gardens and other accoutrements are lavish, but sparsely populated. The reason may be the high price (US$54 a double), the remoteness from town, and the fact that the cottages have only ceiling fans, not air-conditioning.

South of town 3.5 km on the road to San Cristóbal is the *Hotel Nututum Viva* (☎ (934) 5-01-00/61), overlooking the Río Usumacinta just to the left of the road. The modern motel-style buildings are nicely arranged in spacious jungle gardens shaded by palm trees. A glass-fronted restaurant has a fine view of the river and its bathers, as this is a favourite spot for a swim whether you're staying at the hotel or not. Large air-conditioned rooms with bath cost US$40 to US$43 a double. You can also pitch your tent or park your camper here for US$1.50 per person and US$2.25 per vehicle. A swim in the hotel's river *balneario* costs US$0.75.

Places to Eat
As with hotels, so with restaurants: Palenque

is a cow town with tourism, so you should not expect polished service, superb food or low prices. Still, you can do alright here.

Places to Eat – bottom end

Cheapest fare in Palenque is at the taquerías along the western (plaza) side of the block where the church is. Try *Los Faroles* or *El Deportista* for a plate of tacos at US$1.75 to US$2.

Just as cheap, and with a better selection of food, is *Restaurant Arsemio's*, a family-run place at the corner of Jiménez and Hidalgo, to the left of the taco places in front of the church. Everything here seems to cost about US$2.25 to US$3, whether it be filete, chicken, or traditional Mexican antojitos. A few items cost less, a few more. This is a simple, tidy place where Mamá does the cooking and her daughter waits on tables: honest work, honest food, honest prices.

Another family-run place is the *Restaurant Las Tinajas*, 20 de Noviembre at Abasolo, next to the Farmacia 24 Horas and only a few steps from the Posada Charito. The name means Earthen Jars, the building is quaintly woody, and it's run by a family. A few tables set out on the small terrace in front allow you to watch the street action as you eat. At the time of writing, prices are a bit cheaper here than at Arsemio's, but that may change.

Sooner or later you'll probably drop in for a meal at the *Restaurant Maya* (☎ 5-00-42), at the corner of Independencia and Hidalgo at the north-west corner of the plaza, a popular meeting-place for travellers as well as locals 'since 1958', as the menu says. The food is típico, the service Palenque-ish, the hours long (7 am to 11 pm).

Breakfast can be bacon and eggs (US$3) or granola with milk (US$1.15). Lunch and dinner favourites are *enchiladas con mole* (with spicy, bitter chocolate sauce), steak and french fries, and *tamalitos chiapanecos* (little tamales Chiapas-style). Prices range from US$2.50 to US$8 for a full meal; the comida corrida costs less than US$4.

Right next door to the Maya at the corner of Independencia and Juárez, also facing the plaza, is the *Restaurant Chan-Kah*. Stone pillars, wrought iron grillwork, ceiling fans for a breeze and a bit of jungle ambience make this the more atmospheric place to dine, and prices are only slightly higher than at the Maya. A popular choice here is the Mexican variety plate with an assortment of antojitos for US$4.25, but you can also get tacos, tostadas or enchiladas for US$2.50. I had a cheese sandwich which could have had more cheese, and french fries that were fresh but cooked in old oil. There's a bar on the upper floor, and perhaps by the time you arrive, some guest rooms as well.

The Hotel Vaca Vieja's little *Restaurant Yunuen*, corner of 5 de Mayo and Chiapas, has good breakfasts and reasonably priced típico meals, including a comida corrida every day.

The Hotel Casa de Pakal's *Restaurant Castellano* has the advantage of air-conditioning, a rare service among Palenque restaurants. The food is OK and the prices not bad considering the cool air.

For delicious moderately priced pizza, from the plaza walk three blocks west on Juárez to *Piccolini's Pizza* – surprisingly good.

The cheapest meal is the one you make yourself. For this you'll want to drop by the *Expendio de Pan Virginia*, or Virginia's Bakery, across the street from Bancomer on Avenida Juárez, between Abasolo and Aldama.

Places to Eat – middle

The town's two best restaurants are 10 to 15 minutes walk from the plaza near the Mayan statue. Bear left at the statue and walk 100 metres along the road toward the ruins to reach the *Restaurant-Bar Hardy's*, named after owner Zacarias Hardy González, but more commonly known as *La Selva* (☎ 5-03-63).

Beneath its enormous thatched roof are dozens of basket-covered lamps, numerous ceiling fans, and waiters in colourful local garb. The food here is a cut above that available in the rest of Palenque. They offer filete tampiqueña, *fajitas norteñas* and a number of fairly expensive house specialities. Chiapan musicians sometimes play during dinner.

Expect to spend US$5 to US$11 for a full lunch or dinner, though you could spend US$15 for a speciality with wine. Breakfasts are quite expensive. La Selva is open every day from 7 am to 11 pm.

Hotel La Cañada has its own thatched restaurant which is less pretentious than La Selva, but you still get tablecloths, careful service and moderate prices. The restaurant maintains its tradition of attracting travellers with a serious interest in archaeology, who stay after dinner and long into the evening discussing the ruins over cold beer or other drinks from the bar.

Getting There & Away

Air Palenque has a small airstrip north of town, used mostly for air taxi and charter flights. Occasionally there is short-hop scheduled service to and from Tuxtla Gutiérrez, capital of Chiapas. Check with the tourist office or a travel agency in Palenque.

Bus There is less thievery on the bus than on the train, but some bus passengers have reported goods stolen. Don't leave anything of value in the overhead rack, and stay alert.

Both the 1st-class ADO and 2nd-class Autotransportes Tuxtla Gutiérrez bus stations have left luggage (baggage check) rooms.

It's a very good idea to buy your onward ticket from Palenque a day in advance if possible. Though many buses are de paso, originating somewhere else, some (especially 2nd class) originate here, allowing you to reserve your seat in advance.

Here are some distances, times and prices:

Agua Azul Crucero – 62 km, 1½ hours; five 2nd-class buses (US$0.95) by Autotransportes Tuxtla. These buses go on to Ocosingo, San Cristóbal and Tuxtla Gutiérrez; seats are sold to those passengers first. Tickets to Agua Azul go on sale 30 minutes before departure, and if all seats are sold, you must stand all the way to the Agua Azul turn-off. You may also take a combi (see the Getting Around section).

Campeche – 362 km, 5½ hours; one direct 1st-class bus (US$6) by ADO at 7.15 am; you can also catch a bus or combi, or hitchhike the 27 km north to Catazaja, on the main Villahermosa-Escárcega highway, and catch one of the buses which pass every hour or two.

Escárcega – 212 km, three hours; one 1st-class morning bus (US$4.25) by ADO, three 2nd-class buses (US$3.50) by A del Sur

Mérida – 556 km, 10 or 11 hours; one 1st-class bus (US$7.25) by A del Sureste directly to Mérida; one 1st-class ADO morning bus via Campeche. Many more 1st-class buses pass by the main highway junction 27 km to the north of the town.

Misol-Ha – 47 km, one hour; five 2nd-class buses (US$0.50) by Autotransportes Tuxtla. Tickets go on sale 30 minutes before departure, and you may have to stand during the trip.

Mexico City – 1,020 km, 16 hours; one 1st-class bus (US$18) by ADO

Ocosingo – 85 km, two hours; four 2nd-class buses (US$2) by Autotransportes Tuxtla

San Cristóbal de las Casas – 190 km, 5½ hours; five 2nd-class buses (US$3.50) by Autotransportes Tuxtla

Tuxtla Gutiérrez – 275 km, 7½ hours; five 2nd-class buses (US$5) by Autotransportes Tuxtla

Villahermosa – 150 km, 2½ hours; six 1st-class buses (US$2.50) by ADO

Train It's not a good idea to take the train to or from Palenque. There are no dormitorios to lock on board and robberies are common between Palenque and Mérida. So take the bus – it's quicker and you are not as likely to lose your gear.

Getting Around

All of the hotels listed in town are within two to 10 minutes' walk of both bus stations. The train station is six km north of town. Taxis are available at the main plaza and the bus stations.

Colectivos Chambalu, at the corner of Hidalgo and Allende, operates combis (VW minibuses) frequently between Palenque Town and the ruins. Service is every 10 minutes (so they say) from 6 am to 6 pm daily. The minibus will stop to pick you up anywhere along the town-to-ruins road, which makes it especially handy for campers. Fare is US$0.20.

Colectivos Chambalu also operates excursions to Agua Azul and Misol-Ha, departing daily at 10 am, returning at 3.30 pm, costing US$5 per person. Taking the combi tour, though more expensive than the bus, eliminates standing for hours on crowded buses and walking (perhaps with all your luggage) the 1.5 km in from the highway to (and back out from) Misol-Ha, and the 4.5 km walk downhill from the highway to Agua Azul proper – and then back uphill when it comes time to leave.

If you're interested in visiting the ruins at Bonampak or Yaxchilán, you will want to consider Colectivos Chambalu's combi-and-boat tours. See those sections below for details.

RÍO USUMACINTA

The mighty Río Usumacinta snakes its way north-westwards along the border between Mexico and Guatemala, finally flooding into the Laguna de Terminos and the Gulf of Mexico between Villahermosa and Ciudad del Carmen. The river begins as a system of tributaries in the Guatemalan mountains and jungles: Río San Blas, Río de la Pasión, Río Salinas, Río San Pedro. Along its banks stand many ruined Mayan cities and ceremonial centres, for the river was the major means of transport in this region during most of Mayan history. Unlike the flat limestone shelf of Yucatán, where no rivers could run and sacbeob, or sacred roads, had to be built, the Mayan peoples of Chiapas had the ready-made water-road of the Usumacinta.

A journey along the Río Usumacinta today reveals dense rainforest, thrilling bird and animal life, and ruined cities such as Bonampak and Yaxchilán. You can visit these ruins by air if time is short and money plentiful, but a journey by car and boat is cheaper and much more exciting. You can even use the Usumacinta as a waterway to Guatemala, as did the Maya of the past, though there are dangers in doing this.

Tenosique

Tenosique, due east of Palenque on the opposite bank of the Usumacinta, is the last town of any size on the lower part of the river; the next town is Sayaxché, Guatemala, on the

Río de la Pasión, some 150 km to the south-east.

In the past, intrepid travellers would use Tenosique as the jumping-off place for expeditions upriver to Bonampak and Yaxchilán. But now that the road to Bonampak has been improved somewhat, it is more convenient to go via Palenque.

If you are considering going to Tenosique because you've heard that flights to Yaxchilán and Bonampak ruins are cheaper when chartered here, save your time and trouble and fly from Palenque or San Cristóbal – the saving is not enough to warrant a special trip to this humid nonentity of a town.

Flores If you're very adventurous, you can go from Tenosique to Flores, in Guatemala's Petén province near Tikal, by bus and boat in two days of hard travel.

Take an early morning bus from Palenque to the town of Emiliano Zapata, about 40 km north-east of Palenque on the banks of the Usumacinta. From Zapata, take another bus to Tenosique and, after lunch, change for yet another bus (1½ hours, US$1) due east to the riverside town of La Palma.

In La Palma you catch a boat on the Río San Pedro, a tributary of the Usumacinta which runs eastward into Guatemala. Four or five hours on the boat brings you by evening to the border town of El Naranjo where you pass Guatemalan customs. You can spend the night – or at least part of it – in El Naranjo in primitive shelters rented for the purpose. It's best to have your own camping equipment and warm gear as it can actually get cold here at night.

In theory, buses run from El Naranjo to Flores starting at 3 am. This is a tiring, even exhausting and dangerous journey. You're a long way from the long arm of the law in these jungles, which are noted for guerilla activity. Before you attempt this trip it's a good idea to call your consulate and ask about current conditions. The US Consulate in Mérida (☎ (99) 25-50-11) can often provide advice on the safety of this route.

Places to Stay & Eat The best budget hotel in Tenosique is the *Hotel Azuleta*, on Pino Suárez, where singles with fan and bath are US$6, doubles US$8. There are cheap restaurants around the plaza.

Getting There & Away Second-class buses run regularly from Villahermosa, and trains stop here en route to Mexico City and Mérida. The bus station is one km from the centre; the railway station is one km from the plaza.

BONAMPAK & YAXCHILÁN RUINS

The ruins of Bonampak – famous for its frescoes – and the great ancient city of Yaxchilán are accessible on camping excursions from Palenque, or by chartering an aircraft from Palenque, San Cristóbal or Tenosique.

The frescoes at Bonampak have deteriorated greatly since they were discovered and do not provide the expected thrill. Go instead to look at the site, and then examine copies of the murals in books or in the Museo Nacional de Antropología in Mexico City. The site at Yaxchilán is more rewarding, and the trek through the jungle and across the Usumacinta is a thrill in itself.

Bonampak and Yaxchilán have neither food nor water, so make certain you are well supplied if you come on your own. It's bug-infested in these parts – bring insect repellent. Don't leave your gear unattended, as thefts have been reported on previous trips. Finally, carry a torch to see dark parts of the ruins better and for any camping emergencies.

The Mexican government was, until recently, planning to build a dam on the Usumacinta which would have resulted in the inundation of Bonampak and Yaxchilán. The dam proposal has been abandoned, however, and the ruins are preserved for visitors at least for the forseeable future.

Bonampak

Lying about 155 km south-east of Palenque near the Guatemalan frontier, Bonampak was hidden from the outside world by dense

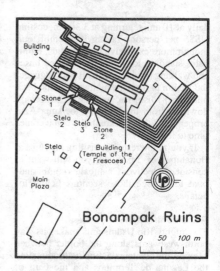

Bonampak Ruins

0   50   100 m

jungle until 1946. A young WW II conscientious objector named Charles Frey fled the draft and somehow wound up here in the Lacandonian rainforest. There he was virtually adopted by local Indians and shown what the Indians told him was a sacred site of their ancestors. Impressed by what he saw, Frey enthusiastically revealed his findings to Mexican officials and archaeological expeditions were mounted. Frey died in 1949 trying to save an expedition member from drowning in the turbulent Usumacinta.

The ruins of Bonampak lie around a rectangular plaza. Only the southern edifices of the plaza are preserved; the rest is little more than heaps of stone. It was the frescoes of a temple in the Southern Group, today designated Building 1, that excited Frey and the archaeologists who followed. They saw three rooms covered with paintings depicting ancient Mayan ways. Painted in profile are warriors decked with quetzal feathers, kings and royal families, priests, shamans, dancers, musicians and war captives. The details of costumes themselves reveal much about Mayan life and the murals are complete with glyphs.

The murals' original colours were brown,

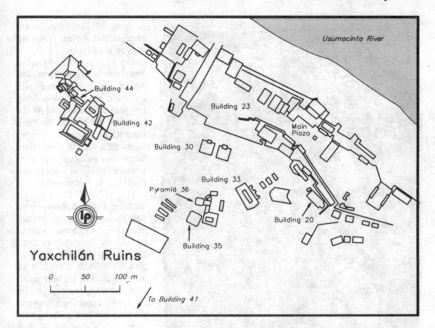

Yaxchilán Ruins

0   50   100 m

To Building 41

green and vermilion, with the figures out-lined in black. Unfortunately, 12 centuries of weather deterioration were accelerated when the first expedition attempted to clean the murals with kerosene. On the positive side, some restoration has been undertaken and reproductions installed for comparison. Generally the murals are so difficult to deci-pher that you may wonder what all the fuss was about. If you look closely (or view the reproductions) though, you may think you are looking at artwork from ancient Egypt.

Some of the murals depict the victory of the Maya over the Olmecs. One panel shows dancing at a celebration, another prisoners waiting to be sacrificed, and a third the giving of thanks to the gods for victory.

To best see what these faded frescoes orig-inally looked like, inspect the Bonampak mural reproductions in the Museo Nacional de Antropología in Mexico City, or the ones at the Museo Regional de Antropología Carlos Pellicer Cámara in Villahermosa.

Tuxtla Gutiérrez's Hotel Bonampak has a full reproduction of the central room's mural in its lobby.

Other than some narrative stelae at the foot of the hill leading to Building 1, the Temple of the Frescoes, the eight other buildings of the Southern Group are badly ruined.

Yaxchilán

Set above the jungled banks of the Usumacinta, Yaxchilán was first inhabited about 200 AD, though the earliest hiero-glyphs found have been dated from 514 to 807 AD. Although not as well restored as Palenque, the ruins here cover a greater extent, and further excavation may yield even more significant finds.

Yaxchilán rose to the peak of its promi-nence in the 8th century under a king whose name in hieroglyphs was translated into Spanish as Escudo Jaguar, or Shield Jaguar. His shield-and-jaguar symbol appears on many of the site's buildings and stelae. The

Limestone lintel of bloodletting rite found at Yaxchilán

city's power expanded under Escudo Jaguar's son, Pájaro Jaguar, or Bird Jaguar (752-70). His hieroglyph consists of a small jungle cat with feathers on the back and a bird superimposed on the head.

Building 33 on the south-western side of the plaza has some fine religious carvings over the northern doorways, and a roofcomb which retains most of its original beauty. At the front base of the temple are narrative carvings of a ball game.

The central plaza holds statues of crocodiles and jaguars. A lintel in Building 20 shows a dead man's spirit emerging from the mouth of a man speaking about him, and stelae of Maya making offerings to the gods.

In front of Building 20 are exceptional stelae featuring Mayan royalty.

Be certain to walk to Yaxchilán's highest temples, which are still covered with trees and are not visible from the plaza. Building 41 is the tallest of these, and the view from its top is one of the highlights of a visit to Yaxchilán. Some tour guides do not want to make the effort to show you Building 41 – insist on it!

Getting There & Away

Air Those with more money than time can charter a small plane to Bonampak and Yaxchilán from Palenque, San Cristóbal, Comitán or Tenosique. For current information on the travel agencies operating these flights, ask at the tourist office in each town.

In San Cristóbal de Las Casas, flights and tours to Yaxchilán and Bonampak can be arranged through Viajes Pakal (☎ 8-28-18/19), at the corner of Hidalgo and Cuauhtémoc, or Amfitriones Turísticos in the Hotel Posada Diego de Mazariegos. The flight option, with a scheduled total of 3½ hours at the two sites, costs from US$80 per person with five in the party up to US$135 each if there are only two. The flights go from Comitán or Las Margaritas (near Comitán) if San Cristóbal airport is out of action; transport to and from the airstrip is included.

Combi & Boat Tours Various travel agencies in Palenque run two-day road and river tours to Bonampak and Yaxchilán, as does Colectivos Chambalu. The rate is US$70 for the two-day venture, including transportation and all meals. A minivan takes you within 10 km of Bonampak and you walk the rest of the way. Tents are provided for overnight. The next morning, you are driven to the Río Usumacinta, where an outboard motor boat takes you for an hour through the jungle to Yaxchilán. Food is included.

There are also one-day trips by Chambalu combi to Bonampak for US$30, or to Yaxchilán and back for US$45 a round-trip.

Viajes Pakal in Palenque offers the following two-day trip for US$82 per person (five or six people), US$115 per person (three or four), or US$214 per person (one or two): drive from Palenque to the Lacandón settlement of Caribal Lacanjá by car, take a two-hour walk to Bonampak (stay 1½ to two hours), walk back to Caribal Lacanjá and sleep in a Lacandón house. Next morning, travel by car to Frontera Echeverría, then boat along the Río Usumacinta to Yaxchilán, stay three hours, and then return to Palenque by boat and car.

Car Despite what you may hear, it is possible to drive to Bonampak and the trip doesn't even require 4WD – although the local car-rental company might not be too pleased if they knew where you intended to take their Volkswagen Beetle. A full tank of fuel might just get you from Palenque to Bonampak, Yaxchilán and back but you'd be safer carrying some additional fuel. The round trip is a bit over 300 km.

The Bonampak turn-off is about 10 km south of Palenque on the Ocosingo and San Cristóbal road. It's marked 'Chancalá', not 'Bonampak', and it's wise to ask directions. It takes about three hours from the main road turn-off to the Bonampak turn-off and the road is passable, although it tends to be dusty and you must beware of rocks and potholes. Eventually you reach the Bonampak turn-off to the right and the road deteriorates to a rougher one-lane track. After about 10 km a sign indicates Bonampak to the left. Despite what the sign may say, the distance is about 15 km.

There's a campsite close to this junction and from here it's wise to walk, particularly if it has been raining, although a Volkswagen

can make it in good weather. There are several streambeds and shaky bridges to be crossed, so be careful if you try to drive all the way to the site.

To continue to Yaxchilán you have to drive on to Frontera Echeverría, a border town to Guatemala which is on the Río Usumacinta upstream from Yaxchilán. From the Bonampak turn-off from the road it's about 20 km to where a sign indicates the direction to the border, from there you travel along another 30 km of rough track. Boats to the ruins can be hired from this sprawling village; you might be asked around US$40 for a complete boat but should be able to knock that down. Yaxchilán is about 20 km downstream, and while you get there quite fast, the return trip against the swift current can take over two hours. Come prepared for the fierce sun.

The comedor (cookshop) above the river in Echeverría is good for dinner or breakfast. Buses occasionally come down the road from Palenque as far as the Bonampak turn-off and sometimes all the way to Echeverría.

PALENQUE TO SAN CRISTÓBAL
According to Captain Dupaix, a Frenchman who trekked along La Ruta Maya in 1807:

Palenque is eight days' march from Ocosingo. The journey is very fatiguing. The roads, if they can be so called, are only narrow and difficult paths, which wind across mountains and precipices, and which it is necessary to follow sometimes on mules, sometimes on foot, sometimes on the shoulders of Indians, and sometimes in hammocks. In some places it is necessary to pass on bridges, or, rather, trunks of trees badly secured, and over lands covered with wood, desert and dispeopled, and to sleep in the open air, excepting a very few villages and huts.

Today the 85-km journey is considerably easier and faster, taking only about two hours by bus. It may take you longer, however, because the entire 190-km journey from Palenque to San Cristóbal de las Casas is dotted with interesting stopovers. Only 20 km from Palenque is the spellbinding tropical waterfall park of Misol-Ha, and another

36 km into the mountains are the many rapids and waterfalls at Agua Azul. Ocosingo, 30 km beyond Agua Azul, is the nearest town to the seldom visited Mayan ruins at Toniná, 14 km east of the town on a side road. From Ocosingo you wind your way higher into the mountains, another 92 km past the Tzotzil and Tzeltal Mayan villages of Huixtán and Oxchuc to the Pan American Highway, meandering through the Jovel Valley. Turn right (north) and after 12 km you're in San Cristóbal de las Casas.

Only 2nd-class buses and colectivo minibuses travel the route, taking about five hours by bus (four hours by car) from San Cristóbal to Palenque if you don't stop over. The road, though narrow, is paved all the way and has little traffic. Not far from Palenque, the road is lined with burnt-out patches of jungle which have been cleared to make way for more cattle pastureland. This destruction of the jungle, though discouraged by the government, is proceeding at an alarming rate.

Misol-Ha Cascades

About 20 km from Palenque, look for signs to the Parque Natural Ejidal Misol-Ha on the right-hand side of the road. Two km along an access road into the *ejido* (collective farm) is a parking area with a small restaurant and a ticket kiosk. Pay US$0.40 per person or US$1 per car, and stroll into the lush jungle 50 metres to where a waterfall plummets nearly 35 metres into a pool safe for swimming. The cascades and jungle surroundings are spectacular enough to be the setting for an Arnold Schwarzenegger epic. Alas, there are no campgrounds here. For tips on how to get to Misol-Ha, refer to the section on Agua Azul.

Agua Azul Cascades

The Agua Azul Cascades are among the wonders of Mexico and should not be missed. Just 61 km south of Palenque, scores of dazzling turquoise waterfalls tumble over white limestone surrounded by jungle. Beyond the rapids, numerous pools of tranquil water offer a refreshing respite from the rainforest's sticky humidity.

On holidays the site will be thronged with local families out for fun; at other times your only companions here will be the ejido workers who staff the ticket kiosk, the snack shops and the camping places. Admission to the ejido costs US$2 per car, US$1 per person (on foot). The cascades are 4.5 km west of the Palenque-Ocosingo road down a steep hill on a bad road.

When swimming, use good judgement and avoid the more rapid areas of the waterfalls, because drownings are all too common here. During the rainy season the currents can be swift and dangerous, the 'turquoise' waters brown with silt, lowering underwater visibility to zero. Under these conditions you, unfamiliar with submerged hazards such as rocks and dead trees, can easily be injured. Crosses set in the upper part of the cascades show where the unlucky met their end.

A trail above the falls takes you over some swaying, less than stable footbridges and up through jungle. Women trekking here should consider taking a male companion. An experienced female traveller reported that she was attacked above the falls, escaping only through a strategically aimed kick to the groin. When she reported the assault to the local authorities, they said they knew the man and that he had jumped tourists before.

Places to Stay & Eat Unless you have a tent or hammock, Agua Azul is likely to be a day trip. There are a few filthy, plain wooden rooms in a shack where you're provided with a blanket and nothing else for the outlandish sum of US$6. You'd do better to string a hammock outside the shack for US$1; or you could rent a hammock from the proprietor for US$3 per night. Those with tents are charged US$1 per night.

Whether you have come here for the day or are overnighting, watch your gear – several travellers reported rip-offs at Agua Azul. There is a small restaurant here, but the food is overpriced and pretty awful. You would be much better off packing a picnic from Palenque.

Getting There & Away It's 56 km, about one hour by bus, from Palenque to the Agua Azul turn-off, or 155 km, about 3½ hours by bus, from San Cristóbal to the turn-off, called Agua Azul Crucero in Spanish. Autotransportes Tuxtla Gutiérrez operates six buses daily from Palenque up into the mountains to Ocosingo, San Cristóbal, and return, stopping at Agua Azul Crucero. Tickets on these buses for Agua Azul Crucero (US$1) go on sale 30 minutes before departure time. This means that most or all of the seats will be sold by the time you're allowed to buy, and you may have to stand for the entire hour-long trip.

From the turn-off you must walk downhill on a potholed road 4.5 km to the cascades. When the time comes to leave, you must return along the same road uphill in the sweltering heat to the turn-off. There are two means of public transport to the falls and each has its drawbacks.

For US$5, Colectivos Chambalu, at Hidalgo and Allende in Palenque, will take you to Misol-Ha, Agua Azul and back. The colectivos (minibuses) depart at 10 am daily (be there by 9.30 am to get a seat), make a 15-minute stop at Misol-Ha and then move on to Agua Azul, where you stay for 90 minutes to two hours. The colectivos have you back in Palenque town about 3.30 pm. If you want to stay longer, you can try to hitchhike back.

If you're not afraid of that 4.5-km jungle walk from the main road to the cascades, hop on a bus travelling between Palenque and Ocosingo. It will drop you at the crucero for less than US$1. When you arrive back at Agua Azul Crucero to catch a bus bound for Palenque, Ocosingo or San Cristóbal, you will most likely have to stand as all seats are generally filled by the time the bus reaches the crucero. Bus traffic dwindles rapidly in late afternoon and disappears in the evening, so start back before 4 pm.

Waiting for the bus at the crucero, you won't be alone. Other readers of this guide-book, along with less fortunate travellers will be there with you, so you'll have someone to talk to. Some travellers have hitched from the crucero, but don't count on this.

Another way to reach Agua Azul is to chat up fellow travellers at the Hotel La Cañada's restaurant, or at the Maya Restaurant near the plaza, and see if you can share a ride and fuel expenses. I expect all car-blessed readers of this book to be sympathetic to the plights of carless readers.

Ocosingo & Toniná

Ocosingo is a small mestizo and Tzeltal Indian valley town on the Palenque-San Cristóbal road, 105 km from San Cristóbal and 85 km from Palenque. It's a friendly, easygoing place but of no particular interest except as an access point for the Mayan ruins of Toniná, 14 km east.

Toniná gets few visitors, partly because it's relatively hard to reach. It doesn't compare with Palenque for beauty or importance but it's a sizable hillside site with some big structures, and fine country roundabout. John L Stephens, visiting in 1840, found Ocosingo to be 'in a beautiful situation, surrounded by mountains, with a large church... In the centre of the square was a magnificent Ceiba tree'. The ceiba tree is long gone, but it's a pretty square nonetheless.

Orientation Ocosingo spreads downhill to the east of the main road. Avenida Central and Avenida 1 Sur run straight down from the main road 350 metres to the pretty main plaza darkly shaded by topiary· umbrella trees and surrounded by porticoed colonial buildings. The bus stations are on Avenida 1 Norte near the highway.

Ocosingo is laid out on the standard Spanish colonial grid plan and divided into quadrants. Street names indicate this (Calle 3 Poniente Norte is the third street west of the plaza on the north side of the plaza), but foster a complexity bewildering for such a small town. The street plan is modelled after that of the Chiapan capital, Tuxtla Gutiérrez. For an explanation of how it all works, refer to the section on Tuxtla.

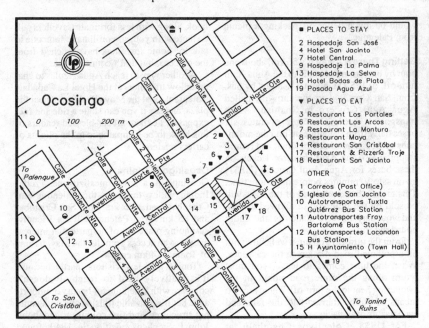

Ocosingo

0   100   200 m

To Palenque

To San Cristóbal

To Toniná Ruins

■ PLACES TO STAY

2   Hospedaje San José
4   Hotel San Jacinto
7   Hotel Central
9   Hospedaje La Palma
13 Hospedaje La Selva
16 Hotel Bodas de Plata
19 Posada Agua Azul

▼ PLACES TO EAT

3   Restaurant Los Portales
6   Restaurant Los Arcos
7   Restaurant La Montura
8   Restaurant Maya
14 Restaurant San Cristóbal
17 Restaurant & Pizzería Troje
18 Restaurant San Jacinto

OTHER

1   Correos (Post Office)
5   Iglesia de San Jacinto
10 Autotransportes Tuxtla Gutiérrez Bus Station
11 Autotransportes Fray Bartolomé Bus Station
12 Autotransportes Lacandon Bus Station
15 H Ayuntamiento (Town Hall)

Everything is within five minutes walk of the plaza. None of the banks in town will change travellers' cheques, but this may change as Ocosingo is put on the tourist map. The postal code here is 29950.

Places to Stay The *Hotel Central* (☎ (967) 3-00-39), Avenida Central 1, on the north side of the plaza, is the best in town, with tidy but simple, clean rooms with ceiling fans, minuscule TV sets and baby-blue tiled private baths for US$10 a single, US$14 a double, US$18 a triple. Some rooms have views of the square and the town, but nothing spectacular. The price is a bit steep for this town, but then all hotels in Ocosingo charge too much.

Posada Agua Azul, two blocks south of the church on the road to Toniná, has rooms of medium size grouped around a courtyard which has a tiny murky swimming pool and a few tightly caged creatures including ant-eaters, hawks and macaws. Single rooms go

for US$7, doubles for US$11 and triples for US$14.

Even cheaper is the *Hospedaje La Palma* on the corner of Calle 2 Poniente and Avenida 1 Norte, just down the hill from the Transportes Tuxtla Gutiérrez station. It's a basic but clean family-run place, with pleasant flowery courtyard and a little comedor (dining room) for meals. Singles/doubles are US$3/US$5 and bathrooms are shared.

Hospedaje San José, Calle 1 Oriente 6, half a block north of the north-east corner of the plaza, has dark, small, musty rooms, but it's clean enough, and family-run. Prices range from US$3.50 for a single with common bath to US$7 for a two-bed room with private bath.

Hotel San Jacinto at Avenida Central 13, half a block east of the north-east corner of the plaza, is bright only on its tiled façade. Inside it's drab, dingy and divey, and over-priced at US$9 a double with bath.

Finally, there's the *Hotel Bodas de Playa*, Avenida 1 Sur just off the square, which reminds one of nothing so much as a cellblock. Many rooms open directly onto the street. The price is an outrageous US$9 a double with shared bath, US$13 a double with private bath.

Places to Eat Ocosingo is famous for its *queso amarillo* (yellow cheese), which comes in three-layered one-kg balls. The two outside layers are like chewy Gruyère, the middle is creamy. If you miss the market, a ball costs US$5 at Mini Super Los Portales on the north-east corner of the plaza.

Restaurant La Montura, Avenida Central 5, in the same building as the Hotel Central, has a prime location on the north side of the plaza, with tables on an outside terrace as well as indoors. It has a sizable menu and is good for breakfast (US$2 to US$3) as well as a lunch or dinner of tacos de bistek (US$3.50) or the plato especial with chorizo (US$3). Chicken is more expensive, at US$5. They'll build you some sandwiches if you want to take a picnic lunch to the ruins at Toniná.

On the opposite (south) side of the plaza, the *Restaurant San Jacinto* is a dark, cheap lonchería, but the *Restaurant & Pizzería Troje* is much nicer. The menu here features the famous queso amarillo: quesadillas (US$2) are cheap, or you can go all out and order the plato especial of *queso fundido con chorizo* (melted cheese with spicy sausage) for US$3. There aren't many pizzas on the menu, but you can choose from many traditional antojitos and soups.

Restaurant Maya, a few steps west on Avenida Central from the Hotel Central and Banamex, is a very tidy, bright, clean little eatery featuring *platos fuertes* (main-course lunch or dinner platters) for US$3.50, fruit salads and antojitos for less.

Restaurant San Cristóbal, Avenida Central 22, a few steps from the Maya, is a simple lonchería where you have to ask what's cooking the day you visit. It may be *pollo en mole* (chicken in a dark sauce) for US$3.

Restaurant Los Portales, Avenida Central 19, facing the north-east corner of the plaza, is a homey but old-fashioned place where you enter through the living room to a light, airy dining room. Several matronly señoras will mother you here, offering various traditional meals for US$3.50 to US$6, all inclusive. The Portales provides an interesting contrast to the neighbouring *Restaurant Los Arcos*, which is more modern but not nearly so pleasant.

Getting There & Away All buses are 2nd class. Autotransportes Tuxtla Gutiérrez (TTG) buses to Palenque (82 km, 1½ hours, US$2.25) via the Agua Azul Crucero (30 km, 45 minutes, US$1), San Cristóbal (108 km, 2½ hours, US$2) and Tuxtla Gutiérrez (193 km, 4½ hours, US$3.50) depart early in the morning. There are also four buses de paso to Palenque and seven in the other direction daily, as well as two daily buses to Yajalón.

Autotransportes Lacandonia (cheaper, older, less comfortable than TTG), has 12 daily buses to San Cristóbal (US$2), five to Yajalón, one to Villahermosa (US$5.50, six hours), and others to Tila, Tumbalá and Sitalá. Autotransportes Maya, located in the same terminal as Lacandonia, has six buses daily to and from San Cristóbal for US$1.75.

Autotransportes Fray Bartolomé de Las Casas (in between the previous two companies for price and comfort) is on the far side of the main road at the top of Avenida 1 Norte. It has five daily departures to San Cristóbal for US$1.50.

Taxis Aereos Ocosingo (☎ (967) 3-01-88) can arrange charter flights to Palenque, Bonampak and Yaxchilán. Sometimes they run air tours to Bonampak and Yaxchilán. The full-day tour (6 am to 6 pm) costs US$125.

Toniná Ruins

Toniná was probably a city-state independent of both Palenque and Yaxchilán, though it declined at the same time as they did, at around 800 AD. Dates found at the site range from 500 to 800 AD but, like Palenque and Yaxchilán, it was at its peak in the last 100 years or so of that period. Toniná is unique because of its huge terraced temple structure built into the side of a hill. Captain Dupaix, Count de Waldeck and John L Stephens and Frederick Catherwood all visited Toniná in the first half of the 19th century. Intermittent excavations go on today but a lot remains covered and only limited restoration has been done – which gives the place a 'lost in the jungle' feel compared to more renowned sites.

The keeper will go round the site with you and explain it (in Spanish), which is helpful since there are very few labels. The track goes past the small museum which holds a surprising number of good carved stones, mostly of local rulers, some of them prisoners of war captured by the forces of Toniná. The high relief of the picture of Chinkultic's ruler, discovered only in 1989, is quite unusual. There are many other statues, bas-reliefs, altars and calendar stones – all, unfortunately, unlabelled.

Past the museum, the path leads over a stream and up a bank to come out in a flat area, from which rises the terraced hillside that supports the main structures. If you're facing this hillside, behind you in a field are an overgrown outlying pyramid and the main ball court.

The flat area at the foot of the hillside contains a small ball court and fragments of limestone carvings. Some of them appear to show prisoners holding out offerings, with dates and other glyphs on the reverse sides. Three large round stones are probably calendar-related.

The two lowest levels of the terraced hillside have some unremarkable mounds. The most interesting part of the site is at the right-hand end of the third and fourth levels. The stone facing of the wall rising from the third to fourth levels here has a zig-zag x-shape, which may represent Quetzalcóatl and also serves as flights of steps. To the right of the base of this are the remains of a tomb, with steps leading up to an altar. Behind and above the tomb and altar is a rambling complex of chambers, passageways and stairways at the third and fourth levels,

believed to have been Toniná's administrative centre.

Over towards the centre of the hillside are remains of the central stairway, which went much of the way up the middle of the hillside.

One level higher than the top of the 'Quetzalcóatl' wall you come upon a grave covered in tin sheeting, which you can lift to see the stone coffin beneath. Here were found the bodies of a ruler and two others. To the left on the same level is a shrine to Chac, the rain god. To the right at the foot of a crumbling temple, a carving shows the earth god, labelled *monstruo de la tierra*. Higher again and to the left are two more mounds. Farthest to the left, the Pyramid of Life & Death may have supported the ruler's dwelling. At the very top of the hill rise two more tall pyramid-temple-mounds.

The unrestored state of the site makes it hard to envisage what most of these structures were like in their heyday, but if you have already visited other Mayan lowland sites like Palenque or Yaxchilán, you can use your imagination to envisage a similar splendour. Many of the stone facings and interior walls were originally covered in plaster, coloured paint or frescoes.

Getting There & Away

The site is 14 km east of Ocosingo along a sometimes rough dirt road. The trip is through pleasant ranch land with lots of colourful birds. In late February and early March 1987, for the first time in living memory, thousands of migrating swallows checked in nightly around 6 pm at a farm on this road – an awesome spectacle: if they make it a habit, it would be well worth trying to synchronise your visit to Toniná with their arrival.

If you have your own vehicle, follow Calle 1 Oriente south from the San Jacinto church on the plaza. Before long it curves left and you pass a cemetery on the right. At the fork a couple of km further on, go left. At the next fork, the site is signposted to the right. Finally a sign marks the entry track to Toniná at Rancho Guadalupe on the left. From here it's another km to the site itself. Stop at the 'Alto Boleto' sign and the keeper will catch up with you (perhaps on horseback) to sell you your ticket (US$2.50). The house opposite the ticket office sells refrescos. The ruins are open from 9 am to 4 pm daily.

Without your own vehicle, you have the option of a taxi (about US$30 a round trip, with a one-hour wait at the ruins), walking, hitching (maybe six vehicles an hour pass Toniná), trying to pick up one of the passenger trucks that head that way, or the buses of Unión de Vehículos de Pasaje y Carga Mixta Ocosingo, which go from Calle 1 Oriente, 3½ blocks south of the plaza near the market. The company has two morning buses to Guadalupe (near the ruins), and two morning returns. The trip costs US$0.90 and takes about 45 minutes. If you can't get back to Ocosingo before nightfall, the Rancho Guadalupe sometimes puts people up for the night or allows them to camp.

VILLAHERMOSA
Population 250,000
Once just a way-station on the long, sweltering road from central Mexico to the savannahs of Yucatán, Villahermosa was anything but a 'beautiful city' as its name implies. Its situation on the banks of the Río Grijalva was pleasant enough, but its lowland location meant it was bathed in tropical heat and humidity every day of every year.

Then several decades ago the petroleum geologists arrived, sure that there was wealth to be found in the boggy land of the region. They were right. Tabasco's oil reserves are among the largest in Mexico, and boosted Mexico's position on the short list of countries with proven oil reserves.

With the boom came money – lots of it – and the people of Villahermosa spent much of it to beautify their city. Today Villahermosa is indeed a beautiful city with wide, tree-shaded boulevards, sprawling parks, fancy hotels (for the oilies) and excellent cultural institutions.

Most travellers along La Ruta Maya go from Palenque directly to San Cristóbal de las Casas (or vice versa) via Ocosingo. A longer loop, from Palenque to Villahermosa, then to Tuxtla Gutiérrez and San Cristóbal, allows you to see the sights in these two provincial capitals. Another way to visit Villahermosa is on a day trip or one-night excursion from a base in Palenque.

If you want to see everything here, you will have to stay at least one night. The open-air Olmec archaeological museum called the Parque-Museo La Venta is one of Mexico's great archaeological exhibits, and will take you most of a morning. The excellent Museo Regional de Antropología (Regional Archaeological Museum) deserves at least an hour or two. And just a short bus ride from the city are the ruins of ancient Comalcalco, complete with a formidable pyramid and temples constructed with mortar made from oyster shells.

With even more time you can relax at beach sites like El Paraíso, El Limón, Pico de Oro and Frontera. Although not on the Caribbean Sea, these beaches are pleasant enough and nearly completely free of tourists. The town of Teapa, an hour from Villahermosa, offers cave exploration, river swimming and a sulphur spa.

History
What is now called the state of Tabasco was once the home of the Olmecs, the first great Mesoamerican civilisation (1200-400 BC), whose religion, art, astronomy and architecture would deeply influence the civilisations that followed in its wake. The Olmec capital, La Venta, was situated in the western part of the state. Major artefacts, including some of the famous gigantic heads, were moved from that site to Villahermosa's Parque-Museo La Venta to save them from damage during oil exploration. The Chontal Maya who followed the Olmecs built a great ceremonial city called Comalcalco outside present-day Villahermosa. By the time the Spanish landed, Comalcalco had long been abandoned and lost in the jungle.

Cortés, who disembarked on the Gulf coast near present-day Villahermosa in 1519,

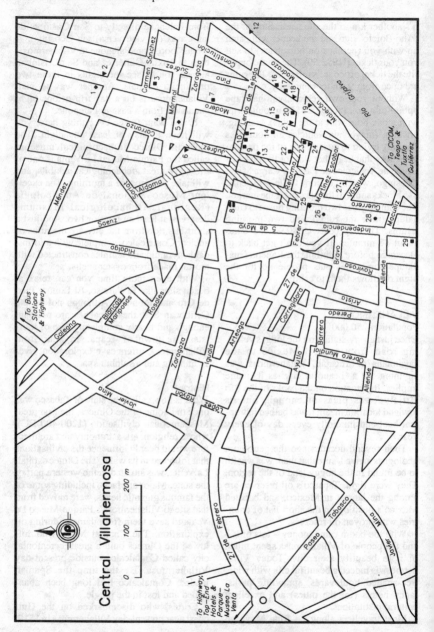

Central Villahermosa

0   100   200 m

To Bus Stations & Highway

To Highway, Top-End Hotels & Parque-Museo La Venta

Río Grijalva

To CICOM, Teapa & Tuxtla Gutiérrez

■ PLACES TO STAY

3   Hotel San Francisco
7   Hotel Palma de Mallorca
9   Hotel Tabasco
10 Hotel San Miguel
11 Hotel Oviedo
14 Hotel Oriente
15 Hotel Don Carlos
16 Hotel Buenos Aires
17 Hotel 'P' (Providencia)
20 Hotel Madan
22 Hotel Miraflores
23 Hotel Madero
29 Hotel Plaza Independencia

▼ PLACES TO EAT

2   Restaurant Geminis

4   Panificadora y Pastelería
6   Panificadora Los Dos Naciones
12 Restaurant-Boat Capitán Beúlo
18 Restaurant La Playita
19 Restaurant Shalymar
21 Restaurant Madan
24 Restaurant El Torito Valenzuela

OTHER

1   Super Lavandería Rex
5   Parque Juárez
8   Post & Telegraph Office
13 Telephone Office
25 Patria es Primo Fountain
26 Palacio de Gobierno (State
    Government Building)
27 Tourist Office & Crafts Shop
28 Plaza de Armas

initially defeated the Maya and founded a settlement called Santa María de la Victoria. The Maya regrouped and offered stern resistance until they were defeated by Francisco de Montejo, who pacified the region by 1540. Nonetheless, the tranquillity was short-lived. The depredations of pirates forced the original settlement to be moved inland from the coast and renamed Villahermosa de San Juan Bautista.

After independence was won from Spain, various local land barons tried to assert their power over the area, causing considerable strife. The 1863 French intrusion under Maximilian of Hapsburg was deeply resisted here and led to regional solidarity and political stability. Nonetheless, the economy languished until after the Mexican Revolution, when exports of cacao, bananas and coconuts began to increase. Then US and British petroleum companies discovered oil, and Tabasco's economy began to revolve around the liquid fuel. During the 1970s Villahermosa became an oil boom town and profits from the state's export of agricultural crops added to the good times. This new-found prosperity has brought a feeling of sophistication that cuts right through the tropical heat, stamping Tabasco as different from neighbouring Chiapas and Campeche.

Geography & Climate

Tabasco's topography changes from flat land near the seaside to undulating hills as you near Chiapas. Due to heavy rainfall – about 150 cm annually – there is much swampland and lush tropical foliage. Outside Villahermosa, the state is rather sparsely populated for Mexico, with a little more than a million people inhabiting about 25,000 square km.

Be prepared for sticky humidity in this tropical zone. Much of the substantial rainfall here occurs between May and October. Outside of Villahermosa, it can be quite bug infested (particularly near the rivers), so bring repellent.

Orientation

Villahermosa is a sprawling city, and you will find yourself walking some considerable distances – in the sticky heat – and occasionally hopping on a minibus (combi) or taking a taxi, unless you have your own wheels.

Bottom-end and middle-range hotel and restaurant choices are mostly in the older commercial centre of the city between the Plaza de Armas, the small main plaza bounded by streets named Zaragoza, Madero and Juárez, and the Parque Juárez, about five

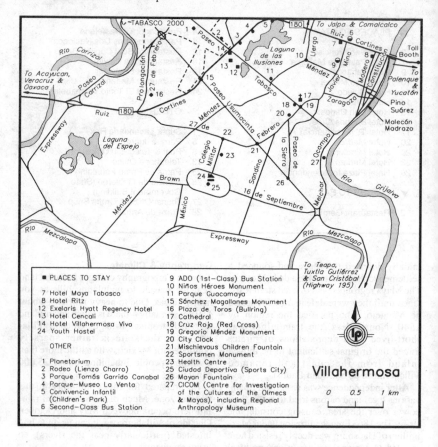

Villahermosa

■ PLACES TO STAY	
7 Hotel Maya Tabasco	
8 Hotel Ritz	
12 Exelaris Hyatt Regency Hotel	
13 Hotel Cencali	
14 Hotel Villahermosa Viva	
24 Youth Hostel	

OTHER	
1 Planetarium	
2 Rodeo (Lienzo Charro)	
3 Parque Tomás Garrido Canabal	
4 Parque-Museo La Venta	
5 Convivencia Infantil (Children's Park)	
6 Second-Class Bus Station	

9 ADO (1st-Class) Bus Station
10 Niños Héroes Monument
11 Parque Guacamaya
15 Sánchez Magallanes Monument
16 Plaza de Toros (Bullring)
17 Cathedral
18 Cruz Roja (Red Cross)
19 Gregorio Méndez Monument
20 City Clock
21 Mischievous Children Fountain
22 Sportsmen Monument
23 Health Centre
25 Ciudad Deportiva (Sports City)
26 Mayan Fountain
27 CICOM (Centre for Investigation of the Cultures of the Olmecs & Mayas), including Regional Anthropology Museum

0   0.5   1 km

blocks to the north. This section has been renovated in recent years and is known, because of those renovations, as the Zona Remodelada (Remodeled Zone) or, more poetically, as the Zona de la Luz (Zone of Lights). The zona is a lively place, busy with people strolling, licking frozen yogurt cones, snacking on fast food, bench-warming and making conversation, and – most of all – shopping. Every Saturday evening is a virtual shopping fiesta, and Madero is its centre.

The city centre can be navigated easily on foot, particularly since a number of its streets

have been closed to vehicular traffic and decorated as pedestrian malls.

Top-end hotels are located on and off the main highway which passes through the city, named Avenida Ruiz Cortines, which is the name you will see on street and directional signs, even though most older maps have this road labelled as Blvd Grijalva. The Parque-Museo La Venta is also on Avenida Ruiz Cortines, several hundred metres north-west of the intersection with Paseo Tabasco.

The Central Camionera de Primera Clase (1st-Class Bus Station, sometimes called the ADO terminal, ☎ (931) 2-89-00) is on Javier

Mina, three long blocks south of Avenida Ruiz Cortines and about 12 blocks north of the city centre. The Central de Autobuses de Tabasco (2nd-Class Bus Station) is right on Avenida Ruiz Cortines near a traffic roundabout marked by a statue of a fisherman; the station is one block east of Javier Mina, four long blocks north of the 1st-class station, and about 16 long blocks from the centre.

Villahermosa's Rovirosa Airport (☎ (931) 2-75-55) is 10.5 km east of the centre on Highway 180, on the other side of the bridge across the Río Grijalva.

Information

Tourist Offices The most convenient tourist office is at Juárez 111, at the back of a government crafts store. It's open Monday to Saturday 9 am to 3 pm and 3.30 to 8 pm, closed Sunday. There's a tourist information booth at the ADO bus station run by the Tabasco Hotel & Motel Association, but its hours are erratic, as are the capabilities of its staff. Similar booths are at Parque-Museo La Venta and Rovirosa airport.

The large, glitzy main Tabasco state tourist office (☎ (931) 5-06-94) is in the new governmental development known as Tabasco 2000, at Paseo Tabasco 1504, half a km north-west of the intersection with Ruiz Cortines, accessible easily only by car. Hours are 9 am to 3 pm and 6 to 8 pm Monday to Friday, 9 am to 1 pm Saturday, closed Sunday. The federal SECTUR office (☎ (931) 6-28-91) is here as well. It's interesting that the tourist offices are in an area convenient to bureaucrats but inconvenient to tourists.

Money Apparently, one of the things they did when they remodelled the Zona Remodelada was to install lots and lots of banks. I counted no fewer than eight within a five-block area bounded by Aldama, Zaragoza, Madero and Reforma. Banamex (☎ (931) 2-89-94) is at the corner of Madero and Reforma; Bancomer (☎ (931) 2-37-00) is at the intersection of Zaragoza and Juárez. Banking hours are 9 am to 1.30 pm.

Cambiaria del Centro (☎ (931) 4-30-53/4), Saenz 222, is a casa de cambio (exchange office) which charges a bit more to change money than banks do, but provides fast and efficient service Monday to Friday from 8.30 am to 2 pm and from 4 to 6.30 pm. Their slogan is 'Where you're treated as you should be', a sentiment absent from most Mexican banks.

Post There's a small post office at the ADO station. The main post office (☎ (931) 2-10-40), is at Saenz 131, corner of Lerdo de Tejada in the Zona Remodelada. Postal hours are Monday to Friday 8 am to 5.30 pm (stamps sold till 7 pm), Saturday 9 am to noon (stamps sold till 1 pm), closed Sunday. Villahermosa's postal code is 86000. The telegraph office (☎ (931) 2-24-94) is near the post office at Lerdo de Tejada 601.

Laundry Try the Super Lavandería Rex (☎ 2-08-15), Madero 705 at Méndez, facing the Restaurant Geminis. Hours are 8 am to 8 pm, Monday to Saturday. A three-kg load costs US$3 for overnight service.

Parque-Museo La Venta

History Parque-Museo La Venta exists thanks to unusual circumstances. Off the Gulf coast some 129 km west of Villahermosa, near Tabasco's border with Veracruz, a great religious site of the Olmec civilisation was first excavated by the archaeologist Frans Blom in 1925. The Olmec city of La Venta, built on an island where the Río Tonalá runs into the Gulf, was originally constructed in about 1500 BC, and flourished from 800 BC to 200 AD. After the original work by Blom, Tulane and California Universities continued the excavations, and many archaeologists took part. M W Sterling is credited with having discovered, in the early 1940s, five massive heads sculpted from basalt.

When, about this time, petroleum engineers drained a nearby marsh, more of the city was revealed. The additional discoveries came to the attention of Villahermosa's 'Renaissance man', Carlos Pellicer Cámara. Pellicer, a poet, historian and archaeologist,

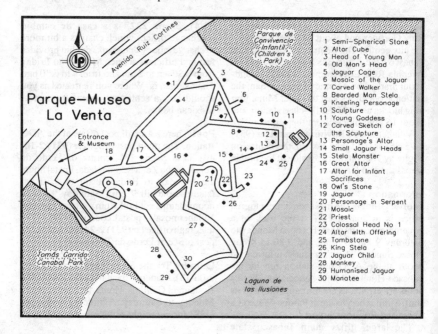

Parque—Museo La Venta

1 Semi–Spherical Stone
2 Altar Cube
3 Head of Young Man
4 Old Man's Head
5 Jaguar Cage
6 Mosaic of the Jaguar
7 Carved Walker
8 Bearded Man Stela
9 Kneeling Personage
10 Sculpture
11 Young Goddess
12 Carved Sketch of the Sculpture
13 Personage's Altar
14 Small Jaguar Heads
15 Stela Monster
16 Great Altar
17 Altar for Infant Sacrifices
18 Owl's Stone
19 Jaguar
20 Personage in Serpent
21 Mosaic
22 Priest
23 Colossal Head No 1
24 Altar with Offering
25 Tombstone
26 King Stela
27 Jaguar Child
28 Monkey
29 Humanised Jaguar
30 Manatee

was appalled when he heard that oil drilling jeopardised the La Venta ruins.

Exerting political pressure and influence on the state's politicians, Pellicer arranged to have the significant finds from La Venta, including several of the gigantic heads, moved to a park on what was then the outskirts of Villahermosa. Today, Parque-Museo La Venta is a monument to Pellicer's efforts; a magnificent museum without walls in a lush green setting that enables your imagination to picture these sculptures in their original Olmec city.

Three colossal Olmec heads, intriguingly African in their facial composition, were moved to the park. The largest weighs over 24 tonnes and stands more than two metres tall. It is a mystery how, originally, the Olmecs managed to move the basalt heads as well as religious statues some 100 km without the use of the wheel.

The influence of the Olmecs on future civilisations throughout Mesoamerica was

substantial. As well as an artistic influence, the divine jaguar represented in statues and even by the thick lips of the huge heads was a major spiritual force imparted to those societies which came later. A number of the great monuments exhibited here were actually found buried, and are thought by some archaeologists to have been sacrificial offerings to the jaguar god.

The park is a maze of paths with numbered artefacts set amidst jungle foliage. As well as the heads, you will see intricately carved stelae and sculptures of manatees, monkeys and, of course, the jaguar. When you visit Parque-Museo La Venta, you'll wonder why other museums haven't placed their nonperishable artefacts in such attractive outdoor settings rather than behind drab walls and alienating glass. Built on the banks of the Laguna de las Ilusiones, the park also has free-ranging deer, monkeys, armadillos and coatimundis, as well as caged crocodiles and jaguars.

Admission Parque-Museo La Venta (☎ (931) 5-22-28) is open every day from 8 am to 4.30 pm. Entry costs US$1. On my most recent visit there were no explanatory leaflets to be had and visitors had to use a guide if they wanted to know anything about what they were seeing. Officially the guides' services are free, but tips are expected, which is the hitch, of course. In the past, self-guidance brochures were available at the entrance for a small charge, or from the tourist office for free. Perhaps they will be available again by the time you visit. In any case, the numbering of the exhibits always seems to be confused.

If your Spanish is up to snuff, come for the evening sound-and-light show (US$1.25) on Tuesday, Thursday, Friday or Saturday, weather permitting, at 7 or 8 pm. Check with the tourist office to make sure the performance will be held, then remember to bring your mosquito repellent.

On the north-east side of Parque-Museo La Venta is the city's children's park, the Parque de Convivencia Infantil. Playgrounds, a small zoo and aviary keep the kids happy here from 9 am to 5 pm any day except Monday, when it's closed. Admission costs a few cents for adults, but is free for children under 12.

Getting There Though this world-famous open-air museum is the city's primary tourist attraction, and though all sorts of important places in this city are well marked, *there is not one single sign* to lead you to the parque, or to point out the entrance! The only way you know you've arrived is when you see the parque's name emblazoned on the wall (obscured by trees) by the entrance – and you won't see this until you are right there.

To reach Parque-Museo La Venta, some three km from the Zona Remodelada, catch any bus or combi heading north-west along Paseo Tabasco, get out before the intersection with Ruiz Cortines, and walk north-east through the sprawling Parque Tomás Garrido Canabal, a larger park which actually surrounds Parque-Museo La Venta. Directional maps are posted at convenient

spots throughout the park. Each has various numbers on it, but the significance of the numbers is identified nowhere, rendering the maps utterly, almost comically, useless.

CICOM & Regional Museum of Anthropology

The Center for Investigation of the Cultures of the Olmecs & Maya (CICOM) is a complex of buildings on the bank of the Río Grijalva one km south of the Zona Remodelada. The centrepiece of the complex is the Museo Regional de Antropología Carlos Pellicer Cámara, dedicated to the scholar and poet responsible for the preservation of the Olmec artefacts in the Parque-Museo La Venta. Besides the museum, the complex holds a theatre, research centre, an arts centre and other buildings.

The Anthropology Museum (☎ (931) 2-32-02) is open 8 am to 7 pm every day; admission costs US$0.50.

Just inside the front door, you're stopped in your tracks by the timeless gaze and regal expression of a massive Olmec head, one of those wonders from La Venta. The best way to proceed with your tour of the museum is to pay your respects to the head, turn left, take the lift to the 2nd (top) floor (3rd floor American style) and work your way down. Although the museum's explanations are all in Spanish, they are often accompanied by photos, maps and diagrams.

On the top floor, exhibits outline Mesoamerica's many civilisations, from the oldest stone-age inhabitants to the more familiar cultures of our millennium. Don't miss the codices by the window on the north side. These are copies of the famous painted books of the Maya; the originals are in repositories outside Mexico. The window here, by the way, offers a nice view of the river and Villahermosa's cathedral.

After you've brushed up on the broad picture, descend one flight to the 1st (middle) floor where the exhibits concentrate on the Olmec and Mayan cultures. Especially intriguing are the displays concerning Comalcalco, the ruined Mayan city not far from Villahermosa, which you may want to visit.

Finally, the ground floor of the museum holds various changing and travelling exhibits.

Getting There CICOM is one km south of the city centre, or 600 metres south of the intersection of Malecón Madrazo and Paseo Tabasco. You can catch any bus or colectivo ('CICOM' or 'No 1') travelling south along Madrazo; just say '¿CICOM?' before you get in, and pay the few cents' fare.

Tabasco 2000 & Parque La Choca

The Tabasco 2000 complex is a testimonial to the prosperity the oil boom brought to Villahermosa, with its modern Palacio Municipal, chic boutiques in a gleaming mall, a convention centre and pretty fountains. There's also a planetarium, where Spanish-language only Omnimax shows are presented Tuesday to Friday at 4, 5.30, 7 and 8.30 pm. Admission is US$1.50, half-price for students. If you are coming from the city centre, take a Tabasco 2000 bus along Paseo Tabasco.

Parque La Choca, just beyond the Tabasco 2000 complex, is the site of a state fair, complete with livestock exhibitions and a crafts festival in late April. It is also a pleasant place to picnic, has a swimming pool and is open Monday to Saturday from 7 am to 9 pm.

Places to Stay – bottom end

Most of Villahermosa's inexpensive hotels are conveniently located in the Zona Remodelada, but there is at least one cheap choice near the 1st-class bus station.

Hotel Palma de Mallorca (☎ (931) 2-01-44/5), Madero 516 between Lerdo de Tejada and Zaragoza, is the best, though not the cheapest, choice in this range. A family-oriented place, its clean, comfortable rooms with ceiling fan rent for US$10/14 a single/double, or US$16 a double with air-conditioning. Good location, good rooms, good prices, but often full. Arrive early if you can.

Hotel Madero (☎ (931) 2-05-16), Madero 301 between Reforma and 27 de Febrero, is in an old building with some character, run by an engaging man who seems to have guests' interests at heart. The clean, pleasant, small rooms are among the best at this price in the city: US$12 a single with ceiling fan and private shower, US$14 a double; air-conditioned rooms cost a few dollars more. Keep street noise in mind when you choose your room.

On Lerdo de Tejada between Juárez and Madero are three small, plain, cheap hotels all in a row, sharing the same excellent location. *Hotel San Miguel* (☎ (931) 2-15-00, 2-14-26), Lerdo 315, in the mall off Madero at Lerdo 315, is perhaps the best of the lot, renting its plain rooms for US$9 a double with one bed, US$13 a double with two beds, or US$20 a double with air-conditioning.

Hotel Oviedo (☎ (931) 2-14-55), Lerdo 303, is a step down from the neighbouring San Miguel, but will do if price is important. Rooms with ceiling fans and sorry beds go for US$9 a double.

Hotel Tabasco (☎ (931) 2-00-77), Lerdo 317, is the worst of the lot, with similar prices for less comfortable, hardly charming rooms.

Hotel Oriente (☎ (931) 2-01-21, 2-11-01), Madero 425 near Lerdo, is very simple and cleanish, with its own good cheap little restaurant on the ground floor. Singles with private shower and ceiling fan go for US$9, doubles for US$11.

Another hotel to try for budget rooms with air-conditioning is *Hotel San Francisco* (☎ (931) 2-31-98), Madero 604 between Zaragoza and María del Carmen. The hotel is a mixed bag: a lift does away with the sweaty hike upstairs; tidy, pleasant hallways lead to the rooms; the bathrooms are neat and tiled, but may not have a seat on the toilet; curtains may be heading earthward. Still, it's pretty good for the price: US$11 for a double with one bed, US$14 for a double with two beds.

Hotel Palomino (☎ (931) 2-84-31) is on Javier Mina at the corner of Pedro Fuentes,

Top: Temple of Inscriptions as seen from the Palace, Palenque, Chiapas (TB)
Left: Stela 1, Parque-Museo La Venta, Villahermosa, Tabasco (TW)
Right: Monument 1, Colossal Head, Parque-Museo La Venta (TW)

Top: Temple of Inscriptions seen from the site entrance, Palenque, Chiapas (TB)
Bottom: Waterfall at Agua Azul, near Palenque, Chiapas (JL)

right across from the main entrance to the ADO (1st-class) bus station. A modern place with well-used facilities, it rents serviceable but sometimes noisy rooms for US$13 a double with ceiling fan and private shower. This may be your first choice if you arrive in Villahermosa late at night by bus in a near-liquid state.

Finally, for the truly desperate, here are two very cheap hotels. *Hotel Providencia* (☎ (931) 2-82-62), Constitución 210, between Lerdo and Reforma has tiny rooms and even tinier baths that are often acceptably clean, and certainly well priced at US$6 per room, single or double. Among the problems here is noise, as the hotel faces busy Constitución, with its back on the even busier Malecón. To find the hotel, look for the odd sign saying 'Hotel P', with an eye peering from a triangle.

Hotel Buenos Aires (☎ (931) 2-15-55), Constitución 216, a few doors north of the Hotel Providencia, offers dispiriting rooms, usually at prices a bit higher than the preferable Hotel P. Singles and doubles here are generally quoted at US$7.

Camping It might be possible to set up a tent or caravan/trailer at the *Ciudad Deportiva* in the southern part of the city. Ask at the field-house adjacent to the Olympic Stadium during the day. The Tamolte bus runs out here. There's trailer parking also at Parque La Choca on Paseo Tabasco north-west of Tabasco 2000, but no tents are allowed.

Places to Stay – middle

Middle-range hotels are also in the Zona Remodelada. Perhaps the best all-round choice is the *Hotel Don Carlos* (☎ (931) 2-24-92/99), Madero 422 between Reforma and Lerdo, facing the Hotel Oriente. The Don Carlos has 116 air-conditioned rooms with private baths, TVs and telephones. The lobby is lavish in its mirrors and marble, and often bustling with tour groups which frequently fill many of its rooms. This is the downtown snazz king, charging US$26 a single, US$30 a double, US$34 a triple, but worth the money.

The well-located *Hotel Miraflores* (☎ (931) 2-00-22/54), Reforma 304 just west of Madero, has nicely appointed air-conditioned rooms with bath for prices identical to those at the Hotel Don Carlos. Here you have the benefits of a relatively quiet pedestrian-street location, and the services of a travel agency and rental car desk.

Hotel Plaza Independencia (☎ (931) 2-12-99), Independencia 123 at the southern end of the Zona Remodelada near the Plaza de Armas, is a pleasant three-star hotel with 90 air-conditioned rooms with TVs, clean private baths, and even balconies to enjoy the view (try for a room on an upper floor). A pleasant restaurant, bar and small swimming pool, plus a car park, add to the hotel's appeal. Prices are the standard three-star ones: US$26 a single, US$30 a double, US$34 a triple. The hotel adds a ridiculous telephone charge of US$0.50 per day to your room bill.

Hotel Madan (☎ (931) 2-16-50, 4-05-24), Pino Suárez 105 just north of Reforma, has 20 nice, modern air-conditioned rooms with bath in a modern, conveniently located building. The hotel entrance is at the eastern end of the building on Pino Suárez; the western end on Madero houses the restaurant (see Places to Eat). Room rates here are US$23 a single, US$26 a double.

For a moderately priced hotel near the bus stations, try the *Hotel Ritz* (☎ (931) 2-16-11), Madero 1013, a modernised three-storey building one block south of Ruiz Cortines (Highway 180), about five blocks east of both the 1st and 2nd-class bus stations. The 62 rooms here all have individual air-conditioners, private baths, and reasonable prices of US$22 a single, US$25 a double. The Ritz is a popular place, so pin down a room early if you can.

Places to Stay – top end

As an oil boom town, Villahermosa has no shortage of luxury lodgings. Three of the best hotels are located near the intersection of Paseo Tabasco and Avenida Ruiz Cortines (Highway 180), a pleasant 10-minute walk from Parque-Museo La Venta.

Poshest of the posh, and a favourite with oil executives and upscale groups, is the *Exelaris Hyatt Regency Villahermosa* (☎ (931) 3-44-44), south-west off Paseo Tabasco on the Laguna de las Ilusiones, south-east of Avenida Ruiz Cortines. The Hyatt is the best in town, with all the expected luxury services at the refreshingly Mexican price of US$90 a double, tax included.

Consider the pretty *Villahermosa Viva* (☎ (931) 2-55-55), right at the the intersection of Paseo Tabasco and Avenida Ruiz Cortines (Highway 180). The comfortable air-conditioned rooms are in two-storey motel-style white stucco buildings placed around a large swimming pool; the restaurant, bar and 'disco' club (sometimes with live entertainment) keep you entertained in the evenings. Singles are US$40 to US$50, doubles US$52 to US$62, tax included.

The price leader in this high-rent area is undoubtedly the *Hotel Cencali* (☎ (931) 5-19-96/97/99; fax 2-18-62), Calle Juárez off Paseo Tabasco, more or less between the Hyatt and the Viva (this is a different Calle Juárez from the one in the city centre!). The Cencali has a nice layout amidst tropical foliage and grassy lawns, a good restaurant, clean swimming pool, and pleasant modern air-conditioned rooms with TVs. It's a favourite with Mexican business travellers and families, and is used by local people for social functions such as weddings and conferences. Prices are a reasonable US$42 a single, US$46 a double, tax included.

Holiday Inn Villahermosa (☎ (931) 3-44-00/24/80), Paseo Tabasco 1407 in the Tabasco 2000 complex, is Villahermosa's newest luxury lodging, a modern slab-like building with very comfortable rooms, a pool, restaurants and bars. Prices are US$80 to US$90, single or double.

What about this: you've arrived by bus, you're tired, or feeling ill, or can't stand the humid heat. You want a cool, safe haven in which to spend the night before heading out the next day. You're ready to spend a bit of money. The place for you is the *Hotel Maya Tabasco* (☎ (931) 2-11-11; fax 2-10-97), four

blocks north of the 1st-class ADO bus station, a block west of the 2nd-class bus station, right near the intersection of Javier Mina and Ruiz Cortines. Its 160 air-conditioned rooms offer TVs with satellite hook-ups; the hotel has a swimming pool, lobby bar, two restaurants (Mexican and international), a discotheque, hairdresser and newsstand. Rates for the refuge are US$38, single or double.

Places to Eat – bottom end

Villahermosa's high humidity is actually good for something: it's likely to take the edge off your appetite. This is fortunate, for Villahermosa has little in the way of exceptional cuisine. There are a number of good, cheap little eateries clustered around the 1st-class bus station on Javier Mina, several right across the street from the main entrance. But the main stem for cheap eateries is undoubtedly Madero; the pedestrian streets of the Zona Remodelada (Lerdo, Juárez, Reforma, Aldama) also have lots of snack and fastfood shops.

El Torito Valenzuela, 27 de Febrero 202 at the corner with Madero, open 8 am to midnight, is perhaps Villahermosa's most popular and convenient cheap taquería. Tacos made with various ingredients are priced at US$0.60 to US$0.80 apiece and similarly varied tortas (sandwiches) go for exactly twice as much. With its corner location, you can watch the busy street life as you munch.

Restaurant Geminis, Madero 704 north of Méndez, is a bit of a walk from the Zona Remodelada, but makes up for it with a variety of dishes at reasonable prices. This very plain little lonchería serves chilaquiles (red or green) with chicken for US$2.50, meat dishes for about US$4, and a variety of breakfasts for US$1.75 to US$3.25. It's open every day, including Sunday.

Panificadora y Pastelería on Mármol facing the Parque Juárez, is the place to go for sweet rolls, bread and pastries for snacks, make-your-own breakfasts, or picnic supplies. Another useful bakery is the

Panificadora Los Dos Naciones, at the corner of Juárez and Zaragoza.

Places to Eat – middle

Madero and Constitución have a number of suitable middle-range dining-places. *Restaurant Madan*, on Madero just north of Reforma, is bright and modern, with plush booths, pseudo-colonial tables and chairs, air-conditioning and a pleasant informal ambience. A genuine espresso machine hisses in one corner, promising an excellent post-prandial cup of coffee. A full meal of fruit cocktail, filete tampiqueña (beef in savoury tomato sauce), dessert, drink, and espresso, costs about US$10 to US$12, though you can easily dine for less. Hours are 8 am to 11.30 pm every day.

Restaurant La Playita, Constitución 202, specialises, as its name suggests, in the seafood which is brought in abundance from the Gulf of Mexico. Clean and pleasant, the restaurant is a good bet whether you're up for fish or not, as it serves beef, pork, chicken and the traditional antojitos as well. Expect to spend US$4.50 for a light meal, US$8 to US$10 for a real tuck-in here.

Restaurant Shalymar, Constitución just south of Reforma, is a similar establishment which you might try in contrast to La Playita.

Safe, pleasant air-conditioned dining in the same price range is yours at the restaurant in the *Hotel Don Carlos*, on Madero north of Reforma.

For a splurge you can cruise the Río Grijalva while eating so-so cuisine on the *Capitán Beúlo* (☎ 3-57-62), a restaurant boat docked on Malecón Madrazo between Lerdo de Tejada and Zaragoza. The meal-and-cruise is most interesting during the day when you can observe life on the river. Evenings you see little, but those who enjoy dinner cruises may find it romantic. Sailings are currently scheduled daily except Monday at 12.30, 3.30 and 9.30 pm, but you'd be wise to reconfirm these schedules and make reservations at least several hours in advance. Prices are higher than in shore restaurants, of course, but not all that bad: steaks for US$9,

shrimp dishes for US$10, full meals for US$20 or so.

Besides the dining rooms of the luxury hotels, there are several garden restaurants along Paseo Tabasco between the river and Avenida Ruiz Cortines. If you get hungry while visiting the Museo Regional de Antropología, try the *Restaurant Los Tulipanes* in the CICOM complex, open for breakfast, brunch and lunch. A full lunch might cost US$15, breakfast a few dollars less.

Entertainment

Teatro Esperanza Iris at the CICOM complex offers folkloric dance, theatre or comedy Wednesday to Saturday at 7 and 9.30 pm. Ask at the tourist office or your hotel for details.

The planetarium at Tabasco 2000 has Omnimax shows and Parque La Venta has sound-and-light shows Tuesday, Thursday, Friday and Saturday; see those sections for details.

Discos can be found in the Villahermosa Viva, Exelaris Hyatt, Cencali and Maya Tabasco luxury hotels, open every evening except Sunday and Monday from about 10 pm on. Cover charge is about US$8. For other cultural goings-on, call the Instituto de la Cultura (☎ 2-79-47) or check their bulletin of events distributed to the museums and bigger hotels.

Getting There & Away

Air Villahermosa's Rovirosa Airport (☎ (931) 2-75-55) is 10.5 km east of the centre on Highway 180, on the other side of the bridge across the Río Grijalva. Aerocaribe and Mexicana operate scheduled flights linking Villahermosa with Mérida, Cancún, and Mexico City. Smaller local airlines fly to Tuxtla Gutiérrez and Oaxaca. For information, contact Turismo Grijalva (☎ (931) 2-25-96, 2-43-94), Zaragoza 911 in the Zona Remodelada.

Bus The 1st-class (ADO) bus station, Javier Mina 297, has a small post office, a tourist information booth, and a selection of little eating places. If you're looking for a hotel near the bus station, refer to Places to Stay and the Hotel Palomino (bottom end), Hotel Ritz (middle) and Hotel Maya Tabasco (top end). While there is no *guardería* for your luggage, you might be able to tip a baggage handler to watch your gear for a few hours.

The two main 1st-class companies serving Villahermosa are ADO and Omnibus Cristóbal Colón. Villahermosa is an important transportation point, but many buses serving it are de paso (they do not originate here, but stop in passing). Seats are therefore often scarce, so buy your onward ticket as far in advance as possible. In any case, don't just blithely wander out to the 1st-class bus station and expect immediately to climb aboard the next bus out.

All of the buses and fares listed below are 1st-class:

Acayucan – 225 km, 3½ hours; several buses by ADO for US$4.50

Campeche – 450 km, seven hours; 14 ADO buses daily for a fare of US$7.50; they'll drop you at Catazaja (Palenque junction) if you like

Cancún – 915 km, 14 hours; several buses daily by ADO for US$18

Chetumal – 575 km, nine hours; several ADO buses daily for US$10

Comalcalco – 53 km, 1½ hours; three buses daily for US$1.25

Mérida – 700 km, 10 hours; 13 by ADO for US$10.50

Mexico City – 820 km, 14 hours; 12 buses daily by Cristóbal Colón for US$17

Oaxaca – 700 km, 13 hours; three buses daily by Cristóbal Colón for US$13

Palenque – 150 km, 2½ hours; four buses daily by ADO for US$2.50

Paraíso – 75 km, two hours; three buses daily for US$1.50

Playa del Carmen – 848 km, 14 hours; several ADO buses daily for US$16

San Cristóbal de las Casas – 308 km, eight hours; one bus daily by Cristóbal Colón for US$6

Tapachula – 735 km, 13 hours; one bus daily by Cristóbal Colón for US$15

Teapa – 60 km, one hour; five buses daily for US$0.75

Tuxtla Gutiérrez – 294 km, six hours; six buses daily by Cristóbal Colón for US$5.50

Veracruz – 475 km, eight hours; several buses daily by ADO for US$9

The 2nd-class Central de Autobuses de Tabasco bus station is on the north side of Avenida Ruiz Cortines (Highway 180) across the highway from the Euzkadi Radial building, just east of the intersection with Javier Mina. It's about five blocks from the 1st-class bus station as the crow flies, but it's almost impossible to cross the busy highway; you may find yourself walking blocks out of the way just to get across!

A number of smaller companies serve local destinations within the state of Tabasco, but there are also 2nd-class buses run by Autobuses Unidos to Acayucan (four a day for US$3.75), Veracruz (one daily for US$10) stopping along the way at Catemaco (US$5), and to Mexico City (three a day for US$15). Buses to La Venta depart four times daily at a fare of US$2.

For Comalcalco, hop on a bus run by Servicio Somellera. They run every 15 minutes throughout the day for US$1.

Train The nearest railhead to Villahermosa is 58 km away at the town of Teapa and it's just as well, as the slow trains through Tabasco are less comfortable and safe than the bus.

Getting Around

To/From the Airport The colectivo airport minibuses charge US$2 per person for the trip into town; a taxi costs US$8. Buy your tickets from a counter in the terminal.

Local Transport From the 1st-class ADO bus station, it's generally about 15 to 20 minutes walk to the recommended hotels (those closer are noted). Ordinarily we'd suggest that you do the journey on foot, but Villahermosa's heat and high humidity may make taking a taxi a better option (figure around US$1.50 in the cheaper Volkswagen Beetle taxis for almost any ride in the city). Local bus fares are only a few cents.

As you exit the front of the ADO station, go left for two blocks to the corner of Mina and Zozaya, where buses stop en route to the Zona Remodelada and Madero, the main thoroughfare. If you are walking, go out the ADO station's front door, cross Mina and follow Lino Merino five blocks to the principal plaza, Parque de la Paz on Madero, and turn right.

Although the major sights listed are far from the centre, there is local bus service to them. See each particular listing for the appropriate bus destination.

Comalcalco Ruins

If you have the time and are interested in archaeology, a day trip from Villahermosa to the ruins of Comalcalco is worth your while. Admission is just US$2.50 and Comalcalco is open daily from 8 am to 5 pm.

Comalcalco was constructed during the Mayan Late Classic period between 500 and 900 AD, when the region's agricultural productivity prompted population expansion. The principal crop which brought Indian peasants from Palenque to this region was the cacao bean, still the chief cash crop (the Comalcalcoans traded it with other Mayan settlements).

Although Comalcalco in many ways resembles Palenque in architecture and sculpture, it is unique in its composition. Because stone was in short supply, the Maya made bricks from clay, sand and – ingeniously – oyster shells. Mortar was provided with lime obtained from the oyster shells. This unique mortar was also used in the sculpting of elaborate stucco façades with multicoloured reliefs, grotesque masks, and human and animal representations. Comalcalco is thought by archaeologists to be among the first cities built of brick.

Due to the passage of time, you will have to look carefully to see some of the stucco sculpture. The government has simplified the task of finding the best carvings by erecting thatch roofs to shelter them. As you enter the ruins, the substantial structure to your left may surprise you, as the pyramid's bricks look remarkably like the bricks used in construction today. Look on the right-hand side of the pyramid and you will see some remains of the stucco sculptures which once covered the pyramid. Then walk through the plaza to the main Acropolis area where, par-

ticularly on the northern section, you will find the remains of fine stucco carvings.

Although the west side of the Acropolis once held a crypt comparable to Palenque's Pakal, the tomb was vandalised before the area was known to the outside world; the sarcophagus was stolen. Continue up the hill to the ruin called the Palace, and from this elevation enjoy the breeze while you gaze down on unexcavated mounds.

Since all the structures are built of stucco and brick, you don't want to assist the erosion process by climbing on them. The 'No Subir' signs are also for your safety; a tourist broke a leg here not long before I visited the site.

Getting There & Away The 55-km journey takes about an hour. A virtual shuttle service operates between Comalcalco and the 2nd-class bus station in Villahermosa, with buses departing every 15 minutes throughout the day; fare is US$1. When you get to the town of Comalcalco, get out at the intersection of Highways 187 and 195, catch a VW minibus (combi) headed south, and mention that you want to get out at *las ruinas*. The driver will charge you US$0.50 and drop you at the access road to the ruins, from whence it is a walk of one km. A taxi from Comalcalco town costs about US$2 each way.

VILLAHERMOSA TO TUXTLA GUTIÉRREZ

Highway 195, the road into the Chiapan mountains, leaves Villahermosa to the southeast, passing CICOM, following Avenida Melchor Ocampo, then heading out of the city to pass through vast banana groves. The road is fairly fast, with wide bends.

At Teapa, 60 km from Villahermosa, you bear right toward Pichucalco rather than enter the town of Teapa proper. Five km past the Teapa turn-off, on the left-hand side, is the Balneario El Azufre (Sulphur Baths), as you can tell by the odour when you descend into the valley to cross a stream and the stink of sulphur rises to meet you.

Just past the bridge over the stream a large sign announces your entry into the state of

Chiapas, 'Siempre México, Siempre Méxicano' (Always Part of Mexico, Always Mexican). The sign and the sentiment may have more to do with the central government in Mexico City than with the Chiapan people, who have been ambivalent throughout history about their links with the lands to the west of the Isthmus of Tehuantepec.

Upon entering Chiapas, the road climbs into the mountains through incredibly lush, beautiful countryside. It's still hot and muggy here, with typical tropical scenes on every side: gigantic ceiba trees, banana groves, Brahma cattle grazing contentedly, and jungle verdure everywhere.

The road passes through a beautiful river gorge *(cañón)*. After passing through the village of Ixhuapan you'll notice that the air is definitely lighter, cooler and less humid.

About 150 km from Villahermosa is the small mountain town of Rayón (population 8500), which has a very basic eatery for travellers and a spartan hostelry for emergencies. Ten km past Rayón is a lookout *(mirador)* named El Caminero. The view would be beautiful, but it's usually obscured by mist and fog.

At Rincón Chamula it is clear by the local people's dress that you've entered Maya country. Besides wearing the traditional clothing, the villagers sell it to travellers at little open-air stands by the roadside.

Pueblo Nuevo (population 10,000) is at 1200 metres altitude, deep in the beautiful mountain country, but still the road climbs.

Past the junction with the road to Simojovel the countryside becomes drier, but it's still very mountainous.

The village of Bochil (population 13,000), 215 km from Villahermosa at an altitude of 1272 metres, is inhabited by Tzotzil Maya. It has two hotels: the tidy *Hotel Juárez* on the main road, and the more modest *Hotel María Isabel* set back a bit from the road. There's also a Pemex fuel station, the only one for many km.

After travelling 264 km from Villahermosa on Highway 195, you come to the junction with Highway 190. Turn left to go directly to San Cristóbal de las Casas (34 km), or right to Tuxtla Gutiérrez (50 km).

Heading toward Tuxtla Gutiérrez, after a few km the road rounds a bend to reveal a breathtaking panorama: you are clinging to a mountainside with a broad valley spread out below. The highway descends the steep slope by a series of switchbacks, then strikes out dead straight across the valley to the capital city of Chiapas, 294 km from Villahermosa.

The valley you're crossing is the wide, warm, fairly dry Río Grijalva valley, also called the Central Depression of Chiapas, at 500 to 1000 metres altitude. Three big artificial reservoirs stretch along the Grijalva – the Angostura in the south-east, the Malpaso or Nezahualcóyotl in the north-west and the Chicoasén in between. The state capital, Tuxtla Gutiérrez, lies towards the west end of this central valley.

Highland & Pacific Chiapas

TUXTLA GUTIÉRREZ
Population 250,000

Many travellers simply change buses in Chiapas' state capital (altitude 542 metres) as they head straight through to San Cristóbal de las Casas. But if you're not in a hurry this surprisingly lively modern city has several things worth stopping for. Among them are probably Mexico's best zoo (devoted solely to the fauna of Chiapas), a good new museum and, a few km outside Tuxtla, the 1000-metre-deep Cañón del Sumidero through which you can take an exhilarating boat ride. Cheap accommodation in Tuxtla is mainly on the rough side, though there are plenty of decent middle-range places. If the canyon is all you're after, you can stay in the smaller, quieter riverside town of Chiapa de Corzo, jumping-off point for the boat trips.

History

The name Tuxtla Gutiérrez comes from the Indian Nahuatl language *tuchtlán*, meaning 'where rabbits abound', which was in turn a translation of the Zoque Mayan *coyatocmo*. The conquistadors pronounced tuchtlán as Tuxtla (TOOSHT-lah), and in the 19th century the family name of Joaquín Miguel Gutiérrez was added. Gutiérrez was a liberal politician, Governor of Chiapas, and leading light in Chiapas' early 19th-century campaign not to be part of Guatemala.

San Cristóbal was capital of the state until 1892, when the title went to Tuxtla Gutiérrez. This was apparently because of hostility in San Cristóbal toward Mexico's dictator at the time, Porfirio Díaz, who encouraged the takeover of peasant land by big landowners. In the same era the Soconusco coffee plantations were notorious for the near-slavery of their Indian workers.

The question of which city was to be the state capital was not taken lightly. In 1911 there was a mini-war between the two rivals, with Tuxtla victorious and many Tzotzil Indians massacred.

There's little of historic interest in Tuxtla, which was of minor importance until it became state capital. Since the 1970s Tuxtla has benefited from the oil discovered in north-west Chiapas.

Orientation

The centre of Tuxtla Gutiérrez is the large Plaza Cívica, several hectares of marble paving shaded by umbrella-like topiary trees and surrounded by modern hotels, official buildings, cinemas and, on its south side, the cathedral. On Sunday the plaza is thronged with Tuxtlans relaxing on the benches, playing games, listening to traders selling their wares, strolling and generally enjoying the heart of their city.

The city's main east-west artery runs across the south of the main plaza, in front of the cathedral. At this point it's called Avenida Central. Further west the same road becomes Boulevard Dr Belisario Domínguez; to the east it becomes Avenida 14 de Septiembre, then Blvd Ángel Albino Corzo.

Street Numbering System Calle Central runs down the west side of the main plaza, and its junction with Avenida Central is the central point for Tuxtla's street-numbering system. This system is logical by comparison with some Mexican cities, but still needlessly complex and potentially confusing.

East-west streets are called avenidas, north-south streets are calles. Avenidas are called 1 Sur, 2 Sur, etc as you go south from Avenida Central, and 1 Norte, 2 Norte, etc going north. Calles are 1 Poniente, 2 Poniente and so on going west from Calle Central; 1 Oriente, 2 Oriente, etc going east. The abbreviations Nte (Norte), Pte (Poniente) and Ote (Oriente) are used frequently on street signs and maps.

Where it all gets a bit complicated is with

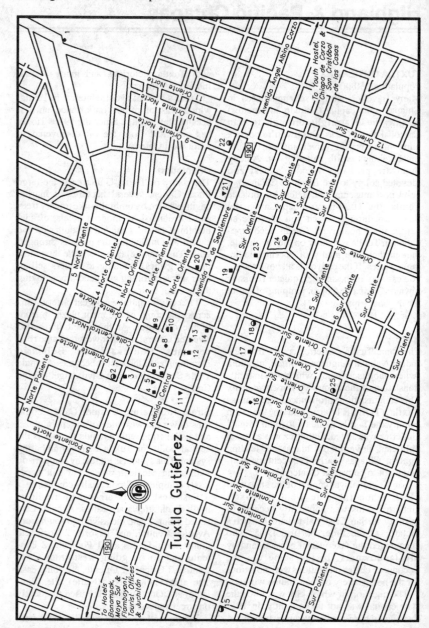

■ PLACES TO STAY

3   Hotels Santo Domingo & María Teresa
4   Hotel Avenida
6   Hotel Esponda
7   Gran Hotel Humberto
9   Hotel Posada del Rey
14 Hotel Regional San Marcos
17 Gran Hotel Olimpo
19 Hotel La Posada
20 Hotel María Eugenia
23 Casa de Huéspedes Ofelia

▼ PLACES TO EAT

4   Restaurant El Gran Cheff
5   La Boutique del Pan Bakery
11 Restaurant Flamingo
13 Cafetería San Marcos
20 Restaurant María Eugenia
21 Restaurant Las Pichanchas

    OTHER

1   Parque Madero Complex
2   Cristóbal Colón (1st-Class) Bus Station
8   Plaza Cívica
10 Post Office
12 Cathedral
15 ADO Bus Station
16 Market
18 Autotransportes Chiapa-Tuxtla Bus Station
22 Transportes Cañón del Sumidero Bus Station
24 Autotransportes Tuxtla Gutiérrez Bus Station
25 Bus to Zoo

the addition (sometimes) of secondary names: each avenida is divided into a Pte part (west of Calle Central) and an Ote part (east of Calle Central) – thus 1 Sur Ote is the eastern half of Avenida 1 Sur. Likewise calles have Norte and Sur parts: 1 Poniente Nte is the northern half of Calle 1 Poniente. The address 1 Poniente Nte 412 would be on the northern part of Calle 1 Poniente, close to the corner of Avenida 4 Norte.

Bus Stations & Hotels The Cristóbal Colón (1st-class) bus station is at the corner of

Avenida 2 Norte and Calle 2 Poniente, one block north and two west of the main plaza's north-west corner. The main 2nd-class bus station, Autotransportes Tuxtla Gutiérrez, is on Avenida 3 Sur Ote just west of Calle 7 Oriente Sur, which from the south-east corner of the main plaza is four blocks east, two south, then half a block west.

Most cheap accommodation is south-east of the main plaza. More expensive hotels are dotted all round the central area, and on the outskirts, particularly on the western outskirts along Highway 190.

Information

There are two helpful tourist offices but both are almost two km west of the main plaza on Avenida Central/Belisario Domínguez/Highway 190. Take any bus or colectivo westwards along this road and mention 'oficina de turismo' or the Hotel Bonampak to the driver to be let off at the proper place.

Of the two, people at the federal tourist office (☎ (961) 2-45-35, 2-55-09) at Blvd Dr Belisario Domínguez 1498, just east of the Hotel Bonampak, usually speak better English. It has information on other parts of Mexico as well as Chiapas and is open 8 am to 8 pm Monday to Friday and 10 am to noon Saturday.

The Chiapas state tourist office (☎ (961) 3-48-37) is on the 2nd floor of the Edificio Plaza de las Instituciones, a tall yellow building beside Bancomer opposite the Hotel Bonampak. It's open 9 am to 8 pm, Monday to Friday.

Post & Telecommunications The post office and telegraph offices are in an alley running off the middle of the east side of the main plaza. The post office is open 8 am to 6 or 9 pm Monday to Saturday for all services, and 9 am to noon Sunday for stamps only. Tuxtla's postal code is 29000.

There are Lada (long-distance phone) casetas at the corners of Avenida 1 Sur and Calle 2 Oriente and at Avenida 4 Sur Ote 234, both open 9 am to 10 pm.

Laundry Laundromats include one at Ángel

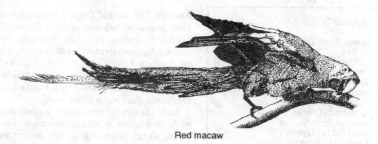

Red macaw

Albino Corzo 1508, three blocks from the Youth Hostel, and the Gaily II, Avenida 1 Sur Pte 575, a block south of the Plaza Cívica, then five blocks west. A three-kg load of washing gets clean for US$3.50. Hours are 8 am to 8 pm, with a siesta break from 2 to 4 pm, Monday to Saturday.

Zoo

Chiapas, with its huge range of environments, claims the highest concentration of animal species in North America – among them several varieties of big cat, 1200 types of butterfly and 641 bird species. You can see a good number of them in Tuxtla's excellent Zoológico Miguel Alvárez del Toro, where the creatures are kept in relatively spacious enclosures in an unspoiled hillside woodland area just south of the city. Also pleasing about this zoo is its evident concern for conservation; most species are accompanied by charts showing their range of habitat and chances of avoiding extinction. (Whether this message has sunk in with all Chiapas citizens is doubtful: shortly after visiting the zoo I was invited to join a jaguar shoot by a hotel manager.)

Among the creatures you'll see are ocelot, lynx, jaguar, puma, polecat, tapir, red macaw, boa constrictor and some meanlooking scorpions and spiders. And there's a special display of 'the most dangerous species, destroyer of nature and probably of itself'.

To reach the zoo take a 'Cerro Hueco' bus (US$0.20) from the corner of Calle 1 Oriente Sur and Avenida 7 Sur Ote. They leave about every 20 minutes and take 20 minutes to get there. Alternatively, a taxi from the city centre costs US$1, and taxis are also quite easy to pick up coming back.

The zoo is open 8 am to 5.30 pm daily except Monday and entry is free. It has a bookshop and a restaurant – try *taxcalate*, a maize-based chocolate-cinnamon drink.

Parque Madero Complex

This museum-theatre-park area is north-east of the city centre, located around the junction of Avenida 5 Norte Ote and Calle 11 Oriente Nte. If you don't want to walk, take a colectivo along Avenida Central/14 de Septiembre/Ángel Albino Corzo to Parque 5 de Mayo at the corner of Calle 11 Oriente and then a combi north along Calle 11 Oriente.

The Museo Regional de Chiapas is the highlight of the complex, with fine archaeological exhibits, colonial history, costume and craft collections all from Chiapas, plus often interesting temporary exhibitions. It's open 9 am to 4 pm daily except Monday. Next door is the 1200-seat Teatro de la Ciudad.

Nearby there's a shady botanical garden, with many species labelled and a solitary, sad manatee in a shallow pond in the middle (it'll probably be dead by the time you get there). The garden is free and open 9 am to 2 pm and 4 to 6 pm except Monday.

Also in Parque Madero are a public swimming pool (US$0.35) and an open-air children's park, the Centro de Convivencia Infantil, which adults may enjoy too. It has models and exhibits on history and prehistory, a mini-railway, pony and boat rides and mini-golf (children's park open 9.30 am to

8.30 pm Tuesday to Friday, 9.30 am to 9.30 pm Saturday, Sunday and holidays; games and rides open from 3.30 to 8 pm Tuesday to Friday, 9.30 am to 8 pm Saturday, Sunday and holidays).

Cañón del Sumidero

The best way to see this natural spectacle is by boat along the Río Grijalva, which flows through the canyon from Chiapa de Corzo. You can stay in Chiapa (see that section), or easily do the trip in a day from Tuxtla. If you want to see Sumidero from the top, you can get combis from Tuxtla to some of the *miradores* (look-out points) on the canyon edge. They're operated by Transportes Cañón del Sumidero (☎ (961) 2-06-49) at Avenida 1 Norte Ote 1121, 7½ blocks east of the north-east corner of the main plaza. Fare is US$1 and they run from about 8 am to 3.30 pm daily, passing miradores La Ceiba, La Coyota, Los Tepehuajes, El Roblar and Los Chiapas/La Atalaya. Vehicles saying 'La Atalaya' (the restaurant at the last of the five miradores) or 'Sumidero' are the ones you want.

El Aguacero

Time for a swim? Make your way to this waterfall on the Río de la Venta River where you can fulfill your desire. If you're not in the mood for a swim, a trip to the falls makes an off-the-beaten-track day trip – though it's busy with local sightseers and picnickers at weekends. A three-km road leading to the falls goes north off Highway 190, 53 km west of Tuxtla between Ocozocoautla and Cintalapa. At the end of the road you walk down a path that has 800 steps. Rodulfo Figueroa buses from 6 Sur Pte between 3 and 4 Pte will get you to the road junction.

Places to Stay – bottom end

The cleanest place in this category is the *Albergue CREA Youth Hostel* (☎ (961) 3-34-05) at Blvd Ángel Albino Corzo 1800, just under two km east of the main plaza. For a bed in one of the small, clean separate-sex dormitories you pay US$2 (plus US$0.50 deposit) and you don't need a Youth Hostel card. There's a small area out the back where you can pitch a tent for US$1.50. Breakfast is available for US$1, lunch and dinner for US$1.75 each. To get there from the Plaza Cívica take a colectivo east along Avenida Central/14 de Septiembre/Ángel Albino Corzo to where a yellow footbridge of steel gridwork crosses over the highway. The hostel is on the right-hand (south) side of the road by the footbridge, just before the black statue of Ángel Albino Corzo standing on a white base in the middle of the road. Enter the gate of the compound and turn left to reach the hostel portion (there are other youth and athletic facilities here as well). Coming from San Cristóbal, you could get off your bus here and save the trek back from the city centre.

Two centrally located bargains, both quite close to the Autotransportes Tuxtla Gutiérrez bus station, are small and often full. One is the *Casa de Huéspedes Ofelia* (☎ (961) 2-73-46), Avenida 2 Sur Ote 643 near the corner of 5 Ote. Rooms are well kept, the management is friendly and the place has its own dining room, but the bathrooms could be cleaner and the mosquitoes can be vicious. The best thing is the price: US$3.50 per person.

The other place is the *Hotel La Posada* (☎ (961) 2-29-32), Avenida 1 Sur Ote 555. Rooms here are around a small courtyard, the family is friendly and rooms with bath are US$9 a single, US$13 a double (US$17 with two beds), US$19 a triple.

The *Gran Hotel Olimpo* (☎ (961) 2-02-95, 3-17-70), Avenida 3 Sur Ote 215, in the same part of town, is a large, absolutely no-frills place where the 187 small, plain rooms are arranged around a bare interior courtyard. On my last visit there was lots of fresh paint in evidence, which is a good sign. In any case, it's fairly cheap. Singles, or doubles with one bed, go for US$9, doubles with two beds for US$12.

Just outside the Cristóbal Colón bus station, on Avenida 2 Norte between 1 and 2 Pte, are the *Hotel Santo Domingo* (☎ (961) 3-48-39), Avenida 2 Norte Pte 259-A, and the *Hotel María Teresa* (☎ (961) 3-01-02),

Avenida 2 Norte Pte 259-B – both dingy, noisy and ill-kept, but you'll see them as you exit the bus station, so I thought I'd let you know. The price for a room is at least fairly low, at US$9 a double.

Camping *La Hacienda Hotel* (☎ (961) 2-79-86), Belisario Domínguez 1197, at the west end of town, has a 20-space trailer park with swimming pool, cafeteria and all hook-ups, as well as space for tents, but beware of noise from the busy boulevard. The rate to park a caravan is US$9 a double (same as a cheap hotel!) and slightly cheaper for two persons in a tent.

Places to Stay – middle
This city has a number of suitable (though not beautiful) middle-range hotels within a few blocks of the Plaza Cívica.

Hotel Avenida (☎ (961) 2-08-07), Avenida Central Pte 224 at Calle 1 Poniente Nte, next to the Mexicana Airline office 1½ blocks west of the main plaza, has only a few rooms but they're decent value at US$11/13 for singles/doubles – quite big and clean, with fans and private baths. Be careful to get a room off the noisy street and preferably one well away from the lobby with its high-volume TV.

Hotel Regional San Marcos (☎ (961) 3-18-87, 3-19-40), Calle 2 Oriente Sur 176, on the corner of Avenida 1 Sur one block from the Plaza Cívica, gives a mediocre first impression in its lobby, but is actually a fine place to stay. The 40 tidy rooms in this modern building have colourful bedspreads and neat tiled bathrooms, there's a small restaurant off the lobby and a huge bottle of agua purificada in the upstairs lounge. With either ceiling fan or air-conditioner, the rooms cost US$16 a single, US$21 a double and US$28 a triple.

Hotel Esponda (☎ (961) 2-00-80), Calle 1 Poniente Nte 142, just north of Avenida Central a block from the Plaza Cívica, is no great shakes, but it's convenient and moderately priced, with double rooms going for US$20. It must have something good about it as 'Rotary Meets Here'.

Gran Hotel Humberto (☎ (961) 2-20-80, 2-25-04), Avenida Central Pte 180 at the corner of Calle 1 Poniente Nte, a block west of the main plaza, has big, bright, spotless rooms with air-con, TV, phone, large showers, even a bottle-opener fixed to the bathroom wall. Singles are US$24; doubles are US$28 with one bed, US$30 with two – which all adds up to good value for this central location. There's underground car parking, the Restaurant Magally (one flight up), a bar and a nightclub on the 9th floor.

Hotel Posada del Rey (☎ (961) 2-29-11), Calle 1 Oriente Nte 310, on the north-east corner of the main plaza, costs about the same as the Humberto – US$30 for a double room with air-conditioning and TV. Upkeep is a bit lax, though, and the hotel building has an alarming 10° list to port when viewed from the front. Rooms are light and clean, and some overlook the main plaza, but they could be bigger and need some new plaster. Still, the location is quite good.

Places to Stay – top end
Most of the city's best hotels are actually motels on the western outskirts, but there is one fine place to stay in the centre.

Hotel María Eugenia (☎ (961) 3-37-67/8/9), Avenida Central Ote at the corner of Calle 4 Oriente Nte, three blocks east of the Plaza Cívica, has a restaurant featuring a good daily comida corrida for US$4.50, a bar, swimming pool, car park, and room service. The comfortable air-conditioned rooms come with TVs and tidy baths, and cost US$36 a single, US$44 a double and US$53 a triple.

Hotel Bonampak (☎ (961) 3-20-47/50), Belisario Domínguez 180, 1.7 km west of the Plaza Cívica, is among the city's oldest 'luxury' hotels, but is renovated and comfortable with air-conditioned singles/doubles priced reasonably at US$32/38, plus 15 bungalows, three suites, a video singles bar and two swimming pools. There's a reproduction of the famous Mayan prisoner mural from Bonampak in the lobby (much more vivid and interesting than the badly faded originals!) and a pleasant restaurant and cafeteria. The tourist offices are right across the street.

Tuxtla's most luxurious hostelry is the 119-room *Hotel Flamboyant* (☎ (961) 2-93-11, 2-92-59), Belisario Domínguez Km 1081, on the south side of the boulevard four km west of the Plaza Cívica. The hotel certainly lives up to its name, with modern-Arabesque architecture draped in hanging foliage, with the Disco Sheik (get it?) set apart in its own little 'mosque' (is there a message here?). The rooms are set round a large swimming pool, with tennis courts, restaurants and bars nearby. Rooms are priced at US$56 a single, US$70 a double, US$84 a triple. High? You'd pay several times more for the same in Cancún.

Hotel Maya Sol (☎ (961) 2-34-85/13), Belisario Domínguez 1380 (Apdo Postal 872), between the Hotel Bonampak and the Flamboyant, on the north side of the boulevard at a traffic roundabout three km west of the Plaza Cívica, doesn't look like much from the highway, but enter and you find three floors of rooms set back from the busy road and draped in lush greenery. You can park near your room, enjoy the coffee shop, disco, restaurant, bar and swimming pool, and pay a moderate US$34 a single, US$40 a double, US$46 a triple for an air-conditioned room with one or two double beds, TV, bath and balcony.

Places to Eat

Many visitors find themselves sitting sooner or later at one of the cafés or restaurants alongside the cathedral. These aren't the cheapest but they're a good place to sample the city's atmosphere. The *Cafetería San Marcos* is always busy.

It's well worth making the short trek eastwards for six blocks along Avenida Central to the *Restaurant Las Pichanchas* (☎ 2-53-51), Avenida 14 de Septiembre Ote 857 (look for the sign with a black pot on a pink background and the words 'Sientase Chiapaneco'). This is an open-air restaurant round a small plant-filled courtyard with live marimba music each afternoon and evening

(except Monday), a menu of local specialities several pages long – and hardly anything over US$4. Friendly and efficient waiters will explain it all for you. Try the *chipilín*, a cheese-and-cream soup on a maize base; and, for dessert, *chimbos*, made from egg yolks and cinnamon. In between you could go for any of six types of tamales, among other things. There are lots of snacks too. Las Pichanchas is open daily from 2 pm to midnight.

The *Restaurant Flamingo* (☎ 2-09-22), Calle 1 Poniente Sur 168, a few yards down a passage in the Zardain building, is a quiet, air-conditioned, slightly superior place with dependably good food and service. Sandwiches cost US$2, more elaborate dishes such as puntas de filete or half a chicken *ala mexicana* or *con mole* are US$5 or US$6. The long menu also includes salami, snapper and lobster. Popular with families, the Flamingo is open every day of the week.

As for good comidas corridas, one of the best values for the money is the one served in the dining room of the *Hotel María Eugenia* (☎ 3-37-67), Avenida Central Ote at the corner of Calle 4 Oriente Nte, three blocks east of the Plaza Cívica. The deluxe comida here goes for only about US$4.50.

Restaurant El Gran Cheff, Avenida Central Pte 226 at Calle 1 Poniente Nte, to the left of the Hotel Avenida, is a fairly nice, modern place serving a daily comida corrida priced from US$3.75 to US$6.25, depending upon what's cooking. On Sunday there are two comidas, one at each of those prices.

If you're visiting the tourist offices or the Instituto de la Artesanía Chiapaneca on Belisario Domínguez, you can get a decent meal in the cafetería of the nearby *Hotel Bonampak*. Spaghetti costs US$1.75 to US$2.50, tamales chiapanecos US$2.50; there are also grilled meats, sandwiches and antojitos. The hotel has a fully fledged restaurant as well.

Among the prettiest, fanciest panaderías I've ever seen is *La Boutique del Pan*, Calle 1 Poniente Nte 121, across the street from the Hotel Esponda half a block north of Avenida Central. The baked goods sold here are as fancy as the shop itself, so stop here before your breakfast, picnic, or bus trip.

Entertainment

There's live music in the Plaza Cívica every Sunday night. On other nights, you can look for live music in the hotels. The nightspot in the Hotel Regional San Marcos had a guitarist when I was last there. Disco Sheik at the Hotel Flamboyant is reputed to be the best. Entrance costs US$3 but it's only open a few nights a week.

Things to Buy

Tuxtla's main market occupies the block bounded by Calles Central Sur and 1 Poniente Sur and Avenidas 3 and 4 Sur Pte.

The Instituto de la Artesanía Chiapaneca has a Chiapas crafts exhibition and shop in the Edificio Plaza de las Instituciones out west on Belisario Domínguez. It's the yellow building beside Bancomer opposite the Hotel Bonampak. Hours are 9 am to 2 pm and 5 to 9 pm, Monday to Saturday.

If for some reason you're hankering for back issues (way back) of magazines like *Rolling Stone, Mad, House & Garden* or *Dirt Rider*, go to Al Caravan Bazar, a small shop on Calle 2 Oriente between Avenidas 1 and 2 Sur.

Getting There & Away

Air Because of its remote location high in the Chiapan mountains, far from most other cities by bus, Tuxtla has good air service. There are two airports, the larger Aeropuerto San Juan (☎ (961) 2-06-01), 35 km west of the city, a 40-minute ride along Highway 190. San Juan handles the large aircraft going to Mexico City. Aeropuerto Terán (☎ (961) 2-29-20), also on Highway 190, but much closer to the city, handles smaller planes such as the ones to Villahermosa, Mérida and Cancún, and intrastate flights to Tapachula and Palenque. Planes can be chartered from Aeropuerto Terán – contact the tourist offices for details.

Mexicana (☎ (961) 2-00-20, 2-54-02) has an office at Avenida Central Pte 206, corner of Calle 1 Poniente Nte. Mexicana has a daily late-morning flight to Mexico City and on some days another flight in the early afternoon.

Aerocaribe (☎ (961) 2-20-22), a short-haul carrier owned by Mexicana and included in its schedules, operates daily flights between Tuxtla and Cancún via Villahermosa and Mérida.

Aviacsa (☎ (961) 3-09-18), Avenida 1 Norte Pte 1026, flies daily to Mexico City, Oaxaca, Palenque, Tapachula and Villahermosa.

Bus Each busline serving this city has its own terminal, and the bus stations are scattered all across town. Ticket queues may be long, so buy your tickets as far in advance as possible except for the very frequent buses (such as to San Cristóbal).

The most important line is the 1st-class Omnibus Cristóbal Colón (☎ (961) 2-16-39), with its terminal at the corner of Avenida 2 Norte Pte and Calle 2 Poniente Nte.

The other 1st-class line is Autobuses de Oriente (ADO, ☎ (961) 2-87-25), which has a terminal at Calle 9 Poniente Sur at Avenida 5 Sur Pte. ADO has two buses daily to Mexico City, one to Puebla, and several buses per week to Oaxaca and Veracruz. Fares are similar to those of Cristóbal Colón.

Of the 2nd-class lines, the most useful is Autotransportes Tuxtla Gutiérrez (☎ (961) 2-02-30), at Avenida 3 Sur Ote 712, half a block west of Calle 7 Oriente Sur.

Here are the details for a variety of destinations; all 1st-class buses below are by Cristóbal Colón, 2nd class by Autotransportes Tuxtla Gutiérrez:

Acayucan – 550 km, eight hours; morning and evening 1st class (US$8)

Ciudad Cuauhtémoc (Guatemalan border) – 255 km, four hours; two morning 1st-class buses (US$5)

Comitán – 168 km, 3½ hours; 10 1st class (US$3) by Cristóbal Colón and hourly 2nd-class buses between 4 am and 5 pm (US$2.90)

Mexico City – 1000 km, 19 hours; five 1st class (US$20)

Oaxaca – 550 km, 10 hours; morning and evening 1st class (US$11), four 2nd class per day (US$9)

Palenque – 275 km, six hours; one 2nd class (US$5.50), which makes a stop at Ocosingo

Salina Cruz – 315 km, five hours; morning and evening buses for US$5.50

San Cristóbal de las Casas – 85 km, two hours; 14 1st class (US$1.75), 2nd-class buses every 30 minutes between 4 am and 9 pm (US$1.50)

Tapachula (Guatemalan border) – 456 km, seven hours; three nightly 1st class (US$7), five 2nd class (US$6)

Tehuantepec – 300 km, 4½ hours; two morning 1st class (US$5)

Villahermosa – 294 km, six hours; six 1st class (US$5.50), three 2nd class (US$4.75)

For the 20-minute trip to Chiapa de Corzo, it's easiest to take a Transportes Chiapa-Tuxtla combi (US$0.30) from Calle 3 Oriente Sur, near the corner of Avenida 3 Sur Ote. They run from 4.30 am to 10 pm.

Getting Around
All colectivos (US$0.15) on Belisario Domínguez/ Avenida Central/14 de Septiembre/Ángel Albino Corzo/Highway 190 run at least as far as the tourist offices and the Hotel Bonampak in the west, and Calle 11 Oriente in the east. Taxis are abundant and rides within the city usually cost US$1.

To/From the Airport Transportes al Aeropuerto runs combis (US$3 per person) to and from Aeropuerto San Juan each morning. They'll pick you up or drop you at hotels in the city. Contact them in the Gran Hotel Humberto (☎ 2-20-80).

Car Rental Budget (☎ 2-55-06) is at Belisario Domínguez 2510, Gabriel Rent-a-Car (☎ 2-07-57) is at Belisario Domínguez 780, Renta de Autos Badia (☎ 2-92-59, extension 174) is in the Hotel Flamboyant at Belisario Domínguez Km 1081. Dollar (☎ 2-89-32) is also on Belisario Domínguez.

CAÑÓN DEL SUMIDERO & CHIAPA DE CORZO
Though it looks like a short distance on a map, the 85-km ride from Tuxtla to San Cristóbal takes about two hours. First you've got to negotiate the system of switchbacks climbing from the valley floor up into the mountains, then you must twist and turn along foggy roads to reach San Cristóbal in its mountain fastness.

The only significant settlement along the way is Chiapa de Corzo, jumping-off place for explorations of the breathtaking Cañón del Sumidero.

The Cañón del Sumidero is a daunting fissure in the countryside a few km east of Tuxtla Gutiérrez, with the Río Grijalva (also called the Río Grande de Chiapas) flowing along at the bottom. Since the Chicoasén Dam was completed at the canyon's northern end in 1981, the waters are now deep enough for fast passenger launches to make the 35-km trip through the canyon, whose nearly sheer walls rise to heights somewhere between 900 and 1200 metres (no-one's quite sure of the exact height!). The two-hour ride costs around US$4.50 – a bargain for a crocodile's-eye view of some of Mexico's most awesome scenery. You can also see the canyon from above by travelling out from Tuxtla to one of several lookout points (see under Tuxtla Gutiérrez).

Highway 190, going east from Tuxtla Gutiérrez, crosses the mouth of the canyon at Cahuaré, shortly before the colonial town of Chiapa de Corzo; you can embark for the boat trip at either Cahuaré or Chiapa de Corzo. Either way the outing can be done in an easy day from Tuxtla Gutiérrez – but since Chiapa de Corzo is an interesting little place in its own right, many people start from there.

History
Chiapa de Corzo, on the east bank of the Río Grijalva, holds an eminent position on the archaeologist's map of Mexico because it has been occupied almost continuously since about 1500 BC. Though it never reached great heights and the ruins today are less than spectacular, its uninterrupted sequence of different cultures – in a crossroads area where Olmec, Monte Albán, Mayan, Kaminaljuyú and Teotihuacán influences were all felt – makes it invaluable to specialists trying to trace pre-Hispanic cultural developments.

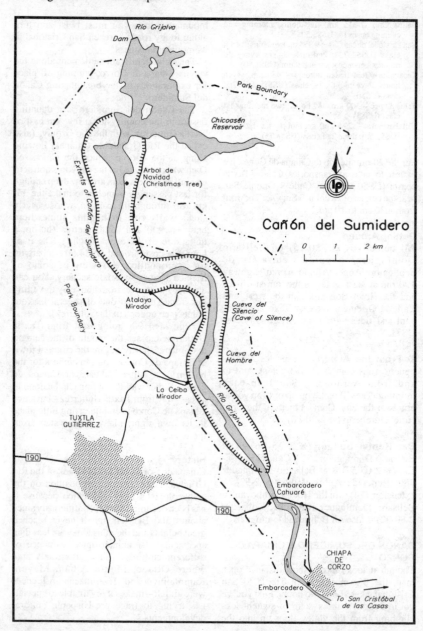

In the couple of centuries before the Spanish arrived, the warlike Chiapa – the most dominant of the peoples in western Chiapas at the time – had their capital, Nandalumí, a few km downstream from Chiapa de Corzo, on the opposite bank of the river and near the canyon mouth. The first Spanish expedition to the area, under Luis Marín in 1524, was aided in its conquest of Nandalumí by the Zapotec slaves of Chiapas, who supplied canoes for the Spanish to cross the river and fought off the Chiapa when they attacked in midstream.

On that occasion the Spanish didn't stay to occupy the area, but a second, more serious expedition under Diego de Mazariegos arrived in 1528. This time the Chiapa, seeing that defeat was inevitable, apparently hurled themselves by the hundreds – men, women and children – to death in the canyon rather than surrender.

Mazariegos then founded Chiapa de Corzo – called Chiapa de los Indios in its early days – but a month later (March 1528) he transferred his headquarters and most of the settlers to a second new settlement, Villa Real de Chiapa (now San Cristóbal de las Casas), where the climate and the Indians were less hostile. The Chiapa Indians rebelled in 1532 and 1534 but that didn't stop Dominican monks from settling in Chiapa de Corzo in the 1540s. Their monastery was built between 1554 and 1572.

In 1863 Chiapa de Corzo was the scene of the decisive battle for control of Chiapas between anticlerical liberals, supporting national president Benito Juárez, and pro-Church conservatives, supporting the French invasion of Mexico. The conservatives, led by Juan Ortega, had already taken San Cristóbal de las Casas, but their defeat by forces from Chiapa de Corzo and Tuxtla Gutiérrez, organised by liberal governor Ángel Albino Corzo and led by Salvador Urbina, marked the end of their attempt to install a reactionary government in Chiapas. In 1888 Chiapa de los Indios was renamed Chiapa de Corzo in honour of the liberal governor.

Orientation & Information

If you want to start your canyon trip at Cahuaré, get off your bus where it crosses the bridge over the wide Río Grijalva, about 11 km out of Tuxtla Gutiérrez. The *embarcadero* (embarkation point) is by the bridge, on the west (Tuxtla) side of the river.

Just about everything of interest in Chiapa de Corzo itself is within a couple of blocks of the large, slightly sloping main plaza, Plaza General Ángel Albino Corzo. Buses will let you out on 21 de Octubre, at the top end of the main plaza as you enter the town. For boats into the canyon, walk down the right-hand side of the main plaza (the street's called 5 de Febrero) and straight on for a couple of blocks until you reach the embarcadero on the river front. There's a post office on the way down, opposite the large church. The market is on La Mexicanidad, the street running down the other side of the main plaza, opposite the other end of the church.

There are a few artesanías' shops in the portales at the bottom of the main plaza.

Cañón del Sumidero

The fast, open, fibreglass launches leave from the embarcaderos on the Río Grijalva at Chiapa de Corzo and Cahuaré. From either place a return trip costs US$35 for a whole boat, or US$4.50 per person for six or more in one craft. If you haven't already got five others with you, just wait until a few more people come along and share a boat with them. Even on weekdays, you shouldn't have to wait more than an hour or so if you get there by, say, 10 am. Chiapa de Corzo is busier than Cahuaré. From both places the launches operate between roughly 7 am and 4 pm. They travel pretty fast so take a layer or two of warm clothing.

It's about 40 km from Chiapa de Corzo to the Chicoasén Dam at the far end of the canyon, and the return trip takes about two hours. The sides of the canyon start to rise once you pass Cahuaré and soon they're beetling up an amazing 1000 metres above you. Along the way you'll see a great variety of bird life – herons, egrets, cormorants, vultures, kingfishers – plus probably a croc-odile or two. The boatmen point out a few odd formations of rock or vegetation, includ-ing one cliff face covered in a growth of thick, hanging moss making it resemble a gigantic Christmas tree.

At the end of the canyon the fast brown river opens out into the broad reservoir behind the Chicoasén hydroelectric dam. The water beneath you is 260 metres deep.

Things to See in Chiapa de Corzo

There are several points of interest around Chiapa's main plaza. The Spanish fountain called La Pila is a fine eight-sided *mudéjar* structure at the bottom end of the main plaza. Built in 1562, it's said to have been inspired by the Spanish royal crown.

The Museo de Laca (Lacquer Museum), dedicated to the craft of lacquered wooden objects or gourds (*jícaras*), faces the main plaza on 5 de Febrero. Exhibits explain the practical and symbolic importance of gourds (the *Popol Vuh* says the sky is a big, blue, upside-down gourd) and there are examples of lacquerwork from other centres like Uruapan, Pátzcuaro and Olinalá, showing the variety of styles and techniques and the influence of Asian motifs going back to the 18th century. The museum also has masks of the type used in Chiapas' January festivities. You might see some of the fine woodcarving of local master Francisco Jiménez. Hours are Tuesday to Sunday 9 am to 7 pm, Monday 1 to 4 pm; admission is free.

The Palacio Municipal, on La Mexicanidad, across the main plaza from the Museo de Laca, has a map of the battle of 1863 on its stairway and a mural of local history culminating in the same battle.

Churches A block beyond the bottom end of the main plaza, the large church of Santo Domingo dates from the mid-16th century. Part of the adjacent ex-monastery has been converted into a Casa de la Cultura. One of the church towers has an enormous gold, silver and copper bell of famed sonority, made in 1576 (one of the earliest in Latin America).

Three other churches crowning small hills around the top of the town were fortified by the liberals as defence points in 1863. You can get good views from all of them. They are shown in the Palacio Municipal mural.

Pre-Hispanic Ruins

Though important to archaeologists, these will interest only the most enthusiastic of visitors. You can reach one small restored pyramid, Montículo 32, by going about a km east along 21 de Octubre (the road which forms the top side of the main plaza – go to the right if facing uphill on the main plaza). It contained a tomb and is located where the road from the town centre meets the bypass.

There are some other stone-faced pyra-mids and stairways, mostly dating from 100 BC to 200 AD, through some backstreets south-east of here. Ask for las ruinas.

Festivals

Fiesta de Enero A succession of some of Mexico's most colourful and curious fiestas, generally known as the Fiesta de Enero, is held in Chiapa de Corzo from 9 to 22 January every year. The main events are:

From 9 January, young men dressed as women and known as *las Chuntá* dance through the streets nightly. This custom is said to derive from a distribution of food to the poor by the maids of a rich woman of colonial times, Doña María de Angulo.

Processions and dances of *los Parachicos* take place on 15 January (the day of Señor de Esquipulas), 17 January (San Antón Abad) and 20 January (San Sebastián Martir). The Parachicos are men with wooden masks and 'hair' made from ixtle – a fibre derived from agave – representing the features and fair hair of Spanish conquista-dors. They wear Saltillo-style sarapes, shake tin *maracas* and are accompanied by little girls. In part, the Parachico tradition is thought to go back to the same Doña María de Angulo, whose crippled son was miracu-lously cured by a Chiapa de Corzo *curandero*. The curandero told her to provide some entertainment for the boy (*para el chico)* in his convalescence, so she got some of her employees to shake maracas for him.

There's a musical parade of just about everyone on 19 January, when the formal announcement of the Fiesta Grande is made.

The most renowned event of all is the Combate Naval on the night of 21 January. This is an hour-long mock battle on the river, enacted by people in canoes, with hosts of spectacular fireworks. It goes back to early colonial times – the Irish traveller Thomas Gage recorded something similar in 1626 – and probably stems from waterborne encounters between Spanish conquistadors and local Indians; the modern version was inspired by a film of the battle of Port Arthur in the Russo-Japanese War, seen locally in 1905.

The celebrations usually close with a parade of *carros alegóricos* (parade floats) and general merrymaking on 22 or 23 January. Local women dress up in highly colourful and exquisitely worked dresses.

Places to Stay & Eat

There's just one hostelry in Chiapa de Corzo – the *Hotel Los Angeles* (☎ (961) 6-00-48), Julián Grajales 2 at La Mexicanidad, at the bottom corner of the main plaza. It's nothing special but it's clean and the rooms, around a courtyard where you could park a car, are quite sizable. Hot water is intermittent and mosquito nets would be a distinct improvement. Cost is US$11 a single, US$14 a double.

There are several restaurants by the embarcadero but more appealing is the friendly *Restaurant Jardines de Chiapa*, in a garden off the La Mexicanidad side of the main plaza. The menu is limited (and tamales are only available at night) but the fare isn't bad. Sopa Fiesta (US$1.25) contains macaroni, egg, avocado and chicken. *Pollo entomatada* (chicken in tomato sauce) is US$3.50.

Getting There & Away

Some buses between Tuxtla Gutiérrez and San Cristóbal de las Casas pass through Chiapa de Corzo, but from Tuxtla it's easier

to take a Transportes Chiapa-Tuxtla combi (see the Tuxtla Gutiérrez section).

Chiapa de Corzo's bus terminals are on 21 de Octubre, the street running east from the top end of the main plaza. Seats on 1st-class buses to San Cristóbal are sometimes in short supply, so book ahead if you can. Alternatively, you could go back to Tuxtla first. Omnibus Cristóbal Colón (1st class) is a block east of the main plaza at 21 de Octubre 26. There are three buses each morning to San Cristóbal (US$1.50, 1½ hours) and Comitán. Autotransportes Tuxtla Gutiérrez is a little farther up the same street. It runs buses half-hourly to San Cristóbal; to Palenque via Ocosingo three times daily; and to Villahermosa, Comitán and Motozintla.

SAN CRISTÓBAL DE LAS CASAS

Population 82,000

San Cristóbal (cris-TOH-bal), nestled in the small Jovel Valley at an altitude of 2110 metres, is in the heart of the Chiapas Highlands, or Sierra Norte de Chiapas, known to locals simply as Los Altos, which are mostly 2000 to 3000 metres high and which also stretch down into Guatemala. The weather here is cool with temperatures between high single figures and the low 20° Cs all the year round. Rainfall in San Cristóbal is negligible from November to April, but about 110 cm falls in the remaining half of the year. It's not unusual for it to rain hard at some time between 3 and 6 pm for several days in succession.

For years now San Cristóbal has been one of the most loved travellers' haunts in Mexico. This tranquil Spanish-built town with its massive, well-kept colonial buildings standing high in a temperate pine-clad valley doesn't have a long list of postcard-type 'sights' but it's surrounded by distinctly mysterious Indian villages, is endlessly intriguing to explore and is full of good food, accommodation and company.

Beyond that, it has a unique, even magical, atmosphere that seeps into many people after a few days, something to do perhaps with the smell of wood smoke, the unrivalled clarity of its light or the Indians padding quickly

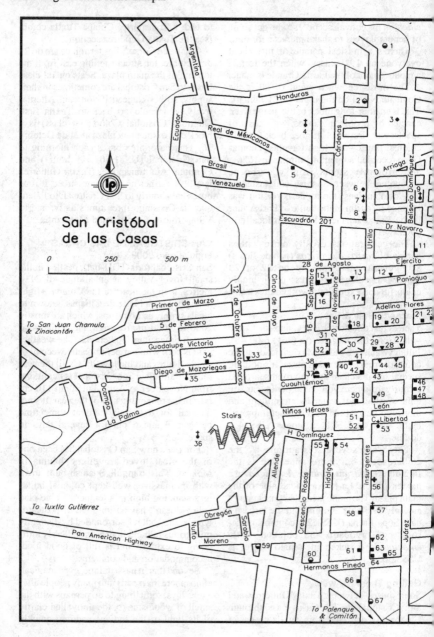

San Cristóbal
de las Casas

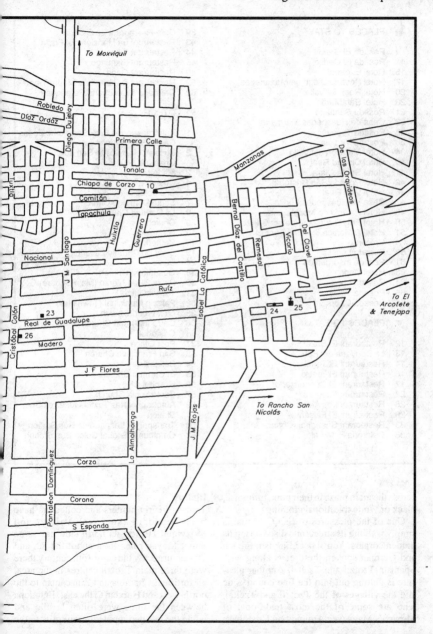

■ PLACES TO STAY

4	Posada El Candil
11	Posada El Cerillo
15	Hotel Español
17	Hotel Posada Diego de Mazariegos
20	Hotel Real del Valle
20	Hotel San Martín
21	Posada Santiago
22	Casa de Huéspedes Margarita
23	Posada Tepeyac
26	Posada Virginia
34	Hotel Mansión del Valle
40	Hotel Ciudad Real
41	Hotel Santa Clara
42	Hotel Posada San Cristóbal
46	Hotel Villa Real
47	Casa de Huéspedes Lupita
48	Hotel Palacio de Moctezuma
50	Hotel Fray Bartolomé de las Casas
51	Hotel D'Monica & Restaurant El Unicorno
58	Posada Lucella
61	Posada Insurgentes
63	Hotel Capri
64	Posada Lupita
65	Posada Vallarta
66	Posada Capri

▼ PLACES TO EAT

12	Restaurant El Bazar
13	La Boutique del Pan
14	Restaurant El Trigal
16	Restaurant El Teatro
17	Restaurant El Conquistador
27	Restaurant Fulano's
28	Restaurant Los Arcos
29	Restaurant El Faisán
33	Restaurant Shanghai (Chang-Gai)
38	Cafetería El Mural
39	Café-Restaurant La Galería
43	Restaurant La Mansión del Fraile
44	Restaurant Tuluc
45	Restaurant Flamingo
49	Restaurant Capri
52	Restaurant & Panadería Madre Tierra
62	Cafetería & Lonchería Palenque

OTHER

1	Autotransportes Fray Bartolomé de las Casas Bus Station
2	Buses/Colectivos to San Juan Chamula
3	Market
4	Church
6	Sna Jolobil
7	Santo Domingo Church
8	La Caridad Church
9	Church
10	Na Bolom
18	Cathedral
19	Casa de Cambio Lacantún
24	Steps
25	Guadalupe Church
30	Plaza 31 de Marzo (Main Square)
31	Tourist Office
32	Palacio Municipal (Town Hall)
35	La Merced Church
36	Cerro (Hill) and Church of San Cristóbal
37	Post Office
53	San Francisco Church
54	Bellas Artes
55	El Carmen Church
56	Hospital Civil
57	Santa Lucía Church
59	Autotransportes Tuxtla Guitérrez Bus Station
60	Transportes Lacandonia Bus Station
67	Omnibus Cristóbal Colón Bus Station

across the main plaza in their pink, turquoise, black or white traditional clothing.

One of the pleasures of San Cristóbal is simply walking its streets and discovering its hidden corners. You'll hear English, French and German spoken these days along with Spanish, Tzotzil and Tzeltal. Another pleasure is getting out into the fine countryside and the villages of the Tzotzil and Tzeltal, who are some of the most traditional of Mexico's Maya (see Around San Cristóbal).

History

Traces of early hunters and collectors have been found in the Jovel Valley, and Moxviquil Hill on its north side has some minor Mayan ruins from about the 8th and 9th centuries. By the early 16th century there were three main Tzotzil centres in the area, all fortified: Chamula and Zinacantán to the north-west and Huixtán to the east. Relations between the three were often hostile and while the last two reputedly sent gifts to the

Spanish who arrived in Chiapas in 1524, the invaders had to conquer Chamula by force. Bernal Díaz del Castillo, author of a famed first-hand chronicle of the Spanish conquest of Mexico, was apparently the first Spaniard to enter Chamula, for which he was awarded the place as his encomienda (estate).

The Spanish didn't settle in the area until four years later, when Diego de Mazariegos founded San Cristóbal (at first called Villa Real de Chiapa) as their regional headquarters. The Spanish occupied the area round the main plaza, known as El Recinto, around which was El Barrio, where Indians and mestizos lived. There were also special *barrios* for Spain's Aztec, Tlaxcalan and Oaxacan allies.

Early in the Spanish period, the Church was a force for protection of the Indians against the excesses of the colonists. Dominican monks first arrived in Chiapas in 1545 and made San Cristóbal their main base. Bartolomé de las Casas (after whom the town is now named), who was appointed Bishop of Chiapas the same year, and Juan de Zapata y Sandoval, bishop from 1613 to 1621, are the most fondly remembered prelates.

For most of the colonial era San Cristóbal was a neglected outpost governed ineffectively from Guatemala. Its Spanish inhabitants made their fortunes – usually from wheat – at the cost of the Indians, who suffered diseases, taxes, loss of their lands and forced labour. They rose up several times, the most famous occasion in colonial times being the Cancuc rebellion of 1712 by the Tzeltal people, provoked by taxes levied to build a church and hospital in San Cristóbal.

San Cristóbal remained the chief Spanish town in Chiapas throughout colonial times, and in 1778 its population count, including the Indian barrios, was 4812, of whom 564 were Spanish. It became the state capital when Chiapas joined recently independent Mexico in 1824.

In the mid-19th century Yucatán was embroiled in the War of the Castes, echoes of which came to Chiapas within a generation. The Chiapan Maya, oppressed just as much as their lowland kin, took inspiration from a religious cult surprisingly similar to the famous Talking Cross of Chan Santa Cruz.

One day in 1867, at a place called Tzajalhemel, only 17 years after the Talking Crosses began their blabber, a Chamula girl called Agustina Gómez Checheb found three pieces of obsidian which seemed to talk. She entrusted them to a local Indian official, Pedro Díaz Cuzcat, who said they woke him at night with their noise inside a wooden box. Tzajalhemel rapidly became an Indian pilgrimage centre where Agustina and Díaz would interpret the 'oracles' of the stones and of a clay figure to which Agustina had allegedly given birth. Díaz even baptised 12 Indians as saints of the new cult, which soon had more followers than the Catholic Church in many Tzotzil and Tzeltal villages north of San Cristóbal. This alarmed the Church and civil authorities and in December 1868 the pair were imprisoned in San Cristóbal.

Enter the revolutionary Ignacio Fernández Galindo. Identifying himself with San Salvador or the Tzotzil god Cul Salik, he came from San Cristóbal to rouse the Chamulas to win back their lands and stop burdensome taxes. In June 1869 the schoolmaster and the Catholic priest in Chamula were murdered and the rebels went through the countryside killing more mestizos. Arriving at San Cristóbal, they successfully demanded the release of Agustina and Díaz but were persuaded to leave Galindo and his wife as hostages.

When the hostages were not released, Díaz led a new attack on San Cristóbal, joined by many other Tzotzil villagers, but the authorities had enough time to gather reinforcements and the rebels were beaten – though resistance lingered a bit longer in the northern area round Simojovel. Galindo was sentenced to death, and other rebels were shot or deported to remote parts of Mexico. Díaz survived to lead a further short-lived uprising of hacienda servants in 1870.

Despite its lively and important history, San Cristóbal has always been something of a mountain outpost. The first paved road from Tuxtla Gutiérrez didn't arrive until the 1940s. Only in the 1970s was a tunnel built to provide adequate drainage for the Jovel Valley and stop the floods which had periodically struck the town since its founding.

Orientation

San Cristóbal is a small place, easy to find your way around, with straight streets rambling up and down several gentle hills. The Pan American Highway (Highway 190) passes along the south side of town, and just off it are the main bus stations. From these terminals, walk north (slightly uphill) to reach the main plaza, Plaza 31 de Marzo, named for the day upon which the town was founded. The cathedral is on the north side of the plaza.

Though straightforward, the town's plan has its pitfalls. For instance, each street seems to have at least two names. The western portion might be named Primero (1°) de Marzo, and the eastern portion Paniagua. South of the main plaza the name is Juárez, but north of the plaza it's Belisario Domínguez. And speaking of Domínguez, there are two streets with that name: Belisario Domínguez and Hermanos (Hnos) Domínguez. Likewise for Adelina Flores and Dr Felipe Flores, Velasco Suárez and Pino Suárez, and perhaps others.

From the Omnibus Cristóbal Colón terminal it's just six blocks up Insurgentes to the main plaza; from Autotransportes Tuxtla Gutiérrez it's five blocks up Allende, then two to the right along Mazariegos.

Places to stay and eat are scattered all around town, but there are clutches of hotels and casas de huéspedes on Insurgentes and on Real de Guadalupe at the north-east corner of the main plaza.

Information

Tourist Office Turismo (☎ (967) 8-04-14) is at the right-hand end of the Palacio Municipal on the west side of the main plaza. It's open 8 am to 2 pm and from 3 to 8 pm Monday to Saturday, 9 am to 2 pm Sunday, give or take a few minutes. Some of the staff speak good English and have a lot of infor-

mation on hand, but how much they'll tell you depends on how busy they are and how energetic they feel.

There is no Guatemalan Consulate in San Cristóbal, but there is one in Comitán (see that section).

Money There are several banks on and near the main plaza. Most of them only exchange foreign currency from 10 to 11 or 11.30 am. The staff of any bank will do their best to ignore you for hours. As the time allotted to exchange transactions is so short and tourists so many, get in line early. Have patience, or take your exchange business to the Casa de Cambio Lacantún (☎ 8-25-87), Real de Guadalupe 12-A, less than half a block east of the main plaza. Lacantún changes money (minimum of US$50) at competitive rates, but charges 2.5% commission on the deal (US$2.50 to change US$100). The commission seems high, but you can be in and out with your money in two minutes. Hours are 8.30 am to 2 pm and 5 to 8 pm Monday to Saturday, 9 am to 1 pm Sunday.

Post & Telecommunications The post office (☎ (967) 8-07-65) is on Cuauhtémoc between Hidalgo and Crescencio Rosas, one block south and one west of the main plaza's south-west corner. It's open 8 am to 7 pm Monday to Friday, 9 am to 1 pm Saturday, Sunday and holidays. San Cristóbal's postal code is 29200.

For telegrams go to Diego de Mazariegos 19, 2½ blocks west of the main plaza. There's also a public telex office near the post office.

Phone calls to the outside world often involve long waits and you'll have to be very patient to place a call to another country. You can attempt to make them at the farmacia on the south side of the main plaza, at the Autotransportes Tuxtla Gutiérrez bus station, and at Diego de Mazariegos 19.

Bookshops For newspapers and magazines, both Mexican and foreign, try the newsstand on the east side of Diego de Mazariegos at No 20-D between Allende and

16 de Septiembre. Librería Soluna, Real de Guadalupe 24-D, less than a block east of the main plaza, has mostly Spanish books, but some are in English. Bring two you've read and trade them for one you haven't. Cafetería El Mural at Crescencio Rosas 4 has some English and Spanish books and magazines for sale, plus several daily newspapers to browse through.

Medical Services San Cristóbal Centro de Salud (also called the Hospital Civil; ☎ (967) 8-07-70), Insurgentes 24 facing the Parque Fray Bartolomé, provides emergency care 24 hours a day. The Red Cross (Cruz Roja; ☎ (967) 8-07-12) is on Insurgentes next to the Centro Recreativo Municipal.

Supermarkets Conasuper San Francisco is next to the San Francisco Church on Insurgentes at Hermanos Domínguez; there's another right next to the Pemex station a few steps to the north; and another, the Supermercado Jovel, on Utrilla at the corner with Real de Guadalupe, just off the north-east corner of the main plaza.

Festivals
San Cristóbal's calendar has a plentiful sprinkling of festivals – some involving just one barrio, others the whole town. Processions, parades and fireworks feature in most of them. Ask at the tourist office for what's on while you're there.

In spring there's a two-week-long fiesta period covering Semana Santa (Holy Week, before Easter), and the Fería de la Primavera y de la Paz (Spring & Peace) the following week. Semana Santa includes processions on Good Friday and the burning of 'Judas' figures on Holy Saturday. The second week features more parades, bullfights and so on. Sometimes the celebrations for the anniversary of the town's founding (31 March) fall in the midst of it all too!

Other fiestas can go on several days before and after the specific date in question. look out for events celebrating the feast of San Cristóbal (17 to 25 July), the anniversary of Chiapas joining Mexico in 1824 (14 Septem-ber), National Independence Day (15 and 16 September), the Day of the Dead (2 November), the Feast of the Virgin of Guadalupe (10 to 12 December) and preparations for Christmas (16 to 24 December).

Festivals are also a feature of life in the Indian villages outside the town – see the Around San Cristóbal section.

Plaza 31 de Marzo
Used as a marketplace until early in this century, the main plaza is the old Spanish centre of the town. It's a fine place to sit and watch the life of the town happen around you. The steps on the east side are a favourite evening gathering place for locals and Indians from outlying villages. The cathedral, on the north side, was begun in 1528, but was completely rebuilt in 1693. Its gold leaf interior has a baroque pulpit and altarpiece. The south-east corner of the plaza is taken up by the former house of Diego de Mazariegos, the Spanish conqueror of Chiapas. Now the Hotel Santa Clara, Mazariegos' house is one of the few nonecclesiastical examples of the Plateresque style in Mexico. The Palácio Municipal on the west side of the square is a 19th-century neoclassical structure.

Santo Domingo Church
Of San Cristóbal's many churches, the Church of Santo Domingo is certainly the most beautiful – especially when its pink façade is floodlit at night. Santo Domingo is in the north-west of town opposite the corner of Utrilla and Chiapa de Corzo. Together with the adjoining monastery, it was built from 1547 to 1560. The church's baroque façade (on which can be seen the double-headed Hapsburg eagle, symbol of the Spanish monarchy) was added in the 17th century. There's plenty of gold inside, especially on the ornate pulpit.

Just south of Santo Domingo, the Church of La Caridad dates from 1712. Taxes levied on Indians for the building of La Caridad and an adjoining hospital for the poor sparked off the Tzeltal rebellion of Cancuc in the same year.

Sna Jolobil Weavers' Cooperative

Anyone interested in Chiapas Indian textiles – and that probably includes just about every visitor to San Cristóbal – should stop by Sna Jolobil. Its Tzotzil Indian name means Weavers' House, and it's located in the old monastery buildings next to the Church of Santo Domingo, with another shop in the Plaza de la Calle Real shopping complex at Real de Guadalupe 5, across the street from the Hotel San Martín half a block east of the plaza.

Sna Jolobil is an organisation of 650 women backstrap-loom weavers from 20 Tzotzil and Tzeltal villages, which aims at fostering this important folk art both for income and to preserve Indian identity and tradition. The showroom is open daily except Sunday from 9 am to 2 pm and 3.30 to 7 pm. Here you can see a fine range of huipiles, generally priced at about US$25 but going up to US$775 and US$1160 for the finest ceremonial garments from Santa Magdalena and Santa Rosario. There are always numerous weavers at their work in and around the former monastery.

Weaver with
backstrap loom

Founded in the late 1970s, Sna Jolobil's aims include the revival of forgotten techniques and designs and the development of natural dyes. One important revival is the weaving of brocade, in which the decorative motifs are worked in when the fabric is woven, unlike embroidery where decoration is added after weaving.

Each village in the Chiapas highlands has its own distinctive dress and modern Western garb is worn less here than it is among most Mexican Indians.

The designs and techniques are derived from many stages of the Indians' history. Most seemingly abstract designs are in fact stylised snakes, frogs, butterflies, dog pawprints, birds, people, saints and so on. Some go back to pre-Hispanic times: for instance the rhombus shape on some huipiles from San Andrés Larráinzar is also found on the garments of one of the figures on Lintel 24 from Yaxchilán. The shape represents the old Mayan universe, in which the earth was cube-shaped and the sky had four corners. Some designs can still perform a religious/magical function: scorpion motifs, for example, can be a symbolic request for rain, since scorpions are believed to attract lightning. The sacredness of traditional costume is shown by the dressing of saints' images in old and revered garments at festival times.

The typical men's costume from Chamula – long-sleeved shirt, wool tunic, belt and long trousers – stems from the Spanish, who objected to the relative nudity of the loincloth and cloak that Chamulan men used to wear. Other patterns have been invented or reinvented more recently as an expression of Indian identity. The square, coloured patch on men's costumes from Cancuc and Oxchuc was originally an Aztec motif, brought to the area by the Aztec allies of the 16th-century Spanish conquistadors. Early this century these villages lacked any special costume, but they used the Aztec idea, which had survived among Chamulans, to help create one.

Na Bolom

A visit to this fascinating house on Guerrero

at the corner of Chiapa de Corzo, six blocks north of Real de Guadalupe, should be high on anyone's list. For several decades it has been the home of Swiss anthropologist and photographer Gertrude (Trudy) Duby-Blom and, until his death in 1963, of her husband, Danish archaeologist Frans Blom.

The pair shared a passion for Chiapas and particularly its Indians. While Frans explored, surveyed and dug at ancient Mayan sites including Toniná, Chinkultic and Moxviquil, Trudy has devoted much of her life to studying and campaigning for the tiny Lacandón Indian population of eastern Chiapas. One building at Na Bolom is reserved for Lacandones to use when they visit San Cristóbal.

In Europe Trudy Blom had been a socialist journalist who survived a Nazi concentration camp. Her energy has continued into old age, with recent emphasis on campaigning to save the endangered Lacandón rainforest and starting a tree nursery for Indian villagers.

The house – whose name is Tzotzil for Jaguar House as well as a play on the owner's name – is full of photographs, archaeological and anthropological relics and books, and is a treasure-trove for anyone with an interest in Chiapas. Visits are only by guided tour (US$1.25), but these are some of the least formal, most open-ended guided tours you'll find anywhere. They are conducted in English and Spanish daily except Monday at 4.30 pm by volunteers from several countries who spend a year at Na Bolom and are happy to chat with visitors. The house also has an artist-in-residence programme. The 14,000-book library, including one of the world's biggest Mayan collections and a wealth of other material on Chiapas and Central America, is open separately from 9 am to 1 pm daily.

If you're interested in the sorts of things Na Bolom offers, you can stay here (US$55 a double) – or just dine with the assembled company.

Other Sights

The Church of El Carmen lies at the corner of Hidalgo and Hermanos Domínguez. Formerly part of a nunnery, it has a distinctive tower resting on an arch. The nunnery was built in 1597, the tower in 1680 to replace one destroyed by floods 28 years earlier. Next door is the Casa de Cultura, containing art galleries, a library with a good English collection, and the Bellas Artes auditorium where regular musical and theatrical performances are held.

The Church of La Merced, located on Diego de Mazariegos 3½ blocks west of the main plaza, was largely reconstructed this century, but there's a pleasant plaza in front of it.

At the Centro de Investigaciones Ecológicas del Sureste, on the corner of Cuauhtémoc and Crescencio Rosas, there are displays on the vegetation, geology and ecology of Chiapas, plus a library and a good local map collection. Open Monday to Friday 3 to 7 pm, Saturday 10 am to 1 pm.

Museo Zul-Pepen is a private butterfly and archaeological museum (!) at Guadalupe Victoria 47. It's open daily except Monday from 4 to 8 pm and costs US$1. The butterfly collection contains many incredibly colourful (if dead) specimens from all over the world. The archaeological section features pieces from several pre-Hispanic cultures but no particular treasures. Compulsory and enthusiastic guided tours in Spanish increase the interest of the displays if you've got the stamina.

You can have an hour's Turkish bath for US$2, or an hour's plain steam for US$1.50, at Baños Mercedarios at Primero (1°) de Marzo 55 (open 6.30 am to 7.30 pm Monday to Saturday, 6.30 am to 6 pm Sunday).

Walks near the Town

The most prominent of the several small hills over which San Cristóbal undulates are the Cerro (Hill) de San Cristóbal in the southwest quarter of town, reached by steps up from Allende, and the Cerro de Guadalupe, seven blocks east of the main plaza along Real de Guadalupe. Both are crowned by churches and afford good views over the town – but there have been reports of attempted rapes on the Cerro de San Cristóbal.

The Cerro de Moxviquil, about 1.5 km north of the town, has some Mayan ruins which were excavated by Frans Blom but have now been grown over again. They lie about 200 metres above the Ojo de Agua on the unpaved Periférico Norte (Northern Ring-Road). If you want to look for them, ask in Na Bolom or elsewhere for directions. The ruins themselves require imagination if they're to provide much interest, but the walk is pleasant.

Cerro Ecatepec is south of the town and a trail leads up it from Los Sumideros, which are the caves that drain the Jovel Valley's small rivers. Los Sumideros are on the Periférico Sur, about two km west of its junction with the continuation of Insurgentes south of the Pan American Highway. A tunnel made in the 1970s to increase Los Sumideros' drainage capacity and prevent flooding also starts near Los Sumideros.

You can ascend Cerro Huitepec (2750 metres), west of the town, either from the church in the south-western barrio of San Felipe or by striking up from the western Periférico, between the Pan American Highway and the road to Chamula.

Places to Stay – bottom end

San Cristóbal is well supplied with clean, cheap places to stay, in all parts of town.

Near the Bus Stations Many hostelries line Calle Insurgentes, the main street heading north from the Cristóbal Colón bus station to the main plaza. The cheaper ones are mainly of the dingy, uncared-for variety. The better ones include the *Posada Vallarta* (☎ (967) 8-04-65), half a block east off Insurgentes at Hermanos Pineda 10 (the first street to the right as you go up Insurgentes from the Cristóbal Colón bus station). It's clean and modernish, plain but neat, and quiet. Singles/doubles with private bath cost US$10/13. (Some rooms have three double beds.) There's also off-street parking.

The *Posada Capri* (☎ (967) 8-30-18), Insurgentes 99, just around the corner from the Cristóbal Colón bus station, is plain and basic but convenient and cheap. Common bathrooms could be cleaner, that's for sure. Singles without bath go for US$4.50, doubles for US$7, triples for US$9.50. Note that there is also a Hotel Capri, a completely different establishment in the middle price range.

The friendly *Posada Insurgentes* (☎ (967) 8-24-35), Insurgentes 73, is located 1½ blocks north of the Cristóbal Colón bus station across the street from the Hotel Capri. It's clean, has newer beds and furnishings than the others on the street, and has plenty of hot water in the common bathrooms. Rate is US$4.50 to US$5.50 per person, depending upon demand.

Posada Lupita, Insurgentes 46, opposite the Posada Insurgentes, is plain to the point of severity, but is OK for the price at US$6.50 a double without private bath. Note that there's also a Casa de Huéspedes Lupita (different management, much nicer) on Juárez.

Posada Lucella (☎ (967) 8-09-56), Insurgentes 55, directly across from the Santa Lucia Church, used to be named the Posada Hueyzacatlán, but the owner changed the name because it was too difficult for many foreigners to pronounce! Now we're left to wonder whether to say 'loo-SELL-ah' or 'loo-SEY-ah', so what's the difference? Serviceable rooms here – nothing special but perfectly OK – cost US$8.50 double with shared bathroom and US$2 more with private bath.

On Calle Real de Guadalupe Another street with a strong concentration of good little casas de huéspedes is Calle Real de Guadalupe, heading east from the plaza. The *Casa de Huéspedes Margarita* (☎ (967) 8-09-57), Real de Guadalupe 34, 1½ blocks east of the main plaza, has long been one of the most popular budget travellers' halts in Mexico – and justifiably so. It's a fine single-storey courtyard house where the señora and her family live in the back while about 18 rooms in the front are let to visitors, and they fill up quickly. The rooms are bare but clean, and the beds are comfortable. Each room takes two, three or more people; if you're alone ask for a *dormitorio* bed (US$4), or find other travellers to share with you (usually easy). A private room with shared bathroom costs US$6.50 a single, US$9 a double. There's a good restaurant and a noticeboard where lifts are sometimes offered.

Just beyond the Margarita is the *Posada Tepeyac* (☎ (967) 8-01-18), Real de Guadalupe 40, corner of Colón. Small and modest, basic but clean, it's a rambling place with birds in the courtyard; rooms at the back get more light. With common bath, singles are US$4.50, doubles US$7; doubles with private bath cost US$8.50.

Posada Santiago (☎ (967) 8-00-24), Real de Guadalupe 32 at Colón, is a warren of passageways and spiral staircases, but offers decent rooms for US$13 a double with private shower. There's a minuscule cafeteria here. Around the corner at Calle Colón 1, corner of Real de Guadalupe, is the *Posada Virginia* (same phone), under identical management as the Santiago. The Virginia is the better of the two: the recently modernised rooms are larger, brighter, and carpeted; some have one double and one single bed. You get more, and you pay more: US$17 a double. There's off-street parking.

Hotel Real del Valle (☎ (67) 8-06-80), Real de Guadalupe 14, half a block east of the plaza, is nice if simple, with clean rooms arranged around a courtyard occupied by the hotel's café and by guests' parked cars. Doubles with bath go for US$13.

On Juárez *Casa de Huéspedes Lupita*, Juárez 12 between León and Felipe Flores, charges US$4.50 per person (singles available). The rooms aren't huge and need a coat of paint but the place is clean (including the bathrooms), family-run and friendly. Don't confuse the Casa de Huéspedes Lupita with the Posada Lupita on Insurgentes.

Hotel Villa Real (☎ (967) 8-29-30), Juárez 8 between León and Felipe Flores, right next to the Lupita, is a step up in quality and comfort. Rooms are arranged around the rear courtyard on three tiers. They're small and

modern, with tiny clean baths; some have one double and one single bed, a good arrangement for families or threesomes. Rates are US$11 a single, US$15 a double.

Farther Out *Posada El Candil* (☎ (967) 8-27-55), Real de Mexicanos 7, two blocks west of the Church of Santo Domingo, is simple, spartan, and a bit of a walk from the plaza, but its location on the outskirts allows you to trade convenience for a low price. Rooms without baths go for US$4.50 a single, US$5.50 a double, US$8 a triple – an indisputable bargain.

Another good budget place is the small *Posada El Cerrillo*, Belisario Domínguez 27, just north of Ejercito Nacional, four blocks north of the main plaza. It's clean and bright with a pleasant little courtyard. Rooms cost US$6.50 with one double bed, US$7 with two beds. Bathrooms are shared, as you'd expect at these prices.

Camping The *Rancho San Nicolás* camping and trailer park (☎ (967) 8-00-57) is two km east of the main plaza: go east along León for a km after it becomes a dirt track. Cost is US$1 per person in a tent, US$2.50 in a cabin, US$4 per person in a caravan or camper with full hook-ups. There's hot water in the showers.

Places to Stay – middle
San Cristóbal has many hotels in charming colonial buildings. Most of them are in the middle price range, and represent excellent value for money.

Hotel Ciudad Real (☎ (967) 8-01-87, 8-04-64), Plaza 31 de Marzo 10, on the south side of the main plaza, is a colonial mansion with a lofty interior court (now covered) which functions as the dining room, complete with log fire in the baronial fireplace for chilly San Cristóbal evenings. The 31 small rooms have been renovated and modernised, and rent for US$16 a single, US$20 a double with TV and private bath. Conversation from the covered court can annoy, so take a room higher up if possible.

Hotel Santa Clara (☎ (967) 8-11-40, 8-08-

71; fax 8-10-41), Avenida Insurgentes 1, near the Ciudad Real on the south side of the plaza, was built in the 1500s and once served as the home of Diego de Mazariegos, the Spanish conqueror of Chiapas. Rooms are mostly big and comfortable and equipped with TV sets. There's a pleasant courtyard brightened by some red macaws (in cages), plus a restaurant, a large bar/lounge, and even a swimming pool. Singles/doubles are US$19/23.

The *Hotel Español* (☎ (967) 8-04-12, 8-00-45), Primero de Marzo 16 near the corner of 16 de Septiembre (Apdo Postal 12)), two blocks north of the cathedral, is another quiet place dripping with colonial charm. Its lovely oasis of a central garden has Talavera tiles and a fountain. The 30 rooms around two courts are comfortable but a little dark and moderate in size; baths are modern, with locally handpainted tiles. Rooms around the first courtyard come with fireplaces complete with *leña* (firewood) and *ocote* (fatwood sticks for lighting the fire). Singles/doubles are US$20/25.

Hotel D'Mónica (☎ (967) 8-13-67, 8-29-40), Insurgentes 33 near León, across from San Francisco Church and the Parque Fray Bartolomé, offers surprisingly good value. Pass through the unimpressive lobby to the nice lounge with fine murals on Indian themes. Behind the lounge is a large open court with three tiers of rooms, 58 in all, each with two double beds, TV, fireplace, and shiny tiled bath. Rates are US$14 a single, US$18 a double. The recently remodelled Restaurant El Unicorno is in the same building, off the lobby.

Hotel Fray Bartolomé de las Casas (☎ (967) 8-09-32), Niños Héroes 2, across from the Pemex station at the corner of Insurgentes, two blocks south of the main plaza, is one of the most characterful places in this range. It's a fine old house with a lovely pillared courtyard (used for parking). The 27 clean, well-kept, quite big singles/doubles with private bath are priced at US$13/17. The hotel has its own little café for breakfast.

A block further up Insurgentes at the corner of Cuauhtémoc, the *Hotel Posada San Cristóbal* (no phone), Insurgentes 3, is another wonderfully atmospheric hostelry. The airy old rooms each have two double beds with reading lights on the walls above them, and showers obviously added on recently. Wrought-iron tables and chairs are set around a fountain in the courtyard, beautified with lots of potted plants. The tidy little Restaurant Kukulcán is part of the hotel. Rooms go for US$13 a single, US$18 a double.

Hotel Palacio de Moctezuma (☎ (967) 8-03-52, 8-11-42), Juárez 16, corner of León, three blocks south-east of the main plaza, is another pleasant place with flowery courtyards, but more modern than most. The 38 clean but small rooms are priced at US$20 a single, US$24 a double. The hotel has its own restaurant, bar, and car park.

Hotel San Martín (☎ (967) 8-05-33), Real de Guadalupe 16, half a block east of the main plaza just beyond the Hotel Real del Valle, has a neat slot-like courtyard with tiers of rooms rising above. A little comedor (dining room) occupies the centre of the court. The 27 rooms are tidy, clean and convenient if spartan, and priced reasonably at US$12 a single, US$14 a double, US$16 a triple.

The *Hotel Mansión del Valle* (☎ (967) 8-25-82/83; fax 8-25-81), Diego de Mazariegos 39, 3½ blocks west of the main plaza, is an old house renovated and updated with three tiers of rooms that are very quiet except for the occasional burst of activity from the school next door. The comfortable rooms come with two double beds, TV, shower with doors, and indigenous weavings to decorate the walls. It's nice, and the person who sets the rates knows it: US$25 a single, US$32 a double.

Not too far north of the Cristóbal Colón bus station, the *Hotel Capri* (☎ (967) 8-00-15, 8-31-18)), Insurgentes 54, has modern, clean, quite bright and fairly quiet rooms round a narrow but flowery courtyard for US$14 a single, US$19 a double, but a bit of haggling does wonders for the price. This is the place to go if you arrive exhausted late in the day, or if you must get up early to catch an early bus onward. The restaurant on the upper floor offers a good five-course comida corrida for US$4.50.

Places to Stay – top end

San Cristóbal's top-end place is not all that much fancier nor higher priced than some of the middle-range hotels. The *Hotel Posada Diego de Mazariegos* (☎ (967) 8-18-25, 8-05-13), 5 de Febrero 1 at Utrilla, is just over a block north of the plaza; 5 de Febrero changes names here and is called Adelina Flores east of the corner. The hotel's 80 charming rooms and suites are the best in town, outspokenly but not oppressively colonial but with modern bathrooms. The posada has the services you'd expect of the best hotel in town: good restaurant (named El Patio), cosy bar, solarium, travel agency, rental car desk, car park, and souvenir shop. Prices for all this are quite reasonable at US$27 a single, US$36 a double. The hotel occupies two buildings on the same corner, and some rooms are much larger than others, so ask to see several before you decide.

Places to Eat

San Cristóbal's popularity among foreign travellers has spawned a large number and variety of restaurants. Among them are numerous places serving natural foods such as wholemeal bread and vegetarian fare. Though the town's restaurants put on a façade of worldly sophistication, this is certainly not Mexico City, or even Mérida. Even though you may encounter slow service and the occasional dull meal, eating in San Cristóbal is usually enjoyable.

Two streets, Madero and Insurgentes, hold many restaurants. The quickest way to acquaint yourself with what the town has to offer is to stroll along them, peering into doorways and examining menus.

On Calle Madero Calle Madero, heading east from the plaza, is the first place to explore. It holds no fewer than 10 eating establishments which can provide breakfast, lunch, dinner, coffee and snacks.

Restaurant El Faisán at Madero 2, just off the main plaza and opposite the Restaurante Tuluc, used to be a cheap hangout where you could make a lemon tea last for several games of chess. Now it's glassed-in and tarted up but still friendly, though the food is high priced. Humble quesadillas cost almost US$3, and the US$5 comida corrida is pretty sparse. Note that they add the 15% IVA (VAT) to your bill when it's totalled, raising prices even more.

Next door, the *Restaurant Los Arcos* has prices lower by up to 30%. The daily comida corrida at US$3.50 to US$4 is well worth the money. You can choose your dessert at the *dulcería* (sweet shop) next door to Los Arcos.

The pine-clad interior of the *Restaurant Flamingo* (☎ 8-13-12), Madero 7, is charmed by soft lights and soft music in the evening. The booths and chairs fill with a mixed crowd come to enjoy sandwiches for US$1.50, plates of spaghetti for US$2.25, and meat dishes for US$3 to US$4. A real espresso machine provides after dinner cappuccino. This Flamingo gets up early, opening at 6 am for breakfast, closing at 10 pm.

Restaurant Fulano's, next along Madero, also has good prices and a menu printed in both English and French. The daily comida corrida might be something like vegetable soup or beef in a pastry crust followed by fish fillet or *puntas de filete* of beef, with dessert and coffee, for US$4. Most substantial meat plates cost about US$4.50.

On Insurgentes *Cafetería & Lonchería Palenque*, Insurgentes 40, is tidy, good, cheap, and only 1½ blocks north of the Cristóbal Colón bus station. They serve the local equivalent of a Big Mac, called a *hamburguesa con queso y doble carne* for US$1.50; other sandwiches are cheaper. A plate of *bistec a la Mexicana* with fried potatoes costs only US$2.25. Hours are long: 8 am to 10.30 daily.

Restaurant La Mansión del Fraile, on Insurgents at the corner of Flores one block south of the plaza, has high-beamed ceilings and bits of tile roofing here and there to give it a colonial mountain town ambience. All three meals are served every day of the week. For breakfast, try a *huarache*, literally a 'sandal', an oblong tortilla spread with various toppings, the Mayan version of a breakfast pizza. For lunch various enchiladas, tacos, sandwiches and soups are served, and a full meal might come to US$4 to US$6. Dinner is more substantial, as is its price of US$6 to US$8.

Among restaurants in San Cristóbal, the little *Restaurante Tuluc* (☎ 8-20-90) comes high on most people's list. It's at Madero 9, 1½ blocks south of the main plaza, and uses herbs as well as anywhere in Mexico. Roquefort salad is a delight – a plate of very lightly boiled potatoes, beetroot and carrots, with fresh tomato and Roquefort cheese on top. The French onion soup comes with real Parmesan, parsley and other herbs in seemingly bottomless bowls, and the *filete Tuluc* is a steak wrapped in bacon and stuffed with cheese and green vegetables. Breakfast can be the Americano of juice, toast, bacon, eggs and coffee for US$2.50; it's served from 6.15 am. The daily comida corrida is an indisputable bargain: 'vanilla foam' as an appetiser, then carrot soup, *albóndigas pibil* (meatballs marinated and baked) or fish fillet with Hollandaise sauce, and dessert with coffee, all for US$4.

For excellent pizza go to the *Restaurant El Unicorno* at Insurgentes 33A, next to the Hotel D'Mónica. Pizza prices here range from US$5 to US$8 but feed two people. Sunday there's paella (US$6), and any lunchtime you can order an avocado stuffed with tuna for US$3.50. Steaks are a speciality. Cocktails are served.

Restaurant Capri, on the east side of Insurgentes at Niños Héroes/León opposite the Hotel Fray Bartolomé de las Casas, is a spruced-up lonchería good for decently priced snacks such as guacamole or *platanos fritos* (fried bananas) for US$1 to US$2, but they do serve more substantial fare like chicken and chips or *filete miñón* for US$3.50 to US$4.50.

Restaurant & Panadería Madre Tierra

(Mother Earth), Insurgentes at Hermanos Domínguez, across from the San Francisco Church and Conasuper San Francisco, 2½ blocks south of the plaza, is a haven of good, healthy food and friendly service in pleasant surroundings. Locally woven cloth covers the tables, and music (traditional Indian, classical, jazz, soft folk or reggae) fills the air. At breakfast you'll smell – and you must taste – the fresh bread. It will also be served with your 'lasagna' (US$4), beef and chopped vegetables in a bowl beneath a crust of noodles and cheese. Wholemeal sandwiches, pizzas and lots of salads (beetroot and parsley, brown rice, pineapple and green pepper) fill out the menu. An espresso machine provides fragrant coffee. Hours are 8 am to 9.30 pm. The bakery is open for purchases from 9 am to 8 pm (Sunday 9 am to 2 pm).

On Primero de Marzo You'll see the street name written as '1° de Marzo', but it's pronounced 'Primero de Marzo', and it harbours several good eating places. Most are close to the intersection with 20 (Veinte) de Noviembre.

Restaurant El Teatro (☎ 8-31-49), Primero de Marzo 8, on the upper floor, is among the few top ranking restaurants in town. The menu, based on French and Italian cuisine, lists chateaubriand, crepes, fresh pasta, *el mejor filete de San Cristóbal* (the best beef fillet in San Cristóbal), and pizzas baked in a wood-fired oven. At lunch, enjoy the view of the town from the windows; candlelit tables and soft music set the mood at dinner. There's live music on Friday and Saturday evenings. Expect to spend US$6 to US$9 for a full dinner here. El Teatro is open from 11 am to 11 pm daily.

Restaurant El Trigal, Primero de Marzo 13-B, just off 20 de Noviembre two blocks north of the plaza, is a simple, mainly vegetarian restaurant. A sample comida corrida (US$3.25) is vegetable soup, brown rice, potato tacos filled with soya meat, fruit salad with cream and a melon licuado.

La Boutique del Pan, Primero de Marzo 5, west off 20 de Noviembre two blocks from the plaza, is the San Cristóbal branch of that delicious-looking bakery/pastry shop in Tuxtla Gutiérrez. Come here to buy snacks, do-it-yourself breakfasts or picnic supplies.

Elsewhere San Cristóbal has a Chinese restaurant, the *Restaurant Shanghai* (or Chang-Gai), Diego de Mazariegos 35 at Matamoros, three blocks west of the plaza. The popular favourites are all on the menu, including wonton soup, fried wonton, chow mein and chop suey (including a vegetarian version). Price for a full meal would be US$6 to US$9. Bits of Chinese restaurant decor put you in the mood for this culinary change of pace.

Café-Restaurant La Galería (☎ 8-15-47) upstairs at Hidalgo 3, a few doors south of the main plaza, has perhaps the most restful ambience in town with its soft New Age music wafting through the wonderful green courtyard of a house built in 1540 and once inhabited by Francisco de Montejo. This meeting-place has English magazines and chess to pass the time. Breakfast can be standard items such as hotcakes or a fruit salad for less than US$2; at lunch choose from four complicated, filling salads or have *chilaquiles* with cheese for less than US$3, or the US$5 comida corrida. Interesting dinner specials (chicken in peanut sauce, chicken baked with honey and soy sauce) go for US$5. Hours are 9 am to 9 pm.

Cafetería El Mural, Crescencio Rosas 4, half a block south of Diego de Mazariegos has crepes as its speciality. Try banana and rompope (US$2). There are plenty of succulent cakes too, including superbly gooey lemon meringue pie. Mint and cinnamon tea are available, and the *licuado de frutas revueltas con leche* is a treat (ask for it, it's not on the menu). El Mural is open from 9 am until 10 or 11 pm Monday to Saturday (later than most places in San Cristóbal), 5 to 10 pm Sunday, and has a bookstall and newspapers to read.

The *Casa de Huéspedes Margarita* at Real de Guadalupe 34 has a popular little restaurant serving everything from Mexican standards to egg breakfasts and oat porridge *(avena)*, yoghurt *(leche bulgara)*, pan integral and peanut butter *(crema de cacahuate)*. It's open until 10.30 pm.

Restaurant El Bazar, Paniagua 2, a half block east of Utrilla and three blocks north of the plaza, is an open-air place inside the building marked 'Plaza San Cristóbal'. They have over a page of breakfast ideas including yoghurt, granola, fruit and honey for US$1.75, plus typical Mexican dishes at US$2 to US$4 and about 20 types of coffee – some with liqueurs. More substantial meals are served as well. It's open from 8 am to 11 pm daily.

Restaurant El Conquistador, Adelina Flores 2, in the Hotel Posada Diego de Mazariegos, is the high-status place to dine. Food and service are good, prices quite moderate for what you get, and the surroundings are a bit of old San Cristóbal. A full lunch or dinner ranges in price from US$8 to US$12, all inclusive.

Entertainment

San Cristóbal's an early-to-bed town, and conversation in cafés, restaurants or rooms will occupy many of your evenings.

Otherwise, there are regular musical and theatrical performances at the Casa de Cultura/Bellas Artes at the corner of Hidalgo and Hermanos Domínguez. La Galería and El Bazar cafés sometimes have live music in the evenings. The *Hotel D'Mónica* restaurant at Insurgentes 33 has Latin American music on Friday nights. There are two discos – the Crystal and the Princess – down near the Pan American Highway (to the left (east) from the southern end of Insurgentes). Entry to either costs US$3; Friday, Saturday and Sunday are the busy nights.

Things to Buy

San Cristóbal's market is between Utrilla and Belisario Domínguez, eight blocks north of the main plaza. It has indoor and open-air sections. Many of the traders are Indian villagers, and fresh food is the main stock-in-trade. One local speciality is cream cheese. The mercado functions daily except

Sunday, when markets are held in outlying villages.

Chiapas' Indian crafts are justifiably famous and there are now hosts of shops in San Cristóbal selling them. The heaviest concentrations are along Calle Real de Guadalupe (where prices go down as you go away from the main plaza) and Utrilla (towards the market end). Other places to look include the shop beneath La Galería at Hidalgo 3, and the Plaza San Cristóbal on Paniagua between Utrilla and Belisario Domínguez.

Textiles – huipiles, rebozos, blankets – are the outstanding items, for Tzotzil weavers are some of the most skilled and inventive in Mexico. To see the very best and compare the styles of different villages (and get an idea of prices), go to either of the Sna Jolobil weaving cooperative shops (see the Sna Jolobil section). Indian women also sell textiles in the plaza around Santo Domingo.

You'll also find some Guatemalan Indian textiles and plenty of the appealing and inexpensive pottery from Amatenango del Valle (animals, pots, jugs, etc) in San Cristóbal. Leather is another local speciality.

Always bargain unless prices are labelled (though there's no harm in trying even then), and don't imagine that apparently meek Indians are any softer than anyone else when it comes to haggling.

Getting There & Away

Air San Cristóbal has an airport, south of the Pan American Highway, but at the time of writing it was out of use. There are plans, however, to form a pilots' cooperative to start flying charters again to Tuxtla Gutiérrez, Palenque, Yaxchilán, Bonampak, etc. A few charters, which can be booked in San Cristóbal, operate from the airstrips at Ocosingo (see that section), Comitán and Las Margaritas, 17 km east of Comitán (see the Tours section under Getting Around).

Bus First-class buses to and from San Cristóbal aren't as frequent as you might hope; wherever you're coming from or going to, even Oaxaca, book ahead. A reminder:

'local' on the schedules means the bus originates here, and ticket-sellers can assure you a seat if you buy your ticket early enough. 'De paso' means the bus originates somewhere else, and may or may not have seats available when it stops here.

Omnibus Cristóbal Colón (1st class, ☎ (967) 8-02-91) is at the junction of Insurgentes and the Pan American Highway. Ticket windows are open from 6 am to 9 pm. All 1st-class buses listed below are by Cristóbal Colón.

Autotransportes Tuxtla Gutiérrez (2nd class, ☎ (967) 8-05-04), on Allende half a block north of the Pan American Highway, has the only buses to the Agua Azul junction (four km from the falls) and Palenque. All 2nd-class buses below are by Autotransportes Tuxtla Gutiérrez unless otherwise noted.

Autotransportes Lacandonia (☎ (967) 8-14-55), Pino Suárez 11-A, on the highway between Hidalgo and Crescencio Rosas two blocks west of the Cristóbal Colón terminal, specialises in 2nd-class buses to Ocosingo and Palenque, but has buses to Villahermosa and Mérida as well.

Here are distances, times and prices from San Cristóbal:

Agua Azul – 138 km, 4½ hours; only 2nd-class buses (US$2.75) going to Palenque (see below) stop here

Ciudad Cuauhtémoc (Guatemalan border) – 170 km, three hours; three 1st class (US$3.25) at 6.45 am (local), 9.30 am and 1.45 pm (de paso). You really should take the 6.45 am bus so you can make it to Huehuetenango or farther by nightfall; buy your ticket at least a day in advance.

Comitán – 83 km, 1½ hours; 10 1st class (US$1.75), all de paso. One 2nd class (US$1.50) at 1.30 pm

Mérida – 746 km, 15 hours; one evening 2nd-class bus (US$13) by Autotransportes Lacandonia.

Mexico City – 1085 km, 21 hours; three 1st class (US$22); the locales depart at 2 pm (via Puebla) and at 6.30 pm (via Córdoba)

Oaxaca – 718 km, 12 hours; one 1st class (US$12) at 4.45 pm

Ocosingo – 108 km, three hours; 2nd-class ATG buses (US$1.75) going to Yajalon or Palenque (see below) stop here; the 5.30 pm bus terminates at Ocosingo. Autotransportes Lacandonia runs frequent buses (17 a day) at the same 2nd class fare.

Palenque – 190 km, 5½ hours; five 2nd-class ATG (US$3.50). The 6 am ATG bus is by reservation; plan to take this one, and buy your ticket a day in advance. The 12.30 pm ATG bus is by reservation as well; the other three buses are de paso. Autotransportes Lacandonia runs six buses daily to Palenque at the same fare.

Tapachula (via Arriaga) – 541 km, nine hours; one 1st class (US$9) at 8 am. Three 2nd class (US$2). Buses to Tapachula all take the Tuxtla Gutiérrez-Arriaga route. For the other route, via Ciudad Cuauhtémoc, Motozintla and Huixtla, you have to change buses at least once, probably twice or more, and are unlikely to save time.

Tuxtla Gutiérrez – 85 km, two hours; 13 1st class (US$1.75); locales depart at 6.30, 7.20 and 8 am, the rest of the buses throughout the day (until 8.30 pm) are de paso. Nineteen 2nd class (US$1.50).

Villahermosa – 308 km, eight hours; one 1st class (US$6) at 10 am. One 2nd class (US$5.75) by Autotransportes Lacandonia.

Getting Around

For buses to the Indian villages near San Cristóbal, see the Around San Cristóbal section. Taxis are fairly plentiful – one stand is on the north side of the main plaza.

Car Rental Rental cars are in high demand and short supply in San Cristóbal, which means prices are high and waiting lists often long. There's just one international agency in town – Budget (☎ (967) 8-05-13, 8-06-21) in the Hotel Posada Diego de Mazariegos at the corner of Utrilla and Flores. For other companies you must contact their offices in Tuxtla Gutiérrez.

Horse *Casa de Huéspedes Margarita* at Real de Guadalupe 34 offers guided rides to Chamula or the Grutas de San Cristóbal for US$18 (book the previous day), but it's also possible to hire your own nag for less from the stables used by the Margarita. The stables are somewhere down near the Pan American Highway at the west end of town. José Hernández (☎ 8-10-65) at Elías Calles 10, in the north-east of the town off Huixtla just north of Chiapa de Corzo, also advertises horses for hire. Check with the tourist office for current availability.

Tours A lady named Mercedes conducts walking tours of San Cristóbal in English and Spanish every day beginning at 9 am by the kiosk in the centre of the main plaza. Be sure to ask the price before you start. Posetur (☎ (967) 8-07-25/28; fax 8-08-27), 5 de Febrero 1 in the Hotel Posada Diego de Mazariegos, also offers tours of the town and of sights in the region.

A few travel agencies in San Cristóbal offer tours to nearby Tzotzil villages or the remote Mayan sites like Yaxchilán and Bonampak. The local village tours don't usually go anywhere you can't reach by ordinary bus, but if you're planning a long or hectic itinerary round several villages, an agency might be able to arrange a special trip. Try Agencia de Viajes las Casas (☎ 8-27-27) at Real de Guadalupe or the others mentioned below – though car rental is probably a better bet.

Making your own way to remote, jungle-bound Yaxchilán, Bonampak or Lacandón Indian settlements is an infinitely less practical proposition. There's a frequently impassable road from Palenque to Bonampak – but according to Hilary Bradt & Rob Rachowiecki's guide *Backpacking in Mexico & Central America* you can take a 10-day walk from Montebello Lakes to this road at certain times of year. However, most people either fly in or take escorted river-road-foot tours. Both the latter choices can be arranged in San Cristóbal and they're only marginally dearer than from Palenque.

Viajes Pakal (☎ 8-28-18/19) at the corner of Hidalgo and Cuauhtémoc, and Amfitriones Turísticos in the Hotel Posada Diego de Mazariegos, both offer the day-trip flight option. Pakal gives you two hours at Yaxchilán and 1½ hours at Bonampak; prices range from US$125 per person, with five in the party, up to US$165 each if there are only two. The flights go from Las Margaritas near Comitán if the San Cristóbal airport is out of action.

Amfitriones supposedly gives you 30 minutes less at Bonampak and 30 minutes more at Yaxchilán, for US$97 per head (minimum four people), and its flights go from Comitán. In both cases transport to and from the airfield is included.

For air tours to Bonampak and Yaxchilán from Ocosingo by Taxis Aereos Ocosingo, telephone 8-25-74 in San Cristóbal.

Pakal in San Cristóbal also offers a two-day trip starting from Palenque for US$125 per person (five or six people), US$155 each (three or four), US$245 each (one or two). The itinerary: travel from Palenque to the Lacandón settlement of Caribal Lacanjá by car, take a two-hour walk to Bonampak (stay 1½ to two hours), walk back to Caribal Lacanjá and sleep in a Lacandón house. Next morning, travel by car to Frontera Echeverría, then a boat along the Rio Usumacinta to Yaxchilán (stay three hours), and finally return to Palenque by boat and car.

Onward to Comitán

A scenic 1½-hour, 83 km drive south-east along the Pan American Highway (Highway 190) from San Cristóbal brings you to Comitán. The highway passes through pine forests rooted in red earth and peopled with woodcutters. The men of Teopisca, a town along the way, cut wood in a forest near Tulanca, 12 km past their town, and ride their loads downhill on little freewheeling carts for almost that entire distance. The women who cut wood in the same forest seem to eschew this flashy and perhaps perilous means of transport, continuing instead to hump it on their backs for the long distance.

AROUND SAN CRISTÓBAL

Unlike in the muggy, hot lowlands of Tabasco and Yucatán, it's a pleasure to walk or make combined walking-bussing excursions to sites outside San Cristóbal in the cool, fresh mountain air. Several features of natural beauty make good destinations for excursions, and the many nearby villages allow you to visit the present day Maya.

Of Chiapas' approximately 2.5 million people, an estimated 20% – 500,000 – are Indians, the pure-blooded successors of the Maya and others who were here before the Spanish came. The Indians of highland

Chiapas are among Mexico's most traditional, with some distinctly pre-Hispanic elements in their nominally Catholic religious life, for whom Spanish is very much a second language.

Along with highland Guatemala, Chiapas is among the best places to explore the fascinating traditional life of today's Mayan peoples. A visit to San Cristóbal gives you the opportunity to do this by using the city as your base and making excursions – on foot, on horseback, by bus, car or tour – into the hinterland to meet the Maya. The best day to go is on Sunday, when churches are open and markets in progress. On other days there may be little to see.

Highest Point in Chiapas

Cerro Tzontehuitz, 10 km north-east of the town, is the highest point in the Chiapas Highlands at 2900 metres. Mountain hikers take note.

El Arcotete

Seven km east of town, the natural limestone arch called El Arcotete spans the Río Quinta in pleasant country. Follow Madero east from the town centre and continue along the Tenejapa road. About 4.5 km from the town centre a sign points to El Arcotete down a dirt road. From the end of the road a path leads a further quarter km to the site, a popular spot for an outing.

Grutas de San Cristóbal

Amateur spelunkers will want to visit this huge, long cavern nine km south-east of San Cristóbal. The gruta's first 350 metres are quite narrow but paved and lit; the entire cavern is thought to be about 3.5 km long. You can enter it for US$0.60 from 9 am to 5 pm daily, and though the cave itself doesn't take long to visit, there are some walking trails in the lovely country beyond. Take a Comitán bus and ask for las grutas (US$0.50). The half-km track to the cave leads south from the Pan American Highway about 10 minutes out of town. Alternatively, you can go on horseback (see the Getting Around section).

To Palenque
Tila (Chol)
Tumbaló (Chol)
Agua Azul
To Pichucalco & Villahermosa
Huitiupón (Tzotzil)
Yajalón (Tzeltal)
Simojovel (Tzotzil)
199
Chilón (Tzeltal)
195
El Bosque (Tzotzil)
Jitotol
Bachajón (Tzeltal)
Temo
Bochil (Tzotzil)
Chalchihuitán (Tzotzil)
Pantelhó (Tzotzil)
195
Santa Magdalena (Tzotzil)
Cancuc (Tzeltal)
Ocosingo
Toniná
Soyaló (Tzotzil)
San Andrés Larrainzar (Tzotzil)
San Pedro Chenalhó (Tzotzil)
Ixtapa (Tzotzil)
Mitontic (Tzotzil)
San Juan Chamula (Tzotzil)
Tenejapa (Tzeltal)
Oxchuc (Tzeltal)
Abasolo (Tzeltal)
Zinacantón (Tzotzil)
Tzontehuitz 2900 m
199
Altamirano
To Chiapa de Corzo & Tuxtla Gutiérrez
190
El Arcotete
Huixtán (Tzotzil)
Chanal (Tzeltal)
San Cristóbal de las Casas
Ecatepec 2750 m
Grutas de San Cristóbal
190
Amatenango del Valle (Tzeltal)
Chiapas Highlands
Villa de Chiapilla
Teopisca
0   10   20 km
To Las Rosas & Venustiano Carranza
To Comitán

Indian Culture

In the traditional Mayan villages of Chiapas and highland Guatemala, men hold the community leadership positions, often in the form of traditional *cargos* or temporary posts which bring prestige but cost a lot, making it very difficult for individuals to accumulate wealth. Senior cargo-holders among the Tzotzil are called *mayordomos* and are responsible for the care of saints' images in the churches. These saints are often identified with pre-Hispanic deities, and their saint's days are marked by important ceremonies. The cargo of an *alférez* (plural *alfereces*) involves organising and paying for these fiestas. Of lower rank are the *capitanes*, whose job is to dance and ride horses at fiestas. *Principales* are men who have carried out important cargos and entered the ranks of 'village elders'. Among the most important festivals are those of the patron saint of each village, Carnival, Semana Santa, the Day of the Dead (2 November) and the day of the Virgin of Guadalupe (12 December).

Women are generally restricted to domestic work, including weaving. In some cases increased sales of textiles have recently enabled them to bring in cash and improve their status.

Indians come into San Cristóbal mainly to buy and sell. They keep their distance from the mestizo population, the result of centuries of exploitation at Spanish hands and treatment as second-class citizens – a state of affairs which even today is changing only slowly. Though shy, Indians can also be friendly and humorous once they get talking, and they can be hard bargainers if you're trying to buy something. Above all, they have a quiet dignity which contributes much to the villages' atmosphere.

Not surprisingly, some Indians remain suspicious of outsiders, and are resentful of any interference in their lives – especially in their religious practices. Many particularly dislike having their photos taken, so ask if you're in any doubt. A tale circulating for some years goes that two tourists were killed for taking photos in the church at Chamula. Whether or not it's true, it's certainly an indication of the hostility that can be aroused by insensitivity to local ways.

Spanish is no more than a second language to the Indians and in some villages only a few people speak it. Market day in most villages is Sunday; proceedings start very early and wind down by lunch time. You can find basic accommodation in some villages.

Here is a quick look at some of the more important indigenous groups living in Chiapas.

Indigenous Peoples

Choles Around 80,000 Choles live in the villages of Tumbalá, Tila and Salto de Agua near Palenque, with a further 20,000 or so in neighbouring Tabasco. Many Choles have to leave their homes to work in towns for at least part of the year. The Corpus Christi Festival in June brings thousands of people to honour the Black Christ image in the church at Tila.

Lacandones For centuries the Lacandones were Mexico's most untouched Indian people, the last true inheritors of ancient Maya traditions living deep in the eastern

Lacandonian man

Chiapas rainforest, called La Selva Lacandona. The past four decades have wrought more changes in their way of life than the previous four centuries: 100,000 land-hungry settlers have arrived in the selva, and North American missionaries have succeeded in converting some Lacandones to Christianity. With these newcomers have arrived radios, watches, aeroplanes – and death. Diseases brought by these outsiders cut into Lacandón numbers until they were in danger of extinction. Today only 300 to 400 Lacandones remain, but the population has not declined for the past 20 years or so.

Tojolabals Around 25,000 Tojolabals – also called Chañabals – live in south-east Chiapas in the Comitán/Las Margaritas/Itamirano area, which includes tropical forest, dry plains and cool highlands. They pay homage to the Christian god as well as to the sun as creator and protector (represented by fire), and to the moon, which rules life and agriculture and is associated with water.

Tzotzils Most of the Indians round San Cristóbal are Tzotzil but like the Tzeltals they are strongly differentiated from place to place. You'll notice this most obviously in their strikingly different costumes: for instance men from Zinacantán wear pink while those of Chamula go for woolly black or white tunics. Tzotzil textiles are among the most varied, colourful and elaborately worked in Mexico.

The total Tzotzil population is around 140,000 and their homeland stretches from Venustiano Carranza in the south to Simojovel in the north, with San Cristóbal roughly in the middle. Some have moved to the Selva Lacandona in search of land. They guard their traditions fiercely; approach them with respect.

Tzeltals After the Tzotzils, the 220,000-strong Tzeltals are the Indian group that travellers are most likely to encounter in Chiapas. They inhabit the region east, north-east and south-east of San Cristóbal. Amatenango del Valle, Aguacatenango, Tenejapa, Cancuc, Oxchuc, Abasolo, Bachajón, Chilón and Yajalón are all Tzeltal villages. Some Tzeltals also live in Ocosingo and in the Selva Lacandona. Each village has its own strong identity and Tzeltals tend to regard themselves primarily as citizens of a particular village. Thanks partly to their large numbers, tradition is strong among the Tzeltals.

San Juan Chamula

The Chamulans have always defended their independence fiercely: they put up strong resistance to the Spanish in 1524 and launched a famous rebellion in 1869. Today they are one of the most numerous of the Tzotzil groups – 40,000-strong – and their village 10 km north-west of San Cristóbal is the centre for some pre-Christian religious practices. Cameras are forbidden in the church and at festivals.

A sign on the church door tells visitors to ask at the 'tourist office', also on the plaza, for permission to enter. People stand or kneel on the ground amid thick clouds of incense, sometimes chanting rhythmically, their faces to the floor. Candles, often hundreds of them, seem to burn incessantly. The floor may be carpeted with pine branches, and saints' images are surrounded with mirrors and dressed in sacred garments.

The Chamulans believe that Christ rose from the cross to become the sun. Christian festivals are interwoven with older ones: the pre-Lent Carnival celebrations, which are among the most important and last several days in February or March, also mark the five 'lost' days *(uayeb)* of the ancient Mayan Long Count calendar (see Facts about the Region under The Vague Year).

Apart from Carnival, local festivals include ceremonies for San Sebastián (mid to late January); Semana Santa; San Juan, the village's patron saint (22 to 25 June); and the annual change of cargo (30 December to 1 January).

On some of these occasions a strong alcoholic brew called *posh* is drunk and you may see groups of men, carrying flags and in ceremonial attire, moving slowly round in tight, chanting circles. At Carnival troops of strolling minstrels wander the roads strumming guitars and wearing sunglasses (even when it's raining) and pointed 'wizard' hats.

More usually, men wear white tunics; those holding cargos have black ones. Chamula women make many of the wool skirts which are worn by women of other villages as well as themselves.

Zinacantán

This Tzotzil village of 15,000 is 11 km north-west of San Cristóbal. The road to it forks left off the Chamula road, then down into the valley where the village lies. It has two churches. Like the Chamulans, the people here are particularly sensitive about photographs; make sure you ask the village authorities if you want to take any.

The men wear very distinctive red-and-white striped tunics (which appear pink), and flat, round, beribboned palm hats. Unmarried men's hats have longer, wider ribbons. Zinacantán isn't a major market centre like Chamula because the market is usually held only at fiesta times. The most important celebrations are for the patron saint, San

Lorenzo, between 8 and 11 August, and for San Sebastián in January.

You'll probably notice many crosses dotting the Zinacantán countryside. These usually mark entrances to the abodes of the important ancestor gods or of the Señor de la Tierra (Earth Lord), all of whom have to be kept happy with offerings at the appropriate times.

In addition to the temporary cargo-holders, there are groups of people with more permanent prestige, like the *sacristanes*, who teach the sacred incantations to mayordomos, and the *músicos*, who preserve the knowledge of the duties of alfereces.

Tenejapa

A quite busy market fills the main street (round behind the church) early on Sunday mornings in this Tzeltal village 28 km northeast of San Cristóbal. The village is set by a river in a pretty valley. More interesting than what's on sale in the market are the people's costumes, particularly those of the village authorities, who wear wide, colourfully beribboned hats and chains of silver coins round their necks. The women wear brightly brocaded or embroidered huipiles. According to tradition they were taught to brocade by women from Larráinzar and Chenalhó after several Tenejapanecas dreamt that Santa Lucía, the patron saint of weavers, asked them to make her a brocade costume.

Tenejapa has a few comedores in the main street and one basic posada, the *Hotel Molina*, which is not always open. The main festival is for the village's patron saint, San Ildefonso, on 23 January.

Amatenango del Valle

The women of this Tzeltal village, 37 km from San Cristóbal down the Pan American Highway towards Comitán, are renowned potters. What's different about Amatenango pottery is that it's still fired by the pre-Hispanic method of burning a wood fire around the pieces, rather than putting them in a kiln. In addition to the pots, bowls, urns, jugs and plates that the village has turned out for generations, young girls in the last 15 years

or so have made *animalitos* (little animals) which find a ready market with tourists. These are small, appealing and cheap, but fragile.

If you visit the village, expect to be surrounded within minutes by girls selling pots. Persuade them to bring some better examples, as they'll try to get rid of their worst pieces first. Many of the better pieces are sold to shops in San Cristóbal.

The women wear white huipiles embroidered with red and yellow, wide red belts and blue skirts. Amatenango's patron saint, San Francisco, is feted on 4 October.

San Pedro Chenalhó

In another village beyond San Juan Chamula, the 1300 Tzotzils of San Pedro Chenalhó live in a valley with a stream running through it, 37 km north of San Cristóbal. Go to San Juan Chamula and then on up the same road for another 27 km. Chenalhó is 1500 metres high, which means quite a descent from Chamula.

There's a weekly Sunday market and though the bus from San Cristóbal takes about 2½ hours, one of Chenalhó's advantages is that it has at least three accommodation possibilities, making it a good destination if you want more than a day out of San Cristóbal. One is a pink house with green pillars, opposite a green house with pink trimmings, along the street which forks right at the three crosses as you enter the village. The same house also serves meals (eggs, rice and tortillas, US$1.50).

A second is Señora Consuelo Aguilar Gordillo's house, on the corner of the third street on the left along Avenida Central (the grandly named main street – don't fork right at the three crosses). Señora Gordillo charges about US$2.50 for a bed.

If neither of these places can take you, look up the friendly priest, Padre Miguel Chanteau, a Frenchman with a St Bernard dog who has been here since 1965. His house is immediately to the right of the church in the main square, and it has a dormitory where he says travellers can stay. If you get the chance to chat with Padre Chanteau, he's a fascinating source of information on the area. As well being the priest, he acts as the village pharmacist, and even brings parties of French schoolchildren over to Chenalhó.

Chenalhó men, if they haven't turned to Western styles, wear black tunics, leather belts, white trousers and sometimes ribboned hats. The main fiestas are for San Pedro (27 to 30 June), San Sebastián (16 to 22 January) and Carnival.

Huixtán

One of the main pre-Hispanic Tzotzil centres, Huixtán has a 16th-century church. The village is just to the left of the San Cristóbal-Ocosingo road, 32 km from San Cristóbal and 20 km from the turn-off from the Pan American Highway.

Huiztecan women wear attractive white shawls with delicate floral patterns. Some men still wear the village's characteristic extremely baggy white trousers, sometimes pulled up to the thighs and tied with a red belt, as well as wool tunics, embroidered cotton shirts and red-banded hats.

A number of mestizos also live in Huixtán. The patron saint is San Miguel Arcángel, whose day is celebrated in late September.

Getting There & Away

Bus Always double check schedules before leaving San Cristóbal. Transport schedules are designed to accommodate early-morning marketeers travelling from the villages into San Cristóbal early, and back home not too long thereafter. The last bus back to San Cristóbal often leaves a village surprisingly early in the day.

Buses and colectivos to the villages nearest to San Cristóbal leave from Utrilla, a block north of the town's market. They leave for San Juan Chamula and Zinacantán every 20 minutes or so and run up to 5 pm; the cost is US$0.40. They leave for Tenejapa hourly, take an hour to get there and cost US$1. Return services from Tenejapa start getting scarce after 12 noon.

From San Cristóbal to Amatenango del Valle, take a Comitán bus from the Autotransportes Tuxtla Gutiérrez terminal

down near the Pan American Highway. The fare is US$1.

Transportes Fray Bartolomé de las Casas is on the north side of town. Go along Utrilla past the market and the local village bus terminus, over a small bridge and round a corner. The station's on the right. From here there are buses to Ocosingo, San Andrés Larráinzar, Bochil, Chenalhó, Pantelhó, Cancuc, Yajalón, Oxchuc and Mesbiljá.

COMITÁN

Population 85,000

Comitán (altitude 1600 metres) is a pleasant enough town, but most visitors who come here are on their way to the Montebello Lakes or to Ciudad Cuauhtémoc, the border crossing point for Guatemala.

The first Spanish settlement in the area, San Cristóbal de los Llanos, was established in 1527. It was from Comitán that the Plan de Chiapas Libre, a successful campaign for Chiapas to be allowed to decide its own political future in the turbulent years following independence from Spain, was launched in 1823. Today the town is officially called Comitán de Domínguez, after Belisario Domínguez, a local doctor who was also a national senator during the presidency of Victoriano Huerta. Domínguez had the cheek to speak out in 1913 against Huerta's record of political murders and was himself murdered for his pains.

Comitán is a commercial centre for local maize, banana, forestry and livestock products.

Orientation

Comitán is set amid hills, so you'll find yourself walking up and down, up and down – with your gear. The 1st-class Cristóbal Colón bus station is out on the Pan American Highway, which passes through the western edge of the town, about 20 minutes' walk from the town centre. To reach the main plaza, turn left out of the bus station and along the highway, take the first right down a hill, then the sixth left (Avenida Central Sur) and go three blocks.

Autotransportes Tuxtla Gutiérrez (2nd

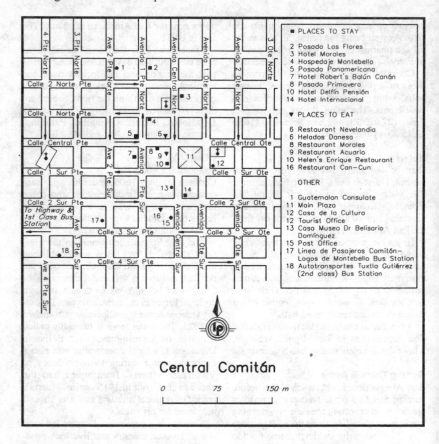

Central Comitán

0   75   150 m

class) is at the corner of Calle 4 Sur Pte and Avenida 3 Poniente Sur; for the main plaza go left out of the entrance on Calle 4 Sur Pte for 3½ blocks, and then three blocks to the left.

Buses for Lagos de Montebello go from Avenida 2 Poniente Sur between Calles 2 and 3 Sur Pte; from Cristóbal Colón follow the directions from there to the main plaza but take the fourth left (not the sixth) and go 1½ blocks. From ATG go 1½ blocks left and then turn left for another 1½ blocks.

The wide and attractive main plaza is bounded by Calle Central on its north side,

Avenida Central on the west, Calle 1 Sur on the south and Avenida 1 Ote on the east. The street numbering scheme resembles that of Tuxtla Gutiérrez in its complexity and confusion. The north-south streets are Avenidas, east-west are Calles. Avenida Central is also called Avenida Belisario Domínguez in honour of the town's most famous son.

Information

Tourist Office There's a tourist office (☎ (963) 2-00-26) in the Casa de la Cultura on the east side of the main plaza, open 8 am to 8 pm (Sunday 9 am to 2 pm) – maybe. The

Casa de la Cultura also has a small museum, an art gallery and an auditorium. The adjacent church, Santo Domingo, dates from the 16th century.

Bancomer is on the south side of the main plaza, Banamex is at the corner of Calle 2 Sur Ote and Avenida 1 Oriente Sur.

The post office (☎ (963) 2-04-27) is on Avenida Central Sur between Calles 2 and 3 Sur, 1½ blocks south of the main plaza; it's open Monday to Friday 8 am to 7 pm, Saturday 8 am to 1 pm. Comitán's postal code is 30000.

You can make long-distance and international telephone calls from the caseta at Avenida 1 Poniente Sur 2-C (corner of Calle Central Pte) or from either of the better hotels in town.

The Guatemalan Consulate (☎ (963) 2-26-69) is at Avenida 2 Poniente Nte 28, almost six blocks from the plaza; it's open 8 am to 2 pm and 3 to 5 pm Monday to Friday, 8 am to 2 pm Saturday, except on Mexican and Guatemalan holidays. You can stop here and pick up your Guatemalan tourist card (see Facts for the Visitor under Visas), which may save you a bit of time and hassle at the border.

Casa Museo Dr Belisario Domínguez

Streets and squares in towns all over Mexico are named after Dr Belisario Domínguez, the local boy who became famous. His story is heroic but sad. A local doctor known for helping the poor people of his native town, he went on to gain national respect for his medical expertise. As senator for Chiapas during the presidency (1911-13) of Francisco Madero, he took his beneficent cause to a national audience. Madero was assassinated in 1913, some say at the orders of his successor, Victoriano Huerta. Senator Domínguez arose in the senate and spoke out eloquently against Huerta's abuses of power. He became the victim of an assassin's bullet soon thereafter.

The Comitán home of the martyred senator at Avenida Central Sur 29, only a few steps south of the plaza, is now a museum, open from 10 am to 2 pm and from 5 to 7 pm Tuesday to Saturday, 9 am to 2 pm Sunday,

closed Monday. Admission costs US$0.15. A tour of the house provides fascinating insights into the medical practices and the life of the professional classes in turn-of-the-century Comitán.

Places to Stay

Comitán has quite a few hotels since a lot of people pass through en route to or from Guatemala. Most are within two blocks of the plaza.

Hotel Delfín Pensión (☎ (963) 2-00-23), Avenida Central on the west side of the main plaza, is one of the better-value places. Its spacious rooms have private baths (hot water intermittent) and those at the back are modern and overlook a leafy courtyard. Singles/doubles are US$9/13.

Hotel Morales (☎ (963) 2-04-36), Avenida Central Norte, 1½ blocks north of the main plaza, resembles an aircraft hangar with rooms perched round an upstairs walkway. Small singles/doubles with private bath but in need of paint are officially priced at US$12/15, but the management granted a 20% discount without any haggling whatsoever.

Comitán also has several cheap posadas with small, often dingy rooms, most of them OK for a night. *Posada Primavera*, Calle Central Pte 4, only a few steps west of the plaza, is the tidiest of three similar hostelries in this area. All charge US$5.25 per bed for rooms without bath and often without windows, arranged around courtyards. The others to look at are the *Hospedaje Montebello* (☎ (963) 2-17-70), Calle 1 Norte Pte 10, and the *Posada Panamericana*, at the corner of Calle Central Pte and Avenida 1 Poniente Nte. The Panamericana has some rooms with private bath; and the rooms upstairs at the back are on a balcony and get more breeze.

Posada Las Flores (☎ (963) 2-33-34), Avenida 1 Poniente Nte 15, half a block north of Calle 2 Norte, has rooms round a quiet courtyard; beds are rented for US$5.25 per person. The less comfortable *Posada San Miguel* right next door takes the overflow if Las Flores is full, and charges the same price.

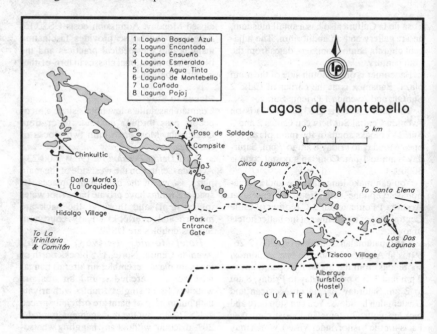

Lagos de Montebello

1 Laguna Bosque Azul
2 Laguna Encantada
3 Laguna Ensueño
4 Laguna Esmeralda
5 Laguna Agua Tinta
6 Laguna de Montebello
7 La Cañada
8 Laguna Pojoj

0   1   2 km

Cave
Paso de Soldado
Campsite
Chinkultic
Doña María's
(La Orquidea)
Cinco Lagunas
Hidalgo Village
To Santa Elena
To La Trinitaria & Comitán
Park Entrance Gate
Los Dos Lagunas
Tziscoo Village
Albergue Turístico (Hostel)
GUATEMALA

There are two more comfortable places in the central area. The *Hotel Internacional* (☎ (963) 2-01-10/12), Avenida Central Sur 16, a block south of the main plaza at the corner of Calle 2 Sur Ote, has clean, bright singles/doubles for US$13/16, plus its own restaurant. It's not what you'd call fancy, but it's pleasant enough.

Hotel Robert's Balún Canán (☎ (963) 2-10-94/95/99), Avenida 1 Poniente Sur 5 between Calle Central and Calle 1 Sur Pte, is the best place in town, a modern red brick and white stucco building with 37 rooms and one suite; all have private baths and colour TVs hooked up to a satellite dish antenna. Prints of Frederick Catherwood's 1844 drawings of Mayan ruins line the stairs. There's a comfy restaurant and bar, and the town's major discotheque. Rates are US$20 a single, US$26 a double.

Places to Eat

Several reasonable cafés line the west side of the main plaza. Prime among them is *Helen's Enrique Restaurant*, in front of the Hotel Delfín. With a porch and pretensions to decor, Helen's charges US$3 to US$5 for main-course platters. Too much? Food is a bit cheaper at the other eateries on this side of the plaza, the *Restaurant Acuario* and *Restaurant Yuly*, which share the portico with a video game den. Slow service is the rule at all these restaurants.

For more familiar fare, the *Restaurant Nevelandia* (☎ 2-00-95), Calle Central Pte at Avenida Central Nte, on the north-west corner of the main plaza, has liveried waiters, tablecloths, and a filling five-course comida corrida for US$5.50. Most meat or chicken dishes cost US$5 to US$7, but sandwiches and burgers are cheaper. *Helados Danesa* next door serves up good ice cream for dessert.

Restaurant Morales, Calle Central Pte 4 next to the Posada Primavera, is small, simple, tidy and cheap with main-course plates costing as little as US$2.50 to US$3.25.

Restaurant Can-Cun, Calle 2 Sur Ote, half a block west of Avenida Central Sur more or less across the street from the Hotel Internacional, is located in a vast and fairly dingy covered courtyard. The longish menu lists enchiladas for US$3, chicken for US$4.50, and meat dishes for US$4.75 to US$6.

For a more expensive meal amid international-style surroundings go to the Hotel Robert's Balún Canán, where *El Escocés Restaurant* is open until 11 pm and the *Grill Bar* until 1 am.

Getting There & Away

Comitán is 83 km down the Pan American Highway from San Cristóbal. The international border at Ciudad Cuauhtémoc is 87 km south of Comitán. It takes 1½ to two hours to either place by bus. For directions to the bus stations, see Orientation above.

Cristóbal Colón (1st class), on the Pan American Highway, and Autotransportes Tuxtla Gutiérrez (2nd class), Calle 4 Sur Pte 53 between Avenidas 3 and 4 Poniente Sur, are the most active bus companies here.

Ciudad Cuauhtémoc (Guatemalan border) – 87 km, 1½ hours; four 1st class (US$1.75) at 6, 8 and 11 am and 3 pm by Cristóbal Colón; 13 2nd class (US$1) by Autotransportes Tuxtla Gutiérrez

Mexico City – 1168 km, 22½ hours; one 1st class (US$24) by Cristóbal Colón

San Cristóbal de las Casas – 83 km, 1½ hours; 11 1st class (US$1.75) by Cristóbal Colón, and 14 2nd class (US$1.50) by Autotransportes Tuxtla Gutiérrez

Tuxtla Gutiérrez – 168 km, 3½ hours; 10 1st class (US$3) by Cristóbal Colón and hourly 2nd-class buses between 5 am and 9 pm (US$2.90) by Autotransportes Tuxtla Gutiérrez

LAGOS DE MONTEBELLO

The temperate forest along the Guatemalan border south-east of Comitán is dotted with about 60 small lakes – the Lagos or Lagunas de Montebello. The area is beautiful, refreshing, not hard to reach, quiet and eminently good for hiking. Some Mexican weekenders come down here in their cars, but the rest of the time you'll see nobody except the few resident villagers and a small handful of visitors. There are two very basic hostelries and a campground. And at one edge of the lake district are the rarely visited Mayan ruins of Chinkultic. What more could you ask for?

Getting There & Away

The paved road to Montebello turns east off the Pan American Highway 16 km south of Comitán, just before the town of La Trinitaria. Running first through flat ranch and ejido land, it passes the track to Chinkultic after 27 km, entering the forest and Montebello National Park five km further on. At the park entrance (no fee) the road splits. The paved section continues four km ahead to the Lagunas de Colores, where it ends at two small houses 50 metres from Laguna Bosque Azul. To the right from the park entrance a dirt road leads past tracks to several more lakes, then to the village and lake of Tziscao (nine km) and on to Los Dos Lagunas (14 km) before leaving the lake area for the village of Santa Elena (about 45 km) and beyond.

Buses and combis from Comitán to the lakes area depart from the terminal of Linea de Pasajeros Comitán-Lagos de Montebello on Avenida 2 Poniente Sur between Calles 2 and 3 Sur Pte. One or another form of transport leaves every hour or half-hour up to about 4 pm.

Vehicles have a number of different destinations so make sure you get one that's going your way. Most people head initially for Chinkultic, Doña María's (La Orquidea), Lagunas de Colores, Laguna de Montebello or Tziscao. Combi and bus fares are pretty well identical; it's US$1 to the Chinkultic turn-off, Doña Maria's or Lagunas de Colores, US$1.25 to Tziscao. By bus it's an hour to Doña María's, 1¾ hours to Tziscao. Combis are quicker.

Returning to Comitán, the last bus from Tziscao leaves about 3.30 pm, and the last combi from Lagunas de Colores at about the same time. Be sure to confirm this early in your wanderings.

There's a steady trickle of vehicles

through the lakes area, and hitching is possible. The many little-used vehicle tracks through the forest provide some excellent walks.

Chinkultic

These dramatically sited ruins lie two km along a track leading north off the La Trinitaria-Montebello road 27 km from the Pan American Highway at the village of Hidalgo. A sign, 'Chinkultic 3', marks the turning. Doña María at La Orquidea restaurant, half a km further along the road, has a map and book on Chinkultic (see Places to Stay) .

Chinkultic is on the extreme western edge of the ancient Mayan area, but is still regarded as a Mayan site. Dates carved by the Mayan inhabitants here extend from the equivalent of 591 to 897 AD – the last of which is nearly a century after the latest dates at Palenque, Yaxchilán and Toniná. These years no doubt span Chinkultic's peak period, but occupation is thought to have started in the late Pre-Classic (around 200 AD) period and continued until after 900. It was a sizable place – some 200 mounds are scattered over a wide area – but only a few parts have been cleared. These are well worth the effort.

The track from the road brings you first to a gate with a hut on the left. Here take the path to the left, which curves round to the right. On the overgrown hill to the right of this path stands one of Chinkultic's major structures, called simply E23. The path leads to a long ball court where several stelae lie on their sides under thatched shelters. Other stelae – some carved with Mayan-looking human figures – lie in the vicinity.

Follow the track back to the hut and turn left, passing what could be a car parking area, soon after which you can spot a few stone mounds in the undergrowth to the right. The hillside ahead of you shortly comes into full view and on it the partly restored temple called El Mirador. The path goes over a stream and steeply up to El Mirador, from which there are good views of the surrounding lakes and a smaller cenote.

The Lakes

Lagunas de Colores The paved road straight on from the park entrance leads through the Lagunas de Colores, so called because their colours range from turquoise to deep green. The first of these, on the right after about two km, is Laguna Agua Tinta. Then on the left come Laguna Esmeralda followed by Laguna Encantada, with Laguna Ensueño on the right opposite Encantada. The fifth and biggest of the Lagunas de Colores is Laguna Bosque Azul, on the left where the road ends. One of the two small houses here sells drinks and food, and there's a lakeside campsite.

Two paths lead on from the end of the road. Proceeding straight on for 800 metres brings you to the gruta – a cave shrine where locals make offerings to ward off illness and so on (take a torch with you). Taking the path to the left, you reach Paso de Soldado, a picnic site beside a small river after 300 metres. The track goes on; according to an old man who was sitting beside it, it reaches a village called Ojo de Agua after '1½ leagues'.

Laguna de Montebello About three km along the dirt road towards Tziscao (which turns right at the park entrance), a track leads 200 metres left to Laguna de Montebello. This is one of the bigger lakes, with a flat, open area along its shore where the track ends. About 150 metres to the left is a stony area which is better for swimming than the muddy fringes elsewhere.

Cinco Lagunas A further three km along the Tziscao road another track leads left to these 'five lakes'. Only four of them are visible from the road, but the second, La Cañada, on the right after about 1.5 km, is probably the most beautiful of all the Montebello Lakes – nearly bisected by two rocky outcrops. The track eventually reaches the village of San Antonio and, amazingly, is a bus route.

Laguna Pojoj A further km along the Tziscao road, a track to the left leads to this lake one km off the road.

Laguna Tziscao This comes into view on the right a further km along the road. Continue on to the junction for Tziscao village on the right. The village has pleasant grassy streets, friendly people and a hostel (see Places to Stay).

Beyond Tziscao

The road continues five km to Las Dos Lagunas on the edge of the national park, then on east to Santa Elena, a village about 30 km from Tziscao. Yet remoter villages lie north of Santa Elena; *Backpacking in Mexico & Central America* describes a 10-day hike through these villages and plenty of jungle to the Palenque-Bonampak road 45 km from Bonampak. Buses certainly go from Comitán to Santa Elena; trucks or buses may now go beyond it.

Places to Stay

Half a km past the Chinkultic turn-off, you can camp or rent a cabin at *La Orquidea*, a small restaurant on the left of the road. The owner is Señora María Domínguez de Castellanos, better known simply as Doña María, a remarkable woman who with help from Amnesty International bought a nearby farm and turned it over to Guatemalan refugees. She also has a map and book on Chinkultic. For the small cabins, which have electric light but no running water, you pay US$3.

Inside the national park, camping is officially allowed only at Laguna Bosque Azul, the last and biggest of the Lagunas de Colores, where the paved road ends. There are toilets and water here.

Tziscao village has a hostel – the *Albergue Turístico* – where you pay US$3 per person for a dormitory bunk or a wooden cabaña. You can also camp for US$1. The hostel lies on the shore of one of the most beautiful lakes and Guatemala is just a few hundred metres away. To reach the hostel, turn off the 'main road' and into the village. Just after you pass the small church on the hill to your right, turn right at the store on the corner and follow this track down towards the lake, where you go to the left. At the hostel you can rent a rowboat by the hour. The señora will cook up eggs, frijoles and tortillas (US$1.50) and there's a fridge full of refrescos, but if you want any variety in your diet, bring it with you. When I visited, the toilets were in bad need of a good clean.

THE GUATEMALAN BORDER

Despite its name, Ciudad Cuauhtémoc is just a few houses and a comedor or two, but it's the last/first place in Mexico on the Pan American Highway (Highway 190). Comitán is 87 km and San Cristóbal 168 km north-west of Ciudad Cuauhtémoc along the Pan American Highway. There are several buses a day to and from both these places (see those sections for details).

Another road from Ciudad Cuauhtémoc runs 69 km south-west to Motozintla. There are 2nd-class buses to Motozintla, and from there buses run to Huixtla (about three hours away) on the Chiapas coastal plain north of Tapachula, providing an unusual but spectacular route across the Sierra Madre.

The Mexican border post – where you must hand in your tourist card if you're heading into Guatemala – is at Ciudad Cuauhtémoc. The Guatemalan post is about four km south at La Mesilla. If your bus from Comitán or San Cristóbal isn't going on to La Mesilla, there are combis, trucks (US$0.50) and the occasional tourist to take you across the no-man's-land.

Travellers have reported that you can get Guatemalan visas/tourist cards at La Mesilla, but these things have a way of changing and you might prefer to get your paperwork sorted out in advance at the Guatemalan Consulate in Comitán or even the embassy in Mexico City.

The Guatemalan border post is officially open from 9 am to noon and 2 to 6 pm. You can usually go through outside these hours but will probably have to pay an extra dollar or so on top of the regular US$5 for your tourist card.

There's no bank at this border. Individual moneychangers operate here but they give you fewer quetzals than a bank would. Try to get some in Mexico before you head for the border.

Guatemalan buses depart La Mesilla for main points inside Guatemala like Huehuetenango (84 km, 1½ hours), Quetzaltenango (also known as Xela, 174 km, 3½ hours) and Guatemala City (349 km, seven hours). Lake Atitlán (245 km, five hours) and Chichicastenango (244 km, five hours) both lie a few km off the Pan American Highway. Before boarding a bus at La Mesilla, try to find out when it's leaving and when it reaches your destination. This could save you several hours of sitting in stationary buses.

THE SOCONUSCO

Along the Pacific coast of Chiapas is the hot, fertile plain known as the Soconusco, 15 to 35 km wide, with quite heavy rainfall from June to October, especially in July and August. Inland and parallel to the coast is the range of the Sierra Madre de Chiapas, mostly between 1000 and 2500 metres but higher in the south where the Tacaná volcano on the Guatemalan border reaches 4092 metres. The Sierra Madre continues into Guatemala, where it includes numerous volcanoes.

Coastal Chiapas, a rich source of cacao, was conquered by the Aztecs at the end of the 15th century and became their empire's most distant province, under the name Xoconochco (from which the area's present name, Soconusco, is derived). Soconusco was the first part of Chiapas to be subdued by the Spanish, lying as it did on Pedro de Alvarado's route to conquer Guatemala in 1524.

Arriaga

The usual reason for travellers going to the small town of Arriaga is to leave. It's where the Juchitán-Tapachula road meets the Tuxtla Gutiérrez-Tapachula road and you might have to change buses here. Coming from Oaxaca or Tuxtla Gutiérrez, Arriaga is the first place you reach on the Soconusco.

Orientation Arriaga uses the now-familiar Chiapan version of the Mexican street grid

(see Orientation in the Tuxtla Gutiérrez section for how it works). Until the new Central de Autobuses is completed on Highway 200 at the edge of the town, the bus stations are on Calle 2 Oriente, between the highway and the main plaza. Should you need food or a bed, there are several places within a couple of blocks.

Places to Stay For the better places in town, first go two blocks towards the centre (away from the highway) from the Cristóbal Colón bus station. A left turn here takes you to the clean *Hotel Colón* (☎ (966) 2-01-20), Calle 3 Norte 8, where singles/doubles cost US$10/14 with private bath and ceiling fan, US$14/18 with air-conditioning as well.

A right and then a left brings you to the *Hotel Albores* (☎ (966) 2-03-96), Calle 4 Oriente 17, and the *Hotel Panamericana* (☎ (966) 2-03-57), both clean, on opposite sides of Calle 4 Oriente. The Panamericana is friendly and slightly better kept though the rooms have less light. Singles/doubles with ceiling fans and private baths are US$9/12 in both places.

Slightly cheaper is the *Hotel Colonial* (☎ (966) 2-08-56), in Callejón Ferrocarril 2, the narrow street running down beside the Autotransportes Tuxtla Gutiérrez bus station. Small but clean rooms with private bath cost US$7 with one bed, US$9 with two beds.

The only top-end place is the *Hotel El Parador* (☎ (966) 2-01-64/99), a motel at the edge of town on the Tonalá road at Km 467.

Places to Eat Several reasonable café-restaurants line Calle 2 Oriente in the bus station area. *Restaurant Lupita*, opposite the Cristóbal Colón station, offers fish or seafood for US$2 to US$3.25, meat dishes for US$1.75 to US$3, plus eggs, tacos, enchiladas and good flan. Slightly grander is the *Restaurant Barkly*, Calle 4 Norte 6 – to reach it from Cristóbal Colón, go a block away from the highway, then take the first right. It's on the right. Chicken soup, a plate of rice, a chile relleno, a refresco and coffee costs US$3.75.

The *Hotel El Parador* restaurant has an international menu.

Getting There & Away By Highway 200, Juchitán is 145 km west of Arriaga, Tonalá is 23 km south-east and Tapachula 245 km south-east. Another paved road strikes 42 km north to meet the Pan American Highway (Highway 190) between Tuxtla Gutiérrez (142 km from Arriaga) and Juchitán.

Bus Quite a few buses, for some reason, end their runs in Arriaga – which is probably why you're here. Happily, the same number start their runs here, increasing your chances of getting a seat leaving the town – though it's pretty likely to be 2nd class. To Tonalá, buses (US$1) by one company or another and colectivo taxis leave every 20 to 30 minutes from Calle 2 Oriente.

Cristóbal Colón (1st class) has two local and six de paso buses daily to Tapachula (US$4.50, four hours) and 11 buses daily to Tuxtla Gutiérrez (US$3, three hours); three local buses to Mexico City (US$19, about 17 hours), and one daily evening bus to Oaxaca (US$8.50, eight hours).

Cristóbal Colón (2nd class), from the same building on Calle 2 Oriente, has services to Tonalá and Tapachula about hourly; plus local buses to Mexico City (four daily), Coatzacoalcos (three daily), Salina Cruz (twice) and Veracruz (once) as well as other de paso services.

Autotransportes Tuxtla Gutiérrez (2nd class), Calle 2 Oriente, across the street from Cristóbal Colón, has eight buses daily to Tapachula (US$4, 4½ hours), 15 to Tuxtla Gutiérrez, six to Juchitán and four to Oaxaca.

Fletes y Pasajes/Autotransportes México-Istmo (2nd class), 1½ blocks towards the highway from Cristóbal Colón, has some buses to Juchitán plus one or two daily to Tuxtepec, Córdoba, Veracruz, Orizaba, Puebla and Mexico City.

Train Trains from Arriaga are slow, 2nd class and very unreliable. For the masochistic or the incurable railway buff, the station is just a couple of blocks from the bus stations.

From Cristóbal Colón, go two blocks towards the town centre, then turn left. Theoretically, there are scheduled departures, but even station staff don't pretend to expect any train until they see it.

Tonalá
Twenty-three km south-east of Arriaga on Highway 200, Tonalá has only marginally more intrinsic appeal but is the jumping-off point for the laid-back beach spot of Puerto Arista and other places on the lagoon-studded nearby coast. A tall pre-Hispanic stela in the Tonalá main plaza appears to depict Tláloc, the central Mexican rain god. There's also a small regional museum at Hidalgo 77, with some archaeological pieces found in the region. Neither is likely to keep you in the town long; if like most people you've come to Tonalá to get to the nearby beaches, you can do so until about 8 pm.

Orientation & Information Highway 200 runs north-south through the middle of Tonalá under the name Avenida Hidalgo, forming the west side of the main plaza or parque central. Bus stations are at each end of the town on this road.

The tourist office (☎ (966) 3-01-01) is on the ground floor of the Palacio Municipal (look for its clock), on the Hidalgo side of the main plaza. Staff are knowledgeable and helpful, and can even tell you the advantages and disadvantages of the various nearby beaches. It's open 9 am to 3 pm and 6 to 8 pm Monday to Friday, and 9 am to 2 pm Saturday.

Bancomer and Banamex both have branches on Hidalgo a few doors from the main plaza.

The post office is a block north of the main plaza at Hidalgo 148.

Places to Stay Tonalá has no great accommodation deals. Get to Puerto Arista if you can. The best place in Tonalá centre is the *Hotel Galilea* (☎ (966) 3-02-39) Avenida Hidalgo on the south side of the main plaza. Rooms are clean and air-conditioned but a bit overpriced at US$16 a single, US$19 a double with private bath. In a similar bracket but slightly better value is the *Hotel Grajandra* (☎ (966) 3-01-44) at Hidalgo 108 near the Cristóbal Colón bus station.

The *Hotel Tonalá* (☎ (966) 3-04-80) at Hidalgo 89, roughly halfway from Cristóbal Colón to the main plaza, has decent doubles for US$16 (US$19 with air-con), but the singles (US$13) are either grotty or hideously close to the roaring of the heavy trucks which grind through Tonalá all night.

A block down from the west side of the main plaza at 6 de Septiembre 24, the *Hotel El Farro* (☎ (966) 3-00-33) is in desperate need of a scrub, some paint and some care. Barely tolerable rooms are US$11 a single, US$15 a double with two beds.

Places to Eat The *Hotel Galilea* on the south side of the main plaza has a restaurant with quite a long menu. On the opposite side of the main plaza, at the corner of Hidalgo, the *Café Samborn's* is no relation to the up-market restaurant chain of a similar name, but it serves respectable chicken *al carbón* and seafood. *Filete de pescado empanizado* (fish fillet fried in breadcrumbs) with salad costs US$5. Don't expect tranquillity here; they fail to drown out the traffic noise even when they turn the TV to full volume.

Several cafés and small restaurants line Hidalgo as it heads north from the main plaza towards the Cristóbal Colón bus station.

Getting There & Away If you're heading for Tapachula, it's often easier to wait in the main plaza for a bus – they come every half an hour or so – rather than make your way out to one of the bus stations, though you're a bit less likely to get a seat this way. You can also get off buses in the main plaza.

Cristóbal Colón (☎ (966) 3-05-40) is on Hidalgo six blocks north of the main plaza. It has six 1st-class locales daily to Tapachula (US$4, 3½ to four hours), five to Tuxtla Gutiérrez (US$4, 3½ hours), two each to Mexico City (US$19, 17 hours) and Villahermosa, and one to Oaxaca (US$8.50, eight hours), plus numerous de paso services,

as well as buses to Juchitán, Tehuantepec, Acayucan, Coatzacoalcos and Tuxtepec. Second-class buses go to most of the same places plus Salina Cruz for about 10% less. Second-class services to Tapachula are hourly between 5.30 am and 9 pm.

Autransportes Tuxtla Gutiérrez (2nd class) has about 15 buses daily to Tapachula from its station on Hidalgo several blocks south of the main plaza, plus about five to Tuxtla Gutiérrez and others to Arriaga, from where there are more frequent services to Tuxtla Gutiérrez, Juchitán and Oaxaca. There are also colectivo taxis from Tonalá to Arriaga.

For transport to the beaches near Tonalá, see the following section.

Beaches near Tonalá

Puerto Arista A half-km collection of palm shacks and a few more substantial buildings in the middle of a 30-km grey beach: that's Puerto Arista. In Puerto Arista, the food's mostly fish, they say there are scorpions, you get through a lot of refrescos, and nothing else happens except the crashing of the Pacific waves while the batteries on your Walkman go down with the sun until the weekend, when a few hundred Chiapanecos cruise in from the towns, or until Semana Santa and Christmas, when they come in the thousands. Then every second palm hut becomes a restaurant or lodging, or both, and the residents make their money for the year.

The rest of the time, the most action you'll see is when an occasional fishing boat puts out to sea, or a piglet breaks into a trot if a dog gathers the energy to bark at it. The temperature's usually sweltering if you stray more than a few yards from the shore, and it's humid in summer.

The sea is clean here but don't go far from the beach: there's an undertow, and riptides known as *canales* can sweep you a long way out in a short time.

Puerto Arista is 18 km south-west of Tonalá. The paved road forks right off Highway 200, three km south-east of Tonalá, then passes through some flat but pretty farmland before crossing a lagoon area inhabited by birds and reportedly a few alligators. The landmark is the lighthouse, where the Tonalá road meets Puerto Arista's only street, running parallel to the shore.

Places to Stay & Eat Turn left at the lighthouse, then take the first right and you come to the *Restaurante Playa Escondida*, one of the few places with year-round accommodation. Palm-roofed mud cabanas with mosquito nets cost US$4 (shower and toilet separate) or US$8 (private bath). The family is friendly and will serve up salad or vegetable soup, or sometimes beefsteak, as well as usually excellent fish. You can also sling your own hammock here for about US$2.

A few other places are open for sleeping and eating when the crowds are away. Two blocks in the opposite direction from the lighthouse, then left towards the sea, *Las Brisas del Mar* has rooms with two double beds and common baths for US$7.50.

Boca del Cielo About three km before Puerto Arista, a road turns left to this little fishing settlement at the mouth of an *estero* (estuary) 17 km away. There's a small seafood restaurant and you can take a launch across the estuary to a sandspit on the ocean front.

Paredón Twelve km west of Tonalá on the large, nearly enclosed lagoon called the Mar Muerto, this is another fishing settlement with plenty of small seafood restaurants. The water immediately around is pretty dirty, but according to the Tonalá tourist office you can rent boats which go to a clean, quiet beach not far away.

Getting There & Away Buses, colectivo taxis and private taxis from Tonalá provide the options unless you have your own vehicle. The Paulino Navarro company runs 2nd-class buses from Tonalá market to Puerto Arista and Boca del Cielo. To reach the market go a block west (downhill) from the Hidalgo side of the main plaza, then turn left a few short blocks along Independencia. You hit the market at the corner of Independencia and Matamoros. The buses start from the opposite corner of the market (Juárez and 5 de Mayo). To Puerto Arista (30 minutes, US$0.50) they leave about hourly until around dark; to Boca del Cielo (US$1, about 1¼ hours) they're erratic but supposedly leave at 5 and 11 am and 3 pm. The last stays overnight at Boca del Cielo.

For Puerto Arista, colectivo taxis are faster, not much dearer and probably more frequent. They're also likely to operate an hour or two after the last bus. They go from the Independencia side of the market, leave when they're full and cost US$1. A private taxi from Tonalá's main plaza costs around US$5 to Puerto Arista, US$10 to Boca del Cielo. From Puerto Arista to Boca del Cielo it's US$7.50.

To Paredón, there are buses and colectivos from the corner of Madero and Allende, a few blocks north-west of the Tonalá main plaza.

Tapachula

Most travellers come to Mexico's southernmost city only because it's a gateway to Guatemala, though for ruin buffs Izapa, 11 km east, is worth a visit. The proximity of Guatemala is quickly apparent from the abundance of quetzals (banknotes, not birds) and strange vehicle number plates. Guatemalans hop over the border for three main purposes: business (which may involve smuggling), shopping, and refuge from the fighting in their own country. Tapachula's population in 1980 was around 100,000 but refugees (some from El Salvador) have greatly swelled that number, leading among other things to local complaints of increased crime and prostitution.

As well as being a border city, Tapachula is the 'capital' of the Soconusco, Chiapas' coffee and banana-growing coastal plain, and a busy commercial centre. You'll notice quite a few blonde Mexicans in Tapachula; they are mostly the descendants of German immigrants from a few decades ago. There are also numerous Chinese citizens, Kuomintang supporters who fled the Chinese revolution in the 1940s. All this,

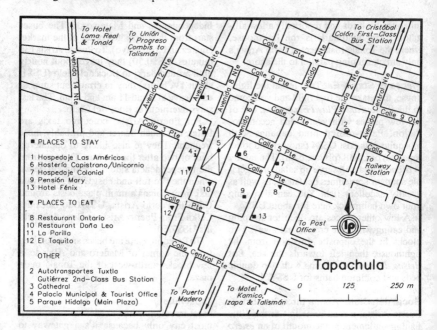

PLACES TO STAY

1 Hospedaje Las Américas
6 Hostería Capistrano/Unicornio
7 Hospedaje Colonial
9 Pensión Mary
13 Hotel Fénix

PLACES TO EAT

8 Restaurant Ontario
10 Restaurant Doña Leo
11 La Parilla
12 El Taquito

OTHER

2 Autotransportes Tuxtla
  Gutiérrez 2nd-Class Bus Station
3 Cathedral
4 Palacio Municipal & Tourist Office
5 Parque Hidalgo (Main Plaza)

Tapachula

0   125   250 m

plus the heat, give the place a livelier atmosphere than most Chiapas towns; even women go around in shorts, a rarity in Mexico outside beach resorts.

Tapachula is overlooked by the 4092-metre Tacaná volcano to its north-east, the first of a chain of volcanoes stretching down into Guatemala. The village of Unión Juárez, 40 km from Tapachula, reportedly provides good views of the volcano, and the surrounding country has hiking possibilities.

Tapachula holds an international fería in late February and early March each year.

Orientation Tapachula's street grid is aligned more or less with the four compass points. The key axes are Avenida Central running north-south and Calle Central (east-west). Avenidas run north-south, are even-numbered west of Avenida Central, odd-numbered east of it, and have the suffix Norte (Nte) or Sur depending on whether you're north or south of Calle Central. Calles run east-west and are even-numbered south of Calle Central, odd-numbered north of it, with the suffix Oriente (Ote) or Poniente (Pte) indicating east or west of Avenida Central. Tapachula's large main plaza, the Parque Hidalgo, is between Avenidas 6 and 8 Norte, with Calle 5 Poniente on its north side. Bus stations are scattered north-east and north-west of the main plaza.

Information Tapachula has a good range of services for the traveller.

Tourist Office The tourist office (☎ (962) 6-35-43) is in the Palacio Municipal on the west side of the main plaza. It's open from 8 am to 8 pm daily. There's also the small, intermittently open Museo Regional del Soconusco in the same building, with some archaeological exhibits.

Money There are several banks around the city centre where you can change dollars and quetzals. If you're going to Guatemala try to get some quetzals in Tapachula; rates at the borders are usually lower. Outside bank hours, some shops and restaurants in Tapachula will accept cash dollars or quetzals at a lower rate than you'd get in banks.

Post The post office is several blocks from the centre at the corner of Calle 1 Oriente and Avenida 9 Norte. It's open 8 am to 6 pm Monday to Friday, 8 am to noon Saturday. Tapachula's postal code is 30700.

Consulate The Guatemalan Consulate (☎ (962) 6-12-52) is at Calle 1 Oriente 33. Hours are 8 am to 4 pm Monday to Friday.

Places to Stay – bottom end In the lower bracket, Tapachula has little except the functional and overpriced. It may be worthwhile to spend some extra pesos for the quiet and comfort of the *Hospedaje Colonial* (☎ (962) 6-20-52), which is better than some middle-range places. It's at Avenida 4 Norte 31, half a block north of Calle 3 Poniente and just 1½ blocks from the main plaza. Clean, bright rooms with private baths line an upstairs balcony round a garden full of plants. Singles are US$9. Doubles are US$14 with one double bed, US$16 with two beds. Ring the bell to enter.

Among the best values in town is the *Hospedaje Las Américas* (☎ (962) 6-27-57), Avenida 10 Norte 47. A single with fan and private bath is US$7 and doubles cost US$9.50.

Pensión Mary, Avenida 4 Norte 28, half a block south of Calle 3 Poniente, charges US$4.50 per person in clean rooms with shared baths, and serves meals too, but is often full.

Places to Stay – middle *Hotel Santa Julia* (☎ (962) 6-31-40), Calle 17 Oriente 5, next door to the Cristóbal Colón 1st-class bus station, has good, clean singles/doubles with TV, telephone and private bath for US$16/19.

Hotel Fénix (☎ (962) 5-07-55), Avenida 4 Norte 19 near the corner of Calle 1 Poniente,

a block west of the plaza, has spacious rooms and open courtyards with plants, and is quite pleasant. Rooms with private bath are US$17 a single, US$22 a double, US$4 more for air-conditioning.

The town's two top hotels, both with air-conditioned rooms and swimming pools, are the *Motel Kamico* (☎ (962) 6-26-40 to 48) on Highway 200 east of the city (singles/doubles US$34/45) and the *Hotel Loma Real* (☎ (962) 6-14-40 to 45) just off Highway 200 on the west side of town, where singles/doubles are US$33/43. There is also the *Hotel Don Miguel* (☎ (962) 6-11-43 to 49), Calle 1 Poniente 18, where rooms are US$23/29, and the *Hotel San Francisco* (☎ (962) 6-14-54) at Avenida Central Sur 94, with the same prices.

Places to Eat *Machacado* – chopped fruit with ice, water and sugar – is a popular, refreshing drink in steamy Tapachula. Another cooler is frozen yogurt *(helado de yogurt)*.

Several restaurants line the south side of the main plaza. *Restaurant Doña Leo* specialises in roast chicken and salad (US$4 for a quarter-bird, US$6 for half a bird) and does a US$2 breakfast of eggs with ham, frijoles, orange juice, coffee and pan dulce.

On Avenida 8 Norte at the south-west corner of the main plaza, *La Parrilla* has quicker service than most places in the centre; it offers antojitos for US$1 to US$3, meat dishes for US$3 to US$5, plus such everyday fare as tacos and queso fundido, but also the once-in-a-lifetime opportunity to sample their *tortas ultrasónicas siglo XXI* (21st-century ultrasonic sandwiches).

For minor pretensions to style go to the *Hostería Capistrano/Unicornio* (☎ 6-24-69), overlooking the east side of the main plaza at the corner of Avenida 6 Norte and Calle 3 Poniente. It serves wine plus Italian and other food. Good pizzas of various sizes cost US$5 to US$11 and a sandwich with salad is US$3.50. Decoration consists of some framed posters and enormous red plastic bows. Imitation Sades, Paul Youngs and Springsteens thump out of the ghetto-blaster. The entrance is unimposing; go through the red gate beside a Coca-Cola sign and up two floors.

The *Mandarin*, a Chinese restaurant on the main plaza, has also been recommended by travellers.

For cheaper chicken, grilled this time, try the very busy *El Taquito*, a block south of the main plaza at the corner of Avenida 8 Norte and Calle 1 Poniente. A quarter-bird goes for US$3.50, a half for US$4.50. The *Restaurant Ontario*, at Calle 3 Pte 12A between Avenidas 2 and 4 Norte, is popular for its range of reasonably priced breakfasts and meals.

Getting There & Away Transport to the Guatemalan border is covered in the Talismán & Ciudad Hidalgo section.

Tapachula is near the south end of Highway 200, 222 km from Tonalá, 245 km from Arriaga, 410 km from Tehuantepec and 660 km from Oaxaca. To Tuxtla Gutiérrez, for which you branch north-east off Highway 200 at Arriaga, it's 400 km.

The road to Guatemala heads 20 km east past the Izapa ruins to the border point at Talismán Bridge. A branch south off this road leads to another border crossing at Ciudad Hidalgo (38 km from Tapachula). From Huixtla, 40 km north of Tapachula on Highway 200, a road heads east across the Sierra Madre to Motozintla and Ciudad Cuauhtémoc.

Bus Cristóbal Colón (1st class) is at the corner of Calle 17 Oriente and Avenida 3 Norte. From the entrance go west (left) two blocks, then six blocks south (left) and three more west (right) to reach the main plaza. There are 20 buses daily to Tonalá (US$4, 3½ hours) and Arriaga (US$4.50, four hours), most of them leaving on the hour. There are 15 buses to Huixtla, 18 to Tuxtla Gutiérrez (seven hours), eight to Tuxtepec and Mexico City (21 hours), three to Córdoba, two to Villahermosa; and one each to San Cristóbal de las Casas (via Tuxtla Gutiérrez, nine hours), Oaxaca (11 hours) and Puebla.

Cristóbal Colón (2nd class) is at the corner of Calle 11 and Avenida Central Norte. There are fairly frequent services to Tonalá, Arriaga, Juchitán and Tehuantepec, plus two or three daily each to Salina Cruz (seven hours), Oaxaca, Coatzacoalcos and Mexico City.

Autotransportes Tuxtla Gutiérrez (2nd class) at Calle 7 Poniente 5, just west of Avenida Central Norte, has four buses daily to Huixtla, Tonalá, Arriaga and Tuxtla Gutiérrez, and one via Tuxtla to San Cristóbal de Las Casas and Comitán.

Buses to Motozintla depart from Huixtla and take about three hours. There are buses from Motozintla to Ciudad Cuauhtémoc, Comitán, San Cristóbal de Las Casas and Tuxtla Gutiérrez, but this route won't save time except to Ciudad Cuauhtémoc and possibly Comitán. Going from Guatemala to central Chiapas, it's much better to cross the frontier at Ciudad Cuauhtémoc/La Mesilla.

Train The station lies just south of the intersection of Avenida Central Sur and Calle 14. Only masochists, the dull-witted and the hopelessly idealistic take the train.

Getting Around Tapachula airport is south of the city off the Puerto Madero road. Combis Aeropuerto (☎ (962) 6-12-87) charge US$2.75 to the airport and will pick you up from any hotel in Tapachula.

Izapa Ruins

If this site was in a more visited part of Mexico it would have a constant stream of visitors, for it's not only important to archaeologists as a link between the Olmecs and the Maya but interesting to walk around. It flourished from approximately 200 BC to 200 AD.

Northern Area Most of this part of the site has been cleared and some restoration has been done. There are a number of platforms, a ball court, and several of the stelae and altars whose carvings provide Izapa's main interest for archaeologists. The platforms and ball court were probably built some time after Izapa was at its peak.

Southern Area This is less visited than the northern area. Go back about 1.75 km along the road towards Tapachula and take a dirt road to the left. Where the vehicle track ends, a path leads to the right. There are three areas of interest and you may have to ask the caretaker to find and explain them, as they are separated by foot trails that are less than obvious. One is a plaza with several stelae under thatched roofs. The second is a smaller plaza with more stelae and three big pillars topped with curious stone balls. The third has just one item – a carving of the jaws of a jaguar holding a seemingly human figure.

Getting There & Away Izapa is 11 km east of Tapachula on the road to Talismán. You can reach it by the combis of Unión y Progreso from Calle 9 Poniente, a block west of Avenida 12 Norte in Tapachula. The main (northern) part of the site is marked on the left of the road. The second (southern) part lies less than one km back towards Tapachula on the other side of the road.

Puerto Madero

This not very attractive beach resort is 25 km south-west of Tapachula. An undertow restricts swimming to just a few areas. There's some accommodation at Puerto Madero but it's not inviting and the beach is said to be dangerous at night because of refugees who sleep on it. If you're desperate for a beach, head for Puerto Arista, a few hours up the coast.

Talismán & Ciudad Hidalgo (Guatemalan Border)

There are two crossing points into Guatemala near Tapachula. Talismán is 20 km east, Ciudad Hidalgo is 38 km south. The Guatemalan border posts on the other side are called El Carmen and Ciudad Tecún Umán respectively. Bridges span the river at both frontier points but it's a long walk at Ciudad Hidalgo. There's more public transport on both sides of the border from Ciudad

Hidalgo/Ciudad Tecún Umán, but many travellers head for Talismán/El Carmen, which is nearer to Tapachula, has a few long-distance bus connections into Mexico and has a more direct road link (via San Marcos) with Quetzaltenango inside Guatemala. Some buses from El Carmen take the longer route to Quetzaltenango via Coatepeque, joining the road from Ciudad Tecún Umán in any case.

A bus all the way through from Talismán to Guatemala City takes about five hours. If you're heading for Lake Atitlán or Chichicastenango, take a bus that's following the highland route via the Pan American Highway to Guatemala City and not the lowland route via Escuintla. Los Encuentros is the junction on the Pan American where the roads for Atitlán and Chichicastenango head off south and north respectively. You can get connections for these places in Quetzaltenango if there isn't one from the border.

At the time of writing it was possible for travellers (including British) to obtain Guatemalan visas at the border, but check in advance to see whether this has changed. There's a Guatemalan Consulate (☎ 8-01-84) at Central Norte 12 in Ciudad Hidalgo, as well as the one in Tapachula. The Guatemalan border posts may insist that you pay for your tourist card in US dollars or quetzals; try to get some before you leave Tapachula.

Getting There & Away

From Tapachula there are six Cristóbal Colón 1st-class buses daily to Talismán (US$0.75). Autobuses Unión y Progreso on Calle 9 Poniente, a block west of Avenida 12 Norte, also runs combi minibuses (US$0.60) about every 10 minutes to Talismán. A taxi from Tapachula to Talismán takes 20 minutes and costs US$5. Autotransportes Tuxtla Gutiérrez covers the 45-minute journey to the frontier at Ciudad Hidalgo (US$0.50, every 15 minutes).

There are three daily Cristóbal Colón 1st-class buses from Talismán to Mexico City (US$24).

Ciudad Hidalgo is also the southern terminus of the Mexican railway from Juchitán, Arriaga, Tonalá and Tapachula. It's possible to get a train from Ciudad Hidalgo all the way to Veracruz but it's 2nd class only, unreliable and very slow.

GUATEMALA

Guatemala City

Population 2 million

Guatemala's capital city, the largest urban agglomeration in Central America, sprawls across a range of flattened mountains (altitude 1500 metres), scored by deep ravines. Its situation is splendid, as the intrepid American archaeologist and explorer John L Stephens discovered when he approached the city from the east in November 1839:

Late in the afternoon, as I was ascending a small eminence, two immense volcanoes stood up before me, seeming to scorn the earth, and towering to the heavens. They were the great volcanoes of Agua and Fuego, forty miles distant, and nearly fifteen thousand feet high, wonderfully grand and beautiful. In a few moments the great plain of Guatimala (sic) appeared in view, surrounded by mountains, and in the centre of it the city, a mere speck on the vast expanse, with churches, and convents, and numerous turrets, cupolas, and steeples, and still as if the spirit of peace rested upon it; with no storied associations, but by its own beauty creating an impression on the mind of a traveller which can never be effaced.

Guatemala City would hardly be described in such glowing words today. In our century it has expanded to cover the entire 'great plain', even tumbling into the valleys surrounding it. The clear air through which Stephens viewed the sunset is now sullied with pollution. Bustle and noise have driven away the 'spirit of peace'. Even so, the city's site is impressive.

When you first get to know it, this city of two million people bears resemblances to Mexico City, its great Latin sister to the north. But the superficial resemblances soon give way to purely Guatemalan impressions. There's the huge and chaotic market, typically colourful and disorganised as though Guatemala City was just a gigantic village. There are the ramshackle city buses, without windows, without lights, without paint, sometimes without brakes, which trundle citizens about with surprising efficiency, though hardly in comfort. And there are the thousands of guards in blue clothing carrying very effective-looking firearms. Wherever there's money or status – banks, offices, private clubs, even McDonald's – there are armed guards.

Despite Stephens' description, Guatemala City today has few colonial buildings to beautify its aggressive urban sprawl. The colonial buildings are all in nearby Antigua Guatemala, the former capital. What you see here is mostly concrete, but at least the buildings are generally only five or six storeys high, allowing light to flood the narrow streets.

There is probably no reason for you to spend lots of time in Guatemala City. The few interesting sights may be seen in a day or two. But you must know your way around because this is the hub of the country, where all transportation lines meet and where all services are available.

HISTORY

Many cities in this part of the world have seen their histories end with an earthquake. For Guatemala City, it was the terrible *temblor* (earthquake) of 29 July 1773 which began its history. There was no city here at that time. The Spanish capital of Central America was at La Ciudad de Santiago de los Caballeros de Guatemala, known today as Antigua Guatemala, in the Panchoy Valley. The earthquake destroyed much of the colonial capital, and the government decided to move its headquarters to La Ermita Valley, the present site of Guatemala City, hoping to escape any further such terrible destruction. On 27 September 1775 King Carlos III of Spain signed a royal charter for the founding of La Nueva Guatemala de la Asunción, and Guatemala City was officially born.

The fervent hopes for a quakeless future were shaken in 1917, 1918 and 1976 as temblors did major damage to buildings in the capital – as well as in Antigua. The city's comparatively recent founding and its history of earthquakes have left little to see in the way of grand churches, palaces, mansions, or quaint old neighbourhoods.

ORIENTATION
Street Grid System
Guatemala City, like all Guatemalan towns, is laid out according to a street grid system which is logical and fairly easy to use. Avenidas run north-south; Calles run east-west. Streets are usually numbered from north and west (lowest) to south and east (highest); building numbers run in the same directions, with odd numbers on the left-hand side and even on the right as you head south or east. The city is divided into 15 *zonas* (zones); each zona has its own separate version of this grid system.

Addresses are given in this form: '9a Avenida 15-12, Zona 1', which is read '9th Avenue above 15th Street, No 12, in Zone 1'. The building you're looking for (in this case the Hotel Excel), will be on 9th Avenue between 15th and 16th Streets, on the right-hand side as you walk south.

Though some major thoroughfares such as 6a Avenida and 7a Avenida cross through several zones, keeping the same name, most zones have their own unique grid systems. Thus 14 Calle in Zona 10 is a completely different street several miles distant from 14 Calle in Zona 1.

Short streets may be numbered 'A', as in 14 Calle A, a short street running between 14 Calle and 15 Calle.

Because of its size and uneven topography, Guatemala City's street grid has a number of anomalies as well: diagonal streets called *rutas* and *vías*, wandering boulevards called *diagonales*, etc. Though you can get lost here, you needn't if you refer to a map from time to time. In smaller Guatemalan cities and towns this street grid system allows you to pinpoint destinations effortlessly.

Landmarks
The ceremonial centre of Guatemala City is the Plaza Mayor (sometimes called the Parque Central) at the heart of Zona 1, surrounded by the Palacio Nacional, the Catedral Metropolitana and the Portal del Comercio. Beside the Plaza Mayor to the west is the large Parque Centenario, the city's central park. Zona 1 is also the retail commercial district, with shops selling clothing, crafts, film, and a myriad of other things. The Mercado Central, a market selling lots of crafts, is behind the cathedral. Most of the city's good cheap and middle-range hotels are in Zona 1. 6a Avenida running south and 7a Avenida running north are the major thoroughfares which connect Zona 1 with other zonas.

Zona 4, south of Zona 1, holds the modern Centro Cívico (Civic Centre) with various government buildings. In south-western Zona 4 is the city's major market district and chaotic bus terminals.

Zona 9 (west of Avenida La Reforma) and Zona 10 (east of Avenida La Reforma), are south of Zona 4; Avenida La Reforma is the southerly extension of 10a Avenida. These are the fancier residential areas of the city, also boasting several of the most interesting small museums. Zona 10 is the poshest, with the Zona Viva (Lively Zone) arrayed around the deluxe Camino Real Guatemala and Guatemala Fiesta hotels. The Zona Viva holds many of the city's better restaurants and nightclubs. In Zona 9, convenient landmarks are the mini-Eiffel Tower called the Torre del Reformador at 7a Avenida and 2 Calle, and the Plazuela España traffic roundabout at 7a Avenida and 12 Calle.

Zona 13, just south of Zona 9, has the large Parque Aurora, several museums, and the Aeropuerto Internacional La Aurora (La Aurora International Airport).

INFORMATION
Tourist Office
The tourist office is in the lobby of the INGUAT headquarters (Guatemalan Tourist Commission), (☎ (2) 31-13-33 to 47; fax 31-88-93), 7a Avenida 1-17, Centro Cívico, Zona 4. Look for the blue-and-white sign with the letter 'i' on the east side of the street, next to a flight of stairs a few metres to the south of the railway viaduct which crosses above 7a Avenida. Hours are from 8 am to

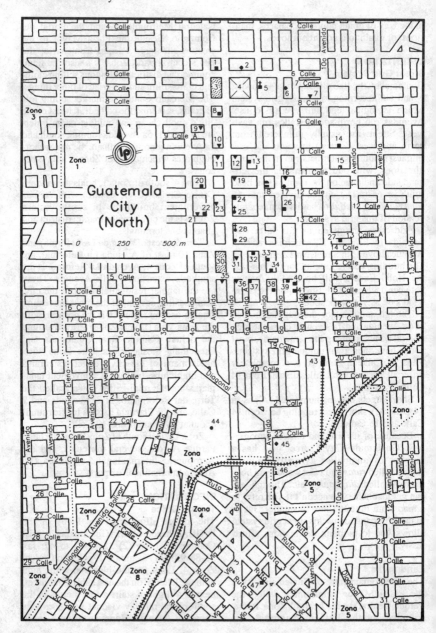

Guatemala
City
(North)

0   250   500 m

Guatemala City (North)

■ PLACES TO STAY

1	Hotel Centenario
8	Hotel Pan American
13	Hotel Ritz Continental
14	Pensión Meza
15	Hogar del Turista
15	Hotel Casa Real
20	Hotel Lessing House
22	Hotel Del Centro
24	Hotel-Apartamentos Guatemala Internacional
26	Spring Hotel
27	Posada Belén
32	Hotel Chalet Suizo
33	Hotel Colonial
34	Hotel San Diego
37	Hotel Hernani
38	Hotel Ajau
39	Hotel Bilbao
40	Hotel Excel
41	Hotel Belmont
42	Hotel Capri
47	Hotel Conquistador Sheraton

▼ PLACES TO EAT

7	Pollo Campero
9	Pollo Campero
10	Multirestaurantes
11	McDonald's
12	Restuarant Bologna
16	Café Bohemia
19	Restaurant Picadilly
21	El Gran Pavo
23	Restaurant Altuna
31	Restaurant Cantón
35	Delicadezas Hamburgo
36	Pollo Campero

OTHER

2	Palacio Nacional
3	Parque Centenario
4	Plaza Mayor
5	Catedral Metropolitana
6	Mercado Central
17	Guatel (Telephone Company Long Distance Station)
18	Correos (Post Office)
25	Iglesia Santa Clara
28	Iglesia San Francisco
29	Policia Nacional
30	Parque Concordia (Parque Gómez Carrillo)
43	FEGUA Railway Station
44	Centro Cultural Miguel Ángel Asturias
45	Centro Cívico
46	INGUAT Tourist Office

4.30 pm, on Saturday from 8 am to 1 pm, closed Sunday. Staff here are friendly and helpful, with lots of good information at their fingertips.

The American Society of Guatemala (☎ (2) 37-14-16), Edificio Rodríguez, Diagonal 6 No 13-08, Zona 10, Office 408, publishes a monthly newsletter entitled *Aquí Guatemala* which covers events in the expatriate community.

Money

Normal banking hours are 8.30 am to 2 pm (until 2.30 pm on Friday), closed weekends, but several banks have *ventanillas especiales* (special teller windows) open longer; ATM cash machines are also making their appearance. Banquetzal has an office, (☎ (2) 51-21-53, 51-20-55), at 10 Calle 6-28, Zona 1, near the Hotel Ritz Continental,

that's open from 8.30 am to 8 pm Monday to Friday, and on Saturday from 9 am to 1 pm.

The airport terminal office of Banco de Guatemala is open 7.30 am to 6.30 pm, Monday to Friday.

American Express is represented in Guatemala by Banco del Café S A (☎ (2) 31-13-11, 34-00-40; fax 31-14-18), Avenida La Reforma 9-00, Zona 9.

Post

The city's main post office (☎ (2) 2-61-01 to 05) is at 7a Avenida 12-11, Zona 1, in the huge pink building. There's no sign, but by the racks of postcards shall ye know it. It's open from 8 am to 7 pm on weekdays, 8 am to 3 pm on Saturday, closed Sunday. Don't expect much from the mail here. Mail service is undependable, especially when sending urgent messages or valuable items, and local citizens and businesses often use private

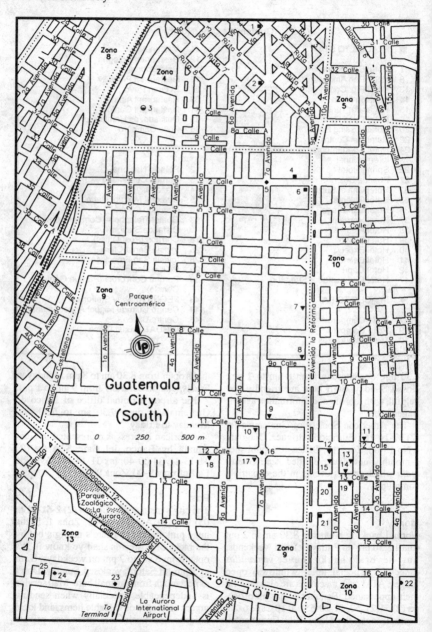

Guatemala City (South)

0   250   500 m

Guatemala City (South)

■ PLACES TO STAY

1 Hotel Conquistador Sheraton
2 Hotel Plaza
4 Hotel Villa Española
6 Hotel Cortijo Reforma
20 Hotel Guatemala Fiesta
21 Hotel Camino Real Guatemala

▼ PLACES TO EAT

7 Restaurant El Parador
8 Pastelería Las Américas
9 Puerto Barrios
10 Palacio Royal
11 Hacienda del los Sánchez
12 La Brisa Seafood Bar
13 Restaurante Excellent
14 La Trattoria
15 Siriaco's
17 Restaurant Picadilly
18 El Gran Pavo
19 Restaurant Bologna

OTHER

3 Market & Terminal de Autobuses
5 Torre del Reformador
8 Museo Popol Vuh
16 Plazuela España
22 Museo Ixchel del Traje Indígena
23 Mercado de Artesanía
24 Museo Nacional de Arte Moderno
25 Museo Nacional de Arqueología y
   Etnografía

National Police	120
Inter-City Long Distance Calls	121
Fire	123
Directory Assistance	124
Red Cross	125
Correct Time	126
To Send a Telegram	127
Ambulance	128
International Calls	171
USADirect (AT&T)	190

Embassies

Remember that embassies *(embajadas)* and their consular sections *(consulados)* often have strange, short working hours. Call ahead to be sure the place will be open before you venture out to find it. (Note that some Guatemala City telephone numbers have six digits, some only five; both work equally well.)

Austria
   Embassy, 6a Avenida 20-25, Zona 10, Edificio Plaza Marítima (4th floor) (☎ (2) 68-11-34, 68-23-24)
Belgium
   Embassy and Consulate, Avenida La Reforma 13-70, Zona 9, Edificio Real Reforma (2nd floor) (☎ (2) 31-65-97, 31-56-08)
Canada
   Embassy and Consulate, 7a Avenida 11-59, Zona 9, Edificio Galerías España (☎ (2) 32-14-11 to 13)
Costa Rica
   Embassy, Avenida La Reforma 8-60, Zona 9, Edificio Galerías Reforma offices 320 and 902 (☎ (2) 31-96-04, 32-15-22)
Denmark
   Consulate-General, 7a Avenida 20-36, Zona 1 (☎(2) 8-10-91, 51-45-47)
El Salvador
   Embassy, 12 Calle 5-43, Zona 9 (☎ (2) 32-58-48, 36-24-21)
Finland
   Consulate-General, Ruta 2 (24 Calle) 0-70, Zona 4,(☎ (2) 31-31-16/17, 36-26-56)
France
   Embassy and Consulate, 16 Calle 4-53, Zona 10, Edificio Marbella (☎ (2) 37-40-80, 37-36-39)
Germany
   Embassy, 20 Calle 6-20, Zona 10, Edificio Plaza Marítima (☎ (2) 37-00-28/29)
Honduras
   Embassy, 15a Avenida 9-16, Zona 13 (☎ (2) 37-39-19, 37-19-21)

courier companies such as King's Express instead.

Telephone

The national telephone network is operated by a private company called Guatel. If you are calling Guatemala City from outside the country, the city code is (2); for any other city or town it's (9). Most telephone numbers in Guatemala City have six digits, but a few old ones have only five; they still work. If the five-digit number you're dialling doesn't work, try putting a '3' in front of it.

A coin-operated telephone in Guatemala is called a *telefono monedero*. Information and emergency telephone numbers have only three digits. Here they are:

Israel
   Embassy, 13a Avenida 14-07, Zona 10 (☎ (2) 37-13-34, 32-53-05)
Italy
   Embassy and Consulate, 8 Calle 3-14, Zona 10 (☎ (2) 6-21-28, 6-54-32)
Mexico
   Embassy, 16 Calle 0-51, Zona 14 (☎ (2) 68-07-69, 68-24-95); Consulate, 13 Calle 7-30, Zona 9 (☎ (2) 6-65-04)
Netherlands
   Embassy, 12 Calle 7-56, Zona 9 (4th floor) (☎ (2) 31-35-05); Consulate, 15 Calle 1-91, Zona 10 (☎ (2) 37-40-92)
Nicaragua
   Embassy, 2 Calle 15-95, Zona 13 (☎ (2) 6-56-13)
Norway
   Consulate, 6a Avenida 7-02, Zona 9 (☎ (2) 31-00-64, 31-67-27)
Panama
   Embassy, Vía 5 No 4-50, Zona 4, Edificio Maya (☎ (2) 32-50-01)
South Africa
   Consulate, 10a Avenida 30-57, Zona 5 (CIDEA) (☎ (2) 36-28-90, 34-15-31/35)
Spain
   Consulate, 4 Calle 7-73, Zona 9, Edificio Seguros Universales (☎ (2) 31-87-84, 32-53-19)
Sweden
   Embassy, 8a Avenida 15-07, Zona 10 (☎ (2) 37-05-55, 33-65-36)
Switzerland
   Embassy and Consulate, 4 Calle 7-73, Zona 9, Edificio Seguros Universales, Apdo Postal 1426 (☎ (2) 36-57-26, 31-37-25)
UK
   Embassy, 7a Avenida 5-10, Zona 4 (7th floor) (☎ (2) 32-16-01/02/04)
USA
   Embassy and Consulate, Avenida La Reforma 7-01, Zona 10 (☎ (2) 31-15-41).

Immigration Office

If you need to extend your tourist card for a longer stay, contact the Dirección General de Migración (☎ (2) 53-52-82, 53-41-58/71/83), 8a Avenida 12-10, Zona 1.

Medical Services

This city has many private hospitals and clinics. One such is the Centro Médico, (☎ (2) 32-35-55), 6a Avenida 3-47, Zona 10; another is Hospital Herrera Llerandi, (☎ (2) 36-67-71/75, 32-04-44/48), 6a Avenida 8-71, Zona 10. For the names and addresses of others, consult your embassy or consulate, or

the yellow pages of the telephone directory under Hospitales.

The Guatemalan Red Cross (☎ (2) 125) is at 3 Calle 8-40, Zona 1. Guatemala City uses a duty-chemist *(farmacia de turno)* system with designated pharmacies remaining open at night and weekends. Ask at your hotel for the nearest farmacia de turno, or consult the farmacia de turno sign in the window of the closest chemist/pharmacy.

ZONA 1

Most of what you'll want to see is in Zona 1 near the Plaza Mayor, bounded by 6 and 8 Calles and 6a and 7a Avenidas.

Plaza Mayor

According to the standard Spanish colonial town-planning scheme, every town in the New World had to have a large plaza for military exercises, reviews and ceremonies. On the north side of the plaza was to be the *palacio de gobierno*, or colonial government headquarters. On another side, preferably the east, there was to be a church (if the town was large enough to merit a bishop then it was a cathedral). On the other sides of the square there could be other civic buildings, or the large and imposing mansions of wealthy citizens. Guatemala's Plaza Mayor is a good example of the classic town plan.

To appreciate the Plaza Mayor, you've got to visit it on a Sunday when it's thronged with thousands of citizens who have come to stroll, lick ice cream cones, play in the fountains, take the air, smooch on a bench, listen to *salsa* music on boom-boxes, and ignore the hundreds of trinket vendors. If you can't make it on a Sunday, try for lunchtime or late afternoon.

Palacio Nacional

On the north side of the Plaza Mayor is the country's Palacio Nacional, built during the dictatorial presidency of General Jorge Ubico (1931-44) at enormous cost. It replaced an earlier palace called El Centenario, which burnt down in 1925. El Centenario had replaced an even earlier

Top: Shop on Avenida Utrilla, San Cristóbal de las Casas (TW)
Left: Cañón del Sumidero, Chiapas (JN)
Right: Lagos de Montebello, Chiapas (JN)

Top: The commercial centre of Guatemala City (TB)
Bottom: Palacio Nacional with crowds and ice-cream vendor, Guatemala City (TB)

palace which was destroyed in the earth-quake of 1917.

The palace is where the President of Guatemala has his executive offices. Visit is by free guided tour (Monday to Friday, 8 am to 4.30 pm). The tour takes you through a labyrinth of gleaming brass and polished wood, carved stone and frescoed arches. The frescoes are by Alberto Gálvez Suárez. When you're finished inside, walk around to the rear (north side) of the palace for a look at the bulletproof cars, shrouded in smoked glass and bristling with antennas (and automatic weapons?), of various executive officers.

Catedral Metropolitana

Built between 1782 and 1809 (the towers were finished later, in 1867), the Catedral Metropolitana has survived earthquake and fire much better than the Palacio Nacional, though the quake of 1917 did a lot of damage, and that of 1976 did even more. All has been restored. It's not a particularly beautiful building, inside or out. Heavy proportions and spare ornamentation make it look severe, though it does have a certain feeling of stateliness. Dark old 17th and 18th-century paintings on the walls teach Bible lessons to the recently converted. Little chandeliers and a baldachin over the altar add a formal touch. The cathedral is supposedly open every day from 8 am to 7 pm, though you may find it closed, especially at siesta time.

Mercado Central

Until it was destroyed by the quake of 1976, the central market on 9a Avenida between 6 and 8 Calles behind the cathedral was a place to buy food and other necessities. Reconstructed in the late 1970s, the modern market specialises in tourist-oriented items such as cloth (hand-woven and machine-woven), carved wood, worked leather and metal, basketry and other handicrafts. Necessities have been moved aside to the streets surrounding the market. As you will be visiting the Plaza Mayor, you should take a stroll through here, though there are better places to buy crafts.

Market hours are 6 am to 6 pm Monday to Saturday, 9 am to noon Sunday.

The city's true 'central' food market is in Zona 4.

ZONA 2
Parque Minerva

Zona 2 is north of Zona 1. Though mostly a middle-class residential district, its most northern extent holds the large Parque Minerva, itself surrounded by golf courses, the rod-and-gun club, sports grounds and the buildings of the Universidad Mariano Gálvez.

Minerva, goddess of wisdom, technical skill and invention, was a favourite of President Manuel Estrada Cabrera (1898-1920), who fancied himself the country's 'Great Educator'. He accomplished little in the way of educating Guatemala's youth, but he built lots of sylvan parks named for the goddess and quaint little temples in her honour. Otherwise, his presidency is notable for the amount of Guatemalan territory he turned over to the gigantic United Fruit Company for the cultivation of bananas.

For all that, the Parque Minerva is a pretty place, good for just relaxing, strolling among the eucalyptus trees and sipping a soft drink. If you want to stroll with the soft drink, the vendor will obligingly pour it from its bottle (worth a few centavos' deposit) into a small plastic bag equipped with a straw.

Mapa En Relieve

The prime sight to see in Zona 2 is the Relief Map of Guatemala, called simply the Mapa En Relieve, in the Parque Minerva. Constructed in 1904 under the direction of Francisco Vela, the map shows the country at a scale of 1:10,000, but the height of the mountainous terrain has been exaggerated to 1:2000 for dramatic effect. Little signs indicate major towns and topographical features. Viewing towers afford a panoramic view. This place is odd but fun, and costs only a few centavos for admission (free on Sunday); hours are 8 am to 5 pm every day.

Getting There The Mapa En Relieve and

Parque Minerva are two km north of the Plaza Mayor along 6a Avenida, but that street is one-way heading south. You can catch a northbound bus (No 1, 45 or 46) on 5a Avenida in Zona 1.

ZONA 4

Pride of Zona 4 is the Centro Cívico, constructed in the 1950s and '60s. Here you'll find the Palace of Justice, the headquarters buildings of the Guatemalan Institute of Social Security (IGSS), the Banco de Guatemala, the city hall, and the headquarters of INGUAT. The Banco de Guatemala building bears high-relief murals by Dagoberto Vásquez depicting the history of his homeland; in the city hall is a huge mosaic by Carlos Mérida completed in 1959.

Behind INGUAT is the Ciudad Olímpica sports grounds, and across the street from the Centro Cívico on a hilltop are the Centro Cultural Miguel Ángel Asturias (the national theatre, chamber theatre, open-air theatre and a small museum of old armaments). The Centro Cívico is hardly a tourist attraction, though the useful INGUAT tourist office is here. Zona 4 is known mostly for its markets and its bus stations, all thrown together in the chaotic south-western corner of the zona near the railway.

ZONA 10

Lying east of Avenida La Reforma, Zona 10 is the upscale district of posh villas, luxury hotels, embassies, and several important museums.

Museo Popol Vuh

If you're at all interested in Mayan and Spanish colonial art you must make a visit to this museum (☎ (2) 31-89-21), named for the famous mythic chronicle of the Quiché Maya. Well-chosen polychrome pottery, figurines, incense burners, burial urns, carved wooden masks and traditional textiles fill several exhibit rooms. Others hold colonial paintings, gilded wood and silver objects. A faithful copy of the Dresden Codex, one of the precious 'painted books' of the Maya, is among the most interesting pieces.

A tortoise, symbol of the summer solstice, from the Dresden Codex

The collection, assembled by Jorge and Ella Castillo, was donated to the Universidad Francisco Marroquín in 1977. It's housed on the 6th level of the Edificio Galerías Reforma, Torre 2, Avenida La Reforma 8-60, Zona 9. Hours are 9 am to 4.30 pm, Monday to Saturday (closed Sunday); admission costs US$0.75 for adults, US$0.25 for students, US$0.10 for children. If you visit around lunchtime, you might want to have a sandwich at the Pastelería Las Américas, or a meal at the Restaurante El Parador, both described in the Places to Eat section.

Museo Ixchel (Indian Costumes)

The Museo Ixchel del Traje Indígena (☎ (2) 68-07-13) is named for Ixchel, wife of Mayan sky god Itzamná and goddess of the moon and of women in childbirth, among other things. As you approach the museum at 4a Avenida 16-27, Zona 10, you'll see groups of village women in their wonderful traditional dress with their woven artwork spread out around them for sale. Within the museum, photographs and exhibits of textiles and other village crafts show the incredible richness of traditional arts in Guatemala's highland towns. If you enjoy seeing Guatemalan textiles at all, you must make a visit to the Museo Ixchel.

The museum is open Monday to Saturday 9 am to 5.30 pm. Admission costs US$0.75 for adults, US$0.25 students, and US$0.10 for children. You can walk to the Museo Ixchel from the Museo Popol Vuh. Walk south along Avenida La Reforma for seven blocks; you'll pass the Hotel Camino Real on the left. At 16 Calle turn left and walk a few blocks to 4a Avenida, turn right (south) and the museum is only a few metres farther along.

ZONA 13

The major attraction in the southern reaches of the city is the Parque Aurora with its zoo, children's playground, fairgrounds, and several museums offering free admission.

The Moorish-looking Museo Nacional de Arqueología y Etnología (☎ (2) 72-04-89) has a collection of Mayan sculptures, ceramics and jade, plus some displays of traditional handicrafts. Facing the Museo Nacional de Arqueología y Etnología is the Museo Nacional de Arte Moderno (☎ (2) 72-04-67), with a collection of 20th-century Guatemalan art, especially painting and sculpture. Hours at both museums are Monday to Friday from 9 am to 4 pm, Saturday and Sunday from 9 to noon and 2 to 4 pm.

Several hundred metres east of the museums is the city's official handicrafts market, the Mercado de Artesanía (☎ (2) 72-02-08), on 11a Avenida, just off the access road to the airport. Like most official handicrafts markets it's a sleepy place in which shopkeepers display the same sorts of things which you find for sale in hotel gift shops. The place livens up when a tour bus rolls in, but commits itself to slumber again when the bus pulls out. Hours are officially 9 am to 6 pm Monday to Saturday, 9 am to 1 pm Sunday.

KAMINALJUYÚ

Several km west of the centre lie the extensive ruins of Kaminaljuyú, a Late Preclassic/Early Classic Mayan site which has provided archaeologists with tantalising insights into the early centuries of Mayan florescence. Kaminaljuyú was conquered by the armies of Teotihuacán (near Mexico City), and the resulting culture shows both Mexican and Mayan influences. Unfortunately, much of Kaminaljuyú has been covered by urban sprawl. What has not been covered is presently being excavated. Though you are allowed to visit from 8 am

to 6 pm daily, your time would be better spent looking at the artefacts recovered here which are on display in the city's museums.

PLACES TO STAY

Guatemala City has a good range of lodgings in all price ranges. Those at the very bottom end of the price scale, as well as those at the very top, often fill up, but there are usually plenty of rooms to be had at prices in-between. Taxes totalling 17% are added to hotel bills in Guatemala. I've already included those taxes in the prices quoted here.

PLACES TO STAY – BOTTOM END

Perhaps the greatest concentration of low-budget hotels in the city is about eight blocks south of the Plaza Mayor near the Policia Nacional (National Police Headquarters) and the Correos (Post Office), in the area bounded by 6a Avenida 'A' and 9a Avenida, and 14 and 16 Calles. There are at least a dozen decent hotels to choose from, and several handy little restaurants as well. It's very important to keep street noise in mind as you search for a budget room.

Hotel Chalet Suizo (☎ (2) 51-37-86), 14 Calle 6-82, Zona 1, has been a popular stopping place for adventurous international travellers for decades. Swiss travel posters greet you as you enter, but the courtyard is tropical Guatemalan with lots of plants. The 25 rooms are clean and quite presentable, though some are darker and more claustrophobic than others. Rates are US$9 a double, or US$12 a double with private shower. Although more rooms have recently been added in a new wing, you should book in advance, as the hotel is usually full.,

Hotel Lessing House (☎ (2) 51-38-91), 12 Calle 4-35, Zona 1, is run by an efficient señora who offers seven tidy rooms for rent. A few simple handicraft decorations brighten them up considerably. An advantage here is that rooms can accommodate one (US$5.50), two (US$9), three (US$11.50) or four (US$15); the larger rooms have private showers. Hot water is trustworthy, as is the welcome at this well-regarded pension.

Spring Hotel (☎ (2) 51-42-07, 51-48-76), 8a Avenida 12-65, Zona 1, is often *completo* (full up) with budget travellers, so it's best to stop by and reserve a room a day or two in advance if possible. The location is good, the 28 rooms presentable, the courtyard sunny, and the price right: US$9 a double with private shower. Bathless rooms are even cheaper.

Hotel Capri (☎ (2) 51-37-37/18), 9a Avenida 15-63, Zona 1, offers good value for money. The desk clerk is well groomed, the staff is busy energetically sweeping and dusting, the 18 rooms are simple but clean and usable, and the prices are only US$6.50 a single, US$11 a double; if you want a private shower the price rises to US$12 a double. By the way, the *Hotel España* (☎ (2) 2-91-13), 9a Avenida 15-59, nearby, is quite large (74 rooms) and very cheap but it's pretty beat-up. You do much better at the Capri.

Hogar del Turista (☎ (2) 2-55-22), 11 Calle 10-43, Zona 1, is a simple city house which has become a 'home for tourists', as its name says. Two narrow courtyards allow in some sun, and two hard-working señoras keep everything tidy. The 14 rooms are decorated with local crafts, and most of the rooms have windows opening onto the courtyards to provide light. (Look at your prospective room before you register; can you bear one without a window?) Prices are a bit higher here, at US$13 a single, US$16 a double, for a room with private shower. Breakfast is available at a small extra charge, and there's free parking.

Right next door is the *Hotel Casa Real* (☎ (2) 2-11-42), 11 Calle 10-57, Zona 1, a casa de huéspedes operated by the aged Señora Blanca v de Beteta. If the Hogar del Turista is full, many travellers find a home here. None of the eight rooms has any plumbing, but some are quite large, with skylights to let in the sun; some rooms are better than others, so look around a bit before choosing. There's a tidy garden courtyard. The reasonable rate is US$3.50 per person.

Hotel Excel (☎ (2) 53-27-09), 9a Avenida 15-12, Zona 1, is a real find, a bright and modern place with 17 rooms on three levels around an L-shaped court used as a car park. It's simple but clean and pleasant, with double rooms with bath going for US$16 and triples for US$22. Most rooms have colour TVs.

Hotel San Diego (☎ (2) 2-29-58), 15 Calle 7-37, Zona 1, is a good, very cheap, family-oriented hotel with a selection of 16 rooms, all without private bath. Prices are: US$2.50 to US$3 a single, US$4 to US$5 a double, US$6 to US$7.50 a triple, US$10 for four.

Hotel Ajau (☎ (2) 2-04-88), 8a Avenida 15-62, Zona 1, is fairly clean, somewhat cheaper, and a lot quieter than many 9a Avenida hotels. You pay US$6.75 a double without private shower, US$9 with.

The 16-room *Hotel Hernani* (☎ (2) 2-28-39), 15 Calle 6-56, Zona 1, is a small, well-located, dignified old hotel without a lot of charm but with decent rooms. Most rooms have private showers, but the shower for your room is not necessarily *in* your room; it may be a few steps down the hall. Prices are US$7/12/15.50 a single/double/triple with shower.

Hotel Bilbao (☎ (2) 2-92-03), 15 Calle 8-45, Zona 1, is spartan but serviceable, renting rooms at the low rates of US$6.75 a double without shower, US$8.75 with. The *Hotel Bilbao 2*, half a block away at the corner of 15 Calle and 8a Avenida, charges slightly more.

Hotel Belmont (☎ (2) 51-15-41), 9a Avenida 15-30, Zona 1, is a fairly large establishment of 62 rooms with so much wrought-ironwork dividing the lobby from the outside that you may think you're going to jail – but don't get the wrong idea, this is a fine place to stay. Rooms cost US$10.50 a double with shared bathroom, or US$12 for a double with its own bath. The *Hotel Belmont 2* a few steps down the street is similar. 9a Avenida is a very noisy street, so be sure to get rooms well away from it.

Pensión Meza (☎ (2) 2-31-77), 10 Calle 10-17, Zona 1, has seen very hard use, and refurbishment is infrequent, but it's often busy with international budget travellers who like the sunny courtyard, the camaraderie, the helpful old proprietor, and the low price of US$4 per person. Shared baths only here. The adjoining restaurant serves cheap meals.

PLACES TO STAY – MIDDLE

Guatemala City's middle-range lodging-places offer excellent value for money. All are comfortable, some quite charming. There are many locations from which to choose.

Posada Belén (☎ (2) 2-92-26, 53-45-30, 51-34-78), 13 Calle 'A' 10-30, Zona 1, is on a little side street, and is therefore quiet. A charming, quiet hostelry with a longstanding reputation for good hospitality, the Belén now consists of three neighbouring houses. To preserve the quiet, children under five years of age are not accepted. Each of the three houses has a nice little sunny courtyard with tropical plants, some have fountains, and all have plentiful local textiles as decoration. The price is US$9 to US$11 per person in a room with bath.

Hotel Villa Española (☎ (2) 36-54-17, 36-56-11), 2 Calle 7-51, Zona 9, is a colonial motel set in its own walled compound in the midst of a tree-shaded residential and commercial district. White stucco, red-brick arcades and dark wood make this the place Pedro de Alvarado would have stayed if he had been a tourist rather than a conquistador. Built on three levels with motel-style open walkways, the 67 rooms are very comfortable; all have private baths (with tubs), many have large beds and some have TVs. The courtyard serves as a safe car park and there's a good dining room and bar. Rates are surprisingly reasonable, at US$40 a double.

Hotel Ritz Continental (☎ (2) 8-08-89, 2-10-85; fax 2-46-59), 6a Avenida 'A' 10-13, Zona 1, is a large hotel of 202 rooms decorated in 1960s style. Once the city's finest hostelry, its marble-paved lobby still bustles with tourists and bellhops because the rooms are comfy (if less than stylish) and the prices are moderate. Services include a swimming pool, games room (billiards, chess, backgammon, cards, dominoes), restaurant and a bar with live entertainment. The rooms have

colour cable TVs and, of course, private baths. The location, three blocks south of the Plaza Mayor, is quiet and convenient. The rate is US$50 a double. A good set-price lunch in the Ritz's dining room costs less than US$4.

Hotel Pan American (☎ (2) 2-68-07/8/9, 2-64-02, 53-59-91), 9 Calle 5-63, Zona 1, was this city's luxury hotel between WW I and WW II. It still attracts many faithful return visitors and new ones who want to experience a bit of its faded charm. The interior courtyard, once busy with coffee traders and banana growers, is now set up as the dining room and decorated with colourful *huipiles*; waiters wear traditional Guatemalan highland costumes. In keeping with the 1930s ambience, there is only one elevator, complete with elevator operator. The 60 rooms are all Art Deco and Biedermeyer, but surprisingly plain, though comfortable enough. The clean private bathrooms have tubs and showers, and each room has a large colour cable TV. Avoid rooms facing the noisy street. Rates are US$40 a single, US$48 a double.

Hotel Plaza (☎ (2) 36-31-73, 31-63-37; fax 2-27-05), Vía 7, 6-16, Zona 4, is about one km south of the Centro Cívico and a 15-minute walk east of the market and bus station area. Though called a hotel, it might best be described as a Spanish Bauhaus motel with colonial appointments. The 57 comfortable rooms on two floors are arranged facing the enclosed parking lot or the courtyard's heated swimming pool. There's a nice restaurant and a bar with live entertainment. Room prices are US$38 a single, US$48 a double.

Hotel Del Centro (☎ (2) 2-55-47, 2-59-80, 8-15-19; fax 2-27-05), 13 Calle 4-55, Zona 1, is a good, solid tourist and business travellers' hotel that's been providing dependable service and comfortable accommodation for decades. The 60 large, airy guestrooms come with shiny bathrooms, colour TVs, and often with two double beds; there's a bit of street noise in some. The price, US$52 a double, is quite reasonable for what you get. The 2nd-floor dining room offers good, reasonably-priced table d'hôte lunches for about US$4.

Hotel Colonial (☎ (2) 2-67-22, 2-29-55, 8-12-08), 7a Avenida 14-19, Zona 1, is a large old city house converted to a hotel. Refurbishment has been done with a weighty colonial hand – lots of stucco and heavy furniture – but the covered interior court is pleasant, the 47 rooms clean and serviceable, with tidy bathrooms. Some rooms are better than others, so inspect several. Rates are US$14 a single, US$23 a double.

Hotel-Apartamentos Guatemala Internacional (☎ (2) 8-44-41 to 45), 6a Avenida 12-21, Zona 1, offers 18 fully furnished apartments for the price of normal hotel rooms. Each apartment has a bedroom (one double bed and one single), a small living room with a day bed, table and chairs for dining or working, tiled bathroom with tub and shower, a kitchen with a full-sized refrigerator-freezer, four-burner cooker, sink, and kitchen utensils. It's the perfect place for families or two congenial couples, the location is convenient, and the price is good: for two people, rates range from US$26 to US$34, depending upon the apartment.

Hotel Centenario (☎ (2) 8-03-81 to 83), 6 Calle 5-33, Zona 1, on the north side of the Parque Centenario and just west of the Palacio Nacional, has a very plain façade and entrance, but 43 comfortable rooms, many with a double and a single bed, plus well-worn but clean showers. There's also a sauna. Prices for this central location are US$20 a single, US$28 a double.

PLACES TO STAY – TOP END

Most luxurious of this city's hotels is the *Hotel Camino Real Guatemala* (☎ (2) 33-46-33; fax 37-43-13; in the USA (800) 228-3000), Avenida La Reforma at 14 Calle, Zona 10, in the midst of the Zona Viva. This is the capital's international-class hotel, with all of the comforts, including restaurants, bars, nightclub, swimming pools and lush gardens. Double rooms cost US$130 to US$150.

Also in the Zona Viva is the 230-room *Hotel Guatemala Fiesta* (☎ (2) 32-25-55 to -66), 1a Avenida 13-22, Zona 10, almost as posh as the Camino Real, with all the services (including a heated swimming pool), but lower prices. A very comfortable double room here costs US$100.

Several hundred metres north of the Zona Viva stands the *Hotel Cortijo Reforma* (☎ (2) 36-67-12 to 16), Avenida La Reforma 2-18, Zona 9, a block east of Guatemala City's version of the Eiffel Tower. This all-suite building offers accommodation decorated in earth tones, with bedroom, living room, minibar, tiled bathroom with tub and shower, space for a kitchenette, and a tiny balcony with a view (from some rooms) of the volcanoes which surround Guatemala City. Price for two persons in a suite is a reasonable US$85.

Hotel Conquistador Sheraton (☎ (2) 6-46-91, 31-22-22; in the USA (800) 325-3535), Vía 5 No 4-68, Zona 4, 200 metres south of the Centro Cívico, is pleasant and attractive with an obliging staff, nice little swimming pool, good restaurant, and 170 bright, modern rooms decorated in white stucco and natural wood. As it is located between busy 7a and 6a Avenidas, many rooms are noisy. Rates are very reasonable for a Sheraton: US$60 to $85 a double.

PLACES TO EAT – BOTTOM END

It is not difficult to find cheap eats in this city. Fast-food and snack shops abound. But to really save money, head for Parque Concordia bounded by 4a and 5a Avenidas and 14 and 15 Calles in Zona 1. The west side of the park is lined with little open-air food stalls serving sandwiches and snacks at rock-bottom prices from early morning to late evening. A meal for US$1 is the rule here.

Delicadezas Hamburgo (☎ 8-16-27), 15 Calle 5-34, Zona 1, on the south side of Parque Concordia, provides a long list of sandwiches at lunch and dinner, as well as German, Guatemalan and American platters at moderate prices. It has a pleasant delicatessen atmosphere and efficient service. Breakfasts go for US$1 to US$2. Hours are from 7 am to 10 pm every day.

Restaurant Cantón, 6a Avenida 14-20,

Zona 1, facing the park on its east side, is the place to go for cheap Chinese food. When you see the prices – wonton soup for US$3, plates of chow mein or chop suey for US$3 and US$4 – you may think I'm wrong. But sit down in this pleasant little place and order only one item from the long menu and it may be more than you can eat. That bowl of wonton soup is easily a meal in itself, and the platters are absolutely enormous. Two people can easily split one platter. The *Canton* is open from 9 am to 5 pm and from 5.30 pm to midnight every day of the week.

There are numerous other Chinese restaurants near the corner of 6a Avenida and 14 Calle, Zona 1. The city's other rich concentration of Chinese restaurants is in the blocks west of the Parque Centenario along 6 Calle, where you'll find the *Restaurant Long Wah* (☎ 2-66-11), 6 Calle 3-70, Zona 1, along with several other places such as *Felicidades, Palacio Real* and *China Hilton*.

6a Avenida between 10 and 15 Calles has dozens of restaurants and fast-food shops of all types: hamburgers, pizzas, pasta, Chinese, fried chicken. You'll have no trouble eating well for US$2 to US$3.

9a Avenida between 15 and 16 Calles, in the midst of the cheap hotel area, has several good little restaurants. There's the *Cafetín El Rinconcito*, 9a Avenida 15-74, facing the Hotel Capri, which is good for tacos, and the restaurant in the Hotel Capri itself, 9a Avenida 15-63, Zona 1, for more substantial meals. The *Hotel Colonial*, 7a Avenida 14-19, Zona 1, has a slightly better and pricier restaurant.

You might also want to try the *Cafetería El Roble*, 9 Calle 5-46, Zona 1, facing the entrance to the Hotel Pan American. This clean little café is very popular with local office workers who come for breakfast (US$1), lunch and dinner (US$2).

Pollo Campero (Country Chicken) is the name of Guatemala's Kentucky Fried Chicken clone. You can find branches of the chain on the corner of 9 Calle and 5a Avenida, and at 6a Avenida and 15 Calle, and at 8 Calle 9-29, all in Zona 1. Cheerful chicken colours of orange and yellow pre-

dominate in these bright, clean places. Two pieces of chicken, french fries (chips), and a soft drink or coffee costs only US$2; three pieces of chicken with salad costs just slightly more.

McDonald's (☎ 51-98-62), complete with Big Macs and armed guards, is at 10 Calle 5-30, Zona 1. Order a Big Mac, *papas fritas*, and a soft drink for about US$2. A *queso-burguesa* is a cheeseburger, and a *quarto de libra* is a Quarter-Pounder. Breakfasts of scrambled eggs or pancakes *(panqueques)* are served here as well.

Multirestaurantes, at the corner of 10 Calle and 6a Avenida, Zona 1, is a spacious covered courtyard with a fountain, and wooden picnic tables at which you can eat Guatemalan, North American, Chinese, or Italian dishes bought from the fast-food shops which surround the court. Full meals for under US$3 are easy to find.

If you're visiting the Museo Popol Vuh and need a bite, try the *Pastelería Las Américas* (☎ 32-56-54), in the same building as the museum, at the corner of Reforma and 9 Calle. Sandwiches and burgers are priced at US$1.75, and you can eat at outdoor café tables. Hot and cold drinks are served.

PLACES TO EAT – MIDDLE

Most middle-range hotels in Zona 1 offer excellent set-price lunches for US$4 to US$6. Try the *Hotel Del Centro, Hotel Pan American*, and *Hotel Ritz Continental*. My favourite for ambience is definitely the Pan American, 9 Calle 5-63, Zona 1.

Restaurant Altuna (☎ 2-06-69, 51-71-85), 5a Avenida 12-31, Zona 1, is a large place with many dining rooms located just a few steps north of the Hotel Del Centro. Dark wood furniture, white tablecloths, and a formal but pleasant decor complement the excellent service. Specialities are seafood and Spanish dishes, both traditional and with Guatemalan touches. Full cost for a meal is about US$10 per person; it's open for lunch and dinner every day of the week.

Restaurant Bologna (☎ 51-11-67), 10 Calle 6-20, Zona 1, just around the corner from the Hotel Ritz Continental, is very small but attractive, serving tasty pizzas, spaghetti, ravioli, and lasagna for US$2 to US$3 per plate, or more substantial grilled meats for about US$4 and US$5. Hours are 10 am to 10 pm Tuesday to Sunday, closed Monday. The Zona Viva branch, at Plaza Rosa No 2, 13 Calle 1-62, Zona 10, is much fancier.

Café Bohemia (☎ 8-24-74), 11 Calle 8- 48, Zona 1, is the place to go for Central European pastries and baked goods. It's appropriately homey with dark wood and aproned staff. A cup of coffee and a pastry need cost only US$1.

Several other good restaurants have their main establishments in Zona 1, and branches in Zona 9 or 10.

El Gran Pavo (The Big Turkey, ☎ 2-99-12, 51-09- 33), 13 Calle 4-41, Zona 1, is just to the left (west) of the Hotel Del Centro's entrance. Large and spare, the dining rooms are the salons of an old town house. The menu seems to include every Mexican dish imaginable, from seafood Veracruz-style to mole poblano, from panuchos yucatecos to cabrito al horno. The *birria*, a spicy-hot soup of meat, onions, peppers and *cilantro* (coriander leaf), served with tortillas, is a meal in itself at US$2. Order the huge Mexican combination plate and your dinner bill might total US$5, but you can dine for more or less as you like. Service here is slow. The Big Turkey is open seven days a week from 11.30 am to 1 am. There's another branch (☎ 32-56-93) at 12 Calle 5-54, Zona 9.

Restaurant Piccadilly (☎ 51-42-68, 53-92-23), 6a Avenida 11-01, Zona 1, is among the capital's most popular eateries with everyone, young and old, ordering from a menu that might have been taken straight from the United Nations cafeteria: *churrasco*, shish kebab, hamburgers, Guatemalan sausage, lots of pastas and chicken cacciatore are all served. Most main courses cost US$3 or less. There's another branch of the Piccadilly on the Plazuela España, 7a Avenida 12-00, Zona 9.

PLACES TO EAT – TOP END

The most elegant dining in the city is to be found in the Zona Viva, the several blocks surrounding the Camino Real Guatemala Hotel and the Hotel Guatemala Fiesta. The dining rooms of these two top hotels provide good food in elegant surroundings with polished service. *La Fonda del Camino* in the Camino Real serves dinner Monday to Saturday from 6.30 pm to midnight.

La Trattoria (☎ 31-06-12), 13 Calle 1- 55, Zona 10, is the place to go for good Italian specialities. The façade is lined with potted geraniums, the pleasant dining room with old prints. Service is attentive. You can expect to spend about US$10 or US$12 per person for dinner with wine.

Restaurante El Parador (☎ 32-00-62), Avenida La Reforma 6-70, Zona 9, a block from the Museo Popol Vuh, is an attractive Guatemalan steakhouse. Rough dark wood, hand-woven textiles and basketwork lampshades set the mood. At dinner, meats are priced from US$5 to US$9, fish at US$5 (shrimp costs more), but luncheon is cheaper. It's a pleasant place open for lunch and dinner every day of the week.

Hacienda de los Sánchez (☎ 36-52-40), 12 Calle 2-25, Zona 10, is where Guatemalan meat-eaters come to pig out. The ambience is aggressively *ranchero*, with a huge tent-pavilion framed by royal palms. Inside, honey-coloured wood tables and benches, menus with heavy leather covers, and the smell of woodsmoke are gathered around an old chuck wagon. Steaks and ribs are priced about US$7 to US$8. The parking lot is full of shiny American pickup trucks. This is where the Marlboro Man eats. It's open every day from noon to midnight.

Puerto Barrios (☎ 34-13-02, 36-56-46), 7a Avenida 10-65, Zona 9, is aggressively nautical the way Hacienda de los Sánchez is aggressively ranchero. This ship-shaped restaurant comes complete with waiters in knee-breeches and frogged coats, oil paintings of buccaneers, portholes for windows, and a big compass by the door. The manager is not even the manager, he's El Capitán. The long menu is not cheap, perhaps because you're paying for all the theatrics. Ceviches go for US$6 or US$7, soups for a bit less, fish for US$8 to US$12. You can easily spend US$16 to US$30 per person here. Come aboard any day from noon to 10 pm.

Siriaco's (☎ 34-63-16), 1a Avenida 12-12, Zona 10, very near the Hotel Guatemala Fiesta, is flashy but informal with a sunken dining room and bar, a skylighted patio courtyard, and a menu of the favourite continental specialities. Expect to spend US$15 or so per person for dinner.

La Brisa Seafood Bar, at the corner of 1a Avenida and 12 Calle, Zona 10, a block from the Hotel Guatemala Fiesta, next door to Siriaco's, is a simple place with lots of windows, Brazilian music (when I was there), and interesting seafood dishes such as shrimp ravioli, in addition to the more traditional preparations. Fish is priced from US$7 to US$8, shrimp up to US$10. On Monday and Saturday there's paella a la Valenciana.

Palacio Royal (☎ 31-42-73, 32-38-57), 7a Avenida 11-00, Zona 9, just off the Plazuela España, is among the best Chinese restaurants in the city. It's a lavish layout encompassing several buildings around the obligatory Chinese garden. Dining rooms are simple but pleasant. Waiters in black and white scurry around carrying choices from a very long menu printed in Chinese, Spanish and English. You can dine frugally (US$6) or lavishly (US$18). The Royal Palace is open for lunch and dinner every day.

For equally good food in more modest surroundings, try the *Restaurante Excellent* (☎ 36-42-78), 2a Avenida 12-74, Zona 10, in the Zona Viva. Beef with mangoes, sweet-and-sour prawns with lychee, Peking duck and similar items are yours to choose from. Prices are similar to those at the Palacio Royal. Hours are noon to 10 pm every day.

ENTERTAINMENT

Wining and dining the night away in the Zona Viva is what many visitors do. If that's beyond your budget, take in a movie at one of the cinemas along 6a Avenida between the Plaza Mayor and Parque Concordia. Walk along the street to see what's playing. Tickets sell for about US$1.25.

GETTING THERE & AWAY
Air

Deregulation of air service in Guatemala has resulted in the founding and expansion of several new Guatemalan airlines. There is more convenient air service than ever before, but some of these airlines and routes will no doubt disappear in the next few years, while others will expand. Contact a travel agent or the airline for the latest news.

Here are the companies:

Aerocaribe, a Yucatán regional carrier owned by Mexicana, flies between Cancún and Santa Elena (near Tikal), then on to Guatemala City. There may soon be a change in the airline's name; enquire at any Mexicana office.

Aeronica (☎ 32-55-41, 31-67-59; fax 32-56-49), 10 Calle 6-20, Zona 9, Guatemala City, is a Nicaraguan airline serving Central America, Canada and Europe. They have an office in Antigua (☎ (3) 2-07-48) at 2 Calle Oriente No 2.

Aeroquetzal (☎ (2) 31-11-73, 34-76-80/85/88; fax 34-76-89), Avenida Hincapié y 18 Calle, Zona 13, Hangar 8, Aeropuerto Internacional La Aurora, Guatemala City, was once a small domestic airline, but it has begun to expand into international service, and now flies nonstop between Los Angeles and Guatemala City, carrying mostly tour groups. The airline plans to begin flights between Guatemala City and Chicago, Managua, Miami, New Orleans, San José (Costa Rica), San Pedro Sula (Honduras), San Salvador (El Salvador) and Tapachula. There are Aeroquetzal offices in Santa Elena, Petén (near Tikal; ☎ (9) 81-15-94; fax 81-15-63), and in Cancún at AVISA (☎ (988) 4-02-38, 4-49-28, 4-26-04, 4-19-68; fax 4-41-19), Avenida Yaxchilán 31-8.

Aerovías (☎ (2) 31-69-35, 31-96-63, 32-56-86), Avenida Hincapié and 18 Calle, Zona 13, Guatemala City, on the eastern side of the runways of La Aurora International Airport, operates medium-sized propeller aircraft between Belize City and Santa Elena (near Tikal), onward to Guatemala City and return. Aerovías has a representative in the USA (☎ (305) 883-1345). The central office (☎ (2) 6-42-81/85) in Guatemala City is at 9a Avenida 12-38, Zona 1. In Belize City, there is an office at the airport, and another at the Mopan Hotel (☎ (2) 7-54-45).

Air France (☎ (2) 36-73-71, 36-76-67), Avenida La Reforma 9-00, Zona 9, Edificio Plaza Panamericana, 8th floor, Guatemala City

Aviateca (☎ (2) 8-13-72, 8-14-15/79, and 8-15-79), 10 Calle and 6a Avenida, Zona 1, Edificio Plaza Vivar, 3rd floor, offices 1 and 2, Guatemala City.

For information and reservations call them at La Aurora International Airport (☎ (2) 6-41- 81/85). The Guatemalan national airline has been privatised and is expanding its international routes. In the USA, call Aviateca at (800) 327-9832.

British Airways (☎ (2) 31-25-55), Avenida La Reforma 8-60, Zona 9, Edificio Galerías Reforma, Torre II, Guatemala City

Continental (☎ (2) 31-20-51 to 55), La Aurora International Airport

COPA Compañía Panameña de Aviación SA (☎ (2) 6-62-56, 31-68-13, 31-84-43) is a Panamanian airline serving Central and South America.

Iberia (☎ (2) 37-39-14/15, 53-65-55), Avenida La Reforma 8-60, Zona 9, Edificio Galerías Reforma

Japan Air Lines (☎ (2) 31-85-97; fax 31-85-31), 7a Avenida 15-45, Zona 9, Guatemala City

KLM Royal Dutch Airlines (☎ (2) 37-02-22), 6a Avenida 20-25, Zona 10, Edificio Plaza Marítima, Guatemala City

LACSA Líneas Aéreas Costarricenses SA (☎ (2) 37-39-05 to 07, or 31-87-47), 7a Avenida 14-44, Zona 9, Edificio La Galería, Guatemala City, is a Costa Rican airline.

Lufthansa German Airlines (☎ (2) 37-01-13 to 16), 6a Avenida 20-25, Zona 10, Edificio Plaza Marítima, Guatemala City

Mexicana (☎ (2) 6-20-84 to 87), 12 Calle 4- 55, Zona 1, Guatemala City

Pan American World Airways (☎ (2) 53-25- 23), 6a Avenida 11-43, Zona 1, Guatemala City

SAHSA (☎ (2) 32-10-71/2/3), 12 Calle 1-25, Zona 10, Edificio Geminis 10, Office 208, Guatemala City, is a Honduran airline.

TACA International Airlines (☎ (2) 80-00-61 to 64), 10 Calle 5-00, Zona 1, Guatemala City, is a Costa Rican airline.

TAPSA Transportes Aereos Profesionales SA (☎ (2) 31-48-60), Avenida Hincapié, Zona 13, Guatemala City, on the eastern side of the runways at La Aurora International Airport, operates small propeller planes on flights to and from Santa Elena (near Tikal).

International air routes to Guatemala usually go through Dallas/Fort Worth, Houston, Los Angeles, Miami, Mexico City or San Salvador. If you begin your trip in any other city, you will probably find yourself stopping in one of these 'hub' cities. There are a few exceptions, mostly flights from cities in the region operated by smaller local airlines. Here are the cities with direct and nonstop flights to and from Guatemala City, and the airlines which fly them:

Belize City – Aerovías has three flights weekly via Santa Elena (Tikal); TACA has daily flights via San Salvador

Cancún – Aerocaribe (Mexicana) and Aeroquetzal have daily flights

Houston – Continental has direct flights daily, and Aviateca three flights per week via Mérida

Los Angeles – daily flights are by American, Aviateca, Mexicana, Pan Am and TACA; most of these flights make at least one stop along the way

Mérida – three flights weekly by Aviateca (see Houston)

Mexico City – Mexicana and Aviateca have daily nonstop flights

Miami – lots of daily flights by American, Aviateca, Pan Am and TACA; many European airlines connect through Miami

New York (JFK) – there is one direct flight by TAN; all other flights connect through Miami, Houston or Dallas/Fort Worth

San José (Costa Rica) – daily nonstops by American, Continental and Medellín, and a direct flight with one stop by LACSA three times per week

San Salvador (El Salvador) – daily nonstops by COPA and TACA

Santa Elena (near Tikal) – Aerocaribe, Aeroquetzal, Aerovías, Aviateca and TAPSA operate daily flights. Note that some flights to Santa Elena (Tikal) depart from the east side of the airport (the main terminal is on the west side); to reach the TAPSA terminal, for instance, you must take a taxi to the east side.

Bus

Unfortunately, Guatemala City has no central bus terminal, even though many Guatemalans talk about the Terminal de Autobuses. Ticket offices and departure points are different for each company. Many are near the huge and chaotic market in Zona 4. If the bus you desire is one of these, the only thing to do is go to the market and ask until you find the bus.

Here is bus route information for most of Guatemala:

Antigua – 45 km, one hour; Transportes Unidos (☎ (2) 2-49-49), 15 Calle 3-65, Zona 1, makes the trip every half-hour for US$0.50 from 7 am to 7 pm stopping in San Lucas Sacatepéquez. Buses Inter-Hotel y Turismo (BIT, ☎ (9) 32-00-11/15 at the Ramada Hotel Antigua) runs new, comfortable minibuses between the airport and Antigua, departing from the airport at 7.15 am and 6.15 pm, arriving in Antigua 45 minutes later. The fare is US$8.

Chichicastenango – 146 km, 3½ hours; Veloz Quichelense, Terminal de Buses, Zona 4, runs buses every half-hour from 5 am to 6 pm, stopping in San Lucas, Chimaltenango and Los Encuentros for a fare of US$2.25

Chiquimula – 169km, three hours; Rutas Orientales (☎ (2) 53-72-82, 51-21-60), 19 Calle 8-18, Zona 1, runs buses via El Rancho, Río Hondo and Zacapa to Chiquimula every 30 minutes from 4 am to 6 pm, for US$2 to US$2.75, depending on the bus. If you're heading for Copán, Honduras, change to a Vilma bus at Chiquimula; see El Florido for details.

Cobán – 219 km, four hours; Escobar Monja Blanca (☎ (2) 51-18-78), 8a Avenida 15-16, Zona 1, has buses at 5, 7, 8, 9, 10 am and noon, 2, 2.30, 4 and 4.30 pm stopping at the Biotopo del Quetzal, Purulhá, Tactic and San Cristóbal for US$2.75.

Copán (Honduras) – see El Florido

El Carmen/Talisman (Mexico) – 278 km, five hours; Transportes Galgos (☎ (2) 53-48-68, 2-36-61), 7a Avenida 19-44, Zona 1, runs buses along the Pacific Slope road to this border-crossing point, stopping at Escuintla (change for Santa Lucía Cotzumalguapa), Mazatenango, Retalhuleu and Coatepeque, at 5.45 and 10 am, noon, 3.30 and 5.30 pm, for US$3.20.

El Florido/Copán (Honduras) – 280 km, seven hours; Rutas Orientales (☎ (2) 53-72-82, 51-21-60), 19 Calle 8-18, Zona 1, runs buses via El Rancho, Río Hondo and Zacapa to Chiquimula every 30 minutes from 4 am to 6 pm, for US$2 to US$2.75, depending on the bus. In Chiquimula you transfer to a Vilma bus for the remaining 58-km, 2½-hour trip via Jocotán and Camotán to this border-crossing point. From the border you must take a minibus to Copán village and the ruins. Refer to the Copán section for more details.

Esquipulas – 222 km, four hours; Rutas Orientales (☎ (2) 53-72-82, 51-21-60), 19 Calle 8-18, Zona 1, has buses departing every half-hour from 4 am to 6 pm, with stops at El Rancho, Río Hondo, Zacapa and Chiquimula. The trip costs US$2.75.

Flores (Petén) – 506 km, 14 hours; Fuentes del Norte (☎ (2) 8-60-94, 51-38-17), 17 Calle 8-46, Zona 1, runs buses at 1, 2, 3 and 7 am, and 11 pm on this gruelling, bone-bashing journey. If your finances can at all afford it, fly instead of taking the bus. Stops are made at Morales, Río Dulce, San Luis, and Poptún. A one-way ticket costs US$6 or US$12, depending upon the comfort (such as it is) of the bus.

Huehuetenango – 270 km, five hours; Los Falcones (☎ (2) 8-19-79), 7a Avenida 15-27, Zona 1, runs two buses a day (7 am and 2 pm) up the Pan American Highway to Huehue, stopping at Chimaltenango, Patzicía, Tecpán, Los Encuentros, and San Cristóbal Totonicapán. The fare is US$3.

La Democracia – 92 km, two hours; Chatia Gomerana, Muelle Central, Terminal de Buses, Zona 4, has buses every half-hour from 6 am to 4.30 pm, stopping at Escuintla, Siquinalá (change for Santa Lucía Cotzumalguapa), La Democracia, La Gomera and Sipacate. The fare is US$1.

La Mesilla/Ciudad Cuauhtémoc (Mexico) – 342 km, seven hours; El Condor (☎ (2) 2-85-04), 19 Calle 2-01, Zona 1, goes to La Mesilla, on the Pan American Highway at the border with Mexico, at 4, 8 and 10 am, and 1 and 5 pm daily for US$3.

Panajachel – 147 km, three hours; Rebulli (☎ (2) 51-65-05), 3a Avenida 2-36, Zona 9, departs for Lake Atitlán and Panajachel every hour from 6.45 am to 4 pm, stopping at Chimaltenango, Patzicía, Tecpán Guatemala (for the ruins at Iximché), Los Encuentros, and Sololá, for US$1.75.

Puerto Barrios – 307 km, six hours; Litegua (☎ (2) 2-75-78), 15 Calle 10-42, Zona 1, has regular buses every hour from 6 am to 5 pm, and Pullman express buses (faster and more comfortable) at 10 am and 5 pm. Stops are at El Rancho, Teculután, Río Hondo and Los Amates (Quiriguá); fare is US$3.50 or US$4.

Quetzaltenango – 203 km, four hours; Transportes Galgos, (☎ (2) 2-36-61), 7a Avenida 19-44, Zona 1, makes this run at 5.30, 8.30 and 11 am, and 2.30, 5, 7 and 9 pm, stopping at Chimaltenango, Los Encuentros and Totonicapán, for US$2.50.

Quiriguá – see Puerto Barrios

Retalhuleu – see El Carmen and Tecún Umán

Río Dulce – see Flores

Río Hondo – see Chiquimula, Esquipulas and Puerto Barrios

San Salvador (El Salvador) – 268 km, five hours; Melva Internacional (☎ (2) 36-72-48), 4a Avenida 1-20, Zona 9, runs buses from Guatemala City via Cuilapa, Oratorio and Jalpatagua to the Salvadoran border at Valle Nuevo and onward to San Salvador at 6, 7.30, 9, 10 and 11 am, noon and 1 pm, for US$3.25

San Vicente Pacaya – 46km, two hours; Cuquita, Muelle Central, Terminal de Buses, Zona 4, heads off to this volcano village south-west of the capital at 10.30 am, 12.30 and 2.30 pm daily, stopping at Amatitlán, for US$1

Santa Lucía Cotzumalguapa – see El Carmen, La Democracia and Tecún Umán

Tecún Umán/Ciudad Hidalgo (Mexico) – 253 km, five hours; Fortaleza (☎ (2) 51-79-94), 19 Calle 8-70, Zona 1, has buses at 5.30 and 9.30 am, stopping at Escuintla (change for Santa Lucía Cotzumalguapa), Mazatenango, Retalhuleu and Coatepeque

Tikal – see Flores

GETTING AROUND
To/From the Airport

La Aurora International Airport is in Zona 13, the southern part of the city, 10 or 15 minutes from Zona 1 by taxi, half an hour by bus. Car rental offices and taxi ranks are outside, down the stairs from the arrivals level. For the city bus stop you must go up to the departures level and make your way to the small park in front of the terminal. The No 5-Aeropuerto bus comes by every now and then, and will take you through Zonas 9 and 4 to Zona 1.

Taxi fares to various points in the centre are established, and are quite high: from the airport to Zona 9 or 10, US$4; to Zona 4, US$4.80; to Zona 1, US$6. A tip is expected. Be sure to establish the destination and price before getting info the taxi.

If you are going directly from the airport to Antigua, you may want to take the minibus run by Buses Inter-Hotel y Turismo (☎ in Antigua (9) 32-00-11/15), which makes the 40-minute trip daily at 7.15 am and 6.15 pm. The minibus drops passengers at several top hotels in Antigua. The fare (US$8), though much more than that of a local bus leaving from Zona 1, is much less than a taxi (US$40).

Bus & Jitney

Guatemala City buses are often pitiful to look at, lacking windows, paint and any padding on seats, but they work, they're unbelievably cheap, they're frequent, and though very crowded sometimes, they're useful. 6a Avenida (southbound) and 7a Avenida (northbound) in Zona 9 are loaded with buses traversing the city; in Zona 1 these buses tend to swing away from the commercial district and travel along 4a, 5a, 9a and 10a Avenidas. Most useful north-south bus routes are Nos 2, 5 and 14. Note that modified numbers (2A, 5-Bolívar, etc) follow different routes, and may not get you where you expect to go. Any bus with 'Terminal' in the front window stops at the inter-city bus 'terminal' near the market in Zona 4.

City buses stop running about 10.30 pm,

the city's traffic signals are turned off (yes!), and jitneys (ruleteros) begin to run up and down the main avenues. The jitneys run all night, until the buses resume their rattling rides at 4 am; hold up your hand as the signal to stop a jitney.

Taxi

Taxis are quite expensive, US$3 or US$4 for a normal ride – even a short one – within the city. Be sure to agree on the fare before entering the cab; there are no meters.

Car Rental

Major international companies have offices both at La Aurora Airport and in the city centre. The cost is high, about US$60 to US$75 per day total (including rental charges, insurance, charges per km and fuel) for even the cheapest car. Insurance does not protect you from all losses by collision or theft. You will usually be liable for $600 to $1500 of damage, after which the insurance covers any loss. Drive safely, park in a secure area at night, and you should do alright.

You must show your passport and driving licence when you rent, and you must normally be 25 years or older. If you do not have a valid credit card for the rental, a very large cash deposit may be required; check in advance to avoid disappointment.

As Guatemala grows in popularity as a tourist destination, rental cars become scarcer during the busiest times of year. Reserve a car ahead of time if possible.

Note that if you wish to drive a Guatemalan rental car to Copán in Honduras, you must obtain an official letter of permission from the car rental agency to give to the Guatemalan customs official at the border. Without such a letter, you must leave the car at the border and proceed by public transport.

Avis de Guatemala (☎ (2) 31-69-90, 36-74-69), 12 Calle 2-73, Zona 9
Budget (☎ (2) 32-25-91, 31-65-46), Avenida La Reforma 15-00, Zona 9
Dollar Rent a Car (☎ (2) 36-77-96, 31-02-59), 7a Avenida 7-28, Zona 9

Hertz (☎ (2) 32-22-42, 31-54-12), 7a Avenida 14-76, Zona 9

Rentalsa (☎ (2) 34-14-16), 11 Calle 2-18, Zona 9

Tabarini Rent-a-Car (☎ (2) 31-61-08, 31-98-14), 2 Calle 'A' 7-30, Zona 10

Tally Renta Autos (☎ (2) 51-41-13, 2-33-27), 7a Avenida 14-60, Zona 1

Tikal (☎ (2) 36-78-32), 2 Calle 6-56, Zona 10

Driving

Except in Guatemala City, major roads in this country are delightfully free of heavy traffic. The capital city is just the opposite. Automotive speed and daring are expressions of machismo. There are surprisingly few accidents, however. Drive carefully, expect the unexpected, and be aware that at night, when the traffic signals are not working, traffic on Avenidas has priority over traffic on Calles (if you're travelling on a Calle, stop and look at every Avenida you cross). The rule at night is not to trust any other driver to do what's expected.

Guatemala's Highlands

The highlands, stretching from Antigua to the Mexican border north-west of Huehuetenango, are Guatemala's most beautiful region. The verdant hills are clad in lush carpets of emerald green grass, fields of tawny corn and towering stands of pine. All of this lushness comes from the abundant rain which falls between May and October. If you visit during the rainy season, be prepared for some dreary, chilly, damp days. But when the sun comes out, this land is glorious.

Highlights of the region include: graceful old Antigua, Guatemala's most beautiful colonial city; Lake Atitlán, a perfect mirror of blue surrounded by Fuji-like volcanoes; the town of Chichicastenango, where traditional Mayan religious rites blend with the Catholicism introduced by the Spanish; Quetzaltenango, the commercial and market centre of the south-west; and Huehuetenango, jumping-off place for the cross-border journey to Comitán and San Cristóbal de las Casas in Mexico.

Every town and village in the highlands has a story to tell, usually beginning more than a thousand years ago. Most towns here were already populated by the Maya when the Spanish arrived. The traditional values and ways of life of Guatemala's indigenous peoples are strongest in the highlands. Mayan is the first language, Spanish a distant second.

The age-old culture based on maize is still alive; a sturdy cottage set in the midst of a thriving *milpa* (field of maize) is a common sight, a sight as old as Maya culture itself. Woodsmoke wafts through the red roof tiles and beneath the eaves of these chimneyless cottages, and on every road one sees men and women carrying loads of *leña* (firewood) to be used for heating and cooking. Many carriers still use a tumpline, a band of cloth or rope looped beneath the load, up the back and around the forehead. The tumpline shifts some of the stress of the load from the lower back, where it can do harm, to the spine, which is better able to support it.

Each highland town has its own market and festival days. Life in a highland town can be *muy triste* (sad, boring) when there's not a market or festival going on, so you should try to visit on those special days.

If you have only three or four days to spend in the highlands, spend them in Antigua, Panajachel and Chichicastenango. With more time you can make your way to Quetzaltenango and the sights in its vicinity such as Zunil, Fuentes Georginas, San Francisco El Alto, Momostenango and Totonicapán. Huehuetenango and the ruins nearby at Zaculeu are worth a visit only if you're passing through, or if you have lots of time; the towns and villages high in the Cuchumatanes mountains north of Huehuetenango offer wonderful scenery and adventures for intrepid travellers.

A NOTE ON SAFETY

As this book goes to press, there are reports of increased incidence of robberies of tourists in the highlands. One incident at the Pacaya volcano in February 1991 resulted in the robbery, rape and murder of tourists by a group of well-dressed armed men allegedly carrying what looked like police credentials. The tourist group was a large one, accompanied by official guides.

The situation may well have changed by the time you arrive. I've travelled the highlands for years and have never had a problem, but I'm always cautious, and I always find out about current conditions. Before you travel in the highlands it is important to contact your embassy or consulate in Guatemala City and get information on the current situation, and advice on how and where to travel in the highlands. Don't rely on local authorities for safety advice as they may downplay the dangers. For embassy phone numbers, see the chapter on Guatemala City.

GETTING AROUND

Guatemala City and the Guatemalan-Mexican border station at La Mesilla are connected by the Pan American Highway, known also as the Carretera Interamericana or as Centroamérica 1 (CA-1). It is a curvy mountain road that must be travelled slowly in many places. Driving the 266 km between Guatemala City and Huehuetenango can take five hours, but the time passes pleasantly amidst the beautiful scenery. (The Pacific Slope Highway (CA-2) via Escuintla and Retalhuleu is straighter and faster, and is the better route to take if your goal is to reach Mexico as quickly as possible.)

Many buses of different companies rumble up and down the highway; for an idea of the service, refer to Getting There & Away in the Guatemala City chapter. As most of the places you'll want to reach are some distance off the Pan American Highway, you may find yourself waiting at major highway junctions such as Los Encuentros and Cuatro Caminos in order to connect with the right bus. Travel is easiest on market days and in the morning. By mid or late afternoon, buses may be dif-

■ PLACES TO STAY		OTHER	
3	Pensión El Arco	1	La Merced
5	Pensión La Antigüenita	2	Convento de Santa Teresa
6	Posada de Don Rodrigo	4	Iglesia de Santa Catalina
10	Hotel Aurora	7	El Carmen
15	Hotel El Descanso	8	Convento de las Capucinas
15	Restaurant Ceniciento	9	Iglesia y Convento de Santo
22	Posada Doña Angelina		Domingo
24	Posada Refugio	12	Museo de Santiago
46	Casa de Santa Lucía	12	Palacio del Ayuntamiento
47	Hospedaje El Pasaje	20	Convento de la Compañía de Jesús
50	Ramada Hotel Antigua	25	Correos (Post Office)
52	Hotel Antigua	26	Mercado
55	El Rosario Lodge	27	Terminal de Buses
		28	Cementerio General
▼ PLACES TO EAT		29	Mercado
		30	Monumento a Landívar
11	Restaurant Doña Luisa Xicotencatl	31	Iglesia de San Agustín
13	Restaurant San Carlos	34	Parque Central
14	El Fondo de la Calle Real	35	Catedral de Santiago
16	Restaurant Café Café	38	Casa Popenoe
17	El Churrasco	39	Iglesia y Convento de Santa Clara
18	Gran Muralla	40	Museo de Arte Colonial
18	Pizzería Martedino	40	Universidad de San Carlos
18	Pollo Campesino	41	INGUAT Tourist Office
19	Capri Antigua Cafetería	42	Palacio de los Capitanes
21	Vaikuntha Centro Yoga	43	Cinema
23	La Tertulia de Doña Beatriz	44	Guatel (Telephone Office)
32	Restaurant Italiano El Capuchino	48	Iglesia del Espíritu Santo
33	La Hamburguesa Gigante	49	Iglesia de Santa Lucía
36	Doña Maria Gordillo Dulces Típicos	51	Iglesia de San José
37	Mistral	53	Iglesia de San Francisco
45	El Sereno	56	Escuela de Cristo
54	Casa de Café Ana		

ficult to find, and all short-distance local traffic stops by dinnertime.

Antigua Guatemala

Population 28,000
Experienced Guatemala travellers spend as little time in Guatemala City as possible, preferring to make Antigua their base. La muy Noble y muy Leal Ciudad de Santiago de los Caballeros de Goathemala, as it was first known, is among the oldest and most beautiful cities in the Americas. Its setting is superb, amidst three magnificent volcanoes named Agua, Fuego and Acatenango. Fuego (Fire) is easily recognisable by its plume of smoke and – at night – by the red glow it projects against the sky.

Founded in 1542, Antigua Guatemala has weathered 16 damaging earthquakes, floods and fires. The handsome, sturdy colonial buildings which survive have proved their worth over and over again, and Antigua today might be said to be the result of Darwinian Architecture: survival of the fittest buildings. The survivors continue to be strengthened (nowadays with steel beams and reinforced concrete); the rubble of the weakest has long since been swept away.

Antigua is a wonderful place to live in or to visit, and lots of people do both. On weekends a long stream of cars and buses brings

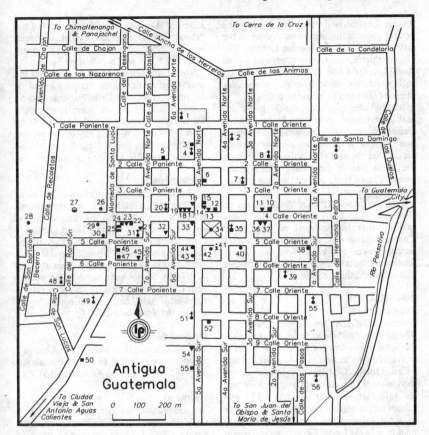

Antigua Guatemala

0   100   200 m

To Chimaltenango & Panajachel
To Cerro de la Cruz
To Guatemala City
To Ciudad Vieja & San Antonio Aguas Calientes
To San Juan del Obispo & Santa María de Jesús

the citizens of Guatemala City up the serpentine route into the mountains for a day of strolling, shopping and sipping in the former capital. On Sunday evening, traffic jams Antigua's cobbled streets as the day trippers head home.

If you have the opportunity to be in Antigua during Holy Week – especially on Good Friday – seize it; but make your hotel reservations months in advance, as all hotels will be full.

ORIENTATION

Volcán Agua is south-east of the city and visible from most points within it; Volcán Fuego is south-west, and Volcán Acatenango is to the west. The three volcanoes which appear on the city's coat of arms provide easy reference points.

Antigua's street grid uses a modified version of the numbering system used in Guatemala City. (For details on that system, see Orientation in the Guatemala City chapter.) In Antigua, compass points are added to the avenidas and calles. Calles run east-west, and so 4 Calle west of the Parque Central is 4 Calle Poniente; avenidas run north-south, and 3a Avenida north of the

Parque Central is 3a Avenida Norte. The central point is the north-east corner of the city's main plaza, the Parque Central. The city is thus divided into quadrants by 4a Avenida and 4 Calle. (Points of the compass in Spanish are norte (north), sur (south), oriente (east) and poniente (west).

The old headquarters of the Spanish colonial government, called the Palacio de los Capitanes, is on the south side of the plaza; you'll know it by its double (two-storey) arcade. On the east side is the cathedral; on the north side is the Palacio del Ayuntamiento (Town Hall); and on the west side are banks and shops.

Intercity buses arrive at the Terminal de Buses, a large open lot just north of the market, four blocks west of the Parque Central along 4 Calle Poniente. Buses serving towns and villages in the vicinity leave from the terminal as well, or from other points around the market.

INFORMATION
Tourist Office
Antigua's INGUAT tourist office (☎ (9) 32-07-63) is in the Palacio de los Capitanes, at the south-east corner of the Parque Central, next to the intersection of 4a Avenida Sur and 5 Calle Oriente. Go here (8 am to 5 pm, seven days a week) for answers to questions and for information about guided hikes and climbs on the volcanoes. Other good sources of local information include the bulletin boards at Doña Luisa Xicotencatl restaurant and Casa Andinista.

Money
Banks in Antigua, as elsewhere in Guatemala, tend to be open from 9 am to 2 pm Monday to Friday (till 2.30 pm Friday), but the Banco del Agro, on the north side of the Parque Central, has a ventanilla especial (special teller window) open longer hours, as well as on Saturday. Lloyd's Bank is at the north-east corner of the Parque Central, on the corner of 4a Avenida and 4 Calle.

Post & Telecommunications
The post office (Correos) is at 4 Calle Pon-

iente and Alameda Santa Lucía, west of the Parque Central near the market. It's open Monday to Saturday from 8 am to noon and from 2 to 8 pm, and is closed on Sunday.

The Guatel telephone office is just off the south-west corner of the Parque Central, at the intersection of 5 Calle Poniente and 5a Avenida Sur. Hours are 7 am to midnight daily. Those wanting to call the USA using AT&T can dial 190 from any telephone (no need to stand in line at Guatel) and reverse the charges or use a credit card number.

Bookshops
Un Poco de Todo, at the north-west corner of the Parque Central, has English and Spanish books. It's open Monday to Friday from 9.30 am to 1 pm and 3 to 6 pm. Casa Andinista, 4 Calle Oriente No 5, just a few steps off the Parque Central, sells Spanish books, postcards and maps. Librería del Pensativo (☎ 32-07-29), 5a Avenida Norte 29 between 1 and 2 Calle, just north of the arch on the right-hand side, has some English books among the Spanish ones.

Medical Services
The local hospital is named for Antigua's great healer: Hospital Pedro de Betancourt (☎ (9) 32-03-01) is at 3a Avenida and 6 Calle.

Laundry
Try the laundromat named Lava Rápido, 5 Calle Poniente No 7, half a block west of the Parque Central. There are several others as well.

Toilets
Public toilets are at 4a Avenida and 4 Calle, at the north-east corner of the Parque Central.

SEMANA SANTA
By far the most interesting time to be in Antigua is during Semana Santa (Holy Week), when the city celebrates by dressing up hundreds of its people in deep purple robes as pseudo-Israelites to accompany daily religious processions in remembrance of the Crucifixion. Streets are covered in

breathtakingly elaborate and colourful *alfombras* (carpets) of coloured sawdust and flower petals. These beautiful but fragile works of art are destroyed as the processions shuffle through them, but recreated the next morning for another day.

In 1992, Semana Santa begins on 13 April and runs until 19 April (Easter Sunday); in 1993, it begins on 5 April and continues until 11 April; in 1994 the dates are 28 March to 3 April. Have ironclad hotel reservations well in advance of these dates, or plan to stay in another town, or in Guatemala City, and commute to the festivities.

Pick up a schedule of events at the tourist office. Traditionally, the most interesting days are Palm Sunday, when a procession departs from La Merced (see Churches) in midafternoon; Holy Thursday, when a late afternoon procession departs the Iglesia de San Francisco; and Good Friday, when an early morning procession departs from La Merced, and a late afternoon one from the Escuela de Cristo.

On a secular note, beware of pickpockets. It seems that Guatemala City's entire population of pickpockets (numbering in the hundreds, perhaps) decamps to Antigua for Semana Santa. In the press of the emotion-filled crowds lining the processional routes they home in on foreign tourists especially. Razor blades silently slice pocket and bag, and gentle hands remove contents seemingly without sound or movement.

PARQUE CENTRAL

In 1839 when John L Stephens visited, Antigua was still largely in ruins, even though the great earthquake of 1773 had occurred 66 years earlier. The city had been only partially rebuilt, and the seat of government had been moved to Guatemala City. Even so, the Parque Central was impressive:

The great volcanoes of Agua and Fuego look down upon it; in the centre is a noble stone fountain, and the buildings which face it, especially the palace of the captain general,...and the majestic but roofless and ruined cathedral,...show at this day that La Antigua was once one of the finest cities of the New World...

After the great earthquake of 1773, the archbishop slept in his carriage in the parque, afraid that an aftershock would bring down the roof of his house on him. Likewise, when I visited several months after the terrible earthquake of February 1976, many *antigüeños* were still encamped in the parque in makeshift tents and shelters of plastic sheeting because their homes had been destroyed.

Today the parque is the gathering place for citizens and foreign visitors alike. On most days the periphery is lined with villagers who have brought their handicrafts – cloth, dolls, blankets, pottery – to sell to tourists; on Sunday the parque is mobbed with marketeers, and the streets on the east and west sides of the parque are closed to traffic in order to give them room. The best prices are to be had late on Sunday afternoon, when the market is winding down. You'll know the time is right to deal when you see the day trippers from Guatemala City form their cars into a 30-km-long metal snake that inches its way back to the capital in a concerto of hooters.

The Palacio de los Capitanes, built in 1543 as the Palace of the Royal Audiencia & Captaincy-General of Guatemala, has a stately double arcade on its façade which marches proudly across the southern extent of the parque. The façade is original, but most of the rest of the building was reconstructed a century ago. From 1543 to 1773, this building was the governmental centre of all Central America, in command of Chiapas, Guatemala, Honduras and Nicaragua.

The Catedral de Santiago, on the east side of the parque, was founded in 1542, damaged by earthquakes many times, badly ruined in 1773, and only partially rebuilt between 1780 and 1820. In the 16th and early 17th centuries, Antigua's churches had lavish baroque interiors, but most lost this richness when they were rebuilt after the earthquakes. The cathedral shares this fate. Its chief distinction today is as the resting place (in the crypt) of Bernal Díaz del Castillo, historian of the Spanish conquest, who died in 1581.

On the north side of the parque stands the Palacio del Ayuntamiento, Antigua's Town Hall, which dates mostly from 1743. In addition to town offices, it holds the Museo de Santiago, which houses a collection of colonial furnishings, artefacts and weapons. Hours are 9 am to 4 pm Tuesday to Friday, 9 am to noon and 2 to 4 pm on Saturday and Sunday, closed Monday; admission costs US$0.10. Next door is the Museo del Libro Antiguo (Old Book Museum), which has exhibits of colonial printing and binding; hours are the same.

The Universidad de San Carlos was founded in 1676, but its main building (built in 1763) at 5 Calle Oriente No 5, half a block east of the parque, now houses the Museo de Arte Colonial (same hours as the Museo de Santiago).

CHURCHES

Once glorious in their gilded baroque finery, Antigua's churches have suffered indignities from both nature and humankind. Rebuilding after earthquakes gave the churches thicker walls, lower towers and belfries, and unembellished interiors; and moving the capital to Guatemala City deprived Antigua of the population needed to maintain the churches in their traditional richness. Still, they are impressive.

From the parque, walk three long blocks up 5a Avenida Norte, passing beneath the arch of Santa Catalina, built in 1694 and rebuilt in the 19th century. At the northern end of 5a Avenida is the Iglesia y Convento de Nuestra Señora de La Merced (Church & Convent of Our Lady of Mercy), known simply as La Merced, Antigua's most striking colonial church. Its baroque façade dates from the mid-1800s.

The next most notable church is the Iglesia de San Francisco, 7 Calle Oriente and 2a Avenida Sur. Dating from the mid-1500s, little of the original building remains. Rebuilding and restoration over the centuries has given us a handsome building; reinforced concrete construction added in 1961 protected the church from serious damage in the 1976 earthquake. All that remains of the original church is the Chapel of Hermano Pedro, resting place of Fray Pedro de Betancourt, a Franciscan monk. Hermano Pedro (Brother Peter) arrived in Antigua in the mid-1600s, promptly founded a hospital for the poor, and earned the gratitude of generations. His intercession is still sought by the ill, who pray fervently by his casket. When their prayers are answered they put testimonials by his tomb: crutches no longer needed, little ornaments in the shape of the afflicted – and healed – limb, medals and pictures.

The Convento de las Capuchinas, 2a Avenida Norte and 2 Calle Oriente, was a convent founded in 1736 by nuns from Madrid. Destroyed repeatedly by earthquakes, it is now a museum, with exhibits of the religious life in colonial times.

Other churches include the ruined Convento de Santa Teresa, 4a Avenida Norte between 1 and 2 Calles Oriente, ruined in 1773; the Iglesia y Convento de Santa Clara, 2a Avenida Sur No 27, corner of 6 Calle Oriente, founded in 1700, rebuilt in 1734, and destroyed in 1773; the Iglesia y Convento de Santo Domingo, corner of 1a Avenida Norte and Calle de Santo Domingo, founded in 1664 and ruined – guess when? – in 1773. The same fate awaited the Convento de Nuestra Señora de la Concepción, at the corner of 4 Calle Oriente and Calle del Hermano Pedro, founded in 1577, ruined in 1773, and the ruins ruined somewhat more in 1976. You might also want to see the Escuela de Cristo, Calle de Fray Rodrigo de la Cruz and Calle del Hermano Pedro, in the south-eastern part of town, built as a church and restored in the mid-1800s.

CASA POPENOE

At the corner of 5 Calle Oriente and 1a Avenida Sur stands this beautiful mansion built in 1636 by Don Luis de las Infantas Mendoza y Venegas. Ruined by the earthquake of 1773, the house stood desolate for 1½ centuries until it was bought in 1931 by Dr and Mrs Popenoe. The Popenoes' painstaking and authentic restoration yields a fascinating glimpse of how the family of an important royal official (Don Luis) lived in the Antigua of the 1600s. The house is open Monday to Saturday from 3 to 5 pm; the guided tour costs US$0.25.

MARKET & MONUMENTO A LANDÍVAR

At the western end of 5 Calle Poniente is the Monumento a Landívar, a structure of five colonial-style arches set in a little park. Rafael Landívar, an 18th-century Jesuit priest and poet, lived and wrote in Antigua for some time. Landívar's poetry is esteemed as the best of the colonial period, even though much of it was written in Italy after the Jesuits were expelled from Guatemala. Landívar's Antigua house was nearby on 5a Calle Poniente.

Around the Monumento a Landívar on the west side of Alameda de Santa Lucía sprawls the market – chaotic, colourful and always busy. Morning, when all the village people from the vicinity are actively buying and selling, is the best time to come.

CEMETERY

If you have never visited a Mexican or Guatemalan cemetery, you can take the opportunity to stroll through Antigua's large Cementerio General, west of the market and bus terminal. Hints of ancient Mayan beliefs are revealed in the lavishly decorated tombs, many of which also have homey touches, and often fresh flowers or other evidence of frequent visits.

PLACES TO STAY – BOTTOM END

Visitors who come to Antigua to attend one of the many Spanish-language schools usually stay in cheap family pensions at low prices – about US$30 per week. The tourist office has information on how to get in touch with willing families.

Some of the best cheap lodgings in town are on the east side of the Alameda de Santa Lucía, across from the market and the bus terminal. *Posada Doña Angelina*, 4 Calle Poniente 33, is actually two hotels in one. The older section on 4 Calle a few steps off the Alameda de Santa Lucía charges US$2.50 per person in waterless rooms arranged around a bare courtyard. The newer

section of the hotel, also around a courtyard, charges US$11 to US$14 a double for a room with shower.

Nearby on the Alameda de Santa Lucía, between 5 and 6 Calles Poniente, are two more cheap lodging-places. *Casa de Santa Lucía* charges US$7 for double rooms with shower and a bit of pseudo-colonial atmosphere; ring the bell to call the attendant. The friendly *Hospedaje El Pasaje*, Alameda de Santa Lucía Sur 3, charges only US$3 per person in waterless rooms; an annexe four blocks away takes the overflow when the main hospedaje is full.

Pensión El Arco, 5a Avenida Norte 32, just north of the Santa Catalina arch, is in part of an old colonial building. The smiling señora makes you feel safe and welcome, and rents plain and sometimes claustrophobic but nevertheless tidy rooms without bath for US$2 per person. Look at the room before you say yes.

Hotel El Descanso (☎ (9) 32-01-42), 5a Avenida Norte 9, '50 steps from the central plaza', has 14 small rooms in the building facing the restaurant called Café Café. It's clean and pleasant, certainly convenient, and low priced. A double room with hot shower goes for US$6.50 to US$11.

Despite its popularity with budget travellers, *Posada Refugio*, 4 Calle Poniente 30, is not particularly beautiful, comfortable or clean. The price is US$2.50 per person in waterless rooms. Likewise the *Pensión La Antigüenita*, 2 Calle Poniente 25, which at least has the virtue of very low prices: US$1.50 to US$3 per room.

Be warned though, that as demand increases, prices at budget places may rise; these prices were accurate at the time the book was researched, but don't be surprised if some rates in a prime tourist town like Antigua have risen markedly by the time you arrive.

PLACES TO STAY – MIDDLE

Antigua's middle-range hotels allow you to wallow in the city's colonial charms for a very moderate outlay of cash.

Hotel Aurora (☎ (9) 32-02-17), 4 Calle Oriente 16, is the best choice in the moderate range. The grassy courtyard is decorated with flowers and graced by a fountain, surrounded by a colonial arcade set with wicker furniture and paved in shiny tiles. The formal sitting room has a fireplace for those chilly mountain evenings, and the grand old-fashioned dining room echoes with the chatter of evenings long past. The 17 rooms have tall ceilings but few windows and, though dark, are comfortable in a colonial way. The Aurora used to be cheap, but the price has risen dramatically in recent years. Still, I believe you'll think that US$26 is a reasonable price for a room here.

El Rosario Lodge (☎ (9) 32-03-36), 5a Avenida Sur 36, is actually an old coffee finca which has turned to renting rooms to travellers. The coffee bushes still produce, and the roasted beans are sold right on the premises where they were grown. Rooms come in a variety of shapes and sizes, with locally made blankets and craftwork as decorations. Several rooms have terraces and fireplaces. Although it's a slight walk from the parque, you'll like the peace and quiet here; meals can be taken in the little Casa de Café Ana in the same building as the lodge, at the corner of 5a Avenida Sur and 9 Calle Poniente. Rates are US$10 to US$12 for a double room with bath; apartments are also available.

The most elaborate of Antigua's moderately priced hotels is the *Posada de Don Rodrigo* (☎ (9) 32-02-91, 32-03-87), 5a Avenida Norte 17. Two courtyards, both very beautiful, form the core of the hotel; the forecourt is the scene of free marimba concerts each afternoon; the rear court has a tinkling fountain to entertain diners in the terrace restaurant. The 33 rooms, all with private bath, have colonial-style furnishings, many of them a century or more old: brass or carved wood bedsteads, beamed ceilings, woven floor mats and other antique or 'antiqued' furnishings. Room rates are US$38/44/50 a single/double/triple, 17% tax included. If you'd like all three meals, add US$12 per person per day.

PLACES TO STAY – TOP END

Hotel Antigua (☎ (9) 32-03-31, 32-02-88; in Guatemala City ☎ (2) 53-24-90, 2-75-75; fax 53-54-82), 8 Calle Poniente 1, between 4a and 5a Avenidas Sur, is a Spanish colonial country club which takes up an entire city block, with another block just to the north serving as its car park. Beautiful lawns and a large heated swimming pool, terraces set with cafe tables, a children's playground, sundecks, and red-tiled porticos over the low buildings surrounding the courtyard make this a very charming place. From the main courtyard you can see the ruined Iglesia de San José, across the street to the west. The 60 rooms have private baths and fireplaces, and many have two double beds. There's a large, elegant colonial-style dining room and a watering hole, the Conquistador Bar, decorated in lots of dark wood. Room rates are quoted in US dollars: US$90/100/110 a single/double/triple, tax included. You might want to come for a drink in the bar even if you can't afford to splurge on a room.

Ramada Hotel Antigua (☎ (9) 32-00-11 to 15; fax 32-02-37), 9 Calle and Carretera a Ciudad Vieja, is the largest and most modern hotel in town, with 155 rooms and suites. The modern buildings have many elements which echo colonial times, such as red-tiled roofs and tile floors. Rooms have balconies, fireplaces (with firewood), modern tiled bathrooms with tubs and showers, and colour TVs with English-language stations. The restaurant surrounds a huge fireplace kept ablaze on chilly evenings. Rates are a reasonable US$55/65 a single/double, tax included. The Ramada is about seven long blocks south-west of the Parque Central.

PLACES TO EAT – BOTTOM END

Eating cheaply in Guatemala is easy, even in touristy Antigua.

The first place everyone tries is *Restaurant Doña Luisa Xicotencatl*, 4 Calle Oriente No 12, 1½ blocks east of the parque. A small central courtyard is set with dining tables, with more dining rooms on the upper level. The menu lists a dozen sandwiches made with Doña Luisa's own bread baked on the premises, as well as yogurt, chilli, cakes and pies, and heartier meat dishes, all priced from about US$1.50 to US$3. Alcoholic beverages are served, as is excellent Antigua coffee. The restaurant is open every day for breakfast (priced from US$1 to US$2), for lunch and dinner well into the evening, and it is usually busy. The useful bulletin board by the entrance is Antigua's unofficial daily newspaper.

Mistral, 4 Calle Oriente 7, across the street from Doña Luisa, serves freshly squeezed fruit and vegetable juices, good coffee and sandwiches, with most items priced at US$1 or less. Behind the streetside juice bar is the courtyard dining area where you can order meat loaf, rabbit stew, steaks, Breton crepes, and other dishes not often found on Guatemalan menus. Most cost US$1.75 to US$2.50. A slice of cake and a soft drink costs just over US$1. In the evening, return for American video movies in the little bar off the courtyard.

Doña María Gordillo Dulces Típicos, 4 Calle Oriente 11, across the street from the Hotel Aurora, is filled with traditional Guatemalan sweets, desserts and confections to take away, often with a crowd of antigüeños lined up to do just that. Delicacies made from milk, fruit, eggs, marzipan, chocolate and sugar compete for customers' affections. Local handicrafts are for sale here as well.

If your pocket is as empty as your stomach, head for 4 Calle Poniente just west of the Parque Central. Within the first block are half a dozen cheap eating places. *La Hamburguesa Gigante*, 4 Calle Poniente 1, will sell you a giant burger for US$0.75. *Restaurant Emilio*, despite its name, is a bar and offers sustenance of another kind. *El Churrasco*, 4 Calle Poniente 16, serves a quarter roast chicken for US$1.10, hamburgers for US$0.50, and steaks (not all that tender) for US$1.25 to US$3. *Pollo Campesino*, 4 Calle Poniente 18, will provide similar roast chicken in more modern surroundings.

Restaurant Pizzería Martedino, 4 Calle Poniente 18, in the same building as Pollo Campesino, is a big place with attractive decor. Good pizzas sell for US$2 to US$5 depending upon size and ingredients; dishes of pasta are less. The *almuerzo del día* (daily set-price lunch) is a bargain at US$2. This place is particularly popular with thrifty Guatemalan families and is especially crowded on Sunday. *Restaurant Gran Muralla*, also in the building at 4 Calle Poniente 18, serves a Guatemalan highland version of Chinese food.

Capri Antigua Cafetería, 4 Calle Poniente 24, near the corner with 6a Avenida Norte, is a simple, modern place that's very popular with younger diners and budget travellers. They usually fill its little wooden benches and tables, ordering soup for less than US$0.50, sandwiches for only slightly more, *platos fuertes* (substantial platters) for US$1.50 to US$2.75.

Perhaps the best bargain in a full restaurant is the *Restaurant Italiano El Capuchino* (☎ 32-06-13), 6a Avenida Norte 10, between 4 and 5 Calles Poniente, a block west of the Parque Central. In the pleasant glass-covered courtyard, the jovial owner speaks good English and proudly shows off two fish tanks, one containing a barracuda. I had a big plate of vegetable soup, a huge serving of spaghetti, bread and mineral water for US$3; the daily four-course set-price lunch costs about the same. About the most you can spend is US$8. There's also a well-stocked bar serving both domestic and foreign wines.

Not far from the market and bus terminal on 4 Calle Poniente between the Alameda de Santa Lucía and 7a Avenida Sur are several *comedores*, family-run cookshops specialising in simple food at rock-bottom prices. There's the *Comedor Antigua* at No 21, the *Cafetería y Comedor San José* at No 30, and the best of all, *La Tertulia de Doña Beatriz* at No 32, which has a pretty little shaded patio with ornate white cast-iron tables and chairs at the back. Individual pizzas, burgers, cakes and other light dishes go for US$0.60 to US$1.10. Doña Beatriz's *tertulia* (club, circle of friends, coterie) usually includes equal numbers of locals and foreign visitors.

Vaikuntha Centro Yoga, 7a Avenida Norte

between 4 and 5 Calle Poniente, just north of the ruined church of San Agustín, has limited offerings of vegetarian fare, as well as yogurt and granola.

Restaurant San Carlos, in the arcade on the north side of the Parque Central, is stark, bare and darkish inside, but offers some views of the parque from a few tables, as well as huge platos fuertes featuring beef, chicken and pork served with salad, rice and potatoes for US$2 to US$3. The *almuerzo económico* (economical lunch) is served daily for US$1.50.

In a corner of El Rosario Lodge (see Places to Stay – middle) is the *Casa de Café Ana*, 5a Avenida Sur and 9 Calle Poniente, well away from the parque and thus lower in price, quiet and pleasant.

PLACES TO EAT – MIDDLE

Even the better restaurants in Antigua have agreeably low prices.

Walk north along 5a Avenida Norte between 2 and 4 Calles Poniente, and in two blocks you'll pass half a dozen good places to eat. *Restaurant Café Café*, 5a Avenida Norte 14, on the left-hand side in the building called La Casa de las Gárgolas, has a big canvas-covered courtyard crowded with potted plants and rough wooden dining tables around a fountain filled with tropical flowers. There is always a daily set-price meal offered, described and priced on a signboard by the door. The huge and colourful *plato típico* for US$3 includes refried black beans, yellow rice, fried bananas, stuffed pepper in spicy red sauce, an enchilada, salad and white cheese. Try the *pepián antigüeño* (US$2) and also the *churrasco de lomito* (US$4).

Half a block farther north is *Ceniciento*, 5a Avenida Norte 9, mostly for cakes, pastries, pies and coffee, but the blackboard menu often features quiche lorraine and *quiche chapín* (Guatemalan-style), yogurt and fruit as well. A slice of something and a hot beverage cost less than US$1.

El Fondo de la Calle Real, 5a Avenida Norte 5, appears to have no room for diners, but that's because all the tables are upstairs.

Roast chicken, fondues, steaks and chops are priced from US$2.50 to US$5, but the filling soups go for much less.

The dining room in the *Posada de Don Rodrigo*, 5a Avenida Norte 17, is one of the city's most pleasant and popular places for lunch or dinner. Many tables are set outside with views of the gardens and the city and the others are in colonial-style rooms. The menu has Guatemalan and North American dishes (including at least one vegetarian dish) at moderate prices. Order the *platillo chapín* of Guatemalan specialities for US$5, or even *lomito* (beef tenderloin), and the most you'll pay for the complete meal is US$8 or US$9. A marimba band plays most afternoons and every Sunday.

PLACES TO EAT – TOP END

El Sereno (☎ (9) 32-00-73), 6 Calle Poniente 30, between the Alameda de Santa Lucía and 7a Avenida Sur, next door to the Tecún Umán School of Spanish, is Antigua's most exclusive restaurant. A colonial house has been nicely restored and modernised somewhat to provide a traditional wooden bar, plant-filled court and several small dining rooms hung with oil paintings. Cuisine is international, leaning heavily on French dishes; the menu changes every week. The short wine list is good but expensive. Expect to pay US$15 to US$22 per person for dinner. Make reservations for lunch or dinner, Wednesday to Sunday from noon to 3 pm, and 6.30 to 9.30 pm; (closed Monday and Tuesday). Don't let the armed guard by the steel door startle you – I mentioned that this place was exclusive.

Your other top-class choice is the dining room of the *Hotel Antigua*, 8 Calle Oriente at 5a Avenida Sur. The large, pleasant dining room has a more festive atmosphere than the smaller, intimate spaces of El Sereno. Prices are similar.

ENTERTAINMENT

Dinner, drinks with friends, a video movie in the bar at Mistral, 4 Calle Oriente 7, a stroll through Antigua's colonial streets – these are the pleasures of the evening here. Bars for music and dancing open and close frequently; ask around for the current favourite.

The cinema half a block south of the Parque Central on 5a Avenida Sur mostly has movies in Spanish, but occasionally has something with subtitles.

THINGS TO BUY

In 1958 an ancient Mayan jade quarry near Nejar, Guatemala, was rediscovered. When it was shown to yield true jadeite (with a hardness of 6.5 to seven) equal in quality to Chinese stone, the mine was reopened. Today it produces jade both for gemstone use and for carving.

When buying jade you must have a fat wad of money, as beautiful well-carved stones can cost US$100 or much more. Look for purity and intensity of colour, translucency, and absence of flaws. Try to scratch the stone with a pocketknife; if it scratches, it's not true jadeite, but an inferior stone. (Of course, as a matter of courtesy, you should ask the merchant beforehand before you carry out this test.)

Antigua has two shops specialising in jade, *La Casa de Jade* (jade is pronounced HAH-deh), 4 Calle Oriente 3, and *Jades* (HAH-dess), 4 Calle Oriente 34.

GETTING THERE & AWAY

Bus connections with Guatemala City are frequent, and there are direct buses several times daily to Panajachel on Lake Atitlán. To go directly to other highland towns such as Chichicastenango, Quetzaltenango and Huehuetenango you may have to take one of the frequent minibuses to Chimaltenango (US$0.20), on the Pan American Highway, and catch an onward bus from there.

Guatemala City – 45 km, one hour; Transportes Unidos (☎ (2) 2-49-49), 15 Calle 3-65, Zona 1, in Guatemala City, makes the trip every half an hour from 7 am to 7 pm stopping in San Lucas Sacatepéquez, for US$0.50. Buses Inter-Hotel y Turismo (BIT, ☎ (9) 32-00-11/15 at the Ramada Hotel Antigua) runs comfortable minibuses between La Aurora International Airport and Antigua, departing from the airport at 7.15 am

and 6.15 pm and arriving in Antigua 45 minutes later. The fare is US$8.

Panajachel (Lake Atitlán) – 80 km, two hours; several buses daily from Antigua's Terminal de Buses, even more from Chimaltenango. Buses Inter-Hotel y Turismo (BIT, ☎ (9) 32-00-11/15 at the Ramada Hotel Antigua) also runs its minibuses between Antigua and Panajachel on Tuesday, Thursday and Sunday, departing from the Ramada Hotel Antigua at 8.30 am, arriving in Panajachel at 10.30, returning from Panajachel (departing from the Hotel del Lago) at noon and arriving in Antigua at 2.30 pm. One-way fare is US$10.

GETTING AROUND

Buses to outlying villages such as Santa María de Jesús (US$0.15, 30 minutes) and San Antonio Aguas Calientes (US$0.10, 25 minutes) depart from the Terminal de Buses west of the market. It's best to make your outward trip early in the morning, and your return trip by midafternoon, as services drop off dramatically as late afternoon approaches.

New motorbikes (Yamaha 200cc) are available for hire for US$15 per day from the Hotel Los Capitanes, next to the Los Capitanes cinema, 9a Avenida Sur.

AROUND ANTIGUA GUATEMALA
Ciudad Vieja & San Antonio Aguas Calientes

Six and a half km south-west of Antigua along the Escuintla road (the one which passes the Ramada Antigua Hotel) is Ciudad Vieja (Old City), site of the first capital of the Captaincy General of Guatemala. Founded in 1527, it was destroyed in 1541 when the aptly named Volcán Agua loosed a flood of water pent up in its crater. Cascading down the steep volcano's side, the water carried tonnes of rock and mud over the city, leaving only a few ruins of the Church of La Concepción.

Past Ciudad Vieja, turn right at a large cemetery on the right-hand side; the unmarked road takes you through San Miguel Dueñas to San Antonio Aguas Calientes. (In San Miguel Dueñas, take the first street on the right – between two houses – after coming to the concrete-block paving;

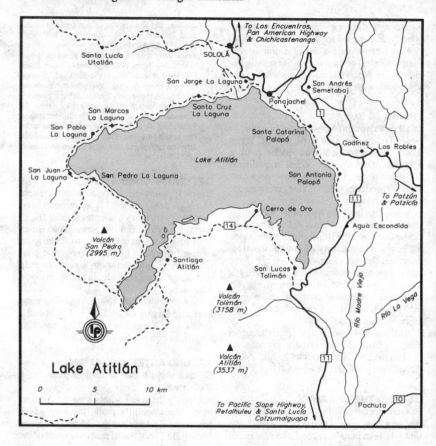

To Los Encuentros,
Pan American Highway
& Chichicastenango

SOLOLÁ

Santa Lucía
Utatlán

San Jorge La Laguna

San Andrés
Semetabaj

Panajachel

Santa Cruz
La Laguna

San Marcos
La Laguna

Santa Catarina
Palopó

Godínez   Los Robles

San Pablo
La Laguna

Lake Atitlán

San Juan
La Laguna

San Pedro La Laguna

San Antonio
Palopó

To Patzún
& Patzicía

Cerro de Oro

14

Agua Escondida

Volcán
San Pedro
(2995 m)

Santiago
Atitlán

San Lucas
Tolimán

Volcán
Tolimán
(3158 m)

Río Madre Vieja   Río La Vega

Lake Atitlán

Volcán
Atitlán
(3537 m)

0   5   10 km

To Pacific Slope Highway,
Retalhuleu & Santa Lucía
Cotzumalguapa

Pochuta

10

this, too, is unmarked. If you come to the Texaco station in the centre of San Miguel, you've missed the road.)

The road winds through coffee *fincas*, little vegetable and corn fields and hamlets of farmers to San Antonio Aguas Calientes, 14 km from Antigua. As you enter San Antonio's plaza, you will see that the village is noted for its weaving. Market stalls in the plaza sell local woven and embroidered goods, as do shops on side streets (walk to the left of the church to find them). If you decide to buy, it's customary to haggle like crazy for a good price.

Santa María de Jesús & Volcán Agua

Follow 2a Avenida Sur or Calle de los Pasos south toward El Calvario (two km), then continue onward via San Juan del Obispo (another three km) to Santa María de Jesús, nine km south of Antigua. This is the jumping-off point for treks up the slopes of Volcán Agua (3766 metres), which rises dramatically right behind the village.

Santa María (altitude 2080 metres, population 11,000) is a village of unpaved streets, bamboo fences, a church and Municipalidad on the main plaza, which is also the bus terminal. Down the street from the church towards the white church in the distance is the *Comedor & Hospedaje El Oasis*, a tidy little pension where you can get a meal or a bed for the night.

Casa Andinista, 4 Calle Oriente No 5A in Antigua, can arrange to rent you camping gear, and can furnish details about the climb. Start very early in the morning, as it can take five hours to reach the summit. Don't hike alone; a group of three or four people is best. If you are not an experienced hiker in good physical condition, don't plan to go all the way. You'll need water, warm clothing and good lungs as the air gets mighty thin at 3766 metres.

Lake Atitlán

The road westward from Antigua makes its way 17 km up to the ridge of the Continental Divide, where it meets the Pan American Highway at Chimaltenango, capital of the Department (province) of Chimaltenango. This was an old town to the Cakchiquel Maya when the conquistadors arrived in 1526 to found their own Spanish settlement. Many of the buildings here were badly ruined in the earthquake of 1976, and there is little to detain you. Chimaltenango is mostly a place to change buses.

A na, a Mayan thatch-roofed hut

Westward 32 km along the highway takes you past the turning for the back road to Lake Atitlán via Patzicía and Patzún. The area around these two towns has been notable for high levels of guerrilla activity in recent years. The road is in poor condition in any case, so it's advisable to stay on the Pan-American Highway to Tecpán Guatemala, the turning-point for a visit to the ruined Cakchiquel capital city of Iximché.

IXIMCHÉ
Set on a flat promontory surrounded by steep cliffs, Iximché was well sited to be the capital city of the Cakchiquel Maya, founded in the late 1400s. The Cakchiquels were at war with the Quiché Maya, and the city's natural defences served them well. When the conquistadors arrived in 1524, the Cakchiquels made an alliance with them against their enemies the Quichés and the Tzutuhils. The Spanish set up their headquarters right next door to the Cakchiquel capital at Tecpán Guatemala. But Spanish demands for gold and other loot soon put an end to the alliance. In the ensuing battles the Cakchiquels went down in defeat.

As you enter Tecpán you will see signs pointing to the unpaved road leading through fields and pine forests to Iximché, less than six km to the south. If you don't have your own vehicle, you can walk the distance in about an hour, see the ruins and rest (another hour), then walk back to Tecpán, for a total of three hours. If you're going to walk, it's best to do it in the morning so that you're back at the highway by early afternoon. Bus traffic dwindles by late afternoon.

Enter the archaeological site (open 9 am to 4 pm daily), pass the small museo (museum) on the right, and you come to four ceremonial plazas surrounded by grass-covered temple structures and ball courts. Some of the structures have been cleaned and maintained; on a few the original plaster coating is still in place, even with some traces of the original paint.

LOS ENCUENTROS
Another 40 km westward along the Pan

American Highway from Tecpán brings you to the highway junction of Los Encuentros. There is no real town here, just a lot of people waiting to catch buses. The road to the right heads north to Chichicastenango and Santa Cruz del Quiché; the road to the left descends 12 km to Sololá, capital of the department of the same name, and then to Panajachel on the shores of Lake Atitlán.

If you are not on a direct bus to Panajachel, you can usually catch a bus or minibus, or even hitch a ride, from Los Encuentros down to Panajachel.

SOLOLÁ

Population 9000

Though the Spanish founded Sololá (altitude 2110 metres) in 1547, there was a Cakchiquel town called Tzoloyá here before they came. Sololá's importance comes from its geographic position on trade routes between the Tierra Caliente (hot lands of the Pacific Slope) and Tierra Fría (the chilly highlands). All the traders meet here, and Sololá's Friday market is one of the best in the highlands.

On market days, the plaza next to the cathedral is ablaze with the colours of costumes from a dozen surrounding villages and towns. Displays of meat, vegetables and fruit, housewares and clothing are neatly arranged in every available space as tides of buyers ebb and flow along the spaces in between. Boys grind coffee in an old-fashioned mill, girls mix up fruit drinks to refresh thirsty marketers, and shoppers haggle over prices of bright new potatoes, tiny tomatoes, all sorts of greens, spices, oranges and fresh garlic. Several elaborate stands are well stocked with brightly coloured yarn and sewing notions to aid in making the traditional costumes you see all around you.

If you can't be here on Friday, the main market day, try to make it on Tuesday, which is almost as good. On Sunday mornings the officers of the traditional religious brotherhoods (*cofradías*) parade ceremoniously to the cathedral for their devotions. On other days, Sololá sleeps.

Sololá to Panajachel

The road from Sololá descends more than 500 metres through pine forests in its eight-km course to Panajachel. You should try to get a seat on the right-hand side of the bus because all of the sights and views are on your right.

Along the way the road passes Sololá's colourful cemetery, and a Guatemalan army base. The fantastic guardpost by the main gate is in the shape of a huge helmet resting upon a pair of soldier's boots. Soon the road turns to snake its way down the mountainside to the lakeshore, offering breathtaking views of the lake and its surrounding volcanoes.

PANAJACHEL

Nicknamed Gringotenango (Place of the Foreigners) by locals and foreigners alike, 'Pana' has long been discovered by tourists. In the hippy heyday of the 1960s and '70s it was crowded with laid-back travellers in semi-permanent exile. When the civil war of the late 1970s and early '80s made Panajachel a dangerous – or at least unpleasant – place to be, many moved on. But in recent years the town's tourism has boomed again, not just with North Americans and Europeans, but with Central American tourists escaping the rigours of civil war in El Salvador and Nicaragua.

There is no notable colonial architecture in this town, no colourful indigenous market. It is a small and not particularly attractive place which has developed haphazardly according to the demands of the tourist trade. Compared to the geometric layout and architectural harmony of colonial highland towns, it is nothing. The lake, however, is absolutely gorgeous, and one wants nothing better than to sit for hours watching the play of colours and shadows on the lake's surface and on the slopes of the proud volcanoes as the sun runs its daily course and the clouds provide their evanescent entertainment. At moments like this you can ignore the village lad strolling along the lakeshore with an armful of newspapers shouting 'Miami Herald! Miami Herald!'

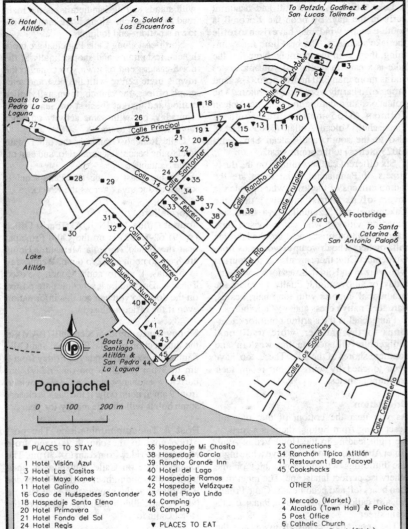

Panajachel

0   100   200 m

■ PLACES TO STAY

1 Hotel Visión Azul
3 Hotel Las Casitas
7 Hotel Maya Kanek
11 Hotel Galindo
16 Casa de Huéspedes Santander
18 Hospedaje Santa Elena
20 Hotel Primavera
21 Hotel Fonda del Sol
24 Hotel Regis
26 Mini Hotel Riva Bella
27 Hotel Tzanjuyú
28 Cacique Inn
29 Hospedaje Santo Domingo
30 Hotel Monterrey
31 Hospedaje Vista Hermosa
32 Hospedaje Santa Elena 2
33 Mario's Rooms

36 Hospedaje Mi Chosita
38 Hospedaje Garcia
39 Rancho Grande Inn
40 Hotel del Lago
42 Hospedaje Ramos
42 Hospedaje Velázquez
43 Hotel Playa Linda
44 Camping
46 Camping

▼ PLACES TO EAT

7 Rancho Mercado Bakery & Deli
8 Al Chisme
10 La Unica Deli
12 La Posada del Pintor
   & Circus Bar
13 Restaurant La Laguna
22 La Hamburguesa Gigante

23 Connections
34 Ranchón Típica Atitlán
41 Restaurant Bar Tocoyal
45 Cookshacks

OTHER

2 Mercado (Market)
4 Alcaldía (Town Hall) & Police
5 Post Office
9 Centro de Salud (Clinic)
14 Bus Stop
15 Banco Agricola Mercantil
17 Billboard Map of Panajachel
19 INGUAT Tourist Office
25 Texaco Fuel Station
35 Guatel Telephone Office
37 Gaby Bicycle Rentals

Lake Atitlán is often still and beautiful early in the day. By noon the Xocomil, a south-easterly wind, may have risen to ruffle the lake's surface. The best time for swimming, then, is in the morning. Note that the lake is a caldera (collapsed volcanic cone) and is more than 320 metres deep. The land drops off sharply very near the shore. The volcanoes surrounding the lake are: Volcán Tolimán (3155 metres), due south of Panajachel; Volcán Atitlán (3505 metres), also to the south; and Volcán San Pedro (3025 metres) to the south-west.

Six different cultures mingle on the dusty streets of Panajachel. First there are the ladino citizens of the town who operate the levers of its tourist industry; then the Cakchiquel and Tzutuhil Maya from surrounding villages who come to sell their handicrafts to tourists; next are the lakeside villa owners who drive up at weekends from Guatemala City; there are also group tourists who whiz in and out in buses for a few hours, a day, or an overnight; finally, there are the 'traditional' hippies with long hair, beards, bare feet, native dress and VW minibuses.

Panajachel is the starting point for excursions to the smaller, more traditional indigenous villages on the western and southern shores of the lake. These, too, have been touched by tourism, but retain their charm nonetheless.

Orientation

As you near the bottom of the long hill descending from Sololá, there is a road on the right leading to the Hotel Visión Azul, Hotel Atitlán and those obtrusive white high-rise buildings which form a blot on the otherwise perfect landscape. The main road then bears left and becomes the Calle Principal, also called Calle Tzanjuyú, Panajachel's main street.

The geographic centre of town, and the closest thing it has to a bus station, is the intersection of Calle Principal and Calle Santander, where you will see the Banco Agrícola Mercantil, the town's only bank, as well as the INGUAT tourist office and the Mayan Palace Hotel. Calle Santander, lined with stands selling handicrafts, is the main road to the beach. Along it are many of the town's bottom-end lodgings.

North-east along Calle Principal are more hotels, restaurants and shops; finally at the north-eastern end of town you come to the town's civic centre with the post and telegraph offices, the church, town hall, police station and market (busiest on Sunday and Thursday, but with some activity on other days from 9 am to noon).

Calle Rancho Grande is the other main road to the beach; it's parallel to, and east of, Calle Santander.

The area east of the Río Panajachel is known as Jucanyá (Across the River).

Information

Tourist Office The INGUAT Tourist Office (☎ (9) 62-13-92) is on the Calle Principal near the Banco Agrícola Mercantil. Hours are 8 am to noon and 2 to 6 pm, Wednesday to Sunday, 8 am to noon Monday, closed Tuesday. Bus and boat schedules are posted on the door, so you can get this information even if the office is closed.

Money Banco Agrícola Mercantil (BAM), at the intersection of Calle Principal and Calle Santander, is open Monday to Friday from 9 am to 3 pm (till 3.30 pm on Friday), but currency exchange services are provided from 9 am to noon only. If the bank is closed, some hotels will change money for you.

Post & Telecommunications The post office next to the church is open from Monday to Friday from 8 am to 4.30 pm. The Guatel office on Calle Santander is open from 7 am to midnight every day. Fax service is available at the shop called Que Hay de Nuevo, on Calle Principal to the left of the Hotel Galindo.

Bookshops Right next door to the tourist office is The Book Exchange, where you can buy used books in English, and also some in French, German, and Spanish. The American-born owner sells coffee, tea, some snacks, and also useful maps of the area.

There's another good bookshop on Calle Los Arboles, up one flight of stairs.

Places to Stay – bottom end

Luckily for low-budget travellers, Panajachel has numerous little family-run *hospedajes* (pensions). They're very simple – perhaps just two rough beds and a bedside table in a room of bare boards with one light bulb – but quite cheap. The best of the hospedajes provide clean toilets, hot showers and even perhaps some meals at a patio comedor. Prices average US$3 for a double, with a US$0.30 charge for a hot shower. The first place to look for hospedajes is along Calle Santander midway between Calle Principal and the beach. Signs along the street point the way down narrow side streets and alleys to the various hospedajes.

Hospedaje Santa Elena 2, off Calle Santander on the road to the Hotel Monterrey, is typical of Pana's hospedajes. Each tidy room has a bed, one sheet, no blankets, one light bulb, and a small table, period. The little courtyard is planted with bananas and noisy with macaws; the showers provide cold water only. The original *Hospedaje Santa Elena* is in an alley off Calle Principal opposite the INGUAT Tourist Office, closer to the centre but farther from the beach.

Hospedaje Vista Hermosa has simple rooms on two levels around a small, pretty courtyard decorated with flowers in a car battery casing. Blue and white, the Guatemalan national colours, predominate. There are no hot showers. *Hospedaje Santo Domingo* is a step up in quality but a few steps off the street; follow the road toward the Hotel Monterrey, then follow signs along a shady path. This backpackers' motel has rough timber rooms built around a nice yard that's quiet, being well away from the noise on Calle Santander. Cold showers, laundry sinks and toilets are available; the price, as usual, is US$3 a double.

Casa de Huéspedes Santander, in an alley off Calle Santander, has clean beds in tidy, bare rooms around a verdant garden for US$3/5/6 a single/double/triple. It's pleasant and convenient.

Mario's Rooms (☎ (9) 62-13-13), just south of the Guatel office on Calle Santander, is popular with young, adventurous travellers, and is among the best of the hospedajes. Rates for each of the 20 rooms are US$2.25 a single, US$3 a double, and there's a tiny little restaurant-bar for meals, drinks, and conversation. *Hospedaje Mi Chosita*, on Calle 14 de Febrero (turn at Mario's Rooms), is tidy and quiet. *Hospedaje Garcia*, farther east along the same street toward Calle Rancho Grande, is a bit fancier.

Overlooking the beach near the Hotel Playa Linda are two more places, *Hospedaje Ramos* and *Hospedaje Velázquez*, both renting rooms US$3 a double. Both hostelries have cold showers only, some beach views and little comedores.

Moving upscale in both price and comfort, *Hotel Las Casitas* (☎ (9) 62-12-24), across from the market near the church and town hall, rents little brick bungalows with tile roofs. Señora Dalma Gutiérrez is always smiling, cleaning or cooking (all three meals) to keep her guests happy. Double rooms cost US$4 without water, US$7 with private (hot) shower.

Hotel Fonda del Sol (☎ (9) 62-11-62), Calle Principal, is a two-storey building on the main street across from the Asamblea de Dios church, west of the intersection with Calle Santander. The 15 simple rooms on the upper floor are well used but fairly decently kept, and low priced at US$5 to US$7 a double, US$7.50 to US$9 a triple; the higher prices are for rooms with private showers. Downstairs is a cheap restaurant, and the hotel can do your laundry for you. The Asamblea de Dios church across the street rocks with gospel music some evenings, but not too late into the night.

Hotel Maya Kanek (☎ (9) 62-11-04), Calle Principal just down from the church, is a motel-style hostelry with rooms facing a cobbled court with a small garden; the court doubles as a secure car park. The 20 rooms, though simple, are a bit more comfortable than at a hospedaje, and cost US$5 a single, US$8.50 a double. It's quiet here.

Hotel Galindo (☎ (9) 62-11-68), Calle Principal north-east of the Banco Agricola Mercantil, has a large and airy restaurant facing the street, and behind it a surprisingly lush jungle of a garden surrounded by modest rooms which rent for US$4.50 per person with private shower.

Mini Hotel Riva Bella (☎ (9) 62-13-48, 62-11-77), Calle Principal, is a collection of neat two-room bungalows, each with its own parking place. Señora María Gertraude E de Benini oversees maintenance and management of the bungalows with the assistance of a cageful of noisy macaws outside the office. The location is convenient and the price US$12 a double with private shower.

As with Antigua, prices of budget accommodation in Panajachel are subject to increase as demand rises; only a few months after the research for this book was completed, the price of a double room at one hotel increased by 100%.

Camping Many people, particularly those with camper vans, camp on the public beach at the end of Calle Santander and Calle Rancho Grande. This is sometimes discouraged, especially now as the beach area is being reconstructed. If you are allowed to camp, you can use the toilets and sinks at one of the little beachfront restaurants. Several public water taps provide water as well (look for them near the signs for the Hotel Paradise Inn, near the riverbed). Another tap and primitive toilet is in front of the Hotel del Lago just up from the beach.

If you're not allowed to camp on the beach, try setting up on the east side of the Río Panajachel; this is usually allowed.

For a formal campground with electrical and water hook-ups, go to the Hotel Visión Azul on the western outskirts of town.

Places to Stay – middle
Panajachel Middle-range lodgings are located all over town, and come in all sizes, shapes and prices.

Rancho Grande Inn (☎ (9) 62-15-54), Calle Rancho Grande, was established decades ago by Milly Schlesier, who built

German country-style villas in a tropical Guatemalan setting. Marlita Hannstein bought Rancho Grande in 1975 and did some renovation, but preserved the high standards of cleanliness and maintenance. The seven white stucco bungalows, set in emerald lawns beneath towering palm trees, have red tile or thatched roofs and small sitting porches, and can sleep up to five people. The location is convenient both to the town and the beach, it's quiet, and prices are very reasonable at US$25 a double, breakfast included. Reserve in advance, or be disappointed.

Hotel Primavera (☎ (9) 62-11-57), Calle Santander just a block south of Calle Principal, offers you eight good, clean, pleasant rooms in a stone and stucco building trimmed with honey-coloured wood. The ground floor has a nice little restaurant, and there's a garden terrace behind the hotel. Laundry service is provided. Rooms cost US$14 to US$15 a double.

Hotel Regis (☎ (9) 62-11-49), Calle Santander across from Guatel, is a group of villas in colonial style set back from the street across a lush lawn shaded by palms. The lobby and dining room are decorated with lots of local crafts. The 14 guestrooms with private bath are in separate bungalows, each with a porch facing the lawn, which has a small swimming pool and playground for children. Obviously this is a choice for families with small children. Rates are US$14/18/22 a single/double/triple.

Hotel Monterrey (☎ (9) 62-11-26), Calle 15 de Febrero, down an unpaved road going west from Calle Santander (look for the sign), is a blue-and-white, two-storey motel-style building facing the lake across lawns which extend down to the beach. The Monterrey offers you clean and cheerful if fairly simple accommodation with satellite TV and private bath for US$14 a single, US$16 a double.

Hotel Playa Linda (☎ (9) 62-11-59), facing the beach at the end of Calle Rancho Grande, has an assortment of rooms, a few with nice views of the lake. Room Nos 1 to 5 have views, rooms 6 to 14 do not; most

Top: Market in the Parque Central, Antigua Guatemala (TB)
Bottom: Lake Atitlán and Tolimán Volcano seen from Santa Catarina Palopó,
Guatemala (TB)

Top: Market at Sololá, Guatemala (TB)
Left: Wooden masks on sale in the market at Chichicastenango, Guatemala (TB)
Right: The idol at Pascual Abaj shrine, Chichicastenango, Guatemala (TB)

have private baths with hot water, some have TVs with satellite programmes. A small restaurant in the front garden can provide sustenance as the macaws by the office provide natural audio. The rate for a double is US$24 to US$32, the higher price being for rooms with views.

Cacique Inn (☎ (9) 62-12-05), Calle Embarcadero off Calle Principal at the western edge of town, is an assemblage of pseudo-rustic red tile-roofed buildings arranged around verdant gardens and a swimming pool. The 33 large, comfortable rooms have double beds, fireplaces, locally made blankets, clean private baths, and odd sliding glass and wrought-iron doors that take some getting used to. Señora Adela Morales Schuman is the *cacique* (leader) here, and she charges US$22/24/28 a single/double/triple, tax included.

Hotel Visión Azul (☎ (9) 62-14-19/26; in Guatemala City ☎ (2) 76-14-83), on the Hotel Atitlán road, is built into a hillside in a quiet location looking toward the lake through a grove of trees. The big, bright rooms in the main building have spacious terraces festooned with bougainvillea and ivy. Modern bungalows a few steps away provide more privacy for families. There's a swimming pool, and the lakeshore is only a minute's walk away across the lawns mown by cattle grazing. Prices are US$39 a double, US$45 a triple. If you arrive when the hotel is not busy (busiest times are weekends and holidays), discounts may be offered.

Hotel Tzanjuyú (☎ (9) 62-13-18; in Guatemala City ☎ (2) 31-07-64), off Calle Principal at the western edge of town, has seen better days, but the gardens are still nice, the flower-bedecked porch is still a good place to sit, and the rooms with bath are serviceable. Prices are high for what you get, at US$24/30/37 a single/double/triple.

Santa Catarina Palopó If you'd like to get away from the tourist bustle of Panajachel (low-key as it is), stay at the *Villa Santa Catarina* (☎ (9) 62-12-91; in Guatemala City ☎ (2) 31-98-76, fax 34-62-37). Most of the 30 comfortable rooms with bath have views

of the lake, and rooms 24, 25, 26 and 27 (partly) face west and have fine views of Volcano San Pedro; all overlook the pretty swimming pool and grounds right on the shore. The village of Santa Catarina Palopó, four km south-east of Panajachel along an unpaved road, is untouristed as the hotel is the only tourist-oriented business here. The dining room serves mostly groups, but also provides moderately priced table d'hôte meals. To stay at the Villa Santa Catarina you pay US$26 a single, US$30 a double, tax included.

Farther along the same road, in between Santa Catarina Palopó and San Antonio Palopó, is the *Hotel Bella Vista* (☎ in Guatemala City (2) 2-68-07/08/09, 51-04-32; fax 2-64-02), 8.5 km from Panajachel. Little bungalows, each with private bath, share gardens with a swimming pool, restaurant, private beach and boat dock. There's even satellite TV and a heliport (some people want to get away from it all, and then back to it all, very quickly). For reservations, contact the Hotel Pan American in Guatemala City.

Places to stay – top end
The best hotel in town is the *Hotel Atitlán* (☎ (9) 62-14-16/29/41), on the lakeshore two km west of the centre. Spacious gardens of bougainvillea, ivy, geraniums and tropical flowers surround this rambling three-storey colonial-style hotel. Inside are gleaming tile floors, antique wood carvings and exquisite handicraft decorations. The staff are experienced and efficient, the dining room pleasant, with a nice open-air patio looking across the heated swimming pools to the lake. The 42 rooms with private bath have twin beds, local craft decorations and shady balconies with views of the grounds or the lake. For what you get, rates are very reasonable at US$40 a single, US$48 a double.

Hotel del Lago (☎ (9) 62-15-55 to 60, fax 62-15-62; in Guatemala City ☎ (2) 31-69-41, 31-74-61, fax 34-80-16), at the beach end of Calle Rancho Grande, is a modern six-storey building which seems out of place in low-rise, laid-back Panajachel. Each of its 100 rooms has two double beds, marble-topped dressing table and vanity, shiny marble bathrooms with tub and shower, plus a balcony with a view of the lake. Besides the beach, the hotel has two swimming pools (one for children), a large restaurant, two elevators, rental bicycles, table tennis, and nice gardens. The del Lago, operated by Biltmore Internacional, charges US$55 to US$60 a double, tax included.

Places to Eat

Panajachel is one of the few places in Guatemala which has some restaurants which cater specifically to foreigners.

The cheapest places to eat are the little cookshacks on the beach with names such as *El Nuevo Cayuco, El Pescador, Los Pumpos, Brisas de Lago* and *Comedor Emilio*. Not only is the food cheap (US$2 for a fill-up), but the view of the lake is a priceless bonus.

Calle Santander has a number of popular restaurants. *La Hamburguesa Gigante*, down toward the beach on the west side of the street, serves a *quarto de libro* (quarterpounder) cheeseburger for US$1, as well as grilled chicken and other dishes at similarly low prices. Try the substantial Desayuno Chapín (Guatemalan breakfast) of ham, eggs, beans and fried bananas for US$1.50.

Right next door is *Connections*, a wonderful meeting-place where you can enjoy a drink (hot, cold, hard or soft), read one of their books, play backgammon, look at their maps, or order pastry or food. Adjoining Connections is *The Video Bar*, with a full programme of videos daily from 2 to 11 pm.

On Calle Santander opposite the Hotel Regis is *Ranchón Típica Atitlán*, a place of rough-hewn log walls, floors paved in stones, fresh fish and roast chicken. Daily set-price meals here go for US$2 to US$3.

Calle Los Arboles, on the north-west side of Calle Principal, also holds numbers of good restaurants. *La Posada del Pintor* and its *Circus Bar* have walls hung with old circus posters, and quiet jazz and rock as background music. Pizzas, boeuf bourguignon, potato salads, steaks, pastas and desserts all share space on the menu. You can expect to spend US$4 to US$10 for a full

dinner. There's live entertainment in the bar some evenings.

A few doors away is *Al Chisme* (The Gossip), a favourite with regular Pana foreign visitors and residents, with its shady streetside patio for dining, as well as a nice interior room. It's a good place to take a break and wind down, with soft music and good breakfasts of English muffins, Belgian waffles and omelettes priced from US$1.50 to US$3. For lunch and dinner Al Chisme offers lots of sandwiches, soups, salads, crepes and chicken pot pie for US$1.15 to US$2.25, or curried shrimp, pork chops, pasta alfredo and tenderloin of beef for US$3 to US$4.50. Alcoholic beverages are served.

La Unica Deli, on Calle Principal next to the Hotel Galindo, has nice gardens with lots of roses, simple tables and chairs, and breakfasts of pancakes and other good things for US$1.50.

Rancho Mercado Bakery & Deli, on Calle Principal next to the Hotel Maya Kanek, advertises 'the best chizburger in town, french fries too' for US$1.25. But last time I visited, it also had a sign by the door which read 'Se necesita cocinera con experiencia' ('We need an experienced cook'), which doesn't bode well for their hamburger reputation.

Restaurant Bar Tocoyal, just across the street from the Hotel del Lago at the southern end of Calle Rancho Grande, is a tidy, modern little thatch-roofed place overlooking the beach. Waiters in white and black glide across the tiled patio in the shade of palms. A lunch of tomato soup, fillet of fish with chips, green beans and sliced tomatoes, bread, a slice of fruit pie, coffee and a soft drink might cost US$6.

Restaurant La Laguna, Calle Principal at the intersection of Calle Los Arboles, has a pretty front patio and garden with umbrella-covered tables. The cooking here is a step above most Panajachel places, and prices are still reasonable. Have the *sopa de frijoles* (black bean soup), *gazpacho* or *guacamole* (avocado purée), a *ceviche* (marinated seafood), then a plato típico of Guatemalan foods, perhaps with *puyaso* (barbecued sirloin), and your bill should be between US$4 and US$6. A reader also recommends their breakfasts (especially the pancakes), which cost US$1.50 per person.

If your budget allows you to spend more, go to the dining room of the *Hotel Atitlán* or, as a second choice, that of the *Hotel del Lago*.

Getting There & Away

The town's main bus stop is where Calle Santander meets Calle Principal, across from the Mayan Palace Hotel and the Banco Agricola Mercantil, but buses leave from other parts of the town as well, depending upon the company.

Antigua – 80 km, two hours; several direct buses daily, even more if you take any bus stopping at Chimaltenango, and change to an Antigua-bound minibus there. Buses Inter-Hotel y Turismo (BIT, ☎ (9) 32-00-11/15 at the Ramada Hotel Antigua) also runs its minibuses between Panajachel and Antigua on Tuesday, Thursday and Sunday, departing the Ramada Hotel Antigua at 8.30 am, arriving in Panajachel at 10.30, returning from Panajachel (departing from the Hotel del Lago) at noon, arriving in Antigua at 2.30 pm. One-way fare is US$10.

Chichicastenango – 29 km, one hour; buses (US$0.75) depart Panajachel at 6.45, 7.45, 8.45 and 9.45 am

Guatemala City – 147 km, three hours; Rebulli (☎ (2) 51-65-05), 3a Avenida 2-36, Zona 9, departs Guatemala City for Lake Atitlán and Panajachel every hour from 6.45 am to 4 pm, stopping at Chimaltenango, Patzicía, Tecpán Guatemala, Los Encuentros, and Sololá, for US$1.75. Departures from Panajachel are at 5, 5.30, 7, 8, 9.30, 11.30 am and 1 and 2.30 pm; on Saturday there's also an 11 am bus.

Huehuetenango – 159 km, 3½ hours; catch a bus or minibus to Los Encuentros, and wait for a Huehue-bound bus there; see the Guatemala City chapter under Getting There & Away for a schedule of Huehue-bound buses; or catch a Morales bus from Panajachel to Quetzaltenango, get out at Cuatro Caminos, and wait for a Huehue bus.

La Mesilla (Mexican border) – 241 km, five hours; see Huehuetenango

Quetzaltenango – 99 km, two hours; buses run by Morales or Rojo y Blanco depart at 5.30, 5.45 and 11.30 am and 2.30 pm, for US$1.25

Getting Around

You can rent bicycles from Alquiler de Bicycletas Gaby, on Calle 14 de Febrero between Calle Santander and Calle Rancho Grande. Otherwise, most people get around Pana on foot. For information on buses and boats to other lakeside villages, see Around Lake Atitlán.

AROUND LAKE ATITLÁN

Various lakeside villages, which can be reached on foot, by bus or motor launch, are interesting to visit. The most popular destination for day trips is Santiago Atitlán, directly across the lake south of Panajachel, but there are others. Some villages even have places for you to stay overnight.

Santa Catarina Palopó to San Lucas Tolimán

Four km east of Panajachel along a winding, unpaved road lies the village of Santa Catarina Palopó. Narrow streets paved in stone blocks and adobe houses with roofs of thatch or corrugated tin huddled around a gleaming white church: that's Santa Catarina. Chickens cackle, dogs bark and the villagers go about their business dressed in their beautiful traditional costumes. Except for exploring village life and enjoying views of the lake and the volcanoes, there's little in the way of 'sightseeing'. For refreshments, there are several little comedores on the main plaza, one of which advertises 'Cold beer sold here'. If your budget allows, a drink or a meal at the village's only hotel, the *Villa Santa Catarina*, is pleasant (for details on the hotel, see Places to Stay in the Panajachel section).

The road continues past Santa Catarina five km to San Antonio Palopó, a larger but similar village. Three km along the way you pass the *Hotel Bella Vista* (three km) and, in San Antonio, the *Hotel Terrazas del Mar*.

High up on the steep hillside east of these villages is the town of Godínez. Many visitors make a loop excursion by bus and on foot to see these three villages. Take a bus from Panajachel bound for Godínez along the high road well up the slope, but get off at the *mirador* (lookout) about one km before

Godínez. From the mirador, paths lead down the mountainside to the shore road, San Antonio and Santa Catarina, from which you can walk back to Panajachel (or you may be lucky enough to catch a bus). The entire excursion takes the better part of a morning.

Beyond San Antonio and Godínez lies San Lucas Tolimán, busier and more commercial than most lakeside villages. Set at the foot of the dramatic Volcán Tolimán, San Lucas is a coffee-growing town and a transport point on the route between the Pan American Highway and the Pacific Slope Highway. Market days are Monday, Tuesday, Thursday and Friday. From San Lucas, a rough, badly maintained road goes west around Volcán Tolimán to Santiago Atitlán, then around Volcán San Pedro to San Pedro La Laguna (see below).

Getting There & Away A bus leaves daily except Saturday for Guatemala City via Santa Catarina (four km) and San Antonio (11 km) at 9 am, but returns by another route. Buses leave Panajachel daily for San Lucas Tolimán via Santa Catarina and San Antonio at 6.30 am and 4 pm.

Santiago Atitlán

South across the lake from Panajachel, on the shore of a lagoon squeezed between the towering volcanoes of Tolimán and San Pedro, lies the small town of Santiago Atitlán. Though it is the most visited village outside Panajachel, it clings to the traditional lifestyle of the Tzutuhil Maya. The women of the town still weave and wear huipiles with brilliantly coloured flocks of birds and bouquets of flowers embroidered on them. The best day to visit is market day (Friday, with a lesser market on Tuesday), but in fact any day will do.

Santiago is also a curiosity because of its reverence for Maximón (MAH-shee-MOHN), a local deity who is probably a blend of ancient Mayan gods, Pedro de Alvarado the fierce conquistador of Guatemala, and the biblical Judas. Despised in other highland towns, Maximón is revered in San-

tiago Atitlán, and his effigy with wooden mask and huge cigar is paraded triumphantly during Holy Week processions (see Holidays & Festivals in the Facts for the Visitor chapter for the dates of Holy Week).

Children from Santiago greet you as you disembark at the dock in Santiago, selling little embroidered strips of cloth and clay whistles. They'll be right behind, alongside and in front of you during much of your stay here.

Walk to the left from the dock along the shore to reach the street into town. This is the main commercial street. As every tourist who's come to visit walks up and down it between the dock and the town, it's lined with shops selling woven cloth, other handicrafts and souvenirs.

On the right as you walk uphill is a sign: 'Visite la casa de la escultura y pintura, visit the house of sculpture and paintings'. This is the studio of Diego Chavez and his sons Diego and Nicolás, the village's self-trained artists. The entire family joins in the artistry, making paintings, figurines carved from wood, relief carvings, and weaving traditional designs into cloth.

At the top of the slope is the main square, with the town office and huge church, which dates from the time, several centuries ago, when Santiago was an important commercial town. Within the stark, echoing church are some surprising sights. Along the walls are wooden statues of the saints, each of whom gets a new shawl embroidered by local women every year. On the carved wooden pulpit, note the figures of corn (from which humans were formed, according to Mayan religion), of a quetzal bird reading a book, and of Yum-Kax, the Mayan god of corn. There is similar carving on the back of the priest's chair. The walls of the church bear paintings, now covered by a thin layer of plaster. A memorial plaque at the back of the church commemorates Father Stanley Francis Rother, a missionary priest from Oklahoma, who was beloved by the local people but despised by ultra-rightist 'death squads', who murdered him right here in the church during the troubled year of 1981.

Places to Stay & Eat Best in town is *Hotel Chi-Nim-Yá*, a simple, basic place with several advantages. The best room in the place is No 106, large and airy, with lots of windows and excellent lake views, for US$4 a double. Smaller, less desirable rooms cost only half that much. A shop adjoining the hotel provides snacks and cold drinks.

Pensión Rosita, to the right of the school and behind the basketball court off the main plaza, has very stark, bare rooms for US$2 per person. The plumbing is primitive.

Restaurant Santa Rita, a few steps from the northeast corner of the plaza past Distribuidor El Buen Precio, boasts *deliciosos pays* (delicious pies).

Getting There & Away An unpaved road in bad repair connects Santiago and San Lucas Tolimán (16 km), but most visitors reach Santiago by motor launch from Panajachel. Two different launches cross between Panajachel and Santiago daily; both depart from the public beach at the foot of Calle Rancho Grande, near the Hotel del Lago. The voyage takes 1¼ to 1½ hours each way, depending upon the winds, and costs US$2 a round trip.

Naviera Santiago departs from Panajachel at 8.45 and 10 am and 4 pm, returning from Santiago at 11.45 am and 1 pm. Naviera Santa Fe leaves Panajachel at 9 and 9.30 am, returning from Santiago at 12.30 and 1 pm.

San Pedro La Laguna

Perhaps the next most popular lakeside town to visit, after Santiago, is San Pedro La Laguna. Its ranking as Number Two means that fewer flocks of *muchachos* will swirl around you as you stroll its narrow cobblestone streets and wander to its outskirts for a dip in the lake.

Places to Stay & Eat Right near the boat dock is *Hospedaje Chuasinahu*, the best place in town, with beds for US$1 per night. The *Ti-Kaaj* next door is not quite as good, but takes the overflow if the Chuasinahu is full. The *Pensión Johanna*, on the other side

of the village near another dock, is another choice at similar rates.

Getting There & Away The rough road from San Lucas Tolimán to Santiago Atitlán continues 18 km to San Pedro, making its way around the lagoon and Volcán San Pedro. Coming from Panajachel, you should take a motor launch, of which there are two. Naviera Pato Poc departs from the public beach in Panajachel, at the foot of Calle Rancho Grande near the Hotel del Lago, at 10 am, 1 and 5 pm, returning from San Pedro at 11.30 am and 3 pm. Naviera Santa María departs from a dock near the Hotel Tzanjuyú, at the western edge of Panajachel, each day at 9.30 am and 2.30 pm, returning from San Pedro at 1 pm only. The voyage costs US$2 a round trip.

Quiché

The Departamento del Quiché is famous mostly for the town of Chichicastenango, known for its bustling markets on Thursdays and Sundays. Beyond Chichi to the north is Santa Cruz del Quiché, the capital of the department. On its outskirts lie the ruins of K'umarcaaj (or Gumarcaah), also called Utatlán, the last capital city of the Quiché Maya.

The road to Quiché leaves the Pan American Highway at Los Encuentros, winding its way through pine forests and cornfields, down into a steep valley and up the other side. Women sit in front of their little roadside cottages weaving yet another gorgeous piece of cloth on their simple back-strap looms. Half an hour after leaving Los Encuentros, you've travelled the 17 km north to Chichicastenango.

CHICHICASTENANGO
Population 8000

Surrounded by valleys, with nearby mountains looming overhead, Chichicastenango (altitude 2030 metres) seems isolated from the rest of Guatemala. It can also seem

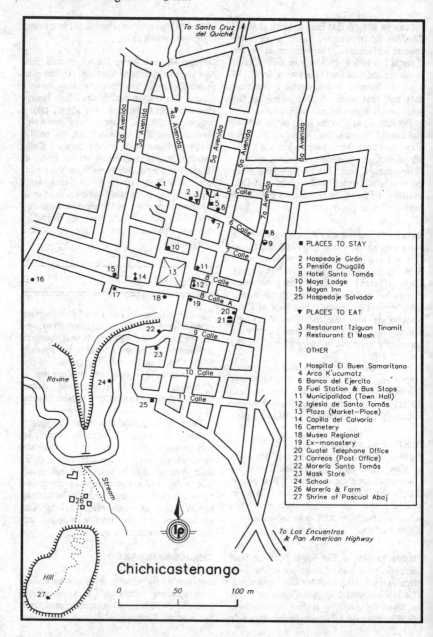

To Santa Cruz
del Quiché

2a Avenida
3o Avenida
4o Avenida
5a Avenida
6a Avenida
7a Avenida
8a Avenida

5 Calle
6 Calle
7 Calle
8 Calle
8 Calle A
9 Calle
10 Calle
11 Calle

Ravine

Stream

Hill

■ PLACES TO STAY

2 Hospedaje Girón
5 Pensión Chugüilá
8 Hotel Santo Tomás
10 Maya Lodge
15 Mayan Inn
25 Hospedaje Salvador

▼ PLACES TO EAT

3 Restaurant Tziguan Tinamit
7 Restaurant El Mash

OTHER

1 Hospital El Buen Samaritano
4 Arco K'ucumatz
6 Banco del Ejercito
9 Fuel Station & Bus Stops
11 Municipalidad (Town Hall)
12 Iglesia de Santo Tomás
13 Plaza (Market–Place)
14 Capilla del Calvario
16 Cemetery
18 Museo Regional
19 Ex–monastery
20 Guatel Telephone Office
21 Correos (Post Office)
22 Morería Santo Tomás
23 Mask Store
24 School
26 Morería & Farm
27 Shrine of Pascual Abaj

To Los Encuentros
& Pan American Highway

Chichicastenango

0   50   100 m

magical when its narrow cobbled streets and red-tiled roofs are enveloped in mists, as they often are. Chichi is a beautiful, interesting place, and not even the many shiny tourbuses parked near the market, not even the gaggles of camera-toting 'It's Thursday this must be Chichi' tour groups can change that. If you have a choice of days, come for the Sunday market rather than the Thursday one, as the cofradías (religious brotherhoods) often hold processions on Sundays. It's best to arrive in town the day before market day to pin down a room and a bed, and to be up early for the market.

Though isolated, Chichi has always been an important market town. Villagers from throughout the region would walk for many hours carrying their wares to participate in the commerce here – and that was in the days before good roads.

Today, though many traders come by bus, others still arrive on foot. When they reach Chichi's main square they lay down their loads, spread out a blanket and go to sleep in one of the arcades which surround the square. At dawn on Thursday and Sunday they spread out their vegetables, fruits, chunks of chalk (ground to a powder, mixed with water and used to soften dried maize), balls of wax, handmade harnesses, etc and wait for customers.

Many ladino business types also set up fairly touristy stalls in the Sunday and Thursday markets. Somehow they end up adding to the colour and fascination, not detracting from it.

Besides the famous market, Masheños (citizens of Chichicastenango) are famous for their adherence to pre-Christian religious beliefs and ceremonies. You can readily see survivals of these old rites in and around the church of Santo Tomás and at the shrine of Pascual Abaj on the outskirts of town.

History

Once called Chaviar, this was an important Cakchiquel trading town long before the Spanish conquest. Not long before the con-quistadors arrived, the Cakchiquels and the Quichés (based at K'umarcaaj near present-

day Santa Cruz del Quiché, 20 km north) went to war. The Cakchiquels abandoned Chaviar and moved their headquarters to Iximché, which was easier to defend. The conquistadors came and conquered K'umarcaaj, and many of its residents fled to Chaviar, which they renamed Chugüilá (Above the Nettles) and Tziguan Tinamit (Surrounded by Canyons). These are the names still used by the Quiché Maya, although everyone else calls the place Chichicastenango, a foreign name given by the conquistadors' Mexican allies.

Government

Chichi has two religious and governmental establishments. The Catholic Church and the Republic of Guatemala appoint priests and town officials to manage their interests, but the local people elect their own religious and civil officers to deal with local matters.

The Indian town government has its own council, mayor and deputy mayor, and court which decides cases involving local Indians exclusively. Chichi's religious life is centred in traditional religious brotherhoods called cofradías. Membership in the brotherhood is an honourable civic duty; leadership is the greatest honour. Leaders are elected period-ically, and the man who receives the honour of being elected must provide banquets and pay for festivities for the cofradía throughout his term. Though it is very expensive, a cofrade (member of the brotherhood) happily accepts the burden, even going into debt if necessary.

Each of Chichi's 14 cofradías has a patron saint. Most notable is the cofradía of Santo Tomás, Chichicastenango's patron saint. The cofradías march in procession to church on Sunday morning and during religious festi-vals, the officers dressed in costumes showing their rank. Before them is carried a ceremonial staff topped by a silver crucifix or sun-badge which signifies the cofradía's patron saint. Indian drum and flute, and perhaps a few more modern instruments such as a trumpet, may accompany the pro-cession, as do fireworks. During major Church festivals, effigies of the saints are brought out and carried in grand processions, and richly costumed dancers wearing the traditional carved wooden masks act out legends of the ancient Maya and of the Spanish conquest. For the rest of the year, these masks and costumes are kept in storehouses called *morerías*; you'll see them, marked by signs, around the town.

Orientation

Though supposedly laid out to the Spanish colonial street grid plan, Chichi's hilly topography defeats the logicality of the plan, and lack of street signs often keeps you wondering where you are. Use our map, identify some landmarks, and you should have little trouble, as Chichi is fairly small.

Information

There is no official tourist information office. Ask your questions at the museum on the main square, or at one of the hotels. The Mayan Inn is perhaps the most helpful and best informed.

Money The Banco del Ejercito, across from the Restaurant El Mash on 6 Calle, is open Monday to Friday from 9 am to noon and 2 to 5 pm and on Saturday from 10 am to 1 pm.

Post & Telecommunications The post office (Correos) is at 7a Avenida 8-47, two blocks north-west of the Hotel Santo Tomás on the road into town. Very near it is the Guatel telephone office, at 7a Avenida 8-21, on the corner of 8 Calle.

Market Day

A hundred years ago, intrepid travellers made their way to this mountainbound fastness to witness Chichi's main square packed with Indian traders attending one of Guatemala's largest indigenous markets. Today the market has stalls aimed directly at tourists as well as those for local people.

On Wednesday and Saturday evenings you'll see men carrying bundles of long poles up the narrow cobbled streets to the square, then stacking them out of the way. In the evening the arcades around the square are

alive with families cooking supper and arranging their bedding for a night's sleep out of doors.

Between dawn and about 8 or 9 am on Sunday and Thursday the stacks of poles are erected into stalls and hung with cloth, furnished with tables and piled with goods for sale. In general, the tourist-oriented stalls selling carved wooden masks, lengths of embroidered cloth and garments are around the outer edges of the market in the most visible areas. Behind these very visible ranks of stalls, the centre of the square is devoted to things that the villagers want and need: vegetables and fruit, baked goods, macaroni, soap, clothing, spices, sewing notions and toys. Cheap cookshops provide lunch for buyers and sellers alike.

The market continues into the afternoon; most of the stalls are taken down by late afternoon. Prices are best just before the market breaks up, as traders would rather sell than carry goods away with them.

Iglesia de Santo Tomás

This simple colonial church dates from about 1540. Though dedicated to the Catholic rite, it is more often the scene of rituals which are slightly Catholic and highly Mayan. The front steps of the church serve much the same purpose as did the great flights of stairs leading up to Mayan pyramids. Much of the day (especially on Sunday) the steps smoulder with incense of copal resin, while indigenous prayer leaders called *chuchkajaues* (mother-fathers) swing censers (usually tin cans poked with holes) containing *estoraque* incense and chant magic words in honour of the ancient Mayan calendar and of their ancestors.

It's customary for the front steps and door of the church to be used only by important church officials and by the chuchkajaues, so you should go around to the right and enter by the side door.

Inside, the floor of the church may be spread with pine boughs and dotted with offerings of maize kernels, bouquets of flowers, bottles of liquor wrapped in corn husks, and candles, candles everywhere.

Many local families can trace their lineages back centuries, some even to the ancient kings of Quiché. Many of their ancestors are buried beneath the church. The candles and offerings on the floor are in rememberance of the ancestors lying directly beneath.

On the west side of the plaza is another little whitewashed church, the Capilla del Calvario, which is similar in form and function to Santo Tomás, but smaller.

Museo Regional

In the arcade facing the south side of the square is the Museo Regional (Regional Museum), open from 8 am to noon and 2 to 5 pm (closed Tuesday). In the two large rooms of the museum you can see ancient clay pots and figurines, arrowheads and spearheads of flint and obsidian, copper axeheads, and *metates* (grindstones for maize). The museum also holds the Rossbach jade collection with several beautiful necklaces, figurines and other objects. Indefonso Rossbach served as Chichi's Catholic priest for many years until his death in 1944.

Shrine of Pascual Abaj

Before you have been in Chichi very long, some village lad will offer to guide you (for a tip) to a hilltop on the outskirts to have a look at Pascual Abaj (Sacrifice-Stone), the local shrine to Huyup Tak'ah (Mountain-Plain), the Mayan earth god. Said to be hundreds – perhaps thousands – of years old, the stone-faced idol has suffered numerous indignities at the hands of outsiders, but local people still revere it. Chuchkajaues come here regularly to offer incense, food, cigarettes, flowers, liquor and Coca-Cola to the earth god, and perhaps even to sacrifice a chicken. The offerings are in thanks and hope for earth's continuing fertility.

Sacrifices do not take place at regular hours. If you're in luck, you can witness one. The worshippers will not mind if you watch, or even if you take photographs, though they may ask if you want to make an offering (of a few quetzals) yourself. If there is no ceremony, you can still see the idol and enjoy the walk up to the pine-clad hilltop and the views of the town and valley.

You don't really need a juvenile guide to find Pascual Abaj. Walk down the hill on 5a Avenida from the Santo Tomás church, turn right onto 9 Calle and continue downhill along this unpaved road, which bends to the left. At the bottom of the hill, when the road turns sharply to the right, bear left and follow a path through the cornfields, keeping the ditch on your left. Walk to the buildings just ahead, which include a farmhouse and a morería. Greet the family here. If the children are not in school you may be invited to see them perform a local dance in full costume on your return from Pascual Abaj (a tip is expected).

Walk through the farm buildings to the hill behind, and follow the switchback path to the top and along the ridge of the hill to a clearing in which you will see the idol in its rocky shrine. The idol looks like something from Easter Island. The squat stone crosses near it have many levels of significance for the Maya, only one of which pertains to Christ. The area of the shrine is littered with past offerings; the bark of the pines here has been stripped away in places to be used as fuel in the incense fires.

Places to Stay

Chichi does not have a lot of accommodation, and most of what it has is in the higher price range. As rooms are scarce, it's a good idea to arrive early on Wednesday or Saturday to secure a room for the Thursday and Sunday markets. Safe parking is available in the courtyard of each hotel mentioned below.

Places to Stay – bottom end

Of the cheap hotels, *Hospedaje Salvador*, two blocks south-west of the Santo Tomás church along 5a Avenida, is about the best. This maze-like warren of red bricks, tiles and white stucco has 35 rooms on three floors reached by obscure routes. Rooms without bath offer the better value as the private baths – particularly those on the lower floors – smell quite strongly. Bathless doubles cost US$3, twice that much with private bath.

Note the football finials on the newel posts of the stairways.

Hospedaje Girón, on 6 Calle next to the Restaurant Tziguan Tinamit, is at the rear of the commercial Girón building; walk through to the back. Spartan and a bit drab except for the colourful blankets, the 16 rooms are clean and priced at US$3 a double without running water, just a bit more for a room with private cold shower.

Maya Lodge (☎ (9) 56-11-67), in the main plaza, has 10 rather dark rooms with clean add-on showers in the very midst of the market. Fairly plain despite some colonial touches, it is comfortable nonetheless, though a bit overpriced. Rates have recently risen to US$30 a double, tax included.

Pensión Chugüilá (☎ (9) 56-11- 34), on 5a Avenida two blocks north of the plaza, is charming and cheap. The cobblestone courtyard is surrounded by an arcade set with chairs, tables and tropical plants. Most of the 25 colonial-style rooms have private baths, some have fireplaces, and there are even a few two-room suites (bedroom and sitting room with fireplace). For what you get here, the price is very reasonable at US$4/5/6 a single/double/triple for rooms without bath, or US$8/10/12 a single/double/triple for rooms with private bath. (A reader reports that the cost of *his* double room was US$22, though, so be aware that prices may change.) There's a pleasant dining room off the portico and, in the dry season, an outdoor dining area in the courtyard.

Places to Stay – top end
The best hotel in town is one of the most pleasant in Guatemala. It's the lovely old *Mayan Inn* (☎ (9) 56-11-76), 8 Calle and 3a Avenida, on a quiet street one long block south-west of the plaza. Founded in 1932 by Alfred S Clark of Clark Tours, it has grown to include several restored colonial houses, their courtyards planted with exuberant tropical gardens, their walls festooned with brilliantly coloured indigenous textiles. The 30 rooms, all with fireplaces, are absolutely charming, with antique furnishings including carved wooden bedsteads, headboards

painted with country scenes, heavily carved armoires and rough-hewn tables. The private bathrooms (many with tubs) may be old-fashioned, but they are decently maintained. A staff member in traditional costume is assigned to help you carry your bags, answer any questions you may have, and even serve at your table in the dining room, as well as to look after your room – there are no door locks. Rates are US$50/60/68 a single/double/triple, tax included, modest for a hotel of this quality.

Hotel Santo Tomás (☎ (9) 56-10-61, 56-13-16), 7a Avenida at 6 Calle two blocks east of the plaza, is colonial in architecture and decoration but modern in construction and facilities, and thus a favourite with bus tour operators. Each of the 43 rooms has private bath and fireplace; all the rooms are grouped around pretty courtyards with colonial fountains. There's a good bar and dining room as well. Rates are US$45 a single, US$60 a double, tax included.

Places to Eat
Finding a meal at a decent price is no problem. Market days offer the best possibilities for rock-bottom cheap meals.

Places to Eat – bottom end
On Sundays and Thursdays, eat where the marketers do – at the cookshops set up in the centre of the market. These are the cheapest in town. On other days, look for the little comedores near the post office and Guatel office on the road into town (7a Avenida).

Restaurant El Mash, 6 Calle near 5a Avenida, at the back of a little flowered courtyard, is modern (for Chichi). I had asparagus soup, salad, fried chicken with rice and vegetable, bread and a drink for US$3.

Restaurant Tziguan Tinamit, at the corner of 6 Calle and 5a Avenida, takes its name from the Quiché Mayan name for Chichicastenango. Modern and bright, it's popular with locals and foreigners alike. Full four-course meals cost about US$3, sandwiches US$1, full breakfasts only slightly more.

Pensión Chugüilá is one of the most pleasant places to eat, and there are always a few other travellers to talk with about life on the road. Main course plates are priced at just over US$1. I had soup, *bistec con papas* (small steak with fried potatoes), orange juice and tea for US$3.50.

Places to Eat – top end

The two dining rooms at the *Mayan Inn* have pale yellow walls, beamed ceilings, red-tiled floors, stocky colonial-style tables and chairs, and decorations of colourful local cloth. Waiters wear traditional costumes which evolved from the dress of Spanish farmers of the colonial era: colourful head-dress, sash, black tunic with coloured embroidery, half-length trousers, and squeaky leather sandals called *caïtes*. The daily set-price meals are the best way to order here, costing US$3.50 for breakfast, US$8 for lunch or dinner, plus drinks and tip. A typical dinner might be cream of tomato soup, roast lamb or grilled beef, or beef tongue in a savoury sauce, followed by salad, and rhum baba or ice cream, and coffee.

The *Hotel Santo Tomás* has a good dining room, but it's often crowded with tour groups. Try to get one of the pleasant courtyard tables where you can enjoy the sun and the marimba band which plays at lunchtime. Set-price meals are priced about the same as at the Mayan Inn, perhaps a bit higher.

Getting There & Away

Chichi has no bus station. The closest thing to a bus stop is the corner of 7a Avenida and 6 Calle, but buses depart from various points around the market, particularly near the Hotel Santo Tomás. Ask any bus driver or police officer by naming your destination, and you'll be directed to the proper spot.

Any bus heading south can drop you at Los Encuentros, where you can catch a bus to your final destination. There are direct buses to Quetzaltenango (94 km, two hours, US$1.25) and to Guatemala City (Veloz Quichelense, 146 km, 3½ hours, US$2.25).

SANTA CRUZ DEL QUICHÉ

Population 13,000

The capital of the Department of Quiché (altitude 2020 metres) is 19 km north of Chichicastenango. As you leave Chichi heading north along 5a Avenida, you'll pass beneath Arco K'ucumatz, an arched bridge built in 1932 and named for the founder of K'umarcaaj.

Without the bustle of the big market and the big tourism buses, Santa Cruz – which is usually called 'El Quiché' – is quieter and more typical of the Guatemalan countryside than is Chichi. If you visit El Quiché, it is probably because you want to visit the ruins of K'umarcaaj (Utatlán). This is best done early in the morning, as you may have to walk to the ruins and back.

K'umarcaaj

The ruins of the ancient Quiché Mayan capital are three km west of El Quiché along an unpaved road. Start out of town along 10 Calle and ask the way frequently. No signs mark the way, and no transport runs regularly. Consider yourself very lucky if you succeed in hitching a ride with other travellers who have their own vehicle. Admission to the site costs a few pennies.

The kingdom of Quiché was established in Late Post-Classic times (about the 1300s) from a mixture of indigenous people and Mexican invaders. Around 1400, King K'ucumatz founded his capital at K'umarcaaj and conquered many neighbouring cities. During the long reign of his successor Q'uikab (1425-75), the kingdom of Quiché extended its borders to Huehuetenango, Sacapulas, Rabinal and Cobán, even coming to influence the peoples of the Soconusco region in Mexico.

The Cakchiquels, a vassal people who once fought alongside the Quichés, broke away from their former overlords and established their capital at Iximché during the 1400s.

Pedro de Alvarado led his conquistadors into Guatemala in 1524, and it was the Quichés, under their king, Tecún Umán, who organised the defence of the country. In the

Santa Cruz del Quiché

1 Restaurant Lago Azul
2 Banco de Guatemala
3 Cafetería Maya Quiché
4 Dominican Church
5 Municipalidad (Town Hall)
6 Main Plaza
7 Restaurant 2000 No 2
8 Small Church
9 Hotel San Pascual
10 Bus Station

0   25   50 m

To Chichicastenango   To K'umarcaaj

decisive battle fought near Quetzaltenango on 12 February 1524, Alvarado and Tecún found one another and locked in mortal combat. Alvarado won, and Tecún was killed. The defeated Quichés invited the victorious Alvarado to visit their capital, where they secretly planned to kill him. Smelling a rat, Alvarado, with the aid of his Mexican auxiliaries and the anti-Quiché Cakchiquels, captured the Quiché leaders instead, burnt them alive, took K'umarcaaj (called Utatlán by his Mexican allies) and destroyed it.

The history is more interesting than the ruined city, of which little remains but a few grass-covered mounds. Of the 100 or so large structures identified by archaeologists, only half a dozen are at all recognisable by us mere mortals, and these are uninspiring. The site itself is a beautiful place for a picnic, shaded by tall trees and surrounded by its defensive ravines, which failed to save the city from the conquistadors. Local prayermen keep the fires of ancient Quiché

burning, so to speak, by using ruined K'umarcaaj as a ritual site. A long tunnel (cueva) beneath the plaza is a favourite spot for prayers and chicken sacrifices.

Places to Stay & Eat
El Quiché has a few little hotels, pensions and restaurants, though if you're looking for comfort rather than price you may find it more convenient to make Chichicastenango your base.

Hotel San Pascual (☎ (9) 55-11-07), 7 Calle 0-43, 1½ blocks south-east of the plaza, has 40 serviceable rooms for US$4 to US$6 a double; the more expensive rooms have private bath. The newest rooms have TVs as well as private baths, and cost a bit more. The whole place is run by a dynamo señora who also runs a typing school for local children in a room off the lobby.

Near the bus station are even cheaper lodging places, such as *Hospedaje Tropical* and *Hospedaje Hermano Pedro*, charging

US$1 per bed; look at the room first and decide if you think it's worth it.

Restaurant 2000 No 2, two blocks west of the square, is simple and cheap. *Restaurant Lago Azul* is second best.

Getting There & Away

Many buses from Guatemala City to Chichicastenango continue to El Quiché (look for 'El Quiché' or just 'Quiché' on the signboard); on market days (Sunday and Thursday) there may be a bus every hour in the morning. The last bus from El Quiché headed south to Chichicastenango and Los Encuentros leaves mid-afternoon, so don't tarry too long here unless you want to spend the night.

El Quiché is the transport point for the sparsely populated and somewhat remote reaches of northern Quiché, which extends all the way to the Mexican border. Ask at the bus station for details. The bus trip over a rough road to Sacapulas, for instance, takes five hours.

South-Western Highlands

The departments of Quetzaltenango, Totonicapán and Huehuetenango are more mountainous and less frequented by tourists than regions closer to Guatemala City. The scenery here is just as beautiful and the indigenous culture just as colourful and fascinating. Travellers going to and from the border post at La Mesilla find these towns offer welcome breaks from long hours of travel, and some interesting possibilities for excursions as well.

Highlights of a visit to this area include Quetzaltenango, Guatemala's second largest city; the pretty nearby town of Zunil, with its Fuentes Georginas hot springs; Totonicapán, a department capital noted for its handicrafts; the Friday market at San Francisco El Alto, the blanketmakers of Momostenango;

and the restored Mayan city of Zaculeu near Huehuetenango.

CUATRO CAMINOS

Following the Pan American Highway westward from Los Encuentros, the road twists and turns ever higher into the mountains, bringing still more dramatic scenery and cooler temperatures. After 58 km you come to another important highway junction known as Cuatro Caminos (Four Roads). The road east leads to Totonicapán (12 km); west to Quetzaltenango (13 km); and north (straight on) to Huehuetenango (77 km). Buses shuttle from Cuatro Caminos to Totonicapán and Quetzaltenango about every 30 minutes from 6 am to 6 pm.

TOTONICAPÁN

Population 9000

If you want to visit a pleasant, pretty Guatemalan highland town with decent services for the traveller but with few other tourists in sight, Totonicapán (altitude 2500 metres) is the place to go. Buses shuttle into the centre of town from Cuatro Caminos frequently throughout the day.

The ride from Cuatro Caminos is along a beautiful pine-studded valley. As you approach the town you pass a large hospital on the left. Turn around the enormous Minerva fountain and enter town along 17a Avenida.

Totonicapán's main plaza has the requisite large colonial church, and also a municipal theatre in neoclassical style, which has recently been restored. Buses go directly to the parque, as the plaza is called, and drop you there.

Wander about the town as you like, sitting in the shady parque, listening to the dull clank of the churchbells, shopping for food or a few travel necessities with the local people. This may give you an idea of what it's like to be a Guatemalan in Guatemala.

Places to Stay

As you make your way into town, one block before coming to the parque on the left, stands the *Hospedaje San Miguel* (☎ (9)

66-14-52), 3 Calle 7-49, Zona 1. It's a tidy place, not what you'd call Swiss-clean, but good for the price, which is US$3 a double with common bath, US$4.50 with private shower. The rooms with showers tend to be larger, with three beds. Flash heaters provide the hot water, which is thus fairly dependable.

QUETZALTENANGO

Population 96,000

Called Xelajú or simply Xela by its Quiché Mayan citizens, Quetzaltenango (altitude 2335 metres) is the commercial centre of south-western Guatemala. Its good selection of hotels in all price ranges makes it an excellent base for excursions to the nearby towns and villages noted for their handicrafts and hot springs.

History

Quetzaltenango came under the sway of the Quiché Maya of K'umarcaaj when they began their great expansion in the 1300s. Before that it had been a Mam Maya town. Tecún Umán, the powerful leader of the Quichés, met Pedro de Alvarado on the field of battle near Quetzaltenango on 12 February 1524. The prize was Guatemala, much of which Tecún controlled, all of which the conquistadors wanted. Alvarado struck a mortal blow, Tecún Umán fell dead, and Guatemala was open to the Spanish.

In the mid-1800s, when the Central American Federation was founded, Quetzaltenango initially decided on federation with Chiapas and Mexico instead of with Central America. Later changing its mind, the city joined the Central American Federation, and became an integral part of Guatemala in 1840.

With the late 19th-century coffee boom, Quetzaltenango's wealth increased. This is where the finca owners came to buy supplies and where the coffee brokers had their warehouses. Things went along fine with the city getting richer and richer until a dual calamity – an earthquake and a volcanic eruption – brought mass destruction and an end to the boom.

The city's position at the intersection of the roads to the Pacific Slope, Mexico and Guatemala City guarantees it some degree of prosperity. Today it's busy again with commerce, both Indian and ladino.

Orientation

The heart of Xela is the Parque Centroamérica, shaded by old trees, graced with neoclassical monuments, and surrounded by the town's important buildings: cathedral, banks, tourist office, government headquarters, museum, Guatel telephone office, and one of the best hotels.

Quetzaltenango has several bus stations. The largest and busiest is the Terminal Minerva, on the western outskirts near the Parque Minerva on 6 Calle in Zona 3, next to the market. City buses 2 and 6 run between the terminal and Parque Centroamérica – look for 'Terminal' and 'Parque' in the front window of the bus.

Buses to several nearby places (Cuatro Caminos, San Francisco El Alto, Totonicapán and Zunil) use a terminal conveniently located at 10a Avenida and 8 Calle, Zona 1, beside the little market.

Some 1st-class lines have their own terminals separate from the common ones. For locations, see Getting There & Away.

A ticket office beneath the tourist office in the Casa de la Cultura on Parque Centroamérica sells bus tickets to Guatemala City on the Transportes Higueros line.

Information

Tourist Office The tourist office (☎ (9) 61-49-31) is in the right-hand wing of the Casa de la Cultura (also called the Museo de Historia Natural) at the lower (southern) end of the Parque Centroamérica. It's open Monday to Friday from 8 am to noon, and from 2 to 6 pm, on Saturday from 8 am to noon and closed on Sunday.

Money The Parque Centroamérica is the place to look for banks. Normal hours for most are 8.30 am to 2.30 pm Monday to Friday. Banco Industrial, facing the Parque at 11a Avenida and 5 Calle, is open on week-

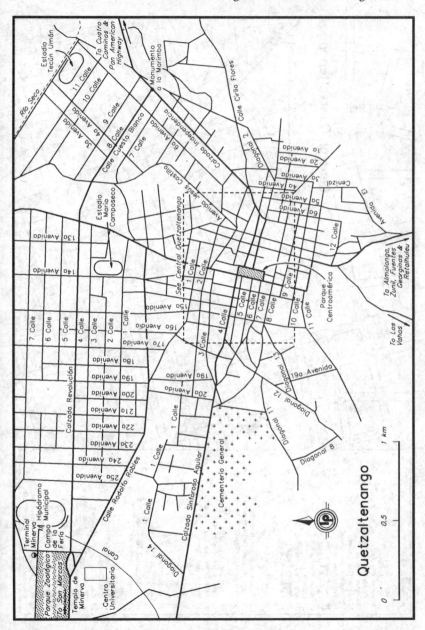

Quetzaltenango

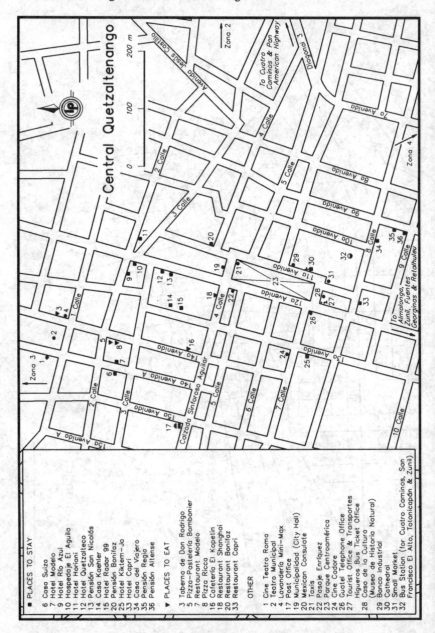

Central Quetzaltenango

■ PLACES TO STAY

6 Casa Suiza
7 Hotel Modelo
9 Hotel Río Azul
10 Hospedaje El Aguila
11 Hotel Horiani
12 Hotel Quetzalteco
13 Pensión San Nicolás
14 Casa Kaehler
15 Hotel Radar 99
20 Pensión Bonifaz
25 Hotel Kiktem–Ja
33 Hotel Capri
34 Casa del Viajero
35 Pensión Regia
36 Pensión Altense

▼ PLACES TO EAT

3 Taberna de Don Rodrigo
5 Pizza–Pastelería Bombonier
7 Restaurant Modelo
8 Pizza Ricca
16 Cafetería El Kopetin
18 Restaurant Shanghai
20 Restaurant Bonifaz
33 Restaurant Capri

OTHER

1 Cine Teatro Roma
2 Teatro Municipal
4 Lavandería Mini–Max
17 Post Office
19 Municipalidad (City Hall)
20 Mexican Consulate
21 Taxis
22 Pasaje Enríquez
23 Parque Centroamérica
24 Cine Cadore
26 Guatel Telephone Office
27 Tourist Office & Transportes
   Higueros Bus Ticket Office
28 Casa de la Cultura
   (Museo de Historia Natural)
29 Banco Industrial
30 Cathedral
31 Small Market
32 Bus Station (for Cuatro Caminos, San
   Francisco El Alto, Totonicapán & Zunil)

days until 3 pm; a ventanilla especial, or special teller window, is open from 3 to 6 pm on weekdays, and from 8.30 am to 12.30 pm on Saturday.

Post & Telecommunications The post office is at 15a Avenida and 4 Calle, Zona 1. The Guatel telephone office is on 12a Avenida between 7 and 8 Calle, at the south-western corner of the Parque Centroamérica, only steps from the tourist office.

Mexican Consulate You can get your Mexican tourist card at the Consulate which is located in the Pensión Bonifaz near the north-east corner of Parque Centroamérica, open Monday to Friday from 8 am to noon.

Laundry Lavandería Mini-Max, 14a Avenida C- 47, at 1 Calle, faces the neoclassical Teatro Municipal, five blocks north-west of the parque.

Parque Centroamérica

The parque and the buildings surrounding it are pretty much what there is to see in Xela. Start your tour at the southern (lower) end and walk around the square anticlockwise. The Casa de la Cultura holds the Museo de Historia Natural, with some Mayan exhibits and others focusing on the Liberal revolution in Central American politics and on the Estado de Los Altos, of which Quetzaltenango was the capital. Marimbas, the weaving industry and other local lore all claim places here. It's fascinating because it's funky.

Just off the south-eastern corner of the parque is a small market devoted largely to handicraft items and daily necessities, a convenient spot for a little shopping.

The once-crumbling cathedral has been rebuilt in the last few decades. The façade of the colonial building was preserved, and a modern sanctuary built behind it.

The city's Town Hall, or Municipalidad, at the northern end of the parque, follows the grandiose neoclassical style so favoured as a symbol of culture and refinement in this wild mountain country. To its right is the Pensión Bonifaz, the best hotel in the centre.

On the west side of the parque between 4 and 5 Calles is the palatial Pasaje Enriquez, built to be lined with elegant shops, but as Quetzaltenango has few elegant shoppers, it has suffered decline. One local tourism brochure defined it well by means of malapropism: 'The outstanding characteristic of the western arch is its grafitti'.

Other Sights

Walk north on 14a Avenida to 1 Calle, to see the impressive neoclassical Teatro Municipal. Inside are three tiers of seating, the lower two of which have private boxes for prominent families; each box is equipped with a vanity for the ladies.

Mercado La Democracia, in Zona 3, is about 10 blocks north-west of the Parque Centroamérica. Walk along 14a Avenida to 1 Calle (to the Teatro Municipal), turn left, turn right onto 16a Avenida, cross the major street called Calle Rodolfo Robles, and the market is on your right. It's an authentic Guatemalan city market with fresh produce and meat, foodstuffs and necessities for city dweller and villager alike.

Less than a km west of the Parque Centroamérica near the Terminal Minerva is the Parque Minerva with its neoclassical Templo de Minerva, built to honour the classical goddess of education and to inspire Guatemalan youth to new heights of learning. Many historians note that lots of Minerva temples got built during the presidency of Manuel Estrada Cabrera (1898-1920), but few schools.

Places to Stay

Most of Xela's lodging places are within a few blocks of the Parque Centroamérica, though one middle-range hotel is on the outskirts.

Places to Stay – bottom end

Two concentrations of cheap hostelries are at the northern end of the Parque Centroamérica along 12a Avenida and south of the parque more or less behind the Casa de la Cultura.

Walk up 12a Avenida from the parque with the Municipalidad on your right and the Cantel textile shop on your left to find the *Pensión San Nicolás*, on the left between 4 and 3 Calles. No one would call it beautiful, but it provides beds for US$1 per person, only steps from the parque. Look at the room before you pay.

A few steps farther up the hill is the *Hotel Quetzalteco*, which was under construction on my last visit, but should be open now. Cross 3 Calle to find the *Hospedaje El Aguila*, just past it, which is very dark, but priced as cheaply as the San Nicolás.

At 2 Calle there are nicer places. Turn right for the *Hotel Horiani*, officially at 12a Avenida 2-23, though you enter on 2 Calle. This tidy place charges US$1.25 a single, US$2.50 a double, but they're willing to haggle if it's not full.

Turn left (west) at 2 Calle to find the *Hotel Río Azul* (☎ (9) 61-48-27), 2 Calle 12-15, Zona 1, which offers luxury compared to its neighbours. All rooms here have private showers with hot water, and some even have colour TVs. Prices are excellent for what you get: US$4.50 a single, US$7.50 a double, US$9 a triple. There's even a car park.

Two more good places are on 13a Avenida. Follow 2 Calle westward half a block from the Hotel Río Azul and turn left to find the *Casa Kaehler* (☎ (9) 61-20-91), 13a Avenida 3-33, Zona 1, an old-fashioned European-style family pension with seven rooms of various shapes and sizes. Room 7 is the most comfortable, as it has its own bath. Prices here are US$3 a single, US$5 a double, US$6 a triple, US$8 a quad for rooms with common bath; for private bath, add about a dollar. This is an excellent, safe place for women travellers; ring the bell to gain entry.

Next door to the Casa Kaehler is the *Hotel Radar 99*, 13a Avenida 3-27, Zona 1, a simple place a la Guatemala, with 15 rooms going for US$2.50 a double with common bathrooms.

Two streets west of Casa Kaehler is *Casa Suiza* (☎ (9) 61-43-50), 14a Avenida 'A' 2-36, Zona 1, with 18 basic rooms grouped around a big courtyard in a fairly convenient location. There's an airy, cheap comedor as well, and a dozen clean rooms priced at US$3.50 to US$5 a single, US$5.75 to US$6 a double, US$8 to US$9.50 a triple. Bathless rooms have sinks for your morning splash; the more expensive rooms have private showers. 14a Avenida 'A', by the way, is a short, narrow street between 14a and 15a Avenidas.

South-west of the parque is the huge old *Hotel Kiktem-Ja* (☎ (9) 61-43-04), in the Edificio Fuentes, a colonial-style building at 13a Avenida 7-18, Zona 1. The 20 rooms are on two levels around the courtyard which also serves as car park. Locally made blankets are inscribed with the hotel's name, and fireplaces are available in each room for a comforting blaze. Double rooms cost US$8.50 with private hot shower.

Another group of budget hotels is south of the Casa de la Cultura. *Hotel Capri* (☎ (9) 61-41-11), 8 Calle 11-39, Zona 1, a block from the Parque Centroamérica behind the Casa de la Cultura, offers rooms in a convenient location for US$2.50 a double with common bath. It has a cheap comedor as well. Other places in Zona 1 charging similar rates are *Casa del Viajero*, 8a Avenida 9-17, *Pensión Altense*, at the corner of 9a Avenida and 9 Calle, and *Pensión Regia*, 9a Avenida 8-26.

Places to Stay – middle

If you want to spend a little more for a lot more comfort, head straight for the family-run *Hotel Modelo* (☎ (9) 61-27-15), 14a Avenida 'A' 2-31, Zona 1. The airy lobby with large fireplace is often occupied by families or Guatemalan business travellers, who favour the hotel. Pleasant small rooms with tiled showers rent for US$12 a single, US$15 a double; an extra person in a room pays US$5. The hotel's good dining room serves breakfast (7.15 to 9.30 am), lunch (noon to 2.30 pm) and dinner (6 to 9 pm) daily.

Pensión Bonifaz (☎ (9) 61-42-41/29/59),

Indians from Guatemala's highlands playing traditional music

4 Calle 10-50, Zona 1, near the north-east corner of the Parque Centroamérica, is the city's social centre, a longstanding favourite accommodation for Guatemalans and foreigners alike. The 62 rooms with private baths (some with tubs) are not what you'd call fancy, but they're comfortably old-fashioned, and some have two double beds. They're divided between the original colonial-style building (the one you enter), and the adjoining modernised building with wood panelling and Danish Modern-style furniture. Rooms in the original building are preferable. The hotel has a good dining room, a TV lounge that fills up quickly on football match days, a cheery bar patronised by Quetzaltenango's gilded youth, a gift shop and a car park. Rates are US$28 a single, US$30 a double.

Hotel del Campo (☎ (9) 61-20-64, 61-80-82), Km 224, Camino a Cantel, is Quetzaltenango's largest and most modern hotel with 104 rooms with showers and TVs decorated in natural wood and red brick. There's an all-weather swimming pool.

Rooms on the lowest floor can be dark; get a room in the 50s (51, 52, etc.). Prices are reasonable at US$20 a single, US$24 a double. The 'Country Hotel' is 4.5 km east of the Parque Centroamérica a short distance off the main road between Quetzaltenango and Cuatro Caminos; watch for signs for the hotel and for the road to Cantel.

Places to Eat

As with hotels, Quetzaltenango has a good selection in all price ranges. Cheapest are the food stalls in and around the small market to the left of the Casa de la Cultura, where snacks and substantial main course plates are sold for US$1 or less. Nearby is the good little restaurant in the *Hotel Capri*, 8 Calle 11-39, behind the Casa de la Cultura, which serves three set-price meals a day, all priced below US$2.

For sit-down eateries serving everything from tacos to pizza and back, go to the corner of 14a Avenida and 3 Calle, then walk north (uphill) along 14a Avenida to find the following places.

Cafetería El Kopetin (☎ 61-24-01), 14a Avenida 3-31, is pleasant and modernish with red tablecloths, natural wood and a family atmosphere. The long and varied menu ranges from hamburgers to Cuban-style sandwiches to filet mignon. Full meals need cost no more than US$1.50; but may go as high as US$4. Alcoholic drinks are served, and El Kopetin is open every day.

Pizza Ricca (☎ 61-81-62), 14a Avenida 2-52, has a busy white-coated staff baking pizzas in a wood-fired oven and serving them to hungry customers waiting patiently in comfy booths. Pizzas come in various sizes and prices from US$1.25 to US$5; hamburgers and plates of spaghetti cost US$0.75 to US$1.50. Beer is served, and Pizza Ricca is open all day, every day.

Pizza-Pastelería Bombonier (☎ 61-62-25), 14a Avenida 2-20, serves more pizzas and hamburgers than bonbons despite its name; many customers order to take away, as there are only a few tables. Both the burgers and pizzas here are cheaper than at Pizza Ricca.

Taberna de Don Rodrigo, 14a Avenida C-45 facing the Teatro Municipal, is a favourite hangout for local youth who, judging from the menu, enjoy consuming American-style fast food (hamburgers, hot dogs, cakes and Cokes) at low prices (US$1 for a burger and drink).

Restaurant Shanghai (☎ 61-41-54), 4 Calle 12-22, Zona 1, is the most convenient Chinese place to the parque, only half a block west of the Cantel shop. The staff is ladino not Chinese, the food is Guatemalan Oriental, but there are a few bits of chinoiserie to put you in the mood, and the restaurant does provide a welcome change of cuisine. They serve *pato* (duck), *camarones* (shrimp) and other Chinese specialities for about US$1.50 to US$2.50 per plate. The Shanghai is open from 8 am to 9:30 pm, seven days a week.

The dining room of the *Hotel Modelo*, 14a Avenida 'A' 2-31, has good set-price lunches and dinners for US$3.

Places to Eat – middle
The dining room of the *Pensión Bonifaz*, at the north-east corner of the parque, is the best in town. This is where the local social set comes to dine and be seen. Food is good and prices, though expensive by Guatemalan standards, are low when compared to those even in Mexico. Soup, main course, dessert and drink can run to US$7 or US$8, but you can spend about half that much if you order only a sandwich and a beer.

Entertainment
Evening entertainment possibilities are limited, as you might expect. It gets chilly when the sun goes down, so you won't want to sit out in the Parque Centroamérica enjoying the balmy breezes – there aren't any.

One of the city's two convenient cinemas (the Cadore at 7 Calle and 13a Avenida, off the south-west corner of the parque, or the Teatro Roma on 14a Avenida 'A' facing the Teatro Municipal) might be playing an interesting movie – perhaps even in English with Spanish subtitles. The bars at the Pensión Bonifaz and Hotel Modelo are good for a drink, a chat and a snack. The Bonifaz features delicious cakes and pastries to go with your coffee or drink.

Getting There & Away
For most 2nd-class buses, head out to the Terminal Minerva on the western outskirts near the Parque Minerva on 6 Calle in Zona 3, next to the market. City buses 2 and 6 run between the terminal and Parque Centroamérica (look for 'Terminal' and 'Parque' in the front window of the bus). This busy terminal has almost hourly buses to many highland destinations.

For buses to Cuatro Caminos (13 km), San Francisco El Alto (17 km), Totonicapán (25 km) and Zunil (10 km), go to the bus parking lot at 10a Avenida and 8 Calle, Zona 1, beside the little market.

Transportes Higueros (☎ (9) 61-22-33), 12a Avenida and 7 Calle, Zona 1, has a ticket office beneath the tourist office in the Casa de la Cultura facing Parque Centroamérica. They run two buses daily to Guatemala City via Panajachel for US$2.50.

Rutas Lima and Autobuses América, two

1st-class lines, have their own terminals on Calzada Independencia, the wide boulevard which is the north-easterly continuation of Diagonal 3 (Zona 1) leading out of town to the Cuatro Caminos road; in Zona 2 it is called 7a Avenida.

Autobuses Galgos (☎ (9) 61-22-48) is at Calle Rodolfo Robles 17-43, Zona 1, about a dozen blocks north-west of the parque.

Chichicastenango – 94 km, two hours; direct buses on market days cost US$1.25. If you don't get one of these, change at Los Encuentros.

Guatemala City – 203 km, four hours; lots of companies have plenty of buses departing frequently from Terminal Minerva. Transportes Galgos has seven 1st-class buses daily (US$2.50) stopping at Totonicapán, Los Encuentros (change for Chichicastenango or Panajachel) and Chimaltenango (change for Antigua).

Huehuetenango – 90 km, two hours; hourly buses from Terminal Minerva; for first class, see La Mesilla

La Mesilla (Mexican border) – 170 km, four hours; Rutas Lima has two first-class buses daily to Huehuetenango (US$2.75) and La Mesilla (US$4) departing from Quetzaltenango at 5 am and 6.30 pm. Or, get a 2nd-class bus from Terminal Minerva to Huehuetenango and change there.

Panajachel – 99 km, two hours; direct buses run by Morales or Rojo y Blanco depart four times daily for US$1.25, or you can take any bus bound for Guatemala City and change at Los Encuentros. Transportes Higueros has Guatemala City-bound buses which stop at Panajachel as well.

Retalhuleu – 67 km, two hours; hourly buses from Terminal Minerva (US$1). Rutas Lima has one daily bus to the border station at Talisman which will drop you in Retalhuleu.

AROUND QUETZALTENANGO

The beautiful volcanic countryside around Quetzaltenango has numerous possibilities for outings. The natural steam baths at Los Vahos are very primitive, but the outing into the hills surrounding the city can be fascinating whether you take a steam bath or not. The hot springs at Almolonga are very basic but also cheap and accessible. Those at Fuentes Georginas are idyllic, still pretty cheap, but not easily accessible unless you have your own transport.

Take note of the market days: Sunday in Momostenango, Monday in Zunil, Tuesday in Totonicapán, Friday in San Francisco El Alto, Saturday in Totonicapán.

Buses from Quetzaltenango to Almolonga, Los Baños and Zunil depart several times per hour from Terminal Minerva; some buses stop at the corner of 10a Avenida and 10 Calle, Zona 1, to take on more passengers.

Los Vahos

If you're a hiker and if the weather is good you might enjoy a trip to the rough-and-ready steam baths at Los Vahos (The Vapours), 3.5 km from Parque Centroamérica. Take a bus headed for Almolonga, and ask to get out at the road to Los Vahos. If you're driving, follow 12a Avenida south from the parque to its end, turn left, go two blocks and turn right up the hill; this turn is 1.2 km from the parque. The remaining 2.3 km of unpaved road is steep and rutted, a thick carpet of dust in the dry season, of mud in the rainy season (when you may want a 4WD vehicle). The first turn along the dirt road is a sharp right (unmarked); at the second you bear left (this is badly marked). Views of the city on a clear day are remarkable. The road ends at Los Vahos, where you can have a steam bath for only a few quetzals and, if you've brought food with you, a picnic.

Zunil

Zunil is a pretty market town in a lush valley framed by steep hills and dominated by a towering volcano. As you approach it along the road from Quetzaltenango you will see it framed as if in a picture, with its white colonial church gleaming above the red-tiled and rusted tin roofs of the low houses.

On the way to Zunil the road passes by Almolonga, a vegetable-growing town four km from Quetzaltenango. Just over one km beyond Almolonga, on the left side of the road, is Los Baños, with natural hot springs. The bath installations are quite decrepit, but if a hot bath at low cost is your desire you may want to stop. Tomb-like enclosed concrete tubs rent for a few quetzals per hour.

Winding down the hill from Los Baños,

the road skirts Zunil and its fertile gardens on the right side before intersecting the Cantel-to-El Zarco road. A bridge crosses a stream to lead into the town; it's one km from the bridge to the plaza.

Zunil is a perfectly typical Guatemalan country town with a particularly pretty church. The church's ornate façade with eight pairs of serpentine columns is echoed inside by a richly worked altar of silver. On market day (Monday) the plaza in front of the church is bright with the predominantly red traditional garb of local people buying and selling.

From Zunil, which is 10 km from Quetzaltenango, you can continue to Fuentes Georginas (nine km), return to Quetzaltenango via the Cantel road (16 km), or take the jungle-bound toll road down the mountainside to El Zarco junction and the Pacific Slope Highway. Buses depart every half hour or so on the return trip to Quetzaltenango.

Fuentes Georginas

Imagine a steep, high wall of tropical verdure – huge green leaves, ganglions of vines, giant ferns, spongy moss, profusions of tropical flowers – at the upper end of a lush mountain valley. At the base of this wall of greenery is a limpid pool of naturally warm mineral water. A pure white statue of a Greek goddess gazes benevolently across the misty water as families happily splash and play, then clamber out for a drink or a snack at a rustic restaurant right at the pool's edge. This is Fuentes Georginas, the prettiest spa in Guatemala. Though the setting is intensely tropical, the mountain air currents keep it deliciously cool all day.

The pools were built during the presidency of General Jorge Ubico (1931-44) and named in his honour; the present installations date from 1964, when they were restored by INGUAT.

Besides the restaurant, there are three sheltered picnic tables with cooking grills (bring your own fuel). Down the valley a few dozen metres are seven cottages for rent at US$9 per night. Each cottage has a hot shower and a fireplace to ward off the mountain chill at night. Admission to the site costs US$0.30, the same again to park a car. Bring a bathing suit, which is required.

Getting There & Away Because Fuentes Georginas is so beautiful, the question is not whether to go but how. A half-day tour using one of the taxis parked in the Parque Centroamérica in Quetzaltenango costs US$15 per carload (US$3 to US$5 per person), and includes a visit to Zunil as well as two hours' swimming time at the spa. This is not a bad price, but it doesn't give you much time there. You might want to take the taxi to the baths, bring a picnic, and walk back to Zunil to catch a late afternoon bus. Hitchhiking is not good on the Fuentes Georginas access road as there are few cars, and they are often filled to capacity with large Guatemalan families. The best days to try for a ride are Saturday and Sunday, when the baths are busiest.

If you're driving or hitching, go uphill from Zunil's plaza to the Cantel road (about 60 metres), turn right and go downhill 100 metres to a Pepsi sign ('Baños Georginas'). On the left, an unpaved road heads off into the mountains; the baths are nine km from Zunil's plaza. You'll know you're approaching the baths when you smell the sulphur in the air.

San Francisco El Alto

High on a hilltop (2610 metres) overlooking Quetzaltenango (17 km away) stands the market town of San Francisco El Alto. Six days a week it's a sleepy sort of place, but on Friday it explodes with activity as thousands of country people pour into the sloping plaza for the huge market. Soon the large plaza, surrounded by the requisite church and Municipalidad and centred on a cupola-like mirador (lookout), is covered in country goods. Stalls spill into neighbouring streets, and the press of traffic is so great that a special system of one-way roads is established to avoid monumental traffic jams. Vehicles entering the town on market day must pay a small fee.

San Francisco's market is not heavy with handicrafts as are those in Chichicastenango and Antigua, though you will find some nice crafts here, such as Momostenango blankets. Rather, this is a real people's market at which you'll find anything and everything needed by a Guatemalan highland villager. If you're not particularly excited by markets and you've seen one of the others, you can give this one a miss. If you love markets, come. Buses depart° from the parking lot at 10a Avenida and 8 Calle, Zona 1, in Quetzaltenango frequently throughout the day.

Places to Stay & Eat The lodging and eating situation here is dire. If you're in need of a bed you'll have to suffer the *Hotel y Cafetería Vista Hermosa* (☎ (9) 66-10-30), 3a Avenida 2-22, Zona 1. The 25 rooms here are ill kept (though a few on the front enjoy good views), service is nonexistent, and the cafeteria rarely has any food to serve. Other than that, it's disappointing. Rates are US$3 a double with common bath, US$3.50 to US$4.50 with private shower.

As for eating, the *Comedor San Cristóbal*, near the Hospedaje San Francisco de Assis, may be your best bet, but that's not saying much.

Momostenango

Beyond San Francisco El Alto, 22 km from Cuatro Caminos (35 km from Quetzaltenango) along a fairly rough unpaved country road is this village in a pretty mountain valley. Momostenango is Guatemala's famous centre for the making of *chamarras*, the thick, heavy woollen blankets which you have no doubt already used to protect yourself from the chill of a highland night. They also make ponchos and other woollen garments. As you enter the village square after an hour of bashing over the bad road, you will see signs inviting you to inspect blanket-making as it happens, and to purchase the finished products. The best time to do this is on Sunday, which is market day; haggle like mad. You might also want to hike three km north to the hot springs of Pala Chiquito,

where the blankets are washed and the dyes fixed.

Momostenango is also noted for its adherence to the ancient Mayan calendar, and for observance of traditional rites. Hills about two km west of the plaza are the scene of these ceremonies, coordinated with the important dates of the calendar round (see Facts about the Region for details on the Mayan calendar). Unfortunately, it's not as easy to witness these rites as it is to visit the Shrine of Pascual Abaj at Chichicastenango.

Places to Stay & Eat *Casa de Huéspedes Paclom* is perhaps the better of the two simple hostelries in town, the other one being *Hospedaje Roxana* on the plaza. Paclom has its own restaurant, and there are several basic comedores on the plaza as well.

Getting There & Away Catch an early bus from Quetzaltenango's Terminal Minerva, or at Cuatro Caminos, or at San Francisco El Alto. There are five or six buses daily, the last one returning from Momostenango by about 3 pm.

HUEHUETENANGO
Population 40,000
Separated from the capital by mountains and a twisting road, Huehuetenango (altitude 1902 metres) has that self-sufficient air exuded by many mountain towns: we may be small, but we're the centre of everything here. Coffee growing, mining, sheep raising, light manufacturing and agriculture are the main activities in this region. The lively Indian market is filled daily with traders who come down from the Sierra de los Cuchumatanes, the mountain range (highest in Central America) which dominates the Department of Huehuetenango. Surprisingly, the market area is about the only place you'll see colourful traditional costumes in this town, as most of its citizens are ladinos who wear modern clothes.

For travellers, Huehuetenango is usually a stage on the journey to and from Mexico. After leaving San Cristóbal de las Casas or Comitán, taking an hour or so at the border,

Huehuetenango

0   100   200 m

■ PLACES TO STAY

2 Auto Hotel Vásquez
3 Hospedaje El Viajero
4 Hotel Zaculeu
5 Hotel Central
6 Pensión Astoria
7 Hotel Mary
8 Mansión El Paraíso
14 Hotel Roberto's
21 Hotel Maya

▼ PLACES TO EAT

1 Doña Estercita Cafetería
7 Pan Delis Bakery-Café
  & Restaurant Regis
13 Ebony Restaurant & Maxi Pizza
16 Los Pollos
21 Rico Mac Pollo
25 Panadería del Trigo
28 Pizza Hogareña

OTHER

9 Post Office
10 Guatel Telephone Office
11 Municipalidad (Town Hall)
12 Parque Central
15 Servicios Sanitarios (Toilets)
17 Bancafé (Banco de Café)
18 Farmacia Berlin
19 Banco del Ejercito
20 Taxis
22 Market
23 Farmacia Ruiz
24 Servicios Santiarios (Toilets)
26 Farmacia Del Río
26 Mexican Consulate
27 Banco de Guatemala

Huehuetenango is the logical place to spend your first night in Guatemala. It's a good introduction to Guatemalan highland life: a pleasant town with a selection of hotels, an interesting market and the ruins of ancient Zaculeu on the outskirts.

History

Huehuetenango was a Mam Maya region until the 1400s when the Quichés, expanding from their capital at K'umarcaaj near present-day Santa Cruz del Quiché, pushed them out. Many Mam fled into neighbouring Chiapas, which still has a large Mam- speaking population near its border with Guatemala. In the late 1400s, weakness of Quiché rule brought about civil war which engulfed the highlands and provided a chance for Mam independence. The troubles lasted for decades, coming to an end in the summer of 1525 after the arrival of Gonzalo de Alvarado, brother of Pedro, who conquered the Mam capital of Zaculeu for the king of Spain.

Orientation

The town centre is five km north of the Pan American Highway. The new bus station and new market are three km from the highway along the road to the centre (6 Calle), on the east side; it is thus two km from the bus station to the main plaza. The new market has not really caught on yet, and much of the space is vacant. City buses running north along 6 Calle will take you to the centre.

Almost every service of interest to tourists is in Zona 1 within a few blocks of the plaza. The old market, bordered by 1a and 2a Avenidas and 3 and 4 Calles in Zona 1, is still the busy one, especially on Wednesday, which is market day. Four blocks west of the market on 5a Avenida between 2 and 3 Calles is the main plaza, called the parque, the very centre of town and reference point for finding any other address. Hotels and restaurants are mostly near the parque, except for one or two small hotels near the new bus station and one motel out on the Pan American Highway.

The post office is at 2 Calle 3-54, right next to the Guatel telephone office across the street from the Hotel Mary, half a block east of the plaza. The Mexican consulate is in the Farmacia Del Río at the corner of 5a Avenida and 4 Calle. Town-operated *servicios sanitarios* (toilets) are on 3 Calle between 5a and 6a Avenidas, only a few steps west of the plaza. Farmacias (chemists) and banks are dotted around the centre, as shown on our map.

Parque Central

Huehuetenango's main plaza is shaded by nice old trees and surrounded by the town's imposing buildings: the Municipalidad, with its band shell on the upper floor; and the huge colonial church. The plaza has its own little relief map of the Department of Huehuetenango, which is interesting because of the Cuchumatanes Mountains.

Zaculeu

Surrounded by natural barriers – ravines and a river – on three sides, the Late Post-Classic religious centre of Zaculeu occupies a good defensive location which served its Mam Maya inhabitants well. It only failed in 1525 when Gonzalo de Alvarado and his conquistadors laid seige to the site. Good natural defences are no defence against starvation, and it was this that defeated the Mam.

The current wisdom about Zaculeu is that it is boring; a bad restoration left its pyramids, ball courts and ceremonial platforms covered in a thick coat of greying plaster. It's too stark, too clean. The restoration work was sponsored by the United Fruit Company which had extremely powerful interests and influence in Guatemala during the first half of the 20th century. The company's business was heavy-handed, and so was its restoration.

Though some of the construction methods used in the restoration were not authentic to the buildings, the work goes farther than others in making the site look like it might have to the eyes of Mam priests and worshippers when it was still an active religious centre. We have become so used to seeing

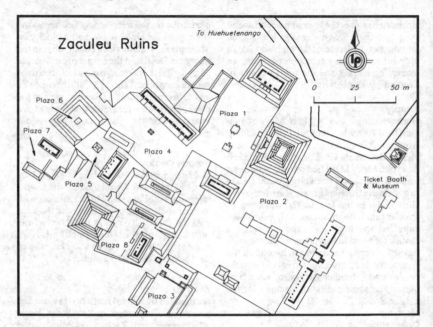

ruddy bare stones and grass-covered mounds that the tidiness of Zaculeu is unsettling.

When Zaculeu flourished, its buildings were coated with plaster, as they are now. What is missing is the painted decoration which must have been applied to the wet plaster. The buildings show a great deal of Mexican influence, and were probably designed and built originally with little innovation. Zaculeu is no Palenque, no Tikal, and never was. Imagine some painted figures on the walls, and you can almost see the Mam priests mounting the steep staircases.

The park-like archaeological zone of Zaculeu is four km north of Huehuetenango's main plaza. It's open daily from 8 am to 6 pm; admission is US$0.20 after you sign the register. Cold soft drinks are available. The small, modern museum has drawings of scenes from the Spanish conquest, a Mam burial urn and potsherds. You're allowed to climb on the restored structures as much as you want, but it's forbidden to climb the grassy mounds which await excavation.

Getting There There are several routes by which to reach Zaculeu from the Parque Central. Jitney trucks and vans depart the corner of 3a Avenida and 4 Calle (between the church and the market) near Rico Mac Pollo heading north along 5a Avenida toward Zaculeu. Some go fairly close to the ruins, others do not, so ask. Another route goes west via 3 Calle and out past the Campo de la Fería (fairgrounds). To walk all the way from the main plaza takes about 45 minutes.

Places to Stay
Huehuetenango has a useful selection of low-budget places to stay, but nothing fancy. Your first explorations should be along 2 Calle between 3a and 7a Avenidas, just off the plaza; there are four little hotels and six eating-places in this three-block stretch, and two more hotels half a block off 2 Calle.

Hotel Central (☎ (9) 64-12-02, 64-14-67), 5a Avenida 1-33, facing the Hotel Zaculeu half a block north-west of the plaza, has been an old favourite of thrifty travellers for decades. Its 17 largish rooms are very simple and well used. Showers are shared, but the water is hot. Two people pay US$3 in a double room; some rooms have three and four beds. The hotel's comedor provides good, fairly tasty, cheap meals; you might want to come and enjoy them even if you don't stay here. It opens for breakfast at 7 am, earlier than most other places in town.

Hotel Roberto's (☎ (9) 64-15-26), 2 Calle 5-49, half a block west of the plaza, is another tidy place in a convenient location with 21 rooms around a courtyard. Rates are a low US$1 per person in rooms without running water. The *Hospedaje El Viajero* across the street is not as good.

Hotel Mary (☎ (9) 64-15-69), 2 Calle 3-52, is a block east of the plaza facing Guatel. It's a cut above the other places: the 25 small rooms have bedspreads and other nice touches. The ground-floor *Restaurant Regis* is handy, as is the *Panadería Pan Delis* bakery-café next door. The price for a room at the Mary is US$3.50 to US$4 a single, US$5 to US$6 a double, US$7 to US$8.50 a triple; the higher priced rooms have private baths.

Auto Hotel Vásquez (☎ (9) 64-13-38), 2 Calle 6-67, has a car park in the front, and 20 small, fairly cheerless but usable rooms at the back for US$1.75 per person, with private bath.

Hotel Maya, 3a Avenida 3-55, behind the church and just to the left of Rico Mac Pollo, resembles a barracks in its cinder-blockiness, but manages to be a bit more cheerful than lower priced places. The location is convenient. Rates are US$1.50 per person in rooms without bath, US$2 per person in rooms with bath.

Even lower in price are places such as the *Mansión El Paraíso*, 3a Avenida 2-41, in the block behind the Municipalidad. This vision of Paradise is fairly gloomy, very barracks-like, but family operated and very cheap at less than US$1 per person; cold water com-

munal showers only. *Pensión Astoria* (☎ (9) 64-11-97), 4a Avenida 1-45, is similar.

The best place in town is the *Hotel Zaculeu* (☎ (9) 64-10-86), 5a Avenida 1-14, facing the Hotel Central half a block north-west of the plaza. This colonial-style place has a lovely garden courtyard and a good dining room that was under renovation the last time I looked in. Rooms near the hotel entrance open onto the courtyard and are preferable to those at the back of the hotel; all 20 rooms have private showers and rent for US$10 a double.

Out on the Pan American Highway two km north-west of the turnoff to Huehuetenango is the *Hotel Pino Montano* (☎ (2) 31-07-61 in Guatemala City), Carretera Panamericana Km 259 (Apdo Postal 20), Huehue's interpretation of an American roadside motel. Boxy bungalows housing 18 rooms are arranged behind a glass-enclosed restaurant and office. Though modern, it manages to be dreary, the only cheer coming from the gospel singing at revival meetings held in a nearby field on some evenings. Double rooms with bath and lots of hot water cost US$9.

Places to Eat

Again, it's 2 Calle between 3a and 6a Avenidas where you should look first. Cheapest eats are at the market, of course. Other than that, start at the plaza and walk west along 2 Calle to find the *Ebony Restaurant*, 2 Calle 5-11, just around the corner from the plaza. The Ebony is Huehue's beach-theme eatery with bamboo walls and basket lamps. The menu lists the standard beef, pork and chicken cuts which sell for US$1 to US$1.50. They make good *licuados* of fresh fruit here. Next door is *Maxi Pizza*, which makes pretty good and pretty cheap pizza.

Next along 2 Calle is *Especialidades Doña Estercita Cafetería y Pastelería*, across the street from the Auto Hotel Vásquez. A tidy place that's much more cheerful than the Ebony, it serves pastries as well as more standard dishes.

Already mentioned were the *Restaurant*

Regis and *Panadería Pan Delis* next to the Hotel Mary at 2 Calle 3-52. Another good bakery is the *Panadería del Trigo*, at the corner of 4a Avenida and 4 Calle.

Los Pollos, 3 Calle between 5a and 6a Avenidas, half a block west of the plaza, advertises that it is open 24 hours a day. Two pieces of chicken, salad, chips and a soft drink cost US$1.50. Burgers and smaller chicken meals are even cheaper.

Rico Mac Pollo, 3a Avenida between 3 and 4 Calles, next to the Hotel Maya, is a similar chicken place.

Just a bit farther from the plaza are *Pizza Hogareña*, 6a Avenida 4-45, and *Restaurante Rincón*, 6a Avenida 'A' 7-21, serving fairly good pizza as well as churrasco (Guatemalan-style beef), cheap sandwiches, and delicious fruit licuados. Getting a meal for under US$2 is easy; it's possible to eat for US$1.

Probably the best restaurant in town is the dining room of the *Hotel Zaculeu*, where a full meal should cost no more than US$3 or so.

Getting There & Away

The new bus terminal is in Zona 4, two km south of the plaza along 6 Calle. Second-class buses run between the terminal and the Guatemalan border post at La Mesilla (84 km, 1½ hours, US$1.25) about every hour between 5 am and 4 pm. There are also a few 1st-class buses for slightly more money. Hourly buses head down the Pan American Highway to Cuatro Caminos (74 km, 1¾ hours, US$1.75) and Quetzaltenango's Terminal Minerva (90 km, two hours, US$2.25). Los Falcones (☎ (2) 8-19-79), 7a Avenida 15-27, Zona 1 in Guatemala City, runs two buses a day on the 270-km, five-hour run down the Pan American Highway to Guatemala City. The fare is US$3.

LA MESILLA

There are a few simple services at this Guatemalan customs and immigration post on the Mexican border. You'll be able to get a simple meal and even an emergency bed for the night. By far the best plan, however, is to get to the border, through it, and on your way as early as possible in the day, no matter whether you're going to Mexico or to Guatemala. When you're done with border formalities, take the next bus out. If it's going directly to your chosen destination, so much the better. If not, go as far as Huehuetenango or Comitán and change buses. There is more onward bus traffic from these cities than from the border; any later bus leaving the border and heading past these cities will no doubt stop in town to pick up passengers anyway.

TODOS SANTOS CUCHUMATÁN
Population 2000

If you're up for a trek into the Cuchumatanes, two buses per day depart around lunchtime from the corner of 1a Avenida and 4 Calle, near the Pensión San Jorge in Huehuetenango on the back-breaking 40-km ride to Todos Santos Cuchumatán. The road is rough, the mountain air chilly, the journey slow, but the scenery is spectacular.

The picturesque town of Todos Santos Cuchumatán (altitude 2450 metres) is one of the few in which the traditional Mayan tzolkin calendar is still remembered and (partially) observed. Saturday is market day in the mountain village of Todos Santos. It's possible to take some good walks from the village.

Accommodation consists of two very primitive, very cheap hospedajes, *Los Olguitas* and *La Paz*, plus a few small comedores for food. You'll need these places because the buses – which are run to take villagers into Huehue for shopping and then home again – don't return there until early the next morning.

Guatemala's Pacific Slope

Guatemala's Pacific Slope is the south-easterly continuation of Mexico's Soconusco, a lush, humid region of tropical verdure. The volcanic soil is rich and good for growing coffee at the higher elevations, palm oil seeds and sugar cane at the lower. Vast fincas (plantations) exploit the land's economic potential, drawing seasonal workers from the highland towns and villages where work is scarce. Along the Pacific shore are endless stretches of beaches of dark volcanic sand. The temperature and humidity along the shore are always uncomfortably high, day and night, rainy season and dry. The few small resorts attract mostly local – not foreign – beach-goers.

To travellers, the Pacific Slope is mostly the fast highway called the Carretera al Pacífico (CA-2) which runs from the border crossings at Ciudad Hidalgo/Tecún Umán and Talismán/El Carmen to Guatemala City. The 275 km between the Mexican border at Tecún Umán and Guatemala City can be covered in about four hours by car, five by bus D much less than the 342 km of the Pan-American Highway through the south-western highlands between La Mesilla and Guatemala City, which takes seven hours. If speed is your goal, the Pacific Slope is your route.

Most of the towns along the Carretera al Pacífico are muggy, somewhat chaotic, and hold little of interest for travellers. The beach villages are worse – unpleasantly hot, muggy and dilapidated. There are exceptions, though. Retalhuleu, a logical stopping-place if you're coming from the Mexican border, is pleasant and fun to visit. Nearby is the active archaeological dig at Abaj Takalik. The pre-Olmec stone carvings at Santa Lucía Cotzumalguapa, eight km west of Siquinalá, and those at La Democracia nine km south of Siquinalá, are unique, and if you travel the Carretera al Pacífico you must stop to see them. The port town of Iztapa and its beach resort of Likín can fill the need if you simply must get to the beach. Near Guatemala City, Lake Amatitlán is the citified version of the more beautiful Lake Atitlán.

The Carretera al Pacífico is good and very fast, which is exactly how the 1st-class buses drive it.

EL CARMEN

A toll bridge across the Río Suchiate connects Talismán, Mexico and El Carmen, Guatemala. The border crossing posts are open 24 hours every day. Minibuses and trucks run frequently between Talismán and Tapachula, half an hour (20 km) away.

There are few services at El Carmen, and these are very basic. The *Hotel Buena Vista* has 10 rooms priced at US$4.50 a single, US$8 a double. *Hotel El Paso* is marginally better, its four rooms going for US$6 a single, US$8.50 a double. Cheapest is the *Hotel Hipp*, with 15 rooms without running water going for US$2.50 a single, US$4.50 a double. The 15 rooms at the *Hotel Handall* are more expensive and not as good.

There is good bus service from El Carmen to Malacatán, on the San Marcos-Quetzaltenango road, and to Ciudad Tecún Umán 39 km to the south. There are also fairly frequent 1st-class buses to Guatemala City along the Carretera al Pacífico (278 km, five hours, US$3.20). Transportes Galgos (☎ (2) 53-48-68, 2-36-61), 7a Avenida 19-44, Zona 1, Guatemala City, is only one company operating along this route. It runs five buses daily from El Carmen stopping at Ciudad Tecún Umán, Coatepeque, Retalhuleu, Mazatenango and Escuintla (change for Santa Lucía Cotzumalguapa). Rutas Lima has a daily bus to Quetzaltenango via Retalhuleu and El Zarco junction.

CIUDAD TECÚN UMÁN

This is the busier and more commercial of the two Pacific Slope border-crossing points, with a bridge linking Ciudad Tecún Umán,

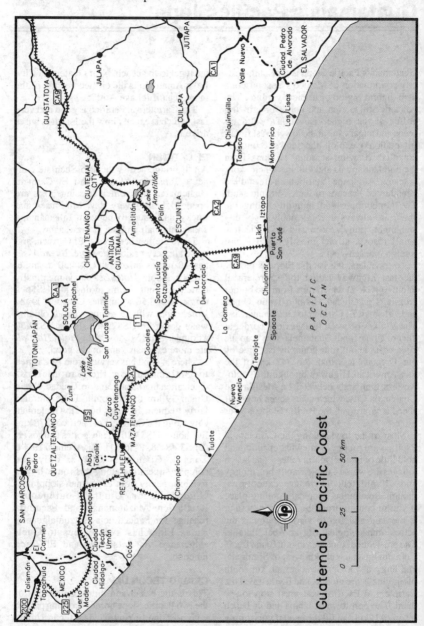

Guatemala's Pacific Coast

Guatemala with Ciudad Hidalgo, Mexico. The border posts are open 24 hours a day. Basic hotels and restaurants are available, but you'll want to get through the border and on your way as soon as possible.

Minibuses and buses run frequently between Ciudad Hidalgo and Tapachula, 38 km to the north (see the Soconusco section for details). From Ciudad Tecún Umán there are frequent buses heading east along the Carretera al Pacífico, stopping at Coatepeque, Retalhuleu, Mazatenango and Escuintla before climbing into the mountains to Guatemala City. If you don't find a bus to your destination, take any bus to Coatepeque or, preferably, Retalhuleu, and change buses there.

COATEPEQUE

Set on a hill in the midst of lush coffee plantations, Coatepeque is a brash, fairly ugly and chaotic commercial centre, noisy and humid at all times. The town is several km north of the Carretera al Pacífico, and there is no reason to stop here unless you're a coffee broker, or you have an emergency.

Of the town's hotels, the 24-room *Hotel Europa* (☎ (9) 75-13-96), 6 Calle 4-01, Zona 1, just off the main plaza, is about the best, with double rooms priced at US$18 with private bath. It has a restaurant. *Hotel Virginia* (☎ (9) 75-18-01), Carretera al Pacífico Km 220, on the Carretera al Pacífico, has 15 air-conditioned rooms for US$11 a single, US$14 a double.

EL ZARCO JUNCTION

About 40 km east of Coatepeque and nine km west of Retalhuleu on the Carretera al Pacífico is El Zarco, the junction with the toll road north to Quetzaltenango. The road winds up the Pacific Slope, carpeted in tropical jungle, rising more than 2000 metres in the 47 km from El Zarco to Quetzaltenango. The toll is less than US$0.50. Just after the upper toll booth the road divides at Zunil: the left fork goes to Quetzaltenango via Los Baños and Almolonga (the shorter route); the right fork via Cantel. For information on these places and the beautiful Fuentes Geor-

ginas hot springs near Zunil, see Around Quetzaltenango in the Guatemala's Highlands chapter.

RETALHULEU

Population 40,000

The Pacific Slope is a rich agricultural region, and Retalhuleu (altitude 240 metres) is its clean, attractive capital – and proud of it. Some years ago the citizens erected a sign on the highway which read 'Welcome to Retalhuleu, Capital of the World'. Most Guatemalans refer to Retalhuleu simply as Reu (RAY-oo).

If Coatepeque is where the coffee traders trade, Retalhuleu is where they come to relax, splashing in the pool at the Posada de Don José and sipping a cool drink in the bar. You'll see their expensive Range Rovers and big 4WD vehicles parked outside. The rest of the citizens get their kicks strolling through the plaza between the whitewashed colonial church and the wedding-cake government buildings, shaded by royal palms.

The balmy tropical air and laid-back attitude are restful. In the evening the parque (plaza) is alive with strollers and noisy with blackbirds. Tourists are something of a curiosity in Reu, and are treated very well. You'll like this place.

Orientation

The town centre is four km south-west of the Carretera al Pacífico along a grand boulevard lined with towering palm trees. The bus station is near the market and the fairgrounds, 700 metres south-west of the plaza along 5a Avenida 'A'. To find the plaza, look for the twin church towers and walk toward them. The railway station is two blocks north-west of the plaza very near the Posada de Don José.

Most of the services you may need are within two blocks of the plaza, including banks, public toilets, cinemas, hotels and restaurants. There is no official tourist office, but people in the Municipalidad, on 6a Avenida facing the east side of the church,

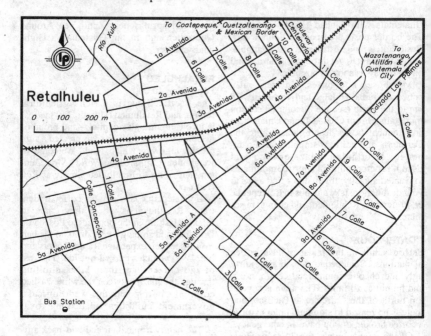

will do their best to help with vexing problems.

Abaj Takalik

There's nothing to see in Retalhuleu proper, but about 30 km to the west is the active archaeological dig at Abaj Takalik (ah-BAH tah-kah-LEEK), where exciting finds have already been made. Large 'Olmecoid' stone heads have been discovered, along with many other objects, which date the site as one of the earliest in all of the Mayan realm. The site has yet to be restored and prettified for tourists, so don't expect a Chichén Itzá or Tikal. But if you're truly fascinated with archaeology and want to see it as it's done, make a visit.

It's difficult to reach Abaj Takalik without your own vehicle; you may have to hire a taxi from Retalhuleu (US$20 to US$30). To do it by bus, early in the morning take any bus heading west towards Coatepeque, go about 15 km west along the Carretera al Pacífico

and get out at the road, on the right, to El Asintal. It's five km to El Asintal (you may have some luck hitching); Abaj Takalik is four km beyond El Asintal along an unpaved road.

Places to Stay

There are few rock-bottom low-end places to stay in Reu, though there are several low-priced, central hotels. Two of the most convenient are just half a block west of the plaza. The better of the two is the *Hotel Astor* (☎ (9) 71-04-75), 5 Calle 4-60, Zona 1, with a pretty courtyard, nine well-kept if simple rooms with showers, and its own parking lot. Rates are US$4.50/8.50/11 a single/double/triple with private shower, US$3.75 per person in bathless rooms. *Hotel Modelo* (☎ (9) 71-02-56), 5 Calle 4-53, Zona 1, just across 5 Calle from the Hotel Astor, is a similar big old place with seven rooms on two floors around a cavernous central court. The rooms are not beautiful, they're of dif-

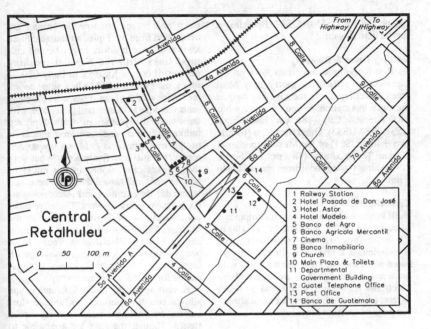

Central Retalhuleu

0   50   100 m

1   Railway Station
2   Hotel Posada de Don José
3   Hotel Astor
4   Hotel Modelo
5   Banco del Agro
6   Banco Agricola Mercantil
7   Cinema
8   Banco Inmobiliario
9   Church
10 Main Plaza & Toilets
11 Departmental
    Government Building
12 Guatel Telephone Office
13 Post Office
14 Banco de Guatemala

ferent sizes, and they have small add-on showers and ceiling fans. Prices are the same as at the Astor.

For even cheaper rooms, look at the *Hospedaje San Francisco*, 250 metres along 6a Avenida from the church on the right-hand side, at 8 Calle.

The nicest place in town is the *Hotel Posada de Don José* (☎ (9) 71-01-80, 71-08-41), 5 Calle 3-67, Zona 1, across the street from the railway station and two blocks north-west of the plaza. On weekends the Don José is often filled with finca owners in town for relaxation; at other times you can get an air-conditioned room with private bath for US$11/20/24 a single/double/triple; sometimes reductions are offered. The 35 rooms are on two levels overlooking the swimming pool and the café and restaurant tables beneath an arcade surrounding the pool. There's a nice bar as well. Out on the Carretera al Pacífico are several other hotels. These tend to be 'tropical motels' by design,

with bungalows, swimming pool and restaurant. *Hotel Siboney* (☎ (9) 71-03-72, 71-01-49), Cuatro Caminos, San Sebastian, is at the eastern end of town where Calzada Las Palmas meets the Carretera al Pacífico. The 24 air-conditioned, bath-equipped rooms here are priced about the same as at the Posada de Don José. *Hotel La Colonía* (☎ (9) 71-00-54/38), Carretera al Pacífico Km 178, is one km east of the Siboney. This is a fairly luxurious layout with 45 rooms with private baths (but no air-con) in bunga-lows around the swimming pool. Prices are as at the Posada de Don José.

Places to Eat

Several little restaurants facing the plaza – *Cafetería Nuevos Horizones, Restaurant El Patio*, etc – provide meals at cheap prices (under US$2). For the best meal in town, head for the *Posada de Don José*, where the pleasant restaurant serves beef and chicken plates for US$3 to US$4, and a big, full meal can be had for US$5 to US$7. Breakfast is served here as well.

Getting There & Away
As Reu is the most important town on the Carretera al Pacífico, transport is easy. Most buses travelling along the highway stop at the city's bus station, so you can catch a bus to Guatemala City (186 km, four hours, US$2.25 to US$3), Quetzaltenango (67 km, two hours, US$1) or the Mexican border at Ciudad Tecún Umán (78 km, 1½ hours, US$1) almost every hour from about 7 am to 5 pm.

CHAMPERICO
Built to serve as an exit route for shipments of coffee during the boom of the late 1800s, Champerico, 38 km south-west of Retalhuleu, is a tawdry, sweltering, dilapidated place that sees few tourists – and with good reason. Though there are several cheap hotels and restaurants, you would do better to reserve your seaside time for more attractive parts of La Ruta Maya.

MAZATENANGO
Population 38,000
East of Retalhuleu 26 km along the Carretera al Pacífico, is Mazatenango (altitude 370 metres), capital of the department of Suchitepéquez. It's a centre for farmers, traders and shippers of the Pacific Slope's agricultural produce. There are a few serviceable hotels if you need to stop in an emergency.

SANTA LUCÍA COTZUMALGUAPA
Population 20,000
Another 71 km eastward from Mazatenango brings you to Santa Lucía Cotzumalguapa (altitude 356 metres), an important stop for anyone interested in Mayan art and culture. In the sugar cane fields and fincas near the town stand great stone heads carved with grotesque faces, fine relief scenes in stone, and a mystery: who carved these ritual objects, and why?

The town itself, though pleasant, is unexciting, with little to keep you. The people in town and in the countryside around are descended from the Pipils, an Indian culture known to have historic, linguistic and cultural links with the Nahuatl-speaking peoples of central Mexico. In Early Classic times, the Pipils who lived here grew cacao, the 'money' of the time. They were obsessed with the Mayan/Aztec ballgame, and with the rites and mysteries of death. Pipil art, unlike the flowery and almost romantic style of the true Maya, is cold, grotesque and severe, but still very finely done. What were these 'Mexicans' doing in the midst of Mayan territory? How did they get here, and where did they come from? Archaeologists do not have many answers. There are other concentrations of Pipils, notably in the Motagua Valley of south-eastern Guatemala, and in western El Salvador. Today these people share a common lifestyle with Guatemala's other indigenous groups, except for their mysterious history.

A visit to Santa Lucía Cotzumalguapa allows you to examine this unique 'lost culture' by visiting a number of its carved stones. Though the sites are accessible to travellers without their own transport, a car certainly simplifies matters. In your explorations you may get to see a Guatemalan sugarcane finca in full operation.

Orientation
Santa Lucía Cotzumalguapa is north-west of the Carretera al Pacífico. In its main square (el parque), several blocks from the highway, are copies of some of the famous carved stones to be found in the region.

There are three main archaeological sites to visit: Bilbao, a finca right on the outskirts of Santa Lucía; Finca El Baúl, a large plantation farther from the town, at which there are two sites, a hilltop site and the finca headquarters; and Finca Las Ilusiones, which has collected most of its findings into a museum near the finca headquarters. Of these sites, Bilbao and the hilltop site at El Baúl are by far the most interesting. If time and energy are short, make for these.

If you have a car, good. If you don't, and you want to see the sites in a day, haggle with

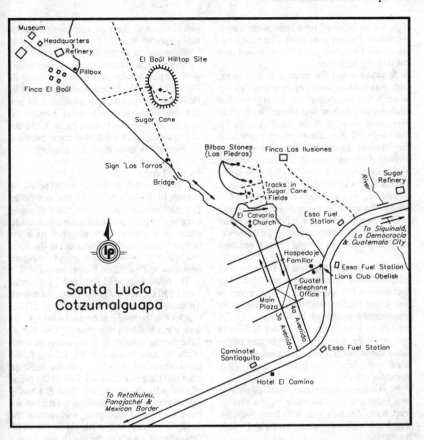

a taxi driver in Santa Lucía's main square for a visit to the sites. It's hot and muggy, the sites are several km apart, and you will really be glad you rode at least part of the way. If you do it all on foot and by bus, pack a lunch so you won't have to return to town. The perfect place to have a picnic is the hilltop site at El Baúl.

Bilbao

This site was no doubt a large ceremonial centre which flourished about 600 AD. Ploughs have unearthed (and damaged) hun-dreds of stones during the last few centuries; thieves have carted off many others. In 1880 many of the best stones were removed to museums abroad, including nine stones to the Dahlem Museum in Berlin.

Known locally as simply *las piedras* (the stones), this site actually consists of several separate sites deep within tall stands of sug-arcane. The fields come right to the edge of the town. From Santa Lucía's main square, go north uphill on 3a Avenida to the outskirts of town. Pass El Calvario church on your right, and shortly thereafter turn sharp right. A hundred metres along, the road veers to the right but an unpaved road continues straight on; follow the unpaved road. The canefields are on your left, and you will soon see a path cut into the high cane.

At times when the cane is high, finding your way around would be very difficult if it weren't for the swarms of local boys that coalesce and follow you as you make your way along the edge of the canefields. At the first sign of bewilderment or indecision they'll strike: *Las piedras? Las piedras?* You answer *Así!* and they'll lead you without hesitation into the sea of waving cane along a maze of paths to each site. A tip is expected, of course, but it needn't be large and it needn't be given to every one of the multitude of guides. The boys are in school many days, but dependably at the ready on weekends, holidays and during school vacation time.

The boys may lead you to the sites in a different order from that which follows. The first stone is flat with three figures carved in low relief; the middle figure's ribs show prominently, as though he were starving. A predatory bird is in the upper left-hand corner. Holes in the middle-right part of the stone show that thieves attempted to cut the stone apart in order to make it more easily portable.

Next is an elaborate relief showing players in a ballgame (an obsession of the Pipils), fruit, birds, animals and cacao bean pods, for which this area was famous and which made it rich.

Farther into the fields are more stones, several of which are badly weathered and worn so that the figures are difficult to make out. The last stones the boys show you are a 10-minute walk from the starting-point. These bear Mexican-style circular date glyphs and other mysterious patterns which resemble closely those used by people along the Gulf coast of Mexico near Villahermosa. These two peoples must have had close relations, but just how they did so is a mystery.

Finally, the boys lead you along a broad unpaved track in the canefields back to the dead end of the unpaved road from which you began. If you go south from this point

you can join 4a Avenida and continue to the main square.

To go on to El Baúl, however, you can save time by backtracking to the point where you turned sharp right just beyond El Calvario church. Buses heading out to El Baúl pass this point every few hours; or you can hitchhike with any other vehicle. If you're driving, you'll have to return to the centre along 4a Avenida and come back out 3a Avenida as these roads are one-way.

Finca El Baúl

Just as interesting as las piedras is the hilltop site at El Baúl, which has the additional fascination of being an active place of pagan worship for local people. This is an excellent place for a picnic. Some distance from the hilltop site on another road, next to the finca headquarters, is the finca's private museum of stones uncovered on the property.

The hilltop site at El Baúl is 4.2 km northwest of El Calvario church. From the church (or the intersection just beyond it), go 2.7 km to a fork in the road just beyond a bridge; the fork is marked by a sign reading Los Tarros. Take the right-hand fork, an unpaved road. From the Los Tarros sign it's 1.5 km to the point where a dirt track crosses the road; on your right is a tree-covered 'hill' in the midst of otherwise flat fields. The 'hill' is actually a great ruined temple platform which has not been restored. Make your way across the field and around the south side of the hill, following the track to the top. If you have a car, you can drive to within 50 metres of the top.

If you visit on a weekend, you may find several worshippers paying their respects to the idols here. They will not mind if you visit as well, and are usually happy to pose with the idols for photographs in exchange for a small 'contribution'.

Of the two stones here, the great grotesque half-buried head is the most striking. The elaborate headdress, 'blind' eyes with big bags beneath them, beak-like nose and idiotic 'have a nice day' grin seem at odds with the blackened face and its position, half-buried in the ancient soil. The head is stained with wax from candles, with liquor and other drinks, and with the smoke and ashes of incense fires built before it, all part of worship. The idol may have reason to be happy. People have been coming here to pay homage for over 1400 years.

The other stone is a relief carving of a figure surrounded by circular motifs which may be date glyphs. A copy of this stone may be seen in the main square of Santa Lucía Cotzumalguapa.

From the hilltop site, retrace your steps 1.5 km to the fork with the Los Tarros sign. Take the other fork this time (what would be the left fork as you come from Santa Lucía), and follow the paved road three km to the headquarters of Finca El Baúl. (If you're on foot, you can walk from the hilltop site back to the unpaved road and straight across it, continuing on the dirt track. This will eventually bring you to the asphalt road which leads to the finca headquarters. When you reach the road, turn right.) Buses trundle along this road every few hours, shuttling workers between the refinery and the town centre.

Approaching the finca headquarters (six km from Santa Lucía's main square), you cross a narrow bridge at a curve, continue uphill, and you will see the entrance on the left, marked by a machine-gun pillbox. Beyond this daunting entrance you pass workers' houses, a sugar refinery on the right, and finally come to the headquarters building guarded by several men with rifles. The smell of molasses is everywhere. Ask permission to visit the museum, and a guard will unlock the gate just past the headquarters building.

Within the gates, sheltered by a palapa, are numerous sculpted figures and reliefs found on the plantation, some of which are very fine. Unfortunately, nothing is labelled.

Behind the palapa are several pieces of machinery once used on the finca but now retired. One of these is a small Orenstein & Kopdel steam locomotive manufactured in Berlin in 1927; there is an even smaller, older, more primitive locomotive as well.

Finca Las Ilusiones

The third site is very close to Bilbao – indeed, this is the finca which controls the Bilbao canefields – but, paradoxically, access is more difficult. Your reward is the chance to view hundreds of objects, large and small, which have been collected from the finca's fields over the centuries.

Leave the town centre by heading east along Calzada 15 de Septiembre, the boulevard which joins the highway at an Esso fuel station. Go north-east for a short distance, and just past another Esso station on the left is an unpaved road which leads, after a little more than one km, to Finca Las Ilusiones and its museum. If the person who holds the museum key is to be found, you can have a look inside. If not, you must be satisfied with the many stones collected around the outside of the museum.

Places to Stay & Eat

The selection of services in this small town is not good, but it is sufficient. *Hospedaje Familiar*, Calzada 15 de Septiembre, across the street from Guatel, is a tidy little family-run place a few blocks east of the main square and a few blocks west of the highway. Rooms with private shower cost US$4.50 a single, US$7 a double.

Out on the highway, a few hundred metres west of the town, is the *Caminotel Santiaguito* (☎ (9) 74-54-35 to 38), Km 90.4, Carretera al Pacífico, 'famous since 1956', a fairly lavish layout (for Guatemala's Pacific Slope) with spacious tree-shaded grounds, a nice swimming pool, and a decent restaurant. The pool is open to non-guests upon payment of a small fee. Motel-style air-conditioned rooms with private baths cost US$11 a single, US$14 a double. They're liable to be full on weekends as the hotel is something of a resort for local people. In the spacious restaurant cooled by ceiling fans you can order a cheeseburger, fruit salad and soft drink for US$3, or an even bigger meal for US$4.50 to US$6.

Across the highway from the Caminotel is the *Hotel El Camino*, with much cheaper rooms that are hot and somewhat noisy because of highway traffic. Prices are similar to those at the Hospedaje Familiar, but you get less for your money here.

Getting There & Away

Esmeralda 2nd-class buses shuttle between Santa Lucía Cotzumalguapa and Guatemala City (4a Avenida and 2 Calle, Zona 9) every half an hour or so between 6 am and 5 pm, charging US$1 for the 90-km, two-hour ride. You can also catch any bus travelling along the Carretera al Pacífico between Guatemala City and such points as Mazatenango, Retalhuleu or the Mexican border.

To travel between La Democracia and Santa Lucía, catch a bus running along the Carretera al Pacífico between Santa Lucía and Siquinalá (eight km); change in Siquinalá for a bus to La Democracia.

Between Santa Lucía and Lake Atitlán you will probably have to change buses at Cocales junction, 23 km west of Santa Lucía and 58 km south of Panajachel.

LA DEMOCRACIA

Population 4200

South of Siquinalá 9.5 km along the road to Puerto San José is La Democracia (altitude 165 metres), a nondescript Pacific Slope town that's hot both day and night, rainy season and dry. Like Santa Lucía Cotzumalguapa, La Democracia is in the midst of a region populated from early times with – according to some archaeologists – mysterious cultural connections to Mexico's Gulf coast.

At the archaeological site called Monte Alto, on the outskirts of the town, huge basalt heads have been found. Though cruder, the heads resemble those carved by the Olmecs near Veracruz several thousand years ago. The Monte Alto heads could be older than, as old as, or not as old as the Olmec heads. We just don't know.

Today these great 'Olmecoid' heads are arranged around La Democracia's main plaza. As you come into town from the highway, follow signs to the *museo*, which will cause you to bear left, then turn left, then turn left again. Stroll around the plaza admir-

ing these interesting, mysterious objects. After seeing the heads, you might like to enjoy the shade of the huge tree in the plaza's centre. Facing the plaza, along with the church and the modest Palacio Municipal, is the small, modern Museo Rubén Chevez Van Dorne with other fascinating archaeological finds. The star of the show is an exquisite jade mask. Smaller figures, 'yokes' used in the ballgame, relief carvings and other objects make up the rest of this important small collection. On the walls are overly dramatic paintings of Olmecoid scenes; there's more drama than meaning or accuracy. A rear room has more of the dramatic paintings, and lots of potsherds only an archaeologist could love. The museum is open from 8 am to noon and 2 to 5 pm; admission costs US$0.10.

La Democracia has no places to stay and few places to eat. The eateries are very basic and ill-supplied, and it's best for you to bring your own food and buy drinks at a place facing the plaza. *Café Maritza*, right next to the museum, is a picture-perfect hot-tropics hangout with a *rockola* (jukebox) blasting music, and a small crew of semisomnolent locals sipping and sweltering. The road south continues 42 km to Sipacate, a small and very basic beach town. The beach is on the other side of the Canal de Chiquimulilla, an intra-coastal waterway. Though there are a few scruffy, very basic places to stay, you'd be better off saving your beach time for Puerto San José, 35 km farther to the east, reached via the road from Escuintla.

Getting There & Away

Chatia Gomerana, Muelle Central, Terminal de Buses, Zona 4, Guatemala City, has buses every half an hour from 6 am to 4.30 pm on the 92-km, two-hour ride between the capital and La Democracia. Buses stop at Escuintla, Siquinalá (change for Santa Lucía Cotzumalguapa), La Democracia, La Gomera and Sipacate. The fare is US$1.

ESCUINTLA

Set amidst lush tropical verdure, Escuintla should be an idyllic place where people swing languidly in hammocks and concoct pungent meals of readily-available exotic fruit and vegetables. But it's not.

Escuintla is a hot, dingy, dilapidated commercial and industrial city that's very important to the Pacific Slope's economy, but not at all important to you. It is an old town, inhabited by Pipils before the conquest, but now solidly ladino. Though it does have some fairly dingy hotels and restaurants, it provides no reason why you should use them.

You may have to change buses in Escuintla. The main bus station is in the southern part of town; this is where you catch buses to Puerto San José. For Guatemala City, you can catch very frequent buses in the main plaza.

PUERTO SAN JOSÉ, LIKÍN & IZTAPA

Guatemala's most important seaside resort leaves a lot to be desired, even when compared to Mexico's smaller, seedier places. But if you're eager to get into the Pacific surf, head south from Escuintla 50 km to Puerto San José and neighbouring settlements.

Puerto San José (population 14,000) was Guatemala's most important Pacific port in the latter half of the 19th century and well into the 20th. Now superseded by the more modern Puerto Quetzal to the east, Puerto San José languishes and slumbers; its inhabitants languish, slumber, play loud music and drink. The beach, inconveniently located across the Canal de Chiquimulilla, is reached by boat.

A smarter thing to do is head west along the coast five km (by taxi or private car) to Balneario Chulamar, which has a nicer beach and also a suitable hotel or two.

About five km to the east of Puerto San José is Balneario Likín, Guatemala's only upscale Pacific resort. Likín is much beloved

by well-to-do families from Guatemala City who have seaside houses on the tidy streets and canals of this planned development.

About 12 km east of Puerto San José is Iztapa, Guatemala's first Pacific port, first used by none other than Pedro de Alvarado in the 1500s. When Puerto San José was built in 1853, Iztapa's reign as the port of the capital city came to an end, and it relaxed into a tropical torpor from which it has yet to emerge. Having lain fallow for almost a century and a half, it has not suffered the degradation of Puerto San José. Iztapa is comparatively pleasant, with several small, easily affordable hotels and restaurants on the beach. The bonus here is that you can catch a bus from Guatemala City all the way to Iztapa, or pick it up at Escuintla or Puerto San José to take you to Iztapa.

LAKE AMATITLÁN

A placid lake backed by a looming volcano, situated a mere 25 km south of Guatemala City – that's Amatitlán. It should be a pretty and peaceful resort, but unfortunately it's not. The hourglass-shaped lake is divided by a railway line, and the lakeshore is lined with industry at some points. On weekends people from Guatemala City come to row boats on the lake (its waters are too polluted for swimming), or to rent a private hot tub for a dip. Many people from the capital own second homes here.

There's little reason for you to spend time here. If you want to have a look, head for the town of Amatitlán, just off the main Escuintla-Guatemala City highway. Amatitlán has a scruffy public beach area where you can confirm your suspicions. If you have a car and some spare time, a drive around the lake offers some pretty scenery. Perhaps one day the lake will be returned to its naturally beautiful state.

Central & Eastern Guatemala

North and east of Guatemala City is a land of varied topography, from the misty, pine-covered mountains of Alta Verapaz to the hot, dry-tropic climate of the Río Motagua Valley.

The Carretera al Atlantico (Highway to the Atlantic, CA-9) heads north-east from the capital and soon descends from the relative cool of the mountains to the dry heat of a valley where dinosaurs once roamed. Along its course to the Atlantic are many interesting destinations, including the beautiful highland scenery around Cobán; the palaeontology museum at Estanzuela; the great pilgrimage church at Esquipulas, famous throughout Central America; the first-rate Mayan ruins at Copán, just across the border in Honduras; the marvellous Mayan stelae and zoomorphs at Quiriguá; and the tropical lake of Izabal and jungle waterway of Río Dulce. The Carretera al Atlantico ends at Puerto Barrios, Guatemala's Caribbean port, from which you can take a boat to Lívingston, a laid-back hideaway peopled by Black Afro-Guatemalans.

The departments of Baja Verapaz and Alta Verapaz were once known for their bad hospitality. In the time before the conquest, this mountainous highland region was peopled by the Rabinal Maya, noted for their warlike habits and merciless conquests. They battled the powerful Quiché Maya for a century, but were never conquered by that imperial nation.

When the conquistadors arrived they too had trouble defeating the Rabinals. It was Fray Bartolomé de las Casas who convinced the Spanish authorities to try peace where war had failed. Armed with an edict which forbade Spanish soldiers from entering the region for five years, the friar and his brethren pursued their religious mission, and succeeded in pacifying and converting the Rabinals. From a land of constant battle, these highlands became a region of peace. It

was renamed Verapaz (True Peace), and is now divided into Baja Verapaz, with its capital at Salamá, and Alta Verapaz, centred on Cobán.

The two departmental capitals are easily accessible along a smooth, fast, asphalted road which winds up from the hot dry valley through wonderful scenery into the mountains, through long stretches of coffee-growing country. Along the way to Cobán is one of Guatemala's premier nature reserves, the Biotopo del Quetzal. Beyond Cobán, along rough unpaved roads, are the country's most famous caverns.

SALAMÁ
Population 11,000

Highway 17, also marked CA-14, leaves the Carretera al Atlantico near El Rancho and heads west up into the hills. After 48 km you turn left, and another 12 km brings you to Salamá (altitude 940 metres), capital of Baja Verapaz, an attractive town with some reminders of colonial rule. The main plaza boasts a big old colonial church that's presently being restored. A colonial bridge on the outskirts once carried all the traffic to this rich agricultural region, but today is used only by pedestrians. If you find reason to stop in Salamá, try to do so on a Sunday, when the market is active.

Should you want to stay the night, the *Hotel Tezulutlán*, Barrio El Centro, has 15 rooms with private showers for US$4 a single, US$7 a double. A hostelry in the grand old style, its rooms are arranged around a pleasant courtyard. The *Hotel Juárez*, 10a Avenida 5-55, Zona 1, is larger, with 26 rooms, and somewhat cheaper as well.

As this is a departmental capital there are frequent buses to and from Guatemala City. Salamateca (☎ (2) 81716), 9a Avenida 19-00, Zona 1 in Guatemala City, has buses running about every two hours from 5.45 am

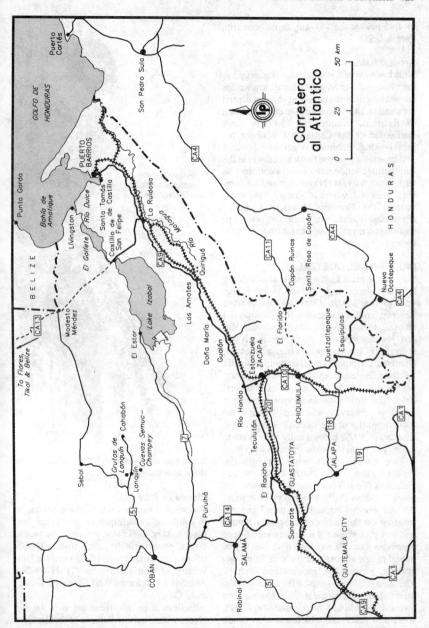

to 4.45 pm on the 151-km, three-hour trip. Fare is US$1.

Around Salamá

Nine km west of Salamá along Highway 5 is the village of San Miguel Chicaj, known for its weaving. Continue along the same road for another 18 km to reach the colonial town of Rabinal, founded in 1537 by Fray Bartolomé de las Casas as a base for his proselytising. Rabinal has gained fame as a pottery-making centre (look especially at the handpainted chocolate cups), and for its citrus fruit harvest (November and December). Market day here is Sunday. Two small hotels, the *Pensión Motagua* and the *Hospedaje Caballeros*, can put you up, though you might decide to return to Salamá instead.

BIOTOPO DEL QUETZAL

Stay on the main highway instead of turning left for Salamá, and another 34 km brings you to the Mario Dary Rivera Nature Reserve, commonly called the Biotopo del Quetzal, Guatemala's quetzal reserve at Km 161, just east of the village of Purulhá. If you stop here intent on seeing a quetzal, Guatemala's national bird, you will probably be disappointed, because the birds are rare and elusive. Stop instead to explore and enjoy the lush high rainforest ecosystem which is preserved here, and which is the natural habitat of the quetzal. The reserve, founded in 1977, is open daily from 6 am to 4 pm (you must leave the grounds by 5 pm).

Two nature trails wind through the reserve, the 1800-metre Sendero los Helechos (Fern Trail), and the Sendero los Musgos (Moss Trail), which is twice as long. As you wander through the dense growth, treading on the rich, dense, spongy humus and leaf-mould, you'll see many varieties of epiphytes (air plants) which thrive in the humid jungle atmosphere: lichens, ferns, liverworts, bromeliads, mosses and orchids. The Río Colorado cascades through the forest along a geological fault. Deep in the forest is Xiu Ua Li Che (Grandfather-Tree), some 450 years old, which was alive when

A quetzal, the national bird of Guatemala

the conquistadors fought the Rabinals in these mountains.

Places to Stay

The reserve has its own camping places, so if you have the equipment, this is the best place to stay. Officially, you are supposed to obtain permission to camp from CECON (Center for Conservation Studies of the University of San Carlos; ☎ (2) 31-09-04), Avenida La Reforma 0-63, Zona 10, Guatemala City.

Believe it or not, there are two lodging places within a short distance of the Biotopo.

Just beyond the Biotopo, another 200 metres up the hill toward Purulhá and Cobán, is the *Pensión Los Ranchitos*, a rustic hospedaje with two little wooden cabins. They sleep seven and eight people, and cost US$2 per person. The family which runs the cabins can provide simple, cheap meals as well.

Should you be looking for more comfort, the *Posada Montaña del Quetzal* (☎ (2) 31-41-81 in Guatemala City during business hours), Carretera a Cobán Km 156, Purulhá, Baja Verapaz, is five km back along the road toward the Carretera al Atlantico. This attractive hostelry has 18 little white stucco tile-roofed bungalow-cabins, each with a sitting room and fireplace, a bedroom with three beds, and a private bathroom. The cabins are off the road, very quiet and set in nice grounds. There are marvellous mountain views from the restaurant. Cost for a bungalow (two persons) is US$10. You can usually catch a bus to shuttle you between the Biotopo and the posada, or hitch a ride with some other vehicle.

Onward to Cobán

The asphalt road is good, smooth and fast, though curvy, with light traffic. Even as you ascend into the evergreen forests, tropical flowers are still visible here and there. Signs by the roadside advertise the services of brokers willing to buy farmers' harvests of cardamom and coffee and dairy cattle. As you enter the town, a sign says 'Bienvenidos a Cobán, Ciudad Imperial', referring to the charter granted in 1538 by Emperor Charles V. About 126 km from the Carretera al Atlantico, you enter Cobán's main plaza.

COBÁN

Population 20,000

The town now called Cobán (altitude 1320 metres) was once the centre of Tesulutlán (Tierra de Guerra in Spanish), The Land of War. Alvarado's conquistadors overran western Guatemala in short order, but the Rabinal Maya of Verapaz fought them off until Fray Bartolomé and his brethren came and conquered them with religion.

A later conquest came in the 19th century

when German immigrants moved in and founded vast coffee fincas. Cobán took on the aspect of a German mountain town as the finca owners built town residences with steeply pitched roofs, elaborate gingerbread bargeboards and other decoration, and gathered to exchange the morning's news in Central European-style cafés. The era of German cultural and economic domination ended during WW II, when the USA prevailed upon the Guatemalan government to deport the powerful finca owners, many of whom actively supported the Nazis.

Today Cobán can be a pleasant town to visit, though much depends upon the season. During most of the year it can be overcast, dank, chill and cheerless; in the midst of the dry season (January to March) it can be misty, or bright and sunny with marvellous clear mountain air. The departmental festival is held in Cobán during the first week of August.

There is not a lot to do in Cobán except enjoy the local colour and the mountain scenery, and use the town as a base for visits to the Grutas de Lanquín and Cuevas Semuc-Champey nearby.

Orientation

The main plaza (el parque) bears a disconcertingly modern concrete bandstand. Most of the services you'll need – banks, hotels, restaurants, bus stations – are within a few blocks of the plaza and the cathedral, as shown on our map. The shopping district is around and behind the cathedral.

Places to Stay

The *Pensión Familiar*, near the main plaza, is very simple and fairly beat-up, but the price is good at US$1.50 per person. The shared bathrooms have cold water only. *Hotel La Paz*, 6a Avenida, Zona 1, 1½ blocks north of the plaza, charges US$2.50 per person but it's much better kept. To get a room, ask at the shop to the right of the hotel.

A step up in quality and price is the *Hotel Oxib Peck* (☎ (9) 51-10-39), 1 Calle 12-11, Zona 1, six blocks (750 metres) west of the plaza on the road out of town. By Guatema-

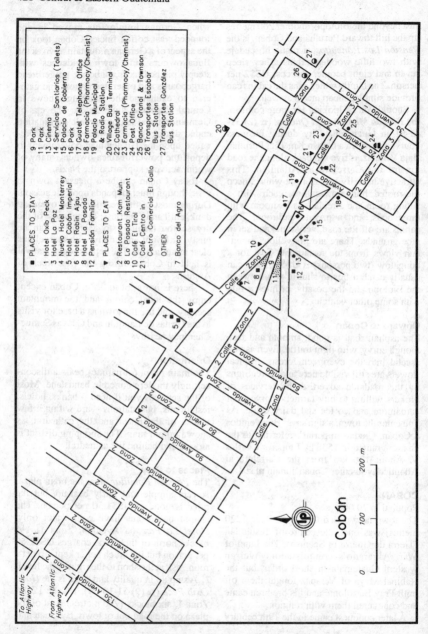

PLACES TO STAY
- Hotel Oxib Peck
1 Hotel La Paz
4 Nuevo Hotel Monterrey
5 Hotel Cobán Imperial
6 Hotel Rabin Ajau
8 Hotel La Posada
12 Pensión Familiar

▼ PLACES TO EAT
2 Restaurant Kam Mun
8 La Posada Restaurant
10 Café El Tirol
21 Café Centro in
Centro Comercial El Gallo

OTHER
7 Banco del Agro
9 Park
11 Park
13 Cinema
14 Servicios Sanitarios (Toilets)
15 Palacio de Gobierno
16 Park
17 Guatel Telephone Office
18 Farmacia (Pharmacy/Chemist)
19 Palacio Municipal
20 Village Bus Terminal
22 Cathedral
23 Farmacia (Pharmacy/Chemist)
24 Post Office
25 Banco Granai & Townson
26 Transportes Escobar
Bus Station
27 Transportes González
Bus Station

To Atlantic Highway
From Atlantic Highway

200 m
100
0   100   200 m

Cobán

lan standards it's clean and bright, with a nice little garden in front, plus a dining room. The 11 rooms are tidy, though plain, with clean tiled showers. Most rooms inspire a bit of claustrophobia as they have no windows to the outside. Still, the hotel offers good value for money at US$4.75 per person.

Hotel Cobán Imperial (☎ (9) 51-11-31), 6a Avenida 1-12, Zona 1, 250 metres from the plaza, is a maze of seven well-used but fairly tidy rooms hidden behind Burgers Bings (enter through the restaurant). Most rooms have add-on tiled baths, and also TVs, which are necessary for a 'view' as few rooms have windows to the outside. It's OK for the price of US$5 a single, US$8 a double, US$10 a triple.

Hotel Rabin Ajau (☎ (9) 51-22-96), 1 Calle 5-37, Zona 1, facing the main plaza, advertises that it is *el unico en su clase en Cobán* (the only one in its class in Cobán), which may be true. Though old-fashioned, well located and fairly well kept, it has no charm and the downstairs disco can be noisy. Rooms facing the street (Nos 1 to 5), on the right side of the hallway, have partial views of the mountains. Instead of the Gideon Bible, each room has its own copy of *El Libro de Mormón (The Book of Mormon)*. There's a restaurant and parking. Rooms with private shower cost US$7 a single, US$13 a double.

Best in town is the *Hotel La Posada* (☎ (9) 51-14-95), 1 Calle 4-12, Zona 2, just off the plaza in the very centre of town. Colonial in style, its colonnaded porches are festooned with tropical flowers and furnished with easy chairs and hammocks from which to enjoy the mountain views. The rooms have nice old furniture, fireplaces, and wall hangings of local weaving, and rent for US$8.50 a single, US$13 a double with private bath.

Places to Eat

Café El Tirol, near the Hotel La Posada, advertises 'the best coffee' in four languages. Facing a bust of Fray Bartolomé de las Casas is a cosy room in which to take pastries and coffee for US$0.75 to US$1.25. Other drinks are served as well, but no meals.

Café Centro (☎ 51-21-92), 1 Calle between 1a and 2a Avenidas, alongside the cathedral in the building called the Centro Comercial El Gallo, has a varied menu, and a nice, light, modern dining room with views through large windows. Substantial plates of chicken (US$2) and beef (US$3) are offered along with a variety of sandwiches (US$0.50 to US$2). For dessert there's lots of ice cream.

You have to walk almost 500 metres from the plaza to reach the *Restaurant Kam Mun*, 1 Calle at 9a Avenida, on the road out of town. When you reach the restaurant you can sample Chinese food in a pleasant, clean little place and pay US$4 to US$6 for a full meal.

The most pleasant dining room in town is that of the *Hotel La Posada*, where you can have a serving of churrasco (tough beef in tomato sauce), rice, spinach, avocado, bread, salad and a soft drink for US$3.

Getting There & Away

Transportes Escobar Monja Blanca (☎ (2) 51-18-78), 8a Avenida 15-16, Zona 1 in Guatemala City, runs about 10 buses a day from 4 am to 4 pm on the 219-km, four-hour trip to Guatemala City, stopping at the Biotopo del Quetzal, Purulhá and Tactic, for US$2.75. You can catch these buses at El Rancho, the intersection of the Carretera al Atlantico and the highway to Cobán.

Around Cobán

If you don't mind bumping over bad and/or busy roads, the best excursion to make from Cobán is to the caves near Lanquín, a pretty village 61 km to the east.

The Grutas de Lanquín are a short distance north-west of the town, and extend for several km into the earth. Have a powerful torch (flashlight) or two, and ask at the Municipalidad (Town Hall) in Lanquín to make sure that the attendant is on duty at the caves to turn on the lights for you. It's also a good idea to ask what the fee will be; haggling may be in order.

Though the first few hundred metres of cavern has been equipped with a walkway and electric lights powered by a diesel generator, the major extent of this subterranean system is untouched. If you are not an experienced spelunker you should think twice about wandering too far into the caves.

The Río Lanquín runs through the caves before coming above ground to run down to Lanquín, offering swimming possibilities at several points. If you have camping equipment you can spend the night near the cave entrance. Otherwise, there are a few very simple hostelries in Lanquín.

Ten km south of Lanquín along a rough, bumpy, slow road is Semuc-Champey, famed for a natural wonder: a great limestone bridge 300 metres long on top of which is a series of pools of cool, flowing river water good for swimming. The water is from the Río Cahabón, most of which passes beneath the bridge underground. Though this bit of paradise is difficult to reach, the beauty of its setting and the perfection of the water make it all worth it.

Getting There & Away From Cobán, take a bus to San Pedro Carchá, six km to the east along the Lanquín-Cahabón road; buses leave very frequently from the village bus terminal down the hill behind the Town Hall in Cobán. From San Pedro Carchá, buses leave three times daily (starting at 5.30 am) on the three-hour ride to Lanquín. The last of three return buses departs Lanquín for San Pedro Carchá in the early afternoon, so you should probably plan to stay the night, either camping at Grutas de Lanquín or Semuc-Champey, or staying in a small hospedaje in Lanquín.

There are no buses to Semuc-Champey. It's a longish, hot walk unless you have your own vehicle, in which case it's a slow, bumpy drive.

RÍO HONDO

Continuing north-eastwards along CA-9, 47 km from El Rancho junction (133 km from Guatemala City) is Río Hondo junction, where CA-10 heads south to Chiquimula and Nuevo Ocotepeque (Honduras), with turn-offs to Esquipulas and the ruins at Copán, just across the border in Honduras.

The town of Río Hondo is north-east of the junction, but lodging places hereabouts list their address as Río Hondo, Santa Cruz Río Hondo or Santa Cruz Teculután – it's all the same place. Just a few km west of the junction are several motels right on CA-9 which provide a good base for explorations of this region if you have your own vehicle. Comfortable middle-range accommodation is very difficult to find in central and eastern Guatemala. The best plan, if you're mobile, is to stay at Río Hondo and take day trips to Copán, Esquipulas and Quiriguá.

Those travelling by bus on a low budget can find suitable cheap accommodation at Copán and Esquipulas, though the situation at Quiriguá is more difficult.

Places to Stay & Eat

Motel Longarone (☎ (9) 41-71-26), Carretera al Atlantico Km 126, Santa Cruz Río Hondo, is the old standard in this area, a comfortable place with a fuel station and spacious, airy dining room at the front. The 54 air-conditioned rooms, all with private showers, are in cement-block bungalow buildings behind the restaurant, arranged around the beautiful swimming pool beneath lofty palm trees amidst tropical gardens. Rates are a reasonable US$9 to US$11 a single, US$11 to US$14 a double and US$21 for a room that sleeps four. Food and service in the restaurant are fairly good. Above the bar are two photographs of the Italian town of Longarone, one before it was swept from the face of the earth by a great landslide, one afterwards. A full, standard menu of Guatemalan and North American favourites, with a sprinkling of Italian dishes, is offered. Expect to spend about US$6 to US$8.50 for a full meal here, less for a sandwich (US$1) or a plate of spaghetti (US$3).

Hotel El Atlantico (☎ (9) 41-71-60), Carretera al Atlantico Km 126, just to the west of the Motel Longarone, is a clone of the Longarone, being precisely the same in layout, much the same in decor, and slightly cheaper in price: US$7 a single, US$13 a double, US$16 a triple.

Across the highway from these two, on the north side, is the *Hotel Nuevo Pasabién* (☎ (9) 41-72-01), Carretera al Atlantico Km 126, more rustic than the other two, with some guestrooms in an older two-storey wooden building, and others in the familiar bungalow units. A passable restaurant faces the highway. All rooms have private bathrooms; the more expensive ones are more modern and comfortable, and have fans. Rates are US$8.50 to US$11 a double.

Note that the Río Hondo motels are looked upon as weekend resorts by local people and even residents of Guatemala City. They drive here and take a room for the whole family for the weekend, revelling in the swimming pools, the nice gardens and the meals in the dining room.

Nine km east of these places, right at the junction with CA-10, the road heading south, is the *Motel Río* (☎ (9) 41-12-67), Carretera al Atlantico Km 136, fairly beat-up but certainly convenient, especially if you don't have your own wheels. Double rooms with private shower go for US$3.O

ESTANZUELA

Travelling south from Río Hondo along CA-10 you are in the midst of the Río Motagua Valley, a hot expanse of what is known as 'dry tropic', which once supported a great number and variety of dinosaurs. Three km south of the Carretera al Atlantico you'll see a small monument on the right-hand (west) side of the road. The monument commemorates the terrible earthquake of 4 February 1976 which killed or injured many Guatemalans and destroyed dozens of villages in this area. The Motagua Valley lies along a geological fault line, and the monument makes this graphically evident. On the roadway, one can actually see how the earth shifted during the earthquake: the white centre line has shifted noticeably to one side.

Less than two km south of the earthquake monument is the small town of Estanzuela, with its Museo de Paleontología filled with dinosaur bones. American palaeontologist Bryan Patterson did research in the Motagua Valley for many years; much of what he found has been gathered together in this private museum now managed by Roberto Woolfolk Saravia. Though Señor Woolfolk also works for INGUAT in Guatemala City and is therefore often absent, the museum is still open from 9 am to 5 pm every day except Monday; admission is free. To find the museum, go west from the highway directly through the town for one km, asking along the way for el museo. Next door to the museum is a small shop selling cold drinks and snacks.

Within the museum are most of the bones of three big dinosaurs, including those of a giant (and I mean giant!) ground sloth some 30,000 years old, and a prehistoric whale. Other exhibits include early Mayan artefacts and other objects which Patterson came across during his research.

ZACAPA
Population 18,000

Capital of the department of the same name, Zacapa (altitude 230 metres) is several km east of the highway. It offers little to travellers, though the locals do make cheese, cigars, and superb old rum (aged 21 years). The few hotels in town are basic, and will do in an emergency; but better accommodation is to be had in Río Hondo and Esquipulas.

CHIQUIMULA
Population 24,000

Another departmental capital set in a mining and tobacco-growing region, Chiquimula (altitude 370 metres) is a major market town for all of eastern Guatemala, with lots of buying and selling activity every day. It's also a transportation point and overnight stop for those making their way to Copán in Honduras.

Places to Stay & Eat

Hotel Chiquimulja (☎ (9) 42-03-87), 3 Calle 6-31, Zona 1, on the north side of the plaza between two Chinese restaurants, is the best in town. Rooms come with private showers, with fan or with air-con, and range in price

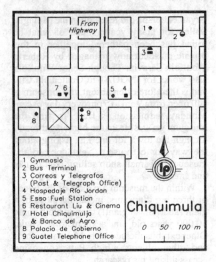

1 Gymnasio
2 Bus Terminal
3 Correos y Telegrafos
  (Post & Telegraph Office)
4 Hospedaje Río Jordan
5 Esso Fuel Station
6 Restaurant Liu & Cinemo
7 Hotel Chiquimulja
  & Banco del Agro
8 Palacio de Gobierno
9 Guatel Telephone Office

Chiquimula

0   50   100 m

from US$2.75 to US$6 a single, US$4 to
US$7 a double.

Two blocks east of the Chiquimulja,
downhill on the same street (3 Calle), is the
Hospedaje Río Jordan, a clean, simple place
renting rooms without running water for
US$1.25 per person, or US$2 per person for
a room with private shower.

As for food, Chiquimula has a surprising
number of little Chinese restaurants, and
many cheap little eateries around the plaza
in the market area and around the bus terminal.

Getting There & Away

Chiquimula is not a destination, it's a transit
point. Your goal is no doubt the fabulous
Mayan ruins at Copán, Honduras, just across
the border from El Florido, Guatemala.

Rutas Orientales (☎ (2) 53-72-82, 51-21-
60), 19 Calle 8-18, Zona 1 in Guatemala
City, runs buses via El Rancho, Río Hondo
and Zacapa to Chiquimula every 30 minutes
from 4 am to 6 pm, for US$2 to US$2.75,
depending on the bus; the 169-km journey
takes three hours.

If you're heading for Copán, change to a
Transportes Vilma bus (pronounced BEEL-

mah; painted silver and black with coloured
stripes on the side) at Chiquimula for the
remaining 58-km, 2½-hour trip (US$1) via
Jocotán and Camotán to El Florido, the
village on the Guatemalan side of the border.
Vilma buses leave Chiquimula for El Florido
at 6.30, 9, 10.30 and 11.30 am, 12.30, 1.30,
2.30, 3.30 and 4.30 pm; return buses depart
from El Florido for Chiquimula at 4, 5.30,
6.30, 7.30, 8.30 and 10.30 am, noon, and
1.30 and 3.30 pm.

After crossing the border at El Florido you
must hitch or take a Honduran minibus to
Copán village and the ruins. Refer to the
Copán section for more details.

It's easy to get back to Río Hondo junction
(35 km) from Chiquimula; just hop on any
bus heading north. From Río Hondo you can
catch buses eastward to Quiriguá and Puerto
Barrios.

You can also easily catch a bus from
Chiquimula's busy bus terminal southward
to Esquipulas (55 km, one hour, US$0.60).

ESQUIPULAS

From Chiquimula, CA-10 goes south into
the mountains where it's cooler and a bit
more comfortable. After an hour's ride
through pretty country the highway
descends into a valley ringed by mountains.
Halfway down the slope there is a mirador
(lookout) from which to get a good view. The
reason for a trip to Esquipulas is evident as
soon as you catch sight of the town: the great
Basílica de Esquipulas towers above the
town, its whiteness shining in the sun.

> Descending, the clouds were lifted, and I looked down
> upon an almost boundless plain, running from the foot
> of the Sierra, and afar off saw, standing alone in the
> wilderness, the great church of Esquipulas, like the
> Church of the Holy Sepulchre in Jerusalem, and the
> Caaba in Mecca, the holiest of temples...I had a long
> and magnificent descent to the foot of the Sierra.
> John L Stephens (1841)

History

This town may have been a place of pilgrimage even before the conquest. Legend has it
that the town takes its name from a noble
Mayan lord who ruled this region when the

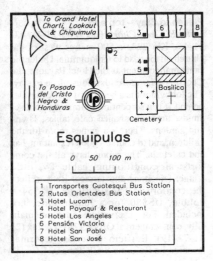

Esquipulas

0   50   100 m

1 Transportes Guotesqui Bus Station
2 Rutas Orientales Bus Station
3 Hotel Lucom
4 Hotel Poyoquf & Restaurant
5 Hotel Los Angeles
6 Pensión Victoria
7 Hotel San Pablo
8 Hotel San José

Spanish arrived, and who received them in peace rather than going to war.

With the arrival of the friars, a church was built, and in 1595 an image of Christ carved from black wood was installed in it. The steady flow of pilgrims to Esquipulas became a flood after 1737, when Pedro Pardo de Figueroa, Archbishop of Guatemala, came here on pilgrimage and went away cured of a longtime ailment. Delighted with this development, the prelate commissioned a huge new church to be built on the site. It was finished in 1758, and the pilgrimage trade has been the town's livelihood ever since. As in Chaucer's day, no one goes on a pilgrimage without spending some money. Stephens said of the church,

Every year, on the fifteenth of January, pilgrims visit it, even from Peru and Mexico; the latter being a journey not exceeded in hardship by the pilgrimage to Mecca. As in the East, 'it is not forbidden to trade during the pilgrimage'; and when there are no wars to make the roads unsafe, eighty thousand people have assembled among the mountains to barter and pay homage to 'our Lord of Esquipulas'.

Orientation
The church is your lodestone and landmark

in Esquipulas, the centre of everything. Most of the good cheap hotels are within a block of it, as are numerous small restaurants. The town's only luxury hotel is on the outskirts, along the road back to Chiquimula.

The Basilica
A grand, massive pile of stone which has resisted the power of earthquakes for almost 2½ centuries, the basilica is approached through a pretty park and up a flight of steps. The impressive façade and towers are flood-lit at night.

Inside, the devout approach El Cristo Negro with great reverence, many on their knees. Incense, the murmur of prayers and the shuffle of sandalled feet fills the air. To get a close view of the famous Black Christ you must enter the church from the side. Shuffling along quickly, you may get a good glimpse or two before being shoved onwards by the press of the crowd behind you. On Sunday, religious holidays, and especially during the festival around 15 January, the press of devotees is intense.

When you leave the church and descend the steps through the park, notice the vendors selling straw hats decorated with artificial flowers and stitched with the name 'Esquipulas'. Just as the devout Muslim grows a beard or takes on the title of Hajji after making the pilgrimage to Mecca, so Central Americans who have seen the Black Christ at Esquipulas buy a flowered hat to let their neighbours know of their pilgrimage.

Places to Stay
Most of the hotels in town have religious names: *Los Angeles* (the angels), *San José* (St Joseph), *Posada del Cristo Negro*, etc. Most are fairly high in price and not especially high in quality; this is a sellers' market because of the press of pilgrims. On holidays and during the annual festival every hotel in town is filled, whatever the price; weekends are fairly busy as well. Numerous cheap hotels are very near the basilica. The two middle-range places are on the outskirts, best reached by private car.

Places to Stay – bottom end

The town's cheap hotels rent tiny, claustrophobic rooms at prices higher than elsewhere in Guatemala. *Hotel San José*, at the northeast corner of the park, is typical, renting tiny waterless rooms for US$1.50 per person, or rooms with showers for US$2.50 per person. *Hotel San Pablo* and *Pensión Victoria*, on the north side of the park, are similar, as are the *Hotel El Ángel* and *Hotel Lucam*.

Hotel Los Angeles (☎ (9) 43-12-54), 2a Avenida 11-94, Zona 1, at the south-west corner of the park, is only a few steps from the church. The hotel's 39 rooms are arranged around a bright inner courtyard, and are kept clean and shiny. Though they are simple, they are not cheap because this is Esquipulas, and the Los Angeles is right next to the church. Doubles without bath cost US$7, or US$10 with bath.

The 34-room *Hotel Montecristo* (☎ (9) 43-14-53), 3a Avenida 9-12, Zona 1, is about the same, though a shade more expensive, with single rooms for US$11, doubles for US$15, triples for US$19, all with private bath.

Places to Stay – middle

Hotel Payaquí (☎ (9) 43-11-43, 43-13-71), 2a Avenida 11-56, Zona 1, only half a block from the church, facing the park, was once the best hotel in Esquipulas, and is still the best in the town centre. Its 40 rooms with bath are still well kept, and the hotel boasts a swimming pool, a car park and a restaurant with a view of the park. As with all Esquipulas hotels, it's priced high at US$23 a double.

Hotel Posada del Cristo Negro (☎ (9) 43-14-82), Carretera Internacional a Honduras Km 224, is two km from the church, out of town on the way to Honduras. It's a lavish, well-kept place by Guatemalan standards, with broad green lawns, a pretty swimming pool, a mirador, a children's playroom (Mundo Infantil) and a large dining room. In the 1960s, this might have been Guatemala's best country-club resort. Comfortable rooms with private bath and TV cost US$18 a double. You get more for your money here.

Places to Stay – top end

Hotel El Gran Chortí (☎ (9) 43-13-71, 43-11-43), Km 222, is 500 metres west of the church on the road to Chiquimula. Under the same management as the Hotel Payaquí, the Chortí is a far more luxurious place to stay. The lobby floor is a hectare of black marble; behind it is a serpentine swimming pool set amidst umbrella-shaded café tables, lawns and gardens. There's a games room for the children, and of course a good restaurant, bar and cafeteria. The rooms have all the comforts: air-conditioning, cable TV, little fridge, telephone and terrace. Rates reflect the comforts: US$45 a single, US$54 a double, US$80 for a junior suite, tax included. For reservations in Guatemala City, contact them at Office 124 (☎ & fax (2) 31-71-49), Edificio Galerías Reforma, Avenida La Reforma 8-60, Zona 9.

Places to Eat

As with hotels, so with restaurants. All are more expensive than in other parts of Guatemala. Low-budget restaurants are clustered at the north end of the park where hungry pilgrims can find them readily. All of the middle-range and top-end hotels have their own dining rooms.

Getting There & Away

Rutas Orientales (☎ (2) 53-72-82, 51-21-60), 19 Calle 8-18, Zona 1 in Guatemala City, has buses departing every half an hour from 4 am to 6 pm, with stops at El Rancho, Río Hondo, Zacapa and Chiquimula. The 222-km, four-hour trip costs US$2.75. If you're going to Copán, take any bus as far as Chiquimula and switch to a Transportes Vilma bus there. See the Chiquimula section for details.

COPÁN

The ancient city of Copán, 12 km from the Guatemalan border in Honduras, is one of the most outstanding Mayan achievements, ranking with Tikal, Chichén Itzá and Uxmal in splendour. To fully appreciate Mayan art and culture you must visit Copán for at least a few hours, and preferably overnight. This can be done on a long day trip by private car,

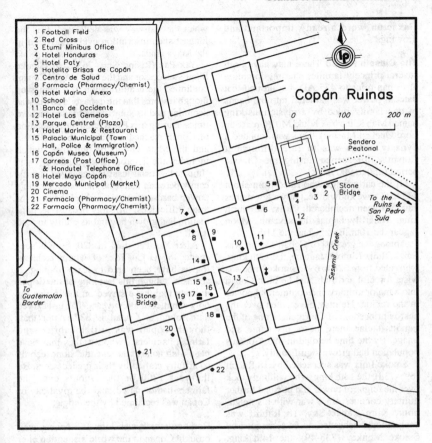

Copán Ruinas

1 Football Field
2 Red Cross
3 Etumi Minibus Office
4 Hotel Honduras
5 Hotel Paty
6 Hotelito Brisas de Copán
7 Centro de Salud
8 Farmacia (Pharmacy/Chemist)
9 Hotel Marina Anexo
10 School
11 Banco de Occidente
12 Hotel Los Gemelos
13 Parque Central (Plaza)
14 Hotel Marina & Restaurant
15 Palacio Municipal (Town
   Hall, Police & Immigration)
16 Copán Museo (Museum)
17 Correos (Post Office)
   & Hondutel Telephone Office
18 Hotel Maya Copán
19 Mercado Municipal (Market)
20 Cinema
21 Farmacia (Pharmacy/Chemist)
22 Farmacia (Pharmacy/Chemist)

0   100   200 m

Sendero Peatonal

Stone Bridge

To the Ruins & San Pedro Sula

Sesemil Creek

To Guatemalan Border

Stone Bridge

public bus or organised tour, but it's better to take two days, staying the night in the village of Copán Ruinas. If you must see Copán in a day, make your base at Río Hondo, Chiquimula or Esquipulas.

History

Early Times Farmers moved into the Copán valley about 1000 BC, enticed by the fertile riverbed land and the reliable supply of fresh water from the Río Copán. Located near important trade routes, Copán must have had significant commercial activity since early times, though little archaeological evidence of this has been found.

In fact, excavations at Copán have yielded surprisingly few clues to the life of these Copanecs between the time when the earliest farmers arrived and the beginning of the Classic period around 450 or 500 AD. There are a few artefacts which suggest that the Copanecs had some trading relationship with the Olmecs of Mexico and/or the Olmecoid peoples of Guatemala's Pacific Slope. But it's surprising to find so little evidence from the Late Preclassic period, when the Mayan ceremonial centres at El Mirador, Tikal and

Uaxactún were already important and growing.

The Classic Period There may have been several princely families sharing dominion at Copán prior to 435 AD, but around that date all power was gathered into the hands of one family ruled by a mysterious king named Mah K'ina Yax K'uk' Mo' (Great Sun Lord Quetzal Macaw). Thus was founded a dynasty which was to rule throughout Copán's florescence during the Classic period (250 to 900 AD).

Of the early kings who ruled from about 435 to 628 we know little. Only a few names have yet been deciphered: Cu Ix, the fourth king, Waterlily Jaguar the seventh, Moon Jaguar the 10th, Butz' Chan the 11th.

Among the greatest of Copán's kings was Smoke Imix (Smoke Jaguar), the 12th king, who ruled from 628 to 695. Smoke Imix was wise, forceful and rich, and he built Copán into a major military and commercial power in the region. He may have taken over the nearby princedom of Quiriguá, as one of the famous stelae there bears his name and image. By the time he died in 695, Copán's population had grown significantly.

Smoke Imix was succeeded by 18 Rabbit (695-738), the 13th king, who willingly took over the reigns of power and pursued further military conquest. In a war with his neighbour, King Cauac Sky, 18 Rabbit was captured and beheaded, to be succeeded by Smoke Monkey (738-49), the 14th king. Smoke Monkey's short reign left little mark on Copán.

In 749, Smoke Monkey was succeeded by his son Smoke Shell (749-63), one of Copán's greatest builders. Smoke Shell, the 15th king, who may have been Copán's Justinian, commissioned the construction of the city's most famous and important monument, the great Hieroglyphic Stairway which climbs the side of Temple 26. The grandeur of his works may have been meant to resurrect the glory – and thus the power – of the reign of Smoke Imix. The stairway immortalises the achievements of the dynasty from its establishment until 755,

when the stairway was dedicated. It is the longest such inscription ever discovered in the Maya lands.

Yax Pac (Rising Sun; 763-820), Smoke Shell's successor and the 16th king of Copán, continued the beautification of Copán even though it seems that the dynasty's power was declining and its subjects had fallen on hard times. During Yax Pac's reign the population of Copán reached a peak of about 20,000, and the Main Group of buildings, which includes the Hieroglyphic Stairway, was 'finished' – or at least not changed significantly between that time and today. Copán's power base crumbled, perhaps because of trade difficulties, probably because its population had grown beyond its ability to feed itself.

After Yax Pac died in 820, he was succeeded by U Cit Tok, of whom archaeologists have been able to learn nothing. It seems as though this last king of the Copán dynasty may have stayed on the throne for only a matter of a few years. The last carved date found at Copán is 822. After that, though Copán was still inhabited and farmed, its rulers – whoever they may have been – left none of the splendid stone records so artfully crafted by their predecessors. By the year 1200 or thereabouts even the farmers had departed, and the royal city of Copán was reclaimed by the jungle.

Rediscovery It was John L Stephens who brought Copán to the world's attention after his visit in the winter of 1841. Stephens relates a story of the Spanish conquest: the ruler of this region, named Copán Calel, was the same one who had received the Spanish peacefully at Esquipulas, which was then under his control. When the Spanish let him know that he was about to be out of a job, Copán Calel reconsidered his earlier benevolence and retreated to Copán (probably close to, but not in, the ruins) to defend his rule. The Spanish attacked, and after a long, fierce battle, they were victorious.

After the conquest, though the ruins at Copán were known, they were ignored. Few good Catholics wanted anything to do with the *ídolos* (idols) that stood in the dense jungle. When Stephens and his colleague Frederick Catherwood arrived to see the idols, they knew that Copán was one of the most significant archaeological sites in all of the Americas.

The jungle growth was thick, the work difficult. 'We could not see ten yards before us, and never knew what we should stumble upon next.' They saw a bit of sculpture buried in the earth.

I leaned over with breathless anxiety while the Indians worked, and an eye, an ear, a foot, or a hand was disentombed; and when the machete rang against the chiselled stone, I pushed the Indians away, and cleared out the loose earth with my hands. The beauty of the sculpture, the solemn stillness of the woods, disturbed only by the scrambling of monkeys and the chattering of parrots, the desolation of the city, and the mystery that hung over it, all created an interest higher, if possible, than I had ever felt among the ruins of the Old World.

After carefully studying and drawing as many stelae, 'altars' and glyphs as possible, Stephens approached the lessor of the land, Don Jose Maria, with an offer to buy the three years remaining on the lease. Stephens knew that as soon as he wrote about Copán, European explorers would come, buy the ruins, and ship them to the great Continental museums. In the three years left of the lease he proposed to explore the ruins fully, ship them to New York first, and to establish a 'great national museum of American antiquities'.

The reader is perhaps curious to know how old cities sell in Central America. Like other articles of trade, they are regulated by the quantity in market, and the demand; but, not being staple articles, like cotton and indigo, they were held at fancy prices, and at that time were dull of sale. I paid fifty dollars for Copan. There was never any difficulty about price. I offered that sum, for which Don Jose Maria thought me only a fool; if I had offered more, he would probably have considered me something worse.

Needless to say, Stephens never prosecuted his claim to Copán, and the city was unclaimed when the English archaeologist Alfred P Maudslay came to do the first sci-

entific investigation of it in 1885. Later research and preservation work was carried out by the Peabody Museum of Harvard University, the Carnegie Institution of Washington, and the Instituto Hondureño de Antropología y Historia.

Orientation & Information

There are two Copáns, the village and the ruins; the village is about 11 km east of the Guatemala-Honduras border. Confusingly, the village is named Copán Ruinas, though the actual ruins are one km east of the village. Minibuses from the border will usually take you onward to the ruins after a stop in the village. If not, there is a footpath *(sendero peatonal)* alongside the road; the walk is a pretty one, past several stelae and unexcavated mounds.

Crossing the Border Allow at least half an hour for border formalities; the border is open from 7 am to 6 pm. Moneychangers will approach you on both sides of the border willing to change Guatemalan quetzals for Honduran lempiras or either for US dollars. The lempira is worth about a third of a US dollar (HL1 = US$0.35). Though quetzals and US dollars may be accepted at some establishments in the village of Copán Ruinas, the clerks at the ruins and the museum feel more comfortable accepting only Honduran currency. You will also have an easier time paying for your minibus ride from the border to the village if you have lempiras. You might want to change at least US$10 into lempiras to pay for customs fees, the minibus ride to the village and return, lunch, and the entrance to the ruins and the museum. If you plan to stay the night, change more.

You must present your passport and tourist card to the Guatemalan immigration and customs authorities, pay a fee of US$1, then cross the border and do the same thing with the Honduran authorities. If you just want a short-term permit to enter Honduras and plan to go only as far as Copán, tell this to the Honduran immigration officer and he will charge you a fee of US$3. With such a permit you cannot go farther than the ruins and you must leave Honduras by the same route. If you want to travel farther in Honduras, ask for a standard visa, which may take a bit more time.

When you return through this border point you must again pass through both sets of immigration and customs and pay the fees. The Guatemalan immigration officer should give you your old tourist card back without charging the full fee for a new one. He'll just stamp 'cancelado' over the exit stamp.

Those driving cars into Honduras will have to pay several other small charges, one of which is for the *fumigación* (insecticide-spraying) of your vehicle to kill Mediterranean flies, the scourge of fruit crops. You should also allow a bit more time if you're bringing a car through.

On the Honduran side of the border are several little cookshacks where you can get simple food and cool drinks while waiting for a minibus to leave.

Visiting the Ruins

The archaeological site is open daily from 8 am to 4 pm; admission costs about US$1.50. The Visitors' Centre (Centro de Visitantes) building at the entrance to the ruins holds the ticket seller, a theatre featuring free audiovisual shows in English, and a bookshop. Nearby are a patio restaurant (*La Cafetería*) with a counter at which you can buy snacks and cold drinks, and souvenir and handicrafts shops in *La Casa del Turista*. Cheaper food is available across the road at the *Comedor Mayapán*. There's a picnic area along the path to the Principal Group of ruins. A nature trail (*sendero natural*) enters the forest several hundred metres from the Visitors' Centre.

You can camp at the ruins, outside the fence; water and toilets are available.

There are at least 4500 mounds containing ruins in the Copán Valley, 3500 of them in the 24 sq km immediately surrounding the Principal Group. Besides the Principal Group, there are two other important concentrations of ruins, El Bosque Residential Zone to the south-west and Las Sepulturas Residential Zone to the east; only Las Sepulturas is open to visitors.

The Principal Group

The Principal Group of ruins is about 400 metres beyond the Visitors' Centre across well-kept lawns, through a gate in a strong fence and down shady avenues of trees.

Stelae of the Great Plaza The path leads to the Great Plaza and what archaeologist and art historian Linda Schele has termed 'a forest of kings' – a 'grove' of huge, intricately carved stelae portraying the rulers of Copán. To the Maya, a stela was reminiscent of a tree, and trees had special religious and political significance as symbols of power and greatness. Only Quiriguá has a comparable collection of great stelae, and even those did not approach the delicate and sensitive high relief renderings of the works at Copán. Most of Copán's best stelae date from 613 to 738, during the reigns of Smoke Imix (628-95) and 18 Rabbit (695-738). All seem to have originally been painted; a few traces of red paint survive on Stela C. Many stelae had vaults beneath or beside them in which sacrifices and offerings could be placed.

Many of the stelae on the Great Plaza portray King 18 Rabbit, including Stelae A, B and 4. Perhaps the most beautiful stela in the Great Plaza is Stela A (731 AD), now in danger of crumbling because of centuries of exposure to the elements. Nearby and almost equal in beauty are Stela 4 (731), Stela B (731), depicting 18 Rabbit upon his accession to the throne, and Stela C (782) with a turtle-shaped altar in front; this last stela has figures on both sides. Stela E (614), erected on top of Structure 1 on the west side of the Great Plaza, is among the oldest stelae.

Stela D (736), at the northern end of the Great Plaza at the base of Structure 2, also portrays King 18 Rabbit. On its back are two columns of hieroglyphs; at its base is an altar with fearsome representations of Chac, the rain god. In front of the altar is the burial place of Dr John Owen, an archaeologist

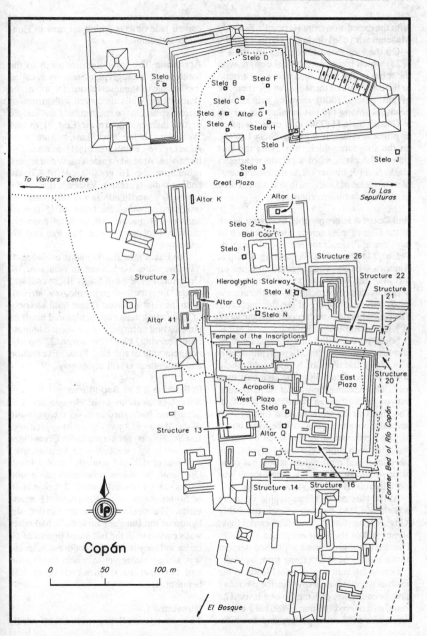

To Visitors' Centre

Stela D

Stela E

Stela B

Stela F

Stela C

Stela 4

Altar G

Stela A

Stela H

Stela I

Stela J

Stela 3

Great Plaza

To Las Sepulturas

Altar K

Altar L

Stela 2

Ball Court

Stela 1

Structure 26

Structure 7

Structure 22

Hieroglyphic Stairway

Structure 21

Stela M

Altar O

Stela N

Altar 41

Temple of the Inscriptions

Structure 20

East Plaza

Acropolis

West Plaza

Stela P

Structure 13

Altar Q

Former Bed of Río Copán

Structure 14

Structure 16

Copán

0   50   100 m

El Bosque

with the expedition from Harvard's Peabody Museum who died during the work in 1893.

On the east side of the plaza are Stela F (721) which has a more lyrical design, with the robes of the main figure flowing around to the other side of the stone, where there are glyphs. Altar G (800), showing twin serpent heads, is among the last monuments carved at Copán. Stela H (730) may depict a queen or princess rather than a king. Stela 1 (692), on the structure which runs along the east side of the plaza, is of a person wearing a mask. Stela J, farther off to the east, resembles the stelae of Quiriguá in that it is covered in glyphs, not human figures.

Ball Court & Hieroglyphic Stairway South of the Great Plaza, across what is known as the Central Plaza, is the ball court *(Juego de Pelota*;731), second largest in Central America. The one you see is the third one on this site; the other two smaller ones were buried by this construction. Note the macaw heads carved at the top of the sloping walls. The central marker in the court was the work of King 18 Rabbit.

South of the ball court is Copán's most famous monument, the Hieroglyphic Stairway (743), the work of King Smoke Shell. Today it's protected from the elements by a roof. This lessens the impact of its beauty, but you can still get an idea of how it looked. The flight of 63 steps bears a history – in several thousand glyphs – of the royal house of Copán; the steps are bordered by ramps inscribed with more reliefs and glyphs. The story inscribed on the steps is still not completely understood because the stairway was partially ruined and the stones jumbled.

At the base of the Hieroglyphic Stairway is Stela M (756), bearing a figure (probably King Smoke Shell) in a feathered cloak; glyphs tell of the solar eclipse in that year. The altar in front shows a plumed serpent with a human head emerging from its jaws.

Beside the stairway, a tunnel leads to the tomb of a nobleman, a royal scribe who may have been the son of King Smoke Imix. The tomb, discovered in June 1989, held a treasure trove of painted pottery and beautiful carved jade objects which are now in Honduran museums.

Acropolis The lofty flight of steps to the south of the Hieroglyphic Stairway is called the Temple of the Inscriptions. On top of the stairway, the walls are carved with groups of hieroglyphs. On the south side of the Temple of the Inscriptions are the East Plaza and West Plaza. In the West Plaza, be sure to see Altar Q (776), among the most famous sculptures here. Around its sides, carved in superb relief, are the 16 great kings of Copán, ending with its creator, Yax Pac. Behind the altar was a sacrificial vault in which archaeologists discovered the bones of 15 jaguars and several macaws which were probably sacrificed to the glory of Yax Pac and his ancestors.

The East Plaza also contains evidence of Yax Pac – his tomb, beneath Structure 18. Unfortunately, the tomb was discovered and looted long before archaeologists arrived. Both the East and West Plazas hold a variety of fascinating stelae and sculptured heads of humans and animals. For the most elaborate relief carving, climb Structure 22 on the northern side of the East Plaza. Excavation and restoration is still under way.

El Bosque & Las Sepulturas

Recent excavations at El Bosque and Las Sepulturas have shed light on the daily life of the Maya of Copán during its golden age. Las Sepulturas, connected to the Great Plaza by a causeway, may have been the residential area where rich and powerful nobles lived. One huge, luxurious residential compound seems to have housed some 250 people in 40 or 50 buildings arranged around 11 courtyards. The principal structure, called the House of the Bacabs ('officials'), had outer walls carved with the full-sized figures of 10 males in fancy feathered headdresses; inside was a huge hieroglyphic bench. Excavation and restoration is proceeding at Las Sepulturas.

Museum

The small, well-organised and well-

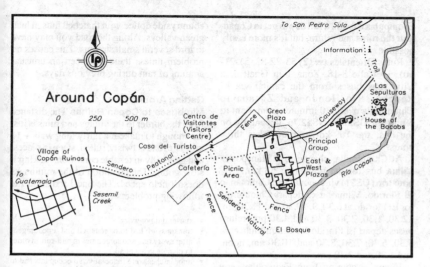

designed Copán Museo on the plaza in the village is worthwhile, if only to see Stela B, portraying King 18 Rabbit, up close and away from the blazing sun. This great builder-king was the one who unfortunately lost his head to the King of Quiriguá. Other exhibits of painted pottery, carved jade, Mayan glyphs and the calendar round are also interesting and informative. The museum is open daily from 8 am to 4 pm; admission costs US$0.35.

Places to Stay & Eat

The village of Copán Ruinas is a small, sleepy, orderly place of white stucco buildings gathered around a pleasant main square. Several inexpensive hotels can provide lodging. *Hotel y Restaurant Paty* is closest to the ruins, right on the village side of the stone bridge. Basic rooms with basic beds go for US$5 a double, or US$9 with a private shower. The restaurant here is the best place, other than the market behind the museum, to eat cheaply.

Just up the street from the Paty is *Hotelito Brisas de Copán*, a bit tidier and more cheerful, managed by a friendly señora; room prices are the same as at the Paty.

Hotel Los Gemelos, half a block south of the Paty on the way to the plaza, is the third place to look, at similar prices. *Hotel Honduras*, diagonally across the street from the Paty, is the last place to look, when all else is full.

Hotel Marina, just off the plaza, is the best in town. It doesn't look like much from the outside, but the flower-filled interior court is pleasant, the rooms sufficiently comfortable, and the dining room the best in town. A double room with private bath rents for US$13. The Marina is sometimes filled by tour groups. To reserve a room, call the Explore Honduras Travel Agency (☎ 31-10-03) in Tegucigalpa, the Honduran capital.

If the Marina is full, try the *Hotel Maya Copán*, which has usable rooms for US$9 a double with shower.

Getting There & Away

Bus It's 280 km (seven hours by bus) from Guatemala City to El Florido, the Guatemalan village on the Honduran border. If you travel by organised tour or private car it's faster and you can make the trip in one day, but it's exhausting and far too rushed. Starting from Río Hondo, Chiquimula or

Esquipulas it is still a full day to get to Copán, tour the ruins and return, but it's more easily possible.

Rutas Orientales (☎ (2) 53-72-82, 51-21-60), 19 Calle 8-18, Zona 1 in Guatemala City, runs buses from the capital via El Rancho, Río Hondo and Zacapa to Chiquimula every 30 minutes from 4 am to 6 pm, for US$2 to US$2.75, depending on the bus; the 169-km journey takes three hours.

At Chiquimula, change to a Transportes Vilma bus for the remaining 58-km, 2½-hour trip (US$1) via Jocotán and Camotán to El Florido. Vilma buses depart Chiquimula for El Florido at 6.30, 9, 10.30 and 11.30 am, 12.30, 1.30, 2.30, 3.30 and 4.30 pm; return buses depart El Florido for Chiquimula at 4, 5.30, 6.30, 7.30, 8.30 and 10.30 am, noon, and 1.30 and 3.30 pm.

If you're coming from Esquipulas, you can get off the bus at Vado Hondo, the junction of CA-10 and the road to El Florido, and wait for a bus there; but as the bus may fill up before departure, it may be just as well to go the extra eight km into Chiquimula and secure your seat before the bus pulls out.

There is no accommodation at El Florido, though you may be able to camp there.

Car If you are driving a rented car, you will have to present the Guatemalan customs authorities at the border with a special letter of permission to enter Honduras, written on the rental company's letterhead and signed and sealed by the appropriate company official. If you do not have such a letter, you'll have to leave your rental car at El Florido and continue to Copán by minibus.

Drive south from Río Hondo and Chiquimula, north from Esquipulas, and turn eastward at Vado Hondo (Km 178.5 on CA-10). A sign marked 'Vado Hondo Ruinas de Copán' marks the way on the 50-km drive from this junction to El Florido. The road is unpaved but usually in good repair and fairly fast (an average of 40 km/h). Twenty km along the way from Vado Hondo are the Chorti Maya villages of Jocotán and Camotán set amidst mountainous tropical

countryside dotted with thatched huts in lush green valleys. Along the road you may have to ford several small streams. This causes no problem unless there has been an unusual amount of rain during previous days.

Getting Around
Minibuses to Copán Ruinas The distance from the border to the village and ruins is just far enough to make it a fairly long walk – 11 km. The road is twisty, rutted, steep in places, and generally in terrible condition, making it slow going. The condition of the minibuses doesn't help speed. The one I took had the following problems:

- starter did not work
- transmission had to be repaired and 'encouraged' after every run, and sometimes in mid-run, in order to change gears at all
- door latches were inoperative so occupants had to hold the doors closed at all times
- springs and shock absorbers neither sprang nor absorbed
- engine was prone to quit abruptly for no apparent reason
- top speed was 15 km/h.

Walking might be just as fast, except on the downhill portions where the minibus's lack of effective brakes helped get us to the village somewhat faster. The fare is US$1 each way. Minibuses and trucks depart from the border periodically throughout the day. You probably won't have to wait more than 30 or 45 minutes – probably less – to catch one.

To return to the border from the village, go to the Etumi Minibus office next to the Hotel Honduras to find out when the next minibus will depart.

QUIRIGUÁ
From Copán it is only some 50 km to Quiriguá as the crow flies, but the lay of the land, the international border and the condition of the roads makes it a journey of 175 km. Like Copán, Quiriguá is famed for its intricately carved stelae. Unlike Copán, the gigantic brown sandstone stelae at Quiriguá rise as high as 10.5 metres. Standing like

sentinels in a quiet tropical park, the stelae of Quiriguá inspire thoughts and questions about the ancient Maya – who they were, how they lived, and what made them erect these tremendous monuments.

A visit to Quiriguá is easy if you have your own transport, more difficult but certainly not impossible if you're travelling by bus. From Río Hondo junction it's 67 km along the Carretera al Atlantico to the village of Los Amates, where there is a hotel and restaurant. The village of Quiriguá is 1.5 km east of Los Amates, and the turn-off to the ruins is another 1.5 km to the east. Following the access road south from the Carretera al Atlantico, it's 3.4 km through banana groves to the archaeological site.

History

Quiriguá's history parallels that of Copán, of which it was a dependency during much of the Classic period. Of the three sites in this area, only the present archaeological park is of interest.

The location lent itself to the carving of giant stelae. Beds of brown sandstone in the nearby Río Motagua had cleavage planes suitable for cutting large pieces. Though soft when first cut, the sandstone dried hard in the air. With Copán's expert artisans nearby for guidance, Quiriguá's stonecarvers were ready for greatness. All they needed was a great leader to inspire them – and to pay for the carving of the huge stelae.

That leader was Cauac Sky (725-84), who decided that Quiriguá should no longer be under the control of Copán. In a war with his former suzerain, Cauac Sky took King 18 Rabbit of Copán prisoner in 737 and later had him beheaded. Independent at last, Cauac Sky commissioned his stonecutters to go to work, and for the next 38 years they turned out giant stelae and zoomorphs dedicated to the glory of King Cauac Sky.

Cauac Sky was followed by his son Sky Xul (784-800), who lost his throne to a usurper, Jade Sky. This last great king of Quiriguá continued the building boom initiated by Cauac Sky, reconstructing Quiriguá's Acropolis on a grander scale.

Quiriguá remained unknown until John L Stephens arrived in 1840. Impressed by its great monuments, he lamented the world's lack of interest in them:

Of one thing there is no doubt: a large city once stood there; its name is lost, its history unknown; and...no account of its existence has ever before been published. For centuries it has lain as completely buried as if covered with the lava of Vesuvius. Every traveller from Yzabal to Guatimala has passed within three hours of it; we ourselves had done the same; and yet there it lay, like the rock-built city of Edom, unvisited, unsought, and utterly unknown.

Stephens tried to buy the ruined city in order to have its stelae shipped to New York, but the owner assumed that Stephens, being a diplomat, was negotiating on behalf of the US government, and that the government would pay. The owner, Señor Payes, quoted an extravagant price, and the deal was never made.

Between 1881 and 1894 excavations were carried out by Alfred P Maudslay. In the early 1900s all the land around Quiriguá was sold to the United Fruit Company and turned into banana groves. The mighty and (some would say) malignant company is gone, but the bananas and Quiriguá remain. Restoration of the site was carried out by the University of Pennsylvania in the 1930s.

The Ruins

The beautiful park-like archaeological zone is open from 7 am to 5 pm daily; admission costs US$0.30. There's a small stand selling cold drinks and snacks near the entrance. You'd do well to bring your own picnic.

Despite the sticky heat and (sometimes) the bothersome mosquitos, Quiriguá is a wonderful place. The giant stelae on the Great Plaza are all much more worn than those at Copán. To impede their further deterioration, each has been covered by a thatched roof. The roofs cast shadows which make it difficult to examine the carving closely, and almost impossible to get a good photograph. But somehow this does little to inhibit one's sense of awe.

Seven of the stelae, designated A, C, D, E,

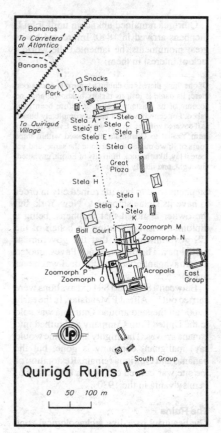

Quirigá Ruins

0   50   100 m

F, H and J, were built during the reign of Cauac Sky and carved with his image. Stela E is the largest Mayan stela known, standing some eight metres above ground, with another three metres or so buried in the earth. It weighs almost 60,000 kg. Note the exuberant, elaborate headdresses, the beards on some of the figures (an oddity in Mayan art), the staffs of office held in the kings' hands, and the glyphs on the stelae's sides.

At the far end of the plaza is the Acropolis, far less impressive than the one at Copán. At its base are several zoomorphs, blocks of stone carved to resemble real and mythic creatures. Frogs, tortoises, jaguars and serpents were favourite subjects. The low zoomorphs can't compete with the towering stelae in impressiveness, but as works of art, imagination and mythic significance, the zoomorphs are superb.

Places to Stay & Eat

There are two places to stay in the immediate vicinity. In the village of Quiriguá, 700 metres south of the highway, is the tidy *Hotel Royal*, a Caribbean-style wooden structure with numerous large, high-ceilinged, well-ventilated rooms with concrete floors on which are arranged four or five beds, a cold-water washbasin and shower, and a toilet, perhaps with a seat. The walls are painted green, there are numerous coat hooks for clothing storage, and sometimes there is a small table. Beds cost US$2 each; doubles with private shower cost US$8.50. If business is slow, you may be able to rent one of the large bathless rooms entirely to yourselves for US$3 a double. Though severely plain, the rooms are clean and the family which runs the place is friendly enough. A little comedor here is the place for basic meals.

At Los Amates, three km west of Quiriguá village, is the eight-room *Hotel y Restaurante Santa Monica*, next to the Texaco fuel station. Though a bit noisy, the price is right, at US$6 for a double room with fan and private shower. About 100 metres east of the Texaco station is the *Ranchón Chileño*, the best restaurant in the area, providing good, filling meals for about US$4.50, light meals for half that much.

Hotel Doña María, Carretera al Atlantico Km 181, at Doña María Bridge, is 24 km west of Los Amates. It looks quite forlorn from the front, but behind the sad façade is an airy dining and sitting area with a fine view of the river and the emerald-green grass and tall palm trees which line its banks. The rooms here are musty, dark, and claustrophobic, but if you spend all of your waking hours swimming in the river, hiking in the mountains, and touring Quiriguá, it might be worth it. Rooms cost US$2 per person in a double with cold-water private bath.

Getting There & Away
The turn-off to Quiriguá is 205 km (four hours) east of Guatemala City, 70 km east of the Río Hondo junction, 43 km west of the road to Flores in El Petén, and 90 km west of Puerto Barrios. Transportes Litegua (☎ (2) 2-75-78), 15 Calle 10-42, Zona 1 in Guatemala City, has regular buses from the capital to Puerto Barrios every hour from 6 am to 5 pm, and Pullman express buses (faster and more comfortable) at 10 am and 5 pm. Stops are at El Rancho, Teculután, Río Hondo and Los Amates (Quiriguá); the fare is US$3.50 or US$4 if you go all the way to Puerto Barrios. The driver will usually oblige if you ask to be dropped off at the access road to the archaeological site rather than three km west at Los Amates.

Waiting at the junction of the Carretera al Atlantico and the Quiriguá access road are men on motorbikes. They run a primitive shuttle service from the highway to the archaeological site and the banana company headquarters, charging a quetzal or two for the 3.4 km ride. You cannot depend upon them to take you back from the archaeological site to the highway unless you establish a time in advance.

Getting Around
If you're staying in the village of Quiriguá or Los Amates and walking to and from the archaeological site, you can take a shortcut along the railway branch line which goes from the village through the banana fields, crossing the access road very near the entrance to the archaeological site.

LAKE IZABAL
This large lake to the north-west of the Carretera al Atlantico has hardly been developed for tourism at all. Head north-west from La Ruidosa junction (Carretera al Atlantico Km 245) along the road to Flores in El Petén, and after 34 km you reach the village of Río Dulce, also known as El Relleno. From beneath the bridge you can hire a motorboat

(you must bargain for a price) to take you to the Castillo de San Felipe, the region's major tourist attraction. Boat owners can also take you downriver to El Golfete, Chocón-Machacas Nature Reserve and Lívingston, but prices for the hire of the boat will be higher than if you do the trip from Lívingston. For details of the trip, see the Lívingston section.

Castillo de San Felipe
The fortress of San Felipe de Lara, about one km west of the bridge, was built in 1652 to keep pirates from looting the villages and commercial caravans of Izabal. Though it deterred the buccaneers a bit, a pirate force captured and burnt the fortress in 1686. By the end of the next century, pirates had disappeared from the Caribbean and the fort's sturdy walls served as a prison. Then it became a tourist attraction.

Places to Stay & Eat
In Río Dulce near the bridge are several cheap hotels. *Hotel Marilú*, on the north side of the bridge, is typical, charging US$2 per person in rooms without private bath. More expensive and comfortable resort hotels are just a few km east on the shores of the river.

Touricentro Marimonte (☎ (9) 47-85-85), on the south bank of the river by the road to Tikal, has a country-club layout with expansive lawns, a wooden main lodge, and little cabañas with two to four beds. You can rent a room in the lodge or in a cabaña for US$30 a single, US$44 a double. Meals are served in the dining room. On weekends the Marimonte is liable to be quite full.

Near the Castillo, the *Hotel Don Humberto* can put you up for US$3 per person if you don't have your own camping equipment.

The Road to Flores
North across the bridge is the road into El Petén, Guatemala's vast jungle province. It's 208 km to Santa Elena and Flores, and another 65 km to Tikal. The road north of Río Dulce is in terrible condition. It's a slow, torturous, bone-jangling ride of some nine

hours to Flores. Some years ago the German government gave the Guatemalan government a grant to improve the road. Once they reached Guatemala City, those millions of Deutschmarks disappeared without a trace – and without a new road being built.

A new grant with stricter controls was approved, but at the last minute the Germans withheld the money, fearing that an improved road would encourage the migration of farmers into El Petén.

The forest here is disappearing at an alarming rate, falling to the machetes of subsistence farmers using the ancient slash-and-burn method of cultivation. Sections of forest are felled and burnt off, crops are grown for a few seasons until the fragile jungle soil is exhausted, and then the farmer moves deeper into the forest to slash and burn new fields. Cattle ranchers, slashing and burning the forest to make pasture, have also contributed to the damage.

Reportedly, the grant for a new road will be approved and the money forthcoming after the Guatemalan government has put controls in place to prevent the destruction of the forest. The people of El Petén are being informed of the threat to their land. Within a decade the forest may either be badly compromised, or may be safely preserved for future generations, or – more likely – will remain an ecological battleground for years to come. Until the forest is safe, the road will probably remain terrible: unpaved, cratered, rutted, with crude ferries of logs to ford rivers, and few services.

Along the way to Flores there are only small jungle hamlets at which simple meals are sometimes available.

Fuentes del Norte (☎ (2) 8-60-94, 51-38-17), 17 Calle 8-46, Zona 1 in Guatemala City, runs buses from the capital to Flores departing at 1, 2, 3 and 7 am, and 11 pm on this gruelling, bone-bashing journey. Stops are made at Morales, Río Dulce, San Luis, and Poptún. The buses reach Río Dulce about five hours after departure. A one-way ticket all the way costs US$6 or US$12, depending upon the comfort (such as it is) of the bus. Those travelling by bus may find,

unfortunately, that every bus is packed full by the time it reaches Río Dulce.

If you're driving, fill your fuel tank before leaving Río Dulce, take some food and drink and start early in the morning.

PUERTO BARRIOS
Population 35,000

Heading eastward from La Ruidosa junction, the country becomes even more lush, tropical and humid until you arrive at Puerto Barrios.

The powerful United Fruit Company, which moved into Guatemala at the beginning of the 20th century, owned vast plantations in the Río Motagua Valley and many other parts of the country. The company built railways to ship its produce to the coast, and it built Puerto Barrios to put that produce onto ships sailing for New Orleans and New York. Laid out as a company town, Puerto Barrios has wide streets arranged neatly on a grid plan, and lots of Caribbean-style wood-frame houses, many on stilts.

When United Fruit's power and influence declined in the 1960s, the Del Monte company became successor to its interests. But the heyday of the imperial foreign firms was past, as was that of Puerto Barrios. A new, modern, efficient port was built a few km to the south-west at Santo Tomás de Castilla, and Puerto Barrios settled into tropical torpor.

Early in the morning, before the sun is high and the humid heat overpowering, Puerto Barrios can be a pleasant place. Children in fresh clothes scamper along the streets to school, men and women off to work greet one another with smiles and chatter. By midday the heat has settled in. In the evening the noisy bars and brothels along 9 Calle get going, and Puerto Barrios takes on an entirely different feeling.

For foreign visitors, Puerto Barrios is little more than the jumping off point for a visit to Lívingston, the fascinating enclave of Black Guatemalans on the north-western shore of the Río Dulce. As the boats for Lívingston leave at odd hours, you may find yourself staying the night in Puerto Barrios.

Orientation

Because of its spacious layout, you must walk or ride farther in Puerto Barrios to get from place to place. For instance, it's 800 metres from the bus terminal by the market to the Muelle Municipal (Municipal Boat Dock) at the foot of 12 Calle, from which boats depart for Lívingston. You are liable to be in town just to take a boat, so you may want to select a hotel because of its closeness to the dock.

Places to Stay & Eat

Motel Miami (☎ (9) 48-05-37), 3a Avenida at 12 Calle, is a relatively new place one block from the dock. Rooms are arranged around a central courtyard used as a safe car park. Rates are US$4.50 a double with private bath, US$7 a double if you want air-conditioning (which you might). If you're driving and need a safe place to leave your car while you visit Lívingston, Señora Lidia Maribel Monjarás, proprietor of the Miami, will allow you to park it in her courtyard for US$1.50 per day.

Hotel Europa (☎ (9) 48-01-27), on 8a Avenida between 8 and 9 Calles, is 1½ blocks from the cathedral and Guatel telephone office (look for the openwork cross on top of the steeple, and the Guatel signal tower). Fairly clean, pleasant and quiet, they charge US$4.50 for one of their 28 double rooms with shower. *Pensión Xelajú*, nearby at 7a Avenida and 9 Calle, charges a bit less for bathless rooms – about US$4 a double – and provides safe parking in its courtyard.

Hotel Canada, 6 Calle between 6a and 7a Avenidas, is also a good place to stay, charging US$3 per person in rooms with fans and private showers.

In a class by itself is the old *Hotel del Norte* (☎ (9) 48-00-87), 7 Calle at 1a Avenida, at the waterfront end of 7 Calle, 1200 metres from the dock (you must walk around the railway yard). In its airy dining room overlooking the Bahía de Amatique you can almost hear the echoing conversation of turn-of-the-century banana moguls, and smell their pungent cigars. Spare, simple and well kept, this is a real museum piece with 38 rooms renting for US$5 a double with shared bath (US$6.50 if you want a view of the bay), or US$10 a double with private bath. Meals are served in the dining room. Service is refined, careful and elegantly old fashioned, but the food can be otherwise. My breakfast consisted of powdered artificial orange juice (in the tropics!), tasteless coffee (in Guatemala!), and two small, dry, day-old pancakes topped with a very weird syrup substitute (in sugar cane country!).

For fancier lodgings you must go out of town. *Hotel Puerto Libre* (☎ (9) 48-04-47, 48-05-60) is at the junction of the Carretera al Atlantico, the road into Puerto Barrios, and the road to Santo Tomás de Castilla, five km from the boat dock. All 34 rooms come with private bath and air-conditioning, and are actually more comfortable than they look at first. A smiling and efficient señora and a crew of hard-working young women keep the place in excellent shape. Rates are US$16 to US$29 a single, US$22 to US$34 a double. The cheapest rooms have central air-con; the most expensive rooms have individual air-con and are located around the swimming pool. The hotel has a good restaurant – perhaps the best in town.

I have yet to come across a recommendable cheap restaurant in Puerto Barrios. If you find one among the dozen or so grubby little places, let me know. Your best bet for cheap eats might well be a shopping trip to the market.

Getting There & Away

Bus Transportes Litegua (☎ (2) 2-75-78), 15 Calle 10-42, Zona 1 in Guatemala City, has regular buses along the Carretera al Atlantico to Puerto Barrios every hour from 6 am to 5 pm, and Pullman express buses (faster and more comfortable) at 10 am and 5 pm. The 307-km journey takes 6 hours, with stops at El Rancho, Teculután, Río Hondo and Los Amates (Quiriguá); fare is US$3.50 or US$4.

Boat Boats to Lívingston depart from the Muelle Municipal at the foot of 12 Calle in Puerto Barrios at 10.30 am and 5 pm daily, arriving in Lívingston 1½ hours later; on very busy days there may be a 3 pm boat as well. Return trips from Lívingston depart at 5 am and 2 pm, with a 7 am boat on some busy days. The one-way fare is an incredible US$0.50. Get to the dock at least 30 minutes prior to departure (45 is better) in order to get a decent seat; otherwise you could end up standing the whole way. If you don't catch one of these cheap boats, try to get aboard the Belize-bound boat (see below) and take it as far as Lívingston. Otherwise you will have to haggle with a boat owner to take you across on a charter trip at a cost of perhaps US$25 to US$40.

Twice-weekly boats from Puerto Barrios to Punta Gorda in southern Belize depart at 7.30 am on Tuesday and Friday, stopping at Lívingston about 9 am. Inquire at the dock for details. If you take this boat, you must pass through Guatemalan Immigration (Migración) and Customs (Aduana) before boarding the boat. Allow some time, and have your passport and tourist card handy.

LÍVINGSTON

The Garifuna (Garinagu, or Black Carib) people of Lívingston and southern Belize are the descendants of Africans brought to the New World as slaves who escaped or were shipwrecked in the Caribbean. Intermarrying with shipwrecked sailors of other races and with the indigenous Maya, they developed a distinctive culture and language incorporating African, Mayan and European elements. They trace their roots through legend to the Honduran island of Roatan, where they were settled by the British after the Garifuna revolt of 1795.

As you come ashore in Lívingston, you will be surprised to meet Black Guatemalans who speak Spanish as well as their traditional language; some speak the musical English of Belize and the islands as well. The town – actually, village – of Lívingston is an interesting anomaly with a laid-back, very Belizean way of life, groves of coconut palms, gaily painted wooden buildings, and an economy based on fishing and tourism.

Orientation

After being in Lívingston for half an hour, you'll know where everything is. Walk up the hill from the dock along the village's main street. The fancy Hotel Tucán Dugú is on your right, several small restaurants on your left. The street off to the left at the base of the hill goes to the Casa Rosada and several other hotels. At the top of the hill another street goes left to several hotels and restaurants. There is no bank in Lívingston, and the rate of exchange for dollars offered in the shops and hotels is not particularly good, so you should come with enough quetzals to cover your stay.

Río Dulce Cruises

Lívingston is the starting point for boat rides on the Río Dulce to enjoy the tropical jungle scenery, have a swim and a picnic, and explore the Chocón-Machacas Nature Reserve, 12 km west along the river. The 7200-hectare reserve was established to protect the beautiful river landscape, the valuable mangrove swamps, and especially the manatees, or sea-cows, which inhabit the waters (both salt and fresh) of the Río Dulce and El Golfete.

There are several ways to make the voyage up the Río Dulce. A mail launch departs from Lívingston for the trip upriver every Tuesday and Friday at about 11 am, charging US$5 per passenger. Motorised dugout canoes called *cayucos* act as tour boats, taking groups of travellers upriver for

Manatee

Top: Main plaza in La Democracia, Guatemala, with Olmecoid basalt heads (TB)
Bottom: Bas-relief from the mysterious Mexican-like Cotzumalguapa culture,
        Santa Lucía Cotzumalguapa, Guatemala (TB)

Top: The basilica of Esquipulas, Guatemala (TB)
Left: Workers building a protective palapa above a stela at Quiriguá (TB)
Right: Stela A on the Great Plaza at Copán, Honduras (TB)

about US$25 or US$30 a boatload (up to four people). If you hire a native canoe for the trip, the cost could be higher. Almost anyone in Lívingston – your hotel clerk, a shop-keeper, a restaurant waiter – can tell you who's currently organising trips up the river.

Shortly after you leave Lívingston, the river enters a steep-walled gorge, its walls hung with great tangles of jungle foliage and bromeliads, the humid air noisy with the cries of tropical birds. A hot spring forces sulphurous water out at the base of the cliff, providing a delightful place for a swim.

Emerging from the gorge, the river even-tually widens into El Golfete, a lake-like body of water that presages the even vaster expanse of Lake Izabal. On the northern shore of El Golfete is the Biotopo Chocón-Machacas. The nature reserve's boat dock is good for swimming. A network of 'water trails' (boat routes around several jungle lagoons) provide ways to see the bird, animal and plant life of the reserve. A nature trail begins at the Visitors' Centre and winds its way through forests of mahogany, palm trees, and rich tropical foliage. Jaguars and tapirs live in the reserve, though your chances of seeing one are slight. The walrus-like manatees are even more elusive. These huge, shapeless, fairly ugly mammals can weigh up to a tonne, yet they glide effort-lessly beneath the calm surface of the river. Even though they are aquatic beasts with flippers rather than arms, they suckle their young.

From El Golfete and the nature reserve, some boats will continue upriver to the village of Río Dulce, where the road into El Petén crosses the river (see the Lake Izabal section). If you didn't stop to visit the Castillo de San Felipe before, now's your chance.

Las Siete Altares

Beaches in Lívingston are mostly disap-pointing, as the jungle comes right down to the water's edge in most places. Those beaches which do exist are often clogged with vegetation as well. The Seven Altars is a series of freshwater falls and pools about five km north-west of Lívingston along the shore of the Bahía de Amatique. It's a pleasant goal for a walk along the beach and a good place for a picnic and a swim. Follow the shore northwards to the mouth of a river. Ford the river, and a path into the woods leads to the falls.

Places to Stay – bottom end

Hotel Caribe, a minute's walk along the shore to the left as you come off the boat dock, is a simple, family-run place right on the water offering double rooms for US$2.50 a double (shared bath).

Casa Rosada (☎ (9) 17-11-21), another 700 metres (a five-minute walk) along the shore just past the auxiliary electric generat-ing plant, has nice little bungalows in a private compound right on the water going for US$10 a double. All three meals are served. It's a good idea to reserve in advance by phone, mail or telegram as there are only five rooms and they're often full.

Up the hill from the boat dock, on the left side of the main street is the *Hotel Río Dulce*, an authentic two-storey wood-frame Carib-bean place painted blue. Bare rooms without running water cost US$3. A bit farther along, turn left down the side street to reach the *Hotel Marina*, which is also cheap.

Turn right at the Catholic church to find the *Parador Flamingo*, on the shore of the Bahía de Amatique, with eight tidy rooms in a walled compound going for US$5 a double. Before coming to the Flamingo you pass the *Lugar Africano*, usually called the African Place, a restaurant with several rooms to rent for US$4.50 a double with common bath.

Places to Stay – middle

Amongst all this laid-back and low-priced Caribbean lodging, the 45-room *Hotel Tucán Dugú* (☎ (9) 48-15-72 to 88), just up from the boat dock on the right, is a luxurious anomaly. Modern but still definitely Carib-bean in style with lots of dark mahogany, bamboo and red tile, it has many conve-niences and comforts, including lush tropical gardens, a pretty swimming pool, and a jungle bar where you might expect to see Hemingway or Bogart. The good restaurant has fine views of the mouth of the Río Dulce. Rooms are fairly large with modern bathrooms, ceiling fans and little balconies overlooking the pool and the gardens. For this comfortable Caribbean hideaway which most of the world knows nothing about, you pay US$45 a single, US$50 a double, tax included. You can book reservations at the office (☎ (2) 32-12-59), in Guatemala City , 1a Avenida 12-77, Zona 10.

Places to Eat

Food in Lívingston is a bit more expensive than in the rest of Guatemala because most of it (except fish and coconuts) must be brought across from Puerto Barrios.

The main street is lined with little comedores, *tiendas* (shops) and *almacenes* (stores). Your best plan may be to choose the place which is currently the most popular. *Restaurant El Malecón*, just up the hill from the boat dock on the left, is airy and rustic, has good views of the water and a loyal local clientele. A full meal of Caribbean-inspired fare can be had for US$4.50. A bit farther up the hill, facing the Guatel telephone office, is the fancier *Restaurant La Cabaña*, which may not be there when you arrive as it had a 'For Sale' sign on it at my last visit. The *Tropic*, a few steps farther along on the right-hand side, is half restaurant and half shop; it's favoured by the thriftiest crowd.

Turn left just beyond the ice plant (Fábrica de Hielo) to find the *Restaurant Saby*, on the left, a typical Caribbean bamboo eatery with local music playing and meals of rice and beans and similar for US$2 to US$3. The

fancier *Restaurant Margoth*, beyond it, was empty at my last visit.

The very funky *African Place*, on the way to the Hotel Flamingo, looks like a miniature Moorish palace and serves a variety of exotic and local dishes; full meals are available for US$5 or less.

For the best (and most expensive) dining in town, head for the dining room of the Hotel Tucán Dugú. A good, complete dinner with drinks goes for US$8 to US$12, depending upon what you order and what you drink.

Entertainment

Some nights of the week, the busiest place in town, with the loudest music, is the Templo Evangélico Iglesia del Nazareno (Evangelical Church of the Nazarene), opposite the Restaurant Margoth. If Caribbean Christianity is not your idea of nightlife, check out the Happy Land bar just a bit farther along the same street, with loud reggae and cheap drinks.

Getting There & Away

The only way to get to Lívingston is by boat. You'll probably be coming from Puerto Barrios, possibly from Punta Gorda, Belize. For details, see the Puerto Barrios section.

Boats from Puerto Barrios to Punta Gorda, Belize, stop at Lívingston on Tuesday and Friday about 9 am. If you plan to catch one of these boats to Belize, be sure that you've contacted the Guatemalan Immigration (Migración) and Customs (Aduana) officials in Lívingston in advance, and have completed all necessary border formalities.

El Petén

In the dense jungle cover of Guatemala's vast north-eastern department of El Petén you may hear the squawk of parrots, the chatter of monkeys and the rustlings of strange animals moving through the bush. The landscape here is utterly different from that of Guatemala's cool mountainous highlands or its steamy Pacific Slope.

The monumental Mayan ceremonial centre at Tikal is a major stop on La Ruta Maya. The ruins of Uaxactún and Sayaxché, though not so easily accessible, are perhaps more exciting to visit for that reason. Several dozen other great cities lie hidden in El Petén's jungles, accessible only to archaeologists with airplanes...and artefact poachers with stone-cutting tools.

The battle for El Petén is raging even as you read this. Will it be left alone and preserved as one vast natural and archaeological zone? Will its forests be cut and cut by farmers and cattle ranchers until the lush green carpet of trees and vines all but disappears, as has happened just across the border in Mexico? Or will the idea of La Ruta Maya – careful environmental and archaeological preservation through managed development with economic benefits for all – triumph? The consciousness of the Petenecos is being raised, and there is some hope that the idea of La Ruta Maya may succeed. In 1990 the Guatemalan government established the one-million-hectare Maya Biosphere Reserve, including most of northern El Petén. The Guatemalan reserve adjoins the vast Calakmul Biosphere Reserve in Mexico and the Orange Jungle Reserve in Belize, forming a huge multinational reserve of over two million hectares.

There are three reasons to penetrate the forests of El Petén. Firstly, to visit Tikal, the greatest Mayan religious centre yet discovered. Secondly, to enjoy the great variety of bird life, including the rare, shy quetzal. The third reason is to see a different Guatemala, one of small farming villages and jungle hamlets, without paved roads or colonial architecture.

GETTING AROUND

The roads leading into El Petén – from the Carretera al Pacifico and from Belize – have been left in a state of bad repair. The reason is partly lack of funds and partly because better roads would encourage migration of farmers and ranchers from other areas of the country. With El Petén's forests already falling to the machete at an alarming rate, good new roads might prove disastrous. Thus road transport in El Petén is slow, bumpy, uncomfortable and sometimes unsafe. There have been several incidents of robbery of buses travelling along the roads between Río Dulce and Flores and the Belizean border at Melchor de Menchos/Benque Viejo de Carmen. For current information on the safety of travelling these roads, call your embassy or consulate in Guatemala City.

The only exception is the road connecting Flores/Santa Elena and Tikal, a good, fast asphalt road built so that tourists arriving by air in Santa Elena can proceed quickly and comfortably to Tikal, 71 km to the north-east. The Guatemalan government long ago decided to develop the adjoining towns of Flores (El Petén's departmental capital), Santa Elena and San Benito, on the shores of Lake Petén Itzá, into the tourism centre of the region. The airport, hotels and other services are here, and it is from this base that visitors can tour the region. Though there are a few small hotels at Tikal, other services are limited, and no more can be built.

FLORES, SANTA ELENA & SAN BENITO

The town of Flores (population 2000) is built on an island on Lake Petén Itzá. A causeway 500 metres long connects Flores to her sister town of Santa Elena (altitude 110 metres, population 17,000) on the lakeshore. Adjoining Santa Elena to the west is the town of San Benito (population 22,000).

Flores, being the departmental capital, is more dignified, with its church, small government building and municipal basketball court arranged around the main plaza atop the hill in the centre of the island. The narrow streets of Flores, paved in cement blocks, hold numerous small hotels and restaurants.

Santa Elena is a disorganised town of dusty unpaved streets, open drainage ditches, small hotels and restaurants. The bus station is at its centre, the airport on its eastern outskirts.

San Benito is even more disorganised, but lively with its honky-tonk bars.

The three towns actually form one large settlement. Most of the time it's referred to simply as Flores.

History

Flores was founded on an island (petén) by the Itzaes after their expulsion from Chichén Itzá, and it was named Tayasal. Though Cortés dropped in on King Canek of Tayasal in 1524 while on his way to Honduras, the meeting was peaceable. Only in March of

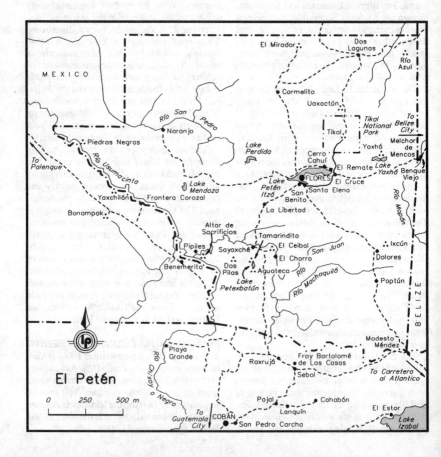

El Petén

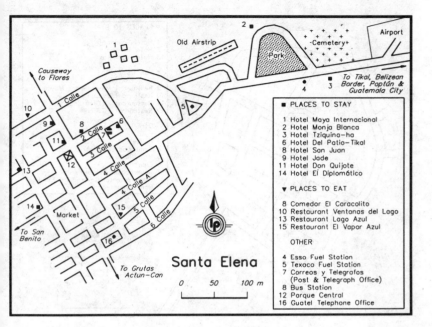

Santa Elena

■ PLACES TO STAY

1 Hotel Maya Internacional
2 Hotel Monja Blanca
3 Hotel Tziquina-ha
6 Hotel Del Patio-Tikal
8 Hotel San Juan
9 Hotel Jade
11 Hotel Don Quijote
14 Hotel El Diplomático

▼ PLACES TO EAT

8 Comedor El Caracolito
10 Restaurant Ventanas del Lago
13 Restaurant Lago Azul
15 Restaurant El Vapor Azul

OTHER

4 Esso Fuel Station
5 Texaco Fuel Station
7 Correos y Telegrafos
  (Post & Telegraph Office)
8 Bus Station
12 Parque Central
16 Guatel Telephone Office

1697 did the Spanish finally bring the Maya of Tayasal forcibly under their control.

At the time of its conquest, Flores was perhaps the last major functioning Mayan ceremonial centre, covered in pyramids and temples, with idols in evidence everywhere. The God-fearing Spanish soldiers destroyed these 'pagan' buildings. Today when you visit Flores you will see not a trace of them, although the modern town is doubtless built on the ruins and foundations of Mayan Tayasal.

When Tayasal was conquered, its Mayan citizens fled into the jungle, giving rise to the myth of a 'lost' Mayan city. John L Stephens, as usual, described it best in 1843:

...in fact, it is not difficult for me to believe that in the wild region beyond the Lake of Peten, never yet penetrated by a white man, Indians are now living as they did before the discovery of America; and it is almost a part of this belief that they are using and occupying adoratorios and temples like those now seen in ruins in the wilderness of Yucatan.

Orientation

The airport is on the eastern outskirts of Santa Elena, about one km from the causeway connecting Santa Elena and Flores. Each bus company has its own terminal, but the main one of interest to foreign travellers is the one in the Hotel San Juan near the causeway in Santa Elena.

Hotels in Flores and Santa Elena are in the bottom-end and middle price ranges. Apart from El Gringo Perdido (which is also in these ranges), hotels several km out of town, along the lakeshore, are all top end.

Information

There is an INGUAT tourist information desk at the airport, open generally from 8 am to 5 pm.

Money Banco Hipotecario in Flores is open from 8.30 am to 2.30 pm, Monday to Friday (till 3.30 pm on Friday). You may also be able to change money at your hotel.

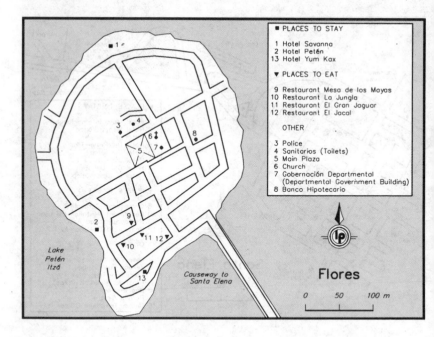

PLACES TO STAY

1 Hotel Savanna
2 Hotel Petén
13 Hotel Yum Kax

PLACES TO EAT

9 Restaurant Mesa de los Mayas
10 Restaurant La Jungla
11 Restaurant El Gran Jaguar
12 Restaurant El Jacal

OTHER

3 Police
4 Sanitarios (Toilets)
5 Main Plaza
6 Church
7 Gobernación Departmental
(Departmental Government Building)
8 Banco Hipotecario

Lake
Petén
Itzá

Causeway to
Santa Elena

Flores

0   50   100 m

Post & Telecommunications The Post and
Telegraph office (Correos y Telegrafos) is
just west of the Hotel del Patio in Santa
Elena.

Grutas Actun-Can

The caves of Actun-Can are only a short walk
south of Santa Elena. Also called La Cueva
de la Serpiente (The Cave of the Serpent),
the caverns are of the standard limestone
variety. No serpents are in evidence, but the
cave-keeper will turn on the lights for you
after you've paid the admission fee
(US$0.35), and may give you the rundown
on the cave formations, which suggest
animals, humans and various scenes.

Lake Petén Itzá

Boat rides on the lake are a major activity.
The people at the bus ticket desk in the Hotel
San Juan can make the arrangements for you,
or your hotel may be willing to do it, or you
can haggle with a boat owner yourself. Stops
on a tour might include the lagoons at La
Guitarra and Petencito, the settlements of
San Andrés and San José, and of course the
Biotopo Cerro Cahuí.

Biotopo Cerro Cahuí

At the north-east end of Lake Petén Itzá,
about 43 km from Santa Elena, the Biotopo
Cerro Cahuí covers 651 hectares of hot,
humid, subtropical forest. Within the reserve
are mahogany, cedar, ramon, broom, sapodilla and cohune palm trees, as well as many
species of lianas (climbing plants), bromeliads (air plants), ferns and orchids. The ramon
trees yielded fodder to the ancient Maya, and
the hard wood of the sapodilla was used in
temple door lintels which have survived
from the Classic period to our own time.

Animals in the reserve include spider
monkeys, howler monkeys, ocelots, bears,

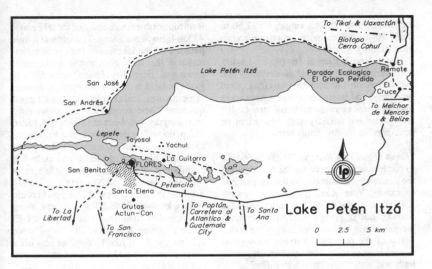

Lake Petén Itzá

white-tailed deer, raccoons, armadillos, and some 21 other beasts. In the water there are 24 species of fish, turtles, snakes, and *Crocodylus moreletti*, the Petén crocodile. The birdlife, of course, is rich and varied. Depending upon the season and migration patterns, you might see kingfishers, ducks, herons, hawks, parrots, toucans, woodpeckers, and the famous ocellated (or Petén) turkey, a beautiful big bird which reminds one very much of a peacock.

The reserve is open daily from 7 am to 5 pm for walking along its nature trails. Parador Ecológico El Gringo Perdido, located on the shore of the lake within the reserve, provides meals, camping sites, dormitories and bungalows. The luxury Hotel Camino Real Tikal is within the reserve as well. See Places to Stay for details.

Getting There Any bus or minibus going north from Santa Elena to Tikal can drop you at the village of El Remate, from where it's a three-km walk along an unpaved road to the reserve. You can also take a Jobompiche minibus from the market in Santa Elena daily at 11 am. Taxis from the airport can take you to the reserve, though this is fairly expensive.

Places to Stay – bottom end

Santa Elena The bottom-end hotels in Santa Elena are cheaper than those in Flores. For locations, refer to the maps.

Hotel San Juan (☎ (9) 81-15-62) is the town's travel centre. Besides being the station for major long-distance bus lines, the travel desk here can make airline reservations for you and arrange tours by minibus to outlying areas of El Petén. The rooms are a bit musty and beat-up but serviceable, with fans, and hot water in the private baths. Some rooms have little TVs. The rate is US$4 a single or a double.

Hotel Jade, very near the causeway, is a longtime favourite with backpackers because of its handy location, washbasin and clothesline for laundry, and its low prices: US$1 a single, US$2.25 a double.

Hotel El Diplomático, a biggish three-storey building in the southern part of town near the market, is fairly beat-up by the marketeers who use it regularly, but it is certainly cheap at US$1 to US$1.50 per person.

Hotel Don Quijote, a few steps west of the Hotel San Juan, is cheaper than the San Juan, though the rooms are nothing special. Rates are US$1.50 to US$3 a single, US$2.50 to US$5.50 a double; more expensive rooms have running water.

Hotel Monja Blanca (☎ (9) 81-13-40), north-west of the park near the cemetery and the airport on the eastern outskirts, offers very basic and badly run-down rooms set in lush gardens away from noisy streets. It's family-run and friendly, and they might be persuaded to let you camp here.

Flores *Hotel Yum Kax* (☎ (9) 81-13-86/68), to the left as you arrive on the island along the causeway, is named for the Mayan god of maize, Yum Kax, (pronounced yoom-KASH). It doesn't look like much from the outside, but it's fairly nice inside, with a pleasant dining room overlooking the water. Many of the plainish 43 rooms have good water views as well. They come with private bath and either fan or air-conditioning for US$10 to US$14 a double.

Hotel Petén (☎ (9) 81-13-92), around the corner from the Yum Kax, looks like a very modest Caribbean town dwelling, but enter the doorway and you will find a small courtyard with tropical plants and a nice brick-and-stucco building of several floors with a pleasant terrace on the roof. Pedro Castellanos, the friendly manager, will show you the 14 comfy if plain double rooms going for US$18 with private shower, electric hot water showerhead, and fan. Try to get a room on the top floor (Nos 33, 34, etc) with a view of the lake.

Hotel Savanna (☎ (9) 81-12-48), on the north side of the island, is quiet, and has a two-storey-high terrace covered by a palapa, the perfect place to sit with a drink and gaze across the lake. Double rooms with bath cost US$18.

Take note that in popular places prices for hotels may sometimes increase in response to demand, which in turn can be affected by increases in the numbers of visitors or by the hotel being listed in a guidebook such as this.

Around the Lake *Parador Ecológico El Gringo Perdido* (The Lost Gringo Ecological Inn; ☎ in Guatemala City (2) 36-36-83) is on the north-eastern shore of the lake about 43 km from Santa Elena. This offbeat jungle paradise on the lakeshore offers good swimming in the lake, nice nature trails, quiet times and tranquility. Shady, rustic hillside gardens hold a little restaurant, a bucolic camping area, and simple but pleasant guest quarters. These consist of bungalows (two sets of bunks, four beds in all), shower, toilet, and patio with palapa cover and hammock; camarotes, smaller rooms with toilet, washbasin and two sets of bunks; and eight-bed dormitories. Rates range from US$3 for a camping-place to US$20 a single or US$24 a double for a bungalow. El Gringo Perdido is three km west of the Tikal highway, along a rough dirt road from the hamlet of El Remate (which is north of El Cruce-Puente Ixlu on the Tikal road). You can hop off a Tikal-bound bus and walk three km, or you can take a taxi from Santa Elena.

Places to Stay – middle

All of these hotels are in Santa Elena.

Hotel Maya Internacional (☎ (9) 81-12-76; in Guatemala City, 31-98-76) is a collection of 10 thatched wooden bungalows built partly on land and partly above the water. The 20 rooms (two to a bungalow) are rustic but interesting, with twin beds and well-used bathrooms with showers (electric showerheads). You must be discreet, as your every word and movement can be heard in the room next door. The hotel dining room is in a separate, larger thatched structure at the end of a short causeway out in the lake. Rates are US$20 a single, US$32 a double.

Hotel del Patio-Tikal (☎ in Guatemala City (2) 32-33-65; fax 37-43-13) looks severe from the outside, but is actually a very nice new colonial-style hotel with a pretty central courtyard planted with tropical flowers and furnished with a stone fountain. The 21 rooms have ceiling fans, cable TVs and private baths, and rent for US$40 a double, offering excellent value.

Hotel Tziquina-ha (☎ (9) 81-13-59; in Guatemala City ☎ (2) 2-05-28), on the south side of the road to the airport, has modern concrete-and-stucco buildings arranged on landscaped lawns, with a swimming pool at the centre of the complex. Though the 36 rooms are comfortable, they smell a bit musty, which is not unusual in humid climates. Each room has a drinks refrigerator, TV, tiled bath (shower) and air-conditioning, and the hotel restaurant serves all meals. If the hotel is not filled by a tour group, you can get a room for US$40 a single, US$54 a double, which is quite expensive for Santa Elena.

Places to Stay – top end

All of Flores' top hotels are well out of town at various sites on the lakeshore. They are designed for tour groups which move at predictable times in their own buses, or for travellers with their own cars. Without your own transport you may spend a frustratingly large amount of time waiting for taxis and shuttle buses.

Hotel Villa Maya, developed and operated by the same people who run the Maya Internacional in Santa Elena, has 84 double rooms with private bath, ceiling fans, hot water, beautiful views of the lake and blissful quiet. The modern architecture uses traditional local elements in a harmonious way. There's a very nice patio restaurant, three tennis courts and two swimming pools. Prices are US$77 a single, US$85 a double. The Villa Maya is located on Petenchel Lagoon, about 10 km east of Santa Elena.

Hotel Camino Real Tikal (☎ in Guatemala City (2) 33-46-33), the fanciest hotel in El Petén, is half an hour's drive around the lake to the north-east shore. Located within the Biotopo Cerro Cahuí, the Camino Real has 120 air-conditioned rooms with all the comforts: private bath, remote-controlled cable TV and mahogany decoration. Two restaurants and two bars keep guests happy, as do tennis courts, swimming pools, water sports on the lake, and all the other top-class services. Rates are US$130 a single, US$141 a double, tax included.

Places to Eat

As with hotels, the restaurants in Santa Elena tend to be cheaper than those in Flores. All

are fairly simple, and open all the time. Beer, drinks, and sometimes even wine, are served. Each hotel in the middle and top-end categories has its own good restaurant.

In Santa Elena, the *Comedor El Caracolito* is conveniently located next to the bus station in the Hotel San Juan. It's good for a quick, cheap meal before or after a bus trip.

Restaurant Lago Azul, 2½ blocks west of the Hotel San Juan, is a good, clean, general-purpose eatery serving breakfast for US$0.75 to US$1.50 and sandwiches for about the same price. Main course plates of meat cost US$3, venison *(venado)* a bit more; vegetarian dishes are featured as well.

Other restaurants include *Ventanas del Lago* (Windows on the Lake), which provides just that with its food; and the very simple *Restaurant El Vapor Azul*, six blocks south of the shore.

On the island of Flores, the *Restaurant Gran Jaguar*, around the corner from the Hotel Petén, has a bold jungle decor of slab-wood walls and lots of plants. The menu includes venado, hamburgers, fish, steaks, spaghetti, and lots of drinks. Full meals cost between US$4 and US$8.

Nearby is the *Restaurant La Jungla*, with a tiny streetside terrace where you can dine from the now-familiar burgers-spaghetti-venison menu. Prices are similar to those at El Gran Jaguar.

The *Restaurant La Mesa de los Maya* is just up the street perpendicular to the one with the other two restaurants. Besides the standard items, the Restaurant La Mesa de los Maya lists *tepezcuintle*, a rabbit-sized jungle rodent, on its menu, as well as armadillo and wild turkey *(pavo silvestre)*. A mixed plate of these exotic meats goes for US$5. Fancy ceiling fans keep you cool, and the pet toucan may perch on the back of your chair, make some wisecrack, and snitch a morsel from your plate.

Getting There & Away

Air Though it is possible to visit Tikal on a one-day excursion by plane from Guatemala City, I encourage you to stay over at least one night in Flores, or even at Tikal itself, for there is a great deal to see and to experience, and a day trip simply cannot do it justice.

The airport at Santa Elena (usually called 'the airport at Flores') is quite busy these days with flights from Guatemala City, Belize City and Cancún. For information on flights to and from these places, see those sections. Aerovías, TAPSA, and Aeroquetzal all charge about US$55 one way for the flight between Flores and Guatemala City.

Four days a week, Aerovías flies between Flores and Belize City for US$50 one way.

Aeroquetzal flies from Flores to Guatemala City, then on to Cancún on Tuesday and Saturday for US$175 one way.

More regional airlines will be opening up routes to and from Flores in the near future. Ask at travel agencies in Cancún, Mérida, Belize City, Guatemala City and other major cities of the region for details. Your travel agent at home may not be able to get up-to-date information on some of these small regional carriers.

When you arrive at the airport in Flores you will be subjected to a cursory customs and immigration check, as this is a special customs and immigration district. If you are arriving from Belize or Mexico, you will, of course, pass through the normal customs and immigration procedures.

Road Travel by bus to or from Flores is slow and uncomfortable, with the exception of the road to Tikal. The main bus station is in the Hotel San Juan in Santa Elena.

Belize City – 222 km, seven hours; Transportes Pinita 2nd-class buses (US$5.50) depart from the Hotel San Juan daily at 5 am, connecting with a Novelo bus (US$3) at the Belizean border

Chetumal (Mexico) – 350 km, nine hours; a special direct 1st-class bus (US$30) departs from the Hotel San Juan each morning, bypasses Belize City and goes straight to Chetumal. At Chetumal it connects with an ADO bus heading north along the coast to Cancún at 2 pm. To go 2nd class you must take the Transportes Pinita and Novelo buses to Belize City (see Belize City), then a Batty bus (US$4) to Chetumal. It's slower, less convenient and less comfortable, but less than half the price of the special 1st-class bus.

El Naranjo – see Palenque

Guatemala City – 506 km, 14 hours; Fuentes del Norte (☎ (2) 8-60-94, 51-38-17), 17 Calle 8-46, Zona 1 in Guatemala City, runs buses departing from the capital at 1, 2, 3 and 7 am, and 11 pm, with stops at Morales, Río Dulce, San Luis and Poptún. A one-way ticket costs US$6 or US$12, depending upon the comfort (such as it is) of the bus. Return buses depart from the Hotel San Juan in Santa Elena for Poptún, Río Dulce, La Ruidosa junction and the Atlantic Highway to Guatemala City at 6 and 10 am, and 1 and 4 pm.

Melchor de Mencos – 101 km, three or four hours; 2nd-class Transportes Pinita buses (US$1.50) depart from the Hotel San Juan at 5 am for this town on the Belizean border. You can walk across the border to Benque Viejo del Carmen, in Belize, once you've cleared customs and immigration on both sides. From Benque there are buses to San Ignacio, Belmopan and Belize City.

Palenque (Mexico) – buses to El Naranjo (seven hours, US$3), on the Río San Pedro, depart from the Hotel San Juan daily at 5 am and 12.30 pm. From El Naranjo you must catch a boat on the river and cruise for about four hours to the border town of La Palma. From La Palma you can go by bus to Tenosique (1½ hours), then to Emiliano Zapata (40 km, one hour), and from there to Palenque. It's best to have camping gear. This can be an exhausting and perhaps even dangerous trip. You may want to consult your embassy or consulate before venturing into the jungle.

Sayaxché – 61 km, two hours; 2nd-class buses (US$1.25) run by Transportes Pinita depart from the Hotel San Juan at 6 am and 1 pm, returning from Sayaxché at these same times

Tikal – 71 km, two hours or more by bus, one to 1½ hours by minibus, one hour by car; buses (US$1.50) depart from the Hotel San Juan daily at 7 am and noon; return trips from Tikal are at similar times, making it necessary to stay overnight (a good idea in any case) or find other means of returning to Flores. Minibuses depart each morning from the Hotel San Juan (6, 8 and 10 am), the Flores airport (meeting all flights), and various middle-range hotels in Flores and Santa Elena for the ride to Tikal. One-way fare is US$3, twice that of the bus. Return trips are made at 2, 4 and 5 pm for the same fare. Your driver will anticipate that you'll want to return to Flores in his minibus that same afternoon; if you tell him which return trip you plan to be on, he'll hold a seat for you, or arrange a seat in a colleague's minibus. If you stay overnight in Tikal and want to take a minibus to Flores, it's a good idea to reserve a seat with one of the minibus drivers when they arrive in the morning. Don't wait until the departure time and expect to find a seat – you might not.

A taxi from the town or the airport to Tikal costs $28 or $32 total, round trip, for up to three people.

Getting Around

Minibus For destinations to small villages around the lake and in the immediate vicinity, there are sometimes seats available in the minibuses which depart from the market area in Santa Elena.

Rental Car Several hotels, car rental companies and travel agencies in Flores/Santa Elena offer vehicles for rent, including cars, 4WD Suzukis, pickup trucks and minibuses. The place to find all the rental car companies is in the arrivals hall at Flores airport. The two companies there are Koka (☎ (9) 81-12-33, 81-15-26) and Los Jades (☎ (9) 81-17-41/34). Basic rates for a car are about US$30 per day, plus US$0.30 per km (the km charge will far exceed the daily rental charge). You should haggle for an all-inclusive, unlimited-km fee, which may be US$50 to US$70 per day.

Boat It is often possible to hire a cayuco (local boat) for cruises and tours on Lake Petén Itzá. Any hotel clerk can help you with this.

TIKAL

There is nothing like Tikal. Towering pyramids rise above the jungle's green canopy to catch the sun. Howler monkeys swing noisily through the branches of ancient trees as brightly coloured parrots dart, squawking, from perch to perch. When the complex warbling song of some mysterious jungle bird is not filling the air, the buzz of tree frogs provides background noise.

Certainly the most striking feature of Tikal is its steep-sided temples rising to heights of more than 44 metres. But Tikal is different from Chichén Itzá, Uxmal, Copán and most other great Mayan sites because it is deep in the jungle. Its many plazas have been cleared of trees and vines, its temples uncovered and partially restored, but as you walk from one building to another you pass beneath the dense canopy of the rainforest. Rich smells of earth and vegetation, peacefulness and animal noises all contribute to an experience not offered by any other major Mayan site.

If you visit from December to February, expect some cool nights and mornings. March and April are the hottest months, and water is scarcest then. The rains begin in May or June, and with them come the mosquitos – have repellent and, for camping, a mosquito net. July to September is muggy and buggy. October and November see the end of the occasional rains, and a return to cooler temperatures.

Day trips by air from Guatemala City to Tikal are popular, and they do allow you to get a glimpse of this spectacular site in the shortest possible time. But Tikal is so big that one needs at least two days to see even the major parts thoroughly.

History

Tikal is set on a low hill, a fact which is difficult to confirm if you fly over, but which is evident as you walk up to the Great Plaza from the entry road. The hill, affording relief from the surrounding low-lying swampy ground, may be why the Maya settled here around 700 BC. Another reason was the abundance of flint, the valuable stone used by the ancients to make clubs, spearpoints, arrowheads and knives. The wealth of flint meant good tools could be made, and flint could be exported in exchange for other goods. Within 200 years the Maya of Tikal had begun to build stone ceremonial structures, and by 200 BC there was a complex of buildings on the site of the North Acropolis.

Classic Period By the time of Christ, the Great Plaza was beginning to assume its present shape and extent. With the dawn of the Early Classic period about 250 AD, Tikal was an important religious, cultural and commercial city with a large population. King Yax-Moch-Xoc, who ruled about 230 AD, is looked upon as the founder of the dynasty which ruled Tikal thereafter.

Under Yax-Moch-Xoc's successor, King

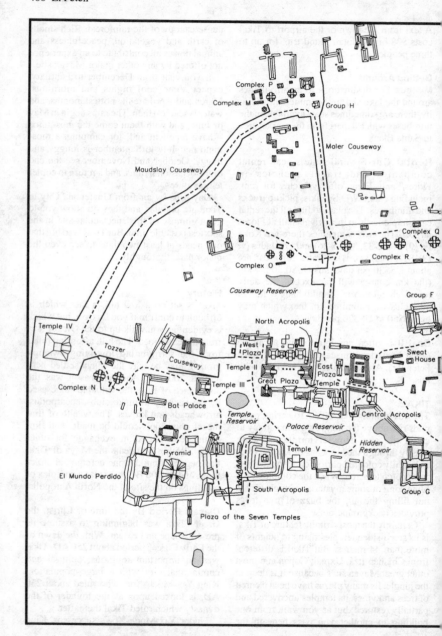

Complex P

Complex M

Group H

Maler Causeway

Maudslay Causeway

Complex Q

Complex R

Complex O

Causeway Reservoir

Group F

Temple IV

North Acropolis

West Plaza

Sweat House

Tozzer

Causeway

Temple II

East Plaza

Complex N

Temple III

Great Plaza

Temple I

Bat Palace

Temple Reservoir

Central Acropolis

Palace Reservoir

Hidden Reservoir

Pyramid

Temple V

El Mundo Perdido

South Acropolis

Group G

Plaza of the Seven Temples

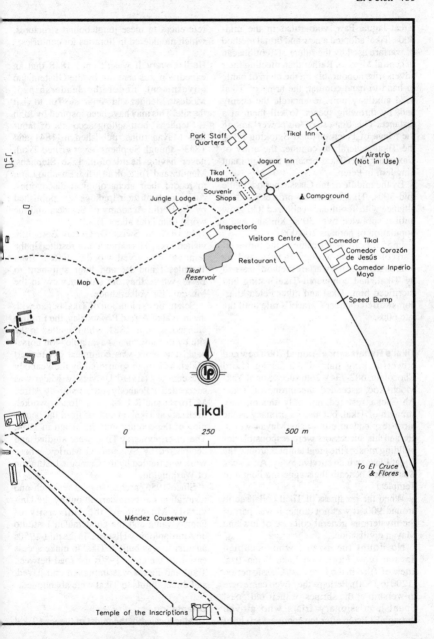

Park Staff
Quarters

Tikal Inn

Jaguar Inn

Airstrip
(Not in Use)

Tikal
Museum

Campground

Souvenir
Shops

Jungle Lodge

Inspectoría

Visitors Centre

Comedor Tikal
Comedor Corazón
de Jesús
Comedor Inperio
Maya

Restaurant

Tikal
Reservoir

Map

Speed Bump

Tikal

0   250   500 m

To El Cruce
& Flores

Méndez Causeway

Temple of the Inscriptions

Great-Jaguar-Paw, who ruled in the mid-300s, Tikal adopted a new and brutal method of warfare used by the rulers of Teotihuacán in central Mexico. Rather than meeting their adversaries honourably on the plain of battle in hand-to-hand combat, the army of Tikal used auxiliary units to encircle the enemy and, by throwing-spears, to kill them at a distance. This first use of 'air power' among the Maya of Petén enabled Smoking-Frog, the Tikal general, to conquer the army of Uaxactún; thus Tikal became the dominant kingdom in Petén.

By the middle of the Classic period, in the mid-500s, Tikal's military prowess and its alliance with Teotihuacán allowed it to grow until it sprawled over 30 sq km and had a population of perhaps 100,000.

In 553, Lord Water came to the throne of Caracol (in south-western Belize), and by 562, using the same warfare methods learned by Tikal, had conquered Tikal's king and sacrificed him. Tikal and other Petén kingdoms suffered under Caracol's rule until the late 600s.

Tikal's Renaissance Around 700 a new and powerful king named Ah-Cacau (Lord Chocolate, 682-734), 26th successor of Yax-Moch-Xoc, ascended the throne of Tikal. Ah-Cacau restored not only the military strength of Tikal, but also its primacy as the most resplendent city in the Mayan world. He and his successors were responsible for building most of the great temples around the Great Plaza, which survive today. Ah-Cacau was buried beneath the staggering height of Temple 1.

When the greatness of Tikal collapsed in around 900, it was not alone; it was part of the mysterious general collapse of lowland Mayan civilisation.

No doubt the Itzaes, who occupied Tayasal (now Flores) on Lake Petén Itzá, knew of Tikal in the Late Post-Classic period (1200 to 1530). Perhaps they even came here to worship at the shrines of their old gods. Spanish missionary friars who moved through El Petén after the conquest left brief references to these junglebound structures, which mouldered in libraries for centuries.

Rediscovery It wasn't until 1848 that an expedition was sent out by the Guatemalan government, under the leadership of Modesto Méndez and Ambrosio Tut, to visit the site. This may have been inspired by John L Stephens' best-selling accounts of fabulous Mayan ruins, published in 1841 and 1843 – though Stephens never visited Tikal, never having heard of it. Like Stephens, Méndez and Tut took an artist, Eusebio Lara, to record their archaeological discoveries. An account of their findings was published by the Berlin Academy of Science, and the world found out about Tikal.

In 1877 the Swiss, Dr Gustav Bernoulli, visited Tikal. His explorations resulted in the removal of carved wooden lintels from Temples I and IV and their shipment to Basel, where they are still on view in the Museum für Völkerkunde.

Scientific exploration of Tikal began with the arrival of Alfred P Maudslay, the English archaeologist, in 1881, who travelled to the site by the only means available – on horseback. His work was continued by Teobert Maler, a German sponsored by the Peabody Museum at Harvard University. Maler was succeeded in Peabody sponsorship by Alfred M Tozzer and R E Merwin. Tozzer worked tirelessly at Tikal on and off from the beginning of the century until his death in 1954. The inscriptions at Tikal were studied and deciphered by Sylvanus G Morley, whose work was funded by the Carnegie Institution of Washington.

Since 1956, archaeological research and restoration has been carried out by the University Museum of the University of Pennsylvania and the Guatemalan Instituto de Antropología y Historia. In the mid-1950s an airstrip was built at Tikal to make access easier. In the early 1980s the road between Tikal and Flores was improved and paved, and direct flights to Tikal were abandoned.

Orientation
Tikal is located in the midst of the vast Tikal

National Park, a 575-sq-km preserve containing thousands of separate ruined structures. The central area of the city occupied about 16 sq km with 3000 buildings.

The road from Flores enters the national park boundaries about 15 km south of the ruins. When you enter the park you must pay a fee of US$2 for the day; if you return the next day, you pay it again.

The area around the Visitors' Centre includes three hotels, a camping area, three small comedores, a tiny post office, a police post, an excellent little museum, and a rarely used airstrip. From the Visitors' Centre it's a 20 to 30-minute walk south-west to the Great Plaza.

The walk from the Great Plaza to the Temple of the Inscriptions is over one km, from the Great Plaza to Complex P one km in the opposite direction. To visit all of the major building complexes you must walk at least 10 km, probably more.

For complete information on the monuments at Tikal, pick up a copy of *Tikal – a Handbook of the Ancient Maya Ruins*, by William R Coe (Philadelphia: University Museum of the University of Pennsylvania, 1967 and later editions). The guide is on sale in Flores and at Tikal, but it may be cheaper if you buy it in your own country; it is cheaper in the USA, for instance.

The ruins are open from 6 am to 5 pm; you may be able to get a special pass to visit the Great Plaza on moonlit evenings by applying to the Inspectorería to the west of the Visitors' Centre.

Great Plaza

Walk along the access road from the Visitors' Centre to a fork in the road. The path to the right goes to Complexes Q and R, the left to the Great Plaza. Approaching the plaza you pass the Sweat House, which may have been used for ritual baths.

The path comes into the Great Plaza around Temple I, the Temple of the Grand Jaguar. This was built to honour – and to bury – King Ah-Cacau; the king may have worked out the plans for the building himself, but it was built above his tomb by his son, who succeeded to the throne in 734. Ah-Cacau's rich burial goods included 180 beautiful jade objects, 90 pieces of bone carved with hieroglyphs, pearls, and stingray spines which were used for ritual bloodletting. At the top of the 44-metre-high temple is a small enclosure of three rooms covered by a corbelled arch. The zapote-wood lintels over the doors were richly carved; one of them is now in a Basel museum. The lofty roofcomb which crowned the temple was originally adorned with reliefs and bright paint. It may have symbolised the 13 realms of the Mayan heaven.

On my last visit the temple was shrouded in scaffolding and closed to climbing, but it should be open again by the time you arrive. The climb up is dangerous (two people have tumbled to their deaths so far), the view from the top magnificent.

Temple II, directly across the plaza from Temple I, was once almost as high, but now measures 38 metres without its roofcomb. This one seems a bit easier to climb, and the view is just as stupendous.

The North Acropolis, while not as immediately impressive as the twin temples, is of great significance. Archaeologists have uncovered about 100 different structures, the oldest of which dates from before the time of Christ, with evidence of occupation as far back as 400 BC. The Maya built and rebuilt on top of older structures, and the many layers, combined with elaborate burials, added sanctity and power to their temples. Look for the two huge wall masks uncovered in an earlier structure, and now protected by roofs. The final version of the Acropolis, as it stood around 800 AD, had more than 12 temples atop a vast platform, many of them the work of King Ah-Cacau.

On the plaza side of the North Acropolis are two rows of stelae. Though hardly as impressive as the magnificent stelae at Copán or Quiriguá, these served the same purpose: to record the great deeds of the kings of Tikal, and to sanctify their memory and add 'power' to the temples and plazas which surrounded them.

Central Acropolis

On the south side of the Great Plaza, this maze of courtyards, little rooms and small temples is thought by many to have been a palace where Tikal's nobles lived. Others think the tiny rooms may have been used for sacred rites and ceremonies, as graffiti found within them suggest. Over the centuries the configuration of the rooms was repeatedly changed, suggesting perhaps that this 'palace' was in fact a noble or royal family's residence changed to accommodate different groups of relatives. A hundred years ago, one part of the acropolis, called Maler's Palace, provided lodgings for archaeologist Teobert Maler when he worked at Tikal.

West Plaza

The West Plaza, north of Temple II, has a large Late Classic-period temple on its north side. To the south, across the Tozzer Causeway, is Temple III, 55 metres high. Yet to be uncovered, it allows you to see a temple the way the last Tikal Maya and first White explorers saw them. The causeway leading to Temple IV was one of several sacred ways built among the temple complexes of Tikal, no doubt for astronomical as well as aesthetic reasons.

South Acropolis & Temple V

Due south of the Great Plaza is the South Acropolis. Excavation has hardly even begun on this huge mass of masonry covering two hectares. The palaces on top are no doubt from Late Classic times (the time of King Ah-Cacau), but earlier constructions probably go back 1000 years.

Temple V, just east of the South Acropolis, is 58 metres high, and was built around 700 AD (again, in the reign of Ah-Cacau). Unlike the other great temples, this one has rounded corners and one very tiny room at the top. The room is less than a metre deep, but its walls are up to 4½ metres thick. The view, as usual, is wonderful, giving you a 'profile' view of the temples on the Great Plaza.

Plaza of the Seven Temples

On the other side of the South Acropolis is the Plaza of the Seven Temples. The little temples, all quite close together, were built in Late Classic times, though the structures beneath must go back a millenium at least. Note the skull and crossed bones on the central temple (the one with the stela and altar in front). On the north side of the plaza is an unusual triple ball court; another, larger version in the same design stands just south of Temple I.

El Mundo Perdido

About 400 metres south-west of the Great Plaza is El Mundo Perdido, the Lost World, a large complex of 38 structures with a huge pyramid in its midst. Unlike the rest of Tikal, where Late Classic construction overlays work of earlier periods, El Mundo Perdido exhibits buildings of many different periods: the large pyramid is thought to be essentially Preclassic (with some later repairs and renovations); the Talud-Tablero Temple (or Temple of the Three Rooms), Early Classic; and the Temple of the Skulls, Late Classic.

The pyramid, 32 metres high and 80 metres along the base, has a stairway on each side, and had huge masks flanking each stairway, but no temple structure at its top. Each side of the pyramid displays a slightly different architectural style. Tunnels dug into the pyramid by archaeologists reveal four similar pyramids beneath the outer face, the oldest (Structure 5C-54 Sub 2B) dating from 700 BC, making the pyramid the oldest Mayan structure at Tikal.

Temple IV & Complex N

Complex N, near Temple IV, is an example of the 'twin-temple' complexes popular among Tikal's rulers during the Late Classic period. These complexes are thought to have commemorated the completion of a katun, or 20-year cycle in the Mayan calendar. This one was built in 711 by King Ah-Cacau – that great builder – to mark the 14th katun of Baktun 9. The king himself is portrayed on Stela 16, one of the finest stelae found at Tikal.

Temple IV, at 64 metres in height, is the highest building at Tikal, and the highest

Indian building known in the western hemisphere. It was completed about 741, in the reign of Ah-Cacau's son. From the base it looks like a steep little hill. Clamber up the path, holding onto trees and roots, to reach the metal ladder which will take you to the top. Another metal ladder, around to the side, lets you climb to the base of the roofcomb. The view is almost as good as from a helicopter, a panorama across the jungle canopy.

Temple of the Inscriptions

Compared to Copán or Quiriguá, there are relatively few inscriptions on buildings at Tikal. The exception is this temple, 1200 metres south-east of the Great Plaza. On the rear of the 12-metre-high roof comb is a long inscription; the sides and cornice of the roof comb bear glyphs as well. The inscriptions give us the date 766 AD. Stela 21 and Altar 9, standing before the temple, date from 736 AD. The stela had been badly damaged (part of it was converted into a *metate* for grinding corn!), but has now been repaired.

Jade mosaic death mask found in the Temple of Inscriptions, Tikal

Northern Complexes

About one km north of the Great Plaza is Complex P, like Complex N a Late Classic twin-temple complex which probably commemorated the end of a katun. Complex M, next to it, was partially torn down by the Late Classic Maya to provide building materials for a causeway now named after Alfred Maudslay, which runs south-west to Temple IV. Group H had some interesting graffiti within its temples.

Complexes Q and R, about 300 metres due north of the Great Plaza, are very Late Classic twin-pyramid complexes with stelae and altars standing before the temples. Complex Q is perhaps the best example of the twin-temple type as it has been mostly restored. Stela 22 and Altar 10 are excellent examples of Late Classic Tikal relief carving, dated 771.

Complex O, due west of these complexes on the western side of the Maler Causeway, has an uncarved stela and altar in its north enclosure. An uncarved stela? The whole point of stelae was to record great happenings. Why did this one remain uncarved?

Tikal Museum

The museum, in a small building between the Jungle Lodge and the Jaguar Inn, is small but has some fascinating exhibits, including the burial goods of King Ah-Cacau, carved jade, inscribed bones, shells, stelae, and other items recovered from the excavations. The museum is open from 9 am to 5 pm (till 4 pm on Saturday and Sunday); admission costs US$0.70 for foreigners, half that price for Chapines (Guatemalans). I expect that soon the museum will be moved to the new Visitors' Centre.

Places to Stay

There are only four places to stay at Tikal, and in the interests of the environment no more lodgings will be built. Water is scarce here, and the land cannot support many more humans.

Most of the places are booked in advance by tour groups, even though most groups (and individuals as well) stay near Lake Petén Itzá and shuttle up to Tikal for the day.

Cheapest of Tikal's lodgings is the official camping area by the entrance road and the disused airstrip. Set in a nice lawn of green grass with some trees for shade, it has simple plumbing and cooking facilities, and is free of charge.

Largest and most modern of the hotels is the 32-room *Jungle Lodge* (☎ in Guatemala City (2) 76-02-94; 29 Calle 18-01, Zona 12), built originally to house the archaeologists excavating and restoring Tikal. Accommodation is in thatched or tin-roofed bungalows, or in the half-timbered main building, which also houses the dining room, bar and reception desk. Rooms without bath cost US$8.50 a double; with bath (no hot water), the cost is US$20. The bungalows with bath are newer than those without, and they must be reserved in advance.

Jaguar Inn, to the right of the museum as you approach on the access road, has only two rooms in airy thatched cottages with wood and local cloth furnishings and simple bathrooms. The price is US$12. Reserve your room by mail or telegram.

Tikal Inn, past the Jaguar Inn as you walk away from the small museum down towards the old airstrip, has 17 rooms in the main building as well as bungalows which are slightly nicer. The swimming pool, dry for years, was fixed up and filled on my last visit. The rooms are quite simple and clean, with walls that extend only partway up to the roof, and thus afford little conversational privacy. Rooms cost US$10 a double in the main building, US$11.50 in the bungalows.

Places to Eat

As you arrive in Tikal, look on the right side of the road to find the three little comedores: *Comedor Imperio Maya, Comedor Corazón de Jesus, Comedor Tikal* and *Tienda Angelita*. The Comedor Imperio Maya, first on the way into the site, seems to be the favoured one. You can buy cold drinks and snacks in the *tienda* (shop) adjoining. All three comedores are similar in comforts and style (there are none), all are rustic and

pleasant, all are run by local people, and all serve huge plates of fairly tasty food at low prices. The meal of the day is almost always a piece of roast chicken, rice, salad, fruit and a soft drink for US$1.75.

Picnic tables beneath shelters are located just off Tikal's Great Plaza, with itinerant soft-drink pedlars standing by, but no food is sold. If you want to spend all day at the ruins without having to make the 20 to 30-minute walk back to the comedors, carry food with you.

The restaurant in the *Visitors' Centre*, across the street from the comedores, serves fancier food at fancier prices. Tenderloin of beef (lomito) is featured, as are other steaks, at US$5 a portion. They do serve decent plates of fruit here for less, though.

Meals at the *Jungle Lodge* are good and not overly expensive. Breakfast is served from 7 to 9 am, lunch from 12.30 to 2 pm, dinner from 7.30 to 8.30 pm. A set-price lunch or dinner is yours for about US$5 or US$6.

The pleasant, rustic dining room at the *Jaguar Inn* also serves all three meals, with good food, good service, and good conversation. A big set-price breakfast costs about US$2, lunch US$2.50 and dinner US$3.50.

Getting There & Away

For details of transport to and from Flores/Santa Elena, see that section. Coming from Belize, you can get off the bus at El Cruce, also called Puente Ixlu, the junction of the Flores-Melchor de Mencos road and the road to Tikal. Wait for a northbound bus or minibus – or hitch a ride with an obliging tourist – to take you the remaining 35 km to Tikal. Note that there is very little northbound traffic after lunch. If you come to El Cruce in the afternoon, it's probably best to continue to Flores for the night rather than risk being stranded at El Cruce.

You don't need a car to get to Tikal, but a vehicle of your own can be useful for visiting less accessible sites such as Uaxactún and the sites around Sayaxché.

Guerrilla Warning Occasionally, armed

guerrillas stop a bus or minibus on the Tikal-Flores road, lecture the passengers on the rightness of the rebel cause, and release them. The few incidents so far have not resulted in physical harm, and only one unconfirmed report has mentioned robbery (American passport holders were allegedly singled out to be relieved of their wallets and cameras). If you are an American citizen staying in Flores or Santa Elena, it might be a good idea to entrust your valuables to the management of your hotel before setting out on the road to Tikal.

The US Department of State's Citizens' Emergency Service (☎ 202-647-5225) in Washington, DC, can provide up-to-date reports through its automatic telephone information service. In Guatemala, ask at your embassy in Guatemala City, or simply ask the locals in Flores for news on the current situation.

UAXACTÚN

Uaxactún (pronounced wah-shahk-TOON), 25 km north of Tikal along a poor unpaved road through the jungle, was Tikal's political and military rival in Late Preclassic times. It was conquered by Tikal's King Great-Jaguar-Paw in the mid-300s, and was subservient to its great sister to the south for centuries thereafter.

During the rainy season from May to October, you will find it difficult to get to Uaxactún. At other times of the year, ask in Flores or Tikal about the condition of the road. You may be advised to make the hour-long drive only in a vehicle with 4WD, whether bus, pickup truck, or rented car. Buses to Tikal sometimes continue to Uaxactún if the road allows.

If you're driving, fill your fuel tank in Flores; there is no fuel available at Tikal or Uaxactún. You might also want to pack some food and drink, though drinks and a few snacks are on sale in the village at Uaxactún.

The road, a jeep track really, winds through the jungle, up and down hills, through sloughs of mud where you'll need that 4WD. You may encounter one or two

other vehicles on this road, in which case you must do some fancy manoeuvering to get by.

When you arrive at Uaxactún, sign your name in the register at the guard's hut at the edge of the disused airstrip which now serves as pasture for cattle. About halfway down the airstrip, roads go off to the left and to the right to the ruins. There's plenty of places to camp, if you have your own equipment.

The Ruins

The pyramids at Uaxactún were uncovered and put in a stabilised condition so that no further deterioration would result; they were not restored. White mortar is the mark of the repair crews, who had patched cracks in the stone to prevent water and roots from entering. Much of the work on the famous Temple E-VII-Sub was done by Earthwatch volunteers in 1974; among them was Jane A Fisher, a Uaxactún-lover who later married the author of this guidebook.

Turn right from the airstrip to reach Group E and Group H, a 10 to 15-minute walk. Perhaps the most significant temple here is E-VII-Sub, among the earliest intact temples excavated, with foundations going back perhaps to 2000 BC. It lay beneath much larger structures, which have been stripped away. On its flat top are holes, or sockets, for the poles which would have supported a wood-and-thatch temple.

About a 20-minute walk to the north-west of the runway are Group A and Group B. At Group A, early excavators sponsored by Andrew Carnegie simply cut into the sides of the temples indiscriminately, looking for graves. Sometimes they used dynamite. This unfortunate work destroyed many of the temples, which are now in the process of being reconstructed.

SAYAXCHÉ & CEIBAL

The little town of Sayaxché, 61 km south-west of Flores, is a base for visiting the Mayan ruins in south-western Petén. There are lots of sites in the area. None even comes close to the grandeur of Tikal, but all provide a fairly adventurous experience.

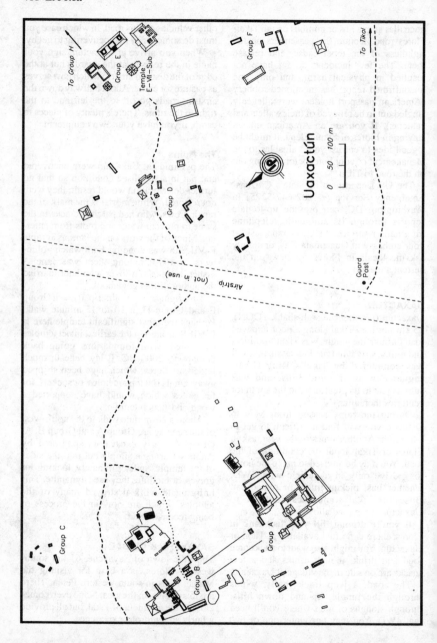

Uaxactún

0   50   100 m

To Tikal

Group F

To Group H

Group E

Temple
E-VII-Sub

Group D

Airstrip (not in use)

Guard
Post

Group C

Group B

Group A

Orientation

The bus drops you on the northern bank of the Río de la Pasión, from which you take a canoe or the car ferry to get across to the town on the other side.

El Ceibal

The most interesting of the sites is El Ceibal, 17 km east of Sayaxché, a city that flourished in the Post-Classic period (around 900 AD), after the golden age of Tikal. Its architecture, carving and stucco decoration suggest strongly that its rulers had come from Mexico, or at least had been influenced by Mexican culture.

As with other sites in eastern Guatemala, the two plazas uncovered so far at El Ceibal are dotted with beautifully carved stelae. The towering ceiba trees which shade the site add a special note of grandeur. The ceiba was a sacred tree to the ancient Maya, and it is Guatemala's national tree today.

Other Mayan sites near Sayaxché are less interesting, but if you have lots of time and an adventurous spirit, you might want to visit Aguateca, Dos Pilas and Tamarindito, south of Sayaxché near Lake Petexbatún.

Places to Stay & Eat

Several small hotels and pensions cater to the needs of travellers heading into the jungle for a look at the more remote ruins.

B & B Carmen Kilkan provides bed and breakfast for less than US$2 per person, and also organises river trips to El Ceibal and other Mayan sites. *Hotel Guayacán* is the lodging-place of long standing in the village, and serves meals as well. Rooms cost US$5 a double. For cheaper lodgings, have a look at the *Hospedaje Mayapán*.

Besides the Guayacán, several little restaurants in town can provide sustenance, including *La Montaña*, which also arranges visits to the ruins roundabout.

Getting There & Away

Transportes Pinita runs two buses daily from the Hotel San Juan in Santa Elena to Sayaxché, at 6 am and 1 pm, with return buses leaving Sayaxché at these same times.

The fare for the two-hour ride along a rough road is US$1.25.

To get to El Ceibal or any of the other ruins in the area, you must arrange transport in Sayaxché as there is no regular service. Instead of walking the 17 km to El Ceibal, hire a boat for about US$30; the boats generally take five or six people. Hotels and restaurants in Sayaxché will help to find other passengers so that you needn't pay for the entire boat yourself. The voyage along the river takes about two hours, after which the walk through the jungle to the site takes less than an hour. Take food and water and your camping equipment if you plan to spend the night.

A route to Mexico from Sayaxché is developing, but is not yet particularly easy to travel. If you have camping equipment, lots of time, and a taste for adventure and (preferably) a companion or two, negotiate with one of the cargo boats which cruises down the Río de la Pasión via Pipiles (where your passport will be checked) to Benemerito, in the Mexican state of Chiapas. From Benemerito you can proceed by bus or boat to the ruins at Yaxchilán and Bonampak, and then onward to Palenque.

EASTWARDS TO BELIZE

It's 101 km from Flores eastwards to Melchor de Mencos, the Guatemalan town on the border with Belize. Of course, Guatemala's official position is that there is no border with Belize, because Belize is a *departamento* of Guatemala.

Transportes Pinita buses depart from the Hotel San Juan in Santa Elena for Melchor at 5 am. The road from Flores to El Cruce is good, fast asphalt. If you're coming from Tikal, start early in the morning and get off at El Cruce to catch a bus or hitch a ride westward. For the fastest, most reliable service, however, it's best to be on that 5 am bus departing from the Hotel San Juan.

East of El Cruce the road reverts to what's usual in El Petén – unpaved mud in bad repair. The trip to Melchor takes three or four hours. There is guerrilla activity along this road, and a remote chance that your bus will be stopped and its passengers lectured on the need for revolution.

At the border you must hand in your Guatemalan tourist card before proceeding to Benque Viejo in Belize, about two km from the border. Buses depart from the market in Benque Viejo for San Ignacio, Belmopan and Belize City. If you arrive in Benque early enough in the day, you may have sufficient time to visit the Mayan ruins of Xunantunich on your way to San Ignacio.

BELIZE

Belize

A tiny English-speaking tropical country with a democratic government and a highly unlikely mixture of peoples and cultures – that's Belize.

Belize is tiny. The population of the entire country is only about 200,000, the size of a small city in Mexico, Europe or the USA. The 23,300 sq km of land within the borders of Belize is slightly more than that of Massachusetts or Wales.

Belize is English-speaking, officially. But the Black Creoles, its largest ethnic group (over half of the population) speak their own fascinating dialect as well as standard English; and when they speak standard English it is with the musical lilt and delightful constructions of the Caribbean. Spanish is a popular second language, and you may also hear Mayan, Chinese, Mennonite German, Lebanese Arabic, Hindi and Garifuna, the language of the Garinagu people of the southern townships.

Belize is a democracy. Some say the political scene here is turbulent, but they are always referring to the purple rhetoric and high emotions of politics. Belize has never had a coup; indeed, it does not have an army, only the tiny Belize Defence Force supplemented by companies of British and Commonwealth soldiers, particularly Gurkhas, as well as fighter-bomber pilots. These forces keep the sovereignty squabble with Guatemala from leaving the halls of diplomacy and emerging on the battlefield.

Belize is many other things. It is friendly, laid-back, beautiful, proud, poor, and hopeful for the future.

TOURISM IN BELIZE

Belize has always been a fascinating place to visit, but in recent years the influx of visitors has grown exponentially. Belize is being 'discovered', and it is changing fast.

It's difficult not to love Belize, but it happens. If a visitor is disappointed, usually it is because of unrealistic expectations. A few points must be kept in mind:

First, Belize is much more expensive than Mexico or Guatemala. Those extremely cheap US$1-a-night hotels so easy to find in Guatemala do not exist in Belize. In fact, the room you get for US$30 in Belize would seem expensive at US$10 in Guatemala, or even in Mexico. Food in Belize can often be mediocre, expensive, or both. Bus fares seem a bit high, taxi fares seem outrageous, and a well-used rental car can cost upwards of US$100 a day.

Second, Belize is not yet fully prepared to receive lots of visitors. Services can be few, far between, and very basic. The country has a small number of hotels, most of which are quite simple, but which may be full when you arrive, leaving you little choice of where to stay. There are only two paved roads in the whole country, so transport can be slow.

If you expect convenience, comfort and ultra-cheapness, you're in for a surprise. But if you are adaptable and adventurous, you'll love Belize.

Belize City

Population 70,000

Ramshackle, funky, fascinating, daunting, homely – these are only a few of the words that can be used to describe the country's biggest city and former capital. The tropical storms which periodically razed the town in the 19th and early 20th centuries still arrive to do damage to its ageing wooden buildings, but they also flush out the open drainage canals, redolent with pollution, which crisscross the town. When there's no storm, Belize City bustles and swelters.

Few people come to Belize City for a holiday; most people pass through while changing buses or planes. If you need a Mexican tourist card, a spare part for a car or

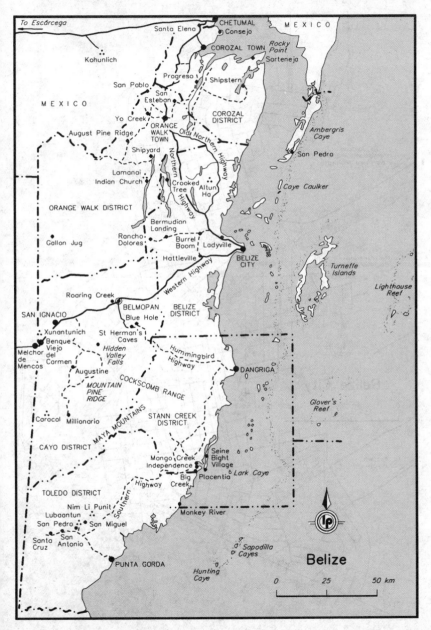

Belize

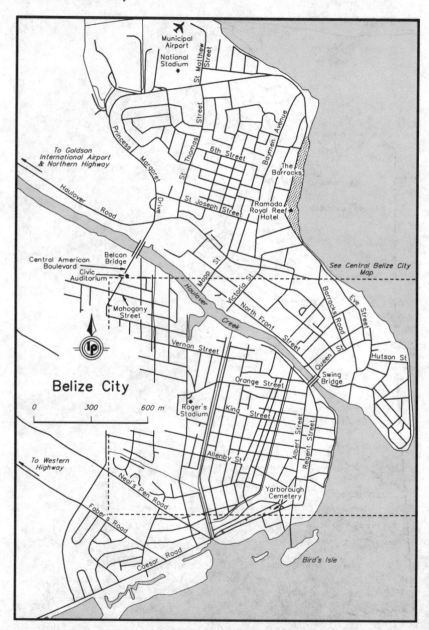

To Goldson
International Airport
& Northern Highway

Municipal
Airport

National
Stadium

St Matthew Street

St Thomas Street

6th Street

Baymen Avenue

The Barracks

Princess Margaret Drive

Haulover Road

St Joseph Street

Ramada
Royal Reef
Hotel

Central American
Boulevard

Belcan
Bridge

Civic
Auditorium

See Central Belize City
Map

Mahogany
Street

Mapp St

Victoria St

North Front Street

Barracks Road

Eve Street

Haulover Creek

Vernon Street

Hutson St

Queen St

Swing
Bridge

Belize City

0   300   600 m

Orange Street

King Street

Roger's
Stadium

Albert Street

Regent Street

To Western
Highway

Allenby St

Neal's Pen Road

Yarborough
Cemetery

Faber's Road

Coesar Road

Bird's Isle

a new sleeping bag, you'll come to Belize City to get it.

Coming into town from the airport or the bus station, your first glimpse of Belize City is likely to be less than inspiring. That intrepid traveller, John L Stephens, passed through 'Balize' in 1839 on his way to Guatemala. He discovered that Belize City, like Istanbul, is best approached from the sea, preferably in the morning:

At seven o'clock the next morning we saw Balize, appearing, if there be no sin in comparing it with cities consecrated by time and venerable associations, like Venice and Alexandrea, to rise out of the water.

There is more petty crime in Belize City than in most other places along La Ruta Maya, so follow some simple rules. Don't walk on back streets alone at night; it's better to walk in pairs or groups and to stick to major streets in the centre, Fort George and King's Park. Don't flash wads of cash, expensive camera equipment or other signs of wealth and don't change money on the street (the professed rate may be a bit better than the official rate, but you also may get mugged and end up with a rate of all you have = BZE$0.00). Don't leave valuables in your hotel room. Don't use or deal in illicit drugs. Follow these rules and you should have no trouble.

ORIENTATION

Haulover Creek, a branch of the Belize River, runs through the middle of the city, separating the commercial centre (Albert, Regent, King and Orange Sts) from the slightly more genteel residential and hotel district of Fort George to the north-east.

Albert St in the centre and Queen St in the Fort George and King's Park neighbourhoods are joined by the Swing Bridge across Haulover Creek. It seems as though everything and everybody in Belize City crosses the Swing Bridge at least once a day. The bridge, a product of Liverpool's ironworks (1923), is swung open daily at 5.30 am and 5.30 pm to let tall-masted boats through. When the Swing Bridge is open,

virtually all vehicular traffic in the centre of the city grinds to a halt in hopeless gridlock.

Each of Belize's bus companies has its own terminal. Most are on the west side of West Collett Canal St near Cemetery Rd. See Getting There & Away for details.

INFORMATION
Tourist Office

The Belize Tourist Board (☎ (02) 77213, 73255), 53/76 Regent St (PO Box 325), next to the Hotel Mopan, is open from 8 am to noon and 1 to 5 pm Monday to Thursday and until 4.30 pm on Friday; it's closed on weekends. They're very pleasant and helpful here, as are the staff at the city's travel agencies.

The Belize Tourism Industry Association (☎ (02) 45538), 99 Albert St (PO Box 62), is an industry group (mostly hotels, rental car companies, etc) which may be able to help with complaints or information about their members.

Money

The Bank of Nova Scotia (☎ (02) 77027/8/9), on Albert St, is open Monday to Friday from 8 am to 1 pm and Friday afternoon from 3 to 6 pm.

The Atlantic Bank Limited (☎ (02) 77124), 6 Albert St, is open Monday, Tuesday and Thursday from 8 am to noon and 1 to 3 pm, Wednesday from 8 am to 1 pm and Friday from 8 am to 1 pm and from 3 to 6 pm.

Also on Albert St is the prominent Belize Bank (☎ (02) 77132/3/4/5), 60 Market Square (facing the Swing Bridge), and Barclay's Bank (☎ (02) 77211), 21 Albert St.

Post & Telecommunications

The main post office is at the northern end of the Swing Bridge, at the intersection of Queen and North Front Sts. Hours are 8 am to noon and 1 to 5 pm daily. If you want to pick up mail at the American Express office, it's at Belize Global Travel Service (☎ (02) 77363/4), 41 Albert St (P O Box 244).

Belize Telecommunications Limited

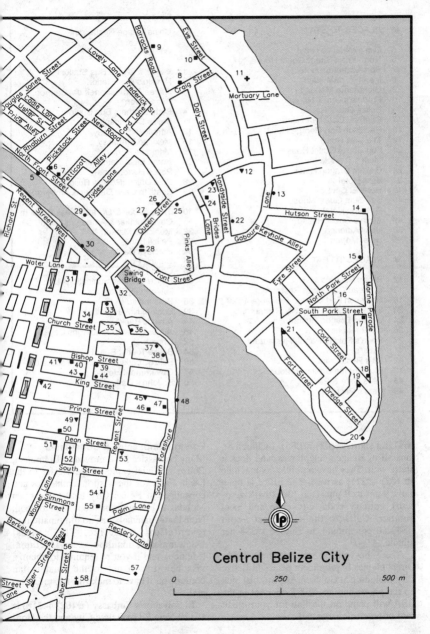

Central Belize City

0   250   500 m

■ PLACES TO STAY

5   Dim's Mira Rio Hotel
6   North Front Street Guest House
7   Bon Adventure Hotel
8   Marin's Travelodge
9   Glenthorne Manor
10 Freddie's Guest House
14 Belize Guest House
17 Chateau Caribbean Hotel
18 Radisson Fort George Hotel
19 The Villa Hotel
21 Fort Street Guest House
22 Mom's Triangle Inn
24 Golden Dragon Hotel
31 Bliss Hotel
40 Hotel El Centro
46 Sea Side Guest House
47 Bellevue Hotel
49 Alicia's Guest House
50 Hotel America
55 Hotel Mopan

▼ PLACES TO EAT

12 Pete's Pastries
17 Chateau Caribbean Restaurant
18 Radisson Fort George Restaurant
23 Shrangri-La & Piccadilly Restaurants
24 Golden Dragon Restaurant
26 Celebrations
27 Shen's Peking Panda Restaurant
41 Macy's
42 Dit's Restaurant
43 Bluebird Ice Cream Parlour
45 Lily's Café & Patio
49 Pete's Pastries

53 China Village Restaurant

OTHER

1   Venus & Z-Line Bus Station
2   Novelo's Bus Station
3   James & Transportes del Carmen
    Bus Station
4   Batty Brothers Bus Station
11 Belize City Hospital
13 American Embassy
15 Mexican Embassy
16 Memorial Park
20 Baron Bliss Memorial
25 Police Headquarters
28 Post Office (Paslow Building)
29 Boats to Caye Caulker & Ambergris
    Caye
30 *Thunderbolt* & *Libra* Express Boats to
    Caye Caulker & Ambergris Caye
32 Municipal Market
33 Belize Bank
34 Barclays Bank
35 Central Park
36 Court House
37 Belize Telecommunications Ltd
    Telephone Office
38 Bliss Institute
39 Bank of Nova Scotia
44 Atlantic Bank
48 *Andera* Boat to Ambergris Caye
52 Church
54 Belize Tourist Board
56 Belize Tourism Industry Association
57 Government House
58 St John's Cathedral

(BTL for short; ☎ (02) 77085), 1 Church St, runs all of Belize's telephones, and does it pretty well. They have a public fax machine (☎ (02) 45211) as well. The office is open daily 8 am to 9 pm. Dial '00' (that's zero-zero), country code, city code and local number. Calls to the USA cost about US$1.60 per minute, to Europe US$3 per minute.

AT&T has placed several of its USA-Direct phones in prominent places in Belize City, including at Goldson Airport. Just pick up the phone and an AT&T operator in the USA will come on the line for your credit card or reverse-charge call.

Foreign Embassies & Consulates
Many embassies have moved to Belmopan, Belize's official capital. Please refer to the list in Facts for the Visitor. Embassies and consulates in Belize City tend to be open Monday to Friday from about 9 am to noon. Note that Guatemala has no diplomatic representation in Belize. The nearest Guatemalan Consulate is in Chetumal (Mexico), and if you're required to obtain a visa before you get to the Guatemalan border, you'll have to make the trip to Chetumal.

El Salvador's Embassy (☎ (02) 44318) is at 120 New Rd in Belize City and the Honduras Embassy (☎ (02) 45889) is at 91 North Front St.

Bookshops

The Book Center (☎ (02) 77457), 114 North Front St, just a few steps north-west of the Swing Bridge, has English-language books, magazines and greeting cards. Hours are Monday to Friday 8 am to noon, 1 to 5 and 7 to 9 pm; Saturday hours are the same except they're closed from 4.30 to 7 pm.; they're closed all day Sunday.

The Belize Book Shop (☎ (02) 72054), Regent St and Rectory Lane, across from the Mopan Hotel, has a larger selection of books.

Medical Services

The Belize City Hospital (☎ (02) 77251) is on Eve St near the corner of Craig St in the northern part of town. Many Belizeans with medical problems travel to Chetumal or Mérida for treatment. A new, modern, private clinic is the Clinica de Chetumal (☎ (983) 26508), Avenida Juárez near the old market and the city's other hospitals. For serious illnesses, Belizeans fly to Houston, Miami or New Orleans.

Laundry

Try the Belize Laundromat (☎ (02) 31117), 7 Craig St near Marin's Travel Lodge, open Monday to Saturday from 8 am to 5.15 pm, closed Sunday. A wash costs US$5 per load, detergent, fabric softener, bleach and drying included. A similar establishment is Carry's Laundry, 41 Hyde Lane, open Monday to Saturday from 8 am to 5.30 pm.

Business Hours

Note that some shops and businesses close early on Wednesday or Thursday and many businesses close on Saturday afternoon. Most establishments close on Sunday, when transport schedules also may be different from the rest of the week.

WALKING TOUR
City Centre

One does not come to Belize City to see the sights, but anyone who comes to Belize City does enjoy a walk around. With one or two hours of walking you can see everything there is to see.

Start – of course – at the Swing Bridge and walk along Regent St, one block inland from the shore. The municipal market to the left just off the Swing Bridge dates from 1820, and looks it. Just past the market is the Mona Lisa Hotel, which appears in Peter Weir's film *The Mosquito Coast*, adapted from Paul Theroux's novel and shot in Belize during 1985.

As you start down Regent St, you can't miss the prominent Court House built in 1926 to be the headquarters of Belize's colonial administrators. It still serves its administrative and judicial functions.

The Central Park is on the right just past the Court House. Always busy with vendors, loungers, con men and other slice-of-life segments of Belize City society, the park offers welcome shade in the sweltering midday heat.

Turn left just past the Court House and walk one long block to the waterfront street, called Southern Foreshore, to find the Bliss Institute. Baron Bliss was an Englishman with a happy name and a Portuguese title who came to Belize on his yacht to fish. He seems to have fallen in love with Belize without ever having set foot on shore. When he died – not too long after his arrival – he left the bulk of his wealth in trust to the people of Belize. Income from the trust has paid for roads, market buildings, schools, cultural centres and many other worthwhile projects over the years.

The Bliss Institute (☎ (02) 77267) is open Monday to Friday from 8.30 am to noon and from 2 to 8 pm, and on Saturday from 8 am to noon; closed Sunday. Belize City's prime cultural institution, it is home to the National Arts Council, which stages periodic exhibits, concerts and theatrical works. There's a small display of artefacts from the Mayan archaeological site at Caracol and, upstairs, the National Library.

On a side street in this neighbourhood is a house with a brass plaque set in the wall. The plaque reads 'On this site in 1897 nothing happened'.

Continue walking south along Southern Foreshore to the end to reach Government House (1814), the former residence of the governor-general. The job disappeared when Belize attained independence (within the British Commonwealth) in 1981. Down beyond Government House is Bird's Isle, a pleasant recreation area.

Inland from Government House, at the corner of Albert and Regent Sts, is St John's Cathedral, the oldest and most important Anglican church in Central America, dating from 1847.

A block south-west of the cathedral is Yarborough Cemetery, with gravestones outlining the turbulent history of Belize back to 1781.

Walk back to the Swing Bridge northward along Albert St. You'll pass the offices of the Belize Tourist Board, the Belize Tourism Industry Association, Continental Airlines (in an unlikely little Hindu fantasy 'temple') and various hotels and restaurants.

Northern Neighbourhoods

Cross the Swing Bridge heading north and you'll come face-to-face with the wood-frame Paslow Building, which houses the city's main post office. Go straight along Queen St to see the city's quaint wooden police station and, eventually, the American Embassy, in a neighbourhood with some pretty Victorian houses.

If you turn right at the Paslow Building and walk along Front St you will eventually pass the Customs House, skirt the luxury hotel district, and emerge at the Baron Bliss Memorial, next to the Fort George lighthouse. There's a small park here and a good view of the water and the city.

Keep walking around the point, pass the Fort George Hotel on your left and walk up Marine Parade to Memorial Park. The park is ill kept but an open patch of green lawn is a welcome sight nonetheless.

PLACES TO STAY – BOTTOM END

The very cheapest hotels in Belize City are often not very safe because of break-ins and drug dealing. I've chosen the places below for relative safety as well as price. If one should prove unsafe, or if you find a good, safe, cheap place, please let me know.

Don't be shocked by these prices. Belize City is expensive for what you get.

Best all round, and often full, is the six-room *Sea Side Guest House* (☎ (02) 78339), 3 Prince St, on the upper floor, between Southern Foreshore and Regent St, more or less behind the Bellevue Hotel. Run by a North American couple who speak German as well as English, the Sea Side has maps and transport schedules on the walls, a bulletin board, one-for-one paperback exchange, the friendly atmosphere and low prices of a youth hostel, a quiet location in one of the city's better districts (even with partial sea views), and clean, decent rooms. Bunks in shared rooms cost US$8, double rooms are US$12.50. Good breakfasts and dinners are served at good prices; book in advance. Arrive early in the morning for the best chance of getting a bed here.

Freddie's Guest House (☎ (02) 44396), 86 Eve St, is the tidiest guesthouse in Belize. Freddie and Tona Griffith keep their three small guestrooms spotless, and the showers positively gleam and shine. Two rooms share one bath and cost US$17.50 a double; the room with private bath costs US$20. The house, set in small, well-kept gardens, is quiet. Neighbours include the Belize Center for Environmental Studies and the Association for Belizean Archeology.

North Front Street Guest House (☎ (02) 77595), 124 North Front St just east of Pickstock St, is also under North American management. Congenial, decent, safe and cheap, this is a favourite of low-budget travellers despite the noisy street and nightclub nearby. Bathrooms are shared, and bunks in the eight rooms cost US$5 to US$6.25. Breakfast and dinner are served if you order ahead. Check out the bulletin board. The location, less than a block from the Shell fuel station where the boats to Caye Caulker tie up, is fairly convenient.

There are other cheap hotels in this area,

Top: The view from the top of Temple II across the Great Plaza at Tikal, Guatemala (TB)

Bottom: Beach and wharf at Caye Caulker, Belize (TB)

Top: British colonial-style house in Orange Walk, Belize (JL)
Bottom: House in Belize City (TB)

including *Dim's Mira Rio Hotel* (☎ (02) 44970), 59 North Front St. The seven rooms here are slightly more expensive, but they come with sink and toilet. The bar overlooks Haulover Creek. *Bon Aventure Hotel* (☎ (02) 44248, 44134; fax 31134), 122 North Front St, right next to the North Front St Guest House, has nine rooms at US$12 a double (shared bath) and US$22 a double (private bath).

Marin's Travelodge (☎ (02) 45166), 6 Craig St, is on the upper floor of a fairly well-kept yellow wooden Caribbean house with a comfy swing on the verandah and seven rooms for rent. Shared showers are clean, and the price for the basic, plain, clean rooms is right at US$6 a single, US$8 a double.

Golden Dragon Hotel (☎ (02) 72817), 29 Queen St, is above the Chinese restaurant of the same name in a cul-de-sac on the south side of Queen St; enter along the left side of the building. Centrally located, fairly quiet, plain but clean, its rooms with private showers offer decent value for US$15 a single or a double with fan, US$27.50 with air-con; a triple with bath and air-con costs US$33.

If you're still looking for a room, try the *Hotel America* (☎ (02) 77384), 11 Dean St at Chapel Lane, above a Chinese restaurant. It is *very* basic for US$10 a double.

PLACES TO STAY – MIDDLE

Glenthorne Manor (☎ (02) 44212), 27 Barracks Rd, is a nice Victorian house with a small garden, high ceilings and lots of furnishings. There are only four rooms, all very atmospheric, and all rented with breakfast included in the tariff: US$30 a single, US$40 a double, US$42.50 for the suite with its own verandah. Reserve in advance, as rooms are often full.

Two blocks east of the US Embassy, facing the sea, stands the *Belize Guest House* (☎ & fax (02) 77569), 2 Hutson St. This big old seafront house is very secure and well maintained, and has fine sea views. The atmosphere is like that of a country inn.

Proprietor Charles Hope, a JP, rents seven rooms, some large and airy, others smaller, all with fans and private baths, for US$33 a single, US$44 a double. VISA and Master-Card are accepted, and Mr Hope can arrange rental cars as well.

Alicia's Guest House (☎ (02) 75082), 8 Chapel Lane at Dean St, has only four rooms on the upper storey above a shop, but the rooms are quite deluxe. All have private bath; the lounge is air conditioned. Rates are US$50 a double, breakfast included.

Fort Street Guest House (☎ (02) 45638; fax 78808), 4 Fort St, is a nice old New England-style house built in 1928 with lots of dark, rich woodwork, and recently restored. The downstairs salons are now a good restaurant; the upstairs has six guestrooms, sitting rooms furnished in wicker, and two bathrooms. A full breakfast is included in the rates which are US$35 a single, US$45 a double, US$60 a triple. Lunch and dinner in the restaurant are very good, and the verandah is a great place for people watching.

Hotel El Centro (☎ (02) 72413, 77739; fax 74553), 4 Bishop St (PO Box 122), has a marble façade and 12 small, tidy, modern guestrooms with cable TV, phone and air-conditioning for US$40 a double. There's a tidy modern restaurant to the left of the hotel. Credit cards are accepted.

Mom's Triangle Inn (☎ (02) 45073, 45523; fax 31975), 11 Handyside St, not far from the US Embassy, has six largeish, carpeted rooms with private showers going for US$28 to US$37 a single, US$37 to US$42 a double; higher priced rooms have air-con. There's a comfortable lounge, a common fridge, lockers for rent and laundry service.

Hotel Mopan (☎ (02) 73356, 77351; fax 45211), 55 Regent St, is a big old Caribbean-style wood-frame place with very basic rooms that are quite expensive for what you get, but the ambience is pure Belize. Some of the city's most interesting people congregate at the bar. Single rooms cost US$30 to US$42, doubles are US$42 to US$58, triples US$49 to US$63; the higher priced rooms have air-conditioning, the rest have fans.

Owners Jean and Tom Shaw are a wealth of information.

Bliss Hotel (☎ (02) 72552, 73310), 1 Water Lane, has 20 rooms, all with private baths, which can be dark and musty, but are clean and usable. There's also a little kidney-shaped swimming pool. Rates are US$27.50 a double with fan, US$40 with air-con.

PLACES TO STAY – TOP END

The city's newest and best is the 120-room *Ramada Royal Reef Hotel* (☎ (02) 31591; fax 31649), Newtown Barracks, in the northern reaches of the city. Opened in the spring of 1991, it has all the luxury facilities, good air-conditioning, and rates of US$170 a single, US$187 a double; these rates include an incredible 25% in tax and service charges. For reservations in the USA, call (800) 228-9898.

Before the opening of the Ramada, Belize City's top place was the *Radisson Fort George Hotel* (☎ (02) 77400, 45600; fax 43820), 2 Marine Parade, just north of the Baron Bliss Memorial. Radisson has given the old Fort George a major facelift, brightening up its public spaces and adding considerable comfort and class to its 76 air-conditioned rooms. Besides a swimming pool, several restaurants and bars, the Fort George has its own boat dock for cruise and fishing craft. Rooms come in three levels of comfort and price, from US$58 to US$138 a single, US$69 to US$173 a double, tax and service included. For reservations in the USA, call (800) 448-8355.

Across the street from the Fort George is *The Villa Hotel* (☎ (02) 455743, 45747; fax 30276), 13 Cork St (PO Box 1240), a smaller 42-room place which is in the midst of expansion. They're big on friendly service here, and their air-conditioned, TV-equipped rooms are certainly up to date and comfortable. High-season (winter) rates are US$83 a single, US$94 a double, US$104 a triple, US$115 a quadruple; low-season (summer) rates can be up to 35% lower.

Chateau Caribbean Hotel (☎ (02) 30800; fax 30900), 6 Marine Parade, by Memorial Park, was once a gracious old Belizean mansion, then a hospital; it's now a comfortable if simple hotel with 25 air-con guestrooms and a good dining room. Rates are US$56 a single, US$67 a double. Rooms in the 'annexe' behind the main building are not quite so pretty, but larger and a bit cheaper.

Unlike these other places, the 35-room *Bellevue Hotel* (☎ (02) 77051/2; fax 73253), 5 Southern Foreshore near King St, is in the city centre not far from the Bliss Institute. The hotel's unimpressive façade hides a tidy modern interior with 35 comfortable, air-conditioned, TV-equipped rooms going for US$87 a single, US$92 a double, and US$11 for an extra person in the same room.

PLACES TO EAT – BOTTOM END

Chances are you won't be eating many meals here, so you won't run out of places to eat them.

Macy's (☎ 3419), 18 Bishop St, has consistently good Caribbean Creole cooking, friendly service, and decent prices. Fish fillet with rice and beans costs about US$4, armadillo or wild boar a bit more. Hours are 11.30 am to 10 pm, closed Sunday.

Mom's (☎ 45073), 11 Handyside St, is the successor – at least in name – to the famous restaurant once located at the south end of the Swing Bridge. The homey, low-ceilinged dining room is usually busy all day during the winter season with travellers coming for huge portions of beans and rice with chicken, beef or fish for US$3, sandwiches and burgers (US$1.50 to US$4), fried chicken, fried fish and T-bone steaks. There's a bar, a blackboard menu, a souvenir and book shop, and a message-laden bulletin board. Mom's is closed on Saturday, and may have shorter hours in summer.

Dit's Restaurant (☎ 33330), 50 King St, is a bright, homey place with powerful fans and a loyal local clientele who come for huge portions and low prices. Rice and beans with beef, pork or chicken costs only US$2.50, and burgers are a mere US$1. Cakes and pies make a good dessert at US$0.75 per slice. Dit's is open from 8 am to 9 pm every day.

Ice cream parlours serving sandwiches and hamburgers are also good places for cheap meals. The menu may be limited, but the prices are usually good and the surroundings are pleasant.

Lily's Café & Patio (☎ 74378), 2-B King St, may be the tidiest little eatery in the city. Arched windows and a tiled floor give it a modern feel, and the pretty patio to the left of the café is the place to eat in good weather. 'The best hamburgers in town' cost less than US$2; big plates of rice and beans with stewed beef, chicken or pork are just US$3.50. Lily's is open from 11.30 am to 2.30 pm and 5.30 to 9 pm (10 pm on Friday and Saturday) and closed Sunday.

Bluebird Ice Cream Parlour (☎ 73918), 35 Albert St, facing the Atlantic Bank, is a very popular place in the commercial centre of town. Besides ice cream there are sandwiches and burgers (US$1 to US$1.50), and fried chicken for twice as much.

Celebrations (☎ 45789), 16 Queen St, not far beyond the post office on the opposite side of the street, is a clean, cheerful and convenient ice cream parlour serving rice and beans for US$2, sandwiches for US$1 and ice cream sundaes for just slightly more.

Pete's Pastries (☎ 44974), 41 Queen St near Handyside St, serves good cakes, tarts, and pies of fruit or meat. A slice and a soft drink costs US$1; my favourite is the raisin pie. You might try Pete's famous cowfoot soup, served on Saturday only, for US$1.50; or a ham and cheese sandwich for US$0.75. Pete's is open 8.30 am to 7 pm (8 am to 6 pm Sunday). There's another store at 71 Albert St, near Dean St, in the centre of town.

PLACES TO EAT – MIDDLE

Go to the corner of Queen St and Handyside to find two more upscale places. *Shangri-La Restaurant* (☎ 45699) invites you to 'dine and relax' in its spacious upper-storey bar overlooking the busy street corner. The menu is Chinese and Belizean, and a full lunch or dinner can be had for US$8 or less. At the *Piccadilly Restaurant*, the menu is eclectic, with tandoori chicken, fish, shish kebab, curries and pizza.

Shen's Peking Panda (☎ 78364), 4 Queen St, upstairs in the same building as the Upstairs Café, serves decent Chinese dishes at moderate prices. It can get noisy in the evening.

China Village, at the corner of Regent and Dean Sts, is the city's most elaborate Chinese eatery, with its own car park, a huge keyhole doorway, numerous dining rooms and a bar. It's the most 'atmospheric' place you'll find in the city. Order soup, a main course, dessert and drink and your bill should be between US$12 and US$18.

Golden Dragon Chinese Restaurant (☎ 72817), in a cul-de-sac off Queen St, is much less decorated, but makes up for it with a very long menu heavy on chow mein and chop suey, wonton soup and sweet-and-sour dishes. Full meals cost US$6 to US$14.

PLACES TO EAT – TOP END

Among the more expensive hotels, the dining room at the *Chateau Caribbean* (☎ 30800), 6 Marine Parade, is particularly notable. Simple but comfortable and pleasant, the upper-storey dining room enjoys a fine view of the Caribbean. Service is smooth and friendly, the dinner menu short but good, with cocktails of conch or shrimp, chicken with mushrooms, fish, steaks and lobster prepared in various ways. A full dinner with superior-quality Belikin Export beer costs US$16 to US$22. At lunch the menu also offers sandwiches and several Belizean dishes, so you can spend less.

Fort Street Guest House (☎ 45638), 4 Fort St, serves tasty food in the cosy atmosphere of a country inn. The menu changes frequently, but is usually enticing. Drop by or telephone to find out what's cooking.

The restaurant at the *Radisson Fort George Hotel* (☎ 77400) is also quite good, with fancier decor and prices. Seafood is the speciality, and a full fish dinner can be had for US$22 to US$26, wine included. To eat for less, order a burger, or chicken or shrimp 'in the basket' (crumbed, deep fried and served in a basket to be eaten with the fingers). The desserts are fancy here.

ENTERTAINMENT

There's lots of interesting action at night in Belize City. The problem is to separate the illegal activities from the legal. Clubs and bars that look like dives probably are. If drugs are in evidence, there's lots of room for trouble, and as a foreigner you'll have a hard time blending into the background.

Clubs

The club called The Big Apple, across from the North Front Street Guest House two blocks north-west of the Swing Bridge, is usually fine. The action depends upon the crowd, of course. The Upstairs Café on Queen St can get rowdy in the evening, but can be fun as well – check it out. The clubs and bars at the upscale hotels – Radisson Fort George, The Villa, etc – are sedate, respectable and safe.

Cinemas

Belize City is one of the very few places along La Ruta Maya that you can enjoy movies in English. The Majestic Theatre (☎ 45006), 17 Queen St, and the Palace Theatre (☎ 77120), 37 Albert St, show mostly action movies (kung fu, gangsters, war, etc). No movies based on a heart-to-heart talk while walking through a meadow need apply.

GETTING THERE & AWAY

Belize City is the country's transport nexus. Buses, boats and planes take you from here to any other part of Belize.

Air

For details on getting to Belize from points outside La Ruta Maya, see the chapters on Getting There & Away and Getting Around. For airport transport, see the Getting Around section below.

Belize City has two airports. Philip S W Goldson International Airport (code: BZE), 16 km north-west of the centre, handles all international flights. (Many domestic flights also originate here, then touch down at the smaller Municipal Airport to pick up passengers.) A new, modern terminal opened in 1990 to replace the tiny old 1960s building.

The terminal has a branch of the Belize Bank (open 8 to 11 am and noon to 5 pm every day) for currency exchange. There's also food service, and AT&T USADirect telephones – just pick up the handset and you're automatically connected with an operator in the USA.

The Municipal Airport (code: TZA) is 2.5 km north of the city centre, on the shore. Most flight schedules pick up passengers at both Goldson and Municipal airports. For many routes, the fare is considerably lower (up to 30%) if you depart from Municipal instead of Goldson.

Except in the busy winter season, it is usually possible to arrive at Goldson Airport and immediately buy a ticket on one of the frequent flights to Ambergris Caye or Caye Chapel. There are less frequent flights to other destinations, so you should find out the schedules and make reservations in advance, if possible. Here are the companies:

Tropic Air (☎ (02) 45671 in Belize City, or (026) 2012, 2117, 2029 in San Pedro, Ambergris Caye; fax (026) 2338), PO Box 20, San Pedro, Ambergris Caye, is the largest and most active of Belize's small airlines. Tropic Air has daily scheduled flights from Goldson Airport to San Pedro (Ambergris Caye, 10 flights), Big Creek/Placentia (one flight), Caye Chapel (10 flights), Corozal (via San Pedro, two flights), Punta Gorda (one flight), and to Cancún (one flight, 1½ hours, US$100 one way), using DeHavilland Twin Otter and Cessna aircraft. They also run day tours to Tikal in Guatemala (US$190 including round-trip flight, overnight in a Flores hotel, all meals and most taxes). For information in the USA call (800) 422-3435 or (713) 440-1867).

Maya Airways (☎ (02) 77215, 72313, 44032), 6 Fort St (P O Box 458), Belize City, has a similar schedule of flights to points in Belize, and adds Dangriga (four flights daily) to the flight roster. For information in the USA call (800) 552-3419.

Island Air (☎ (02) 31140 in Belize City, (026) 2435 in San Pedro, Ambergris Caye) also has service between Belize City and San Pedro.

Aerovías (☎ (02) 75445; in the USA (305) 883-1345) operates several flights per week between Belize City's Goldson Airport and Flores (near Tikal) in Guatemala, with onward connections to Guatemala City. For details, see the El Petén chapter under Flores.

Fares for Tropic Air and Maya Airways flights depend upon which airport you use:

Fare to	From Goldson Int'l	From Municipal
Ambergris Caye (San Pedro)	US$30	US$24
Caye Chapel	US$24	US$15
Corozal	US$48	US$38
Dangriga	US$34	US$23
Punta Gorda	US$61	US$50

The fare between Corozal and Punta Gorda is US$87; between San Pedro and Punta Gorda it's US$69.

International airlines serving Belize City have offices at Goldson International Airport; some have offices or agents in the centre of town as well.

TACA (☎ (02) 77257); in the city centre, contact Belize Global Travel (☎ (02) 77185), 41 Albert St

Continental (☎ (02) 78309); the city centre office is on Albert St between Dean and South in a marvellous little Hindu 'temple'

TAN-SAHSA (☎ (02) 77080)

Belize Trans Air (☎ (02) 77666, 77653, 77663); the city centre office is at 16 Albert St between King and Prince streets

American Airlines (☎ (02) 32522)

Pan American World Airways (☎ (02) 45176,45658)

Bus

Several different companies operate buses on different routes throughout the country. The bus stations are along or near the Collett Canal on West Collett Canal St, East Collett Canal St, or neighbouring streets. This is a rundown area not good for walking at night (take a taxi).

Batty Brothers Bus Service (☎ (02) 77146), 54 East Collett Canal, operates buses along the Northern Highway to Orange Walk, Corozal and Chetumal (Mexico).

Venus Bus Lines (☎ (02) 73354, 77390),

Magazine Rd, operates buses along routes similar to those of Batty Brothers.

Novelo's Bus Service (☎ (02) 77372), 19 West Collett Canal, is the line to take to Belmopan, San Ignacio, Xunantunich, Benque Viejo and the Guatemalan border at Melchor de Mencos.

Z-Line Bus Service (☎ (02) 73937) runs buses south to Dangriga, Big Creek (for Placentia) and Punta Gorda, operating from the Venus Bus Lines terminal on Magazine Rd in Belize City.

James Bus Service, Pound Yard (across from Batty Brothers), runs several buses a week to Dangriga and Punta Gorda.

Transportes del Carmen, Pound Yard (across from Batty Brothers), has several buses daily between Belize City and Benque Viejo via Belmopan and San Ignacio.

Belmopan – 84 km, 1½ hours; see Benque Viejo. James Bus Service buses to Dangriga and Punta Gorda stop in Belmopan as well.

Benque Viejo – 131 km, four hours; Novelo's operates buses from Belize City to Belmopan (US$1.40), San Ignacio (US$1.90) and Benque Viejo (US$2) every hour on the hour daily from 11 am to 7 pm (noon to 5 pm on Sunday). Coming from Benque, the buses start at 6 am and the last bus leaves at 3 pm. Transportes del Carmen also operates several buses daily on this run.

Chetumal – 160 km, four hours (express 3¼ hours); Venus has buses departing from Belize City every hour on the hour from noon to 7 pm for US$3.50; departures from Chetumal are hourly from 4 to 10 am. Batty's has buses every two hours on the hour for the same price.

Corozal – 155 km, 3½ hours; virtually all Batty's and Venus buses to and from Chetumal stop in Corozal, and there are several additional buses as well. There are frequent southbound buses in the morning but few in the afternoon; almost all northbound buses depart from Belize City in the afternoon. The fare between Belize City and Corozal is US$3.

Dangriga – 170 km, five hours; Z-Line has four buses daily for US$4. James Bus Service has several buses per week.

Orange Walk – 94 km, two hours; same schedule as Chetumal

Punta Gorda – 339 km, eight hours; Z-Line has one bus daily at 10 am for US$8.25. James Bus Service has five buses per week.

San Ignacio – 116 km, three hours; see Benque Viejo

Boat

Fast, powerful motor launches zoom between Belize City and the cayes – particularly Caye Caulker – every day. Before you take this trip, provide yourself with a bottle of sunscreen, a hat and/or clothing to protect you from the sun and sea spray. If you sit in the bow there's less spray, but you bang down harder when you come over a wave. Sitting in the stern gives a smoother ride, but you may get dampened by spray. Along the way you pass small cayes engulfed by mangroves and lots of sticks jutting up out of the water. These sticks mark lobster traps.

The traditional starting place for boats to Caye Caulker, and also some boats to Ambergris Caye, is near the A & R Shell fuel station on North Front St, two blocks northwest of the Swing Bridge. Each morning a variety of boats tie up here and wait for passengers. There are con artists working this business, so accept only a seaworthy-looking boat with a big motor (preferably two), and refuse to sail in an overloaded craft. Most boats leave Belize City between 8 and 10 am; after that, outbound boats are more difficult to find.

The fare for the voyage to Caye Caulker is usually US$6, but may be a bit higher depending upon the craft, the season, the number of people, whether Venus is rising or setting, etc. The trip against the wind takes from 40 minutes to one hour, depending upon the speed of the boat. Ask the price before you board the boat, and don't pay until you're safely off the boat at your destination (the legitimate boat owners won't ask you to pay before then).

Across Haulover Creek from the Shell station, just west of the Swing Bridge on Regent St West, is the dock for the Thunderbolt Express and Libra Express boats (☎ in San Pedro (026) 2217, 2159) which make the run between San Pedro on Ambergris Caye and Belize City, stopping at Caye Caulker and Caye Chapel along the way. *Thunderbolt* leaves San Pedro each morning at 7 am, reaches Belize City by 9 am, and departs from Belize City for the voyage back to San Pedro at 4 pm (1 pm on Saturday). *Libra* leaves San Pedro at 7.30 am and returns from Belize City at 1 pm. Fares are US$7.50 from Belize City to Caye Caulker, US$10 to San Pedro. In San Pedro, the Express ticket office is on Almond St.

Andrea departs from Belize City from Southern Foreshore by the Bellevue Hotel for San Pedro, Ambergris Caye, Monday to Friday at 4 pm (1 pm on Saturday, no boat on Sunday); the return trip to Belize City leaves San Pedro at 7 am. Fare is US$10 one way, US$17.50 round trip, and the voyage takes 1¼ to 1½ hours.

Boat owners in Belize can be a strange lot. One boat bears a sign which reads 'You are cordially invited to eat, shit and die'.

GETTING AROUND

Taxi

Trips by taxi within Belize City cost US$1.50 for one person, US$0.50 for each extra person.

To/From the Airport

The taxi fare to or from the airport is a fairly outrageous US$12.50, but there's no alternative except hiking.

Car Rental

Renting a car in Belize is expensive; the insurance available (and required) covers liability if you hit others, but not necessarily collision (if you damage the rental car). A major credit card is usually required and a valid driving licence is always required, in order to rent. The cost of renting is usually more than US$100 per day when the daily fee, kilometrage charges, insurance charges, etc are all added up. Then there's fuel, at US$0.52 per litre (US$2 per US gallon).

Avis rates for 4WD vehicles with insurance and unlimited kilometrage included are US$100 per day or US$600 per week for a Suzuki Samurai or US$138 per day, US$838 per week for an Isuzu Trooper.

For many parts of the country you may need such a 4WD vehicle, especially during the rainy months of summer. Talk over your route with the rental agency.

Agencies in Belize City include these:

Avis Rent-a-Car (☎ (02) 78637), in the Radisson Fort George Hotel, 2 Marine Parade, and at the Esso fuel station at the intersection of Front St and Handyside St

Budget Rent-a-Car (☎ (02) 32435; fax 30237), 771 Bella Vista

National Car Rental (☎ (02) 31586), Goldson International Airport

There are several smaller local agencies as well.

The Cayes

Belize's 290-km-long barrier reef, the longest in the western hemisphere, is the eastern edge of the limestone shelf which underlies most of La Ruta Maya. To the west of the reef the water is very shallow – usually not much more than four or five metres deep – which allows numerous islands called *cayes* (pronounced 'keys') to bask in warm waters.

Of the dozens of cayes, large and small, which dot the blue waters of the Caribbean off the Belizean coast, the two most popular with travellers are Caye Caulker and Ambergris Caye. Caulker is commonly thought of as the low-budget island, where hotels and restaurants are considerably less expensive than on resort-conscious Ambergris.

Both islands have an appealing laid-back Belizean atmosphere. No-one's in a hurry here. Stress doesn't figure in the lives of many islanders. Pedestrian traffic on the sandy unpaved streets moves at an easy tropical pace. The fastest vehicle is a kid on a bicycle. Motor vehicles are few and mostly parked.

Island residents include Creoles, mestizos, and a few transplanted North Americans and Europeans. They run lobster and conch-fishing boats, hotels and pensions, little eateries and a few island businesses which supply the few things necessary in a benevolent tropical climate.

CAYE CAULKER
Population 800
Approaching Caye Caulker on the boat from Belize City, you glide along the eastern shore which is overhung with palm trees. Dozens of wooden docks jut out from the shore to give moorings to boats and swimming possibilities to island residents. Off to the east, about two km away, the barrier reef is marked by a thin white line of surf.

Caye Caulker (called Hicaco in Spanish, sometimes Corker in English) lies about 33 km north of Belize City and 24 km south of Ambergris Caye. The island is about seven km long north to south, and only about 600 metres wide at its widest point. Mangroves cover much of the shore, coconut palms provide shade. The village is on the southern portion of the island. Actually Caulker is now two islands, ever since Hurricane Hattie cut the island in two just north of the village. The cut is called, simply, The Cut. It has a tiny beach, swift currents running through it, and it marks the northern limits of the settlement.

You disembark and wander ashore to find a place of sandy unpaved 'streets' which are actually more like paths. The government has carefully placed 'Go Slow' and 'Stop' signs at the appropriate places, even though there are no vehicles in sight and everyone on Caulker naturally goes slow and stops frequently. The stops are often to get a beer – most right hands on this island spend much of the day wrapped around a cold one. Virtually constant sea breezes keep the island comfortable even in Belize's sultry heat. If the wind dies, the heat immediately becomes noticeable, as do the sandflies and mosquitoes.

Many gardens and paths on the island have borders of conch shells, and every house has its 'catchment', or large wooden cistern to catch rainwater for drinking. Lobster traps are piled everywhere from mid-March to mid-July when it's illegal to catch the beasts. By late July the piles of traps disappear back into the shallow waters surrounding the island.

Orientation
The village has two principal streets, Front

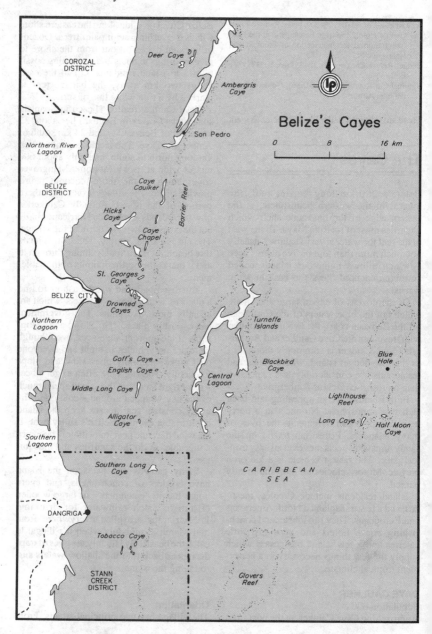

St to the east and Back St to the west. The distance from The Cut in the north to Shirley's Guest House at the southern edge of the village is a little more than one km.

The Belize Telecommunications telephone office is open from 8 am to noon and 1 to 4 pm, Monday to Friday, 8 am to noon on Saturday, closed Sunday.

Water Sports

The surf breaks on the barrier reef, easily visible from the eastern shore of Caye Caulker. A short boat ride takes you out there to enjoy some of the world's most exciting snorkelling, diving and fishing. Boat trips are big business on the island, so you have many to choose from. Ask other visitors to the island about their boating experiences, and use this information to choose a boat. Virtually all of the island residents are trustworthy boaters, but it's still good to discuss price, duration, areas to be visited, and the seaworthiness of the boat. Boat and motor should be in good condition. Even sailboats should have motors in case of emergency (the weather can change quickly here). The cost is usually around US$10 to US$13 per person; sometimes lunch is included.

Underwater visibility is up to 60 metres. The variety of underwater plants, coral and tropical fish is wonderful. Be careful not to touch the coral, both to prevent damage to it and to yourself; coral is sharp, and some species sting or burn their assailants.

Among the more interesting places to dive is in the underwater caves off the western shore of the island. The cave system here is elaborate and fascinating, but cave-diving is a special art. You should not go down without an experienced guide and the proper equipment (strong lights, etc). The dive shops on the island can tell you what – and what not – to do.

Beachgoers will find the water warm, clear and blue, but they won't find much in the way of beach. Though there's lots of sand, it doesn't seem to arrange itself in nice long, wide stretches along the shore. Most of your sunbathing will be on docks or in deck chairs at your hotel. Caulker's finest public

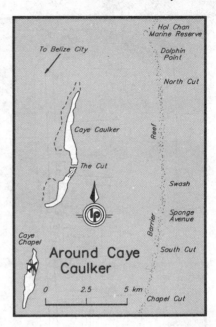

beach, at The Cut to the north of the village, is tiny and crowded, and nothing special to write home about.

Places to Stay

Though hotels on Caulker are among the cheapest in Belize, they are still more expensive than comparable places in Mexico or Guatemala. Among the comforts you pay for on Caulker are shade and pretty grounds.

Cheap, No Shade or Grounds *Lena's Hotel* (☎ (022) 2106) has 11 rooms in an old building right on the water, with no grounds to speak of. Rates are fairly good for what you get: US$8 a double in summer, a dollar or two more during the busy winter season.

Deisy's Hotel (☎ (022) 2123) has 11 rooms in several blue-and-white buildings which get full sun most of the day. Rooms with table or floor fans, sharing common baths, cost US$9 a double; with private shower the rate is US$16.

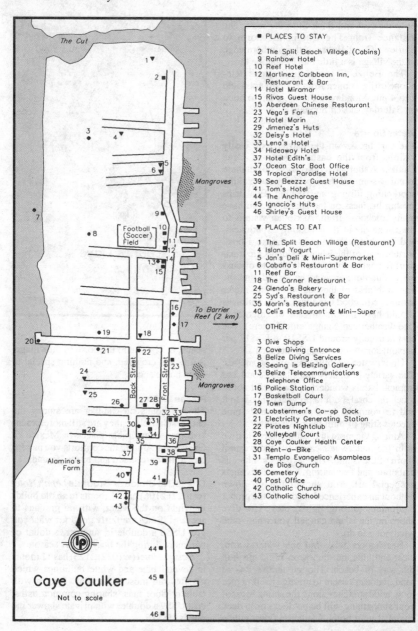

PLACES TO STAY

2 The Split Beach Village (Cabins)
9 Rainbow Hotel
10 Reef Hotel
12 Martinez Caribbean Inn,
    Restaurant & Bar
14 Hotel Miramar
15 Rivas Guest House
15 Aberdeen Chinese Restaurant
23 Vega's For Inn
27 Hotel Marin
29 Jimenez's Huts
32 Deisy's Hotel
33 Lena's Hotel
34 Hideaway Hotel
37 Hotel Edith's
37 Ocean Star Boat Office
38 Tropical Paradise Hotel
39 Sea Beezzz Guest House
41 Tom's Hotel
44 The Anchorage
45 Ignacio's Huts
46 Shirley's Guest House

PLACES TO EAT

1 The Split Beach Village (Restaurant)
4 Island Yogurt
5 Jan's Deli & Mini–Supermarket
6 Cabaña's Restaurant & Bar
11 Reef Bar
18 The Corner Restaurant
24 Glenda's Bakery
25 Syd's Restaurant & Bar
35 Marin's Restaurant
40 Celi's Restaurant & Mini–Super

OTHER

3 Dive Shops
7 Cave Diving Entrance
8 Belize Diving Services
8 Seaing is Belizing Gallery
13 Belize Telecommunications
    Telephone Office
16 Police Station
17 Basketball Court
19 Town Dump
20 Lobstermen's Co-op Dock
21 Electricity Generating Station
22 Pirates Nightclub
26 Volleyball Court
28 Caye Caulker Health Center
30 Rent-a-Bike
31 Templo Evangelico Asambleas
    de Dios Church
36 Cemetery
40 Post Office
42 Catholic Church
43 Catholic School

Hideaway Hotel (☎ (022) 2103), behind the Asambleas de Dios Church, is a hot two-storey cement-block building with six bare rooms on the ground floor; all have table fans (ceiling fans are preferable). No beach, no shade, no grounds, and the church rocks with up-tempo hymns some nights, but prices are fairly good at US$8 a double in summer, US$10 a double in winter.

Hotel Edith's is tidy and proper, with tiny rooms, each of which has a private shower, priced at US$13 a single, US$16 a double (one bed) or US$20 a double (two beds).

Hotel Miramar has rooms on two floors in a building facing the sea, but without sea views from the rooms. The common showers are fairly tidy, and the prices very good at US$5 a double (one bed), US$8 a double (two beds), just slightly more for a triple. Enquire about rooms at the house behind the Belize Telecommunications building.

Riva's Guest House (☎ (022) 2127) has six rooms that are clean, and cheaper than most others in town at US$7 a double.

Martinez Caribbean Inn (☎ (022) 2113) has 16 rooms, all with private bath. The tiny cell-like rooms aren't gorgeous, but the hot water is really hot and the prices moderate at US$18 a double.

Some Shade for Sitting The *Reef Hotel* (☎ (022) 2196) is often considered the centre of the village. The two-storey wood-and-masonry building has a porch for sitting, a bar nearby (it can be noisy, but doesn't go late at night), and rooms with private showers. You pay US$18 a single, US$20 a double for a good location.

Hotel Marin is not on the shore but it has some trees and gardens, and porches off the bungalows for hanging hammocks. Prices are good: US$10 a double with common bath in summer, US$15 in winter; with private shower prices are US$20 in summer, US$25 in winter.

Tom's Hotel (☎ (022) 2102) has nice, tidy, white buildings with 20 rooms priced at US$8 a single, US$10 a double with common bathrooms.

The Split Beach Village has six rooms with private showers in tidy wooden bungalows priced at US$23 a double in summer, US$30 in winter. Here you're only steps from The Cut.

Nice Shady Grounds *Jimenez's Huts* (☎ (022) 2175) has little thatched huts with walls of sticks, each with a private shower. The place is quaint, quiet and relaxing, and constitutes very good value at US$15 to US$18 a double, US$18 a triple, US$23 for four.

Tropical Paradise Hotel (☎ (022) 2124; fax 2225) pretty much lives up to its name. Choose from six tidy panelled rooms in a long wooden building for US$18 to US$27 a double with private shower and ceiling fans; or an equal number of individual yellow cabins with ceiling fans and private baths (some with tubs) for US$23 to US$33. Higher prices apply during the busy winter season. There's a nice modern restaurant and bar, and a big dock for boats or sunning. Owner Ramon Reyes keeps everything in good shape, and all his guests happy.

Shirley's Guest House (☎ (022) 2145), along the south-eastern shore, has nice bungalows with four rooms (two upstairs, two down) boasting mahogany floors, good cross-ventilation and fans. Each pair of rooms shares a bath. Rates are US$19 a single, US$24 to US$27 a double.

The Anchorage closes in the summer, but rents its four thatched, whitewashed bungalows in winter for US$20 a double. Each bungalow has a cold-water shower – but how cold is the water here? Its location at the southern end of town is quiet.

Ignacio's Huts, just south of The Anchorage, is a collection of thatched cottages shaded by dozens of gently swaying palm trees. The cottages are quite simple, but who needs more on Caulker? Rates are satisfying at US$8 to US$15 per hut, with private shower, depending upon the hut and the season.

Sea Beezzz Guest House (☎ (022) 2176) is a solid, two-storey house on the shore with a nice patio garden in front. Safe, secure, comfortable, with hot water in the private

Diving for lobsters

showers and a dining room service for all three meals, its only disadvantage is that it closes down for the summer. Rates are US$35 to US$50 per room.

Rainbow Hotel (☎ (022) 2123), just north of the boat docks on the way to The Cut, is a two-storey concrete building with plain but clean rooms going for US$28 a double with clean tiled private shower, fan, and a window facing eastwards out to sea.

Vega's Far Inn (☎ (022) 2142; fax in Belize City (02) 31580), owned by the congenial Vega family – Antonio ('Tony'), Lydia and Maria – has several very tidy waterless rooms upstairs in a wooden house, with good, clean showers down the hall. Other much bigger rooms with private showers are in a concrete building. All rooms have wall fans; there's some shady space in front of the house for sitting. An adjoining shady camping area is just the place to pitch your tent, for US$6 per person. Prices for rooms are US$10 to US$40 a single, US$20 to US$50 a double, depending upon the room and the season. The Vegas rent

snorkelling equipment, little sailboats (Sunfish), and can sign you up for snorkelling or sport-fishing trips. For reservations, write to them at PO Box 701, Belize City.

Places to Eat

The shallow waters around Caulker are alive with spiny lobsters. During the lobstering season from 15 July to 15 March you'll see boats filled with them draw up to the docks. All the restaurants serve lobster during the season, and it's a bargain. Conch is another island favourite. The season for collecting these hard-shelled creatures is all months except July and August.

Though they serve such 'luxury' items as lobster and conch, there are no fancy restaurants on Caulker. Even so, prices are high as everything except lobster and fish must be brought out from the mainland. The island's simple eateries are supplemented by little shops selling sandwiches, snacks and baked goods.

You expect to find haggis and oatcakes at the *Aberdeen Restaurant* (☎ 2127), just south of the Hotel Martinez, but instead it serves Chinese and Belizean food. The lighting is dim, decor is sparse, music is reggae, servings are generous, and the menu includes fried rice, egg foo yung, curries, T-bone steak and fried lobster. The last page of the long menu lists specialities such as salty pepper shrimp. A full meal costs US$5 to US$12.

Martinez Caribbean Inn is tidy and lighter than the Aberdeen, and features lots of sandwiches, burgers and antojitos (garnaches, tacos, panuchos, etc) as well as rice and beans with chicken or lobster. For breakfast, coffee and a fruit plate costs less than US$3. Lunch or dinner can cost US$2.50 to US$8. They concoct a tasty rum punch that's sold by the bottle (US$5) or the glass (US$1.50).

Marin's Restaurant, a block west of the Tropical Paradise, serves up fresh seafood in its outdoor garden and mosquito-proof screened dining room. Try the lobster with pineapple (Belizean style, sweet-and-sour) for US$7 or whole grilled catch-of-the-day for US$4.

The restaurant at the *Tropical Paradise*

Hotel is busy all day because it serves the island's most consistently good food in big portions at decent prices. In the light, cheerful dining room, breakfast is served from 8 am to noon, lunch from 11.30 am to 2 pm and dinner from 6 to 10 pm. You can order curried shrimp or lobster for US$8, many other things for less.

Delicious aromas waft from the doors of many island houses, and customers for these home-baked treats waft in. Such home-based industries as Glenda's baked goods, Island Yogurt and others provide a welcome – and usually cheap – alternative to restaurant meals.

Entertainment
After one evening on the island, you'll know what there is to do in the evening. The Reef Bar, by the Reef Hotel, has a sand floor and tables holding clusters of bottles (mostly beer) as semipermanent centrepieces. This is the gathering, sipping and talking place. For music, take a look at Pirates, the nightclub.

Getting There & Away
Talk about building an airstrip on Caye Caulker may soon come to action. Right now, the only way to fly is to nearby Caye Chapel, then continue by boat to Caulker. However, transport by fast motor launch from Belize City is so convenient that most people go that way.

Information on boats from Belize City is included in that section. Boats depart from Caye Caulker for Belize City early in the morning, usually between 6 and 8 am. The *Ocean Star*, for instance, leaves Caulker at 6.45 am, arriving at the Shell station in Belize City by 7.30 am. You can buy a ticket (US$5.50) at the boat office next to Hotel Edith's.

Some boats make an afternoon run to Belize City as well, departing from the island between 3 and 5 pm on the 45-minute run. Check on return trips with your boat captain when you arrive on the island.

A number of boats stop at Caulker on their way to San Pedro, Ambergris Caye. Ask around near the docks to see who's doing this, and when.

AMBERGRIS CAYE
Population 2000
The largest of Belize's cayes, Ambergris (pronounced am-BER-griss) lies 58 km north of Belize City. It's over 40 km long, and connected to Mexican land on its northern side. Most of the island's population lives in the town of San Pedro near the southern tip. The barrier reef is only one km east of San Pedro. In the morning, before the workday noises begin, if you stand on one of the docks on the town's eastern side, you can hear the low bass tone of the surf breaking over the reef.

It started life as a fishing town, but San Pedro is now Belize's prime tourist destination with a variety of hotels, restaurants and other services. Prime it may be, but it's certainly no Cancún even though developers have recently moved in to construct and aggressively promote beachfront condominiums. Ambergris is still less developed than Isla Mujeres. Like Caye Caulker, Ambergris has an engaging laid-back atmosphere. (A sign in a local restaurant has it right: 'No shirt, no shoes – *no problem!*') But as word spreads to the outside world of its beauties and its laid-back lifestyle, more tourists will come, and the laid-back lifestyle – their reason for coming – will someday be swept away and replaced with frenetic Cancún-style consumerism.

Right now, though, San Pedro is sandy streets with little traffic, lots of Caribbean-style wooden buildings (some on stilts), and few people who bother to wear shoes. Everyone is friendly, and everyone is looked upon as a person – not a tourist, not a source of dollars, but a person.

Orientation
It's about one km from the Paradise Hotel in the northern part of town to the airport in the south, so everything is within easy walking distance unless you're burdened with lots of luggage.

San Pedro has three main north-south

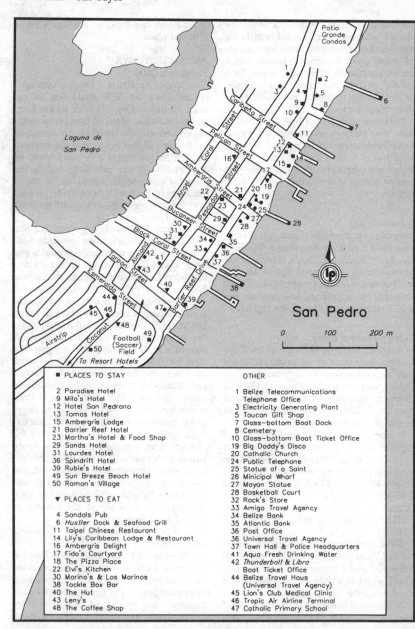

San Pedro

0   100   200 m

■ PLACES TO STAY

2 Paradise Hotel
9 Milo's Hotel
12 Hotel San Pedrano
13 Tomas Hotel
15 Ambergris Lodge
21 Barrier Reef Hotel
23 Martha's Hotel & Food Shop
29 Sands Hotel
31 Lourdes Hotel
36 Spindrift Hotel
39 Rubie's Hotel
49 Sun Breeze Beach Hotel
50 Ramon's Village

▼ PLACES TO EAT

4 Sandals Pub
6 Hustler Dock & Seafood Grill
11 Taipei Chinese Restaurant
14 Lily's Caribbean Lodge & Restaurant
16 Ambergris Delight
17 Fido's Courtyard
18 The Pizza Place
22 Elvi's Kitchen
30 Marino's & Los Marinos
38 Tackle Box Bar
40 The Hut
43 Leny's
48 The Coffee Shop

OTHER

1 Belize Telecommunications
   Telephone Office
3 Electricity Generating Plant
5 Toucan Gift Shop
7 Glass-bottom Boat Dock
8 Cemetery
10 Glass-bottom Boat Ticket Office
19 Big Daddy's Disco
20 Catholic Church
24 Public Telephone
25 Statue of a Saint
26 Minicipal Wharf
27 Mayan Statue
28 Basketball Court
32 Rock's Store
33 Amigo Travel Agency
34 Belize Bank
35 Atlantic Bank
36 Post Office
36 Universal Travel Agency
37 Town Hall & Police Headquarters
41 Aqua Fresh Drinking Water
42 Thunderbolt & Libra
   Boat Ticket Office
44 Belize Travel Haus
   (Universal Travel Agency)
45 Lion's Club Medical Clinic
46 Tropic Air Airline Terminal
47 Catholic Primary School

streets which used to be called Front St (to the east), Middle St, and Back St (to the west). Now these streets have tourist-class names: Barrier Reef Drive, Pescador Drive and Angel Coral Drive, but some islanders might still use the old names.

Information

Money You can change money easily in San Pedro, but keep in mind that US dollars are accepted in many establishments.

Both the Atlantic Bank and the Belize Bank are near the Spindrift Hotel. The Atlantic Bank (☎ (026) 2195) is open Monday, Tuesday and Thursday from 8 am to noon and 1 to 3 pm; Wednesday 8 am to 1 pm; Friday 8 am to 1 pm and 3 to 6 pm; Saturday from 8.30 am to noon.

Belize Bank is open Monday to Thursday from 8 am to 3 pm, Friday 8 am to 1 pm and 3 to 6 pm, Saturday from 8.30 am to noon.

Post & Telephone San Pedro's post office is on the ground floor of the Spindrift Hotel. Hours are 8 am to noon and 1 to 5 pm (4.30 pm on Friday), closed Saturday and Sunday.

The Belize Telecommunications telephone office is open Monday to Friday from 8 am to noon and 1 to 4 pm, Saturday from 8 am to noon; closed Sunday.

Water Sports

Ambergris is good for all water sports: scuba diving, snorkelling, sailboarding, boating, swimming, deep-sea fishing and sunbathing. Many island hotels have their own dive shops to rent equipment, provide instruction and organise diving excursions.

Universal Travel & Tours, in the lobby of the Spindrift Hotel on Barrier Reef Drive, offers a full list of services. Hire a fishing boat for US$135 a day (deep-sea fishing for US$350 a day), or a boat and guide for a two-tank dive (US$45 plus equipment rental costs of about US$36), take a full diving certification course for US$350, or just sign up for a full-day barbecue beach picnic on a remote beach for US$40, lunch included. Rent a canoe for US$30 a day, a snorkel, mask and fins for US$8, take a bird-watching

cruise for US$20, or go sailing and snorkelling for the day for US$35, drinks included.

Among the favourite seafaring destinations near and far are these:

Blue Hole, a deep sinkhole of vivid blue water where you can dive to 40 metres, observing the cave with diving lights

Caye Caulker North Island, the relatively uninhabited northern part of Caulker, with good snorkelling, swimming, and places for a beach barbecue

Glovers Reef, about 50 km east of Dangriga, is one of only three coral atolls in the western hemisphere; the other two, Lighthouse Reef and the Turneffe Islands, are also in Belize

Half Moon Caye, a small island on Lighthouse Reef, 113 km east of Belize City, has a lighthouse, excellent beaches, and spectacular submerged walls teeming with marine flora and fauna. Underwater visibility can extend over 60 metres. The caye is a bird sanctuary and home to the rare Pink-Footed Booby.

Hol Chan Marine Reserve, with submerged canyons 30 metres deep busy with large fish; the canyon walls are covered with colourful sponges

Lighthouse Reef, which includes Half Moon Caye, is one of three coral atolls in the western hemisphere, lying 100 km east of Belize City

Mexico Cave, filled with colourful sponges, lobsters and shrimp

Palmetto Reef, with lots of canyons, surge channels, and many varieties of coral (hard and soft) as well as sponges and fish

Punta Arena, an area of underwater canyons and sea caves teeming with fish, rays, turtles, sponges and coral

San Pedro Cut, the large break in the barrier reef used by the larger fishing and pleasure boats

Tres Cocos Cut, a natural break in the barrier reef which attracts a variety of marine life

Turneffe Islands, a large atoll 30 km east of Belize City teeming with coral and alive with fish and large rays

For those who don't fancy diving or snorkelling, but who still want to see some of the marvellous marine life, glass-bottom boat tours are run by several companies. About the cheapest is the two-hour tour (9 to 11 am or 2 to 4 pm) for US$7.50. Buy your tickets in the house to the left of Milo's Hotel at the northern end of Barrier Reef Drive, and board the boat at the dock due east of there.

Swimming is best off the pier at the Paradise Hotel. All beaches are public and you can probably use their lounge chairs if it's a slow day. At Ramon's Village there is a very nice thatched cabaña for sunset-watching at the end of the pier.

Mainland Excursions

Many visitors to Belize fly to Ambergris and make it their base for flying excursions to other parts of this small country. Tours are available to the Mayan ruins at Altun Ha and Xunantunich, to the Belize Zoo, Crooked Tree Bird Sanctuary, the Baboon Sanctuary, Mountain Pine Ridge, and even to Tikal in Guatemala. Inquire at Universal Travel & Tours (☎ (026) 2031, 2137; fax 2185), Amigo Travel (☎ (026) 2180, 2435; fax 2192), or at any of the more expensive hotels in San Pedro.

Places to Stay – bottom end

Though there are some cheap places to stay here, they are small, few in number, and do not offer particularly good value for money. Wherever you stay, you'll never be more than a minute's walk from the water.

Lourdes Hotel (☎ (026) 2066) on Pescador is very plain and well used – no one would call it beautiful, few would call it pleasant – but cheap at US$10 a single, US$17.50 a double with private shower. Ask at the Lourdes Store, four doors to the left (south) of the hotel.

Milo's Hotel (☎ (026) 2033), on Barrier Reef Drive, has nine small, dark, fairly dismal rooms above a shop in a blue-and-white Caribbean-style building. It's quiet, cheap, and often full for those reasons. Rooms using common showers go for US$10 a double.

Tomas Hotel (☎ (026) 2061), Barrier Reef Drive, offers very good value for money. This family-run place charges US$20 (summer) or US$25 (winter) for eight light, airy double rooms with private baths (some with tubs). Two rooms have double beds, the others have a double and a single, making them good for families or threesomes.

Martha's Hotel (☎ (026) 2053), corner of Ambergris and Pescador, has 16 rooms. All have private bath, and sometimes the wash-basin is in the room because the bathroom is so small. Room Nos 11 and 12 are lighter and airier than the rest. Rates are US$15 to US$24 a single, US$27.50 to US$35 a double, US$37.50 to US$46 a triple, US$50 for four; the higher prices apply during the busy winter season.

Hotel San Pedrano (☎ (026) 2054, 2093), corner of Barrier Reef and Caribeña, has one apartment and seven rooms, all with private bath. Though most rooms don't have ocean views, they do have nice wooden floors and well-maintained patio furniture. The apartment rents for US$150 per week and has a double bed and two single beds, while the rooms rent for US$27 a single, US$33 a double, US$40 a triple in winter; summer prices are a few dollars lower.

Rubie's Hotel (☎ (026) 2063), at the south end of Barrier Reef Drive, is close to the airport and right on the water. Five of the nine rooms here have private showers; not all of the rooms overlook the sea. Rates are US$15 a single, US$25 a double with bath, US$15 a double with shared bath in winter, lower in summer.

Lily's Caribbean Lodge (☎ (026) 2059), off the east end of Caribeña facing the sea, has 10 clean, pleasant rooms; several (especially those on the top floor) have good sea views. At US$15 a double in summer it's a bargain, but the rate rises to US$37.50 in winter. There's a tidy restaurant on the ground floor.

Places to Stay – middle

Many of these hotels cater to divers, who are often willing to pay more for a room – any room – if the diving's good. Note that some of these hotels charge 10% or 15% for service in addition to the 5% government room tax. I've included both of these extra charges in the rates quoted below.

The *Barrier Reef Hotel* (☎ (026) 2075; fax 2192), on Barrier Reef Drive in the centre of town, is a landmark, its attractive Caribbean wood-frame construction captured by countless tourist cameras daily. Most of the 10 rooms are not in this structure, however, but in a newer and less charming concrete-block addition at the back. The bonus here is air-conditioning, good on sticky hot days. The rate is US$50 a double in summer, US$75 in winter.

Places to Stay – top end

Ambergris has many resort hotels, but none are Cancún-style huge high-rises. On Ambergris, a resort is often a collection of thatched bungalows which can house upwards of two dozen people. Here are the best places to stay right in San Pedro.

Paradise Hotel (☎ (026) 2021, 2083), at the northern end of Barrier Reef Drive, is a favourite amongst Ambergris cognoscenti. Its 25 rooms are in thatched cottages shaded by palms, separated by lots of sand set with deck chairs. Rooms, cabañas and villas are large, airy and attractive with clean showers, ceiling fans, and good firm beds. The Palm Restaurant is among the island's better places to eat; the bar a congenial watering hole. The hotel has its own dock and dive shop. Rates range from US$40 to US$75 a single, US$65 to US$115 a double, US$80 to US$130 a triple, tax and service included. For reservations in the USA, call (800) 537-1431 (fax (713) 785-9528), or write to PO Box 888, Belize City.

Spindrift Hotel (☎ (026) 2018, 2174; fax 2251), corner of Bucaneer and Barrier Reef, has a good location right in the centre of town on the beach. It's a modern, fairly attractive building with 24 comfortable rooms ranging from a smaller room with one double bed, ceiling fan, and a view of the street for US$47.50 a double, to a room with two double beds, air-conditioning and a view of the sea for US$90 a double. There are also several apartments priced at US$120 to US$160. All rooms have private showers. The hotel has a good restaurant, and a bar called the Pier Lounge in which 'chicken drops' are held on Wednesday evenings. (You drop a chicken onto a slate with numbers, hoping for it to land on a high number, which becomes your score.)

Sands Hotel (☎ (026) 2040) stretches between Barrier Reef Drive and Pescador. It has recently expanded and increased its number of rooms. Prices have not been set, but should be in the range of US$70 a double for an air-conditioned, bath-equipped room.

Sun Breeze Beach Hotel (☎ (026) 2191, 2345; fax 2346), PO Box 14, at the southern end of Barrier Reef Drive not far from the airport, is a nice, fairly new Mexican-style two-storey concrete building with a sandy inner court opening towards the beach and the sea. Shady tiled porticos set with easy chairs are great for lounging and watching nothing happen; other lounge chairs are arranged down by the shore. The 34 air-conditioned, shower-equipped rooms are attractive and comfortable, and priced at US$92 a single, US$104 a double, US$127 a triple, US$145 for four people in winter; prices in summer are 10% to 15% lower.

Ramon's Village (☎ (026) 2071, 2213; fax 2214), on Coconut Drive south of the Tropic Air terminal, is a charming Caribbean hideaway with two-storey cabañas, thatched Hawaiian-style, facing a good beach. Dive shop, boats for excursions, jet-skis, sailboards, lounge chairs for sunning, swimming pool with bar surrounded by coconut palms...you get the idea. Some cabañas have sea views, many have porches for sitting, and all come with at least a king-size bed, or two double beds. All is very well kept. Rates range from US$115 to US$260 a double; cabañas have private baths and either ceiling fans or air-conditioning. Diving trips and water sports equipment are all available at extra fees. For reservations in the USA call (601) 649-1990; fax (601) 425-2411.

Places to Eat – bottom end

There's not much in the way of cheap food. Even buying your own is no solution as everything's imported and quite expensive. But you needn't starve, just choose carefully.

Leny's, near the airport on Tarpon, has lots of rich, filling soups including *chirmolex*, a black soup much like Mexican pozole. They also serve Mexican salbutes, tostadas, etc, and the inevitable rice and beans. The most expensive item on the menu is Mexican steak *encebollado* (with onions) for US$4. Simple but tidy, it's open every day for every meal.

The Coffee Shop, across Coconut Drive from the Tropic Air terminal, is air-conditioned, and serves sandwiches, burgers, chilli dogs, tostadas and burritos priced from US$2 to US$4. A ham-and-eggs breakfast is yours for US$4, an omelette or huevos rancheros the same, but my favourite breakfast here is a big slice of home-made banana bread and a cup of their good coffee for US$1.50. They open for breakfast at 6.30 am, and serve meals until early evening.

Places to Eat – middle

Elvi's Kitchen (☎ 2126), on Pescador near Ambergris, is typically Belizean, offering substantial servings, prices for every budget, and food cooked to order. A big plate of fish and chips is yours for US$7; rice and beans with fish for US$5. You can spend as much as US$10 for shrimp with garlic cooked in wine, or as little as US$1.75 for a ham and cheese sandwich. The pleasant if plain dining room is open at mealtimes only: 11.30 am to 2 pm and 6.30 to 10 pm (a bit later on the weekends). Sit on picnic tables inside a thatched, screened-in hut with crushed shells and sand under your feet. Fans cool the place nicely.

The Hut, on Tarpon St at the southern end of Barrier Reef Drive, is the place to go when you're bored with other restaurants' menus. Where else can you get a chicken sandwich with melted cheese and sweet potato fries? They have stone crab claws, taco salads, and build-your-own burgers. The Hut doesn't look like much from the outside but is quite nice within, with floral-print tablecloths and plants hanging in macramé. The bar is always well attended by regulars. Hours are 7 am to 10 pm. Expect to pay US$5 to US$12.50 for a full dinner.

Lily's (☎ 2059), in Lily's Hotel off the eastern end of Caribeña, is a family-run place specialising in seafood. A lunch or dinner of lobster, conch or shrimp might cost US$10 to US$15; breakfasts are served for about US$5. It's pleasant, but there's no sea view, even though the building is on the shore.

The Pizza Place, on Barrier Reef near Pelican, has all sorts of pizzas big enough for two or three people and priced from US$10 to US$17. Sit at bar stools to consume them, or take them away. A slice of cheese pizza is US$1.15, and a whole one is US$9. They also serve frozen chocolate bananas, and sandwiches on French bread laden with salami, ham, lettuce, tomato and cheese for US$3.

Enter *Fido's Courtyard* past The Pizza Place and you'll find several eating places, an art gallery and a travel agency around a shady deck area overlooking the sea. The Bar serves drinks such as rum and Coke or beer for US$1.50. The Grill, open from 6 am to 6 pm (closed Wednesday), serves sandwiches, burgers, steaks, fish and lobster for prices ranging between US$8 and US$14. The thatched roof and cool breeze make this a good place to sit, talk and relax anytime. Come for lucky number bingo played here some evenings.

Marino's, on Pescador St near Bucaneer St, is a neat little restaurant with a bar to the left, a dining room to the right. The menu is interesting, with cheap sandwiches, fried chicken and chips, grilled chicken, fish and pork chops, salads of chicken or lobster and shrimp ceviche. The price for lunch or dinner can be anywhere from US$2 to US$15. Don't confuse Marino's with the down-at-heel Los Marinos cantina in the right-hand end of the building.

Barrier Reef Hotel on Barrier Reef Drive has a small restaurant on its ground floor specialising in pizza. An attractive place with checked tablecloths, its menu lists nine, 12 and 16-inch pizzas priced from US$7.50 to US$17, depending upon ingredients. They also serve a few sandwiches, nachos and shrimp cocktails.

Taipei Chinese, at the corner of Barrier Reef and Caribeña, serves Taiwanese dishes at moderate prices. Hours are 11 am to 3 pm and 5.30 pm to midnight.

Ambergris Delight, on Pescador near Pelican, cooks fried chicken and pies to take away, just the thing when you want to have a picnic or relax in your hotel room. This is also the ticket office for the *Andrea*, which plies the waves to Belize City.

Places to Eat – top end

Pier Restaurant at the Spindrift Hotel is among the island's best places to dine. The attractive dining room is breezy, with a fine sea view. When I recently looked in, they were offering a daily special of chicken and rice soup for US$3.25, and coq au vin with herbed rice and a 'medley' of vegetables for US$11.

Palm Restaurant in the Paradise Hotel, at the northern end of Barrier Reef Drive, can start you out right in the morning with a lobster omelette (US$6); or you can have a fruit plate and coffee for US$3.50. For lunch or dinner start with garnachos (fried corn tortillas topped with refried beans, coleslaw and melted cheese), and go on to deep-fried grouper or snapper, lobster or shrimp. For dessert try a piece of caye lime pie (too bad it's so small). Such a three-course dinner costs about US$25, all included.

Self-Catering Rock's Store, at the corner of Pescador and Black Coral, is a modern mini-supermarket with a wide selection of canned and packaged foods, which is what most people on the island eat. Rock's attempt at classical architecture – the Ionic columns at the portal – fails because the capitals are upside down, but hey, this is San Pedro, who cares?

Martha's Hotel has a shop that's well-stocked with food, drink and souvenirs.

Entertainment

Sipping, sitting, talking and dancing are part of everyday life on Ambergris. Many hotels have comfortable bars, often with appropriate sand floors, thatched roofs and reggae music.

Sandals, on Barrier Reef north of Caribeña, is perhaps the cheapest tavern on the island; look for its large sign in the shape of a beach thong. It's a good place to swap stories of adventures and excursions, and seek information about low-priced Ambergris activities.

Tackle Box Bar, on a wharf at the eastern end of Black Coral Drive, is a San Pedro institution. Very popular with divers and boat owners, it's a good place to get the latest info on diving trips and conditions, boat rentals and excursions.

Fido's, on Barrier Reef near Pelican, always has a lively crowd in the evenings, sometimes playing bingo.

Big Daddy's, located right next to San Pedro's church, is the town's hot night spot, often featuring live reggae, especially during the winter.

To drink with the locals in a real cantina at lower prices, head for Los Marinos, on Pescador at Bucaneer. Don't expect a beautiful place, expect a real Mexican-style cantina; women, therefore, may not find the atmosphere particularly welcoming or comfortable.

Getting There & Away

Air San Pedro (code: SPR) is the home of Tropic Air (☎ (026) 2012, 2117, 2029; fax 2338), so flight connections between Ambergris Caye and the mainland are good. Maya Airways and Island Air also operate flights between San Pedro and Belize City.

Tropic Air flies from San Pedro to Caye Chapel, Belize City Municipal Airport (US$24) and Goldson International Airport (US$30) 11 times daily; the flight takes only about 15 minutes. To Corozal (code: CZL; fare: US$27) they run two 20-minute flights daily.

Maya Airways (☎ in Belize City (02) 77215) has eight scheduled flights daily, Monday to Saturday, to and from Belize City; two flights on Sunday. Maya also runs two daily flights in each direction between Corozal and San Pedro.

For Island Air schedules, contact Amigo Travel (☎ (026) 2180, 2435; fax 2192) on Barrier Reef Drive near the Spindrift Hotel. For more details of flights in Belize, see the Belize City section.

Boat Boat service between Belize City and San Pedro, Ambergris Caye, is not as dependable as boat service to and from Caye

Caulker. You may find that some of the information below has changed. Check on boats a day before departure, if possible. Some boats departing from the A & J Shell station on North Front St and headed for Caye Caulker continue as far as San Pedro. See the Belize City section for details.

Andrea departs from Belize City from Southern Foreshore by the Bellevue Hotel for San Pedro, Ambergris Caye, Monday to Friday at 4 pm (1 pm on Saturday, no boat on Sunday); the return trip to Belize City departs from San Pedro at 7 am. The fare is US$10 one way, US$17.50 return, and the voyage takes 1¼ to 1½ hours. Buy your tickets at Ambergris Delight, on Pescador near Ambergris in San Pedro.

Some boats going to Caye Caulker continue to San Pedro on Ambergris Caye. *Thunderbolt Express* departs from San Pedro for Caye Caulker, Caye Chapel and Belize City at 7 am, arriving in Belize City at 8.30 or 9 am, returning from Belize City along the same route at 4 pm (on Saturday at 1 pm); no boats on Sunday. *Libra Express* departs from San Pedro at 7.30 am, follows the same route, and returns from Belize City at 1 pm. Fares are US$7.50 to Caye Caulker, US$10 to Belize City. For tickets in San Pedro, apply at their ticket office on Almond St. You can call for reservations on (026) 2217, 2159.

Miss Belize departs from a dock behind the Court House in Belize City Monday to Friday at 9 am and 4.30 pm on the 75-minute voyage to San Pedro. The fare is US$10 one way, US$19 a round trip. Return trips depart from San Pedro at 7 am and 2.30 pm. On Saturday, the single departure from Belize City is at 7 am, the return from San Pedro at 2.30 pm. On Sunday the departure from San Pedro is at 2.30 pm, from Belize City at 4.30 pm. Check in advance, as these schedules are often changed or cancelled.

Getting Around

If you're travelling heavy, take a taxi from San Pedro's airport to any hotel in town for US$2, slightly more for the more expensive hotels out of town to the south. Otherwise, it's no more than a 10-minute walk to any

place in town from the airport, less from the boat docks.

San Pedranos get around on foot, by bicycle, dune buggy, golf cart and pickup truck. A few huge slab-sided Ford station wagons act as taxis. You can rent a golf cart at Island Rentals, in the Fido's complex on Barrier Reef Drive, for US$15 per hour, US$22.50 for four hours, US$30 for a full day; you'll have to leave a deposit. They also rent mopeds. Bicycles can be rented for US$2.50 per hour.

OTHER CAYES

Though Ambergris and Caulker are the most easily accessible and popular cayes, it is possible to arrange visits to others. Serious divers are the usual customers at camps and resorts on the smaller cayes. Often a special flight or boat charter is necessary to reach the cayes, and this can be arranged when you book your lodgings. Most booking offices are in Belize City as the smaller cayes have infrequent mail service and no telephones (only radios).

Caye Chapel, just south of Caulker, holds the luxurious *Pyramid Island Resort* (☎ (02) 44409; fax 32405; PO Box 192, Belize City).

St George's Caye, 14 km east of Belize City, was the first capital of the Belize settlement between 1650 and 1784, and saw the decisive battle of 1798 between the British settlers and a Spanish invasion force. Today it holds *St George's Lodge* (☎ (02) 44190; fax 30461; PO Box 625, Belize City), a 16-room, moderately priced resort. For reservations in the USA call (800) 678-6871.

The Turneffe Islands, a coral atoll about 30 km east of Belize City, hold numerous lodgings, from low-budget camps like the eight-room *Rendevous Point Camp* and six-room *Turneffe Flats* (☎ (02) 45634), 56 Eve St, Belize City, to the luxury *Turneffe Islands Lodge*, (fax (03) 0276; in the USA ☎ (800) 338-8149; fax (904) 641-5285). PO Box 480, Belize City. The lodge itself only has a radio hookup. It used to have a Belize City office but no longer seems to.

Tobacco Caye's lodging possibilities include *Island Camps* (☎ (02) 72109, (05)

22201), 51 Regent St, Belize City; *Reef End Lodge*, PO Box 10, Dangriga; and *Fairweather & Friends*, PO Box 240, Belize City.

Gallows Point Caye, just off Belize City, has *The Wave* (☎ (02) 73054), 9 Regent St, Belize City.

Western Belize

After you leave Belize City, head westward along Cemetery Road to reach the Western Highway. The road is paved and fairly good all the way to the Guatemalan border. Along the way you pass Hattieville, which was founded in 1961 after Hurricane Hattie wreaked destruction on Belize City. Many residents sought refuge from the storm's violence in this inland spot. Some decided to stay, and Hattieville was born.

BELIZE ZOO
This zoo, 46 km west of Belize City (Mile 29), is home to a variety of indigenous Belizean cats and other animals kept in natural surroundings. The land hasn't been cleared; it's as if cages just appeared from nowhere and then paths were cleared for tourists. A sign marks the turning for the zoo; the entrance is more than one km off the highway. Hours are 10 am to 4.30 pm daily; admission costs US$5, and it goes to a worthy cause.

The Belize Zoo (☎ (02) 45523) had an odd beginning. Sharon Matola was in charge of a number of Belizean animals during the shooting of a wildlife film entitled *Path of the Raingods*. By the time filming was over, her animals were partly tame, and thus might not have survived well in the wild. So Ms Matola founded the Belize Zoo.

A guide takes you on a very personal tour of the zoo, explaining the habitat, introducing the 100 species of animals, and making the case for preservation of Belize's ecological wealth. You'll see Baird's tapir, Belize's national animal, and the gibnut or paca *(tepezcuintle)*, a sort of rodent which appears on some Belizean dinner-tables. Jaguar, ocelot, howler monkey, peccary, vulture, stork, even a crocodile appear during the fascinating tour. People spend a lot of money at Disneyland to see hokey mechanical replicas of such wild creatures; here they're all real, and right at home.

Getting There & Away
Novelo's Bus Service (☎ (02) 77372), 19 West Collett Canal St, Belize City, runs buses from Belize City along the Western Highway every hour on the hour daily from 11 am to 7 pm (noon to 5 pm on Sunday). Coming from Benque Viejo del Carmen, the buses start at 6 am and the last bus leaves at 3 pm (US$1.25). Just ask to get out at the Belize Zoo. Look at your watch when you get out; the next bus will come by in about an hour.

BANANA BANK RANCH
A short distance east of Belmopan, at Km 76 (Mile 47) on the Western Highway, a dirt track heads north to Banana Bank Ranch Lodge & Stables (☎ (08) 23180, after first ring push *123 and say 'calling Banana Bank'; you can also try (02) 22677; fax (08) 22366), PO Box 48, Belmopan. This is the Belizean version of a dude ranch, operated by John and Carolyn Carr. They'll take you on horseback trips into the bush, show you where to swim or paddle a canoe, and introduce you to their pets. Rates for one of the nine rooms and all three meals work out to US$35 per person per day. A 2½-hour trip on horseback costs about US$18 and a river trip is about the same. If you plan to stay for a few days, call and the owners will pick you up from Belmopan.

GUANACASTE PARK
A few km east of Belmopan, at the junction of the Western and Hummingbird Highways, is Guanacaste Park. This small (21 hectare) nature reserve at the confluence of Roaring Creek and the Belize River holds one giant guanacaste tree which survived the axes of canoe makers and still rises majestically in its jungle habitat. The great tree supports a

whole ecosystem of its own, festooned with bromeliads, epiphytes, ferns and dozens of other varieties of plants. Wild orchids flourish in the spongy soil among the ferns and mosses, and several species of 'exotic' animals pass through. Birdlife is abundant and colourful. Stop at the information booth to learn about the short nature trails in the park. If you're in Belize City when you read this, you can get more information from the Belize Audubon Society (☎ (02) 77369), 49 Southern Foreshore, Belize City.

BELMOPAN
I think a large number of people were sceptical when, in 1970, the government of Belize declared its intention of building a model capital city in the geographic centre of the country; in 1961, Hurricane Hattie had all but destroyed Belize City. Certain that killer hurricanes would come again, and that Belize City could never be properly defended from them, the government decided to move.

During its first decade Belmopan was a lonely place. Weeds grew through cracks in the streets, a few bureaucrats dozed in new offices and insects provided most of the city's traffic. But two decades after its founding, Belmopan has begun to come to life. Its population, now over 4000, is growing slowly, some embassies have moved here and when, inevitably, the next killer hurricane arrives, the new capital will no doubt get a population boost.

Orientation
The bus stops are near the post office, police station, the market and telephone office (see the Belmopan map). Unless you need to visit the British High Commission (☎ (08) 22146/7), 34/36 Half Moon Ave, or the US Embassy's Belmopan office (☎ (08) 22617), you'll probably only stay long enough to have a snack or a meal at one of the restaurants near the bus stops.

Things to See
There is one thing to do in Belmopan if you're excited about Mayan ruins – examine the archaeological treasures preserved in the vault at the Archaeology Department (☎ (08) 22106). There is no museum yet, but if you call and make an appointment for a visit on Monday, Wednesday or Friday afternoon from 1.30 to 4.30 pm, you can see many of the artefacts recovered from Belize's rich Mayan sites.

Places to Stay & Eat
Belmopan is a bureaucrats' and diplomats' town, not one for budget travellers. *Circle A Lodge* (☎ (08) 22296), 35-37 Half Moon Ave, is the cheapest at US$30 a double for one of its 14 rooms. The nearby *Bullfrog Inn* (☎ (08) 22111; fax 23155), also with 14 rooms, is slightly more expensive at US$35 for an air-conditioned double. *Belmopan Convention Hotel* (☎ (08) 22130, 22340; fax 23066), 2 Bliss Parade (PO Box 237) is the most expensive, at US$50 for one of its 20 air-conditioned, bath-equipped rooms.

All of these hotels can provide meals, or you can order your own at the *Caladium Restaurant* (☎ 22754), on Market Square just opposite the Novelo's bus stop. *Yoli's*, next to the fuel station, is a less convenient alternative.

Getting There & Away
Bus Novelo's operates buses between Belize City (84 km, 1½ hours, US$1.40), Belmopan, San Ignacio (32 km, 45 minutes, US$1) and Benque Viejo (47 km, one hour, US$1.90) departing from Belize City every hour on the hour daily from 11 am to 7 pm (noon to 5 pm on Sunday). Coming from Benque, the buses start at 6 am and the last bus leaves at 3 pm. Transportes del Carmen also operates several buses daily on this run.

James Bus Service buses to Dangriga and Punta Gorda stop in Belmopan as well.

SAN IGNACIO (CAYO)
San Ignacio, also called Cayo, is a prosperous farming and holiday centre in the lovely tropical Macal River valley. In general it's a quiet place of about 8000 people (counting the population of neighbouring Santa Elena on the east side of the river). At night the

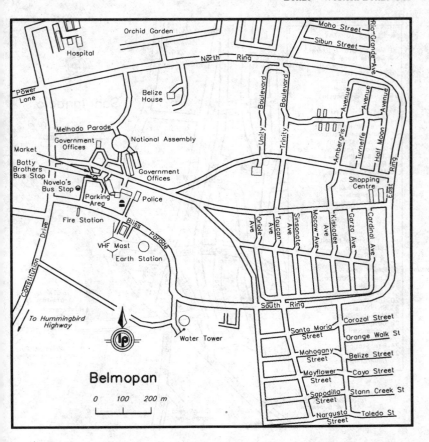

Belmopan

0   100   200 m

Map labels: Orchid Garden, Hospital, Moho Street, Sibun Street, Rio Grande Ave, North Ring, Power Lane, Belize House, Boulevard, Boulevard, Avenue, Avenue, Avenue, Melhado Parade, Government Offices, National Assembly, Unity, Trinity, Ambergris, Turneffe, Half Moon, Market, Batty Brothers Bus Stop, Novelo's Bus Stop, Government Offices, Parking Area, Police, Shopping Centre, East Ring, Fire Station, Bliss Parade, Oriole Ave, Toucan Ave, Sinsonate Ave, Macaw Ave, Kiskadee Ave, Garza Ave, Cardinal Ave, Constitution Drive, VHF Mast, Earth Station, To Hummingbird Highway, Water Tower, South Ring, Santa Maria Street, Corozal Street, Orange Walk St, Mahogany Street, Belize Street, Mayflower Street, Cayo Street, Sapodilla Street, Stann Creek St, Nargusta Street, Toledo St

quiet disappears and the jungle rocks to music from the town's bars, and restaurants which sometimes serve as bars.

There's nothing much to do in town, but San Ignacio is a good base from which to explore the natural beauties of Mountain Pine Ridge. Horseback treks, canoe trips on the rivers and creeks, spelunking in the caves, bird-watching, touring the Mayan ruins of Xunantunich, and hiking in the tropical forests are all popular ways to spend time. This is the district of macaws, mahogany, mangoes, jaguars, and orchids.

Just on the outskirts of town, down Buena Vista Rd from the Hotel San Ignacio, are the unimpressive ruins of Cahal Pech (Place of the Ticks), a minor ceremonial centre dating from the Classic period.

San Ignacio, with its selection of hotels and restaurants, is also the logical place to spend the night before or after you cross the Guatemalan border. Benque Viejo, the Belizean town on the border, has only limited facilities.

Orientation

San Ignacio is west of the river, Santa Elena to the east. The two are joined by the one-

■ PLACES TO STAY

1 Venus Hotel & Store
5 Central Hotel &
  Farmers Emporium
6 Hi-Et Hotel
8 Jaguar Hotel
10 Belmoral Hotel
26 Hotel San Ignacio

▼ PLACES TO EAT

2 Serendib Restaurant
4 The Place Restaurant
7 Eva's Restaurant & Bar
8 Jaguar Restaurant & Bar
11 Tai San Chinese
   Restaurant
13 Maxim's Chinese
   Restaurant
17 New Lucky Chinese
   Restaurant
18 Oriental Restaurant
   & Bar

OTHER

3 San Ignacio Hospital
9 Bus Station
12 Taxi Rank
14 Church
15 Belize Bank
16 Esso Fuel Station
19 Town Hall,
   Library & Toilets
20 Taxi Rank
21 Shell Fuel Station
22 Market Building
23 Government House,
   Police Station
   & Post Office
24 Fire Station
25 Electricity
   Generating Plant

San Ignacio

0   50   100 m

lane Hawkesworth Bridge, San Ignacio's landmark suspension bridge. As you come off the western end of the bridge, turn right and you'll be on Burns Ave, the town's main street.

Information

There is no information office, but your questions can doubtless be answered by someone at Eva's Restaurant & Bar, or by one of the civil servants at Government House or the police station.

Belize Bank, on Burns Ave, is open Monday to Friday from 8 am to 1 pm (also Friday afternoon from 3 to 6 pm) for money exchange.

The very simple, basic San Ignacio Hospital (☎ (092) 2066), is up the hill off of Waight's St, to the west of the centre.

The post office is on the upper floor of Government House and is open Monday to Friday from 8 am to noon and 1 to 5 pm, Saturday from 8 am to 1 pm.

Belize Telecommunications has an office on Burns Avenue north of Eva's in the Cano's Gift Shop building. Hours are Monday to Friday from 8 am to noon and 1 to 4 pm,

Saturday from 8 am to noon and is closed Sunday.

Market day is Saturday, with the marketeers setting up behind the Hotel Belmoral at the bus station. The small market building beneath Hawkesworth Bridge, built through the largesse of Baron Bliss, has some vegetables and fruits on sale every day.

Places to Stay – bottom end

Central Hotel (☎ (092) 2253), 24 Burns Ave, is the best and cleanest of the town's cheap hotels, and a bargain at US$8 a single, US$10 a double in rooms without running water. It's plain and simple, but the new paint shines like the smiles of the owners. *Imperial Hotel*, next door at 22 Burns Ave (above Eva's Restaurant), is almost as tidy and only a bit more expensive.

Hi-Et Hotel, 12 West St at the corner of Waight's St, is a family-run place, and when you stay here, you have the feeling that you're part of that family. It's more like a pension than a hotel. Two people pay US$10 for a room with shared bathroom.

Jaguar Hotel, across the street from the Central and Imperial at 19 Burns Ave, is plain, basic and well used, though not as well kept as the other two places. Prices are US$8 a single, US$10 a double with shared bath.

Hotel Belmoral (☎ (092) 2024), 17 Burns Avenue at the corner of Waight's St, has 15 rooms with bath, and has recently undergone renovation which has raised prices to US$14 a single, US$20 a double with private shower.

Venus Hotel (☎ (092) 2186), 29 Burns Ave, newish, clean and bright, is the 'luxury' hostelry among bottom-end places. Of its 25 clean rooms, most are without private shower and cost US$11 a single, US$16 a double; the common showers are new and clean, if cramped. Rooms with private shower cost US$18 a single, US$23 a double. All rooms have ceiling fans, and some (especially rooms 10 and 16) have views of the football fields and the river. Cool drinking water is available from the fridge next to the reception desk.

Places to Stay – middle

Hotel San Ignacio (☎ (092) 2034, 2125; fax 2134), PO Box 33, on Buena Vista Rd about one km uphill from the police station, enjoys magnificent views of the jungle and river from its swimming pool and balconies. The large reception area has the feeling of an old colonial outpost or hunting lodge. It's a great place to stay, but is often full, especially on weekends. Rooms cost US$40 a single, US$50 a double, US$55 a triple; suites cost a bit more. The hotel has a restaurant, bar and discotheque.

Las Casitas Resort (☎ (092) 2475), 22 Surrey St, over one km north of San Ignacio at Branch Mouth, has seven rooms priced at US$20 a double, with an extra US$5 for meals. This is the cheapest and closest of the mountain 'ranches' in this area (see below). Besides lodging, Las Casitas offers horses and canoes for hire, and guided hikes in the forest.

For other ranches near San Ignacio, see the section on Mountain Pine Ridge.

Places to Eat

Eva's Restaurant & Bar is the social centre of the expatriate set – temporary and permanent – in San Ignacio. Table tops are formica, conversation turns along with the ceiling fans, and the beer is cold. Daily special plates at US$2.50 are the best value, but there's also *chilmoles* (black bean soup), chicken curry, beef soup, sandwiches and burgers. The most expensive thing on the menu is beefsteak and fried potatoes at US$4. Eva's serves all three meals, and is the nearest thing San Ignacio has to an information centre.

Maxim's Chinese Restaurant, at the corner of Far West and Bull Tree Rds, is several blocks from the centre, but worth the walk. The owner makes the trip into Belize City weekly to get fish and other ingredients to make his fried rice, sweet-and-sour dishes, and vegetarian plates which range in price from US$2 to US$4. Try the Belikin Stout if you like dark beer. The restaurant is small, dark, and open from 11.30 am to 2.30 pm and from 5 pm until midnight. Like all good

Chinese restaurants, you can have food made up to take away.

Chinese restaurants abound in San Ignacio. You might try the *Tai San*, near the Hotel Belmoral and, on Burns Avenue across from the Belize Bank, the *New Lucky* and the *Oriental*.

Across Burns Avenue and north a few metres from Eva's is the *Serendib Restaurant*, serving – of all things – Sri Lankan dishes, here in the Belizean jungle. Service is friendly, the food is good, and prices are not bad, ranging from US$2.50 for the simpler dishes, up to US$7.50 for steak or lobster.

Getting There & Away

Novelo's operates buses to and from Belize City (116 km, three hours, US$1.90), Belmopan (32 km, 45 minutes, US$1), San Ignacio, and Benque Viejo (15 km, 20 minutes, US$0.38) leaving Belize City every hour on the hour daily from 11 am to 7 pm (noon to 5 pm on Sunday). Coming from Benque Viejo, the buses start at 6 am and the last bus leaves at 3 pm. Transportes del Carmen also operates several buses daily on this run.

Horses, canoes and mountain bikes are all used to get around Mountain Pine Ridge, but to get to the horses, canoes and mountain bikes you must sometimes take a taxi. They congregate near the traffic circle at the west end of Hawkesworth Bridge, and charge surprisingly high rates for short trips out of town. A trip of a few km can easily cost US$5 to US$10.

MOUNTAIN PINE RIDGE

Western Belize has lots of beautiful, unspoiled mountain country dotted with waterfalls and teeming with wild orchids, parrots, keel-billed toucans and other exotic flora and fauna. Almost 800 square km to the south and east of San Ignacio has been set aside as the Mountain Pine Ridge Forest Reserve.

The rough forest roads in the reserve are often impassable in the wet season, and not easily passable even when it's dry. Inacces-

sibility is one of Mountain Pine Ridge's assets, for it keeps this beautiful land in its natural state for visitors willing to see it on horseback, on foot or along its rivers in canoes.

Access roads into the Mountain Pine Ridge Reserve go south off the Western Highway in Santa Elena, across the river from San Ignacio, and near Georgeville, about nine km east of San Ignacio.

Suitable goals for forest trips include Hidden Valley Falls, a silver cascade which plunges almost 500 metres into a misty valley; Río On's pools and waterfalls; and Río Frio Caves, near Augustine. Camping here is allowed only with prior permission from the Department of Forestry, and only at Augustine and near the settlement of San Antonio. In the southern reaches of the reserve lies Caracol, a vast Mayan city still engulfed by jungle. The archaeologists are still at work here, and nothing has been restored, but Caracol is obviously of major importance to studies of Mayan archaeology, culture and history. We'll learn much from what's found here. Caracol can be reached on horseback (a four-day trek), or on an overnight trip in a good 4WD vehicle.

Keel-billed toucan

Mountain Pine Ridge

0   5   10 km

Places to Stay

Lodges & Ranches The forests and mountains surrounding San Ignacio are dotted with small inns, lodges and ranches offering accommodation, meals, hiking, horseback trips, spelunking, swimming, bird-watching and similar outdoor activities. All of the lodges below have full programmes of hikes, rides, excursions and activities. Though you can sometimes show up unannounced and find a room, these are small, popular places so it's best to write or call ahead for reservations as far in advance as possible. When you do, ask for information on activities as well.

Just east of Santa Elena (across the river from San Ignacio), an unpaved road going south is marked for *Maya Mountain Lodge* (☎ (092) 2164; fax 2029), 9 Cristo Rey Rd (PO Box 46, San Ignacio). From San Ignacio, it's a five-minute taxi ride. The quaint thatched cottages here have private showers (with hot water), ceiling fans, and local textiles as decoration. Healthful foods are served in their patio restaurant, the Parrot's Perch Lounge is hung with hammocks and furnished with a bar, and the lodge rents mountain bikes and canoes as well as organising many tours and activities throughout the area. Even Spanish instruction is given through their Educational Field Station. The 14 rooms are priced at US$50 a single, US$70 a double for B&B.

Casa Cielo Resort Hotel (☎ (082) 3180; fax (092) 2060), Mile 8, Mountain Pine Ridge Road (Central Farm PO, Cayo District), also has thatch-roofed cabañas with private baths (hot water) and an atmospheric restaurant-bar. The favourite drinks here are cold beer and juices made from exotic fruits grown right on the property. Casa Cielo is part of Mountain Equestrian Trails, a ranch specialising in horseback treks, fishing and caving expeditions around Mountain Pine Ridge. Rooms cost US$50 to US$70 a single, US$70 to US$105 a double, tax and service included; lower prices are for B&B, higher for all three meals.

Chan Chich Lodge (☎ in Belize City (02) 77031; fax 77062), PO Box 37, Belize City, is perhaps the most luxurious of the Mountain Pine Ridge lodges. Its location is incredible: the luxurious thatched cabañas fill the central plaza of a Mayan archaeological site! Very little clearing of the jungle had to be done. (Resident ornithologists have identified more than 260 species of birds here.) Each of the 12 cabañas has a private bathroom, ceiling fan, two queen-sized beds, and a spacious verandah. The central building holds the dining room and bar. Rooms cost US$70 a single, US$85 a double; meals cost US$30 per person per day. This is a very special place. For information and reservations in the USA, call (800) 343-8009.

duPlooys' Riverside Cottages & Hotel (☎ (092) 2188; fax 2057), Big Eddy, San Ignacio, Cayo, has nine rooms in three nice tile-roofed cottages down by the river. All rooms have private baths with hot water and private screened porches. Besides the normal array of Mountain Pine Ridge activities, duPlooys' offers you a white sandy beach for sunning, and swimming on the Macal River. Ken and Judy duPlooy, formerly of Charleston, South Carolina, are proud of their 20-acre spread, and are certain to make your stay enjoyable. Rates are US$30 to US$45 a single, US$45 to US$75 a double, depending upon how many meals you take. To find duPlooys', go 10 km west from San Ignacio to a left turn and then follow the signs.

Chaa Creek Cottages (☎ (092) 2037; fax 2501), PO Box 53, Cayo, Belize, is right on the bank of the creek in the Macal River valley. The 16 thatch-roofed cottages here have adobe walls, Mayan textile wall hangings and private baths. The owners are Mick and Lucy Fleming, an Anglo-American couple. Rates for the cottages are US$30 to US$48 a single, US$48 to US$84 a double, 5% tax and 15% service charge included. The lower prices are for B&B, the higher for all three meals. To find Chaa Creek, go eight km west of San Ignacio to Chial, turn left and follow the signs to Chaa Creek.

Getting There & Away

Unless you have your own transport, you'll have to depend on taxis or the hospitality of your Mountain Pine Ridge ranch hosts to transport you between San Ignacio and the ranches. Sometimes the ranches will shuttle you at no extra cost; sometimes they'll merely arrange a taxi for you.

XUNANTUNICH

Xunantunich (pronounced shoo-nahn-too-NEECH) is Belize's best Mayan site. Though other sites such as Caracol and Lamanai promise to be more important, Xunantunich (Stone Maiden) is currently the archaeological pride of Belize.

Set on a levelled hilltop overlooking the Mopan (or Belize) River, Xunantunich controlled the riverside track which led from the hinterlands of Tikal down to the Caribbean. During the Classic period, a ceremonial centre flourished here. Other than that, not too much is known. The kings of Xunantunich erected a few beautiful stelae inscribed with dates, but we have no full history of their reigns as we have at Tikal, Copán and other sites. Archaeologists have uncovered evidence that an earthquake damaged the city badly about 900 AD, after which it may have been largely abandoned.

Though it is an interesting site, and its tallest building, El Castillo, is impressive as

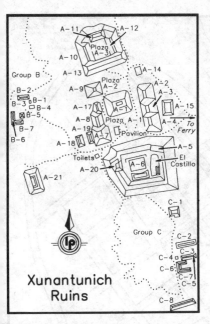

Xunantunich Ruins

The stairway on the north side of El Castillo – the side you approach from the courtyard – goes only as far as the temple building. To climb to the roofcomb you must go around to the south side and use a separate set of steps. On the east side of the temple a few of the masks which once surrounded this structure have been restored.

Getting There & Away

There are no facilities at Xunantunich except picnic tables, pit toilets and a cistern of rainwater for drinking, so bring water and perhaps a picnic or snacks.

Novelo's buses on their way between San Ignacio and Benque Viejo will drop you at the village of San José Succotz, where you catch the ferry to the west side of the river. There are also Shaw's buses shuttling between San Ignacio and Benque Viejo. The bus trip costs US$0.25. Make your excursion to Xunantunich in the morning to avoid the ferryman's lunch break. Ferry hours are 8 am to noon and 1 to 5 pm; the ferry crosses on demand. There is no fee for passengers or cars, except on weekends, when cars pay US$0.50 each way.

From the ferry it's a walk of two km uphill to the ruins.

When you return, cross on the ferry and have a cold drink at the tienda across the road. You can wait for the bus to San Ignacio here. If your goal is Benque Viejo, you can walk there from the ferry in about 15 minutes.

BENQUE VIEJO DEL CARMEN

A foretaste of Guatemala just two km east of the border – that's Benque Viejo del Carmen. The name and lingua franca are Spanish, the people Spanish-speaking Maya or ladinos. Some ambitious maps of the town make it look like a prosperous, orderly place, but it's more like a jungle outpost. Hotels and restaurants are very basic. You're better off staying and eating in San Ignacio if you can.

Benque Viejo stirs from its normal tropical somnolence in mid-July, when the Benque Festival brings three days of music and revelry. Then it's back to sleep.

it rises some 40 metres above the jungle floor, Xunantunich will perhaps disappoint you after you've seen Tikal, Chichén Itzá, Uxmal or Palenque. It has not been extensively restored, as those sites have, and the jungle has grown around and over the excavated temples. But the walk from the ferry beneath arches of palm fronds, the tropical plants and animals and the lack of crowds at the site are compensations.

Xunantunich is open from 8 am to 5 pm; admission costs US$1.50. In the rainy season (June to October), bugs can be a problem; you may need your repellent.

The path from the guardian's hut leads to Plaza A-2, surrounded by low, bush-covered buildings and then on to Plaza A-1, dominated by Structure A-6: El Castillo. A thatched pavilion near El Castillo provides shelter from the sun or rain. On the edges of the grassy plazas, hummingbirds hover in the humid air, sucking nectar from brilliantly coloured tropical flowers.

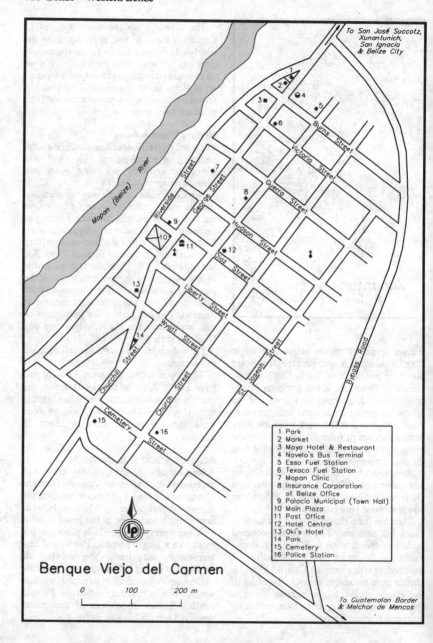

To San José Succotz,
Xunantunich,
San Ignacio
& Belize City

To Guatemalan Border
& Melchor de Mencos

Mopan (Belize) River

Riverside Street
George Street
Guerra Street
Victoria Street
Burns Street
Hudson Street
Diaz Street
Liberty Street
Wyatt Street
Joseph Street
St Joseph Street
Bypass Road
Churchill Street
Church Street
Cemetery Street

1 Park
2 Market
3 Maya Hotel & Restaurant
4 Novelo's Bus Terminal
5 Esso Fuel Station
6 Texaco Fuel Station
7 Mopan Clinic
8 Insurance Corporation
  of Belize Office
9 Palacio Municipal (Town Hall)
10 Main Plaza
11 Post Office
12 Hotel Central
13 Oki's Hotel
14 Park
15 Cemetery
16 Police Station

Benque Viejo del Carmen

0   100   200 m

Places to Stay & Eat

Maya Hotel y Restaurante (☎ (093) 2116), 11 George St, is the best hotel in town, a clean family-run operation with a relaxing atmosphere and a convenient location near the bus terminal. The 10 rooms have lots of bunks; most have no running water, but the communal showers are clean, the restaurant serves all three meals, and there's a billiard table on the ground floor. Rates are US$5.50 to US$6 a single, US$10 to US$19 a double; the higher prices are for rooms with private shower.

Next best is the *Hotel Central*, corner of Churchill and Diaz Sts, with clean waterless rooms above a store. The asking price is US$10 per person, so you've got to haggle here.

Oki's Hotel (☎ (093) 2006), 47 George St, has 11 very basic rooms in a converted village house, some of which are very cramped and dark. The communal showers and toilets are usable, the price US$5 per person.

Getting There & Away

One bus from San Ignacio (usually the 9 am) goes through Benque Viejo all the way to the Belizean border post. Otherwise, there are hourly buses between San Ignacio and Benque. From Benque, taxis shuttle back and forth from the border charging a high US$2.50 for the two-km ride, so you might want to make the 15-minute walk instead.

Crossing the Border

Cross early in the morning so as to have the best chance of catching buses onward. Get your passport (and, if applicable, your car papers) stamped at the Belizean station, then cross into Guatemala. The border station is supposedly open 24 hours a day, but officers are usually only on duty from 6 am to midnight. If you need a Guatemalan visa (see Facts for the Visitor under Visas & Embassies), as citizens of most British Commonwealth countries do, you should obtain it before you reach the border. There are no Guatemalan diplomatic representatives in Belize; the nearest one is in Chetumal, Mexico.

Guatemalan tourist cards (US$5) are obtainable at the border.

The Guatemalan town of Melchor de Mencos has several cheap hotels and restaurants. If you've crossed the border in the morning, you'll be able to catch a Transportes Pinita bus westward to Flores (101 km, three or four hours, US$1.50). To go on to Tikal, get off the bus at El Cruce (Puente Ixlu), 36 km east of Flores, and wait for another bus, minibus or obliging car or truck to take you the final 35 km north to Tikal. Note that northward traffic flow drops dramatically after lunch.

Northern Belize

Low-lying, often swampy, cut by rivers and lagoons, northern Belize is farming country. Sugar cane is a major crop, but many farmers are branching out to different crops rather than be held hostage to the fluctuations of the commodities markets. The shoreline in the north is often vague, a wide band of marshy land edged in dense mangrove.

The north has several significant biosphere reserves. Largest and most significant is the Río Bravo Conservation Area, over 1000 sq km of tropical forests, rivers, ponds and Mayan archaeological sites in the western part of Orange Walk District. Spread along the Mexican and Guatemalan borders, the Río Bravo reserve joins the Maya Biosphere Reserve in Guatemala and the Calakmul Reserve in Mexico to form a vast multinational reserve.

Other reserves include the Shipstern Wildlife Reserve south of Sarteneja on the large peninsula to the south-east of Corozal Town. Shipstern is an excellent place for birdwatching, as is the Crooked Tree Wildlife Sanctuary midway between Orange Walk and Belize City. The Bermudian Landing Community Baboon Sanctuary west of Belize City protects the black howler monkey.

The ancient Maya prospered in northern Belize, scooping up the rich soil and piling it on raised fields, and at the same time creating drainage canals. These *chinampas* (raised growing-beds surrounded by water) supported many a rich coastal trading town. At Cerros, across the bay from Corozal Town, a small Mayan fishing settlement became a powerful kingdom in Late Pre-classic times. At least a dozen other powerful Mayan cities flourished here, but like Cerros they are somewhat difficult to reach, and their largely unrestored temples do not seem particularly impressive to eyes that have seen Tikal, Chichén Itzá, or even Tulum.

BERMUDIAN LANDING COMMUNITY BABOON SANCTUARY

There are no real baboons in Belize, but locally the black howler monkey is given that name. Though there are howler monkeys throughout the Mayan areas, the black howler exists only in Belize, and like so much wildlife in the rapidly developing Mayan lands, its existence is threatened.

In 1985 a group of local farmers were organised to help preserve the black howler and to protect its habitat by harmonising its needs with their own. Care is taken to leave the forests along the banks of the Belize River where the black howler feeds, sleeps, and – at dawn and dusk – howls loudly and unmistakably. You can learn all about the black howler, and the other 200 kinds of animals and birds to be found in the Reserve, at the Visitors Center (☎ (02) 44405) in the village of Bermudian Landing.

For more information about the sanctuary, check with the Belize Audubon Society (☎ (02) 77369), 49 Southern Foreshore, Belize City.

Getting There & Away

Private buses leave Orange St in Belize City (one from the corner of Mussel St, the other the corner of George St) after lunch, Monday to Saturday, for the hour-long ride to Bermudian Landing. Departures from Bermudian Landing for Belize City are at 5.30 pm. The round-trip fare is US$2.50. There is no accommodation at the site, though you may be permitted to camp if you call ahead for permission.

ALTUN HA

Northern Belize's most impressive Mayan ruin is at Altun Ha, 55 km north of Belize City along the Old Northern Highway in the village of Rockstone Pond.

Altun Ha (Mayan for Rockstone Pond) was undoubtedly a small (population about 3000) but rich and important Mayan trading town, with agriculture also playing an important role in its economy. Altun Ha had formed as a community by at least 600 BC, perhaps several centuries earlier, and the town flourished until the mysterious collapse of Classic Mayan civilisation in around 900 AD. Most of the temples you see here date from Late Classic times, though burials indicate that Altun Ha's merchants were trading with Teotihuacán in Preclassic times.

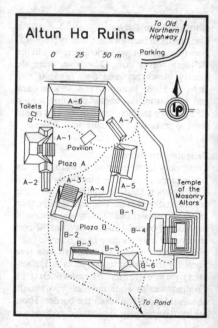

Altun Ha is open daily from 8 am to 5 pm; admission costs US$1.50.

Of the temples arranged around the two plazas here, the largest and most important is the Temple of the Masonry Altars (Structure B-4), in Plaza B. The restored structure you see dates from the first half of the 600s AD, and takes its name from altars on which copal resin was burnt and beautifully carved jade pieces were smashed in sacrifice. Excavation of the structure in 1968 revealed many burials of important officials. Most burials had been looted or desecrated, but two were intact. Among the jade objects found in one of these was a unique mask sculpture portraying Kinich Ahau, the Mayan sun god, the largest known well-carved jade object from the Mayan area.

In Plaza A, Structure A-1 is sometimes called the Temple of the Green Tomb. Deep within it was discovered the tomb of a priest/king dating from around 600 AD. Tropical humidity had destroyed the king's garments and the paper of the Mayan 'painted book' which was buried with him, but many riches were intact: shell necklaces, pottery, pearls, stingray spines used in bloodletting rites, jade beads and pendants, and ceremonial flints.

Getting There & Away

The 'New Alignment' of the Northern Highway passes well inland of Altun Ha, and so does most of its traffic, leaving little activity on the Old Northern Highway. The easiest way to visit the site is on a tour. Many travel agencies run tours daily from Belize City and San Pedro (Ambergris Caye). Otherwise, try hitching, or ask about trucks and buses leaving Belize City's Farmer's Market (on Central American Blvd just north of Haulover Creek) for the town of Maskall, only two km from Altun Ha. You must make it to Altun Ha and back (or onwards) in a day as there is no accommodation at the site. Camping, though not strictly legal, is sometimes permitted; ask at the site.

CROOKED TREE WILDLIFE SANCTUARY

Midway between Belize City and Orange Walk Town, three km west of the Northern Highway, lies the fishing and farming village of Crooked Tree. In 1984 the Belize Audubon Society succeeded in having 12 sq km around the village declared a wildlife sanctuary, principally because of the wealth of birdlife. Migrating birds flock to the rivers, swamps and lagoons here each year during the dry season (November to May – winter up north). Among Crooked Tree's most famous winter visitors is a large group of jabiru storks which come here to nest. With a wingspan of 2½ metres, the jabiru is the largest flying bird in the western hemisphere.

For details about the sanctuary, check with the Belize Audubon Society (☎ (02) 77369), 49 Southern Foreshore, Belize City.

Getting There & Away

Two buses run from Belize City to Crooked Tree daily; ask at the Belize Audubon Society, or the Batty or Venus bus stations, for current times. If you start early from Belize City, Corozal Town or Orange Walk Town, you can bus to Crooked Tree Junction, walk in to the village, learn about the reserve's flora and fauna at the Visitors Center, spend some time bird-watching, and head out again.

A faster, more comfortable but more expensive alternative is to take a day-long tour from Belize City. Several travel agencies organise these for about US$75 per person.

ORANGE WALK

The agricultural and social centre of northern Belize is this town of some 10,000 people, 94 km north of Belize City. It's important to the farmers (including many Mennonites) who till the soil of the region, raising sugar cane, citrus fruit and (ahem!) marijuana. Orange Walk is not very important to visitors unless they're bound for one of the remote archaeological sites or wildlife reserves

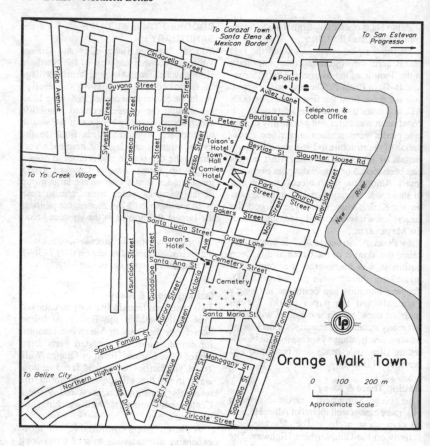

Orange Walk Town

0   100   200 m

Approximate Scale

nearby, in which case the hotels and restaurants in Orange Walk are handy.

Cuello & Nohmul Archaeological Sites

Near Orange Walk is Cuello, a Mayan site with a 3000-year history, but little to show for it. Archaeologists have found plenty here, but you will find only a few grassy mounds. The site is on private property, that of the Cuello Brothers Distillery (☎ (03) 22141), about four km west of Orange Walk along Yo Creek Road. Call and ask for permission before you tramp around the site.

Nohmul, near the village of San Pablo (12 km north of Orange Walk), was a much more important site, with a lofty acropolis looming over the surrounding countryside. Though a vast site, most of it is now covered in grass and sugar cane. To take a look at what there is, walk two km west of San Pablo; you may need a guide to find it.

Lamanai Archaeological Site

By far the most impressive site in this part of the country is Lamanai, in its own archaeology reserve on the New River Lagoon near the settlement of Indian Church. Though most of the site remains unexcavated and unrestored, Lamanai is a good place to see what the archaeologist sees before excavation.

As with most sites in northern Belize, Lamanai (Submerged Crocodile, the original Mayan name of the place) was occupied as early as 1500 BC, with the first stone buildings appearing between 800 and 600 BC. Lamanai flourished in Late Preclassic times, growing to be a major ceremonial centre. Unlike many other sites, Maya lived here until the coming of the Spanish in the 1500s. The Indian church (actually two of them) built nearby attests to the fact that there were Maya here for the Spanish friars to convert. Convert them they did, but by 1640 the Maya had reverted to their ancient forms of worship.

The site is open from 8 am to 5 pm daily; admission costs US$1. Of the many temples here, the grandest is Structure N10-43, a huge Late Preclassic building rising more than 34 metres above the jungle canopy. Also of interest is Structure P9-56, built several centuries later, with huge masks four metres high emblazoned on its flanks. Archaeological work continues at this site.

Getting There & Away The easiest way to see Lamanai is by organised tour from Belize City, but this can be expensive – about US$140 per person (minimum of four) for an overnight trip. In the dry season (generally October to May), you can drive or hitch by truck to the site via San Felipe. If it's been raining that road is usually impassable and you'll have to go from Orange Walk to Guinea Grass or Shipyard by truck and then hire a boat (about US$60) for the one-hour voyage upriver.

Places to Stay

Orange Walk Town has several hotels, among them *Jane's Hotel* (☎ (03) 22473), 2 Baker's St, with eight rooms (most with private shower), and *Jane's Hotel Extension* (☎ (03) 22526), Market Lane, which has six bathless rooms. Rates are US$8 a single, US$11 a double.

Baron's Hotel (☎ (03) 22518, 22847; fax 23472), 40 Belize Rd (also called Queen Victoria Ave), is the class act in town, with 31 rooms with bath, some air-conditioning, a swimming pool, and a rate of US$20 a double.

Taisan's Hotel (☎ (03) 22752), 30 Queen Victoria Ave, north of the plaza, is seven bathless rooms above a Chinese restaurant, each going for US$7 a single, US$10 a double.

Getting There & Away

Transport to or from Orange Walk Town is easy. Southbound buses pass through town at least every hour (usually on the hour, and sometimes on the half-hour as well) from 4.30 am to about 12.30 pm, with a few later buses. Northbound buses pass through at 15 minutes before the hour from 1.45 pm to 8.45 pm. It's 61 km to Corozal Town (1½ hours, US$1.25), and 94 km to Belize City (two hours, US$1.75).

COROZAL TOWN

Population 9000

Corozal is a farming town. Several decades ago the countryside was given over completely to sugarcane (there's a refinery south of the town). Today, though sugar is still important, crops are now diversified. The land is fertile, the climate good for agriculture and the town is prosperous. Many of those who do not farm commute to Orange Walk or Belize City to work.

Corozaleños, most of whom speak Spanish as their first language, are pleasant folks, and you may find that people greet you on the street, or at least offer a smile. The North American expatriate community here is considerable. New retirement developments in Consejo Shores have turned into comfortable gringo ghettos. If you spend any time at all in Corozal, you're sure to hear many personal stories from Yanks and Canadians who left it all behind to pursue the good life in quiet Belize.

History

Corozal's Mayan history is long and important. On the northern outskirts of the town

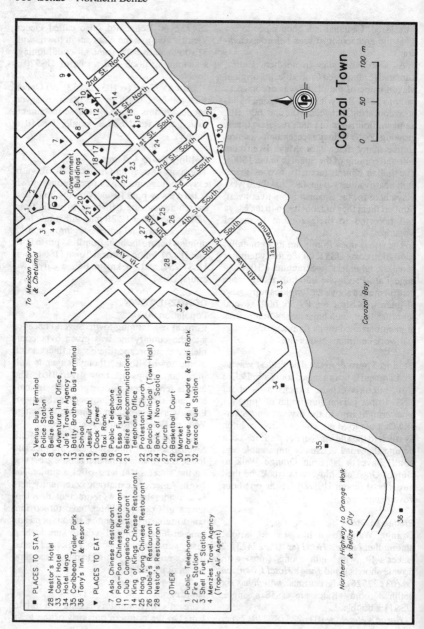

Corozal Town

0   50   100 m

Northern Highway to Orange Walk
& Belize City

To Mexican Border
& Chetumal

Corozal Bay

PLACES TO STAY

28 Nestor's Hotel
33 Capri Hotel
34 Hotel Maya
35 Caribbean Trailer Park
36 Tony's Inn & Resort

PLACES TO EAT

7   Asia Chinese Restaurant
10 Pon-Pon Chinese Restaurant
11 Club Campesino Restaurant
14 King of Kings Chinese Restaurant
25 Hong Kong Chinese Restaurant
26 Dubbie's Restaurant
28 Nestor's Restaurant

OTHER

1   Public Telephone
2   Fire Station
3   Shell Fuel Station
4   Menzies Travel Agency
    (Tropic Air Agent)
5   Venus Bus Terminal
6   Police Station
8   Belize Bank
9   Adventure Inn Office
12 Jal's Travel Agency
13 Batty Brothers Bus Terminal
15 School
16 Jesuit Church
17 Clock Tower
18 Taxi Rank
19 Public Telephone
20 Esso Fuel Station
21 Belize Telecommunications
    Telephone Office
22 Protestant Church
23 Palacio Municipal (Town Hall)
24 Bank of Nova Scotia
27 Church
29 Basketball Court
30 Market
31 Parque de la Madre & Taxi Rank
32 Texaco Fuel Station

are the ruins of a Mayan ceremonial centre once called Chetumal, now called Santa Rita. Across the bay at Cerros is one of the most important Late Preclassic sites yet discovered. Maya have been living around Corozal since 1500 BC.

Modern Corozal Town dates from only 1849, however. In that year, refugees from the War of the Castes in Yucatán fled across the border to safe haven in British-controlled Belize. They founded a town, and named it after the cohune palm, a symbol of fertility. For years it had the look of a typical Caribbean town, but Hurricane Janet roared through in 1955 and blew away many of the old wooden buildings on stilts. Much of Corozal's cinder-block architecture dates from the late 1950s.

As late as the 1970s, when Belize's Northern Highway was a potholed moonscape negotiated only by trucks, Corozal Town enjoyed a prosperous if small tourist trade. Travellers would cross the border from Mexico and relax on the shores of Corozal before taking the punishing trip southward in the back of a truck. Now that the highway is improved, bypasses Corozal, and is served regularly by buses, most travellers leave Chetumal and go all the way to Belize City or beyond.

Orientation & Information

Though founded by Maya, Corozal now resembles a Mexican town with its plaza, its Palacio Municipal and its large church. The bright chimes of the clocktower keep everyone on schedule. You can walk easily to any place in town. Even Tony's Inn & Resort, on the south-western outskirts, is only a 20-minute walk from the plaza.

The Belize Bank on the north side of the plaza is open for currency exchange Monday to Friday from 8 am to 1 pm, and also Friday afternoon from 3 to 6 pm.

Santa Rita Archaeological Site

You can walk to this site, which is less than two km from the bus station. Just follow the main road north-west toward the Mexican border. When it curves to the right, continue straight on, and the site is right there. Though important to archaeologists, there is not a lot to see today.

Cerros Archaeological Site

There is more to see at Cerros, namely a temple more than 20 metres high, but the site is mostly a mass of grass-covered mounds. Negotiate with a boat owner to ferry you across Corozal Bay and back.

Places to Stay – bottom end

Nestor's Hotel (☎ (04) 22354), 125 5th Ave South, is the budget favourite here, and thus is often full. Jake, the owner, has 16 clean, modern, simple rooms with private showers priced at US$7 a single, US$8 a double. Hot water is solar heated. Jake has been in Belize a long time and has many entertaining stories to tell. Arrive as early as possible in the day to pin down a room. The hotel's good, low-priced restaurant is open from 6 am to 11 pm.

Capri Hotel (☎ (04) 22042), at the southern end of 4th Ave, has 30 small, fairly dingy rooms, some with private bath, priced a bit lower than Nestor's. Upkeep is not the best, however, and the noise from the bar can be deafening, so look upon the Capri as a last resort.

Hotel Maya (☎ (04) 22082), PO Box 112, on 7th Avenue (the main road) about 400 metres south of the plaza is very well worn, expensive for what you get, but run by very nice people. The 17 aged rooms are clean and often all occupied despite the trampoline beds, cracked windows and torn insect screens. You may forget about the condition of your room when you relax over a meal or a cold drink in the shady rear patio (service is from 8 am to 2.30 pm and 6.30 to 9 pm). Rates are high, reflecting the dearth of decent low-priced rooms in Corozal: US$16 a single, US$21 a double with private shower. As for meals, sandwiches cost about US$2, burgers a bit more, a full fried chicken dinner US$5. Cold beer is US$1 for Belikin, US$2.50 for Heineken.

Camping *Caribbean Trailer Park* (☎ (04) 22045), PO Box 55, about 500 metres south of the plaza, has large swaths of lush grass shaded by coconut palms, usable toilets and mouldy showers, and all hook-ups. Rates are US$2.50 per person for a tent, US$5 in a camper van (RV). Talk to Jim or Donna, who live at the north end of the park. The park is marked only by a sign reading 'Caribbean Restaurant'.

Places to Stay – middle

About one km south of the plaza on the shore road is *Tony's Inn & Resort* (☎ (04) 22055), an attractive holiday enclave with landscaped grounds and lawn chairs set to enjoy the view of the bay. It has its own swimming lagoon, satellite TV, and an air-conditioned restaurant and bar. The 26 rooms on two floors come with fan or air-conditioner, and cost US$50 to US$70 a double in winter and are about 30% cheaper in summer.

Adventure Inn (☎ (04) 22187; fax 22243), PO Box 35, is 12 km north-east of the centre overlooking the bay in Consejo Shores. The atmospheric bungalows hold 20 rooms with private showers priced at US$45 a double. For more information and reservations, apply to the hotel's office in Corozal, on 4th Avenue 1½ blocks north of the plaza.

Places to Eat

Nestor's Hotel, the *Hotel Maya* and *Tony's Inn* all have decent restaurants. Otherwise, there are many small Chinese restaurants like the *Asia Chinese Restaurant* on 5th Avenue between 1st and 2nd Sts North. Chow mein, chop suey, lobster or fish with rice, and many other items are listed on the menu. Portions cost US$1.75 to US$5, depending upon the ingredients and the size of the portion.

The *Club Campesino* has grilled meats, chicken and the like, but opens only at 6.30 pm for dinner, drinks and late-night socialising.

Getting There & Away

Air Corozal Town has its own little airstrip (code: CZL) several km south of the centre, reached by taxi (US$3 – you can share the cost with other passengers). It is only an airstrip, nothing more, with no shelter and not even so much as a vendor selling soft drinks, so there's no point in arriving too early for your flight. If it's raining, you'll wait in the rain. Taxis meet all incoming flights.

Tropic Air (☎ in San Pedro, Ambergris Caye (026) 2542, 2012) has two flights daily between Corozal Town and San Pedro, Ambergris Caye; the 20-minute flight costs US$27. You can connect at San Pedro with flights to Belize City, and from Belize City to other parts of the country. For information and tickets, apply to Menzies Travel Agency, across the road from the Venus bus terminal.

Maya Airways (☎ in Belize City (02) 77215) also runs two daily flights between Corozal and San Pedro at the same fare. For information and tickets, apply to Jal's Travel Agency (☎ (04) 22163), 49 4th Avenue, half a block north of the plaza.

Bus Venus Bus Lines (☎ (04) 22132) and Batty Brothers Bus Service operate frequent buses between Chetumal (Mexico) and Belize City, stopping at Corozal Town (see those sections for details).

Buses leave Corozal Town and head south via Orange Walk for Belize City at least every hour from 3.30 am to 11.30 am, with extra buses on the half-hour during busy times. From Belize City to Corozal, departures are on the hour between noon and 7 pm.

Belize City – 155 km, 3½ hours; many Venus & Batty Bros buses daily, US$3

Chetumal – 30 km, one hour with border formalities; many Venus & Batty Bros buses daily, US$0.75

Orange Walk – 61 km, 1½ hours; many Venus & Batty Bros buses daily, US$1.25

CROSSING THE BORDER

Corozal Town is about 18 km south of the border-crossing point at Santa Elena/Subteniente López. Most of the Venus and Batty Brothers buses travelling between Chetumal and Belize City stop at Corozal Town. Otherwise, hitch a ride or hire an expensive taxi (US$10) to get you to Santa Elena. From Subteniente López, minibuses shuttle the 12 km to Chetumal (Combi Corner) frequently all day.

Southern Belize

Southern Belize is perhaps the most remote stretch of La Ruta Maya. The roads are long and usually in bad condition, the towns small, and access to sites requires time, energy and – sometimes – money. But if you want to explore off the tourist track, southern Belize is the place to do it.

Among the places to visit are Dangriga (formerly Stann Creek), centre of the Black Carib Garinagu (or Garifuna) culture; the Cockscomb Basin Jaguar Preserve; Placentia, where life is similar to that on the cayes; and Punta Gorda, near several unrestored Mayan sites. From Punta Gorda there are weekly boats across the bay to Lívingston in Guatemala.

THE HUMMINGBIRD HIGHWAY
Heading south from Belmopan, the Hummingbird Highway is well paved as far as the Caves Branch River (19 km), but then degenerates as it bumps and grinds its way south and east to Dangriga. A short distance past the river is a stopping place for a visit to the Blue Hole, a lovely swimming spot in a little canyon. From the Blue Hole, a trail leads several km off the highway to St Herman's Cave, a romantic-looking limestone cavern. (You'll need a torch to explore it.) Another trail leads to an unpaved road that takes you back to the highway some distance from the Blue Hole.

Onward to Dangriga, the road crosses several rivers emptying out of the Maya Mountains to the south, and passes through plantations of cacao, bananas and citrus, before coming to the junction of the Southern Highway and the road into Dangriga.

DANGRIGA
Population 10,000
Once called Stann Creek Town, this is the largest town in southern Belize. It's smaller than Belize City but bears a certain resemblance to the capital with its dilapidated wooden houses and dusty streets. There's not much to do here except spend the night and head onwards – unless it's 19 November. Read on.

History
Dangriga's citizens are descendants of the Black Caribs, people of mixed South American Indian and African blood, who inhabited the island of St Vincent as a free people in the 1600s. By the end of the 1700s, the British colonisers had brought the independent-minded Caribs under their control and transported them from one island to another in an effort to subdue them. In the early 1800s, oppression and wandering finally brought many of the Black Caribs to southern Belize. The most memorable migration took place late in 1832, when on 19 November a large number of Caribs reached Belize from Honduras in dugout canoes. The event is celebrated annually in Belize as Garifuna Settlement Day. Dangriga is the place to be on 19 November as the town explodes in a frenzy of dancing, drinking and celebration of the Garifuna heritage.

Orientation
North Stann Creek empties into the Gulf of Honduras at the centre of the town. Dangriga's main street is called St Vincent St south of the creek and Commerce St to the north. From where the road into town joins St Vincent St, it's about 1.5 km to the northern reaches of Commerce St. The bus station is on St Vincent St at the southern end of the bridge over the creek.

The town's two banks, Barclay's and Bank of Nova Scotia, are on the east side of Commerce St, north of the bridge. The post office is on Caney St near Mahogany Road, east off St Vincent St. The police station is north of the banks on Commerce St: for the Town Hall and the small market, head north across the bridge over North Stann Creek and turn right (east).

Though there is no government tourist office, the Belize Tourism Industry Association has an office of sorts at 3 Lemon St in PJ's gift shop; look for the sign on Commerce St, north of the creek.

Places to Stay & Eat
Dangriga has a selection of cheap hotels which can provide lodgings for a night.

Down near the mouth of the North Stann Creek, on the south bank, are two good choices. *Sophie's Hotel*, 970 Chatuye St, has 10 decent rooms, some with private bath, for US$8.50 a single, US$12 a double. There's a restaurant on the ground floor, and good views of the water from the balcony. Nearby is the *Río Mar Hotel* (☎ (05) 22201), 977 Southern Foreshore at the corner of Waight's St, with nine B&B rooms (with bath) going for US$10 a single, US$15 a double.

The Hub (☎ (05) 22397; fax 22813), 573 South Riverside (PO Box 56), near the bus stop and the southern end of the bridge across North Stann Creek, is a clean place with six rooms (some with private showers) going for US$8 a single, US$12 a double, a few dollars more for a room with bath. *Riverside Hotel* (☎ (05) 22168; fax 22296), 5 Commerce St, on the north side of the bridge, has 12 rooms with common showers going for US$8 a single, US$11 a double.

Among the cheapest places is *Catalina's Hotel* (☎ (05) 22390), 367 Cedar St, which charges US$4 a single, US$7 a double for waterless rooms.

Several of the aforementioned hotels, among them the Hub, the Río Mar, and Sophie's, have their own restaurants. The main street has the usual selection of Chinese eateries as well.

Getting There & Away
Air Maya Airways (☎ (02) 77215, 72313, 44032), 6 Fort St (PO Box 458), Belize City, has four flights daily between Belize City and Dangriga. The one-way fare is US$23 from Belize Municipal Airport.

Bus Z-Line has four buses daily from Belize City via Belmopan to Dangriga (170 km, five hours, US$4). James Bus Service has several buses per week, some of which continue

Jaguar

southwards after stopping in Dangriga. One Z-Line bus per day (departing from Belize City at 10 am) goes on past Dangriga as far as Punta Gorda, 169 km farther south.

SOUTHERN HIGHWAY
The Southern Highway, south of Dangriga, is unpaved and can be rough going, especially in the rainy months. About halfway is the village of Maya Center, where a track goes 10 km west to the Cockscomb Basin Jaguar Preserve. There's no public transport to the reserve, but the walk through the lush forest is a pretty one. At the reserve is a campsite (US$1.50 per person), several simple cabins available for rent (US$8 per person), a Visitors Center, and numerous hiking trails. Though you cannot be assured of seeing a jaguar (though this is their preferred habitat), you will certainly enjoy seeing many of the hundreds of other species of birds, plants and animals in this rich environment.

PLACENTIA
Though it's now accessible by plane from Belize City, Placentia still seems remote. Perched at the southern tip of a long, narrow sandy peninsula, it's almost as good as an island for getting that 'away from it all' feeling. Accommodation, from expensive resort to laid-back and low-priced guesthouse and camping area, is easy to find, though rooms may be full on major holidays.

Buses run south from Dangriga daily to the town of Independence, from which it is usually possible to find a boat going across the bay to Placentia. Faster, more comfortable and more dependable are the daily flights run by both Tropic Air and Maya Airways from Belize City's Municipal Airport to the town of Big Creek, just to the south of Independence. Boats will meet the plane if notified in advance.

PUNTA GORDA
At the southern end of the Southern Highway is Punta Gorda, the southernmost town of any size in Belize. Rainfall and humidity are at their highest, and the jungle at its lushest, in the Toledo District which surrounds Punta Gorda.

Nim Li Punit & Lubaantun
Within the jungle are several Mayan sites, including Nim Li Punit (36 km north of Punta Gorda near the village of Indian Creek), and Lubaantun (27 km north-west near San Pedro Columbia). Though archaeologists have made excavations at both sites, there has been little clearing and no restoration, and there are no services.

Nim Li Punit is less than one km west of the Southern Highway, but getting there by public transport can be difficult. As for Lubaantun, take the bus for San Antonio and get out at the road for San Pedro Columbia; the ruins are about 1½ km past the village (a total of about four km from where the bus drops you). You should have camping equipment, as the only bus departs from Punta Gorda for San Antonio in late afternoon.

Places to Stay & Eat
Punta Gorda is hardly a tourist mecca, but you won't want for a bed. The eight-room *Foster's Hotel* (☎ (07) 22067), 19 Main St, and 10-room *Mahung's Hotel* (☎ (07) 22044, 22016), at the corner of Main and North Sts,

have usable bathless rooms for US$5 per person; Mahung's has several rooms with bath for a few dollars more. *Wahima Hotel*, 11 Front St, is a bit cheaper at US$8 a double for any of its five rooms.

St Charles Inn (☎ (07) 22149, 22197), 23 King St, has a dozen nicer rooms with private shower for US$15 a double.

The restaurant situation is not the best, though it will undoubtedly improve as tourism increases. A few simple restaurants on the main street provide sustenance, though no unforgettable culinary experiences.

Getting There & Away
Air Both Tropic Air and Maya Airways have daily flights from Belize City to Punta Gorda, stopping at Big Creek (for Placentia) along the way. One-way fare is US$50 from Belize City's Municipal Airport, US$61 from Goldson International.

Bus Z-Line has one bus daily at 10 am from Belize City to Punta Gorda, a 339-km, eight-hour journey (US$8.25). James Bus Service has five buses per week on this route.

Boat On Tuesday and Friday, a boat leaves Puerto Barrios in Guatemala at 7.30 am, calls at Lívingston about 9 am to take on and drop off passengers and then continues across the Gulf of Honduras to Punta Gorda. The return trip departs from Punta Gorda on those same days at 2.30 pm, calling at Lívingston on the way to Puerto Barrios. Tickets go on sale in the morning on the day of the voyage. Remember that you must go through Customs and Immigration formalities before boarding the boat.

Glossary

Abrazo – embrace, hug. In particular, the formal, ceremonial hug between political leaders.

Alux, aluxes – Mayan for gremlin, leprechaun, benevolent 'little people'

Apartado Postal – post office box, abbreviated *Apdo Postal*

Ayuntamiento – often seen as *H Ayuntamiento (Honorable Ayuntamiento)* on the front of Town Hall buildings, it translates as 'Municipal Government'.

Barrio – district, neighbourhood

Billete – banknote (unlike in Spain where it's a ticket)

Boleto – ticket (bus, train, etc)

Caballeros – literally 'horsemen', but corresponds to 'gentlemen' in English; look for it on toilet doors

Cacique – Indian chief; also used to describe provincial warlord or strongman

Cafetería – literally 'coffee-shop', it refers to any informal restaurant with waiter service; it is not usually a cafeteria in the American sense of a self-service restaurant

Callejón – alley or small, narrow or very short street

Camión – truck; bus

Casa de cambio – moneychanger. In Mexico it offers exchange rates comparable to or better than banks and is much faster to use.

Caseta de larga distancia – long-distance telephone station, often shortened to *caseta*

Cazuela – clay cooking pot, usually sold in a nested set

Cenote – large natural limestone cave used for water storage (and sometimes ceremonial purposes) in Yucatán

Cerveza – beer

Chac – Mayan god of rain

Chac-mool – Mayan sacrificial stone sculpture

Chapín – a citizen of Guatemala; Guatemalan

Charro – cowboy

Chingar – literally 'to rape' but in practice a word with a wide range of colloquial meanings similar to the use of 'to screw' in English. If you've been 'screwed' then you might ruefully admit that *me chingaron*. Someone who's adept at 'screwing' people is a *chingón*. A *chingadera* is a dirty trick, a *chingadazo* is a heavy blow, *vete a la chingada* means something like 'go to hell' while *no chingues* means 'don't annoy me'. A suggestion to *chinga tu madre*, 'rape your mother', should only be made to someone if you want to meet him outside afterwards.

Chultún – artificial Mayan cistern found at Puuc archaeological sites south of Mérida

Churrigueresque – Spanish baroque architectural style of the early 18th century, with lavish ornamentation; named for architect José Churriguera

Cigarro – cigarette

Cocina – literally 'kitchen', also seen as *cocina económica* (economical kitchen) or *cocina familiar* (family kitchen), it's a cookshop, a small, basic restaurant usually run by one woman, often located in or near a municipal market; see also *lonchería*

Colectivo – jitney taxi or minibus (usually a *combi*, or Volkswagen minibus) which picks up and drops off passengers along its route

Completo – full up, a sign you may see on hotel desks in crowded cities

Conquistador – Spanish explorer-conqueror of Latin America

Correos – post office

Curandero – Indian traditional healer

Damas – ladies, the usual sign on toilet doors

Dzul, dzules – Mayan for foreigners or 'townfolk', that is, not Maya from the countryside

Ejido – in Mexico, communally owned Indian land taken over by landowners but returned to the original owners under a program initiated by President Lázaro Cárdenas

Encomienda – Spanish colonial practice of putting Indians under the 'guardianship' of landowners, practically akin to medieval serfdom

Estación ferrocarril – railway station

Ferrocarril – railway

Galón, galones – US gallons (fluid measure; sometimes used in Guatemala)

Gringo/a – male/female European or North American visitor to Mexico

Gruta – cave

Guayabera – man's thin fabric shirt with pockets and appliquéd designs on the front, over the shoulders and down the back; worn instead of a jacket and tie in hot climates

Guardarropa – cloakroom, place to leave parcels when entering an establishment

Hacienda – estate; also 'Treasury', as in *Departamento de Hacienda*, Treasury Department

Hay – pronounced like 'eye', meaning 'there is', 'there are'. You're equally likely to hear *no hay*, 'there isn't' or 'there aren't'.

Henequen – agave fibre used to make rope, grown particularly around Mérida in Yucatán

Huipil – woven white dress from the Mayan regions with intricate, colourful embroidery

IMSS – Instituto Mexicana de Seguridad Social, the Mexican Social Security Institute; it operates many of Mexico's larger public hospitals. In Guatemala the corresponding institution is the IGSS.
IVA – the *impuesto al valor agregado* or 'ee-vah' is a value added tax which can be as high as 15% and is added to many items in Mexico

Kukulcán – Mayan name for the Aztec-Toltec plumed serpent Quetzalcóatl

Larga distancia – long-distance telephone; see also Caseta de larga distancia
Lavandería – laundry; a *lavandería automática* is a coin-operated laundry (laundromat)
Leng – colloquial Mayan term for coins (Guatemalan highlands)
Libras – pounds (weight; sometimes used in Guatemala)
Lista de correos – poste restante or general delivery; literally 'mail list,' the list of addressees for whom mail is being held, displayed daily in the post office
Lonchería – from English *lunch*; a small, simple restaurant which may in fact serve meals all day (not just lunch). You often see loncherías near municipal markets.
Lleno – full (fuel tank)

Machismo – maleness, masculine virility. An important concept in Mexico.
Manzana – apple; also a city block. A *supermanzana* is a large group of city blocks bounded by major avenues. Ciudad Cancún uses manzana and supermanzana numbers as addresses.
Mariachi – small ensemble of street musicians; strolling mariachi bands often perform in restaurants
Mestizo – people of mixed blood (Spanish and Indian); the word now more commonly means 'Mexican'
Metate – flattish stone on which corn is ground
Millas – miles (distance; sometimes used in Guatemala)
Montezuma's revenge – Mexican version of 'Delhi-belly' or travellers' diarrhoea
Mordida – 'little bite,' or small bribe that's usually paid to keep the wheels of bureaucracy turning. Giving a *mordida* to a traffic policeman may ensure that you won't have a bigger traffic fine to pay.
Mudéjar – Moorish architectural style
Mujeres – women

Onzas – ounces (weight; sometimes used in Guatemala)

Palacio de gobierno – building housing the executive offices of a state or regional government
Palacio Municipal – Town Hall, seat of the corporation or municipal government
Palapa – thatched roof; palm leaves are used for thatch
Parada – bus stop, usually for city buses
Pisto – colloquial Mayan term for money, quetzals (Guatemalan highlands)

Pie, pies – foot, feet (unit of measure; sometimes used in Guatemala)
Plateresque – 'silversmith-like'; the architectural style of the Spanish renaissance (16th century), rich in decoration
Plazuela – small plaza

PRI – Institutional Revolutionary Party. The controlling force in Mexican politics for more than half a century.
Propino, propina – a tip, different from a *mordida*, which is really a bribe
Puro – cigar

Quetzalcóatl – plumed serpent god of the Aztecs and Toltecs

Rebozo – long woollen or linen scarf covering the head or shoulders
Retablo – ornate gilded, carved decoration of wood in a church
Retorno – 'return'; in Cancún, a U-shaped street which starts from a major boulevard, loops around and 'returns' to the boulevard a block away

Sacbé – ceremonial limestone avenue or path between great Mayan cities
Sanatorio – hospital, particularly a small private one
Sanitario – literally 'sanitary'; usually means toilet
Sarape – traditional woollen blanket
Supermercado – supermarket. Can range from a small corner store to a large, American-style supermarket.

Taller – shop or workshop. A *taller mecánico* is a mechanic's shop, usually for cars. A *taller de llantas* is a tyre-repair shop
Telefono monedero – coin-operated telephone (Guatemala)
Templo – in Mexico, a church; anything from a wayside chapel to a cathedral
Tequila – clear, distilled liquor produced, like pulque and mezcal, from the maguey cactus
Tex-Mex – Americanised version of Mexican food
Típico – typical or characteristic of a region; particularly used to describe food
Topes – speed-break ridges found in many Mexican

towns, indicated by a highway sign bearing a row of little bumps

Viajero – traveller

War of the Castes – bloody Mayan uprising in Yucatán during the mid-19th century

Zócalo – Aztec for 'pedestal' or 'plinth', but used to refer to a town's main plaza. The usage comes from Mexico City, where the great pedestal for a monument to Independence was erected in the Plaza de la Constitución, but the monument itself was never finished; the plinth has since been removed. The plaza came to be called 'El Zócalo' and the usage spread to many (but not all) Mexican towns.

Menu Translator

Antojitos

Many traditional Mexican dishes fall under the heading of *antojitos* ('little whims'), savoury or spicy concoctions that delight the palate.

burrito – any combination of beans, cheese, meat, chicken or seafood seasoned with salsa or chilli and wrapped in a flour tortilla

chilaquiles – scrambled eggs with chillis and bits of tortillas

chiles rellenos – *poblano* chillis stuffed with cheese, meat or other foods, dipped in egg whites, fried and baked in sauce

enchilada – ingredients similar to those used in tacos and burritos wrapped in a flour tortilla, dipped in sauce and then baked or fried

machaca – cured, dried and shredded beef or pork mixed with eggs, onions, cilantro and chillis

papadzul – corn tortillas filled with hard-boiled eggs, cucumber or marrow seeds, and covered in tomato sauce

quesadilla – flour tortilla topped or filled with cheese and occasionally other ingredients, and then heated

queso relleno – 'stuffed cheese', a mild yellow cheese stuffed with minced meat and spices

taco – a soft or crisp corn tortilla wrapped or folded around the same filling as a burrito

tamale – steamed corn dough stuffed with meat, beans, chillis or nothing at all, wrapped in corn husks

tostada – flat, crisp tortilla topped with meat or cheese, tomatoes, beans and lettuce

Sopas (Soups)

chipilín – cheese and cream soup on a maize base

gazpacho – chilled vegetable soup spiced with hot chillis

menudo – popular soup made with the spiced entrails (tripe) of various four-legged beasts

pozole – hominy soup with meat and vegetables (can be spicy)

sopa de arroz – not a soup at all but just a plate of rice; commonly served with lunch

sopa de lima – 'lime soup', chicken stock flavoured with lime

sopa de pollo – bits of chicken in a thin chicken broth

Huevos (Eggs)

huevos estrellados – fried eggs
huevos fritos – fried eggs

huevos motuleños – local dish of the Yucatecan town of Motul: fried eggs atop a tortilla spread with refried beans, garnished with diced ham, green peas, shredded cheese and tomato sauce, with fried bananas (platanos) on the side

huevos rancheros – ranch-style eggs: fried, laid on a tortilla and smothered with spicy tomato sauce

huevos revueltos estilo mexicano – 'eggs scrambled Mexican-style' with tomatoes, onions, chillis and garlic

huevos revueltos – scrambled eggs; *con chorizo* (chor-REE-so) is with spicy sausage, con frijoles is with beans

Pescado, Mariscos (Seafood)

The variety and quality of seafood from the coastal waters of Yucatán and Belize is excellent. Lobster is available along Mexico's Caribbean coast and in Belize, particularly on the cayes. Campeche (Mexico) is a major shrimp fishing port, with much of its catch exported.

All of the following types of seafood are available in seafood restaurants most of the year. Clams, oysters, shrimp and prawns are also often available as *cocteles* (cocktails).

abulón – abalone
almejas – clams
atún – tuna
cabrilla – sea bass
camarones gigantes – prawns
camarones – shrimp
cangrejo – large crab
ceviche – raw seafood marinated in lime juice and mixed with onions, chillis, garlic, tomatoes, and *cilantro* (fresh coriander leaf)
dorado – dolphin
filete de pescado – fish fillet
huachinango – red snapper
jaiba – small crab
jurel – yellowtail
langosta – lobster
lenguado – flounder or sole
mariscos – shellfish
ostiones – oysters
pargo – red snapper
pescado al mojo de ajo – fish fried in butter and garlic
pescado – fish after it has been caught (see *pez*)
pez espada – swordfish
pez – fish which is alive in the water (see *pescado*)

sierra – mackerel
tiburón – shark
tortuga or *caguama* – turtle
trucha de mar – sea trout

Carnes y Aves (Meat & Poultry)

asado – roast
barbacoa – literally barbecued, but by a process whereby the meat is covered and placed under hot coals
biftec de res – beefsteak
biftec, bistec – any cut of meat, fish or poultry
birria – barbecued on a spit
borrego – sheep
cabro – goat
carne al carbón – charcoal-grilled meat
carne asada – tough but tasty grilled meat
carnitas – deep-fried pork
chicharrones – deep-fried pork skin
chorizo – pork sausage
chuletas de puerco – pork chops
cochinita – suckling pig
codorniz, la chaquaca – quail
conejo – rabbit
cordero – lamb
costillas de puerco – pork ribs or chops
guajolote – turkey
hígado – liver
jamón – ham
milanesa de res – crumbed beefsteak
milanesa – crumbed
patas de puerco – pig's feet
pato – duck
pavo – turkey, a fowl native to Yucatán, which figures prominently in Yucatecan cuisine
pibil – Yucatecan preparation: meat is flavoured with *achiote* sauce, wrapped in banana leaves and baked in a pit oven, or *pib*
poc-chuc – slices of pork cooked in a tangy sauce of onion and sour oranges or lemons
pollo – chicken
pollo asado – grilled (not roast) chicken
pollo con arroz – chicken with rice
pollo frito – fried chicken
puerco – pork
tampiqueño, tampiqueña – 'in the style of Tampico', a style of cooking meats often using a spiced tomato sauce
tocino – bacon or salt pork
venado – venison

Frutas (Fruit)

coco – coconut
dátil – date
fresas – strawberries, but also used to refer to any berries
guayaba – guava
higo – fig

limón – lime or lemon
mango – mango
melón – melon
naranja – orange
papaya – papaya
piña – pineapple
plátano – banana (suitable for cooking)
toronja – grapefruit
uva – grape

Legumbres, Verduras (Vegetables)

Vegetables are rarely served as separate dishes, but are often mixed into salads, soups and sauces.

aceitunas – olives
calabaza – squash or pumpkin
cebolla – onion
champiñones – mushrooms
chícharos – peas
ejotes – green beans
elote – corn on the cob; commonly served from steaming bins on street carts
jícama – a popular root vegetable which resembles a potato crossed with an apple; eaten fresh with a sprinkling of lime, chilli and salt
lechuga – lettuce
papa – potato
tomate – tomato
zanahoria – carrot

Dulces (Desserts, Sweets)

flan – custard, crème caramel
helado – ice cream
nieve – Mexican equivalent of the American 'snow cone' – flavoured ice with the consistency of ice cream
paleta – flavoured ice on a stick
pan dulce – sweet rolls, usually eaten for breakfast
pastel – cake
postre – dessert, after-meal sweet

Other Foods

achiote – a sauce of chopped tomato, onion, chillis and *cilantro* (fresh coriander leaf) used widely in Yucatán
azúcar – sugar
bolillo – French-style bread rolls
crema – cream
guacamole – mashed avocados mixed with onion, chilli sauce, lemon, tomato and other ingredients
leche – milk
mantequilla – butter
mole poblano – a nationally popular sauce made from more than 30 ingredients, including bitter chocolate, chillis and many spices; often served over chicken or turkey

pimienta negra – black pepper
queso – cheese
salsa – sauce made with chillis, onion, tomato, lemon
or lime juice and spices
sal – salt

At the Table

copa – glass
cuchara – spoon
cuchillo – knife
cuenta – bill
menú – menu; sometimes, fixed price meal, as in
menú del día
plato – plate
propina – the tip, 10 to 15% of the bill
servilleta – table napkin

taza – cup
tenedor – fork
vaso – drinking glass

Café (Coffee)

café sin azúcar – coffee without sugar. This keeps the
waiter from adding heaps of sugar to your cup,
but it doesn't mean your coffee won't taste sweet;
sugar is often added to and processed with the
beans.
café negro or *café americano* – black coffee with
nothing added except sugar, unless it's made with
sugar-coated coffee beans
café con leche – coffee with hot milk
café con crema – coffee with cream served separately
nescafé – instant coffee

Index

ABBREVIATIONS

B-Belize   G-Guatemala   M-Mexico

MAPS

Altun Ha, ruins (B) 512
Antigua Guatemala (G) 369
Belize 473
Belize City (B) 474
  Central Belize City 476-477
Belize's Cayes (B) 488
Belmopan (B) 503
Benque Viejo del Carmen (B) 510
Bonampak, ruins (M) 272
Cañon del Sumidero (M) 304
Campeche (M) 206
  Around Campeche (M) 210
Cancún, (Ciudad Cancún) (M) 105
  Around Cancún 108
Carretera al Atlantico (G) 425
Caye Caulker (B) 490
  Around Caye Caulker 489
Chetumal (M) 220
Chiapas Highlands (M) 325
Chichén Itzá, ruins (M) 148
Chichicastenango (G) 390
Chiquimula (G) 432
Cobá (M), ruins 235
Cobán (G) 428
Comitán, central (M) 330
Copán (Honduras) 439
  Around Copán 441
  Copán, ruins 435
Corozal Town (B) 516
El Petén (G) 452
Escárcega (M) 214

Esquipulas (G) 433
Felipe Carrillo Puerto (M) 227
Flores (G) 454
Guatemala City (G) 348-350
Guatemala's Highlands (G) 367
Guatemala's Pacific Coast (G) 414
Huehuetenango (G) 408
Isla Cozumel (M) 248
Isla Mujeres (M) 126
  Isla Mujeres Town 128
Izamal (M) 156
Kabah, ruins (M) 192
Kohunlich, ruins (M) 226
La Ruta Maya 12-13
Labná, ruins (M) 194
Lagos de Montebello (M) 332
Lake Atitlán (G) 378
Lake Petén Itzá (G) 455
Mérida (M) 162-163
Mountain Pine Ridge (B) 507
Northern Yucatán Peninsula (M) 138
Ocosingo (M) 278
Orange Walk Town (B) 514
Palenque (M) 262-263
Palenque, ruins (M) 264
Panajachel (G) 381
Parque-Museo La Venta (M) 286
Playa del Carmen (M) 243
Progreso (M) 180
Quintana Roo (M) 218
Quiriguá, ruins (G) 444

Quetzaltenango (G) 399
  Central Quetzaltenango 400
Retalhuleu (G) 416
  Central Retalhuleu 417
San Cristóbal de las Casas (M) 308-309
San Ignacio (Cayo) (B) 504
San Miguel Cozumel (M) 250
San Pedro (B) 494
Santa Cruz del Quiché (G) 396
Santa Elena (G) 453
Santa Lucía Cotzumalguapa (G) 419
Sayil, ruins (M) 193
Tabasco & Chiapas (M) 260
Tapachula (M) 340
Ticul (M) 199
Tikal, ruins (G) 460-461
Tizimin (M) 143
Tulum, ruins (M) 229
Turquoise Coast (M) 238
Tuxtla Gutiérrez (M) 296
Uaxactún, ruins (G) 468
Uxmal & the Puuc Route (M) 185
Uxmal, ruins (M) 187
Valladolid (M) 140
Villahermosa (M) 284
  Central Villahermosa 282
Xunantunich, ruins (B) 509
Yaxchilán, ruins (M) 273
Zaculeu, ruins (G) 410

TEXT

Map references are **bold** type.

Acanceh (M) 201
Agua Azul Cascades (M) 276-277
Akumal (M) 240
Amatenango del Valle (M) 328
Ambergris Caye (B) 493-500
Antigua Guatemala (G) 368-377
369

Places to Eat 374-376
Places to Stay 373-374
Arriaga (M) 336-337

Becal (M) 202-203
Belize City (B) 472-487
Places to Eat 482-483
Places to Stay 480-482
Belmopan (B) 502, **503**

Benque Viejo del Carmen (B) 509-511, **510**
Biosphere Reserves, Wildlife Sanctuaries & Zoos
  Bermudian Landing Baboon Sanctuary (B) 512
  Belize Zoo (B) 501
  Biotopo Cerro Cahuí (G) 454-455
  Biotopo del Quetzal (G) 426-427

Chocón-Machacas Nature
  Reserve (G) 448
Cockscomb Basin Jaguar Pre-
  serve (B) 520
Crooked Tree Wildlife Sanctu-
  ary (B) 513
Guanacaste Park (B) 501-502

Boca Paila (M) 234
Bolonchén de Rejón (M) 196-
  197

Calderitas (M) 224
Calkini (M) 202-203
Campeche (M) 196, 204-213,
  206, 210
  Places to Eat 211-212
  Places to Stay 210-211
Cancún (M) 104-136, **105, 108**
  Places to Eat 119-123
  Places to Stay 111-119
Cañón del Sumidero (M) 299,
  303, 305-306, **304**
Caye Caulker (B) 487-493, **489,
  490**
Caye Chapel (B) 500
Cayo (San Ignacio) (B) 502-506
Ceibal (G) 467-469
Celestún (M) 182-183
Champerico (G) 418
Chemuyil (M) 240
Chetumal (M) 215, 219, **220**
Chiapa de Corzo (M) 303-305,
  306-307
Chiapas (M) 295-344, **325**
Chiapas Zoo (M) 298
Chichicastenango (G) 389-395,
  390
Chiquimula (G) 431-432, **432**
CICOM (Villahermosa) (M) 287
Ciudad Cuauhtémoc (M) 335
Ciudad Hidalgo (M) 343
Ciudad Tecún Umán (G) 413-
  415
Ciudad Vieja (G) 377-378
Coatepeque (G) 415
Cobán (G) 427-430, **428**
Comitán (M) 329, **330**
Copán (Honduras) 434-442,
  435, 439, 441
Corozal Town (B) 515-518, **516**
Cozumel (M) 247-258, **248**
Cuatro Caminos (G) 397

Dangriga (B) 519-520

El Aguacero (M) 299
El Carmen (G) 413
El Petén (G) 451-470, **452**

El Zarco Junction (G) 415
Escárcega (M) 214-217, **214**
Escuintla (G) 422-423
Esquipulas (G) 432-434, **433**
Estanzuela (G) 431

Felipe Carrillo Puerto (M) 200,
  226-228, **227**
Flores (M) 271-272, (G) 451-
  459, **454**
Fuentes Georginas (G) 406

Gallows Point Caye (B) 501
Grutas Actun-Can (G) 454
Grutas de Balankanché (M) 152-
  153
Grutas de Loltún (Loltún Caves)
  (M) 195-196
Grutas de San Cristóbal (M) 324
Guatemala City (G) 346-365,
  348, 350
  Places to Eat 358-361
  Places to Stay 355-358

Honduras 434-442
Huehuetenango (G) 407-412,
  408
Huixtán (M) 329

Indian Culture, Mexico (M) 325
Isla Mujeres (M) 126-136, **126**
Iximché (G) 379
Iztapa (G) 423

La Democracia (G) 422
La Mesilla (G) 412
Lagos de Montebello (M) 333-
  335, **332**
Lake Amatitlán (G) 423
Lake Atitlán (G) **378**, 379-387
Lake Izabal (G) 445-446
Lake Petén Itzá (G) 454, **455**
Las Aventuras (M) 240
Likín (G) 423
Lívingston (G) 448-450
Los Encuentros (G) 379-380
Los Vahos (G) 405

Mayan Sites
  Abaj Takalik (G) 416
  Altun Ha (B) 512-513, **512**
  Becan (M) 215-216
  Bilbao (G) 419-420
  Bonampak (M) 272-273, **272**
  Cerros (B) 517
  Chicanna (M) 215-216
  Chichén Itzá (M) 215-216

Chinkultic (M) 334
CICOM (Villahermosa) (M) 288
Cobá (M) 234-237, **235**
Comalcalco (M) 293
Copán (Honduras) 434-441,
  439
Cuello (B) 514
Dzibilchaltún (M) 179-180
Dzibilnocac (M) 197-198
Edzná (M) 198
Edzná Ruins (M) 210
Finca el Baúl (G) 420-421
Finca las Ilusiones (G) 421
Hecelchakan (M) 202-203
Hochob (M) 197-198
Izapa Ruins (M) 342-343
Kabah (M) 191-193, **192**
Kaminaljuyú (G) 355
Kohunlich (M) 225-226, **226**
K'umarcaaj (G) 395-396
Labná (M) 194-195, **194**
Lamanai (B) 514-515
Lubaantun (B) 521
Mayapán (M) 201-202
Monte Alto (G) 422
Nim Li Punit (B) 521
Nohmul (B) 514
Palenque (M) 259-271, **264**
Parque-Museo La Venta (M)
  285-287
Playa Lancheros(M) 129
Puuc Route (M) 184-203
Quiriguá (G) 442-444, **444**
Río Bec (M) 216
Santa Rita (B) 517
Sayil (M) 193-194, **193**
Tikal (G) 459-467, **460-461**
Toniná (M) 277, 279-281
Tulum (M) 228-232
Uaxactún (G) 467, **468**
Uxmal (M) 186-191, **185, 187**
Xlapak (M) 194
Xpujil (M) 215-216
Xtacumbilxunaan (M) 196-197
Xunantunich (B) 508-509, **509**
Yaxchilán (M) 272-272, **273**
Zaculeu (G) 409-410, **410**
Mazatenango (G) 418
Mérida (M) 158-179, **162-163**
  Places to Eat 170-174
  Places to Stay 166-170
Misol-Ha Cascades (M) 276
Momostenango (G) 407
Mountain Pine Ridge (B) 506-
  508, **507**
Museo Popol Vuh (G) 354

Ocosingo (M) 277-281, **278**
Orange Walk (B) 513-515, **514**

Pamul (M) 241-242
Panajachel (G) 380-385, **381**
Placentia (B) 520-521
Playa del Carmen (M) 242, **243**
Progreso (M) 180-182, **180**
Puerto Arista (M) 338-339
Puerto Aventuras (M) 241
Puerto Barrios (G) 446-448
Puerto Morelos (M) 246-247
Puerto San José (G) 423
Punta Allen (M) 234
Punta Gorda (B) 521
Puuc Route (M) 191-196

Quetzaltenango (G) 398-405,
399, 400
Quiché (G) 389-397
Quiriguá (G) 442-445, **444**

Retalhuleu (G) 415, **417**
Río Dulce Cruises (G) 448-449
Río Hondo (G) 430-431
Río Lagartos (M) 144-145
Río Usumacinta (M) 271-272

Salamá (G) 424-426
San Antonio Aguas Calientes
(G) 377-378
San Benito (G) 451-459
San Cristobal de las Casas (M)
307-324, **308-309**
Places to Eat 319-321
Places to Stay 316

San Francisco el Alto (G) 406-
407
San Ignacio (Cayo) (B) 502-506,
504
San Juan Chamula (M) 327
San Lucas Tolimán (G) 387-388
San Miguel Cozumel (M) 249,
250
San Pedro (Ambergris Caye) (B)
493-500, **494**
San Pedro Chenalhó (M) 328-
329
San Pedro la Laguna (G) 389
Santa Catarina Palopó (G) 385,
387-388
Santa Cruz del Quiché (G) 395-
397, **396**
Santa Elena (G) 451-459, **453**
Santa Lucía Cotzumalguapa (G)
418
Santa María de Jesús (G) 378-
379
Santiago Atitlán (G) 388-389
Sayaxché (G) 467-469
Soconusco (M) 336
Sololá (G) 380
St George's Caye (B) 500

Tabasco (M) 259-294
Talismán (M) 343
Tapachula (M) 339-342, **340**
Tecoh (M) 201
Telchaquillo (M) 201

Tenejapa (M) 328
Tenosique (M) 271
Ticul (M) 198-200, **199**
Tizimin (M) 142-144, **143**
Tobacco Caye (B) 500
Todos Santos Cuchumatán (G)
412
Tonala (M) 337-338
Totonicapán (G) 397-398
Turneffe Islands (B) 500
Tuxtla Gutiérrez (M) 293-294,
295-303, **296**
Places to Eat 301, 302
Places to Stay 299-301

Valladolid (M) 137-142, **140**
Places to Eat 141-142
Places to Stay 139-141
Villahermosa (M) 281-293, **284**
Places to Eat 290-291
Places to Stay 288, 290
Volcán Agua (G) 378-379

Xcacel (M) 239-240
Xcaret (M) 242
Xel-Ha Lagoon (M) 239

Yal-Ku Lagoon (M) 241

Zacapa (G) 431
Zinacantán (M) 327-328
Zunil (G) 405-406

Where Can You Find Out.........

HOW to get a Laotian visa in Bangkok?

WHERE to go birdwatching in PNG?

WHAT to expect from the police if you're robbed in Peru?

WHEN you can go to see cow races in Australia?

In the Lonely Planet Newsletter!

Every issue includes:

- *a letter from Lonely Planet founders Tony and Maureen Wheeler*

- *a letter from an author 'on the road'*

- *the most entertaining or informative reader's letter we've received*

- *the latest news on new and forthcoming releases from Lonely Planet*

- *and all the latest travel news from all over the world*

Other Guides to the Region

Argentina - a travel survival kit
This guide gives independent travellers all the essential information on Argentina — a land of intriguing cultures, 'wild west' overtones and spectacular scenery.

Bolivia - a travel survival kit
From lonely villages in the Andes to ancient ruined cities and the spectacular city of La Paz, Bolivia is a magnificent blend of everything that inspires travellers. Discover safe and intriguing travel options in this comprehensive guide.

Brazil - a travel survival kit
From the mad passion of Carnival to the Amazon — home of the richest and most diverse ecosystem on earth — Brazil is a country of mythical proportions. This guide has all the essential travel information.

Chile & Easter Island - a travel survival kit
Travel in Chile is easy and safe, with possibilities as varied as the countryside. This guide also gives detailed coverage of Chile's Pacific outpost, mysterious Easter Island.

Colombia - a travel survival kit
Colombia is a land of myths — from the ancient legends of El Dorado to the modern tales of Gabriel Garcia Marquez. The reality is beauty and violence, wealth and poverty, tradition and change. This guide shows how to travel independently and safely in this exotic country.

Costa Rica - a travel survival kit
This practical guide gives the low down on exceptional opportunities for fishing and water sports, and the best ways to experience Costa Rica's vivid natural beauty.

Ecuador & the Galápagos Islands - a travel survival kit
Ecuador offers a wide variety of travel experiences, from the high cordilleras to the Amazon plains — and 600 miles west, the fascinating Galápagos Islands. Everything you need to know about travelling around this enchanting country.

Mexico - a travel survival kit
A unique blend of Indian and Spanish culture, fascinating history, and hospitable people, make Mexico a travellers' paradise.

Peru - a travel survival kit
The lost city of Machu Picchu, the Andean altiplano and the magnificent Amazon rainforests are just some of Peru's many attractions. All the travel facts you'll need can be found in this comprehensive guide.

South America on a shoestring
This practical guide provides concise information for budget travellers and covers South America from the Darien Gap to Tierra del Fuego. By the author the *New York Times* nominated 'the patron saint of travelers in the third world'.

Also available:
Brazilian phrasebook, *Latin American Spanish* phrasebook and *Quechua* phrasebook.

Lonely Planet Guidebooks

Lonely Planet guidebooks cover every accessible part of Asia as well as Australia, the Pacific, South America, Africa, the Middle East and parts of North America and Europe. There are four series: *travel survival kits*, covering a single country for a range of budgets; *shoestring guides* with compact information for low-budget travel in a major region; *walking guides*; and *phrasebooks*.

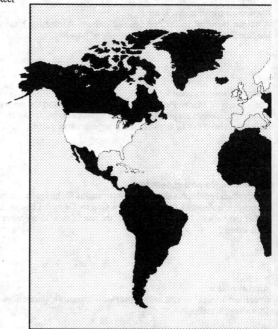

Australia & the Pacific
Australia
Bushwalking in Australia
Islands of Australia's Great Barrier Reef
Fiji
Micronesia
New Caledonia
New Zealand
Tramping in New Zealand
Papua New Guinea
Papua New Guinea phrasebook
Rarotonga & the Cook Islands
Samoa
Solomon Islands
Sydney
Tahiti & French Polynesia
Tonga
Vanuatu

South-East Asia
Bali & Lombok
Burma
Burmese phrasebook
Indonesia
Indonesia phrasebook
Malaysia, Singapore & Brunei
Philippines
Pilipino phrasebook
Singapore
South-East Asia on a shoestring
Thailand
Thai phrasebook
Vietnam, Laos & Cambodia

North-East Asia
China
Chinese phrasebook
Hong Kong, Macau & Canton
Japan
Japanese phrasebook
Korea
Korean phrasebook
North-East Asia on a shoestring
Taiwan
Tibet
Tibet phrasebook

West Asia
Trekking in Turkey
Turkey
Turkish phrasebook
West Asia on a shoestring

Indian Ocean
Madagascar & Comoros
Maldives & Islands of the East Indian Ocean
Mauritius, Réunion & Seychelles

Mail Order

Lonely Planet guidebooks are distributed worldwide and are sold by good bookshops everywhere. They are also available by mail order from Lonely Planet, so if you have difficulty finding a title please write to us. US and Canadian residents should write to Embarcadero West, 112 Linden St, Oakland CA 94607, USA and residents of other countries to PO Box 617, Hawthorn, Victoria 3122, Australia.

Europe
Eastern Europe on a shoestring
Iceland, Greenland & the Faroe Islands
Trekking in Spain

Indian Subcontinent
Bangladesh
India
Hindi/Urdu phrasebook
Trekking in the Indian Himalaya
Karakoram Highway
Kashmir, Ladakh & Zanskar
Nepal
Trekking in the Nepal Himalaya
Nepal phrasebook
Pakistan
Sri Lanka
Sri Lanka phrasebook

Africa
Africa on a shoestring
Central Africa
East Africa
Kenya
Swahili phrasebook
Morocco, Algeria & Tunisia
Moroccan Arabic phrasebook
West Africa

North America
Alaska
Canada
Hawaii

Mexico
Baja California
Mexico

South America
Argentina
Bolivia
Brazil
Brazilian phrasebook
Chile & Easter Island
Colombia
Ecuador & the Galápagos Islands
Latin American Spanish phrasebook
Peru
Quechua phrasebook
South America on a shoestring

Central America
Costa Rica
La Ruta Maya

Middle East
Egypt & the Sudan
Egyptian Arabic phrasebook
Israel
Jordan & Syria
Yemen

The Lonely Planet Story

Lonely Planet published its first book in 1973 in response to the numerous 'How did you do it?' questions Maureen and Tony Wheeler were asked after driving, bussing, hitching, sailing and railing their way from England to Australia.

Written at a kitchen table and hand collated, trimmed and stapled, *Across Asia on the Cheap* became an instant local bestseller, inspiring thoughts of another book.

Eighteen months in South-East Asia resulted in their second guide, *South-East Asia on a shoestring*, which they put together in a backstreet Chinese hotel in Singapore in 1975. The 'yellow bible' as it quickly became known to backpackers around the world, soon became *the* guide to the region. It has sold well over ½ million copies and is now in its 6th edition, still retaining its familiar yellow cover.

Today there are over 80 Lonely Planet titles – books that have that same adventurous approach to travel as those early guides; books that 'assume you know how to get your luggage off the carousel' as one reviewer put it.

Although Lonely Planet initially specialised in guides to Asia, they now cover most regions of the world, including the Pacific, South America, Africa, the Middle East and Eastern Europe. The list of *walking guides* and *phrasebooks* (for 'unusual' languages such as Quechua, Swahili, Nepalese and Egyptian Arabic) is also growing rapidly.

The emphasis continues to be on travel for independent travellers. Tony and Maureen still travel for several months of each year and play an active part in the writing, updating and quality control of Lonely Planet's guides.

They have been joined by over 50 authors, 40 staff – mainly editors, cartographers, & designers – at our office in Melbourne, Australia, and another 10 at our US office in Oakland, California. Travellers themselves also make a valuable contribution to the guides through the feedback we receive in thousands of letters each year.

The people at Lonely Planet strongly believe that travellers can make a positive contribution to the countries they visit, both through their appreciation of the countries' culture, wildlife and natural features, and through the money they spend. In addition, the company makes a direct contribution to the countries and regions it covers. Since 1986 a percentage of the income from each book has been donated to ventures such as famine relief in Africa; aid projects in India; agricultural projects in Central America; Greenpeace's efforts to halt French nuclear testing in the Pacific and Amnesty International. In 1990 $60,000 was donated to these causes.

Lonely Planet's basic travel philosophy is summed up in Tony Wheeler's comment, 'Don't worry about whether your trip will work out. Just go!'